Oxford Socio-Legal Studies

Smart Regulation

SMART REGULATION

Designing Environmental Policy

NEIL GUNNINGHAM
Director, Australian Centre for Environmental Law,
Australian National University
(author of Chapters 1 and 4 and joint author of Chapters 2, 3, 5 and 6)

PETER GRABOSKY
Director of Research, Australian Institute of Criminology
(joint author of Chapters 3 and 5)

with

DARREN SINCLAIR
(joint author of Chapters 2, 3 and 6)

CLARENDON PRESS · OXFORD
1998

Oxford University Press, Great Clarendon Street, Oxford OX2 6DP
Oxford New York
Athens Auckland Bangkok Bogotá Buenos Aires Calcutta
Cape Town Chennai Dar es Salaam Delhi Florence Hong Kong Istanbul
Karachi Kuala Lumpur Madrid Melbourne Mexico City Mumbai
Nairobi Paris São Paolo Singapore Taipei Tokyo Toronto Warsaw
and associated companies in
Berlin Ibadan

Published in the United States
by Oxford University Press Inc., New York

British Library Cataloguing in Publication Data
Data available

Library of Congress Cataloging in Publication Data
Gunningham, Neil.
Smart regulation: designing environmental policy/Neil
Gunningham, Peter Grabosky, with Darren Sinclair.
p. cm. — (Oxford socio-legal studies)
Includes bibliographical references and index.
1. Environmental law.   2. Environmental policy.   I. Grabosky,
Peter N., 1945– .   II. Sinclair, Darren.   III. Title.   IV. Series.
K3585.4.G86   1998   344'.046—dc21   98–24209
ISBN 0-19-826857-2

1 3 5 7 9 10 8 6 4 2

Typeset by Hope Services (Abingdon) Ltd.
Printed in Great Britain
on acid-free paper by
Bookcraft Ltd., Midsomer Norton, Somerset

For Beth, Kate and Sue.

For Bronwyn.

General Editor's Introduction

Twenty or thirty years ago we were secure in our assumption that the most appropriate legislative response to the undesirable consequences of industrialised life for the natural environment was the use of legal regulation backed by the criminal sanction. This reliance upon command and control regulation was, however, soon to be threatened by a growing belief that it was both ineffective and inefficient. Complaints also began to be heard, particularly in the United States, that regulatory agencies acted towards regulated business with an unnecessary, counterproductive, and ultimately costly adversarialism, and some academics in other countries where there may have been a less adversarial approach were nevertheless influenced by these arguments. Neo-liberal writers and politicians simply attacked the whole regulatory enterprise, arguing instead for widespread deregulation.

In practice, however, reliance on command and control regulation has so far been substantially unshaken by these various assaults. Yet there remains a growing concern that something better than this traditional form of regulation needs to be devised. There are demands for less costly regulation and for regulation that is more sensitive to the fact that business has to operate in increasingly competitive environments.

This book addresses the key issue of how regulatory policy is to be developed in the face of such pressures. The authors focus on the problem of environmental regulation and provide a comprehensive and thorough analysis which rises above a simplistic debate about the virtues of regulation or deregulation. Instead they seek a way forward that is both effective and sensitive, one that avoids the inefficiencies of command and control regulation and the problems that deregulation brings. In the chapters that follow the authors argue for what they call 'smart' regulation: a way of achieving the goal of effective environmental protection in an era of constrained public resources through the use of a variety of more flexible, pluralistic approaches. Their book is a welcome addition to a number of monographs on regulation that have already appeared in *Oxford Socio-Legal Studies*.

Keith Hawkins

Preface

In writing this book, we have incurred a number of debts. The greatest of these are to our colleagues at the Australian Centre for Environmental Law at The Australian National University.

Darren Sinclair's contribution to the book extends well beyond the specific chapters of which he is joint author. Darren also read and commented upon the remainder of the manuscript and his insights substantially enriched the quality of the final product. Neil Gunningham wishes to acknowledge a highly productive and stimulating collaboration with him.

Patricia Burritt provided exceptional research assistance and project co-ordination throughout the book's gestation period. In particular, she demonstrated an impressive capacity to unearth relevant material from unlikely sources and to manage and hold together the various strands of the project, and to do all this with understanding and good humour even in the face of the tightest deadlines. Without her efforts, the writing of the book would have been immeasurably more painful.

Maureen Lawrentin provided flawless administrative support and never gave less than 100 per cent, despite demands on her time and tolerance far and beyond the call of duty.

Our thanks and appreciation also go to those who read and commented upon drafts of various chapters, or who in other ways deepened our understanding of a number of critical issues, namely: Ellen Baar; John Braithwaite; Lee Breckenridge; David Cole; Ben Davy; Peter Drahos; Carol Heimer; Bridget Hutter; Sue Holmes; John Horwich; Bob Kagan; Jan Keppler; Nadia McLaren; Kate Short; Laureen Snider; Bill Thomas; Brian Wastle; and Mike Young. We are also grateful to all those who participated in a workshop on the themes of the book in December, 1996.

Finally, we express our appreciation for the patience, support and encouragement of our spouses, Sue (who also provided good counsel and understanding through the various traumas of authorship) and Bronwyn.

The project benefited substantially from a grant provided to Neil Gunningham by the Australian Research Council from 1995–1997, and from the sabbatical leave he spent at the Centre for Socio-Legal

Studies at Wolfson College, Oxford and at the Center for the Study of Law and Society at the University of California, Berkeley.

The majority of Peter Grabosky's contribution was made during his visiting fellowship at the Administrative Compliance and Governability Project, Urban Research Program, Research School of Social Sciences, Australian National University from 1993–1995. He would like to pay particular thanks to Professor Pat Troy for institutional support during that period. Additional institutional support was provided by the Australian Institute of Criminology, particularly the Institute's J. V. Barry Library, during the earlier stages of the project.

The project began as a collaboration initially between Gunningham and Grabosky, and was joined in the later stages by Sinclair. The precise contributions are as set out on page iii. above. In addition to his contribution to chapters three and five, additional material to chapter two was provided by Grabosky.

Some aspects of chapters one and six first appeared in N. Gunningham and J. Rees 'Industry Self-Regulation' (1997) 19(4) *Law and Policy* 363 and D. Sinclair 'Self-Regulation versus Command and Control? Beyond False Dichotomies' (1997) 19(4) Law and Policy 529. Similarly, some of the material in Chapter Three was developed from ideas originally appearing in P. N. Grabosky: 'Green Markets: Environmental Regulation by the Private Sector' (1994) 16(4) *Law and Policy* 420–48; 'Beyond the Regulatory State' (1994) 27(2) *Australian and New Zealand Journal of Criminology* 192–95; 'Using Non-governmental Resources to Foster Regulatory Compliance' (1995) 8(4) *Governance: An International Journal of Policy and Administration* 527–50; 'Regulation by Reward: On the Use of Incentives as Regulatory Instruments' (1995) 17(3) *Law and Policy* 256–281; and 'Counter-productive Regulation' (1995) 23 *International Journal of the Sociology of Law* 347–69.

Portions of the work in Chapter Four first appeared in N. Gunningham 'Environment, Self-Regulation and the Chemical Industry: Assessing Responsible Care' (1995) 17(1) *Law and Policy* 55–107; and 'Environmental Management Systems and Community Participation: Rethinking Chemical Industry Regulation' (1998) 16(2) *UCLA Journal of Environmental Law and Policy*. Some aspects of Chapter Five, relating to biodiversity policy design, draw on ideas developed by Neil Gunningham and Mike Young while writing a report to the Australian Government's Department of Environment Sport and Territories and subsequently elaborated in N. Gunningham and

M. D. Young 'Towards Optimal Environment Policy: The Case of Biodiversity Conservation' (1997) 24(2) *Ecology Law Quarterly* 244–297. Our work was also extensively used by the OECD in *Saving Biological Diversity: Economic Incentives*, Ch 5 (1996) OECD, Paris.

Neil Gunningham
P. N. Grabosky
Canberra
March 1998

Table of Contents

Table of Abbreviations

BAT	Best Available Technology
CCPA	Canadian Chemical Producers' Association
CERCLA	Comprehensive Environmental Response, Compensation and Liability Act (US 1980)
CMA	Chemical Manufacturers Association (CMA)
CRTK	Community Right-to-Know
EMAS	Eco-Management and Audit Scheme (EMAS)
EMS	Environmental Management System
EPA	Environmental Protection Agency
GEMI	Global Environmental Management Initiative
INFOAM	International Federation of Organic Agriculture Movements
INBio	National Biodiversity Institute (Costa Rica)
INPO	Institute of Nuclear Power Operators
IPM	Integrated Pest Management
ISO	International Standards Organisation
NCAP	National Community Advisory Panel
NGO	Non-Government Organisation
NIMBY	Not-In-My-Backyard
OECD	Organisation for Economic Co-operation and Development
OHSA	Occupational Health and Safety Administration
PIM	Printing Industry of Minnesota
RIA	Regulatory Impact Analysis
RSPCA	Royal Society for the Prevention of Cruelty to Animals
SLAPP	Strategic Lawsuits Against Public Participation
SMEs	Small and Medium Sized Enterprises
SOCMA	Synthetic Organic Manufacturers Association
TQM	Total Quality Management
TRI	Toxic Release Inventory
UNEP	United Nations Environment Programme
WWF	World Wide Fund For Nature

PART I

Practice and Potential in
Environmental Regulation

1 Introduction

Neil Gunningham

One of the crucial issues of our time is how to avoid serious, and perhaps cataclysmic, damage to the natural environment. The causes of such damage are both complex and controversial, and arise from a wide variety of social and economic pressures. The results, however, are more readily apparent. The evidence that pollution, land degradation, deforestation, ozone depletion, climate change, and the loss of biological diversity are inflicting serious and in some cases irreversible damage to the planet which sustains us, is increasingly compelling.[1] Indeed, it is arguable that the window of opportunity for averting major ecological disaster is a rapidly shrinking one, and that, in some cases, it may already be too late to prevent ongoing environmental degradation.[2]

For policymakers, a variety of strategies are available that might, subject to political and economic constraints, enable serious environmental

---

[1] See OECD, *Environmental Data 1995: Compendium,* November 1995, OECD, Paris; World Resources Institute, *World Resources 1994–95: A guide to the Global Environment,* Oxford University Press, New York; and OECD, *The State of the Environment* (1991), OECD, Paris. On pollution, see, for example, C. Flavin, 'The Legacy of Rio' in Worldwatch Institute, *State of the World 1997* (1997), Earthscan Publications, London; World Resources Institute (WRI), International Institute for Environment and Development, and World Conservation Union-IUCN, *World Directory of Country Environmental Studies* (1996), WRI, Washington, DC; on land degradation, see L. R. Oldeman *et. al., World Map of the Status of Human-Induced Soil Degradation: an explanatory note* (1991), 2nd ed., International Soil Reference and Information Centre & United Nations Environment Programme, Wageningen, Netherlands and Nairobi; for details of deforestation and biological diversity loss, see World Conservation Monitoring Centre, *Global Biodiversity—Status of the Earth's Living Resources* (1992), Chapman and Hall, London; on ozone depletion, see United Nations Environment Programme, *Environmental Effects of Ozone Depletion: 1994 Assessment* (1994), UNEP, Nairobi and World Meteorological Organization, *Scientific Assessment of Ozone Depletion: 1994* (1995), WMO, Geneva; and on climate change, see S. H. Schneider, *The Planetary Gamble We Can't Afford to Lose* (1997), Basic Books, New York; and Intergovernmental Panel on Climate Change (IPPC), *Climate Change: Second Assessment* (1996), Cambridge University Press, Cambridge, UK.

[2] That is, the integrity of entire ecological systems may have been undermined to such an extent that even if all adverse human inputs were to immediately cease, they would continue on a downward spiral of destruction. See also S. H. Schneider, *The Planetary Gamble We Can't Afford to Lose* (1997), Basic Books, New York; D. H. Meadows; D. Meadows & J. Randers, *Beyond the Limits: Confronting Global Collapse: Envisioning a Sustainable Future* (1992), Post Mills VT, Chelsea Green; and L. R. Brown; C. Flavin, and S. Postel, *Saving the Planet: How to shape an environmentally sustainable global economy* (1991), W. W. Norton, New York.

damage to be slowed down, halted, or, ideally, reversed. This book is about one of the most important of those strategies: environmental regulation. We use this term, deliberately, in the broadest sense, to include not just conventional forms of direct ('command and control')[3] regulation—the staple diet of many politicians—but also to include much more flexible, imaginative, and innovative forms of social control which seek to harness not just governments but also business and third parties. For example, we are concerned with self-regulation and co-regulation, with utilizing both commercial interests and Non-Government Organisations (NGOs), and with finding surrogates for direct government regulation, as well as with improving the effectiveness and efficiency of more conventional forms of direct government regulation itself.

We do not claim that regulation—even broadly defined—is necessarily the most important means (and certainly not the only means) of addressing every major environmental problem. Indeed, so complex are the causes of such problems that their solutions are also likely to be multifaceted, with regulation being but one component. However, we do claim that regulation does have a very substantial role to play in protecting the environment, but that most existing approaches to regulation, are seriously sub-optimal. By this we mean that they are not effective in delivering their purported policy goals; or efficient, in doing so at least cost; nor do they perform well in terms of other criteria such as equity, administrative viability or political acceptability.

The major task of this book is to demonstrate how environmental regulation could be redesigned so that it would perform 'optimally'[4] in terms of those criteria (or at least come a lot closer to it). The central argument will be that, in the majority of circumstances, the use of multiple rather than single policy instruments, and a broader range of regulatory actors, will produce better regulation. Further, that this will allow the implementation of complementary combinations of instruments and participants tailored to meet the imperatives of specific environmental issues. By implication, this means a far more imaginative, flexible, and pluralistic approach to environmental regulation than has so far been adopted in most jurisdictions: the essence of 'smart' regulation.

In this introductory chapter, as indeed in chapters two and three, we

---

[3] The term 'command and control' refers to the prescriptive nature of the regulation (the command) supported by the imposition of some negative sanction (the control).

[4] The word 'optimal' is useful shorthand but subject to misuse. See pp. 25 below.

lay the groundwork for the substantive task of regulatory redesign which we undertake in Parts II and III. First, we provide an overview of the political and ideological debate about the future of regulation that has dominated decision-making for more than a decade. We suggest that this debate has been a largely sterile one that has not substantially advanced the cause of environmental policy. Secondly, we argue that the germ of a far more fruitful approach is contained in recent theoretical work in the sphere of legal pluralism, and in the evolution of more innovative policy instruments in the field of the environment specifically. Thirdly, we show that even these innovations are insufficient to achieve environmental and economic policy goals. Their limitations can only be overcome by invoking a broader vision of regulation and by the pursuit of broader policy mixes, utilizing combinations of instruments and actors, and taking advantage of various synergies and complementarities between them. Fourthly, we describe the structure of the remainder of the book. Finally, we outline our methodology, the normative basis of our enterprise, and the criteria against which we evaluate the success of regulatory design.

Regulation, deregulation, and beyond

In broad terms, the history of environmental regulation involves two phases. The first began around the early 1970s, when governments in most developed countries responded to public environmental concern by introducing a myriad of regulations designed to prohibit or restrict environmentally harmful activities.[5] By and large, these regulatory approaches have tended to follow the United States model of 'command and control' regulation. That is, legislatures have proscribed certain behaviour and set up a regulatory agency to monitor and police compliance with the legal standards. Although this mechanism has never completely displaced other means of social control,[6] it is nevertheless the 'reigning conception' which has guided policy-making for many years.

Yet the strategy of using regulatory agencies to curb the environmental degradation caused by the behaviour of corporations and others

---

[5] R. Kagan, 'Regulatory Enforcement' in D. Rosenbloom & R. Schwartz (eds.), *Handbook of Regulation and Administrative Law* (1994), Dekker, New York.

[6] In respect of some issues, including many involving rural communities (e.g., soil degradation and some aspects of biodiversity loss) education, persuasion and voluntarism have been the dominant responses.

is fraught with difficulty. By the late 1970s, it was evident that much command and control regulation had not turned out the way the policymakers had intended. Some regulatory agencies, particularly in the United States, adopted an adversarial stance towards regulatees which often engendered regulatory resistance and proved counterproductive.[7] Moreover, environmental regulations, both in the United States and elsewhere, were often inflexible, and excessively costly for business to comply with.[8] Centralized, bureaucratic standard-setting—the centrepiece of traditional forms of command and control—is now routinely castigated by its critics for being 'an inherently inefficient and cumbersome way to control pollution'[9] and for failing to deliver many of the environmental benefits it promised.[10]

The critique of command and control legislation can be seriously overstated. Criticism is often directed at the relatively unrepresentative adversarial approach adopted in the United States, and fails to acknowledge a significant movement towards more flexible and cost-effective forms of regulation across a number of developed countries that avoid the worst excesses of highly prescriptive versions.[11] Moreover, some critics conveniently overlook the fact that regulatory agencies are often constrained or prevented from performing their mandate by a lack of resources or other factors entirely beyond their

[7] E. Bardach & R. Kagan, *Going by the Book: The problem of regulatory unreasonableness* (1982), Temple University Press, Philadelphia. See also D. Vogel, *National Styles of Regulation: Environmental Policy in Great Britain and the United States* (1986), Cornell University Press, Ithaca, New York.

[8] D. J. Fiorino, 'Towards a New System of Environmental Regulation: the case for an industry sector approach' (1996) 26(2) *Environmental Law* 457–489; and references cited in E. Bardach & R. Kagan, *Going by the Book: The problem of regulatory unreasonableness* (1982), Temple University Press, Philadelphia. See also D. Vogel, *National Styles of Regulation: Environmental Policy in Great Britain and the United States* (1986), Cornell University Press, Ithaca, New York. For an overview of European approaches, see R. Brinkman; S. Jasanoff; & T. Ilgen *Controlling Chemicals: The politics of regulation in Europe and the United States* (1986), Cornell University Press, Ithaca, New York.

[9] E. D. Elliott, 'Environmental TQM: Anatomy of a pollution control program that works!' (1994) 92 *Michigan Law Review* 1847 and references cited therein.

[10] See, for example, E. D. Elliott & E. M. Thomas, 'Chemicals' in C. Campbell-Smith; B. Breen, J. W. Futrell, J. M. McElfish & P. Grant (eds.), *Sustainable Environmental Law: integrating natural resource and pollution abatement law from resources to recovery* (1993), West Publishing, St Paul, US at 1266–1270; J. Quarles, *Cleaning up America: An insider's view of the Environmental Protection Agency* (1976), Houghton Mifflin, Boston, US; W. E. Orts, 'Reflexive Environmental Law' (1995) 89(40) *Northwestern University Law Review* 1227; B. Commoner, *Making Peace with the Planet* (1990), Pantheon Books, New York; and B. Commoner, 'Failure of the Environmental Effort' (1988) 10 *Environmental Law Reporter* 195.

[11] See further chapter 2 below.

control. Nor should it be forgotten that, notwithstanding the serious difficulties confronting many regulatory agencies, command and control
regulation has achieved some significant victories in halting, or at least
slowing, some forms of environmental degradation.[12] For example,
both water and air quality have been substantially improved in many
jurisdictions over the last thirty years, due in large part to government
regulation.[13]

However, for reasons described more fully in chapter two, many of
the gains have been achieved at an unnecessarily high social and economic cost, and in an increasing number of cases, regulation has been
demonstrably ineffective.[14] There is also considerable evidence that
government regulation, at least in an archetypal form of command and
control, has reached the limits of its technical capacity and cost-
effectiveness.[15] The low-hanging fruit has all been picked. The overall
result is, at best, one of slow progress at excessive cost. Pressures for
governments to reduce outlays and to provide for more competitive
business environments, and for business to keep up with rapidly changing technology, combine to further undermine the effectiveness of
prescriptive government regulation.

Against this backdrop, the neo-liberal critics of the regulatory state,
including in particular some economic rationalists, have been able to
mount a credible case for environmental deregulation. From the late
1970s onwards, they have focused on the shortcomings of traditional
government regulation as a basis for arguing the case for its replace-
ment by market or property-rights approaches.[16]

In some areas of social regulation, where previously the state had
played a central role, the neo-liberals were so successful that some
twenty or so years of conventional government regulation (what may

[12] See, generally, G. Easterbrook, *A Moment On The Earth: The coming of age of environmental optimism* (1995), Viking Press, New York.
[13] S. Cohen, 'EPA: A Qualified Success' in S. Kamieniecki, R. O'Brien & M. Clarke
(eds.), *Controversies in Environmental Policy* (1986), State University of New York Press,
Albany, p. 174. For further discussion, see B. A. Ackerman & R. B. Stewart, 'Reforming
Environmental Law' (1985) 37 *Stanford Law Review* 1333 at 1364.
[14] For example, command and control regulation is not well equipped to deal with diffuse, non-point and multi-media sources of pollution or with ever more complex and systemic environmental problems, such as climate change and the loss of biological diversity,
that demand far more sophisticated policy responses (A. L. Alm, 'A Need For new
Approaches: Command-and-control is no longer a cure-all'(1992) *EPA Journal* 18
May/6–11 June). See further chapter two p. 44.
[15] A. L. Alm, 'A Need For new Approaches: Command-and-control is no longer a
cure-all' (1992) *EPA Journal* 18 May/6–11 June.
[16] See chapter 2.

be termed the 'first phase' of regulation) was followed, in the 1970s and 1980s, by substantial deregulation (the 'second phase'). However, despite their enthusiasm for a wholesale dismantling of the regulatory state, neo-liberal governments met substantial public opposition to deregulation when it came to the environment. Although resources for environmental regulation suffered badly at the hands of the Reagan and Thatcher administrations in particular,[17] the basic regulatory structures and legislation remained largely intact.[18]

Nevertheless, so influential has neo-liberal thinking been at a political level, and so successfully has economic rationalism dominated social policy debates, that the regulatory climate has been substantially changed. Regulators are in retreat, reluctant to argue for new or tougher regulation for fear of alienating either their political masters or influential business lobbies who are never reticent to suggest that such regulation will make them less competitive, or hasten their move to another jurisdiction. The current battle between the United States Environment Protection Agency (EPA) and a number of States which are strongly resisting enforcement of Federal environmental laws, is perhaps one symptom of this regulatory malaise.[19]

Even in the unlikely event that pro-regulators were to win such battles, and the pendulum were to swing back towards more regulation ('bigger and better' regulatory agencies, more standards, tougher enforcement etc.) this would raise as many problems as it would solve. First, there is little evidence that policy-makers have overcome many of the serious limitations of this approach which became evident during the 'first phase' of regulation. Secondly, government resources are necessarily limited. When premises can only be inspected once every few years, when inspectors have to rely on industry to self-monitor, when an agency cannot afford the time or resources to launch prosecutions, then traditional regulatory strategy is inevitably limited.[20] As a result, it may well be that, in many circumstances, traditional regulation is nei-

---

[17] J. A. Lash, *A Season of Spoils: The Reagan administration's attack on the environment* (1984), Pantheon Books, New York.

[18] In the US, a more recent assault on environmental regulation, led by Republican Speaker Newt Gingrich (N. Robinson, 'International Initiatives on Greenhouse' in B. Boer, R. Fowler & N. Gunningham (eds.), *Environmental Outlook No. 2* (1996), The Federation Press, Sydney, p. 240) has been similarly unsuccessful.

[19] J. R. Cushman, 'Virginia Seen as Undercutting US Environmental Rules' (1997) *New York Times* 19 January 11.

[20] See, for example, N. Gunningham, 'Negotiated Non-Compliance: A case study of regulatory failure' (1987) 9(1) *Law and Policy* 69–97.

ther the most efficient nor the most effective strategy. If so, then it is, at best, only a partial solution, which should be used selectively rather than 'across the board'.

Were the pendulum to swing to the opposite extreme, with free market and property-rights approaches substantially replacing regulation, there is little reason to believe that environmental outcomes would be any better.[21] For reasons we explore in chapter two, the limitations of these approaches are also severe. As a result, their capacity to deliver optimal environmental outcomes is, in most cases, even more limited than that of command and control regulation. The crucial question thus becomes: where should one go next in terms of regulatory policy? None of the main players can claim satisfaction with the existing state of affairs. There is a groundswell of dis-satisfaction with traditional strategies: on the one side from the public and environmentalists (because they insufficiently improve environmental outcomes); and on the other from business (because they fail to take account of the pressures of international competition and the need for economic efficiency). There is also a considerable danger of stalemate. On the one hand, the push for deregulation has lost some momentum, having proved a less than adequate solution to many areas of social (as opposed to economic) concern,[22] and there remains considerable public support for direct government intervention regarding the environment. On the other hand, traditional regulatory approaches seem to have reached their limits, and in any event, fiscal constraint and government overload (with demands for policy and services exceeding capacities to respond) combine to threaten efforts to expand such regulation. Moreover, the very approach of couching the debate in terms of *either* regulation *or* deregulation kindles a spurious and sterile ideological divide, which inhibits attempts to find solutions containing the best of both approaches.

---

[21] See further, R. Kuttner, *Everything For Sale: The virtues and limits of markets* (1997), Alfred A. Knopf, New York; and pp. 83 (chapter two) below.

[22] Across the broad spectrum of social and economic policy, deregulation has had some significant successes. Perhaps most noteworthy of these related to interstate trucking and airlines in the United States. Conversely, there occurred some serious failures. The relaxation of prudential controls on small financial institutions in the United States gave rise to the constellation of events known as the Savings and Loan Scandal of the late 1980s (M. Mayer, *The Greatest Ever Bank Robbery: The collapse of the savings and loan industry* (1992), Collier Books, New York; and K. Calavita & H. N. Pontell, 'The State And White Collar Crime: Saving the Savings and Loan (1994) 28(2) *Law and Society Review* 297–324. For a broader analysis, see R. Kuttner, *Everything For Sale: The virtues and limits of markets* (1997), Alfred A. Knopf, New York.

In our view, the challenge for regulatory strategy is to transcend this ideological divide by finding ways to overcome the inefficiencies of traditional regulation on the one hand, and the pitfalls of deregulation on the other. That is, to move beyond the market-state dichotomy to devise better ways of achieving environmental protection at an acceptable economic and social cost. This will involve the design of a 'third phase' of regulation: one which still involves government intervention, but selectively and in combination with a range of market and non-market solutions, and of public and private orderings. Given the political and fiscal constraints under which governments now labour, it will be crucial to harness resources *outside* the public sector in furtherance of government policy. In the following chapters, we will demonstrate ways whereby these goals may be achieved, and opportunities for environmental innovation, regulatory flexibility, and improved environmental performance, but without the use of greater government resources (that is, 'smart' regulation). Among these opportunities are those which flow from naturally occurring market phenomena, and from other commercial influences. These and other mechanisms may be enlisted in furtherance of 'governing at a distance'.[23]

In approaching regulatory strategy in this manner we are not alone. In the broader arena of public policy generally, the substantial failings of both traditional government regulation and market-based solutions have already prompted a search for innovative and more effective alternatives. Osborne and Gaebler's *Reinventing Government* is probably the most well known and influential attempt to devise a new regulatory agenda in these terms.[24] The authors challenge the conventional wisdom that the only way out of our repeated public crises is either to raise taxes or to cut spending. On the contrary, they offer a third option, namely transforming how we go about providing services so as to improve both efficiency and effectiveness. They suggest that the fundamental issue is not *how much* government we have, but what *kind* of government. In their words: 'we do not need more government or less government, we need better government'.[25]

---

[23] P. Grabosky, 'Green Markets: Environmental regulation by the private sector' (1994) 16(4) *Law and Policy* 419–448; and P. Grabosky, 'Using Non-governmental Resources to Foster Regulatory Compliance' (1995) 8(4) *Governance: An International Journal of Policy and Administration* 527–550; and N. Rose & P. Miller, 'Political Power Beyond the State: problematics of government' (1992) 43 *British Journal of Sociology* 173–205.

[24] D. Osborne & T. Gaebler, *Reinventing Government* (1992), Addison-Wesley, Boston.

[25] D. Osborne & T. Gaebler, *Reinventing Government* (1992), Addison-Wesley, Boston, pp. 23–24.

Our quest is, in some respects, a similar one, though the answers we provide are both substantially different from theirs, and addressed to different issues of social policy. We would nevertheless agree with the general sentiment that we need to pursue 'smarter regulation', which, for our purposes, means that which promises improved environmental performance, but at a price acceptable to business and the community.

Building on what we have

In pursuing our quest for 'smart' regulation we draw sustenance from two sources: one theoretical and academic; the other pragmatic and policy-oriented. While both illuminate our search, neither provides the answers we seek.

Turning to the former, there is some evidence that a new paradigm for the analysis of regulation may be evolving: one capable of transcending the regulation-deregulation dichotomy and of providing a much broader perspective of what regulation can involve.[26] The most influential work within this paradigm, is that of Ayres and Braithwaite, who argue the case for 'responsive regulation' capable of providing 'creative options to bridge the abyss between deregulation and proregulatory rhetoric'[27] and of achieving 'win-win' solutions through innovations in regulatory design. In particular, they emphasise the contributions of enforced self-regulation (whereby regulatees develop their own compliance programme, which is then subject to approval by regulatory authorities) and regulatory republicanism (where an enlightened private sector and an informed public, through deliberation and constructive participation, can contribute productively to the regulatory process). We build both on that work and, more generally, on the broader literature on legal pluralism to which it is related.

---

[26] See, for example, I. Ayres & J. Braithwaite, *Responsive Regulation: transcending the deregulation debate* (1992), Oxford University Press, New York; J. Braithwaite, *Crime, Shame and Reintegration* (1989), Cambridge University Press, Cambridge; B. Fisse & J. Braithwaite, *Corporations, Crime and Accountability* (1993), Cambridge University Press, Sydney ; R. Hahn, *A Primer on Environmental Policy Design* (1989), Harwood Academic Publishers, London; R. Hahn, 'Towards a New Environmental Paradigm' (1993) 102 *Yale Law Journal* 1719; C. Sunstein, 'Paradoxes of the Regulatory State' (1990) 57 *University of Chicago Law Review* 407; C. Sunstein, *After the Rights Revolution: Reconceiving the regulatory state* (1990), Harvard University Press, Cambridge, Mass.; and D. F. Kettl, *Sharing Power: public governance and private markets* (1993), Brookings Institution, Washington.

[27] I. Ayres & J. Braithwaite, *Responsive Regulation: Transcending the deregulation debate* (1992), Oxford University Press, New York, p. 14.

Scholars within the legal pluralism tradition focus upon the inter-relationship between state law and private forms of social control and conflict resolution. They recognise that the law is just one element in a web of constraint on behaviour, some of whose strands are barely discernible, and many of which are non-governmental.[28] For our purposes, the central insight of legal pluralism is that, - contrary to conventional wisdom, most regulation is already 'in the hands not of government officials but of the myriad individuals employed in the private sector'[29] and that, often, more can be achieved by harnessing the enlightened self-interest of the private sector than through command and control regulation. It is through the theoretical lens of pluralism, that we will elucidate the relationships which exist between the state, industry, and third parties, and the way in which the law relates to each and operates in the shadow of the other.[30] From this perspective, the limitations of a government-specific approach become readily apparent, as do the virtues of 'de-centering the state' and developing a broader and more inclusive conception of the regulatory process.[31]

However, beyond these general perspectives, there has been little analysis of regulation which assists in addressing the central theme of this book: the design of efficient and effective 'optimal' policy mixes.

---

[28] E. Ehrlich, *Fundamental Principles in the Sociology of Law* (1912) Harvard University Press, Cambridge; G. Teubner, 'Substantive and Reflexive Elements in Modern Law' (1983) 17 *Law and Society Review* 239–286; and P. Fitzpatrick, 'Law and Societies' (1984) 22 *Osgoode Hall Law Journal* 115–138. One of the most influential social thinkers of the late twentieth century, Michel Foucault, observed that the real practice of government was not through the imposition of law, but rather in working with and through the constellation of interests, institutions, and interpersonal relations which are part of civil society (M. Foucault, 'Governability' in G. Burchell, C. Gordon & P. M. Miller, (eds.) *The Foucault Effect: Studies in governmentality* (1991), Harvester Wheatsheaf, London, p. 127). A subsequent interpreter of Foucault referred to this 'as governing in accordance with the grain of things' (G. Burchell, 'Civil Society and the System of Natural Liberty' in G. Burchell, C. Gordon, P. M. Miller (eds.), *The Foucault Effect: Studies in governmentality* (1991), Harvester Wheatsheaf, London, p. 127).

[29] E. Bardach & R. Kagan, *Going by the Book: The problem of regulatory unreasonableness* (1982), Temple University Press, Philadelphia, p. 33.

[30] M. Galanter, 'Justice In Many Rooms' (1981) 19 *Journal of Legal Pluralism* 1–47.

[31] See also the literature on private institutions of social control and new technologies of governance in C. Shearing & P. Stenning, *Private Policing* (1987), Sage Publications, Beverly Hills; N. Rose & P. Miller, 'Political Power Beyond The State: Problematics of government' (1992) 43(2) *British Journal of Sociology* 173–205; J. Di Iulio, G. Garvey & D. Kettl, *Improving Government Performance* (1993), The Brookings Institution, Washington DC; P. Grabosky, 'Using Non-governmental Resources to Foster Regulatory Compliance' (1995) 8(4) *Governance: An International Journal of Policy and Administration* 527–550; and, on the development of reflexive law, W. E. Orts, 'Reflexive Environmental Law' (1995) 89(40) *Northwestern University Law Review* 1227.

For example, little work has been done to assess the relative advantages of different combinations of mechanisms in different institutional, economic, or social contexts. Neither is there any substantial body of literature which assists in addressing specifically environmental issues in the broader manner we envisage. For example, the environmental literature substantially overlooks means by which public agencies may harness commercial institutions and resources residing outside the public sector to further policy objectives, or how governments might foster conditions conducive to the operation of 'naturally occurring' private initiatives. Mitchell's sophisticated analysis of oil pollution and of the role of classification societies in preventing ballast discharges at sea, is perhaps the most striking exception.[32]

Our second source of sustenance in designing smarter regulation is the rapid expansion of different types of environmental policy instruments over the last decade. These policy innovations include: self-regulation and co-regulation; environmental audits; environmental management systems (EMSs); eco-labelling schemes; liability rules for banks and insurers; environmental reporting; community right-to-know legislation (CRTK); and good neighbour agreements.[33]

While these instruments open up a range of policy options far broader than traditional regulation, they have rarely been used to their full potential. This is because most of these developments have been driven by pragmatic policy considerations and the desire to rectify specific problems, rather than by broader theoretical concerns. As a result, they have also tended to develop in an *ad hoc* manner, often without any serious attempt to design them as part of an integrated system. Nor has there been much systematic enquiry into how such instruments might interact with each other and other forms of regulation.[34] Rather, policymakers have commonly fallen into the trap of simply adding a new

[32] R. B. Mitchell, *International Oil Pollution at Sea* (1994), MIT Press, Cambridge. Other exceptions include work on interest groups (T. Bonyhady, *Places Worth Keeping: conservationists, politics and law* (1993), Allen & Unwin, Sydney, Australia; E. Papadakis, *Politics and the Environment: the Australian experience* (1993), Allen & Unwin; Sydney, Australia; D. Farrier, 'Policy instruments for conserving biodiversity on private land' in J. Bradstock (ed.), *Conserving Biodiversity: threats and solutions* (1995), Surrey Beatty & Sons, Chipping Norton, UK.

[33] See further chapter two pp. 50 ff.

[34] For example, there is a burgeoning literature on environmental audit, the 'new generation' regulatory tool. Yet this literature is almost exclusively client oriented (addressing issues of confidentiality, how audits should be conducted, by whom, etc.). What is lacking is any serious evaluation of the implications of environmental audit or any concern to specify how and under what circumstances audit is most likely to make a substantial contribution to environmental protection.

instrument to their arsenal of weapons without giving sufficient thought
to how this will impact on their overall regulatory strategy.

Also introduced, but with a much more coherent and sophisticated
theoretical underpinning, has been a range of economic instruments
including taxes, charges, and tradeable property and pollution rights.[35]
However, even most of the economic literature shows only a limited
appreciation of the extent to which some economic instruments at least
might be viewed not just as a complement to direct regulation (or a
more flexible form of it), but integrated with a range of other policy
instruments.[36]

Overall, there remains a tendency to treat the various policy instruments as alternatives to one another rather than as potentially complementary mechanisms capable of being best used in combination.[37] As
a result, policy analysts have tended to embrace one or other of these
regulatory approaches without regard to the virtue of others. Perhaps
predictably, economists have focused on economic instruments, lawyers
and government regulators on direct regulation, industry on self-
regulation, and scientists on research.[38]

We will argue that such 'single instrument' or 'single strategy'
approaches are misguided, because all instruments have strengths and
weaknesses; and because none are sufficiently flexible and resilient to
be able to successfully address all environmental problems in all contexts. Accordingly, we maintain that a better strategy will seek to har-

[35] See further chapter 2 pp. 69.

[36] Much of the debate between economists and regulators continues to be couched in
terms of economic instruments *versus* regulation rather than in terms of synergies and
complementarities. See, for example, A. Moran, 'Tools of Environmental Policy: Market
Instruments versus Command-and-control' in R. Eckersley (ed.), *Markets, the State and the
Environment: Towards Integration* (1995), Macmillan Education Australia, Melbourne, p. 73;
C. Dieker, *Lessons from Uncle Sam: Regulation v. economic incentives* (1997), a paper delivered
at 16th Australian National Environmental Law Conference, Adelaide, April. For a more
sophisticated and integrated approach, see M. Jacobs *The Green Economy: Environment, sus-
tainable development and the politics of the future* (1991), Pluto Press, UK, pp. 151ff; and also
OECD, *Guidelines for the Use of Economic Instruments in Environmental Policy* (1990), October,
OECD, Paris (40) 23; and OECD, *Applying Economic Instruments to Environmental Policies in
OECD and Dynamic Non-Member Economies* (1994), OECD, Paris. What is lacking even from
the more sophisticated OECD documents is an analysis of how and in what circumstances various instruments and institutions might be combined. See further at pp. 125
below.

[37] T. Swanson 'Book Reviews: J. B. Opschoor & R. K. Turner (eds.) *Economic Incentives
and Environmental Policies: Principles and Practice* (1994)' (1995) 4(1) *Review of European
Community and Environmental Law (RECIEL)* 85.

[38] See, for example, S. Dovers, 'Information, Sustainability and Policy' (1995) 2(3)
Australian Journal of Environmental Management 149. As to the extent to which this 'single
institutions' approach may be changing, see pp. 16 below.

ness the strengths of individual mechanisms while compensating for their weaknesses by the use of additional and complementary instruments. That is, we will argue that in the large majority of circumstances (though certainly not all), a mix of instruments is required, tailored to specific policy goals. Moreover, such a mix of instruments will work more effectively if a broader range of participants are capable of implementing them. This means the direct involvement not only of governments (first parties) but also of business and other 'targets' of regulation (second parties) and a range of other interested actors (third parties), both commercial and non-commercial. To date, the use of third parties has been restricted to public interest and community groups. Commercial third parties, in particular, remain a largely untapped resource in the environmental arena, despite their considerable potential to act both as quasi-regulators and to influence the behaviour of regulatees more generally.

Towards a successful policy mix

The central thesis of this book is that recruiting a range of regulatory actors to implement complementary combinations of policy instruments, tailored to specific environmental goals and circumstances, will produce more effective and efficient policy outcomes. Further, that this approach will reduce the regulatory burden on government, thus freeing up scarce public resources to be allocated to situations where government intervention or assistance is most required.

We place particular emphasis on the potential for second and third parties (business or commercial or non-commercial third parties) to act as surrogate or quasi-regulators, complementing or replacing government regulation in certain circumstances. We do so not to fulfil the ideological agenda of deregulation[39], but because we consider that it will build a more robust and comprehensive policy mix than traditional approaches, at the same time as achieving more cost-effective outcomes for business. We will demonstrate how commercial actors can exert controlling influences in furtherance of environmental protection in addition to (and, at times, in excess of) those which governments may contemplate; how scrutiny on the part of public interest groups can

---

[39] Government would continue to have an ongoing and critical role in establishing regulatory objectives, harnessing other regulatory actors to conform to these objectives, underpinning these broader strategies with a regulatory safety net, or (where better alternatives are not available) directly intervening itself.

often supplement vigilance which might be exercised by government agencies; and also, how the government can facilitate greater third party involvement in support of the public interest, thereby deriving considerable policy leverage by harnessing external resources and by facilitating private orderings in furtherance of environmental protection.

We do not, however, advocate a 'smorgasbord' approach, where the greater the number of different instruments and actors the better. There are limits to government and private sector resources which necessitate a careful selection of the most cost-effective regulatory combinations. There are also limits to the administrative burden that can reasonably be placed on regulatees in satisfying a multiplicity of regulations. Excessive administrative burdens may well divert internal firm resources away from more productive pollution prevention activities. Finally, appropriate mixes of instruments and actors will vary depending on the nature of the environmental problem and industry sector or sectors being addressed, making it difficult if not impossible to generalize concerning optimal combinations.

Nor do we assume that any combinations of instruments will be better than a single instrument approach. On the contrary, different combinations of instruments, or the introduction of a new instrument to an existing policy mix, could have a variety of effects, not all of which are positive. These range from synergy (where two instruments enhance each other's effects) to neutralization (where one instrument negates or dilutes the effects of another). For example, uniform pollution standards for individual firms may well undermine the efficiency of a broad-based pollution tax.[40] What is needed then, is not simply the introduction of a broad range of policy instruments, but the matching of instruments with the imperatives of the environmental issue being addressed, with the availability of different regulatory actors, and with the intrinsic qualities of each other.

We are not alone in advocating the need to design optimal (or at least better) policy mixes. By the mid 1990s, there was a growing recognition that this was a vitally important issue of environmental policy. By this time, dissatisfaction with the regulatory *status quo* and the deregulatory alternatives had spawned a number of suggestions, at international, regional, and national levels, for such an approach. At an international level, references to the concept of regulatory mix (though not how to achieve it) are to be found as early as 1992, in Agenda 21,

---

[40] See further pp. 129 (chapter three) below.

the main policy document to emerge from the Rio Earth Summit.[41] Regionally, the clearest statement is contained in the European Union's Fifth Action Program which aspires to 'create a new interplay between the main groups of actors (government, enterprise, public) and the principal economic sectors (industry, energy, transport, agriculture and tourism) through the use of an extended, and integrated range of instruments'.[42] Similar sentiments have also been expressed at national level in a number of jurisdictions,[43] and by organisations such as the World Business Council for Sustainable Development.[44]

Yet despite these expressions of support for a new approach to regulation involving a broader range of instruments and parties, little attempt has been made to put it into operation. As the OECD put it in 1997: 'instruments, while pervasive, are the least analysed [public management tool]. When they are analysed, they tend to be studied individually rather than comparatively'.[45] In the United States, Europe and elsewhere, there are increasing calls to go 'beyond command and control regulation',[46] but without any clear sense of direction as to what this might mean.[47] And while the United States EPA had, by the late 1990s, introduced a range of more flexible programmes that sought

[41] United Nations Commission on Environment and Development (UNCED), *Agenda 21: Programme of action for sustainable development*, Section 1 Chapter 8 (B) *Providing and Effective Legal and Regulatory* Framework (1992), United Nations Conference on Environment and Development, UNCED, Geneva, p. 55.

[42] Commission of the European Community (CEC*)*, *Towards Sustainability* Fifth Action Program of European Union (1992), Brussels, p. 25.

[43] For example, the first concerns were documented as early as 1990 when the Australian Manufacturing Council Report *Industry and the Environment: Europe and North America* (pp. 1–2) noted 'The complexity of the problems, and the apparent limitations of command and control mechanisms, have made governments reassess their regulatory regimes and seek to meet community standards via a more flexible approach to regulation such as economic mechanisms . . . leading edge businesses, trade unions and industry associations are meeting the challenge in an open and proactive fashion'.

[44] S. Schmidheiny, *Changing Course: A global business perspective on development and the environment* (1992), MIT Press, Cambridge, pp. 30–32.

[45] PUMA/OECD, 'Choices of Policy Instruments' (20 March 1997), 15th Session of Public Management Committee, PUMA/OECD, Paris.

[46] For example, the American Bar Association 16th Annual Conference on Environmental Law in 1997 had this as its theme, and in the same year the theme of an International Conference on Environmental Law and Policy, held in Nigeria (Law Centre, Lagos State University), was 'Towards Flexible, Efficient and Effective Environmental Law'.

[47] The most recent initiative (not yet complete at the time of writing) is the Enterprise For The Environment, which focuses on improving the regulatory process and environmental performance drivers that influence behaviour in the US, and is a policy forum involving The Center for Strategic and International Studies; The Keystone Center; and The National Academy of Public Administration.

continuous improvement and reflect collaboration with stakeholders,[48] these remain marginal to its central mission and have so far produced only very limited results.[49] Similarly, in Europe, there remains heavy reliance on command and control as the basic policy instrument,[50] and only very limited experimentation with instrument and policy mixes.[51] The Fifth Action Program, the vehicle most likely to develop a broader approach, was, according to a report in late 1996, still making extremely slow progress and was nowhere near completion.[52] The record of some individual countries is also disappointing. For example, in the United Kingdom, two high level reports in the same year both identified inertia as the dominant government response to a range of important sustainability issues.[53]

Nor has there been any substantial advance in thinking about regulatory mixes at the theoretical level. Certainly, the Organisation for Economic Co-operation and Development (OECD), long a leader in both monitoring and developing the environmental regulatory agenda internationally, now acknowledges explicitly that combinations may be more valuable than individual instruments acting alone. However, it has not yet engaged in the crucial task of theorizing how this might be brought about.[54] That is, while the breadth of the OECD approach is

[48] D. J. Fiortino, 'Towards a New System of Environmental Regulation: the case for an industry sector approach' (1996) 26(2) *Environmental Law* 457–489. These programmes are described at pp. 56–64 below (chapter two).

[49] See T. Davies & J. Mazurek, *Industry Incentives for Environmental Improvement: Evaluation of US Federal Initiatives* (1996) A Report to the Global Environmental Management Initiative Center for Risk Management, Resources for the Future, Washington, DC. Even the most promising of these innovations, the Environmental Leadership Program, is beset by problems (not least the lack of credible incentives for firms to join) which makes the transition from the pilot phase to full programme an extremely challenging one. See also B. Ward, 'Now at BAT' (July 1997) 14(4) *Environmental Forum* 38.

[50] See J. B. Opschoor & H. B. Vos, *Economic Instruments For Environmental Protection* (1989), OECD, Paris.

[51] For details of EU Fifth Action Program, see H. Joliffe, 'EU Fifth Action Program: progress report on implementation of "Towards Sustainability" ' (1996) 5(4) *Review of European Community and Environmental Law (RECIEL)* 342.

[52] H. Joliffe, 'European Union Fifth Action Program: Progress Report on Implementation of "Towards Sustainability" ' (1996) 5(4) *Review of European Community and Environmental Law (RECIEL)*, 342–343.

[53] Environmental Data Services Ltd., 'Sustainable Development Advisors Take Government To Task' (1997) *ENDS Report* Number 264, p. 7, published by the Environmental Data service.

[54] See, for example, OECD, *Reducing Environmental Pollution: Looking back, thinking ahead* (1994), OECD, Paris; OECD, *Draft Council Recommendations on the Use of Economic Instruments in Environmental Policy*, (1990) Env/EC (90) 23, OECD, Paris; and see also J. B. Opschoor, H. & K. Turner, *Economic Incentives And Environmental Policies: principles and practice* (1994), Kluwer Academic Publishers, Dordrecht.

to be applauded, it has still not taken the next crucial step of identifying *which* complementary combinations of instruments, in conjunction with the use of *what* broader range of regulatory actors, are likely to be complementary rather than counterproductive, or of identifying how to *integrate* different instruments and actors to produce an optimal regulatory mix. It is equally true of sustainability policies more generally that, as Dovers points out, 'rarely have criteria for choosing between different instruments been made explicit and applied rigorously'.[55] Even less attention has been paid to identifying criteria for choosing between different *combinations* of instruments and institutions.

Perhaps the closest approximation to the ideals expressed in this section is to be found in the attempts by a few nations to design individual environmental strategies in ways which, without articulating the importance of mixes in regulatory design, nevertheless embody some important principles of such design. The Dutch approach to Internal Company Environmental Management[56] and to environmental covenants,[57] initiatives in the United States such as Project XL and the Environmental Leadership Program,[58] and the efforts of some Australian States to reform the principles of their pollution legislation are good examples.[59]

In summary, despite a recent and growing recognition of the importance of 'regulatory mix' as a research and policy issue, very little work has been done to put the concept into practice, to show what it would mean in specific circumstances, or to design a set of principles and policy prescriptions to achieve it. The task of this book is to fill that gap.

---

[55] S. Dovers, 'Information, Sustainability and Policy' (1995) 2(3) *Australian Journal of Environmental Management* 149.

[56] M. Aalders, 'Regulation and In-Company Environmental Management in the Netherlands (1993) *Law and Policy* 15(2) 75.

[57] See J. Van Dunne, (ed.), *Environmental Contracts and Covenants: New instruments for a realistic environmental policy?* (1993), Koninklijke Vermande, Netherlands.

[58] See further chapter two pp. 50 below.

[59] In Victoria (Victorian EPA, *Accredited Licenses* (1994), Publication 423, VGPS), firms are rewarded through an accredited licensing scheme with reduced regulatory obligations for demonstrating excellence in environmental management, and achieving significant improvements in waste outputs (A. T. Iles, 'Adaptive management: Making environmental law and policy more dynamic, experimentalist and learning' (1996) 13(4) *Environmental and Planning Law Journal* 288 at 299). Accredited licence-holders are not required to apply for works approval; can have a greatly simplified permit for a premises otherwise requiring many individual permits; and pay reduced licence fees if they can prove use of an environmental management system that is verified by an independent auditor, and produce an environment improvement plan with community input.

The structure of this book

The book is in three parts. Part I (comprising chapters one to three) is introductory and provides a context for the main body of our argument. Before one is in a position to design principles for optimal (or at least better) environmental regulation and regulatory mixes, it is necessary to survey the regulatory terrain. That is, one must identify the range of instruments and actors available for recruitment to the regulatory cause; the policy levers which government can pull to activate their engagement; the underlying properties of instruments and parties which determine complementary regulatory combinations; and the means of avoiding dysfunctional combinations. These issues are addressed in chapters two and three.

Specifically, in chapter two, we review the main instruments available and, in chapter three, the main institutional actors who might be capable of implementing them: the government regulator; the companies and industries which are the targets of regulation; and the 'third party' participants, both commercial and non-commercial. We identify the strengths and weaknesses of these instruments, the circumstances where they have most potential, and the extent and means whereby government might exploit them to optimal effect. We explore the roles which different parties might play in achieving optimal mixes and their broader contribution to environmental policy. We also address the issue of instrument interaction, and discuss some of the forms in which regulatory instruments, broadly defined, might combine with positive or negative consequences.

In Part II (comprising chapters four to five), we explore the issues of regulatory design and policy mix as they relate to the chemical industry and critical aspects of agriculture, drawing our examples from North America, Western Europe, and Australia. The reasons for choosing a sector-specific approach are addressed in the methodology section below. In essence, much richer results are likely to be gained from concrete context-specific study than from an abstract or generic approach. The two sectors upon which we focus have been chosen to provide a representative range of regulatory structures, strategies and actors; of environmental issues and institutional capacities. The threats we examine within these sectors pose different environmental risks, elicit the attention of different institutional actors, and are amenable to different combinations of regulatory instruments. These two sectors, industry and agriculture, are also vitally important in environmental policy terms.

In chapter four, we examine means of reducing point-source pollution in the chemical industry, and in particular, of ameliorating major risks to the environment caused by toxic emissions to air, land, and water. The chemical manufacturing industry is diverse, comprising large multi-national industrial corporations with sophisticated environmental compliance programmes; their buyers and suppliers; and small 'backyard' operations where knowledge of regulatory requirements may be largely lacking. The organizational structure of the industry exists in a network of relationships with insurance and other commercial institutions having a direct interest in the environmental performance of chemical manufacturers. As we shall see, the structure of the chemical industry suggests the possibility of effective co-regulation (utilizing Responsible Care, EMSs and Product Stewardship programmes), of major third-party involvement (buyers and suppliers, local communities, public interest groups, trade unions, and environmental auditors) in conjunction with information-based strategies (CRTK).

In chapter five, we examine means of addressing two crucially important environmental threats as they relate to the agricultural sector: biodiversity loss and non-point source pollution caused by pesticides, fertilisers and agricultural by-products. As we will see, biodiversity has a number of features which distinguish it from more conventional resource management issues and which make it a particularly important subject for policy research. These include the fact that much biodiversity loss is irreversible; that it is subject to threshold effects; and that it, commonly, has no immediate economic value. The use of agricultural pesticides and fertilizers, which may cause serious damage not only to organisms and ecosystems but also to human health, gives rise to a different set of policy challenges. These include the need to remove various perverse incentives which traditionally encouraged unsustainable farming practices; the importance of fostering peer-to-peer education in furtherance of environmentally friendly agriculture; and the potential for fostering consumer demand for low input products.

In both cases, the reach of traditional regulation, and the opportunities of policing it effectively, are likely to be very limited. The alternatives however, differ substantially with the different features of biodiversity and non-point source pollution. One important differentiating factor is whether or not the producer's interest and the public interest converge. Biodiversity conservation, at least those aspects dependent on habitat preservation, will usually entail some degree of sacrifice on the part of the producer. By contrast, agricultural practices based on low inputs, and encouraged by consumer demand, can sometimes be more profitable than 'farming as usual'.

More generally, the agricultural sector provides unusual and promising examples of constructive engagement of interest groups and industry. Markets, both domestic and international, are greater potential instruments of control than governments and investors, and financiers in particular, and may have a profound influence. In addition, the prospective contribution of the environmental services sector to agricultural enterprise may also become important.

In our approach to both the chemical industry and to agriculture, we adopt a common structure. We begin by providing a profile of the industry sector and by identifying those characteristics that are likely to be important in identifying workable instrument and actor combinations. We outline the existing regulatory and policy regimes and their strengths and limitations, and suggest which new instruments and institutional forms might operate constructively there. We then argue the case for redesigning regulation to achieve a policy mix appropriate to the particular circumstances of that industry, and in accordance with the general approach which we outlined above.

Finally, in Part III (chapter six), we distil the conclusions and insights of the previous chapters, and extrapolate from the industry sector studies to draw more general conclusions about regulatory and policy design. Specifically, our central task is to identify a set of processes, principles, and policy prescriptions that can be applied to a wide variety of environmental circumstances, which will guide policymakers in implementing policy mixes of instruments and participants. These policy principles would be capable of matching instruments and potential regulatory participants with each other and with the characteristics of the environmental problem at hand. In particular, we devise a robust theoretical underpinning of regulatory design that transcends the limitations of single instrument and party approaches. Armed with such knowledge, policymakers will be in a much stronger position to devise improved regulatory solutions.

How we approached our task: assumptions, evaluation criteria, and methodology

The normative basis of our study

Our approach to the task of designing regulatory policy is, principally, normative. It is from the standpoint of public policy that we address questions of regulatory strategy: in what circumstances and to what extent can regulation safely be left to industries themselves? When government intervention is necessary, what forms should it take? What are the implications of adopting one form of regulation rather than another? What are the appropriate roles of third parties? How can we achieve smarter and more effective regulation? Our concern in each case is to suggest ways in which policymakers, acting in good faith and intending to design successful environmental regulation, might best approach that task.

This last statement is almost certain to raise the hackles of public choice theorists and to be regarded by them as, at best, naive. These theorists suggest that the process of establishing and implementing regulation is susceptible to corruption; that regulatory officials are vulnerable to capture or prone to engage in rent-seeking behaviour to further their own ends; and that politicians pander to noisy lobby groups at the expense of the community as a whole.[60] Even public interest groups, which ostensibly seek interventionist policies to protect the environment, may, in reality, have much baser, self-serving motives.[61] The public choice solution is to remove, as far as possible, the target of special interest group influence (i.e., government) from the regulatory process.[62] Instead, free market environmentalism and a property-rights approach are favoured.[63]

We do not deny that regulatory agencies are organizational entities with their own agendas, seeking to cope with often turbulent, unpredictable and highly politicized environments.[64] Nor can we offer any

[60] See D. Mueller, *Public Choice II* (1989),Cambridge University Press, Cambridge, New York; and W. F. Shughart II, *Antitrust Policy and Interest-Group Politics* (1990), Quorum, Greenwood Press, UK.

[61] Another related problem which citizens' environmentalist activity may pose is that of policy distortion. Not all environmental issues have the same political 'sex appeal'. Charismatic megavertebrates attract more interest than do worms. Old-growth forests arouse more passions than does soil degradation. The process of agenda setting by environmental groups, their choice of issues, would make a fascinating treatise in its own right. Suffice it to say that preoccupation with a particular ecosystem, issue, or threat almost inevitably entails an opportunity cost, and problems of inconsistency seem destined to remain a fact of democratic life (S. Breyer, *Regulation And Its Reform* (1982), Harvard University Press, Cambridge).

[62] M. S. Greve & F. L. Smith, *Environmental Politics: Public costs, private rewards* (1992), Praeger, New York.

[63] T. L. Anderson & D. Leal, *Free Market Environmentalism* (1991), Westview Press, Boulder, Co.

[64] P. C. Yeager, *The Limits of Law: The public regulation of private pollution* (1991), Cambridge University Press, Cambridge; and N. Gunningham, *Pollution, Social Interest And The Law* (1974), Martin Robertson, UK.

definitive solutions to the democratic and bureaucratic politics ('politics without romance'[65]) identified by public choice scholars and others.[66] However, the public choice critique can be overstated.[67] Indeed, on the basis of a broad review of the evidence, it would be hard to deny that, in some circumstances, broader considerations of the public good do prevail.[68] As Howse, Pritchard and Trebilcock put it:

there appear to be no iron-clad rules of politics that render insurmountable the challenge of devising institutions that allow government to act with speed and flexibility, and that ensure that policies reflect a principled deliberation on the entire range of legitimate interests and values that are at stake.[69]

Moreover, we contend that for government to simply walk away and leave environmental protection to unfettered market forces, as some public choice theorists would advocate, is really no solution at all.[70] Instead, following Yeager,[71] we argue that 'the primary institutional goal is to produce rules that have a reasonable chance of surviving the inevitable political and legal attacks and that are capable to a tolerable degree of effective implementation in the real world'.

We consider that a pragmatic approach to regulatory design, where government is relatively unencumbered by the ideological baggage of the regulation versus deregulation debate, and seeks to harness the resources of a range of potential participants, has the greatest chance of avoiding the types of political and bureaucratic manoeuvring that

[65] J. Buchanan, 'Politics without Romance' in J. Buchanan & R. Tollison (eds.) *The Theory of Public Choice—II* (1994), University of Michigan Press, p. 13.

[66] T. O. McGarity & S. A. Shapiro, *Workers At Risk: The failed promise of occupational safety and health administration* (1993), Praeger, Westport, p. 7; and N. Gunningham, 'Public Choice: Advancing the economic analysis of law' (1992) 21(1) *Federal Law Review* 117–135.

[67] The US Environmental Protection Agency, for example, far from being vulnerable to capture by a single group, is subject to a complex set of constituencies, and can enlist the support of a range of highly vocal and organized environmental organisations in support of controversial decisions (J. R. Lazarus 'The Tragedy of Distrust in the Implementation of Federal Environmental Law' (1991) 54 *Law and Contemporary Problems* (1991) 363–364). More generally, see N. Gunningham, 'Public Choice: Advancing the economic analysis of law' (1992) 21(1) *Federal Law Review* 117–135 and references therein.

[68] See, for example, S. Breyer, *Regulation And Its reform* (1982), Harvard University Press, Cambridge, p. 10; and R. Howse; J. R. S. Pritchard & M. J. Trebilcock, 'Smaller Or Smarter Government?' (1990) 40 *University of Toronto Law Journal* 498 at 533.

[69] R. Howse, J. R. S. Pritchard & M. J. Trebilcock, 'Smaller Or Smarter Government?' (1990) 40 *University of Toronto Law Journal* 498 at 533.

[70] On the limitations of free market environmentalism, see R. Kuttner, *Everything For Sale: the virtues and limits of markets* (1997), Alfred A. Knopf, New York and chapter 2 below.

[71] P. C. Yeager, *The Limits of Law: The public regulation of private pollution* (1991), Cambridge University Press, Cambridge.

public choice theorists so despise. As Mendeloff [72] points out, it is no coincidence that it is 'when creative professionals and politicians have been relatively free to shape programs without strong pressures from either pro- or anti-regulatory ideologies' that many of the most worth-while regulatory measures have been adopted.

By sharing the regulatory burden between a range of participants, the chances of any one participant pursuing an agenda not in the public interest will be minimized. For example, it is unlikely that com-mercial third parties will be influenced by political lobbying. Again, a substantial part of our agenda is to identify opportunities for win-win solutions, and to design policy mixes that maximize these opportunities. To the extent that this can be done, the problem of self-interested lobby groups, seeking to block regulatory reform, necessarily recedes.

Evaluation criteria: what we mean by 'optimal'

Unfortunately, despite substantial analysis and discussion in the litera-ture, it is not immediately obvious how one judges whether or to what extent a particular policy has been 'successful', or, to use the narrower, technical term favoured by economists, 'optimal'. And yet, this is funda-mental to the task of designing optimal policy mixes. Regulatory or social policy goals are rarely spelled out in the statutes themselves, at least in terms that are capable of measuring their relative success or failure. Different groups with an interest in the outcome of legislation will them-selves often disagree sharply about what a successful outcome would be. So how are we to determine what a successful policy would look like?

This problem has, increasingly, occupied the minds of policy-makers and others in recent years. For example, the OECD has iden-tified flexibility, efficiency and cost-effectiveness as important indices of success, not only in its studies of economic mechanisms but also more broadly.[73] Many other policy-making bodies, academic think tanks, and individual writers have come up with other lists, no two of which appar-ently coincide.[74] Indeed, there is almost no limit to the number and

---

[72] J. Mendeloff, 'Overcoming Barriers to Better Regulation' (1993) 18 *Law and Social Inquiry* 711 at 713.

[73] OECD, *Environmental Policy: How to apply economic instruments* (1991), OECD, Paris; OECD, Group on Economic and Environment Policy Integration, Expert Group on Economic Aspects of Biodiversity, *Biological Diversity: Economic incentive measures for conserva-tion and sustainable use* (1995) OECD, Paris; and OECD, *Making Markets Work for Biological Diversity: The role of economic incentives measures* (1995), OECD, Paris.

[74] For example, within Australia, negotiations on a National Strategy for Ecologically Sustainable Development identified several criteria in addition to those selected by the

range of individual characteristics that could be legitimately used to assess regulatory performance.

In the absence of any consensus on precisely what criteria a successful regulatory strategy should satisfy, and with no value-free way of establishing any, it falls upon us to identify our own preferred criteria and our reasons for choosing them. We are influenced in part by pragmatism: we could not develop a set of regulatory design principles that seeks to accommodate a broad range of assessment criteria because using a large number of variables would make it impractical to account for all the various interactions and permutations that would arise.[75] For this reason, we narrowed down the available assessment criteria to four core objectives. The ones we chose are relatively uncontroversial.[76] They begin with the three which find their way into almost all lists:[77] effectiveness (contributing to improving the environment);[78] efficiency (improving the environment at minimum cost within which we include administrative simplicity); and equity showing fairness in the burden-sharing among players to which we add political acceptability (which includes factors such as liberty, transparency, and accountability).

Of these, we chose to make effectiveness and efficiency the pre-eminent criteria, because we believe that, in the majority of cases, the effectiveness of regulatory policy in reaching an environmental target, and its efficiency in doing so at least cost, will be the primary concerns

OECD. These include: equity, environmental effectiveness, community acceptance, the provision of ongoing incentives for technical innovation, and the use of more efficient and environmentally benign production processes (Ecologically Sustainable Development Working Group, *Intersectional Issues Report* (1992), AGPS, Canberra, in M. D. Young *et. al.*, 'Feedlots and Water Quality' (1994) 11 *Australian Journal of Environmental Management* 52). In contrast, a report by the Australian Manufacturing Council, *Best Practice Environmental Regulation* (1993) identifies ten criteria that could form the basis of benchmarking environmental regulation. These are: certainty, communication, consultation, cost effectiveness, efficiency, flexibility, integrity, practicality, responsibility and transparency. The report defines each of these terms and concludes that in order to minimize the adverse effects on industrial competitiveness, while affording maximum environmental protection, the principles should be incorporated into the regulatory design process.

[75] To give an example, fifteen circumstances, each involving two aspects, would produce 32,768 possible settings (H. Bressers & P. J. Klok, 'Fundamentals For A Theory Of Policy Instruments' (1988) 15(3/4) *International Journal of Social Economics* 22–41 at 24.

[76] For a similar list, see M. Jacobs, *The Green Economy: Environment, sustainable development and the politics of the future* (1991), Pluto Press, UK, p. 152.

[77] P. Winsemius & U. Gutram, 'Responding To The Environmental Challenge' (1992) *Business Horizons*, March–April 12.

[78] M. Jacobs, *The Green Economy: Environment, sustainable development and the politics of the future* (1991), Pluto Press, UK, p.152 defines this criterion as concerning: how certainly does the instrument achieve the environmental target set; how quickly; and how flexible it is to changing circumstances.

of policymakers. Certainly, this is not always so, and proponents of environmental justice would, understandably, put equity at the top of their list.[79] However, to follow the latter approach would involve us writing a very different book, with a very different title.

In any case, we consider effectiveness and efficiency to be the two criteria most likely to yield substantial results in terms of improved environmental performance. These criteria are the essence of the term 'optimality', which is concerned with whether instruments will do the desired task and at an acceptable performance level. As economists use these terms in defining optimality:

> By efficiency is meant the static aspects (i.e., what levels of administrative costs are associated with the instruments) and the dynamic ones (e.g., to what extent will the various instruments induce technological innovation or diffusion). By effectiveness is meant the degree to which the determined environmental objectives are achieved through the use of certain instruments.[80]

The term 'optimal' is, therefore, a convenient shorthand to encapsulate our core goals in designing systems of regulation. However, to the extent practicable, we will also be mindful of the remaining two criteria, at least where they are likely to be of major significance. For example, in the circumstances of the chemical industry, we argue the case for greater community participation and oversight, on the basis that participative democracy (and, in terms of our criteria, political acceptability) will be crucial to the credibility, legitimacy, and success of a more flexible co-regulatory regime, while recognizing that this is at odds with economic efficiency.

As a result of our selection and prioritization, our study is not all encompassing: we do not purport to design a quantitative, interactive model of a regulatory system that integrates a wide range of assessment criteria. However, we do provide a framework with the ability to suggest useful generalizations—in Breyer's terms, 'generalisations that are broad enough to cover more than one regulatory programme but specific enough to impart useful knowledge',[81] and in so doing we hope, through the design of policy mixes, to make a significant contribution to the environmental policy debate.

---

[79] See, for example, B. Davy, *Essential Injustice: When legal instruments cannot resolve environmental and land use disputes* (1997), Verlag Springer, Vienna.

[80] H. Opschoor, H. & K. Turner, *Economic Incentives And Environmental Policies: Principles and practice* (1994), Kluwer Academic Publishers, Dordrecht, p.11.

[81] S. Breyer, *Regulation And Its reform* (1982), Harvard University Press, Cambridge.

Even when employing relatively narrow defined assessment criteria such as we have proposed, further thorny questions may arise concerning how one actually quantifies effectiveness and efficiency. In many circumstances, particularly when a policy is comparatively new or untried, no objective measures of success or failure will be available.[82] The use of various cost-benefit assumptions, including the time scales under which they operate, will inevitably be contentious. For example, those who take seriously issues of intergenerational equity are likely to take a very different view from those whose major concern is profit levels in the next five years. Depending upon where one sits on the environmental spectrum, one's views on effectiveness and efficiency will be coloured by different imperatives.

This is also a problem that is easier acknowledged than overcome. When discussing effectiveness and efficiency, we will be mindful of the contentious nature of these concepts and careful how we use them. In doing so, we are influenced by three meta-principles which are increasingly recognized both in international agreements and in national legislation: those of inter-generational equity; the precautionary principle; and the polluter pays principle.[83] We have also striven to take account of the opinions and beliefs of the major players involved—those who have most experience of the impact of particular instruments in particular regulatory settings. Although this does not provide an independent and objective measure of regulatory effectiveness or efficiency, it does both sensitize us to different perspectives, and teach us a great deal about the limitations and potential of different regulatory strategies. Such accounts may be particularly valuable when we have a paucity of independent evidence, as is all too frequently the case.

There is a further and serious difficulty associated with use of assessment criteria that is conveniently avoided by much of the existing literature. There will often be a tension between different criteria, which

---

[82] J. Mendeloff, 'Overcoming Barriers to Better Regulation' (1993) 18 *Law and Social Inquiry* 711 at 722–25.

[83] The concept of inter-generational equity is bound up in the concept of sustainability, defined by the World Commission on Environment and Development (the Brundtland Commission) as: 'development which meets the needs of the present without compromising the ability of future generations to meet their own needs.' The attraction of this definition is its vision of integrating environmental and economic goals. The precautionary principle states that a lack of scientific certainty about the level of environmental harm is not sufficient reason to avoid taking policy action to prevent that harm. The polluter pays principle requires the generator of pollutants to pay fully for the prevention of environmental damage from these pollutants (A. Gilpin, *An Australian Dictionary of Environment and Planning* (1990), Oxford University Press, Melbourne).

existing 'lists' do little to resolve. For example, it is not always possible to reconcile efficiency goals with other public values, such as equity and transparency. And yet, several commentators[84] assume that solutions can be arrived at which simultaneously achieve efficiency, effectiveness, *and* equity, while others ignore the problem entirely. Yet if such tensions cannot always be avoided (and the evidence suggests they cannot) then what principles do we use to make policy trade-offs between them? We face a normative dilemma, and must invoke value-judgments in allocating weightings to different criteria. Our own view is that the weightings of different criteria should vary with different environmental problems. For example, certainty and effectiveness will be more prominent in cases where irreversibility is at stake; transparency and consultation will be highlighted when local communities are put at risk; and efficiency and flexibility will be relatively more important when there are large differences in the capacities of firms to reduce pollution.

To an extent, we can extract ourselves from some of these complex normative dilemmas, by stepping back from the setting of policy goals and putting ourselves in the position of policy advisers. We would claim that, for whatever environmental policy goal a particular decision-maker wishes to achieve, with whatever weightings of different assessment criteria, we can advise how to go about the task of designing it for optimal results (as defined by the decision-maker). If we adopt this role, then we have no need to buy into arguments about, for example, the time frame within which efficiency or effectiveness should be measured, or even how to resolve the largest tension of all, between environmental protection and economic growth.

As to this last issue, for better or worse, the concept of 'sustainable development' has been adopted by governments as the most appropriate policy response. In essence, sustainable development refers to 'development that improves the total quality of life, both now and in the future, in a way that maintains the ecological processes on which life depends'.[85] The reduction of poverty itself is seen as a necessary pre-condition for improved environmental practices.[86]

[84] For example, S. Schmidheiny, *Changing Course: A global business perspective on development and the environment* (1992), MIT Press, Cambridge; and P. Winsemius & U. Gutram, 'Responding To The Environmental Challenge' (1992) *Business Horizons*, March–April 12.

[85] Ecologically Sustainable Development Steering Committee, *National Strategy for Ecologically Sustainable Development in Australia* (1992), AGPS, Canberra. See also President's Council on Sustainable Development, *Sustainable America: A new consensus* (1996), Washington DC.

[86] World Commission On Environment And Development, *Our Common Future* (1987), Oxford University Press, Oxford, UK.

The origin of the concept of sustainable development can be traced back to the United Nations Conference on the Human Environment, Stockholm, 1972, and the World Commission on Environment and Development, 1987, where the central importance of human economic well-being was recognized and entrenched in policy statements. More recently, at the 1992 United Nations Conference on Environment and Development (the 'Rio Earth Summit'), the principle of sustainable development was recognized in the Rio Declaration, and has subsequently been incorporated into several international environmental treaties and the political discourse and legislation of many national governments. The shift from unsustainable to sustainable growth patterns has been identified as probably the most complex policy agenda facing governments today.[87] It is a task that, if it is to be fulfilled, will require a major reorientation of economic, political and other institutional structures and processes.

In this book, while acknowledging the enormity of the task at hand, and the need to address the fundamental drivers of unsustainable development in a multi-faceted way, we maintain that environmental regulation (broadly defined) is and will remain an important part of the policy solution. At a practical level, the vast majority of governments in industrialized countries, and, increasingly, developing countries, will continue to depend on regulatory policy to achieve specific environmental objectives. The challenge we seek to address, therefore, is not to articulate the policies of sustainable development in a broad sense, but rather how best to design successful systems of environmental regulation once those superordinate goals have been established.

Finally, we refer throughout the book to 'optimal policy mixes', and we should clarify what we mean by this concept. We use the term 'optimal policy mix' as a convenient shorthand to signify our aspiration to design the best possible environmental policy (in terms of our core assessment criteria of effectiveness and efficiency), using a broader combination of instruments and actors.

However, we must state plainly that an optimal mix (measured against a particular weighting of social objectives, addressed to a particular environmental problem) is an ideal that may never be attained— not least because of the difficulties of identifying the effects of particular policies at the margin and in combination with each other[88] and

---

[87] S. Dovers, 'Information, Sustainability and Policy' (1995) 2(3) *Australian Journal of Environmental Management* 142.

[88] J. Mendeloff, 'Overcoming Barriers to Better Regulation' (1993) 18 *Law and Social Inquiry* 711 at 722.

because of the political obstacles identified by public choice theorists and others. In practice, it may well be that the best we can do is identify better, rather than best (optimal) strategies. If we do this, we should take care to identify the tensions between efficiency and effectiveness and the importance of any particular trade-off that could be accepted.

It is nevertheless worth striving for, and even when we fall short of fully achieving it, the framework presented will be important in evaluating the strengths and weaknesses of particular regulatory strategies; in suggesting which changes in regulatory policy are likely to be in the right direction, or which sorts of regulatory strategies work best for dealing with certain types of problems; and in identifying which ones are likely to be counterproductive. If, as a minimum, we provide an analysis and a framework which enables policymakers to design mixes which substantially improve the *status quo*, then this in itself will be a useful contribution. Given the underdeveloped nature of the debate about regulatory strategy, and the paucity of our currernt knowledge of effective and efficient regulatory design, what we undertake is still a significant step forward in public policy.

Methodology

Our subject matter is environmental regulatory design and policy mix as it has been, or might be applied, to advanced industrialized countries. It is in western democracies that environmental regulation is most developed, and the array of regulatory and quasi-regulatory institutions most active. The rest of the world will be able to learn from the innovations, the successes, and the failures, of the West. In examining the value of existing and embryonic policy instruments and mixes, and the role of a broader range of institutional actors, we draw on experience in the use of those approaches in North America, Western Europe and Australia. Given inevitable resource constraints, we have necessarily been selective in our approach.

Particular attention is given to the United States (whose regulatory system is at one extreme in terms of its legalistic and adversarial nature), to Australia (which is representative of a very different approach),[89] and to selective examples of innovation in regulation and environmental policy in some Western European countries and Canada, from which there is much to learn. For example, in the case of the chemical industry, the most important development of the last decade has been

[89] N. Gunningham, 'Negotiated Non-Compliance: a case study of regulatory failure' (1987) 9(1) *Law and Policy* 69.

Responsible Care, an advanced and sophisticated self-regulatory programme. Since this is still evolving, our focus is on the three counties
which first adopted it and which have made most progress with it:
Canada; the United States; and Australia. Also in the case of chemicals, the Dutch model, based on an industry sector approach, a national
environmental plan, and environmental covenants, provides particular
insights on innovative regulatory design, while the British approach to
integrated pollution control presents both an opportunity, but also a
particular challenge, to the chemicals sector.[90]

In studying biodiversity within the agricultural sector, our initial
focus is on Australia: the only developed country amongst the twelve
nations which are classified as 'megadiverse', and in part, for this reason, an innovator in seeking means to discharge its responsibilities
under international agreements for the protection of biodiversity. We
compare the Australian approach with that adopted in a number of other
developed countries, in seeking to draw broader lessons for the design
of optimal policy mixes.

In the central chapters of this book we adopt a sector-specific
approach rather than seeking to identify optimal mixes in the abstract.
This is because what works and what does not work is usually highly
dependent on the particular characteristics of the industry or environmental threat at issue. So complex and various are the causes of environmental degradation and the circumstances in which they arise that
no single instrument, and indeed no single mix of instruments, could
conceivably be successful in addressing all or even most of them. As a
result, generalizations are extremely hazardous. In short, the complexities of social, economic and ecological processes preclude simple
broad-brush solutions.[91] The only answer to the question: 'what is the
optimal combination of instruments and mechanisms?' is: 'it all
depends'. As one recent study put it: 'a priori rules are inferior to case-
by-case analysis'.[92]

For these reasons, research needs to address regulatory design at a
lower level of generality: to identify specific policy strategies in specific

[90] See K. Allott, *Integrated Pollution Control: The first three years* (1994), *Environmental Data Services*, London, UK, p.xiv.

[91] J. B. Opschoor, H. & K. Turner, 'Environmental Economics And Environmental Policy Instruments: introduction and overview' in J. B. Opschoor, & K. Turner, *Economic Incentives and Environmental Policies: Principles and practice* (1994), Kluwer Academic Publishers, Dordrecht.

[92] J. B. Opschoor, H. & K. Turner, *Economic Incentives and Environmental Policies: Principles and practice* (1994), Kluwer Academic Publishers, Dordrecht, p.35.

social, economic and institutional contexts. A sector-specific approach is one way (though not the only way) to do so. An equally legitimate approach would have been to take environmental threat(s) (for example, ozone depletion, sulphur dioxide emissions) rather than industry sectors as the focus of study, though within the confines of a single book it was not possible to do both.

There were strong reasons for preferring the first of these options to the second. Crucially, in redesigning environmental regulation, one does not start with a clean slate. There are already layers of existing environmental policy only very limited amounts of which are likely to be dismantled in the future. A sector-specific approach is likely to complement what already exists,[93] whereas a threat-specific approach is likely to confront the problem that existing regulations and policy interventions are commonly not threat-specific. The result is that options that, in the abstract, might be optimal, would (given existing policy distortions), in reality, produce seriously sub-optimal outcomes.

Certainly, we are able to derive lessons of much broader application from these sector-specific studies. They provide important 'testing grounds' enabling the development of policy prescriptions and design principles of general relevance. However, most of the latter will be principle or process-based rather than outcome oriented or concerned with general policy prescriptions, and we have no illusions of being able to identify single policy mix(es) of general application.

In arguing for redesigning regulation, and in particular, in arguing for the construction of broader policy mixes, we both seek to build on lessons from the past, and to design as yet untried approaches for the future. As to the former, (what works, what does not and why) we draw on the history of environmental regulation in a number of jurisdictions, as indicated above, and on our study of particular industry sectors. However, in examining innovative policy mechanisms it must be acknowledged, as the OECD has put it, that: 'little is known about their

---

[93] Moreover, environmental policy in a number of countries, including the United States and the Netherlands, is consciously moving further in a sector specific direction. See D. J. Fiorino, 'Towards a New System of Environmental Regulation: The case for an industry sector approach' (1996) 26(2) *Environmental Law* 457–489 describing the main initiatives of the US EPA from the mid 1990s (the Common Sense Initiative; the Sustainable Industry Project; Project XL; and the Environmental Leadership programme) as part of a broader shift to a sector specific approach. The Dutch have also moved to a sector specific approach under the National Environmental Plan. See M. Gambel, *US Environment Protection Agency, The Dutch Model: Lessons for the US* (1995), US EPA, Washington, DC.

effectiveness, efficiency, or administrative implications compared to traditional regulation, nor about how they can best be implemented'.[94]

As to the latter (what might work in the future), we face the difficulty that it is not possible formally to test our proposals against real world experience.[95] The empirical component of our research was conducted very much with this problem in mind. Every attempt was made, first to glean the experience of the main groups of industry participants as to what sorts of instrument and party combinations might be practicable, and second (at an advanced stage in our research) to anticipate problems with our draft recommendations.

In the case of the chemical industry, (where our principal focus was on Responsible Care and environmental management systems) we relied substantially on interviews with a broad cross section of industry participants. We spoke to corporate executives, industry group officials, regulatory executives, public interest group leaders, environmental auditors, environmental lawyers, financial institutions and members of the insurance industry. We sought to discover how each of these interests perceives the involvement of themselves and of other actors in the regulatory process and how those actors are seen to facilitate or inhibit attaining the goals of efficient and effective environmental policy. We were equally concerned to ascertain how, and in what circumstances, alternative regulatory instruments or combinations were seen as likely to make a contribution to the overall policy mix.

In the case of agriculture, we spoke to producers, industry representatives, regulatory officials, interest group members, as well as participants in the environmental services industry. In addition, we drew significantly from many informants contacted in the course of a related project on the use of incentives for biodiversity conservation in which we were engaged during the period 1994–5.[96]

The principal form of data collection was semi-structured interviews conducted by one or other of the principal investigators. These were conducted with a representative sample of the groups identified above.

---

[94] Alternatives to traditional regulation: a preliminary list in OECD, *Environmental Policy: how to apply economic instruments* (1991), OECD, Paris, p.4.

[95] This is one reason why we have a design principle concerning ongoing evaluation of new instruments and mixes. See chapter six.

[96] M. D. Young, N. Gunningham, J. Elix, J. Lambert, B. Howard, P. Grabosky & E. McCrone, *Reimbursing the Future: An evaluation of motivational, voluntary, price-based, property-right, and regulatory incentives for the conservation of biodiversity* Part 1 and Part 2 Appendices (1996), Department of the Environment, Sport and Territories, Biodiversity Unit, Biodiversity Series, Paper No.9, Canberra.

This sample was supplemented by strategically targeted interviews with other key actors identified on the basis of 'snowball' sampling. Snowballing enables the researcher to identify key players and to 'find the principles underlying the field in the minds and strategies of the people who operate in and around the borders of the field'.[97] In respect of access, much information is on the public record and there was a high response rate. Less than 10 per cent of prospective respondents declined to be interviewed, most commonly through unavailability rather than unwillingness. These interviews provided substantial qualitative data for analysis.[98]

Summing up

The less than satisfactory performance of both direct government regulation and market deregulation has forced a critical re-examination of current regulatory strategies. This, in turn, has led to considerable experimentation throughout the industrialized world, with alternative policy mechanisms such as economic instruments, self-regulation, and co-regulation, and a variety of information-based strategies.

This book offers a new approach: identifying optimal combinations of market and non-market policy instruments which effectively harness the different regulatory participants to meet the twin objectives of economic efficiency and environmental effectiveness. In particular, it establishes a regulatory design process which can guide policymakers in avoiding the excesses and inefficiencies of stand alone command and control regulation on the one hand and the pitfalls of deregulation on the other, while capitalizing on the virtues of each.

The book should be of particular interest to regulators and policymakers seeking to fulfil their mandate of achieving improved

---

[97] Y. Dezalay & B. G. Garth, *Dealing In Virtue: International commercial arbitration and the construction of a transnational legal order* (1996), University of Chicago Press, Chicago.

[98] Responsible Care and the environmental management systems approach are still evolving. Responsible Care is the older of these schemes, having been introduced in the late 1980s and largely developed during the 1990s. While substantial changes continue to be made to it, nevertheless Responsible Care has been in place long enough to lend itself to empirical study. In contrast, ISO 14001 was ratified in 1996 and, at the time of writing, was only in the early stages of implementation. Accordingly, detailed empirical work would be premature. As a consequence, about 3/4 of the 122 interviews we conducted on the chemical industry were concerned with Responsible Care. Our research on environmental management systems, reported in chapter 4, relied on some thirty exploratory interviews. These were conducted principally in the US and supplemented by a small number in Australia, the UK and Scandinavia. This was complemented by desktop research on ISO 14001, which sought to identify its major features; to expose its major flaws; and to specify its crucial characteristics as a potential regulatory tool.

environmental outcomes at an acceptable social and economic cost, and to construct policies which improve outcomes for both the environment and business. In addition to suggesting means of achieving optimal policy mixes (or at least getting closer to them) it will give policymakers an opportunity to explore a broader range of strategies before choosing a solution to a regulatory problem. In particular, it suggests ways to make more effective use of scarce regulatory resources; to develop more efficient regulatory strategies; to 'take the heat' off command and control regulation; to achieve cheaper, more cost-effective means of achieving environmental protection goals without imposing unreasonable costs on business; to treat differently serious violators and occasional non-compliers; to provide better assurances of compliance by regulated entities; and more efficiently use scarce government inspection and enforcement resources by recruiting a range of third parties. By indicating the advantages and limitations of various regulatory and policy options, it should also encourage rational and informed decision-making.

The book should be of equal interest both to business and to environmental and public interest groups. Not only does it provide better means of achieving their often differing social goals but it also holds out the promise of more constructive, creative dialogue and of achieving win-win outcomes than does the *status quo*.

It will also be important to regulatory theorists generally. The latter will find that the research has implications which extend to the range of similar mechanisms that exist in other areas of social regulation such as occupational health and safety, consumer protection, and companies and securities regulation.

2 Instruments For Environmental Protection

Neil Gunningham and Darren Sinclair, with contributions by Peter Grabosky

Introduction

Despite decades of experimentation, the holy grail of optimal environmental regulation has continued to elude policymakers and regulatory theorists. As we saw in chapter one, neither traditional command and control regulation nor the free market provide satisfactory answers to the increasingly complex and serious environmental problems which confront the world. This has led to a search for alternatives more capable of addressing the environmental challenge, and, in particular, to the exploration of a broader range of policy tools such as economic instruments,[1] self-regulation, and information-based strategies.

In this chapter, we review the main categories of environmental instruments, both old and new. We do so not only to provide an overview of the main policy alternatives and to summarize the 'state of the art' in environmental policy making (though this in itself may be valuable for those who are not closely acquainted with the area), but also in order to demonstrate the substantial shortcomings of all current approaches and to argue a case for regulatory redesign.

Specifically, we will demonstrate that, while each of the main categories of instruments has something valuable to offer, it has substantial limitations as a 'stand alone' strategy. Further, we suggest that there are only a restricted range of circumstances in which each category of instrument is likely to work well: no single instrument type works 'across the board'. The success of instruments also depends substantially upon the interests and opportunities of key players and their relationships. To develop these arguments, we identify the main characteristics of each category of policy instrument, and of individual instruments within that category, and their corresponding strengths, weaknesses, and limitations.

Such an account is also a necessary precursor to chapter three, where we will show that both the success of environmental policy generally,

---

[1] Instruments are the tools employed by institutions to do what they wish to do.

and the effectiveness of different instruments or combinations of instruments, can be increased by the recruitment of a much larger range of social actors and by utilizing those actors in a wider range of roles than has so far been the case. In particular, we will demonstrate the considerable contribution that both commercial and non-commercial third parties might make in influencing the environmental performance of regulatees directly and in achieving efficient and effective regulation. Business too may make an important contribution, not just as regulatee, but also as regulator of itself and others.

Varieties of regulatory instruments

There are a range of possible ways of cataloguing the various instruments available for use in environmental policy. We have organized the following account to conform to a fairly standard breakdown of the different categories: command and control regulation; self-regulation; voluntarism; educational and information strategies; economic instruments; and free market environmentalism. This categorization is not intended to be exhaustive; it merely provides a relatively comprehensive summary of the range of environmental policy instruments available. We also acknowledge that the taxonomic distinctions are somewhat artificial. In reality, there is significant overlap between instruments; similar instruments, particularly those involving education and information, are at the disposal of governmental, public interest, and commercial institutions alike. Consequently, it is better to think of the following policy instrument categories as points on a compass, rather than discrete or absolute policy units.

1. Command and control regulation

Since the early 1970s, governments throughout the industrialized world have responded to the rise of environmental degradation and industrial pollution with a myriad of environmental policies. The dominant government response, however (particularly to 'brown' issues such as pollution[2]), has been the application of 'direct' or 'command and control' regulation designed to prohibit or restrict environmentally harmful activities.[3]

---

[2] As we will see in chapter 5, with some issues involving the rural sector, such as aspects of biodiversity, this approach has been less pronounced.

[3] R. Kagan, 'Regulatory Enforcement' in D. Rosenbloom & R. Schwartz (eds.), *Handbook of Regulation and Administrative Law* (1994), Dekker, New York.

Command and control regulation is generally characterized by an environmental target, for example a limit on emissions of a pollutant to water or the air, and subsequent penalties that apply if this target is not met. In the United States, in particular, command and control regulation has tended to rely on the application of 'best available technology' (BAT) or similar technology-based standards.[4] This entails the regulator determining the environmental target or standard on the basis of what is technically feasible at a particular point in time, in a particular industry sector, and in a particular industrial application.[5] A common feature has been the compartmentalization of different media, such as land, air and water, and different industries and natural resource uses, into separate regulations. Only in the 1990s, and only in some jurisdictions, have more integrated approaches become common.

The term 'command and control' has crept into the language of policymakers (in the main replacing the traditional term, 'direct regulation') largely through the writings of neo-classical economists, who used it to encapsulate what they regarded as the negative aspects of direct government intervention compared to the virtues of market mechanisms. In part because the debate concerning market versus government instruments has taken place largely in the United States, it has been possible to treat command and control as almost synonymous with the prevalent form of regulation in that jurisdiction; technology-based standards. This is unfortunate since not all forms of direct regulation are subject to the criticisms that can be levelled at technology-standards.[6] Nevertheless, the term 'command and control' is now almost universally used rather than direct regulation and, with this note of caution, will be adopted in this section and elsewhere in this book.

Not surprisingly, given the breadth of environmental issues it covers, command and control regulation takes a variety of forms, the most common of which is environmental standards.[7]

---

[4] A. S. Miller, 'The Origins and Current Directions of United States Environmental Law and Policy: an overview' in B. Boer, R. Fowler, & N. Gunningham (eds.), *Environmental Outlook: Law and policy* (1994), Federation Press, Sydney.

[5] Although specific technological requirements do not necessarily impede innovation or lock firms into using a particular technology, in practice they often have this effect: permit writers tend to be conservative and are unwilling to authorize new technologies or processes, so agency guidance becomes *de facto* requirement and technological lock-in occurs.

[6] For example, performance based standards focus on outcomes and are not restrictive or rigid in the same way as technology standards can be.

[7] Other specific forms of regulation include: *land use controls* which involve dividing a geographic area into different zones, within which only certain types of activity are

Standards involve the establishment of uniform requirements on broad categories of activities to achieve specific environmental goals. These include: ambient standards; technology-based performance standards; design or specification standards; environment management standards; and product standards. Of these, the major categories are technology-based standards, performance-based standards, and process-based standards.

The various types of standards have fundamentally different *modus operandi*. For example, design or specification standards prescribe an approved technology for a particular industrial process or environmental problem.[8] Such a standard 'is defined in terms of the specific types of safeguarding methods one must use in specific situations and . . . places great emphasis on the design and construction of these safeguards'.[9] In contrast, performance standards define a firm's duty in terms of the problems it must solve or the goals it must achieve. That is, performance standards are outcome-focused and avoid overt prescriptions. Process-based standards address *procedures and parameters* for achieving a desired result, in particular, the processes to be followed in managing nominated hazards.[10] They are most used in respect of haz-

---

permitted. Issues such as land use, the size of buildings, lot sizes, the clearing of vegetation, and population density may be addressed by prescriptive or performance based standards; *environmental impact assessment*, a critical appraisal of the likely effects of a proposed project or activity on the environment. Such assessments are usually carried out by the proponents at the behest of a regulatory authority as a necessary prerequisite for project approval. As such, they fulfil a gatekeeping function and, for this reason, should, arguably, be classified separately. Assessments may take into account: impact on communities; environmental impact on ecosystems of the locality; and diminution of the aesthetic, recreational, scientific, or other environmental quality or value of a locality; and *water use controls* which apply to the exploitation of natural resources or recreational activities, such as fishing and power boating. These controls are, commonly, subsumed within wider management plans for water catchment areas, coastal zones, national parks, and recreational areas (J. Bernstein, *Alternative Approaches to Pollution Control and Waste Management—Regulatory and Economic Instruments* (1993), The World Bank, Washington DC).

[8] In some versions, the regulatee is notionally given considerable discretion to select the most appropriate technology to their circumstances, but in practice, those who depart from the one approved technology run a considerable 'regulatory risk' that the regulatory authority will not deem their choice of technology as complying with the statutory requirement. See J. Atcheson, 'Can We Trust Verification?' (1996) July/Aug *Environmental Forum* 16 at 17.

[9] P. W. McAvoy, *OSHA. Safety Regulation: Report of the Presidential Task Force* (1977), American Enterprise Institute, Washington DC.

[10] See, for example, J. Potter, 'Chemical Accident Prevention Regulation in California and New Jersey' (1993) 20 *Ecology Law Quarterly* 755–815.

ards that do not lend themselves to easy measurement, such as safe working practices, or Environmental Management Systems.[11]

Permits and licenses are often used to implement standards. They tend to be targeted at point sources of pollution. Permits and licenses allow firms to continue to emit pollutants, but generally at levels proscribed in the relevant standards. A permit or license may cover a single point of discharge or an entire industrial facility.

Arguably, *environmental covenants*, which are binding contracts between an industry and government, should also be classified as a form of command and control, at least if they are enforced through the permit mechanism, are implemented within the framework of current environmental laws and are accompanied by an implicit threat of less attractive alternatives if they are not agreed to. We treat the Dutch version (which can be enforced in this way) as an innovative version of command and control. However, the diversity of such agreements makes classification difficult, and other versions may be better classified as 'voluntary agreements'.

Strengths and weaknesses of command and control

The major strength of command and control regulation is its dependability (provided there is adequate monitoring and enforcement).[12] By this, we mean that the behaviour expected of regulatees can be specified with considerable clarity (for example, through the provision of national minimum standards),[13] making it relatively straightforward to identify breaches of the legal standard and to enforce the law.[14] This provides regulators with defined operational parameters and, in turn, firms themselves have a clearer understanding of their regulatory obligations.

---

[11] Industry Commission, *Work, Health & Safety: Inquiry into occupational health and safety* (1995), Volume I. Report No 47, AGPS, Canberra, p.38; and N. Gunningham 'From Compliance to Best Practice in OHS: The role of specification, performance and systems based standards' (1996) 9(3) *Australian Journal of Labour Law* 221–246.

[12] For a comprehensive defence of command and control, see H. Latin, 'Ideal versus Real Regulatory Efficiency: Implementation of uniform standards and "fine tuning reforms" ' (1985) 37 *Stanford Law Review* 1267–332.

[13] The regulator can consider actual technologies, or those that will shortly be introduced, making both information gathering and the standard itself relatively easy to implement. Enforcement is also relatively easy, involving ascertaining whether the prescribed control technology is operating appropriately.

[14] O. McGarity, 'Four Dimensions of Health and Environmental Regulation' (undated), an unpublished paper, *University of Texas Law School*, points out that command regulation is easy to articulate, predictable in impact (the enforcement agency can often know precisely how the regulatee will react), and easy of enforcement (because the agency can structure commands so that it knows exactly how to enforce them).

When coupled with strong community support, command and control regulation has been relatively successful in curbing aspects of point-source pollution,[15] outlawing extremely hazardous substances and the dumping of toxic wastes, and the protection of endangered species.[16] It also sends important moral signals, emphasising that 'tolerance of a polluting activity is a concession, whereas other mechanisms may lead to it being viewed as a right'.[17]

Although the rigidity of command and control regulation, particularly when embodied in uniform technology-based standards, has been criticized for being economically inefficient, Latin argues that there are several advantages to this approach over more particularized and flexible instruments.[18] For example, he cites:

> . . . decreased information collection and evaluation costs, greater consistency and predictability of results, greater accessibility of decisions to public scrutiny and participation, increased likelihood that regulations will withstand judicial review, reduced opportunities for manipulative behaviour by agencies in response to political or bureaucratic pressures, reduced opportunities for obstructive behaviour by regulated parties, and decreased likelihood of social dislocation and "forum shopping" resulting from competitive disadvantages between geographical regions or between firms in regulated industries.[19]

However, command and control is likely to be more successful in some circumstances than in others. The clear, precise standards that command and control can embody, can best be enforced against firms

---

[15] There have been impressive reductions in some airborne pollutants, such as lead concentrations and emissions of ozone depleting substances; and similar successes in water quality have, in many cases, dramatically improved the condition of national rivers (C. Sunstein, 'Paradoxes of the Regulatory State' (1990) 57 *University of Chicago Law Review* 407–41; A. W. Reitze, (1991) 'A Century of Pollution Control Law: What worked; what's failed; what might work' 21 *Environmental Law* 1549–1646; A. L. Alm, 'A. Need For new Approaches: Command-and-control is no longer a cure-all' (1992) *EPA Journal* 18 May/June 6–11; and W. E. Orts 'Reflexive Environmental Law' (1995) 89 *Northwestern University Law Review* 1227.

[16] C. Perrings & D. Pearce, 'Threshold Effects and Incentives for the Conservation of Biodiversity' (1994) 4 *Environmental and Resource Economics* 13–28. For example, endangered species legislation has saved a number of species from extinction (C. Sunstein, 'Paradoxes of the Regulatory State' (1990) 57 *University of Chicago Law Review* 407–41).

[17] Bureau of Industry Economics, *Environmental Regulation: The Economics of Tradeable Permits—A survey of theory and practice*, Research Report 42, (1992), AGPS, Canberra.

[18] H. Latin, 'Ideal versus Real Regulatory Efficiency: Implementation of uniform standards and "fine tuning reforms" ' (1985) 37 *Stanford Law Review* 1267–332.

[19] H. Latin, 'Ideal versus Real Regulatory Efficiency: Implementation of uniform standards and "fine tuning reforms" ' (1985) 37 *Stanford Law Review* 1267–332 at 1271.

which are readily identifiable and accessible.[20] For example, regulators enforcing a United States Federal law requiring limited erosion and site remediation at strip mines were far more successful when dealing with larger firms,[21] which were easier to identify, visit, and keep tabs on than a multitude of more transient smaller firms. Similarly, firms which have in-house environmental expertise and are concerned with their corporate image are also suited to command and control, and are more likely to adopt a cooperative approach to regulatory compliance.[22] Braithwaite and Fisse point out that corporate environmental officers may be powerful advocates for environmental standards as they are often supportive of the regulatory regime which provides a *raison d'être* for their employment.[23]

By and large, command and control has been most effective in reducing pollution from single media, point sources.[24] For example, the United States Clean Water Act of 1972 successfully created effluent discharge standards for all new and existing point source discharges. In doing so, it employed a permit system to ensure compliance with these standards. As a result, water quality visibly improved throughout the country.

Contrary to expectations, and prevailing wisdom, Porter argues that stringent business regulations can inspire technological innovation in furtherance of regulatory compliance, and thus enhance international competitiveness.[25] In Germany, for example, tough command and control regulations have been credited with not only improving the productivity of existing firms through technological and managerial improvements, but also the creation of entire new pollution control industries. These firms are in a competitive position to export their products and services as other countries catch up to Germany's high environmental standards.

---

[20] Kagan refers to the difference between regulating 'elephants' and 'foxes': it is harder for elephants to hide (R. Kagan, 'Regulatory Enforcement' in D. Rosenbloom & R. Schwartz (eds.), *Handbook of Regulation and Administrative Law* (1994), Dekker, New York.

[21] N. Shover, D. A. Clelland & J. Lynxwiler, *Enforcement or Negotiation: Constructing a regulatory bureaucracy* (1986), State University of New York Press, Albany, New York.

[22] P. Grabosky & J. Braithwaite, *Of Manners Gentle: Enforcement strategies of Australian business regulatory agencies* (1986), Oxford University Press, Melbourne.

[23] J. Braithwaite & B. Fisse, 'Self Regulation and the Costs of Corporate Crime' in C. D. Shearing & P. C. Stenning, *Private Policing* (1987), Sage Publications, Beverley Hills, USA.

[24] A. L. Alm, 'A Need For new Approaches: Command-and-control is no longer a cure-all'(1992) *EPA Journal* 18 May/June 6–11.

[25] M. Porter, *The Competitive Advantage of Nations* (1990), Macmillan Press, London.

A discussion of the strengths of command and control regulation inadvertently reveals its corresponding weaknesses (at least in its traditional forms).[26] It is not as effective in dealing with transitory, mobile, and/or remote firms which are difficult to identify and keep track of; diffuse, non-point sources of pollution; the transference of pollution from one medium to another; and rapidly changing technologies and economic circumstances. Unfortunately, many of the most pressing environmental problems fall into one of these categories. There is a long list of largely unresolved environmental problems where command and control has achieved only very modest results. These include deforestation, desertification, agricultural run-off, and urban air pollution.[27] To these are added new and complex problems, in particular, global climate change and the increasingly rapid loss of biological diversity.

A number of serious weaknesses of command and control have contributed to its limited effectiveness. One of the most common criticisms is that it *requires regulators to have comprehensive and accurate knowledge of the workings and capacity of industry*. For example, in establishing BAT standards, regulators are often required to engage in lengthy and intricate information gathering exercises to determine appropriate pollution reduction targets. Apart from the inevitable drain on public resources this inevitably entails, there is a clear imbalance of knowledge between regulators and industry. Even assuming that regulators do get it right, they can only ever provide transitory solutions as populations, technology, and economic activity change and grow, and indeed, new environmental problems arise.[28]

Although certainly not exclusive or inherent to command and control regulation, the use of uniform standards has attracted considerable criticism from economists in particular. This is because firms and industries will invariably differ in the cost of reducing polluting emissions.[29] Uniform standards prevent firms from tailoring their responses, even though some may be able to reduce pollution at much lower costs. The net effect is an increase in the overall cost of regulation.

[26] The means whereby recent innovations seek to overcome these weaknesses is addressed at pp. 47–50 below.

[27] A. L. Alm, 'A Need For new Approaches: Command-and-control is no longer a cure-all'(1992) *EPA Journal* 18 May/June 6–11.

[28] *Ibid*.

[29] R. Hahn, & R. Stavins, 'Incentive-Based Environmental Regulation: A new era from an old idea?' (1991) 18(1) *Ecology Law Quarterly* 1–42; and R. Stewart, (1992) 'Models for Environmental Regulation: Central planning versus market-based approaches' *Boston College Environmental Affairs Law Review* 547–62.

An additional problem, at least of some forms of command and control, *is the absence of incentives* for firms to go beyond minimum standards (especially once a firm has already invested in pollution control technology that meets the required standard).[30] The result is that the onus is always on government to apply stricter standards, a sometimes difficult political process which assumes that governments have detailed knowledge of the most appropriate standards for different industries. A closely related problem is the failure to institute favourable modifications to corporate culture, certainly as it is currently applied.[31] The inability to encourage firms to go 'beyond compliance', through a process of continuous improvement and cultural change, is one of the most serious failings of command and control in its traditional forms.[32]

Another criticism of command and control, given resources constraints, is the cost and difficulty of enforcement. This is critical as it may negatively impact on its purported dependability. Although some authorities may be committed to enforcement, most regulatory regimes have insufficient resources to monitor compliance with any degree of adequacy. As such, they fail to pose a credible deterrent threat. Even when such a threat may be credible, however (as in the United States), the application of traditional regulatory enforcement instruments runs the risk of eliciting defiance and resistance. In their work on nursing home regulation, Makkai and Braithwaite have found just such an effect, where in some contexts a deterrent regulatory posture actually *reduced* compliance.[33] In a very different setting, Terry Anderson has used the expression 'shoot, shovel, and shut up' to describe the response of some western ranchers in the United States to Federal endangered species legislation.[34]

Resistance to what is perceived to be the heavy hand of regulation may be a very rational response where regulations impede efficiency

---

[30] C. Sunstein, 'Paradoxes of the Regulatory State' (1990) 57 *University of Chicago Law Review* 407–41.

[31] W. E. Orts, 'Reflexive Environmental Law' (1995) 89 *Northwestern University Law Review* 1227.

[32] However, contrast the innovation inhibiting effect of technology based standards in the US (see note above) with the operation of such standards in Germany, where the law requires Best Available Technologies (BATs) in such a way as to give incentives to companies to implement innovative and cutting edge environmental technologies (S. Breyer, *Breaking the Vicious Circle: Toward effective risk regulation* (1993), Harvard University Press, Cambridge; and J. Bernstein, *Alternative Approaches to Pollution Control and Waste Management—Regulatory and Economic Instruments* (1993), The World Bank, Washington DC).

[33] J. Braithwaite & T. Makkai, 'Trust and Compliance' (1994) 4 *Policing and Society* 1.

[34] T. Anderson, 'At Home on the Range with the Wolves: Making a Liability into an Asset' (1995) 2 (June) Ecoworld.com.

and competitiveness.[35] When mutual mistrust between government and industry degenerates into adversarial legal combat, efficiency and effectiveness are in even greater jeopardy. In the more litigious jurisdictions, such as the United States, legal challenges to regulatory actions can be a significant drain on the resources of regulator *and* regulatee.[36]

Command and control regulation is also vulnerable to political manipulation. There are many recent instances where some aspect of regulatory policy has been 'hijacked' to serve the interests of individuals or groups with political weight at the expense of good environmental policy.[37] Similarly, regulators themselves may succumb to self-interested behaviour, variously being captured by the very industries they purport to regulate or engaging in 'rent-seeking', whereby the regulatory bureaucracy seeks to extend its own interests at the expense of the public.[38]

Finally, command and control may lead to increasing administrative complexity and a proliferation of law. The sheer volume of environmental statutes and associated regulations in industrialized countries makes it difficult for regulators and industry alike to keep up all their obligations. Industry is subject to a complex web of legislation, agency rules, permit procedures, judicial decisions, and other enforceable policies.[39] This can result in a counterproductive regulatory overload.[40] New entrants into an industry may be discouraged by lengthy regulatory and legal approval proceedings associated with command and control.[41]

In the face of these imperatives, there is a growing consensus that traditional forms of command and control regulation have serious and,

[35] More than one scholar has built a reputation on the identification of regulations which appear senseless, or, if they make any sense at all, are less sensible than a variety of alternatives otherwise available.

[36] J. A. Sigler & J. E. Murphy, *Interactive Corporate Compliance: An alternative to regulatory compulsion* (1989), Quorom Books, New York.

[37] R. Leone, *Who Profits? Winners, Losers and Government Regulation* (1986), Basic Books, New York; and B. A. Ackerman & W. T. Hassler, *Clean Coal/Dirty Air or How the Clean Air Act became a Multibillion-Dollar Bail-Out for High-Sulfur Coal Producers and What Should Be Done About It* (1981), Yale University Press, New Haven.

[38] See, for example, C. Sunstein, 'Constitutionalism after the New Deal' (1987) 101 *Harvard Law Review* 448–451 at 421.

[39] R. A. Harris & S. M. Milkis, *The Politics of Regulatory Change: A tale of two agencies* (1989), Oxford University Press, New York.

[40] See National Law Journal (USA), 1993 Corporate Counsel Survey, Aug 30, 1993 at s1.

[41] B. A. Ackerman, & R. B. Steward, 'Reforming Environmental Law' (1985) 37 *Stanford Law Review* 1333 at 1364.

in some cases, intractable problems and, confronted with new challenges they are ill equipped to meet, have reached the limit of their effectiveness in arresting environmental degradation.[42]

Innovative developments in command and control

Recognizing the substantial limitations of command and control regulation, in its traditional forms, a number of innovative approaches have been developed in recent years. A milestone in this respect was a joint enterprise in the United States between Amoco Corporation and the EPA, known as the Yorktown Project. This project began by documenting the numerous ways in which the conventional system of regulation neither encourages nor rewards innovation. It went on to show that site specific flexibility to achieve environmental objectives fosters innovation and leads to more cost-effective solutions, in a manner which far surpassed the 'one-fits-all' approach. In particular, a key conclusion of the Project was that the objectives of environmental regulations can be achieved more cost-effectively if the regulated community is allowed to devise individualized plant-specific compliance plans. For example, the participants in the Project unanimously selected the most effective pollution prevention options for a particular facility, that solution often being far removed from what the existing regulations prescribed. The project team concluded that 'by prioritising projects in this manner, equivalent release reductions could have been achieved . . . at 25% of the cost'.[43]

Also significant are a number of responses to the Clinton administration's Reinventing Environmental Law initiative.[44] For example, under Project XL, a project designed to reward companies that 'have developed creative, common sense ways of achieving superior environmental performance at their facilities',[45] an enterprise can propose

---

[42] D. J. Fiorino, 'Towards a New System of Environmental Regulation: The case for an industry sector approach' (1996) 26(2) *Environmental Law* 457–489; A. Moran, 'Tools of Environmental Policy: Market instruments versus command and control' in R. Eckersley (ed.), *Markets, the State and the Environment* (1995), Macmillan Press, Melbourne, pp.73–85; and W. E. Orts, 'Reflexive Environmental Law' (1995) 89 *Northwestern University Law Review* 1227.

[43] B. J. Raffle & D. Mitchell, *Effective Environmental Strategies: Opportunities for innovation and flexibility under Federal environmental laws* (1993), Executive Summary, Amoco, Chicago, p1.

[44] W. J. Clinton & A. Gore Jr., *Reinventing Environmental Regulation* (1995), the White House Washington DC.

[45] W. J. Clinton & A. Gore Jr., *Reinventing Environmental Regulation* (1995), the White House Washington DC, p.36.

alternative environmental strategies 'where the company can demonstrate that such strategies will achieve better environmental results than expected to be achieved under existing law'.[46] A second initiative, from within the EPA itself, the Sustainable Industry Project, has the objective 'to develop policies that foster the permanent integration of environmental protection functions into the basic profit-oriented activities of industrial firms'.[47] A third, the Environmental Leadership Program, seeks to use greater information to empower citizens and communities, and focuses on the role of compliance management systems in regulation.

Another important innovation is facility-wide permitting, which, in its 'ideal type', incorporates two elements. First, pollution prevention requirements are outlined in the facility's Pollution Prevention Plan, including an implementation schedule for the identified source reductions, implemented at the facility's discretion. Secondly, permitted emission/discharge limits are set, which ensure compliance with existing single media regulations and eliminate cross-media transfers. The virtue of facility-wide permitting is to enable a facility to focus its resources on achieving the pollution reduction goal rather than undergo the cumbersome process of obtaining several different permits. Because the emphasis is on pollution prevention, the single permit may create incentives for technology innovation.[48]

The Victorian EPA in Australia, under its 'accredited licensing' scheme, has also applied a variation of facility-wide permitting which rewards 'good performers' by relieving them of much of the regulatory burden that would normally apply, such as works approvals and multiple licenses across different sites.[49] To participate, firms must have a commendable environmental record and are expected to have prepared an environmental improvement plan, to conduct periodic environmental audits and to implement an environmental management system. The aim is to provide an incentive for firms to go beyond mere compliance with existing regulations.

[46] W. J. Clinton & A. Gore Jr., *Reinventing Environmental Regulation* (1995), the White House Washington DC, p.36.

[47] US Environmental Protection Agency, *Sustainable Industry: Promoting strategic environmental protection in the industrial sector: Phase 1 Report* (1994), US EPA, Washington DC, p.1.

[48] S. Schuler 'New Jersey's Pollution Prevention Act of 1991: A. regulation that even the regulated can enjoy' (1992) 16 *Seton Hall Legislative Journal* 814–832.

[49] A. T. Iles, 'Adaptive Management: Making environmental law and policy more dynamic, experimentalist and learning' (1996) 13(4) *Environmental and Planning Law Journal* 288–309 at 299.

The Dutch have taken the concept a step further by negotiating pollution reduction targets for specific industry sectors that last well into the next century.[50] These targets go beyond what is currently practised with conventional command and control regulation. Firms negotiate with the government individual agreements, or 'covenants', which incorporate comprehensive management plans and fit within the overall sector target.[51] They are then granted permits accordingly. The benefit to industry is the assurance of long-term regulatory stability, which is crucial for optimal business investment planning.

There is also evidence of a shift, across a range of OECD countries, from *ex ante* to *ex post* controls, and to rewarding good behaviour.[52] In the United Kingdom, the concept of integrated pollution control based on a requirement to use the 'best practicable environmental option' heralds a shift from end-of-pipe approaches towards cleaner production, coupled with greater transparency and public accountability.[53] More recently, the European Union Directive on Integrated Pollution Prevention and Control[54] espouses a very similar holistic approach to pollution control at European level. A further trend, most developed in some European Union directives, is towards process or systems-based regulation, which commonly involves a requirement that hazards must be managed by incorporating three fundamental steps: hazard assessment, risk assessment, and risk control.[55]

Despite their potential, the jury is still out on many of these recent innovations. Concerns are expressed about the principal focus on large firms, upon the intensity of the administrative and resource burden the new initiatives entail, and upon the risks of regulatory capture which is implicit in regulatory flexibility. In the case of the Dutch covenants,

---

[50] R. Gerits & J. Hinssen, 'Environmental Covenant for the Oil and Gas Producing Industry: A. valuable policy instrument?' (1994) 24(6) *Environment Policy and Law* 323.

[51] Netherlands National Environment Policy Plan 2 (1995); J. M. Van Dunne, *Environmental Contracts and Covenants: New instruments for a realistic environmental policy?* (1993), Koninklijke, Vermande.

[52] Organisation for Economic Co-operation and Development (OECD), *Meeting on Alternatives to Traditional Regulation* (1994), May, OECD, Paris.

[53] However, this approach confronted many serious obstacles and was far from successful, at least in its early years. See K. Allott, *Integrated Pollution Control: The first three years* (1994), Environmental Data Services, London, UK.

[54] Council Directive 96/61/EC. This Directive proposed to minimize or eliminate polluting emissions to all media by establishing a unified permitting system in each Member State which complies with a general framework of principles.

[55] This approach is most developed in the related area of occupational health and safety. See N. Gunningham, 'From Compliance to Best Practice in OHS' (1996) 9(3) *Australian Journal of Labour Law* 221–246.

there is also a danger that pushing out targets too far into the future will result in a serious miscalculation of changes in technology and other factors. It will be some time before we know whether, and if so, to what extent, the benefits of the various initiatives outweigh the costs and whether they will, indeed, overcome many of the problems of traditional forms of regulation.

2. Self-regulation

Self-regulation is an important, yet often unacknowledged, component of many regulatory regimes. In both the United States and Europe, self-regulation is prevalent in many areas of social regulation,[56] and this is equally the case in other advanced economies.[57] If anything, self-regulation is likely to play an even more important role in the future, either as an alternative, or as a complement, to direct government regulation. This is because:

(i) the broader problem of regulatory overload makes the continuing use of highly detailed prescriptive regulation problematic, and quite probably counterproductive; and

(ii) shrinking tax bases, an ideological swing against government intervention, and the resistance of multinational companies operating in global markets, all make direct regulation both politically and economically unattractive.

Self-regulation is not a precise concept but, for present purposes, it may be defined as a process whereby an organized group regulates the behaviour of its members.[58] Most commonly, it involves an industry-level organization (as opposed to the government or individual firms) setting rules and standards (codes of practice) relating to the conduct of firms in the industry. One can further categorize industry self-regulation in terms of the degree of government involvement (for as we shall

---

[56] E. Bardach & R. Kagan, *Going by the Book: The problem of regulatory unreasonableness* (1982); Washington and Lee Law Review, 'Regulation Symposium' (1988), 45 *Washington and Lee Law Review* 1245–1390; and G. Teubner, L. Farmer & D. Murphy (eds.), *Environmental Law and Ecological Responsibility* (1994), Wiley, UK.

[57] For example, in Australia, there are at least 500 self-regulatory arrangements administered by industry and professional associations, in areas as diverse as service and advertising standards; information disclosure and customer complaint handling; professional standards; and stock exchange and futures market controls (Trade Practices Commission (TPC) (Australia), *Self-regulation in Australian Industry and the Professions* (1988), AGPS, Canberra).

[58] Organization for Economic Co-operation and Development (OECD), *Meeting on Alternatives to Traditional Regulation* (1994) May, OECD, Paris, p.7.

see, 'pure' self-regulation, without any form of external intervention, is uncommon). Rees, for example, suggests that industry self-regulation might take one of three forms.[59] First, voluntary, or total self-regulation involves an industry or profession establishing codes of practice, enforcement mechanisms, and other mechanisms for regulating itself, entirely independent of government. Secondly, mandated self-regulation involves direct involvement by the state whereby it requires business to establish controls over its own behaviour, but leaves the details and enforcement to business itself, subject to state approval and/or oversight. Finally, mandatory partial self-regulation involves business itself being responsible for *some* of the rules and their enforce-ment but with the over-riding regulatory specifications, though not the details, being mandated by the state.

There is a growing number of increasingly sophisticated self-regulatory schemes in the sphere of environmental protection. Well documented examples include the chemical industry's Responsible Care programme, which applies in over forty countries;[60] safety-regulation of nuclear power plants by the Institute of Nuclear Power Producers (INPO) in the United States;[61] the Brazilian Extractive Reserves system, under which community associations are granted exclusive use of certain lands in order to encourage and facilitate their sustainable use;[62] and the Canadian forest industry's Sustainable Forest Management Certification System.[63] There are also considerably sophisticated self-regulatory programmes in less developed countries.[64]

---

[59] J. V. Rees, *Reforming the Workplace: A. study of self-regulation in occupational health and safety* (1988), University of Pennsylvania Press, US, p.9.

[60] This is explored more fully in chapter 4 below.

[61] J. V. Rees, *Hostages of Each Other: The transformation of nuclear safety since Three Mile Island* (1994), University of Chicago Press, Chicago, US. INPO is a private regulatory bureau-cracy with about 400 employees who develop standards, conduct inspections, and inves-tigate accidents. With an annual budget of nearly US$54 million, INPO has achieved significant improvements in safety and environmental performance within the industry.

[62] A utilization plan is prepared by each association and approved by a government agency. Enforcement of the plan is largely the responsibility of the association. See fur-ther Environmental Law Institute (ELI), *Brazil's Extractive Reserves* (1995), Environmental Law Institute, Washington DC, Ch V. At the time of writing it is too early to assess the success of this scheme.

[63] This code of practice was devised in response to European boycott initiatives and premised on industry awareness that national and international market forces demand independent, reliable certification systems. See further, G. T. Rhone, *Canadian Standards Association Sustainable Forest Management Certification System* (1996), Industry Canada, Ottawa, Canada.

[64] For example, in Alanya, Turkey, overfishing has been very effectively prevented by the introduction of an innovative self-regulatory scheme devised by the locals themselves,

Strengths and weaknesses of self-regulation

In principle, self-regulation offers greater speed, flexibility, sensitivity to market circumstances, efficiency, and less government intervention than command and control regulation. Because standard setting and identification of breaches are the responsibility of practitioners, with detailed knowledge of the industry, this will, arguably, lead to more practicable standards, more effectively policed. There is also the potential for utilizing peer pressure and for successfully internalizing responsibility for compliance. Moreover, because self-regulation contemplates ethical standards of conduct which extend beyond the letter of the law, it may significantly raise standards of behaviour and lead to a greater integration of environmental issues into the management process.[65] It may be regarded as a form of 'responsive regulation':[66] regulation which responds to the particular circumstances of the industry in question, including how effective an industry has been in the past in making private regulation work.

Yet, in practice, self-regulation often fails to fulfil its theoretical promise and commonly serves the industry rather than the public interest. Indeed, self-regulation has an extremely tarnished image, and is often reviled by conservationists, consumer organizations and other public interest groups for being a charade—a cynical attempt by self-interested parties to give the appearance of regulation (thereby warding off more direct and effective government intervention) while serving private interests at the expense of the public.[67] As John Braithwaite has put it:

which allocates fishing rights in particular locations on a rotational basis. According to Elinor Ostrom, 'all fishing boats have an equal chance to fish at the best spots. Resources are not wasted searching for or fighting over a site. No signs of overcapitalisation are apparent' (E. Ostrom, *Governing the Commons: The evolution of institutions for collective action* (1990), Cambridge University Press, Cambridge, p.19. See also F. Berkes, 'Marine Inshore Management in Turkey' in National Research Council, *Proceedings of the Conference on Common Property Resource Management* (1986), National Academy Press, Washington DC, pp.63–83.

[65] See further, N. Gunningham & V. Rees, 'Industry Self-Regulation' (1997) *Law and Policy* (publication of the 1997 issue delayed).

[66] See further, I. Ayres & J. Braithwaite, *Responsive Regulation: Transcending the deregulation debate* (1992), Oxford University Press, New York.

[67] J. Braithwaite & B. Fisse, 'Self Regulation and the Costs of Corporate Crime' in C. D. Shearing & P. C. Stenning, *Private Policing* (1987), Sage Publications, Beverley Hills. USA; M. Blakeney & S. Barnes, 'Advertising Deregulation: Public health or private profit' in R. Tomasic, *Business Regulation in Australia* (1984), CCH Australia, North Ryde, NSW.

Self-regulation is frequently an attempt to deceive the public into believing in the responsibility of an irresponsible industry. Sometimes it is a strategy to give the government an excuse for not doing its job.[68]

According to the critics, self-regulatory standards are usually weak, enforcement is ineffective, and punishment is secret and mild. Moreover, self-regulation commonly lacks many of the virtues of conventional state regulation, 'in terms of visibility, credibility, accountability, compulsory application to all, greater likelihood of rigorous standards being developed, cost spreading, and availability of a range of sanctions'.[69]

As we will argue in chapter four, the extent to which self-regulation, *in practice*, has either the positive or the negative attributes identified by its proponents or detractors, will depend very much on the social and economic context within which an individual self-regulatory scheme operates, and on the particular characteristics of the scheme itself. Generalizations are extremely dangerous. As with other instruments, self-regulation works better in some circumstances than in others. Self-regulation works best where there is a degree of coincidence between the self-interest of the individual company or industry, and the wider public interest.[70] For example, it is in the interests of both the producer and the general public for the producer to adopt new process technology which uses fewer raw materials and energy and generates less waste. Such situations are often referred to as 'win-win'. Improved environmental performance occurs naturally in the quest for an improved 'bottom line'.[71]

---

[68] J. Braithwaite, 'Responsive Business Regulatory Institutions' in C. Cody & C. Sampford (eds.), *Business, Ethics and Law* (1993), Federation Press, Sydney, p.91.

[69] K. Webb & A. Morrison, 'The Legal Aspects of Voluntary Codes', a draft paper presented to the *Voluntary Codes Symposium*, Office of Consumer Affairs, Industry Canada and Regulatory Affairs, Treasury Board, Ottawa, September 1996 and to be included in *Exploring Voluntary Codes in the Marketplace*, edited by D. Cohen & K. Webb, Government of Canada, Ottawa, (due to be published 1998) p1.

[70] Whether it is economically rational for an enterprise to adopt self-regulation is more problematic than it might appear, because there may be a substantial gap between long-term and short-term self interest. For example, it may be in the long-term interests of firms to invest in environment protection measures which would not only demonstrably reduce costs and increase profits of individual enterprises in the long term, but would also enhance the environmental credentials of the entire industry. However, for those who are economically marginal, or for managers whose performance is judged in the short term, such investments may not be practicable in the absence of some form of external pressure.

[71] See further, N. Gunningham & J. V. Rees, 'Industry Self-Regulation' (1997) 19(4) *Law and Policy* 363.

However, where a substantial gap exists between the public interest and the private interest of individual enterprises, then it would be naive to rely upon an individual enterprise or industry association taking steps voluntarily in the public interest unless there is some external pressure to do so. This pressure might come from a variety of sources, the most important of which include the threat (actual or implied) of direct government intervention, broader concerns to maintain credibility and legitimacy (and through this, commercial advantage), and the market itself. The likelihood of self-regulation functioning successfully will necessarily vary with the strength of these pressures.[72]

Not all industries lend themselves to self-regulation through industry associations. Rees uses the term 'community of shared fate' to refer to circumstances in which poor performance on the part of one member reflects adversely upon, and indeed, may jeopardise the interests of, the entire industry.[73] These circumstances facilitate the mobilization of peer pressure to ensure that no one member 'lets the side down'. Other structural factors that may bear upon the likely success of industry self-regulation include:

(i)   enterprises are aware of each others' behaviour and can detect non-compliance (this will be compromised by large numbers of firms which enhances the temptation and opportunity to cheat);[74]

(ii) industries that have a history of effective co-operative action (e.g., an existing association);

(iii) a means of punishing non-compliant behaviour; and

(iv) where consumers, customers, or other clients value compliant behaviour and can identify compliant firms (with the result that free riders can be controlled by markets, particularly where these are driven by consumer demand).[75]

---

[72] See further, N. Gunningham & J. V. Rees, 'Industry Self-Regulation' (1997) 19(4) *Law and Policy* 363.

[73] J. V. Rees, *Hostages of Each Other: The transformation of nuclear safety since Three Mile Island* (1994), University of Chicago Press, Chicago, US.

[74] M. Olson, *The Logic of Collective Action* (1965), Harvard University Press, Cambridge, US. See also J. Q. Wilson, *Political Organisations* (1973), Basic Books, New York, chapter 8.

[75] See D. S. Cohen, 'The Regulation of Green Advertising: The state, the market and the environmental good' (1991) 25 *University of British Columbia Law Review* 225. Cohen cites the case of the Canadian Care Labelling programme, which has few free riders, in part because of active lobbying by consumer groups. He also suggests that the GAP. Inc's Sourcing Principles and Guidelines, and the Canadian Eco-Labelling program, are examples of codes that employ the market to curb free-riders.

Self-regulation may have its best chance of success when activated by external institutions. Government may directly engage in the self-regulatory process by jointly negotiating targets and strategies, and providing, if necessary, external verification and/or ratification. In such cases, self-regulation may be more properly termed co-regulation. Often, negotiations at this level will occur through industry associations on a sectoral basis.[76] One benefit may be that firms participating in the design of regulations will be more committed to abiding by them. Experience in the Netherlands indicates that the very act of negotiating co-regulatory agreements provides industry with a greater insight into better environmental management.[77]

There is considerable evidence, from a variety of jurisdictions, that it is largely fear of government regulation that drives the large majority of self-regulatory programmes.[78] It seems unlikely that they would perform well in the absence of continuing government oversight and the threat of direct intervention in the event of self-regulatory failure.

In addition, third parties are also able to contribute to self-regulation, by exercising vigilance and by voicing criticism, as appropriate. This can move industry to open a dialogue with community groups with the aim of finding mutually beneficial ways to improve environmental performance. As we discuss below in chapter four, the chemical industry, because of its poor public relations record and lack of credibility, has been at the forefront of such moves. For example, under the Responsible Care programme, community groups and outside technical experts are given an important role in overseeing the chemical industry's environmental performance. The independent oversight exercised by third parties may be essential to maintaining the credibility of a self-regulatory regime.

From the above analysis, it will be apparent that there are substantial limits to the contribution of self-regulation. The greater the nexus between environmental improvement and increased costs, the greater the incentive to renege on self-regulatory objectives. Consequently, only rarely can self-regulation alone be relied upon to achieve environmental goals. As we have seen, even effective self-regulation may depend on a degree of inducement. And at least the spectre of coercive state

---

[76] I. Ayres & J. Braithwaite, *Responsive Regulation: Transcending the deregulation debate* (1992), Oxford University Press, New York.

[77] Environment Policy and Law 'Environmental Caveats' (1994) 24(4) *Environment Policy and Law* 191.

[78] See Dutch study in M. Aalders, 'Regulation and In-Company Environmental Management in the Netherlands' (1993) 15(2) *Law and Policy* 75.

intervention may be required in those cases where virtue is lacking. In the words of one government regulatory official: 'If self-regulation worked, Moses would have come down from the Mountain with the Ten Guidelines'.[79]

3. Voluntarism

In contrast to self-regulation, which entails social control by an industry association, voluntarism is based on the individual firm undertaking to do the right thing unilaterally, without any basis in coercion. Commonly, voluntarism is initiated by government, and may involve government playing the role of co-ordinator and facilitator. At a general level, this category embraces voluntary agreements between governments and individual businesses taking the form of 'non-mandatory contracts between equal partners, one of which is government, in which incentives for action arise from mutual interests rather than from sanctions'.[80] However, the variety of such agreements makes precise classification difficult. The words 'non-mandatory' are fundamental, for to the extent that such agreements contain a coercive element (for example, there are strong pressures to enter into it) they might legitimately be regarded as an innovative form of command and control, or co-regulation, as with the Dutch environmental covenants mentioned above.[81]

Among the most important individual instruments in this category are support for projects undertaken by landholders (where the financial support is partial and there is heavy reliance on voluntary effort for successful completion). Voluntary programmes of this nature do not require any commitment to participation for any set period of time on the part of the landholder or resource user. Rather, programme participation relies upon the enthusiasm and goodwill of the landholder or resource user, and withdrawal from a programme only results in a cessation of assistance. For example, all states in Australia have programmes to assist in the voluntary use of land for the protection of wildlife. Some of these carry no financial inducements at all. The

---

[79] Quoted in P. Grabosky & J. Braithwaite, *Of Manners Gentle: Enforcement strategies of Australian business regulatory agencies* (1986), Oxford University Press, Melbourne, p.184.

[80] Organisation for Economic Co-operation and Development (OECD), *Meeting on Alternatives to Traditional Regulation* (1994) May, OECD, Paris, p.7.

[81] Grants to facilitate specific projects are also classified as voluntary instruments notwithstanding that they also provide a financial incentive, provided that the grant is intended to provide only partial financial support for the project, which still relies heavily on the voluntary efforts of the recipients for its successful completion.

Australian Landcare programme is another example of this approach. Landcare reflects a desire to restrict government intervention to ameliorate land degradation through the encouragement of voluntary activity and the provision of extension services. It provides opportunities for joint activities between landholders and community groups by invoking a sense of responsibility for land conservation.

In the areas of land and biodiversity conservation, management agreements with the person responsible for managing an area of land will be of particular significance. These are a form of conditional use right whereby landholders are reimbursed for the incremental cost of providing non-marketable biodiversity services and the capital costs associated with the building of fences, etc. necessary to conserve biodiversity. The normal mechanism used is one whereby landholders are offered the opportunity to agree, in return for a payment, to contribute to the maintenance of biodiversity not expected of that person's market competitors. They are a crucial mechanism for providing on-going protection of habitat. Management agreements generally involve a legally binding contract entered into for a period of time, under which a land user agrees to refrain from certain activities and to undertake other activities in return for reimbursement.[82]

Within the areas of energy efficiency and pollution control, two of the most notable voluntary agreements between government and industry are the United States EPA's 33/50 and Green Lights programmes. Under 33/50, firms are encouraged to reduce the release of toxic chemicals through positive public recognition.[83] Industry participation is completely voluntary and commitments are not enforceable by law. Instead, the programme relies on co-operation between industry and the EPA, and subsequent positive public recognition of environmental achievements. Participating firms are required to develop detailed

[82] See further, J. Bowers, *Incentives and Mechanisms for Biodiversity: Observations and Issues* (1994), CSIRO. Division of Wildlife and Ecology, Canberra, p.14; D. Farrier, 'Conserving Biodiversity on Private Land' (1995) 19(2) *Harvard Environmental Law Review* 304–405; D. B. Botlain, *Discordant Harmonies* (1990), Oxford University Press, New York, pp.195–6; K. L. Wallace & S. A. Moore, 'Management of Remnant Bushland for Nature Conservation in Agricultural Areas of South-Western Australia—Operational and Planning Perspectives' in D. A. Saunders, G. W. Arnold, A. A. Burbidge & A. J. M. Hopkins (eds.) *Nature Conservation: The role of remnants of native vegetation* (1987) , Surrey Beatty and Sons, Chipping Norton, NSW, p.259; Land Use Consultants, *Countryside Schemes and Nature Conservation* (1994), London, UK.

[83] A. S. Miller, 'The Origins and Current Directions of United States Environmental Law and Policy: An overview' in B. Boer, R. Fowler & N. Gunningham (eds.), *Environmental Outlook: Law and Policy* (1994), Federation Press, Sydney.

action plans, but can adapt them to target the least costly abatement measures. An initial evaluation reveals that the 33/50 programme has significantly reduced toxic chemical releases by participating firms.[84] Green Light (whereby firms agree in writing to install energy efficient lighting) has also claimed some success. The programme signed up 5 per cent of all commercial office space in less than three years.[85] Average investment returns are estimated at between 20 and 40 per cent. More recently, the European Commission has sought to promote voluntary environmental agreements in the industrial context, recognizing that they can promote a pro-active attitude on the part of industry, provide tailor-made solutions and allow for a quicker and smoother achievement of objectives. However, it is recognized that these benefits will only be obtained if agreements are carefully designed to ensure their environmental effectiveness. Here the key elements have been identified as: 'the setting of qualitative objectives, a staged approach providing for intermediate objectives, the publication of the agreement, the monitoring and reporting of results'.[86]

Strengths and weaknesses of voluntarism

Voluntarism has the considerable virtue of being non-interventionist, having high industry acceptability and raising minimal equity concerns. It can also promote an ethic of environmental stewardship. Like self-regulation, voluntarism works better in some circumstances than others. Its greatest strength is where landowners or other regulatees perceive their self-interest (short-term as well as long-term) as being to protect the environment.

Unfortunately, in the large majority of circumstances, this is not the case. For example, as we will see in chapter five, there is often a considerable gap between the public interest in environmental protection and the private interests of individual land users in respect of biodiversity conservation.[87] Nevertheless, even in these circumstances, volun-

---

[84] S. Arora & T. N. Cason, 'An Experiment in Voluntary Environmental Regulation: Participation in EPA's 33/50 Program' (1995) 28(3) *Journal of Environmental Economics and Management* 271.

[85] A. S. Miller, 'The Origins and Current Directions of United States Environmental Law and Policy: An overview' in B. Boer, R. Fowler & N. Gunningham (eds.), *Environmental Outlook: Law and Policy* (1994), Federation Press, Sydney.

[86] Communication from the Commission to the Council and the Parliament on environmental covenants Com. (96) s.61.

[87] The basic problem derives from the fact that private landholders (or indeed, other private users of resources) commonly lack any economic incentive to take account of the social costs of their actions. That is, we encounter a classic externalities problem where

tarism still has an important role, particularly where the threats to the environment require active participation to resolve. The challenge in designing voluntary mechanisms is to build, rather than hinder, the development of a custodial ethic, and to make environmental protection part of the 'community norm'.[88] Where this can be done, then voluntary agreements between government and businesses or other interest groups, both in respect of the sort of 'green issues', and in an industrial context, have considerable attractions:

> . . . they avoid adversarial relations; involve businesses or other groups in political processes; improve compliance because rules rest on consensus rather than on coercion; and permit, through negotiation, the development of instruments better adapted to economic and competitive contexts.[89]

Management agreements have similar virtues: they are financially attractive, flexible, co-operative, non-intrusive (where voluntary), and easily targeted. Their most obvious limitation is their high administrative cost associated with negotiation and monitoring. They also require periodic oversight, auditing, or other forms of supervision on the part of government, although this role may, in part, be transferred to local communities.[90] However, as a 'stand alone' mechanism, management agreements are subject to a serious limitation, namely that they need to be periodically renegotiated, and at each renegotiation the person involved has an opportunity to hold the benefits of their work for ransom.[91]

the direct benefits of biodiversity loss (e.g., increased agricultural production from clearing land) go to individual property owners, whereas the costs (in terms of loss of species, ecosystems, genetic resources, and other potential uses) fall on society at large. The problem is that the impact of one landholder clearing their land will make little impact on the overall problem, nor will this individual decision influence the behaviour of other landholders. Accordingly, each landholder will be tempted to take advantage of the willingness of others to protect the environment while continuing to despoil it themselves. See M. Olson, *The Logic of Collective Action* (1965), Harvard University Press, Cambridge, MA.

[88] A. Bennett, G. Backhouse & T. Clark (eds.), *People and Nature Conservation: Perspectives on private land use and endangered species recovery* (1995), Surrey Beatty and Sons, Chipping Norton, UK.

[89] Organisation for Economic Co-operation and Development (OECD), *Meeting on Alternatives to Traditional Regulation* (1994), May, OECD, Paris, p.7.

[90] See further, J. M. Hopkins & D. A. Saunders, 'Ecological Studies as a Basis for Management' in D. A. Saunders, G. W. Arnold, A. A. Burbidge & A. J. M. Hopkins (eds.) *Nature Conservation: The role of remnants of native vegetation* (1987) , Surrey Beatty and Sons, Chipping Norton, NSW, p.15.

[91] Consequently, to achieve dependability, the most effective management agreements are underpinned by a conservation covenant designed to protect the resources in the longer term. For example, a conservation covenant attached to the land title could require the existing landholder and all subsequent landholders to neither damage nor threaten that habitat.

Grants to facilitate specific projects, provided they are well targeted, can also have considerable attractions, not least being high multiplier effects. Because they usually cover only a proportion of the total costs, grants avoid the moral hazard associated with management agreements where people have an incentive to falsify receipts and overstate expenditures. However, they can be difficult to target and monitor without incurring high administrative costs.

4. Education and information instruments

The range of educational and information-based instruments is broad, and in many cases, these instruments may overlap. For the purposes of this chapter, we have attempted to cover the spectrum by breaking them down into the following major categories:

(i)   education and training;
(ii)   corporate environmental reporting;
(iii) community right-to-know and pollution inventories;
(iv)   product certification; and
(v)   award schemes.

(i) Education and training

Education and training are essential to improving the capacity of industry and the community to address pressing environmental issues. They are critical to changing attitudes, behaviour, and expertise to be consistent with environmental policy imperatives.[92] Environmental information delivered through government sponsored education and

---

[92] A great deal of environmentally inappropriate behaviour may arise not from perversity or selfishness, but rather from ignorance. Therefore, the greater one's knowledge of environmental issues and/or action strategies, the greater one's tendency to adopt good environmental and resource management practices (J. Hines, H. Hungerford & A. Tomera, 'Analysis and Synthesis of Research on Environmental Behaviour: A meta-analysis' (1987) 18(2) *Journal of Environmental Education*). Similarly, research-based management advice was identified as a major need in a survey of landholders and managers of remnant lowland native grassland (L. Gilfedder & J. B. Kirkpatrick, *A Survey of Landholder Attitudes and Intentions Towards the Long Term Conservation of Native Lowland Grasslands* (1995), Report to the Grasslands Ecology Unit, Australian Nature Conservation Agency, Canberra). Programmes such as Victoria's Land for Wildlife scheme already address the central role of education and information, through a series of booklets for landowners which provide advice on matters such as native vegetation management, wetlands and waterway management, and weeds control (see M. D. Young, N. Gunningham, J. Elix, J. Lambert, B. Howard, P. Grabosky, E. McCrone, *Reimbursing the Future: An evaluation of motivational, voluntary, price-based, property-right, and regulatory incentives for the conservation of biodiversity* (1996), Biodiversity Series Paper No. 9, Department of the Environment, Sport and Territories, Biodiversity Unit, Canberra, p.107).

training programmes is likely to be an essential supplement to other forms of regulation.[93] Education and training can be tailored to meet the needs of industry, and in particular, to address information gaps that hamper the environmental performance of small and medium sized businesses. A key function of these instruments is to internalize environmental awareness and responsibility into corporate decision-making.

There is considerable evidence that educational instruments deliver improved management practices. They work best, however, when they exploit the self-interest of the target audience.[94] With any education campaign, the critical issue is being able to effectively target and deliver the message to the intended audience. In some cases, this may require lateral solutions. For example, in Australia, it was determined that the most effective way of targeting disparate users of ozone depleting substances in commercial refrigerators was to train and certify private contractors who regularly serviced commercial refrigerators.[95] The benefits were not only improved environmental work practices on the part of service contractors, but the delivery of reliable information on the phase-out process to otherwise unreachable small and medium sized businesses.[96] An alternative approach in targeting industry is to provide toll-free help-lines. For example, the United Kingdom's Department of Trade and Industry (DTI) operates an Environmental Enquiry Point—

---

[93] They are, however, rarely used in isolation. That is, they are a supplementary instrument.

[94] For example, where informed resource users have a self-interest in protecting biodiversity, then educational programmes, appropriately designed, can bring about very substantial benefits. If, for example, eutrophication of a lake is due to farmers using more fertilizer than is necessary to maximize profits, it may only be necessary to bring this to their attention. Enlightened self-interest may then be sufficient to solve, or at least reduce, the problem. Education and information provision can assist to improve management of common-property resources, such as a fishery. Fishers may learn that the continued use of a certain type of net will reduce stocks to such an extent that they would lose their livelihoods (see M. D. Young, N. Gunningham, J. Elix, J. Lambert, B. Howard, P. Grabosky, E. McCrone, *Reimbursing the Future: An evaluation of motivational, voluntary, price-based, property-right, and regulatory incentives for the conservation of biodiversity* (1996), Biodiversity Series Paper No. 9, Department of the Environment, Sport and Territories, Biodiversity Unit, Canberra, p.107).

[95] Australia and New Zealand Environment and Conservation Council (ANZECC*), Revised Strategy for Ozone Protection in Australia* Report No. 30 (1994), AGPS, Canberra.

[96] Often, the only sources of professional expertise which small business proprietors routinely access are their lawyers, their accountants, and, perhaps, their bank managers. These professionals may be useful conduits for information relating to regulatory compliance, particularly as it may affect the nature of professional services in question.

a one-stop-shop for companies wishing to obtain technical information relevant to improving their environmental performance.[97]

(ii) Corporate environmental reports

Increasingly, firms have begun to adopt the practice of environmental accounting and reporting.[98] Corporate environmental reports are a useful way for firms to disseminate information about the environmental record, either as part of an annual report or as a stand alone document, but more than that, they can be used as an internal diagnostic tool to enhance their performance.[99] The very act of compiling a report necessarily entails a degree of introspection that may reveal previously hidden opportunities for abating pollution. Corporate environmental reporting is still in its infancy, however there are some potentially exciting developments. These include the use of 'eco-balance sheets' and full-cost accounting which measure all business inputs and outputs, establish performance indicators, and calculate environmental efficiency per unit of production.[100] Despite the potential of corporate environmental reporting, there are still substantial shortcomings to be overcome. These include consistency and coherence in the reporting format, and importantly, independent verification. [101]

[97] The service covers: technical matters; legal obligations; proposed new standards; and environmental conferences and seminars. If an enquiry is dealt with in less than four hours, no fee is charged (J. Holmes, *Managing into the 1990's—Manufacturing and the Environment: An executive guide* (1992), Department for Enterprise (DTI), London.

[98] D. Owen, 'A Critical Perspective on the Development of European Corporate Environmental Accounting and Reporting (1996), a paper presented at the 1996 Australian Academy of Science, *Fenner Conference on the Environment: Linking Environment and Economy Through Indicators and Accounting Systems*, 30 September to 3 October, The University of New South Wales, Sydney.

[99] Such disclosures may contain: an overall environmental policy statement; an overview of significant environmental impacts; targets for reducing emissions and wastes and quantitative performance against those targets; descriptions of environmental management systems in place; relevant research and development activities; breaches of environmental regulations; and the results of environmental audits (C. Deegan, 'Corporate Environmental Reporting in Australia—a review and critical assessment' (1996), a paper presented at the 1996 Australian Academy of Science, *Fenner Conference on the Environment: Linking Environment and Economy Through Indicators and Accounting Systems*, 30 September to 3 October, The University of New South Wales, Sydney). The reporting is predominantly non-financial in nature.

[100] C. Jasch, 'Environmental Information Systems in Austria' (1993) 13(2) *Social and Environmental Accounting* 7–9.

[101] M. Rae, 'Why Do Corporate Environmental Reporting? If You Don't, Your Company Will Die!' (1996), a paper presented at the 1996 Australian Academy of Science, *Fenner Conference on the Environment: Linking Environment and Economy Through Indicators and Accounting Systems*, 30 September to 3 October, The University of New South Wales, Sydney.

(iii) Community right to know and pollution inventories

Access to information is an essential prerequisite for effective community input into environmental decision-making. In order to address this, a number of countries around the world have introduced laws compelling disclosure of pollution and chemical hazard information. Commonly referred to as 'community right to know' (CRTK), such legislation is intended to inform the community of the environmental impact of a firm's activities and of a firm's pollution abatement policies. The most prominent is the Emergency Planning and Community Right to Know Act (the EPCRA) introduced in the United States in 1986.[102] More recently, Canada has introduced a national pollution inventory,[103] which follows aspects of the United States EPCRA. European jurisdictions, such as the United Kingdom, have adopted different types of laws which compel government to disclose information on pollution control and chemical hazards.[104] These follow a number of European Community directives on Freedom of Access to Information and Control of Major Hazards of Industrial Activities.

The benefits of CRTK are readily apparent from the United States experience.[105] In particular, CRTK:

(i)   provides community groups with increased insight and political leverage;

(ii) exposes government and regulatory agencies' shortcomings, creating pressure for stricter enforcement;

(iii) stimulates pollution prevention by sensitizing companies to community pressure;

(iv) can lead to the establishment of 'good neighbour' agreements between local communities and companies;

(v)   improves the quality of public policy debate;

(vi) lessens the need for environmental regulation via industry commitments to verifiable reduction targets; and

---

[102] Emergency Planning and Community Right to Know Act 1986, 42 USC *et. seq.* Public Law 99–499. A. number of state governments in the United States, such as New Jersey, introduced 'right to know' laws as early as 1983, requiring environmental surveys to be submitted to the State EPA.

[103] See further, *National Pollutant Release Inventory for Canada* (1992), Multi-Stakeholder Advisory Committee, Environment Canada.

[104] M. Purdue, 'Integrated Pollution Control in the Environmental Protection Act 1990: A. Coming of Age of Environmental Law?' (1991) 54 *Modern Law Review* 534 at 538–539.

[105] N. Gunningham & A. Cornwell, 'Legislating the Right to Know' (1994) 11 *Environmental and Planning Law Journal* 274–288.

(vii) can directly influence the price of a firm's stock, serving to reward good environmental performers and punish the bad.[106]

A central component of most CRTK legislation is a pollution inventory which compiles data on the emission of pollutants or chemicals to the air, water, and land. The basic function of a pollution inventory is 'to document the release or transfer of selected chemical pollutants to all media as a basis for developing and monitoring the effectiveness of pollution prevention measures or programs'.[107] In the United States, this strategy, as embodied in the Toxic Release Inventory, has been hailed by the former administrator of the EPA, William Reilly, as 'one of the most effective instruments available'[108] for reducing toxic emissions, a view reinforced by his successor, Carol Browner,[109] and many others.

A major benefit of inventories is to encourage introspection. As Foucault and his followers remind us, the simple process of enumeration and record keeping has a regulatory function.[110] When the phenomenon enumerated is undesirable, as in the case of pollution, the necessity of enumeration focuses managerial attention on the underlying phenomenon.[111] No executive likes to see their company exposed publicly at the bottom of the performance rankings; resulting managerial exhortation is likely to have greater impact than any fixed standard which regulatory authorities might be inclined to impose. When pub-

[106] J. T. Hamilton, 'Pollution as News: Media and stock market reactions to the Capital Toxic Release Inventory Data' (1995) 27(1) *Journal of Environmental Economics and Management* 98–103.

[107] Pollutant Release Transfer Register p.2. Within this broad objective, there are many variables which will dictate the final make-up of the inventory. These include: scope of the inventory; who must report; what substances must be reported; what information must be reported; to whom the information is reported; access to that information; and how the inventory should be enforced (See N. Gunningham 'Issues and Options in Designing an NPI' in Minter Ellison (eds.) *Final report to the Environment Protection Agency for the Development of Legislative Modelling for the National Pollutant Inventory and Associated Community Right to Know in Australia* (1995), Minter Ellison, Melbourne).

[108] W. Reilly, *Aiming Before We Shoot: The quiet revolution in environmental policy* (1990), address to the National Press Club, Washington DC, September 26.

[109] C. Browner, cited in W. E. Orts 'Reflexive Environmental Law' (1995) 89(4) *Northwestern University Law Review* 1227.

[110] N. Rose & P. Miller, 'Political Power Beyond the State: Problematics of government' (1992) 43 *British Journal of Sociology* 173–205.

[111] One must concede that such attention may, at times, be in furtherance of *non*-compliance, as in the case of mining companies which tamper with apparatus for the monitoring of dust levels.

lished, this, in turn, can inform markets, including peers, regulators, or NGOs, which may be in a position to foster compliance.[112]

Notwithstanding the considerable virtues of CRTK and pollution inventories, they are not without their shortcomings and limitations. Firms often fear that disclosure will enable a competitor to gain an unfair advantage, that public interest groups will sensationalize the information or that the public will misunderstand its significance and overreact on the basis of unwarranted anxiety. Another potential problem is the tendency to focus on concentrated toxic 'hot spots' adjacent to local communities, at the expense of more widely dispersed pollutants. For these reasons, CRTK can only ever play a supporting role and must be supplemented by other regulatory instruments. Within this limitation, well structured CRTK legislation can and does provide substantial benefits to government, the community, and responsible firms.

(iv) Product certification

Surveys indicate that many consumers are taking environmental considerations into account when they purchase goods and services.[113] There is evidence, however, that unassisted markets do not provide accurate information to consumers and, in some cases, may mislead them about the environmental performance of specific products.[114] In order to inform the public about the environmental 'soundness' (or otherwise) of various consumer products, governments can contribute to the development of labelling standards, and of eco-labelling schemes. This can help inform consumers, and sustain markets for environmentally appropriate goods and services.[115] Private accreditation schemes, with appropriate safeguards, might achieve similar results.

The experience of establishing eco-labelling schemes within and between nations has been mixed at best. Assessing the full environmental implications and the relative merits of competing products, and then incorporating the results into a single, broad-based labelling

[112] D. Vogel, *Lobbying the Corporation: Citizen Challenges to Business Authority* (1978), Basic Books, New York, pp.131–136; and L. Allan, E. K. Kaufman & J. D. Underwood, *Paper Profits: Pollution in the pulp and paper industry* (1972), MIT Press, Cambridge MA.

[113] S. Dawson & N. Gunningham, 'The More Dolphins There Are the Less I Trust What They're Saying: Can green labelling work?' (1996) 18(1) *Adelaide Law Review* 1–34.

[114] D. S. Cohen, 'The Regulation of Green Advertising: The state, the market and the environmental good' (1991) 25 *University of British Columbia Law Review* 225.

[115] Organisation for Economic Co-operation and Development (OECD), *Environmental labelling in OECD Countries* (1991), OECD, Paris.

scheme is not a simple task.[116] Indeed, criteria and procedures for certification can become so contentious that they may lead to impasse and deadlock. With the notable exception of the German Blue Angel scheme, most national broad-based labelling schemes have experienced strong industry opposition, which has greatly limited their coverage and effectiveness. In addition to design difficulties, there are considerable costs associated with the establishment and ongoing operation of labelling schemes, particularly those that attempt to provide a full 'life-cycle-analysis' of products.[117] Several schemes intended to become self-funding have, in fact, required continued government assistance.[118] There is also cause to doubt whether the information provided under such schemes is necessarily 'full information' and thus not always good.[119] For these reasons, some governments have withdrawn from eco-labelling, leaving the development of labelling criteria for non-governmental bodies.

(v) Award schemes

Award schemes have considerable publicity potential, and as such, can contribute to the education and information strategies of a regulatory regime.[120] The publicity which may accompany an award can serve an educative function, raising public awareness about surrounding circumstances, and focusing attention on critical issues. Through a system of awards, virtuous conduct that might otherwise pass unnoticed can be publicized.[121] The public enunciation of virtuous conduct may have greater impact than the public denunciation of harmful behaviour. Recipients of awards may be presented as role models, with the exem-

[116] For some of the difficulties surrounding eco-labelling programs, see J. A. Grodsky, 'Certified Green: The law and future of environmental labelling' (1993) 10(1) *Yale Journal on Regulation* 147–227.

[117] J. A. Grodsky, 'Certified Green: The law and future of environmental labelling' (1993) 10(1) *Yale Journal on Regulation* 147–227.

[118] S. Dawson & N. Gunningham, 'The More Dolphins There Are the Less I trust What They're Saying: Can green labelling work?' (1996) 18(1) *Adelaide Law Review* 1–34.

[119] See P. Menell, 'Educating Consumers about the Environment: Labels versus Prices' in E. Eide & R. van den Bergh (eds.), *Law and Economics of the Environment* (1996), Juridisk Forlag, Oslo.

[120] J. Gardiner & G. Balch, 'Getting People to Protect Themselves: Information facilitation, regulatory and incentives strategies' in J. Brigham & D. Brown (eds.) *Policy Implementation: Penalties or incentives* (1980), Sage Publications, Beverly Hills CA; and P. N. Grabosky, 'Regulation by Reward: On the use of incentives as regulatory instruments' (1995) 17(3) *Law and Policy* 256–280.

[121] Awards may be conferred in recognition of exemplary behaviour by third parties, as well as by industry.

plary act or pattern of conduct celebrated by the award held out as worthy of emulation by others.

The European Commission administers the high profile European Better Environment Awards for Industry.[122] A trophy and recognition is provided to the winning candidate.[123] The Oregon Governor's Awards for Toxics Use Reduction is another example of a programme which celebrates environmental achievement.[124] Awards can also be conferred by private institutions, such as public interest groups, and by philanthropic organisations. The Goldman environmental prize, which recognizes exceptional achievements by environmental activists, is one example.[125] Despite their obvious merits, award schemes are not without limitations. Most significant of these is their tendency to become debased through overuse. Excessive reliance on award schemes can make recognized achievements less noteworthy, and thus dilute their educative impact.

Strengths and weaknesses of education and information instruments

The provision of information is essential to environmental improvement, for only with adequate information can decision-makers at all levels maximize returns and avoid unintended consequences.

The viability of other regulatory instruments is substantially dependent on the availability and quality of relevant information. The application and enforcement of command and control regulations, in particular, requires regulatory authorities to be aware of technological innovations relevant to, for example, BAT standards and any breaches of emission standards.[126] Similarly, the effectiveness of economic instruments, such as taxes and tradeable permits, will only be maximized if firms are fully cognisant of their environmental performance, and the

[122] J. Elkington, P. Knight, & J. Hailes, *The Green Business Guide* (1992), Victor Gollancz, London.

[123] Even in the absence of a monetary component, symbolic rewards may still have substantial instrumental value (R. Goodin, 'Making Moral Incentives Pay' (1980) 12 *Policy Sciences* 131–145). The reputational capital which can be generated by an award may be worth a considerable amount (C. Stone, 'Choice of Target and Other Law Enforcement Variables' in M. Friedland (ed.), *Sanctions and Rewards in the Legal System* (1989), University of Toronto Press, Toronto).

[124] L. R. Jones & J. H. Baldwin, *Corporate Environmental Policy and Government Regulation* (1994), JAI Press, Greenwich Connecticut.

[125] A. Wallace, *Eco-Heroes: Twelve Tales of Environmental Victory* (1993), Mercury House, San Francisco.

[126] G. Bakkenist, *Environmental Information: Law, policy and experience* (1994), Cameron May, UK.

costs and benefits of various abatement options.[127] If a persuasive case for environmental improvement can be made, firms are more likely to respond positively to the range of other instruments, whether voluntary, economic, or interventionist.[128]

Educational and informational instruments will be more effective when they harnesses self-interest to become financially attractive and self-enforcing, thus providing continuing incentives for environmental protection and sustainability.[129] However, self-interest is not an essential prerequisite to the success of educational campaigns. There is evidence, for example, that some people may be willing to sacrifice their own financial interests if they are made aware of the importance of preventing environmental degradation, and ways in which they might do so.[130] As the OECD puts it:

> . . . people and businesses often care deeply about contributing responsibly to the public good (businesses also care about 'reputation'), and governments can use information, communication, encouragement, peer pressure, and education strategies to convince the public of the need for change.[131]

In most circumstances, education and informational instruments can be implemented with modest administrative burdens, thus improving their cost-effectiveness. However, we do not suggest that this category of instruments is dependable, or that they can be relied upon in isolation, particularly where there is a substantial tension between the public and private interests. Indeed, there is evidence of a considerable gap between attitudes and behaviour. That is, even when people collectively

---

[127] T. Panayotou, *Economic Instruments for Environmental Management and Sustainable Development* (1994) August, a report presented to the UNEP Expert Group Meeting on Use and Development of Economic Policy Instruments for Environmental Management, UNEP, Nairobi.

[128] J. Hines, H. Hungerford & A. Tomera, 'Analysis and Synthesis of Research on Environmental Behaviour: A. meta-analysis ' (1987) 18(2) *Journal of Environmental Education* 31.

[129] Those who have been informed of the advantages of biodiversity conservation in certain contexts (e.g., eco-tourism) will be more inclined to develop self-regulatory mechanisms that seek to maintain biodiversity values by, for example, agreeing not to drop boat anchors on coral reefs and to drive only on designated tracks. Those who have been informed of the financial savings available from energy efficiency measures will be more likely to adopt those measures voluntarily.

[130] A. Bennett, G. Backhouse & T. Clark (eds.), *People and Nature Conservation: Perspectives on private land use and endangered species recovery* (1995), Surrey Beatty and Sons, Chipping Norton, UK.

[131] Organisation for Economic Co-operation and Development (OECD), *Meeting on Alternatives to Traditional Regulation* (1994), May, OECD, Paris, p.8.

perceive the need for environmental protection, each individual will not necessarily take appropriate action if this conflicts with other goals and interests. For example, the South Australian experience has been that, even when people were well informed and were supportive of the need for biodiversity conservation, many still wanted to clear their own land. Only regulation (coupled with compensation) prevented them from doing so.[132] Thus, the main weakness of educational and information instruments is that they contain no precautionary elements and cannot be depended upon to protect the environment when there is a significant gap between private and social objectives.

Predictably, instruments within this category will also be more effective in some circumstances than others. CRTK, for example, relies heavily on the energies of local communities in using the information and pressuring enterprises to improve their environmental performance. Where an environmental hazard involves no immediate threat to human health, or where there is no identifiable local community, or where we are dealing with non-point source pollution, not readily measured and traced back to its origins, then this instrument has far less to offer. Similarly, corporate environmental reporting is dependent upon the willingness of public interest groups to follow through on its results and to both shame bad performers and praise good ones. Finally, eco-labelling relies upon the willingness of consumers to buy 'green' products and upon their capacity to distinguish between these and other classes of product.

5. Economic instruments

The idea of economic instruments was conceived by academic economists, and for many years remained largely of theoretical interest; regulators, environmentalists, and industry alike tended to be more comfortable with the familiar terrain of traditional regulation.[133] In the 1980s, however, the OECD recognized the potential application of economic instruments, and began to give the concept wider circulation amongst policymakers. This, combined with the increasing awareness of the limits of traditional regulatory enforcement, has led to the growing acceptance and use of economic instruments in western industrial

---

[132] Personal communication, John Bradsen 5 October 1995.

[133] S. Kelman, 'Economic Incentives and Environmental Policy: Politics, ideology, and philosophy' in T. Schelling (ed.), *Incentives for Environmental Protection* (1983), MIT Press, US, pp.291–331.

states.[134] Today, economic instruments are regarded by many as 'the hottest growth industry in environmental law'.[135]

Economic instruments may take a variety of forms, some providing positive incentives, and others negative. While there is no single agreed classification, for present purposes, that provided by Panayotou is particularly helpful.[136] Panayotou treats such instruments as belonging to one of the following categories: property-rights; market creation; fiscal instruments and charge systems; financial instruments; liability instruments; performance bonds; and deposit refund systems.

(i) Property-rights

Much environmental depletion and pollution is caused by inadequately defined and insecure property-rights. The classic assertion of this proposition is Garrett Hardin's 'tragedy of the commons'.[137] Hardin describes how, in the case of an unmanaged pasture, herders operate in their own self-interest by overgrazing, since there is insufficient incentive to deter them from doing so. The result is that, over time, the pasture is depleted to an unsustainable level, to the detriment of all. This problem might be avoided either by command and control regulation (directing people how to behave), or by providing for a system of property-rights in such a way that the problem disappears. The latter solution is, generally, preferred by economists on the grounds that it is low in administrative and transaction costs and achieves the internalization of externalities[138] once and for all, without need for policymakers to continually revisit the issue.

For example, if clear and enforceable property-rights and obligations are created for wildlife with commercial value, then an incentive will exist (for those holding the property-rights) to maintain the species and

---

[134] R. Eckersley, *Markets, the State and the Environment* (1995), Macmillan Press, Melbourne; and E. Rehbinder, 'Environmental Regulation Through Fiscal and Economic Incentives in a Federalist System' (1993) 20 *Ecology Law Quarterly* 57–83.

[135] W. E. Orts, 'Reflexive Environmental Law' (1995) 89 *Northwestern University Law Review* 1227 at 1241.

[136] T. Panayotou, *Economic Instruments for Environmental Management and Sustainable Development* (1994), a report to the UNEP. Expert Group Meeting on Use and Development of Economic Policy Instruments for Environmental Management, Nairobi, August 1994.

[137] G. Hardin, 'The Tragedy of the Commons' (1968) 162 *Science* 1243–48.

[138] That is, it requires the full social costs of the environmental harm to be borne by a private party causing the harm rather than being passed on to taxpayers, consumers, or to future generations.

their habitats.[139] Once a right or value is created, the owner has an incentive to maintain that value so that they can maximize the profits that accrue from selling that right. At the same time, funds will be generated, some of which could be used for further conservation measures. In circumstances such as these, property-right mechanisms offer a powerful means to encourage people to conserve environmental resources and limit their use to that which is sustainable.

Experience with the effectiveness of these mechanisms, however, is mixed, and their application may be limited to relatively simple situations.[140] The strengths and weaknesses of the property-rights approach is discussed further at section 6 (Free market environmentalism) of this chapter.

(ii) Market creation

The object of this strategy is for government to create a market where none previously existed. For example, a market might be created through the issue of tradeable pollution rights or tradeable resource rights, which can be bought or sold like any other commodity. This entails regulatory authorities determining an overall level of tolerable activity, based on the assimilative capacity of a particular environmental sector, then allocating tradeable rights or quotas up to this level.[141] In effect, this means creating property-rights, manifested in the form of permit certificates. If the users are then free to trade these certificates amongst themselves, they will be able 'to negotiate solutions to environmental problems upon the property structure instituted by the regulator. In short, this approach allows the regulatory agency to solve the missing market environmental problem by creating a surrogate market in permits'.[142]

[139] Organisation for Economic Co-operation and Development (OECD), *Economic Incentives for the Conservation of Biodiversity: Conceptual framework and guidelines for case studies* (1994), Group on Economic and Environment Policy Integration, Expert Group on Economic Aspects of Biodiversity, OECD, Paris.

[140] Ostrom argues that some commons problems are solved neither by privatization nor centralization but rather by local people getting together to solve their own problems (E. Ostrom, *Governing the Commons: The evolution of institutions for collective action* (1990), Cambridge University Press, New York, p.18). However, she concedes that such solutions are more likely where communities are small, stable, communicate effectively, and have a strong concern for the future.

[141] T. H. Tietenberg, 'Economic Instruments for Environmental Regulation' (1990) 6(1) *Oxford Review of Economic Policy* 17–33.

[142] T. Swanson, 'Economic Instruments and Environmental Regulation: A. critical introduction' (1995) 4(4) *Review of European Community and International Environmental Law* 287 at 289.

The advantage of market creation is that, unlike direct regulation, it gives firms greater flexibility in tailoring responses to their individual circumstances. The assumption is that firms are in a better position than regulatory authorities to identify and specify appropriate action. Government retains effective control of the scheme, however, by determining the allowable emissions and quantity of available permits, and is thus able to set the overall level of polluting emissions or resource exploitation. Government must also be in a position to enforce the allowable emissions of individual permits to prevent abuses by free-riders, in a similar fashion to the enforcement provision of traditional regulatory instruments. Market creation can be envisaged as a hybrid between free market environmentalism and direct regulation.[143]

The economic rationale for creating an artificial market for pollution permits is to effectively exploit differences in the marginal cost of abatement.[144] If the cost of reducing a given pollutant varies between firms, the overall cost of reaching a desired level of pollutant emissions will be minimized if the burden of compliance is shifted to those firms with the lowest marginal costs. Rational behaviour by participating firms would mean that low marginal cost firms continue to reduce emissions until the cost of further reductions is equal to or greater than that of purchasing pollution permits, whilst high marginal cost firms will continue to pollute until the cost of purchasing pollution permits is equal to or less than that of reducing emissions. The benefit in using a market of tradeable permits to achieve such an outcome is that it can be introduced without regulatory authorities needing to know anything about the circumstances of individual firms, in particular their capacity to reduce pollutants. There may also be a further benefit in that firms are encouraged to develop innovative forms of pollution abatement in order to sell off excess permits at a profit.[145]

Although the activity subject to trade has, typically, been one or another form of pollution, the concept can be extended to a variety of

[143] P. Kinrade, 'Towards Ecologically Sustainable Development: The Role and Shortcomings of Markets' in R. Eckersley (ed.) *Markets, the State and the Environment: Towards Integration* (1995), Macmillan Education Australia, Melbourne, p.86 at p.96.

[144] M. Hinchy, S. Thorpe & B. S. Fisher, *A. Tradeable Emissions Permit Scheme* (1992), ABARE Research Report 93.5, ABARE, Canberra.

[145] Bureau of Industry Economics, *Environmental Regulation: The Economics of Tradeable Permits—A survey of theory and practice,* Research Report 42, (1992), AGPS, Canberra. They would then be in a position to sell excess permits for profit. Depending on the type of tradeable permit scheme applied, new entrants may also be required to develop novel non-polluting technologies if they wish to compete with existing firms but are prevented from purchasing permits.

environmentally harmful activities. For example, transferable development rights have been applied as part of comprehensive management plans in New Jersey's Pinelands. Here, development rights operate in conjunction with zoning restrictions so that landholders who own valuable habitat can trade with landholders in zones of land of lesser biological importance. The use of transferable development rights is also allowed under the Resource Management Act 1991 in New Zealand. Tradeable water entitlements and individually transferable fishing quotas are other examples.[146] So too, there are emerging schemes for effluent trading in watersheds, wetland banking mitigation, and conservation banking, all of which adopt some component of tradeable rights.[147]

Despite the substantial theoretical benefits available from utilizing tradeable permits, a number of practical difficulties have emerged in their application. These include:

(i) difficulties in finding a rational basis on which to allocate permits, whether historical use, equity, or individual rights;[148]

(ii) a propensity for schemes to be inequitable if permits are simply allocated to existing polluters—'for new entrants to the market will have to pay the price to achieve rights of discharge';[149]

(iii) limited trading and uncompetitive behaviour, such as hoarding permits, which undermine theoretical cost efficiencies;

(iv) difficulties in monitoring and enforcing permits when there is a large number of small, disparate polluters or there are mobile sources of pollution, such as vehicles, or there are non-point sources of pollution, such as methane emissions from farms;

(v) difficulties in taking into account the transboundary effects and highly localized ambient concentrations pollutants;[150] and

[146] M. D. Young, N. Gunningham, J. Elix, J. Lambert, B. Howard, P. Grabosky, E. McCrone, *Reimbursing the Future: An evaluation of motivational, voluntary, price-based, property-right, and regulatory incentives for the conservation of biodiversity* (1996), Biodiversity Series Paper No. 9, Department of the Environment, Sport and Territories, Biodiversity Unit, Canberra.

[147] For a useful summary, see The Keystone National Policy Dialogue on Ecosystem Management, Final Report (October 1996), Keystone Center, Colorado.

[148] T. Swanson, 'Economic Instruments and Environmental Regulation: A. critical introduction' (1995) 4(4) *Review of European Community and International Environmental Law* 287.

[149] D. James, *Using Economic Instruments for Meeting Environmental Objectives: Australia's experience* (1993), Department of the Environment, Sport and Territories, Canberra, p.22.

[150] Geographical difficulties associated with permit use, such as transboundary pollution or high concentrations of pollutants exceeding ambient limits, may be addressed by attaching a transfer coefficient to each permit. When a trade takes place, the permit value

(vi) difficulties in issuing uniform permits for a mix of pollutants or resources.[151]

Perhaps unsurprisingly, given the array of practical obstacles, only a modest number of market creation schemes have so far been introduced. Some, such as the United States acid rain permit trading programme, have the capability to work with considerable effectiveness.[152] Others have suffered serious design faults, with the result that very few trades have actually taken place and monopolistic and anti-competitive behaviour has emerged.[153] There is a dilemma in increasing the complexity of the design and operation of permit schemes to address unintended consequences, in that they have the potential, through greater administrative and enforcement burdens, to undermine theoretical efficiencies. It is difficult to escape the conclusion that despite potential efficiency gains, market creation may be restricted to applications where the use of permits can be easily monitored and verified, and where there are good trading prospects. In these circumstances, well designed schemes have the capacity to deliver substantially reduced pollution loads and a substantially lower cost to industry.[154]

may increase or decrease depending on the nature of the coefficient attached. Coefficients could be based on, for example, proximity between permit buyers and sellers, concentric zones around a fixed location, or even prevailing wind directions. By manipulating transfer coefficients, regulators are able to engineer regulatory outcomes.

[151] Except where that mix impacts on a common environmental problem, such as ozone depletion, and the relative contributions of different substances have been quantified in the form of transfer coefficients.

[152] Environment Protection Agency, *EPA Acid Rain Program* (1996), Update No. 3 Technology and Information, EPA, Washington DC.

[153] With many permit schemes in operation, the actual number of trades taking place between firms is well below expectations—this has perplexed policymakers. One market for effluent permits experienced only one trade in six years (A. Moran, 'Tools of Environmental Policy: Market instruments versus command and control' in R. Eckersley (ed.), *Markets, the State and the Environment* (1995), Macmillan Press, Melbourne, pp.73–85). Explanations include:

(i)   insufficient players for a competitive market to emerge;
(ii)   too many regulatory controls which inhibit trading by making it costly;
(iii) abatement technologies are limited and require discrete amounts of investment. This results in 'lumpy' investments, which would need to be matched by an equivalent parcel of permits;
(iv)   the initial allocation of permits may be overly generous, resulting in firms which have more than enough permits for their needs and, therefore, no incentive to trade; and
(v)   hoarding of permits to limit new entrants or drive out competitors.

[154] See, in particular, the experience of the South Coast Air Quality Management District, Southern California RECLAIM programme evaluated in P. Leyden, 'Trading in Southern California' (1997), a paper delivered to *American Bar Association 26th Annual Conference on Environmental Law*, Keystone, Colorado, March.

(iii) Fiscal instruments and charge systems

Fiscal instruments are used to encourage environmentally responsible behaviour through full (or partial) cost pricing of consumption or production. That is, rather than establishing property-rights over common or unpriced resources, this approach involves establishing prices on them, as a different way to internalize externalities. For example, a tax might be based on the degree of harm caused, or in proportion to the amount of polluting activity.[155] Economic theory indicates that fiscal instruments, principally taxes and charges, will impose less costs on industry to achieve a given level of pollution reduction than will command and control regulations intended to reach the same goal.[156] As with market creation, this is because taxes and charges can exploit differences in the marginal cost of abatement between firms to lower the overall cost of abatement.[157] There is an ongoing incentive to find new and cheaper ways to reduce pollution or resource consumption and avoid payment, and because taxes and charges are non-prescriptive, there are no limits to the ways in which these can be achieved.

Emission and effluent charges are amongst the most common form of fiscal instrument. They are usually applied to individual point sources or to 'bubbles' (from prescribed areas or zones) and applied per unit of discharge.[158] As each unit of pollution is reduced, so an economic dividend is provided to the polluting enterprise. France, Germany and the Netherlands all have effluent charges on water pollution.[159] Proposed taxes on phosphates would fulfil similar functions. Other applications include charges for the collection and treatment of waste, and charges on potentially hazardous substances such as lubricant oils, fertilisers,

---

[155] Taxes and charges embody the 'Polluter Pays Principle', or in the case of natural resource use, the 'User Pays Principle'.

[156] W. Baumol & W. Oates, *The Theory of Environmental Policy* (1988) (2nd edn.), Cambridge University Press, Cambridge, New York.

[157] In theory at least, the inherent cost effectiveness of tradeable permits and taxes should be identical (K. Hamilton & G. Cameron, 'Simulating the Distributional Effects of a Canadian Carbon Tax' (1994) XX(4) *Canadian Public Policy: Analyse de Politiques* 385–96). If the marginal cost of abatement is known with some degree of certainty, then there is no obvious theoretical reason to choose tradeable emission permits over taxes, or vice versa. However, practical difficulties associated with the enforcement of permits and the number, size, and location of polluters may sway the choice towards taxes.

[158] D. James, *Using Economic Instruments for Meeting Environmental Objectives: Australia's experience* (1993), Department of the Environment, Sport and Territories, Canberra, pp.10–11.

[159] J. B. Opschoor & H. B. Vos, *Application of Economic Instruments for Environmental Protection in OECD Countries* (1989), OECD, Paris, pp.82–88.

pesticides, and batteries. Charges and taxes can be invoked to create incentives for more efficient resource use. Examples include user-pays charges for water, proposals for energy/carbon taxes, and taxing nature-based tourism operators.

It is important to recognize, however, that many tax and charge schemes that have been implemented across the globe are, in reality, revenue raising devices, not serious environmental policy instruments.[160] That is, the size of the price signal to polluters is well below that required to achieve a given environmental objective. In fairness, it may be politically possible only to introduce taxes and charges at low levels, essentially as symbolic measures, and increase them over time until they provide an effective price-based signal to the market. This rationale has been applied to suggestions for a phased introduction of carbon taxes to reduce greenhouse gas emissions in Australia.[161]

Financial subsidies are another form of fiscal instrument. By subsidies, we refer to tax concessions conditional upon desired conduct. For example, tax deductions for the expenses of environmentally responsible activity, such as mine site remediation; or lower tax rates on preferred products or materials, such as energy efficient cars or unleaded petrol. In recent years, such approaches have become increasingly sophisticated. For example, Costa Rica now runs a transferable reforestation tax credit scheme under which landholders receive a tax credit for keeping their land forested or for returning land to native species cover. Subsidies may also be offered by private and non-profit institutions. Defenders of Wildlife operate the Wolf Reward Program which pays $5,000 to private landholders if wild wolves successfully raise a litter of pups on their land.

Objections to using taxes and charges take three basic forms.[162] First, there is considerable difficulty in setting a tax or charge at the right level. This is because the costs and choices facing polluters may not be known to policymakers (and in any case, may be subject to lobbying to minimize business costs). This problem might be overcome by trial and error (which may disrupt investment plans), or by establishing a pro-

---

[160] Project 88, *Project 88—Round II: Incentives for Action* (1991), Washington DC.

[161] R. Eckersley (ed.), *Markets, the State and the Environment* (1995), Macmillan Press, Melbourne.

[162] Further problems include the high administrative (collection) costs, difficulties in tailoring the regional aspects of pollution, and economically regressive impacts on the community.

gressive scale of charges, to be increased over time.[163] Nevertheless, there may remain some circumstances where it is essential to 'get it right' first time, and where failure to do so may cause irreversible loss. Secondly, where prices are relatively inelastic due to limited input substitutability, costs may simply be transferred to final consumers with no consequential environmental benefit. Alternatively, the size of the tax or charge would need to be very large, and thus undermine the cost-effectiveness of the instrument.[164] Firms may also not respond rationally to price signals. Where taxes or charges represent only a small proportion of outlays, costs might simply be ignored or not noticed. And thirdly, taxes and charges may be perceived as legitimating or condoning environmentally harmful behaviour. For the State to allow pollution, at a price, strikes some as an inferior regulatory strategy to one which condemns environmentally deleterious activity outright. In some circumstances, taxes or charges also raise issues of fairness and distribution, because they affect some regions and industries more than others and impact on small business much more substantially than on larger enterprises.

In regard to tax subsidies, abatement incentives may be self-defeating, not for any sinister intent on the part of prospective recipients, but because they might attract new entrants to the industry. A number of these new players may be expected to bring inefficient processes with them, thus increasing the number of potential polluters and, in the long run, the overall level of pollution.[165] Subsidies may also be a drain on public revenue.

(iv) Financial instruments

Financial instruments include such measures as revolving funds, green funds, subsidised interest rates, and soft loans. The intention is to mobilize additional financial resources for conservation and environmental protection. For example, revolving loans enable central governments to provide funds to local governments, small businesses, or other entities,

---

[163] D. James, *Using Economic Instruments for Meeting Environmental Objectives: Australia's experience* (1993), Department of the Environment, Sport and Territories, Canberra, p.12.

[164] For example, the consumption of petrol for private motor vehicle use is very price inelastic: because of the unavailability of alternative fuels, the price of petrol would need to be very high before consumers would substantially change their driving behaviour.

[165] W. Baumol & W. Oates, *The Theory of Environmental Policy* (1988) (2nd edn.), Cambridge University Press, Cambridge; P. Palmquist, 'Pollution Subsidies and Multiple Local Optima' (1990) 66 *Land Economics* 394–401; and R. Kohn, 'When Subsidies for Pollution Abatement Increase Total Emissions' (1992) 59(1) *Southern Economic Journal* 77–87.

enabling them to finance a variety of environmental activities such as sewage treatment, waste water recycling, non-point source pollution control projects, and reforestation. As loans are repaid, they are recycled to make new loans to other entities. Similarly, revolving funds are used to acquire land, attach an easement to it, and then to sell the property so encumbered. Money from the sale of the land is then reused to purchase other property. Loans are commonly made at interest rates lower than the market can offer, thus partially subsidizing particular environmental projects which, although desirable, cannot be justified in strict commercial terms. For example, revolving loan funds are used in China for industrial pollution control.[166] Although financial instruments may indeed be effective for such purposes they do not, however, adhere to the polluter pays principle. There are also dangers that such instruments may be abused. For example, funds might be used for purposes other than those intended (e.g., industrial expansion lacking an environmental rationale), emphasizing the need for transparency and accountability at all stages.

(v) Liability instruments

Imposing civil liability on those who despoil the environment can provide an economic incentive for the management and control of risk, pollution and waste. Enterprises are given an inducement to internalize externalities by the threat that legal action will be used to recover the cost of environmental damages. At the very least, they may be persuaded to take out environmental insurance which, while mitigating the risk, may also expose them to pressure from the insurance company.[167]

It is important to distinguish between inherent and practical problems of liability instruments. In contrast to most other economic instruments, liability systems recover damages *ex post* (although the incentive effect is *ex ante*). This need not make them any less effective, in theory, providing that the liability system impacts upon the resource user in proportion to the harms that their uses are causing. In practice, however, many liability schemes are beset with problems that seriously limit their potential role in environmental protection.[168] These include diffi-

---

[166] World Bank, *China: Southern Jiangsu Environmental Protection Project* (1993), Staff Appraisal Report 11370–CHA, Washington DC.

[167] See further, chapter three pp.118 below.

[168] S. Rose-Ackerman, 'Public Law Versus Private Law in Environmental Regulation: European Union proposals in the light of the United States experience' (1995) 4(4) *Review of European Community and International Environmental Law* 312–319. Proposals for reversal of the onus of proof, or for strict liability, would serve to mitigate some of these problems,

culties in dealing with large numbers of individuals and complex, multifaceted problems; tracking the pathway between industrial activity and harm; and the very high, and potentially unequal, transaction costs of court action (even allowing for the possibility of class actions and other mechanisms to reduce these costs).[169] A deciding factor in the viability of liability instruments is the timing of their introduction: prospective application is likely to be far more successful than retrospective application.

(vi) Performance bonds

Performance bonds require regulatees to post a security deposit which is redeemable upon satisfactory completion of a required task.[170] In the event of non-performance, the deposit is forfeited. The most obvious example would be a performance bond lodged by a mining company which undertakes to rehabilitate land used for mining once an operation is complete. In the event that the company fails to adequately restore the land and its biodiversity, all or part of the bond would be forfeited and deployed for remediation purposes. Performance bonds are equally applicable to pollution reduction and effluent control programmes and might be extended to forestry and fisheries. Performance bonds are best suited to situations where there is one source of potential environmental damage, and where that damage can be reasonably

but would leave others untouched. Even in the litigious United States, in recent years only a small number of tort cases have been used to prevent prospective injuries and only a few cases have provided equitable relief to abate pollution (A. W. Reitze, 'A Century of Pollution Control Law: What worked; what's failed; what might work' (1991) 21 *Environmental Law* 1549–1646). See also P. S. Menell, 'The Limitations of Legal Institutions for Addressing Environmental Risks' (1991) 5(3) *Journal of Economic Perspectives* 93–113.

[169] As E. Brunet, 'Debunking wholesale Private Enforcement of Environmental Rights' (1992) 15 Harvard Journal of Law and Policy 321 puts it, this approach: 'ignores the unequal positions of individuals *vis-à vis* large business organisations, the investigative and litigative expertise of agencies, the economies of scale achievable by an agency, and the consequent deterrent effects which flow from this'. Consequently, the contribution of liability schemes to environmental policy is likely to be modest at best (S. Rose-Ackerman, 'Public Law Versus Private Law in Environmental Regulation: European Union proposals in the light of the United States experience' (1995) 4(4) *Review of European Community and International Environmental Law* 312–319).

[170] An alternative, but related, mechanism is risk insurance. There might, for example, be advantages in compelling the taking out of insurance cover before engaging in a particularly hazardous activity. Widespread applications are limited by difficulties in setting appropriate premiums and no provision for ongoing 'maintenance, repair, administration, monitoring or compensation beyond the life of the project' (R. Ramsay & G. C. Rowe, *Environmental Law and Policy in Australia* (1995), Butterworths, Australia, pp.211–212).

estimated. They are socially acceptable, administratively simple and cost-effective, and incorporate both the polluter pays and precautionary principles.[171] They are, however, only appropriate to address temporary threats.

(vii) Deposit refund systems

Conceptually similar to performance bonds, deposit refund systems provide individuals and/or firms with a financial incentive to dispose of waste in an environmentally preferable way. For example, producers or carriers of hazardous waste could be required to lodge a deposit, redeemable upon presentation of the waste product in question, or upon proof of satisfactory disposal.[172] The most common manifestation of this type of instrument is the deposit refund system for used beverage containers,[173] but its potential application is much wider, extending to batteries, automobiles, and other forms of solid waste. There is considerable debate, however, as to the administrative complexity and cost of operating such systems.

(viii) Removing perverse incentives

The value of many potentially valuable incentive mechanisms may be lost or minimized by the existence of perverse incentives, sometimes referred to as the 'subsidizing of environmental bads'. For example, a carbon tax is unlikely to realise its potential to reduce greenhouse gas emissions while the production of coal-fired electricity remains subsidized as part of a separate government programme. Often perverse incentives occur because the government has intervened in the market to secure social or economic ends, without fully understanding or considering their implications for environmental protection. The World Watch Institute has identified massive environmentally destructive subsidies in highly advanced economies such as Canada, the United States and Australia. The OECD lists administered resource prices, output pricing, irrigation subsidies, below cost timber pricing, subsidized crop insurance, and agricultural support programmes, as examples of government intervention that causes perverse incentives (the perverse envi-

---

[171] D. James, *Using Economic Instruments for Meeting Environmental Objectives: Australia's experience* (1993), Department of the Environment, Sport and Territories, Canberra.

[172] J. B. Opschoor & H. B. Vos, *Application of Economic Instruments for Environmental Protection in OECD. Countries* (1989), OECD, Paris, pp.82–88.

[173] Nine States of the US, several Canadian Provinces, a number of European nations, and South Australia have all introduced deposit refund schemes to recycle beverage containers (Project 88, *Project 88—Round II: Incentives for Action* (1991), Washington DC).

ronmental impact of traditional agricultural policy instruments will be discussed in chapter five). In principle, all such unsustainable market distortions should be removed, or at least reduced, before positive incentives are introduced.[174]

Strengths and weaknesses of economic instruments

In theory, the virtues of economic mechanisms are their ability to:

(i)   influence behaviour through price signals or property systems without the need for direct intervention in the affairs of individuals;

(ii) encourage individuals to seek out the most cost-effective (and innovative) solutions;

(iii) decentralize decision-making to individuals who often have better information on how to solve a problem than regulators;

(iv) reduce the government's enforcement costs as well as the resource user's compliance costs; and

(v)   to give resource users an ongoing incentive to develop better environmental approaches.

Whether, in practice, these virtues are necessarily demonstrated is less clear. Since relatively few economic instruments have been implemented in environmental policy, and most of these only recently, we have very little experience of how they actually work. Significantly, a recent and comprehensive OECD report on this issue has been unable to reach any general conclusions about the effectiveness, efficiency, equity implications, acceptability, or administrative implications of economic instruments.[175] As we will observe in chapter five, the extent to which economic mechanisms can make a positive contribution to environmental protection is likely to depend substantially on the particular contexts in which they are applied, the threats to which they are addressed, their inherent attributes, [176] and their particular design and implementation.

There are, nevertheless, some generalizations that can usefully be made about the role of economic instruments and property-right approaches and about their relationship with regulatory strategies. In theory at least, economic instruments, appropriately designed, are likely

[174] Many perverse incentives have become so entrenched over a long period of time that the recipients now do not regard them as subsidies and thus fiercely resist their removal.

[175] Organisation for Economic Co-operation and Development (OECD), *Making Markets Work for Biological Diversity* (1996), OECD, Paris.

[176] As described in the preceding pages.

to substantially reduce the overall costs imposed on industry. This is because 'regulatory instruments require the central authority to determine the best course of action, whereas economic instruments decentralize much of the decision-making to the single farm or factory or household, which typically has better information for determining the appropriate individual response to given economic conditions'.[177] Each firm can therefore optimize its abatement strategy in response to appropriate market signals. Such signals can also stimulate demand for new abatement technologies.

Unfortunately, and contrary to claims made in some of the earlier literature, economic instruments are not self-enforcing and may involve considerable control costs.[178] Indeed, one recent study concluded that 'there is no reason to expect that the administrative costs of economic instruments are generally lower than those of regulatory instruments'.[179] In any comparison with other regulatory instruments, it is appropriate, therefore, to compare the total regulatory costs, that is the public administrative costs plus the private costs borne by industry. It must also be acknowledged that market-based and property-right instruments are not generally well understood, and perhaps for this reason, do not rate highly in terms of community acceptance.

In the practical application of economic instruments, potential shortcomings include:

(i)   a lack of dependability on the part of property-rights and fiscal instruments in particular (unless underpinned by direct regulation) which may be crucial, for example, in the protection of ecosystems and biodiversity;[180]

(ii) a heavy reliance on information (e.g., about the quantity or quality of emissions). In circumstances where such information is very hard to obtain, a technology-based approach may be more appropriate;

[177] E. B. Barbier, J. C. Burgess & C. Folke, *Paradise lost? The ecological economics of biodiversity* (1994), Earthscan Publications Ltd, London.

[178] J. Bowers, *Incentives and Mechanisms for Biodiversity: Observations and issues* (1994), CSIRO Division of Wildlife and Ecology, Canberra, p.9.

[179] L. S. Lohman, 'Economic Incentives in Environmental Policy: Why are there white ravens?' in H. Opschoor & K. Turner (eds.), *Economic Incentives and Environmental Policies: Principles and practice* (1994), Kluwer Academic Publishers, Dordrecht, p.22.

[180] C. Perrings & D. Pearce, 'Threshold Effects and Incentives for the Conservation of Biodiversity' (1994) 4 *Environmental and Resource Economics* 13–28.

(iii) the risk that markets themselves may fail and that firms may not respond rationally to price signals;[181]

(iv) the risk that subsidies, in particular, will have a 'lulling" effect which reinforces the *status quo* rather than foster innovative pollution controls; and

(v) undesirable distributive impacts. For example, tax incentives operate regressively, they are worth more to the wealthy than to the poor, and they are of no benefit at all to those outside the tax system entirely or to those firms operating at a loss.[182]

Finally, as Cohen points out:

Economic instruments can be used to create incentives to meet or exceed centrally mandated standards. They can perhaps reduce the enforcement and compliance costs associated with criminal justice models of regulation. But they do not transform regulation in the way their original proponents hoped and believed. Most economic instruments require the state to set standards—the difference between this instrument and command and control regulation is that incentives and markets were used to move firms towards compliance. And while levels of compliance were perhaps higher than that achieved with command and control regulation, economic instruments still required public bureaucracies to monitor and ultimately to enforce the standards.[183]

6. Free market environmentalism

Although often billed as alternatives to command and control, economic instruments (excluding property-rights) may, in fact, be considered as market-based *variants of* command and control, in that the

---

[181] For example, markets may not always be conducive to recycling. Many recycling initiatives, worthy from the social/ecological standpoint, have not been economically viable because the price of goods made from raw material with which recycled goods must compete does not reflect the full environmental and other costs of its production. Similarly, poorly designed economic instruments 'can inflict costs on the community that are as high as those associated with command and control systems' (D. James, *Using Economic Instruments for Meeting Environmental Objectives: Australia's experience* (1993), Department of the Environment, Sport and Territories, Canberra, p.5). On the limitations of free markets generally, see R. Kuttner, *Everything For Sale: The virtues and limits of markets* (1997), Alfred A. Knopf, New York.

[182] S. Surrey, 'Tax Incentives as a Device for Implementing Government Policy: A comparison with direct government expenditures' (1970) 83(4) *Harvard Law Review* 705–38.

[183] D. Cohen, 'Voluntary Codes: The Role of the Canadian State in a Privatized Regulatory Environment', a draft paper presented at the Voluntary Codes Symposium, Office of Consumer Affairs, Industry Canada and Regulatory Affairs, Treasury Board, Ottawa, September 1996 and to be included in *Exploring Voluntary Codes in the Marketplace*, edited by D. Cohen & K. Webb, Government of Canada, Ottawa, (publication due 1998), p.2.

regulator still dictates environmental aims through the manipulation of price signals or tradeable permits.[184] Such instruments must be clearly distinguished from the extreme alternatives to environmental regulation which are espoused in sweeping terms by 'free market environmentalists' such as Anderson and Leal.[185] They argue not only in favour of a more precise allocation and specification of property-rights (much as described above), but also for the substitution of free markets for legislative solutions, to regulate the exploitation of virtually all natural resources and sources of pollution.[186]

Free market environmentalism entails allocating property-rights for natural resources to private interests, or liability rules imposed in respect of harm from pollution, then allowing the market to operate unfettered by government intervention. Under this approach, all environmental outcomes can and should be determined by the accumulation of bargains struck between individual owners of natural resource property-rights.[187] There is no role for government in establishing and pursuing environmental objectives. There would, however, be a role for government in monitoring and enforcing the trading of individual property-rights. Free market environmentalism is thus not really an instrument in the sense of a government or some other institution intervening to correct a market failure; rather it is characterized by the substantial absence of interventionist instruments. Such an approach would entail, *inter alia*, broadly defining property-rights to include not only land ownership, but also leases of public land for grazing or timber harvesting; recognizing existing property-rights and removing impediments to the creation of new ones; minimal disturbance on individuals or firms to use their property as they choose; unbundling land-use rights and land ownership so that, for example, water rights are not attached to land; and allowing different conservation and resource rights to be traded.[188]

---

[184] For example, taxes and charges are another form of government regulation: government sets the charge and polices the system, prosecuting those who breach the rules.

[185] T. L. Anderson & D. R. Leal 'Free Market Versus Political Environmentalism' (1992) 15 *Harvard Journal of Law and Public Policy* 297–310.

[186] J. E. Krier, 'The Tragedy of the Commons, Part Two' (1992) 15 *Harvard Journal of Law & Public Policy* 325–47.

[187] M. Jacobs, 'Sustainability and the "Market": A typology of environmental economics' in R. Eckersley (ed.), *Markets, the State and the Environment* (1995), Macmillan Press, Melbourne.

[188] A. G. Chisholm & A. S. Moran (eds.) (1993), *The Price of Preservation* Tasman Institute, Melbourne.

Free market environmentalists allege that it is difficult, if not impossible, for policy-makers to obtain accurate information about the value people place on environmental goods. A better solution is to allow the market to determine these values under a system of well specified property-rights. Anderson and Leal also contend that the free market approach is preferable because the political process of determining government regulation is itself essentially corrupt, with regulatory officials and politicians both vulnerable to special interest group lobbying and conflicts of interest.[189]

Strengths and weaknesses

Each of the main strategies advocated by free market environmentalists has serious limitations. For example, although the property-rights approach is claimed to be widely applicable, in practice it has only been used successfully in a very limited range of circumstances; and even in some of these, can produce unwanted side effects. Take the most common scenario used to promote this approach: endangered species protection. It is argued that because no one owns such species or their habitat, no one has an incentive to protect them. Conversely, if people are granted an exclusive right to and profit from a resource, they have a greater incentive to conserve that resource.[190] Experience with the effectiveness of mechanisms which adopt this 'exclusive rights' approach, however, is mixed. For example, the commercialization of wildlife has had only limited successes,[191] most of which involve charismatic megafauna, or immediate commercial pay-offs.[192] Moreover,

---

[189] T. L. Anderson & D. R. Leal 'Free Market Versus Political Environmentalism' (1992) 15 *Harvard Journal of Law and Public Policy* 297–310.

[190] M. D. Young, N. Gunningham, J. Elix, J. Lambert, B. Howard, P. Grabosky, E. McCrone, *Reimbursing the Future: An evaluation of motivational, voluntary, price-based, property-right, and regulatory incentives for the conservation of biodiversity* (1996), Biodiversity Series Paper No. 9, Department of the Environment, Sport and Territories, Biodiversity Unit, Canberra.

[191] Zimbabwe's CAMPFIRE programme is perhaps the best known and most effective case in its attempt to institute species protection. Under this programme, local communities have been given the right to use wildlife as they wish. The result has been a substantial shift in community attitudes to wildlife and the emergence of many innovative market arrangements. Generally, the people involved see wildlife as an asset worth preserving.

[192] T. M. Swanson & E. Barbier, (eds.) *Economics for the Wild: Wildlife, wildlands, diversity and development* (1992), Earthscan, London; T. M. Swanson, *Intellectual Property Rights & Biodiversity Conservation: An interdisciplinary analysis of the values of medical plants* (1995), Cambridge University Press, New York; and R. Yeager & N. Miller, *Wild Death Land Use and Survival in Eastern Africa* (1986), State University of New York Press in association with the African-Caribbean Institute, Albany, New York.

there may also be serious unforeseen problems with the commercialization approach generally: namely that it encourages illegal use (giving rise to black markets and smuggling operations); that it threatens genetic diversity;[193] and that when specially bred species, such as salmon, escape into the wild this can also cause serious damage to the gene pool.[194]

An alternative free market proposal would be to sell or lease publicly owned land such as national parks or timber reserves to private interests. This would allow those interested in the preservation of an endangered species habitat, such as environmentalists, to purchase the property-rights and prevent any further exploitation. On a similar principle, the Nature Conservancy purchases privately owned land, as well as easements, for conservation purposes. The problem with this approach is that it assumes that private individuals and public interest groups have the necessary resources to compete with potentially large multinational firms in the purchase of the property-rights. Further, environmentalists are unlikely to derive much income from their activities, leaving them at a further competitive disadvantage to firms which are able to use profits from the past exploitation of resources to purchase more property-rights.

Turning specifically to pollution, it is contended by free market environmentalists that common law tort remedies (mimicking the market, in Coasian terms) are a more appropriate and efficient response than command and control regulation.[195] For example, if the owners of private fishing rights in a stream had their property damaged through the actions of an upstream polluter, they would be able to obtain compensation by bringing a liability suit against the polluter. Thus the threat of legal remedy would provide an ongoing incentive to minimize stream pollution. However, as indicated above,[196] there are serious shortcom-

---

[193] M. D. Young, N. Gunningham, J. Elix, J. Lambert, B. Howard, P. Grabosky, E. McCrone, *Reimbursing the Future: An evaluation of motivational, voluntary, price-based, property-right, and regulatory incentives for the conservation of biodiversity* (1996), Biodiversity Series Paper No. 9, Department of the Environment, Sport and Territories, Biodiversity Unit, Canberra, vol. I p.36.

[194] M. D. Young, N. Gunningham, J. Elix, J. Lambert, B. Howard, P. Grabosky, E. McCrone, *Reimbursing the Future: An evaluation of motivational, voluntary, price-based, property-right, and regulatory incentives for the conservation of biodiversity* (1996), Biodiversity Series Paper No. 9, Department of the Environment, Sport and Territories, Biodiversity Unit, Canberra, vol. 2 p.31.

[195] T. L. Anderson & D. R. Leal 'Free Market Versus Political Environmentalism' (1992) 15 *Harvard Journal of Law and Public Policy* 297–310.

[196] See p.78–9.

ings in using liability as an environmental instrument, including difficulty in accommodating complex, multifaceted problems, very high transaction costs, and the inevitable inequities between different litigants. A total reliance on tort liability to enforce property-rights would, therefore, be fraught with dangers.[197] To take another example, some free market economists advocate a property-rights approach to the problem of automobile emissions, involving the privatization of highways and an entitlement to those damaged by pollution to sue highway owners for compensation. Apart from the potential for high transaction costs, there are several unresolved threshold issues, such as who is going to sue,[198] what damages are relevant, and how the source is going to be traced. All these issues are conveniently ignored.[199] In essence, property-rights enforced through liability rules are unlikely to be viable in complex situations involving many different users of a single commodity where the exclusion of other users in not practicable.[200]

The concept of free market environmentalism has been the subject of more comprehensive critiques. Blumm suggests that, because of less than perfect market information, high transaction costs, and difficulties in pricing collective goods and internalizing externalities, privatization fails to generate the promised efficiencies.[201] Further, the evidence from the pre-regulatory era is that unassisted markets systemically failed to provide efficient or fair allocations of environmental resources. He concludes that private rights are expensive to define and enforce, and would rely on *ad hoc* assessments of individual cases under common law. Others suggest that the free market environmentalists ignore the need for markets to be co-ordinated by the very governments whose capacities they doubt.[202]

---

[197] E. Brunet, 'Debunking Wholesale Private Enforcement of Environmental Rights' (1992) 15 *Harvard Journal of Law & Public Policy* 321–22.

[198] Past experience demonstrates that it is more often public interest groups that initiate civil suits, not individuals; this emphasizes the importance of *collective* solutions over narrow private interests (E. Brunet, 'Debunking Wholesale Private Enforcement of Environmental Rights' (1992) 15 *Harvard Journal of Law & Public Policy* 321–22).

[199] W. Funk, 'Free Market Environmentalism: Wonder drug or snake oil?' (1992) 15 *Harvard Journal of Law and Public Policy* 511–12.

[200] B. Schauzenbacher, *Economic Instruments as Policy Instruments for Environmental Management and Sustainable Development* (1995), UNEP, Environment and Economics Unit, Nairobi.

[201] M. C. Blumm, 'The Fallacies of Free Market Environmentalism' (1992) 15 *Harvard Journal of Law & Public Policy* 371–89.

[202] J. E. Krier 'The Tragedy of the Commons, Part Two' (1992) 15 *Harvard Journal of Law and Public Policy*, 325–47.

The purported strengths of free market environmentalism: an absence of political and policy interference and the ability to reflect the true value of environmental goods, are, in fact, largely dependent on efficiently operating markets. That is, markets should, as far as possible, be based on perfect competition and perfect information. The problem is that markets rarely operate this way.[203] There is the inevitability of transactions costs, less than rational behaviour by competitors, and decisions being made in the absence of relevant information and the ability to enforce the internalization of externalities. Private individuals and public interest groups do not have the necessary resources to compete with potentially large multinational firms in the purchase of the property-rights. Further, environmentalists are unlikely to derive much income from their activities, leaving them at a further competitive disadvantage to firms which are able to use profits from the past exploitation of resources to purchase more property-rights. This exposes the central conundrum facing the free market environmentalists: that government intervention, to a greater or lesser extent, is required to minimize these market distortions. As Krier points out, there is no guarantee that government will not fail in establishing and operating a market of resource property-rights, just as it fails in establishing and operating environmental regulatory regimes.[204]

In conclusion, the circumstances in which the free market environmentalism approach is demonstrably viable appear to be limited, in particular, to situations where there is a resource that lends itself to commercial exploitation; where property-rights can be clearly defined and readily enforced; where there is an absence of multiple users; where the users have access to appropriate information; and where the users clearly have an ongoing dependency on the viability of the resource. It is no coincidence that the most convincing examples provided by free market environmentalists conform to just such situations.

7. Conclusion

In this chapter, we have shown that, beyond the confines of the traditional system of regulation, there exists a far richer tapestry of policy instruments than is commonly realized. As the conventional approach to command and control begins to collapse under its own weight,[205] so

---

[203] J. E. Krier, 'The Tragedy of the Commons, Part Two' (1992) 15 *Harvard Journal of Law & Public Policy* 325–47.
[204] *Ibid.*

policymakers have begun to pay increasing attention to the potential of these broader policy options.

As a result, environmental policy is in transition: from command and control towards a much more pluralistic conception of instrument design. Yet these moves towards pluralism have, so far, been hesitant in their approach and uneven in their outcomes. Economic instruments, long hailed by environmental economists as the answer to a broad range of problems, have been introduced only cautiously, in limited areas, and with encouraging,[206] but nevertheless mixed results.[207] Some instruments, for example corporate environmental reporting, and environmental accounting, remain very much at the experimental stage. Others, such as some forms of product certification, have been tried and found wanting. Still others, such as community right-to-know and some forms of co-regulation, have had some marked successes, but only in limited circumstances. Overall, alternative policy instruments are still at an early stage of development in which 'little is known in general about [their] effectiveness, efficiency, or administrative implications, nor about how they may be best implemented'.[208]

Even where policymakers have utilized innovative approaches, this has often been in a manner which is largely incoherent and unreflexive. Single instrument and single category approaches still predominate, commonly driven, as we indicated in chapter one, either by professional myopia or self-interest, and with little awareness of the limitations of those instruments and their incapacity to operate effectively 'across the board'. All too often, the story of the little boy and the hammer remains apposite to policy design. The little boy, having been given a toy hammer as a gift, would use the tool for every task he confronted, regardless of its suitability.

Sometimes, mixes of instruments, or a broader range of institutional actors, are invoked, but often with little awareness of the need for conscious regulatory design. Far worse, some mixes, put together with

---

[205] W. F. Pederson, 'Can Site Specific Pollution Control Plans Furnish an Alternative to the Current Regulatory System?' (1995) 25 *Environmental Law Reporter* 10486.

[206] See, for example, M. Kenny, 'Use of Marketplace Incentives in California to Improve Air Quality' (1997), a paper delivered to *American Bar Association 26th Annual Environmental Law Conference*, Keystone, Colorado, March 1997.

[207] See, for example, E. Rehbinder, 'Environmental Regulation Through Fiscal and Economic Incentives in a Federalist System' (1993) 20 *Ecology Law Quarterly* 57–83. See also Organisation for Economic Co-operation and Development (OECD), *Evaluating Economic Instruments for Environmental Policy* (1997), OECD, Paris.

[208] Organisation for Economic Co-operation and Development (OECD), *Meeting on Alternatives to Traditional Regulation* (1994), May, OECD, Paris, p.4.

insufficient thought as to their likely consequences or undesirable side effects, are likely to be counterproductive or dysfunctional. Many of the most constructive and sophisticated innovations, to date, have been modifications to conventional regulation. These range from a more judicious blend of performance and specification standards, through changing permit and compliance programmes to introduce more flexibility, to the use of process-based standards, reflexive regulation, and incentives for exemplary performance. Some of these innovations to command and control have taken on the characteristics of other instruments and have utilized a broader range of institutional actors. That is, here at least, there is now some conscious mixing of instruments and actors.

However, these broader innovations are the exception rather than the rule and their impact, so far, has been very modest. For example, after almost two years of operation, only one company had taken up an Accredited Licence in Victoria,[209] while a detailed evaluation of Project XL (and a number of other innovations) concluded that too high transactions costs, mutual mistrust, and the lack of a statutory base have resulted in very low participation rates in this and a number of kindred schemes.[210] In any event, these innovations are dwarfed by other new environmental initiatives in the traditional mould which, to quote Marc Landy: 'exacerbate the environmental regime's worst excesses'.[211] Even the European Union's Environmental Management and Audit Scheme (EMAS), the most far reaching of these alternative schemes, has encountered problems, largely a result of the political compromises and dilution necessary to gain industry's acquiescence to its introduction.

Notwithstanding the very modest advances made to date, some of this experimentation nevertheless suggests important themes and insights on which future policy development and design may build. As should now be obvious, there is no such thing as a single, perfect, universal solution to environmental problems. Each of the instruments dis-

---

[209] T. Samson, *An Important Step But No Giant Leap: An assessment of the Victorian Accredited Licensing System*, (1996), October, Australian National University Honours Thesis, Australian National University, Canberra.

[210] T. Davies & J. Mazirek, *Industry Incentives for Environmental Improvement: Evaluation of US. Federal initiatives* (1996), a report to the Global Environmental Management initiative (GEMI), Washington DC.

[211] In the United States, the most important of these are the new 1991 Clean Air Act and RCRA 'Corrective Action'. See also M. Landy, 'National Regulation in a Global Economy: The dynamics of interdependency' (1997), a paper delivered at University of California, Berkeley, February.

cussed above has its shortcomings. Moreover, environmental problems themselves are of such variation and complexity, and the industrial and ecological contexts in which they occur are so varied, that the ideal solution will be context specific. What works best will necessarily vary from case to case.

Our challenge is to envisage what combination of instruments will be most appropriate in a given setting and to design strategies that mix instruments and institutional actors to optimal effect. However, before accepting that challenge, we need to examine the contribution that a broader range of institutional actors could make to optimal environmental policy, and how instruments interact with each other, for better or for worse. These issues are the subject matter of the next chapters.

3 Parties, Roles, and Interactions

Peter Grabosky, Neil Gunningham and Darren Sinclair

Traditionally, the regulatory process has been thought of as a dance between two participants—government and business, with the former acting in the role of regulator and the latter as regulatee. However, beneath the surface of this simplistic image lies a far more complex reality in which a wide variety of instruments can be used by a multiplicity of regulatory participants and where informal social orderings play as significant a role as formal ones. As we will argue, the traditional view of regulation as exclusively a governmental function has become outmoded.

In developing this theme, we will show how the rich array of instruments described in the previous chapter are available not just to government, but also, in many cases, to industry and third party actors, and provide important (but largely unrecognized) opportunities for each of these major institutions to play an important role in environmental protection. Moreover, in addition to their ability to use individual regulatory instruments, third parties can play a number of other roles, acting as agents of informal social control, in a variety of interactions with other regulatory participants.

We will also argue that there are important but largely neglected roles that government can play, over and beyond the conventional one of invoking its own policy instruments. Specifically, the state can enlist the support of a variety of non-governmental institutions in furtherance of the regulatory process. By guiding a range of market forces, and through other unobtrusive forms of activity, government can influence public interest groups, commercial third parties and industry itself to act as quasi-regulators, thereby facilitating innovative and pluralistic regulatory activity.

Finally, we explore instrumental and institutional interaction, building upon the insight derived from chapter two that each of the main categories of instruments has limitations as well as strengths, and that combinations of instruments are likely to work better than individual instruments alone. However, from the present chapter, it will be apparent that more than this is needed, because regulatory space is three dimensional rather than two dimensional. That is, there are a rich variety of third parties as well as first and second parties that can, potentially, be harnessed to perform quasi regulatory functions, and the broader question becomes not just one of mixing instruments with each other but also of mixing instruments *and* institutions. As we will see in part four of this chapter, this is a process with many pitfalls and, unless skilfully done, can result in negative rather than positive policy mixes.

We begin by identifying a number of very different types of third parties and articulating in broad terms the actual and potential techniques which may be employed by each of them, and the factors which determine their effectiveness in influencing environmental outcomes. We also examine the extent and means whereby they may act as surrogate or *de facto* regulators, and the opportunities for constructive interaction with other regulatory actors.

1. Third parties: public interest groups

In most developed countries, public interest groups have become influential participants in the regulatory process. They have been instrumental in placing environmental issues high on the public agenda, and in keeping them there. A significant proportion of environmentally beneficial activity by government and industry only occurs because of the vigilance and the pressure exercised by public interest groups. For present purposes, we focus particularly on the roles they can play in strengthening the effectiveness of environmental policy instruments; as a force of informal social control in their own right; and on how the judicious use of government policy can enhance both these roles.

Despite a common interest, there is often a lack of unity in the environmental movement. Environmental activism exists on a continuum, from 'deep green' fundamentalists, at one extreme, to the most pragmatic partners in the policy process, at the other.[1] Its institutions can be global in membership and concern, such as Greenpeace, or quite limited in focus, for example 'surfers against sewage'. However, the diversity of citizen environmentalism is almost certainly more of a strength than a weakness: a constructive diversity rather than a divisive one. The current division of labour among environmental interest groups entails a set of groups specializing in dramatic action to call attention to particular environmental problems, (such as toxic waste) or

---

[1] C. Manes, *Green Rage: Radical environmentalism and the unmaking of civilisation* (1990), Little Brown, Boston; M. Dowie, *Losing Ground: American environmentalism at the close of the twentieth century* (1996), MIT Press, Cambridge.

issues (such as wilderness preservation); others specializing in the recruitment and socialization of new members of the environmental cause; and those who labour over submissions to public inquiries and engage in face-to-face interaction in policymaking forums. Their energies tend to be focussed on their respective tasks, rather than on internecine conflict.

Among the most important contributions of environmental activists are:

(i) educating the community;
(ii) providing information to regulators and regulatees;
(iii) fulfilling a watchdog role;
(iv) acting as private enforcers;
(v) seeking compensation or preventing harm; and
(vi) reforming the law.

Since these roles are widely understood (unlike the potential roles of commercial third parties below) they will be summarized fairly briefly here.

Public interest groups perform an important *general educative function*. By raising public awareness about policy issues, they contribute to a more informed community. Public interest groups can also contribute to agenda setting—raising an issue and enhancing its priority. By attracting public and governmental attention to particular issues, whether local, national or global, they may elevate these issues from obscurity to political prominence. For example, Greenpeace succeeded in focusing world attention on whaling, and the World Wide Fund for Nature has made endangered species an issue of international concern. In the annals of regulation, entire regimes have been created or restructured in the aftermath of citizen activity which succeeded in placing an issue on the public agenda.[2]

Public interest groups can also be an important *source of information* for government authorities, providing a perspective which might not be otherwise readily available to elected officials and public servants.[3] Public interest group participation in the regulatory process ensures that not only an industry view, but also an environmental standpoint,

---

[2] A. Marcus, *The Adversary Economy: Business responses to changing government requirements* (1980), Quorom Books, Westport CT.

[3] J. Mansbridge 'A Deliberative Theory of Interest Representation' in M. Petracca (ed.) *Interest Groups in the Political Process* (1992), Westview Press, Boulder, Colorado, pp.32–57.

will be forcefully presented. It may, arguably, achieve better policy out-comes, and will certainly enhance the legitimacy of those outcomes which are produced.

Public interest groups are also in a position to act in a *watchdog role*, to identify any shortcomings in the development and implementation of government policy. Their potential to effectively monitor the opera-tions of government has led some observers to call for an institutional-ized role for public interest groups, to enhance the accountability of the public sector.[4] John Braithwaite, in particular, has argued that by giving citizens the right to formally challenge non-enforcement by gov-ernment agencies, one greatly enhances the prospects of industry com-pliance.[5] Public officials, not wishing to be upstaged by members of the public, will be more motivated in securing and monitoring compli-ance.[6] Similarly, action-forcing suits initiated by citizens may compel regulatory agencies to make difficult decisions, as officials of the United States EPA have acknowledged.[7] At the very least, the threat of citizen suits may force government and industry to the negotiating table.[8]

In addition to pressuring regulators to take appropriate action, pub-lic interest groups, and indeed individuals, may assume direct respon-sibility for the *private enforcement* of government regulations.[9] Such citizen enforcement need not pre-empt government enforcement entirely, but rather may serve as a complement to state action. The primary justifi-cation for this form of action is efficiency. Yeager observes that, in the United States, public interest groups have been able to bring a larger

[4] I. Ayres & J. Braithwaite, *Responsive Regulation: Transcending the regulation-deregulation debate* (1992), Oxford University Press, New York.

[5] J. Braithwaite, 'Policies for an Era of Regulatory Flux' in B. Head & E. McCoy (eds.) *Deregulation or Better Regulation?* (1991), Macmillan Press, Melbourne, pp.21–34.

[6] Anon, 'Ruckelshaus Worried Citizen Suits Will Reveal Poor Enforcement Record' (1984), May 11, *Inside EPA*, United States Environment Protection Agency, p.1.

[7] B. Boyer & E. Meidinger, 'Privatising Regulatory Enforcement: A preliminary assess-ment of citizen suits under Federal environmental laws' (1985) 34 *Buffalo Law Review* 833–964 at 863.

[8] In the United States, regulations under the Surface Mining Control and Regulation Act 1977 allow citizens to request an inspection by Federal regulatory authorities. The citizen must submit a signed written statement which would give regulatory authorities reason to believe that a violation exists. The citizen may accompany the inspector in the course of the inspection, and is entitled to receive a copy of the inspector's report. In the event that no inspection is conducted, the citizen is entitled to a written explanation for the decision in question (N. Shover, D. A. Clelland & J. Lynxwiler, *Enforcement or Negotiation: Constructing a regulatory bureaucracy* (1986), State University of New York Press, Albany, New York).

[9] G. S. Becker & G. T. Stigler, 'Law Enforcement, Malfeasance, and Compensation of Enforcers (1974) 3(1) *Journal of Legal Studies* 1.

number of enforcement actions than public regulatory authorities, at a fraction of the cost.[10] Similarly, in the United Kingdom, the generally available right of private prosecution is frequently exercised in the public interest by third parties. For example, the Royal Society for the Prevention of Cruelty to Animals investigates tens of thousands of complaints, successfully prosecuting about 2,000 cases each year.[11]

Some commentators have sought to design optimal combinations of state and third party enforcement. For example, it has been suggested that government should establish baseline standards and then contract out enforcement.[12] An alternative division of labour between government regulatory authorities and citizen litigants would entail the former specializing in the detection of regulatory offences and the latter in litigation.[13]

In contrast with conventional regulation, the role of public interest groups interacting with the use of economic instruments, particularly taxes and charges, is likely to be restricted to influencing policy formation, as opposed to its operation.[14] This is because the primary aim of economic instruments is to place decision-making in the hands of industry itself through the manipulation of price signals, with limited government or third party involvement.

Public interest groups may also initiate litigation in order to *seek compensation* for any previous damage to the environment, or to *prevent impending* harm. Compensation may entail redemption of damage, or payment of monetary compensation. Barriers to compensation for damages resulting from pollution may be formidable. To succeed in a private civil action, a plaintiff must usually prove, on the balance of probabilities, the existence of personal injury or damage to personal property directly attributable to acts or omissions on the part of the polluter. Preventative litigation may be used as a means of gaining time,

---

[10] P. C. Yeager, *The Limits of Law: the public regulation of private pollution* (1991), Cambridge University Press, Cambridge, New York, p.321; and see also W. Landes & R. Posner, 'The Private Enforcement of Law' (1975) 4 *Journal of Legal Studies* 1; and M. Polinsky, 'Private Versus Public Enforcement of Law' (1980) 9 *Journal of Legal Studies* 105.

[11] C. Harlow & R. Rawlings, *Pressure Through Law* (1992), Routledge, London.

[12] M. Cohen & P. Rubin, 'Private Enforcement of Public Policy' (1985) 3(1) *Yale Journal on Regulation* 167–194.

[13] J. Coffee, 'Rescuing the Private Attorney General: Why the model of the lawyer as bounty hunter is not working' (1983) 42 *Maryland Law Review* 215–288.

[14] However, note the existence of radical proposals for private collection of taxes.

of holding off development proposals until their full implications become apparent to the public and to decision makers.[15]

And finally, public interest groups may use litigation to *reform the law*, that is, to make it a more useful instrument in achieving any of the above objectives. Reform-oriented litigation moves beyond matters of prevention and compensation, and is aimed at changing the rules of the game. To this end, litigants may seek to set precedents, develop doctrine, or to contribute to the evolution of rules which may bear upon citizen access to law generally, or other specific objectives.[16]

The use of the legal process can complement other forms of citizen participation in furtherance of environmental interests. Regardless of its immediate goal, litigation can be a form of political expression. As with protest activity and other, more flamboyant, forms of political action, litigation can serve to attract attention to a group and to its cause, to focus public attention upon an issue, or to criticize government or industry. Litigation may have a political impact well beyond the immediate case. Although less dramatic and much less conducive to visual depiction than public protest, legal action, through the attention which it may attract, can serve as a means of mobilizing public support and as a rallying point, to generate or to maintain public momentum for a cause.[17]

---

[15] M. Wilcox, 'The Role of Environmental Groups in Litigation' (1985) 10 *Adelaide Law Review* 41–8.

[16] In the United States, citizen litigation (usually provided for by statute) has been central in the creation and development of environmental law. Here, the law has been an important instrument by which citizens oversee and reinforce the regulatory process. The United States legal system is relatively accessible to citizens who contend that regulatory authorities have failed to fulfil their legislative mandate. Most federal pollution control legislation empowers any person to begin an enforcement action against a polluter (A. Fadil, 'Citizen Suits Against Polluters: Picking up the pace' (1985) 9 *Harvard Environmental Law Review* 23–82; J. Austin, 'The Rise of Citizen Suit Enforcement in Environmental Law: Reconciling the private and public Attorney-General' (1987) 81 *Northwestern University Law Review* 220–62; and M. Greve, 'Environmentalism and Bounty Hunting' (1989) 97 *The Public Interest* 15–29), and citizen enforcement reinforces government regulatory activity.

[17] M. Wilcox, 'The Role of Environmental Groups in Litigation' (1985) 10 *Adelaide Law Review* 41–8 at 42. In Japan, for example, the publicity attracted by citizens' environmental litigation was instrumental in mobilising support for anti-pollution movements (M. McKean, *Environmental Protest and Citizen Politics in Japan* (1981), University of California Press, Berkeley, p.79). Even though the immediate goal of these legal actions is compensation for injury and illness occasioned by pollution, the publicity which they attract tends to focus attention on the dangers of pollution and the inadequacies of prevailing pollution controls.

Public interest group-industry interactions

In addition to the roles of public interest groups outlined above, which, by and large, are indirect means of influencing industry's environmental performance,[18] such groups may also bring pressure to bear directly on companies and industries. This is an important example of the interaction between private parties in the policy mix that may, but need not, include a role for government, and of the potential for these groups to act as informal instruments of social control.

Pressures exerted by interest groups on companies can be formidable—even in the absence of any government facilitation of NGO activity, and sometimes despite strong government opposition. For example, in June 1995, when the British government was content for an obsolete drilling platform to be sunk on site in the North Sea, rather than be transported ashore and dismantled, an international campaign by Greenpeace, aimed directly at the producer, prevailed upon the company to reverse its decision. Public scrutiny and criticism of Dow Chemical, beginning during the Vietnam War and continuing through the 1970s, contributed significantly to the company's improving its environmental performance on a number of fronts, to the extent that it has become one of the more respected corporate citizens of the United States. Thus can well orchestrated publicity campaigns by environmental interest groups influence corporate conduct when governments are unable or unwilling to act.

The relationship between interest groups and industry is not, however, inevitably adversarial.[19] Indeed, some of the most interesting developments in environmental policy during the past decade have involved industry-environmentalist partnerships, a relationship which we refer to as 'constructive engagement'. Such engagement may take a

---

[18] In that they, generally, involve government, regulatory authorities, or the courts as intermediaries.

[19] In some cases, interests between environmentalists and industry converge. In Germany, Greenpeace collaborated with a whitegoods manufacturer in the development of an 'ozone-friendly' refrigerator. In the United States, the Environmental Defence Fund assisted the McDonald's Corporation to develop a plan for the purchase of products made from recycled materials for use in the latter's restaurants. Subsequent environmental gains, including a 40 per cent reduction in solid waste output, significantly benefited McDonalds' corporate image. In Australia, the Australian Conservation Foundation and the National Farmers' Federation share an appreciation for the problem of soil degradation, and have developed an alliance to develop policies for remediation. Their joint involvement in the Landcare programme is, arguably, one of the most impressive examples of such co-operation.

variety of forms. 'Good neighbour agreements' between chemical industry firms and local residents are common in Europe and the United States.[20] They feature means by which concerned citizens have access to information relating to regulatory compliance, and the right to inspect facilities and to review compliance and accident plans. For example, under the United States EPA's Project XL, community organizations and other local stakeholders have the opportunity to shape and vet a company's environmental management strategy.[21] With community support, the strategy becomes a legally enforceable contract.

In Japan, citizen interaction with industry is facilitated by what are termed 'pollution control agreements'. These instruments contain detailed terms and conditions for management of the enterprise, including emission levels, and provisions for monitoring and reporting, and involve a type of contract between management of an enterprise, on the one hand, and local government or citizens' group, on the other.[22]

Environmental interest groups may also directly engage industry through the provision of 'green' endorsements. With firms spending millions of dollars to present themselves (justifiably or otherwise) as environmentally benign, the blessings of environmentalists may be a boon to marketing. As mentioned in the previous discussion of education and information strategies, environmental groups may directly influence the behaviour of industry, as well as individuals, through the provision of prizes and awards, and the operation of eco-labelling schemes. For example, the Banksia Environmental Foundation in Australia presents the Banksia Awards each year, which recognize individuals and corporations for their environmental achievements in such categories as Rural Community Groups, Land Management; and Resource Conservation and Waste Minimisation Management, and the World Wide Fund for Nature carries out licensing arrangements with companies wishing to use its Panda symbol. In Sweden, the forest industries and leading environmental organizations are working jointly

[20] Although less common in Australia, an agreement was reached between industry, state regulatory authorities, and local citizens concerned about environmental and health issues of a chemical facility. The agreement involved the creation of an ongoing monitoring committee comprising representatives of the three parties (D. Robinson, *Pollution Control and Public Interest Litigation* (1991), Environmental Defender's Office, Sydney, p.10.

[21] D. J. Fiorino, 'Towards a New System of Environmental Regulation: the case for an industry sector approach' (1996) 26(2) *Environmental Law* 457–489.

[22] K. Kato, 'The New Frontiers of Environmental Policy in Japan' in P. Thomas (ed.) *Environmental Liability* (1991), International Bar Association Section on Business Law, 7th Residential Seminar on Environmental Law, Graham and Trotman, London, pp.47–62.

towards a forest certification system: a breakthrough of international importance.

In recognition of the fundamental importance of industry co-operation in reducing environmental degradation, public interest groups are increasingly gearing their operations to maintain an active dialogue with business.[23] For example, Greenpeace and the World Wide Fund for Nature both have business units which deal exclusively with business. In the aftermath of its successful engagement with McDonald's, the Environmental Defence Fund and the Pew Charitable Trust (a private philanthropy) co-founded the Alliance for Environmental Innovation, a body specifically designed to develop new partnerships with major corporations in the United States.[24] By strategically engaging highly visible market leaders, particularly those in consumer products industries, public interest groups hope to bring about not only improved environmental performance on the part of individual firms, but also entire industries: the visibility of the process can have an educative effect beyond the immediate participants.

Government support for the role of public interest groups

There are several ways in which government can facilitate the engagement of public interest groups in the regulatory process. First, they may directly subsidize them. The extent to which public interest groups can make a contribution to the design and implementation of environmental regulation depends, at least in part, on their level of resourcing, which in turn may be related to government policy. There is usually a massive imbalance between the resources of environmental NGOs and their adversaries, which government funding can at least begin to mitigate. Although some groups, in order to maintain both the appearance and the reality of independence, refuse to accept government funds, others are often the beneficiaries of government financial assistance, though commonly only to a very limited extent. Any decision to reduce

---

[23] F. K. Long & M. B. Arnold, *The Power of Partnerships* (1995), Harcourt Brace, New York.

[24] The Green Business Letter, 'Grand Alliances: A new network of nonprofits is helping environmental partnerships grow and prosper' (1996) (March) *The Green Business Letter*; and Business and the Environment, 'Alliance for Environmental Innovation to Start First Projects This Spring' (1996) VII(3) (March) *Business and the Environment* 8. On innovative enforcement generally, see M. Squillace, 'Innovative Enforcement Mechanisms in the United States' AIC Conference Proceedings No. 26 (1–3 September 1993), N. Gunningham, J. Norberry and S. McKillop (eds.) (1995), Australian Institute of Criminology, Canberra.

such funding will obviously impinge on the ability of public interest groups to actively participate in the regulatory process.

Secondly, government may supplement direct funding of public interest groups with financial incentives, and through taxation policy (for example, making contributions to such groups tax deductible). They could also, in order to actively encourage private enforcement, offer financial rewards to third parties for successful litigation.[25] In the United States, for example, the Clean Water Act provides a modest incentive for citizen enforcement by allowing for recovery costs incurred in enforcement litigation.[26] It is not difficult to imagine a more attractive reward system facilitating the emergence of regulatory 'bounty hunters'. Indeed, the precursor to modern United States environmental protection legislation, the Refuse Act of 1899, authorized citizen-informants to receive up to half of the amount of fine imposed upon a convicted offender.[27]

Thirdly, government may provide greater access to the prime currency of public interest groups: information. Starved of information about the activities of industry, the state of the environment and government policy, their effectiveness will be severely curtailed. There are several mechanisms by which government can improve access to information. As discussed above, these include community right to know legislation—for example, the United States Toxic Release Inventory (TRI)—state of the environment reporting, environmental accounting, corporate environmental reporting, and product certification. Such information gives community groups increased political leverage both through the media and in plant level negotiations, enabling them to more effectively pressure polluters to reduce emissions.[28] For example, in the United States, some of the worst polluters, conscious of the likely public reaction now that their environmental record is in the public

---

[25] P. N. Grabosky, 'Citizen Co-Production and Corruption Control' (1990) 5 *Corruption and Reform* 125–51.

[26] Mann (1991).

[27] 33 USCA s 411(12).

[28] Data from the US National Toxic Release Inventory indicates that release of toxic chemicals has decreased approximately 20 per cent since 1987 (W. S. Pease 'Chemical Hazards and the Public's Right-to-Know: How effective is California's Proposition 65?' 30(10) *Environment* 9, quoted in P. Adams & M. Ruchel, *Unlocking the Factory Door* (1992), Report of the Coode Island Review Panel by the Hazardous Materials Action Group, Melbourne, Victoria, p.24), which noted that 'on the eve of the first national release of US Toxic Release Inventory data in 1987, Monsanto Corporation went public with a preemptive pledge to reduce by 90 per cent the company's worldwide toxic emissions to air by 1992'.

domain, have voluntarily implemented pollution control measures on a scale far greater than previously contemplated.

Fourthly, government may improve the legal standing—the right to bring an action before a court—of public interest groups. The question of legal standing is central to the issues of private enforcement and compensation. Such a right may be conferred explicitly by statute, or may be inferred by judicial interpretation. The key issue in the determination of standing is the balance between private and public interest. Governments may enhance public interest group activities by widening the legal rights to standing. The notion of private enforcement of public law is more common in some jurisdictions, particularly the United States, than others, such as Europe and Australia.[29] In the latter, the law of standing has tended to favour private parties, those seeking to vindicate a personal stake, as opposed to those seeking to act on behalf of a wider public.[30]

Beyond the impediments entailed by restrictions on standing, citizen participation in the legal process may be inhibited by the expense of accessing requisite legal services. These costs often exceed the financial capabilities of individuals or environmental interest groups. In addition to bearing the costs of a legal action, prospective litigants are faced with the likelihood, if their action should fail, of having their opposing party's costs awarded against them as well. Government could improve public participation in the legal process by changing the costs rules for cases brought forward by private litigants that are demonstrably in the public interest. For example, courts could be given discretion, in such cases, to direct that each party only bear their own costs.

Fifthly, while recognizing that some initiatives between public interest groups and business may take place entirely independent of government, governments may intervene in such a way as to nurture and

[29] One might predict that, all else being equal, litigation would be more common where government activity in furtherance of environmental protection is less. This does appear to be the case in relation to enforcement activity in the United States. An inverse relationship was observed there in the early 1980's between citizen litigation and government enforcement activity. As the deregulatory ethos of the Reagan era was accompanied by a decrease in enforcement activity by the EPA, the number of citizen enforcement actions increased significantly (J. Miller, *Citizen Suits: private enforcement of Federal pollution control laws* (1987), John Wiley, New York, p.12; J. Austin, 'The Rise of Citizen Suit Enforcement in Environmental Law: Reconciling the private and public Attorney-General' (1987) 81 *Northwestern University Law Review* 220–62 at 233; P. C. Yeager, *The Limits of Law: the public regulation of private pollution* (1991), Cambridge University Press, Cambridge, pp.320–321).

[30] According to prevailing legal policy, defence of the common good and supporting the public interest are the responsibilities of government.

facilitate constructive engagement between business and NGOs. Necessarily, what is appropriate will vary with the circumstances of the case, but obvious possibilities include government endorsement and public recognition for such initiatives, tax incentives or other financial support for those engaging in them,[31] regulatory relief and flexibility where alternative means of achieving environmental outcomes can be demonstrated,[32] and providing a formal contractual underpinning for what would otherwise be informal and unenforceable arrangements.[33] There is also ample opportunity for governments to engage environmental representatives in the process of establishing and operating self-regulatory and co-regulatory agreements with industry. For instance, such representatives, as already discussed, could be members of independent audit teams, or participate in wider community consultative fora, as is the case under the United States EPA's Project XL.

Overcoming the shortcomings of public interest group engagement

The contribution of public interest groups to environmental policy is not one of unmitigated virtue. As recent history has shown, there are participants on all sides of contemporary environmental policy debate to whom accommodation and compromise are anathema. In pressing their position, the credibility of public interest groups may be tainted by the use of sensationalism, falsehoods, or distortion. There is also the danger that public interest groups will: (i) focus on 'trendy' environmental issues, such as the loss of mega-vertebrates, at the expense of less popular issues, such as soil erosion; and (ii) encourage the 'NIMBY'[34] syndrome at the expense of sound environmental policy. The challenge of democratic government is to ensure that contending interests receive a fair hearing, that the marketplace of ideas remains a fair marketplace, and that no one interest dominates public discourse. Governments may facilitate this outcome by distributing funding to a variety of public interest groups, by providing genuine opportunities for public interest groups to participate in the regulatory process, at both the planning and implementation stages, and by ensuring that reliable data on environmental issues, such as pollution inventories, is placed on the public record.

Perhaps one of the most commonly voiced objections to public inter-

[31] For example, Australian Landcare.

[32] In Australia, Victoria's accredited licensing scheme contemplates such relief (see pp.48).

[33] See Project XL, above.

[34] 'Not In My Back Yard'.

est group involvement is in relation to private litigation. It is often claimed that widening the law of standing to permit private enforcement of pollution control regulations would open the floodgates to litigation, and invite a gaggle of frivolous and vexatious busybodies to court, at great expense and inconvenience. However, there is precious little evidence to support this allegation, and the experience of environmental law judges and litigators is to the contrary.[35]

There are nevertheless, some genuine problems inherent in private litigation.[36] Citizen suits in the United States, for example, may be directed not at the most serious offenders, but at those most likely to settle; and enforcement which is left entirely to the market may threaten whatever underlying logic exists in environmental policy.[37] Relationships between regulatory agencies and regulated companies tend to be of an ongoing nature, and efficient regulatory outcomes often result from a subtle mix of co-operation and deterrence. Violations occurring within such a relationship may be more appropriately dealt with by informal means. Private enforcement may thus disrupt what might otherwise be a workable regulatory arrangement.

Private enforcement also carries with it the potential for inconsistency and unpredictability.[38] A variety of private enforcers, acting

[35] For example, in the Australian State of New South Wales, where the rules of standing are very liberal, the incidence of third party appeals is quite small, and very few of these could be categorized as frivolous (N. Pain, 'Third Party Rights Public Participation Under the Environmental Planning and Assessment Act 1979 (NSW): Do the floodgates need opening or closing?' (1989) 6(1) *Environmental and Planning Law Journal* 99 26–35; and J. Hodgson, 'Third Party Appeals in South Australia 1972–1993' (1996) 13(1) *Environmental and Planning Law Journal* 8–28); and D. Roe, 'An Incentive-Conscious Approach to Toxic Chemical Controls' (1989) 3(3) *Economic Development Quarterly* 179–187.

[36] M. Greve, 'Environmentalism and Bounty Hunting' (1989) 97 *The Public Interest* 15–29 at 16.

[37] Nor are environmentalists themselves universally enthusiastic about the use of the legal process. As a former president of the Australian Conservation Foundation stated: 'Environmental groups hate getting involved in legal cases. They cost a lot of money. They are very distracting. Environmentalists realise that they do distort the decision making process . . . The environmental movement would much rather debate issues on their merits in public fora' (M. Wilcox, 'Retrospect and Prospect' in T. Bonyhady (ed.) *Environmental Protection and Legal Change* (1992), Federation Press, Sydney pp.206–30 at pp.228–9).

[38] In contrast, the interests of business (not to mention the interests of justice) are best served by a stable, predictable regulatory environment. The absence of any co-ordinating mechanism in a decentralized system of complementary private enforcement may jeopardize consistency and predictability. Contradictory postures of public and private enforcers may impede business planning. This is undesirable, and illustrates the need for the legal process to 'maintain a stable system of signals' (J. Coffee, 'Rescuing the Private Attorney General: Why the model of the lawyer as bounty hunter is not working' (1983) 42 *Maryland Law Review* 215–288 at 226).

independently from what might be a variety of motives, may not be expected to produce consistent enforcement outcomes. Moreover, some citizen enforcers, no matter how well motivated, may lack the competence to prosecute effectively, and may thereby spoil an opportunity for effective enforcement action. Private enforcers are also likely to be unfamiliar with the organizational pathology which underlay the offending behaviour in question, and are thus ill-equipped to prescribe a remedy.[39]

Ideally, citizens would complement, not replace, enforcement by government agencies. The challenge is to harness the constructive elements of private enforcement, neutralize those elements which might be counterproductive, and combine them systematically with public enforcement. On the one hand, it is important that public interest groups be empowered so that they can fulfil legitimate and important roles: challenging government policy; regulatory decision-making; business behaviour; and acting as surrogate regulators. On the other hand, it is also important that public interest groups should not be tempted to abuse their position as a defender of the environmental interest, that there should not be opportunities for excess or to override carefully devised regulatory compliance strategies. The optimal ordering for citizen enforcement would entail some provision for private actions, with safeguards against abuse. 'Gatekeeping' strategies, invoking judicial discretion as to the granting of standing where competing principles are at stake, are likely to play a central role in achieving that balance.[40]

2. Third parties: commercial

The role of commercial interests as *de facto* regulators and as instruments of informal social control, capable of shaping future environmental outcomes, has been largely neglected in the literature on environmental regulation.[41] Yet, as we shall see, their influence can be

---

[39] Corporate behaviour cannot simply be reduced to questions of greed and the bottom line. While some pollution behaviour may arise from deliberate premeditation and calculation, other offending may result from ignorance and negligence (R. Kagan, & J. Scholz, 'The Criminology of the Corporation and Regulatory Enforcement Strategies' in K. Hawkins and J. Thomas (eds.) *Enforcing Regulation* (1984), Kluwer-Nijhoff, Boston, pp.67–96).

[40] Environmental Offences and Penalties Act 1989 NSW, s.13 (2A) allows for third party action.

[41] The most notable exception is the excellent contribution of Ronald Mitchell, *Intentional Oil Pollution at Sea* (1994), MIT Press, Cambridge.

profound. In this section, we identify these interests and explore their potential contribution in determining the environmental performance of industry. Our focus is on significant third-party non-governmental resources which can expand and strengthen the regulatory net; on circumstances where commercial environmentalism can act as a powerful institution of corporate social control; and on the potential roles of government in facilitating or otherwise encouraging such initiatives.

Green consumers

Growing public sensitivity to environmental issues is reflected in consumer behaviour. Consumers who are environmentally aware are inclined to purchase products which they perceive to be environmentally appropriate, and to favour products of manufacturers who have otherwise demonstrated concern for the environment. Collectively, such consumers have the economic muscle to demand that environmentally unsound products are either improved or replaced. Companies which are in a position to demonstrate their credibility as environmentally responsible corporate citizens, and thereby benefit from consumer preferences, will thus enjoy a competitive advantage.[42] Indeed, consumer preferences may be more exacting than government regulatory requirements. Substantial public relations and marketing advantages can flow from a legitimately earned reputation as an environmentally responsible company.[43]

The purchase of environmentally preferable goods and services entails an implicit rejection of less acceptable alternative products. The boycott, or concerted avoidance of certain purchases, may be mobilized against products or producers deemed to be environmentally harmful.[44] An example of a consumer environmental boycott is the boycott of Norwegian fish products organized in 1993 by Greenpeace in protest

[42] R. Stewart, 'Models for Environmental Regulation: Central planning versus market-based approaches' (1992) *Boston College Environmental Affairs Law Review*, 547–62.

[43] P. N. Grabosky, 'Green Markets: Environmental regulation by the private sector' (1994) 16(4) *Law and Policy* 419–448.

[44] For discussions of various aspects of consumer boycotts, see M. C. Smith, *Morality and the Market: Consumer pressure for corporate accountability*, (1990) Routledge, London; M. Friedman, 'Consumer Boycotts: A conceptual framework and research agenda' (1991) 47(1) *Journal of Social Issues* 149–168; P. Fahey, 'Advocacy Group Boycotting of Television Advertisers, and its Effect on Programming Content' (1992) 140 *University of Pennsylvania Law Review* 647–709; C. Joyner, 'The Transnational Boycott as Economic Coercion in International Law: Policy, place and practice' (1984) 17(2) *Vanderbilt Journal; of Transnational Law* 206–286; and M. C. Harper, 'The Consumer's Emerging Right to Boycott: NAACP v. Claiborne Hardware and its implications for American Labor Law' (1984) 93(3) *Yale Law Journal* 409–454).

against that nation's resumption of whaling. Boycott organizers maintained that the loss of foreign markets significantly exceeded the commercial value of Norway's whale catch.[45]

More recently, the establishment of independent certification of 'well managed forests' through the forest stewardship council, a body whose existence owes far more to the initiative of major environmental groups than to government, gives paper and timber buyers considerable leverage over forest methods.

An essential prerequisite to consumers exercising green preferences is access to reliable information which reflect products' relative environmental impact. The inevitable self-interest of manufacturers dictates that the source of such information should come from an independent party. This may be either a third party or government. As we have suggested, government can fulfil this role indirectly by enacting truth in advertising legislation, and directly, by introducing eco-labelling programmes.[46] Environmental public interest groups can also certify 'green' products[47] or organize boycotts, and, in some cases, retailers may provide green lines of products to their customers.[48]

Government can also more directly guide the power of consumption to favour environmentally preferable products through use of economic instruments, such as taxes and charges. A government may tax environmentally harmful inputs or practices.

Direct influence by government on manufacturers can take place through its considerable purchasing power. In many markets, government is, in fact, the dominant purchaser. For example, government consumption of office equipment and motor vehicles far exceeds any other single purchaser. Government may, therefore, provide a leadership role in dictating market preferences for products by developing and implementing a green purchasing policy. The Clinton Administration's acquisition of energy efficient computers is but one example.

---

[45] Boycotts can, however, be a double edged sword. For example, in 1989, representatives of the United States timber industry called for the boycott of a brewer which sponsored a controversial television documentary on forests which had been produced by an environmental group, the National Audubon Society (P. Fahey, 'Advocacy Group Boycotting of Television Advertisers, and its Effect on Programming Content' (1992) 140 *University of Pennsylvania Law Review* 647–709 at 679).

[46] Above pp.65.

[47] See further, S. Dawson & N. Gunningham, 'The More Dolphins There Are The Less I Trust What They're Saying: Can green labelling work?' (1996) 18(1) *Adelaide Law Review* 1–34.

[48] For example, K-Mart has introduced a number of in-house green products, such as recycled motor oil.

There are several limits to consumers exerting their green purchasing power.[49] First, the difficulty for government in establishing workable eco-labelling programmes is well documented. Establishing meaningful criteria for a range of products across a range of environmental issues is an extremely complex and difficult task. Secondly, where there has been comprehensive life cycle analysis of products, the overriding factor in determining overall environmental impact is often how the consumer *uses* a product. For example, although one washing machine may be deemed to be more environmentally benign than a competitor, if the consumer chooses to wash in hot water and overfill the machine, then any advantage will be completely negated. Thirdly, in the absence of reliable eco-labelling requirements, commercial appeals to environmentalism may be designed to pre-empt or to neutralize negative publicity. Finally, it could be argued that green consumer campaigns fail to address the core issue of unsustainability, that of over-consumption. Instead, they merely reinforce existing notions of the right to consume, albeit in a slightly more benign form. These difficulties in effectively exploiting the undeniable power of consumer preferences means that it remains a largely untapped resource.

Buyer-supplier relations

The power of consumer preference is by no means wielded solely by the ultimate purchaser. Companies, driven by their own internal priorities, or mindful of their corporate image and their customers' preferences, commonly affect each others' behaviour. Purchasers often have leverage over suppliers which they may use to influence the latter's environmental performance. The interchange between industrial buyers and suppliers also generates incentives to innovate and to respond to market demands.[50] As one of our interviewees told us: 'When McDonald's says "jump", six hundred suppliers ask, "how high?" '

Large firms, in particular, may be able to use their market power to impose product and process preferences on their smaller upstream suppliers and downstream buyers. This capacity may prove very important, given the difficulties confronting governments in applying conventional regulatory instruments to small enterprises[51] (many of

---

[49] S. Dawson & N. Gunningham, 'The More Dolphins There Are The Less I Trust What They're Saying: Can green labelling work?' (1996) 18(1) *Adelaide Law Review* 1–34.

[50] M. Porter, *The Competitive Advantage of Nations* (1990), Macmillan Press, London, p.590.

[51] The difficulties for government in regulating the environmental performance of small businesses are well documented (R. Kagan, 'Regulatory Enforcement' in

whom will be buyers and suppliers). Some larger firms have taken steps to influence the behaviour of small firms through the practice of 'product stewardship'. This entails taking corporate responsibility for the whole life cycle of a product, from the extraction and consumption of raw materials, through its manufacture, to its final disposal. Firms may exert their purchasing power to ensure that suppliers actually implement environmental safeguards by, for example, requesting information on storage, handling use, and disposal practices, and insisting on the introduction of appropriate environmental management systems.[52]

A related development, in terms of encouraging firms to engage in systemic improvement of their environmental practices, is the growth of 'off the peg' EMSs. As we shall see in chapter four, the adoption of the most widely recognized such system, International Standards Organisation's ISO 14001 environmental management standard, may also come to be driven principally by supply chain pressure. If so, the result will be that many enterprises which would not choose to adopt such a system voluntarily may nevertheless be prevailed upon to do so as a result of third party pressure, even in the absence of legislation mandating such a requirement.

The influence of the retail sector in driving innovation is widely recognized.[53] A supplier's business practices can bear upon a retailer's public image, and buyers are increasingly sensitive to the risk of being tainted by a supplier's questionable environmental performance. To this end, buyers are tending increasingly to scrutinize products from cradle to grave, noting such considerations as energy efficiency in manufacture, minimization and responsible disposal of waste, economical use of materials in packaging, and recyclability of product.[54]

D. H. Rosenbloom & R. D. Schwartz (eds.) *Handbook of Regulation and Administrative Law* (1994), Marcel Dekker, New York, 383–422; and N. Shover, D. Clelland and J. Lynxwiler, *Enforcement or Negotiation: Constructing a regulatory bureaucracy* (1986), State University of New York Press, Albany). Regulators find it easier to keep tabs on and interact with larger firms. But as Alm (A. L. Alm, 'A. Need For New Approaches: Command and control is no-longer a cure-all' (1992) 18 May/June *EPA. Journal* 6) correctly identifies, the accumulative effect of pollution from many small firms may outweigh that from a few large firms.

[52] N. Gunningham, 'Environment, Self-Regulation and the Chemical Industry: Assessing Responsible Care' (1995) 17 *Law and Policy* 55–107.

[53] M. Porter, *The Competitive Advantage of Nations* (1990), Macmillan Press, London, pp.502 and 523.

[54] G. Stuart, 'Marketing Reports on Environmental Concerns in the Packaging Industry' (1992) *Reuters News Service*, 20 August.

In 1990, the McDonald's Corporation began a programme to purchase $100 million worth of products made from recycled materials each year. The British retail chemist, Boots, set a goal to reduce the volume of packaging of its merchandise by 75 per cent by 1997.[55] Another firm in the United Kingdom requires every supplier to have a company environmental policy, affirmed by an audit.[56] The same firm has also developed a comprehensive questionnaire to obtain information from prospective suppliers.[57] Successful suppliers are required to sign codes of conduct and to manage their activity in accordance with specified principles. Non-compliance may lead to the buyer obtaining a new source of supply.

Wal-Mart, a large retailer in the United States, encourages its suppliers to reduce overpackaging, and actively seeks environmentally sound changes to their products.[58] The retailer then actively publicizes their achievements. In the words of one sign, prominently displayed in retail stores:

Our Commitment: Land-Air-Water. Our Customers are concerned about the quality of our air, land and water and want the opportunity to do something positive. Together with our manufacturing partners, we'll provide you with information on products which have been environmentally improved.[59]

The company is even developing prototype 'green' stores, which would be designed and managed consistent with principles of low energy consumption, low waste generation, and recyclability.[60]

---

[55] Reuters, 'It's Green for Go in Boots the Chemist' (1992) *Reuters News Service*, 13 June.

[56] G. Stuart, 'Marketing Reports on Environmental Concerns in the Packaging Industry' (1992) *Reuters News Service*, 20 August.

[57] Similarly, British Telecom encourages prospective suppliers to explain their environmental programmes, and encourages them to be responsible for the environmental impact of their products (G. Stuart, 'Marketing Reports on Environmental Concerns in the Packaging Industry' (1992) *Reuters News Service*, 20 August; and P. N. Grabosky, 'Green Markets: Environmental regulation by the private sector' 16(4) *Law and Policy* 429). A company questionnaire seeks information from prospective suppliers on the use of recycled materials in their products, and the potential for re-use and recycling of products. It further seeks to identify any environmental hazards which may be arise during the course of the product's life, energy consumption entailed in manufacture, and the supplier's plans for improving its overall environmental performance. British Telecom also encourages supplier buy-back of products after their normal life.

[58] J. Elkington, P. Knight & J. Hailes, *The Green Business Guide* (1992), Victor Gollancz, London, p.126.

[59] Quoted in G. Berle, *The Green Entrepreneur* (1991), Liberty Hall Press, New York, p.143.

[60] N. Platt, 'The Rise of the Eco-Consumer Has Big Business Seeing Green' (1992) *Reuters News Service*, 25 May.

By calling public attention to their environmental policies and practices, retailers perform an educative function which extends well beyond the conventional marketing role.[61] This, in turn, can help shape future consumer preferences. For example, it has been suggested that Americans' awareness of, and preferences for, motor vehicle safety design was enhanced significantly by commercial advertising.[62]

The good small business is often able to adapt to changing market opportunities, and to meet the requirements of buyers. In some cases, buyers are willing to assist in this process. For example, the Body Shop cosmetics retailer assists suppliers in self-assessment, and works with them to improve their environmental performance. At other times, the approach of retailers can be more adversarial, and more demanding. For example, the Body Shop advised a supplier that they would consider increasing their purchases if the supplier were to adopt a formal environmental policy, publish a comprehensive audit report, and end 'unnecessary confrontation with environmental groups'.[63]

Scrutiny of suppliers is hardly the sole province of retailers. Manufacturers are also in a position to influence supplier behaviour. Volvo, for example, asks that its suppliers comply with its environmental standards. In the chemicals sector, several prominent companies, such as Dow Chemicals and Du Pont, have introduced relatively sophisticated forms of product stewardship where suppliers are encouraged to meet high environmental standards, and have their performance assessed by independent auditors.[64] Such relationships are inevitably unequal; large manufacturers are able to impose their standards on smaller suppliers and/or buyers. However, this is one of the few potentially effective ways of addressing the chronic weakness of many forms of environmental regulation in targeting small and medium sized firms.

It is important to recognize that the above influences are wielded quite independently of any government authority. There are, nevertheless, several ways in which government can enhance the quasi reg-

---

[61] S. Schmidheiny, *Changing Course: A global business perspective on development and the environment* (1992), MIT Press, Cambridge, p.112.

[62] For a discussion of 'the Volvo effect' and its wider implications, see Harvard Law Review, 'Note: Harnessing Madison Avenue: Advertising and products liability theory' (1994) 107 *Harvard Law Review* 895–912.

[63] Greenpeace, *Community Right-to-Know and the Myth of Self-Regulation'* (1994), Greenpeace, Melbourne.

[64] See further chapter 4 below.

ulatory function of commercial third parties.[65] Innovative regulatory approaches such as EMSs, co-regulation, and flexible license and accreditation schemes may include provisions for product stewardship. For example, government could require accredited EMSs to include provisions that explicitly address buyer-supplier relationships—only those firms that complied would obtain more flexible cost effective forms of accreditation. Similarly, government could place a duty of care on producers to ensure, for example, that their wastes are handled and disposed of in an appropriate manner by registered contractors. Government sponsored 'green' award schemes could also recognize the contribution of upstream suppliers and downstream buyers. Corporate environmental reporting is another avenue where product stewardship could be encouraged through, for example, official government recognition of suitably comprehensive reporting systems. Economic instruments are also a potentially potent tool for sensitizing buyer-supplier relationships to environmental factors. By taxing environmental undesirables, for example the carbon content of fossil fuels, close to the source, an environmental price signal will filter through the entire downstream myriad of buyer-supplier relationships.

Institutional investors

There is a long history of socially responsible investment. For example, the seventeenth century Quakers in Britain and the United States refused to profit from slavery or war. More recently, international investment boycotts of South Africa, arguably, played an important role in the downfall of apartheid.[66] The emergence of specialized environmentally conscious investment funds, over the last two decades, has resulted in the expansion and entrenchment of this approach.[67] Such 'green' institutional investors avoid companies and industries with poor environmental reputations, and/or specialize in environmentally reputable companies. This provides an opportunity for environmental interest groups. For example, in 1993, Greenpeace worked with 'green' fund managers in the United Kingdom to prevent the float of an Indonesian timber company accused of irresponsible forestry practices.[68]

---

[65] P. N. Grabosky, 'Using Non-governmental Resources to Foster Regulatory Compliance' (1995) 8(4) *Governance, an International Journal of Policy and Administration* 527–550.

[66] R. Sparkes, *The Ethical Investor* (1995), Harper Collins, London, chapter 8.

[67] M. C. Smith, *Morality and the Market: Consumer pressure for corporate accountability* (1990) Routledge, London, p.175–6.

[68] R. Sparkes, *The Ethical Investor* (1995), Harper Collins, London, chapter 11, pp.98–9.

Beyond the ethical imperatives behind environmentally responsible investment, there may be sound financial incentives. Environmental performance is increasingly regarded as an indicator of business health. Good environmental management reflects good management in general. To the extent that this perception is shared by financial markets (and there is increasing evidence that it is), pressure on companies to improve corporate environmental citizenship will be that much greater. There is also the desire to avoid businesses that may face costs associated with environmental liability.

As opposed to the relatively limited financial clout of specialised 'green' investment funds, the potential influence of large institutional investors can be substantial. In 1991, the twenty largest pension funds in the United States controlled over $620 billion in assets. Even here, there is considerable scope for leverage. In a number of United States jurisdictions, state pension fund managers are required to give preference in their investment decisions to companies in compliance with the Valdez (now CERES) Principles.[69] One trustee of the New York City Employees Retirement System, with $21 billion in assets, was quoted as saying:

We hold the view that when corporations treat the environment badly, they treat their investors badly—by subjecting the company to harmful publicity and by exposing themselves to enormous liability. The pension funds have become activists in protecting our investments by working to protect the environment.[70]

Market influence is further enhanced by regulatory requirements that shareholders and financial markets must be kept informed of potential environmental liabilities.[71] In the absence of disclosure requirements mandated by government, institutional investors themselves are increasingly in a position to demand that the companies in which they invest account for their environmental performance.

The extent to which investors are able to effectively discriminate between companies that do and do not have a commendable environmental practices will ultimately determine the overall impact of environmentally responsible investment. Government can facilitate the

---

[69] J. Elkington, P. Knight & J. Hailes, *The Green Business Guide* (1992), Victor Gollancz, London, p.71.

[70] Reuters, 'New York City Fund Wants Green Stance from Four Companies' (1992) *Reuters News Service*, 10 December.

[71] For a less optimistic perspective on the effects of ethical investing, see M. Dowie, *Losing Ground: American environmentalism at the close of the twentieth century* (1996), MIT Press, Cambridge.

potential good work of investors by ensuring that there are reliable sources of information about firm environmental performances for the market to access. Relevant examples include CRTK legislation and corporate environment reporting requirements.[72] Of course, if private institutions can require disclosure and contribute to informed markets without assistance from government, so much the better.

The limitations of 'green' institutional investing may be similar to those facing eco-labelling schemes. There are uncertainties in determining what qualifies as a 'green' product or firm. Further, it may be difficult to keep track of a firm's environmental performance if it is a multinational with subsidiaries operating in several different jurisdictions. Despite these potential problems, the enormous financial clout of investment institutions makes them a tantalizing prospect as surrogate environmental regulators. Developing credible assessment criteria that can accommodate the intricacies and complexities of actual performance, potentially across different jurisdictions, would be a constructive step forward, particularly for the large investment institutions which are not ostensibly 'green', and could be developed with the assistance of government, environmental interest groups, and businesses themselves.

Financial institutions

In addition to their activities as institutional investors, banks and other lending institutions are in a position to exercise considerable influence over their clients' behaviour. Lenders have a consistent record as effective regulators of business behaviour—particularly given the central role they play in the economy. Many now recognize the risk to their own commercial well-being posed by questionable environmental practices on the part of a borrower. Beyond the lender's obvious interest in the commercial viability of the borrower, banks must now be concerned about the environmental risks posed by any assets which they might hold as security for a loan. In the event of foreclosure, banks could end up owning a liability rather than an asset.[73]

---

[72] For example, in Australia, the Australian Stock Exchange now requires listed companies to make a statement in their annual report about how they identify and manage environmental risks to their business.

[73] For a comprehensive attempt to examine how financial markets can support the goals of eco-efficiency and sustainable development, see S. Schmidheiny and F. Zorraquin, *Financing Change: The Financial Community, Eco-Efficiency and Sustainable Development* (1996), MIT Press, Cambridge.

The pressures which the banking industry can exert in further-ance of a borrower's environmental citizenship can be considerable. Schmidheiny predicts that an environmental audit report is likely to become an integral part of a loan application.[74] One prospective lender already requires a comprehensive assessment of all risks associated with a proposed loan: a seventeen page environmental compliance checklist comprises part of the loan application.[75] Canadian banks have begun to require detailed information from prospective commercial borrowers regarding all aspects of the latter's environmental exposure.[76]

More broadly, a group of international banks, working with UNEP, has produced the Statement by Banks on Environment and Sustainable Development, which urges banks to:

> . . . expect, as part of our normal business practices, that our customers com-ply with all applicable local, national and international environmental regula-tions [and] will seek for business relations with suppliers and subcontractors who follow similarly high environmental standards.[77]

Not surprisingly, the major way in which government can foster a 'green' lending philosophy amongst financial institutions is through strong liability legislation. A lender can be exposed to liability in a num-ber of ways. For instance, a business that is forced to pay for clean-up costs may find it increasingly difficult to meet loan repayments. A con-taminated property held as security may dramatically reduce in market value and thereby undermine a financial institution's asset base. Certain legislation (e.g., the United States Comprehensive Environmental Response, Compensation and Liability Act 1980 (CERCLA)) may make a lender directly liable for contaminated site remediation expenses. It is also possible for government to subordinate a lender's lien to an unrecorded lien by a government authority. This approach to liability legislation is more common in the United States.

The behaviour of banks in that country has been profoundly influ-enced by the enactment of CERCLA and its interpretation in the case of *United States* v. *Fleet Factors Corp.*[78] CERCLA empowers the EPA to

---

[74] S. Schmidheiny, *Changing Course: A. global business perspective on development and the envi-ronment* (1992), MIT Press, Cambridge, pp.64–5.

[75] *Ibid.* at p. 258.

[76] Deloitte Touche Tohmatsu International, *Coming Clean: Corporate environmental report-ing* (1993), Deloitte Touche Tohmatsu International, London, p.40.

[77] UNEP, Advisory Committee on Banking and the Environment (1992), UNEP, Nairobi, 2.2, p.1.

[78] 901 F2d 1550 (11th Cir 1990).

recover costs for the clean up of contaminated sites from a number of parties beyond the current owners.[79] In *Fleet*, it was held that a bank can be held liable for cleaning up a site if it has 'operated' a site through involvement in the management of a borrower, regardless of whether or not the bank chose to exercise that capacity to influence the borrowers' environmental decisions.

Increased lender liability may eventually lead to a reduction in the number of environmentally damaging activities that are financed and, in turn, to industries or businesses of a particularly environmentally damaging nature being forced from the market. Liability legislation for contaminated sites is, however, not without its critics. CERCLA, in particular, is criticized for having introduced a legal minefield that is a large drain on public and private resources, without having yielded any significant environmental improvements.[80]

Government can also contribute to more environmentally sensitive financial decisions by supplying information. For example, one way banks and other financial institutions might evaluate the environmental credentials of their would-be clients is through environmental reports, and financial institutions are increasingly cited as potential customers of such reports. However, they are, at present, put off by the diversity of reporting styles and lack of consistent and comparable data.[81] By ensuring that enterprises report consistently on actual and potential liabilities (as firms are, to some extent, required to do under United States SEC legislation), the capacity of financial institutions to assess and act upon their client's environmental credentials would be considerably enhanced.

Finally, a note of caution is appropriate for those who would regard finance as a fail-safe instrument for environmental protection. First, the influence of financiers may not always be beneficial. For example, purveyors of agricultural finance may specify the use of ecologically

---

[79] Specifically, to banks, insurance companies, landlords on behalf of their tenants, and successor corporations. Thus bankers, for example, could find themselves liable for the remediation of land contaminated by a client when they foreclose on properties. See G. Anhang, 'Cleaning Up the Lender Management Participation Standard under Comprehensive Environmental Response Compensation and Liability Act 1980 in the Aftermath of Fleet Factors' (1990) 15 *Harvard Environmental Law Review* 235. For background, see (1986) 87 *Stanford Environmental Law Review*. For UK. perspective, note 'Digging Deep: Re-using Contaminated Land' (1991) 87 *Conveyancer & Property Lawyer* 249.

[80] M. K. Landy & M. Hague, 'The Coalition for Waste: Private interests and Superfund' in M. S. Greve & F. L. Smith Jr., (eds.) *Environmental Politics: Public costs, private rewards* (1992), Praeger Publishers, New York.

[81] See, above p.62.

harmful fertilizers and pesticides as a condition of obtaining their product. Thus, where the scope of risk is narrowly defined, finance may be environmentally counterproductive.[82] Secondly, because banks must compete for business, no single lending institution can afford to insist upon its clients having far higher environmental credentials than others, because to do so would be to risk a substantial loss of business. The temptation (tempered by the particular liability rules in force and the degree to which borrowers 'forum shop') will be to relax environmental standards in order to increase the flow of business. Thirdly, large institutions may be able to by-pass banks altogether, for example through the issue of corporate bonds.

Insurance institutions

Provided it is possible to create a viable market, environmental insurance is a powerful policy tool. Just as financial institutions have become sensitive to the environmental performance of their borrowers, so too do insurers have strong incentives to control their policyholders.[83] The availability of insurance, and the cost of insurance premiums, have begun increasingly to reflect a prospective policyholder's environmental record. Schmidheiny has commented that companies with an unfavourable record of environmental compliance 'will find it increasingly difficult and expensive to get insured'.[84]

In many cases, insurers now subject their policyholders to scrutiny beyond that which government authorities can bring to bear, and may hold their policyholders to standards well in excess of that which regulators are in a position to require. With poor environmental performers paying higher insurance premiums, the insurance market provides incentives for responsible corporate conduct, and disincentives for non-compliance.[85] The influence of insurers is by no means limited to private sector policyholders. Yandle observed that smog problems confronting the city of Los Angeles were a cause of concern to those

[82] D. T. Hornstein, 'Lessons from Federal Pesticide Regulation on the Paradigms and Politics of Environmental Law Reform' (1993) 10 *Yale Journal on Regulation* 369–446.

[83] The insurance industry has another reason to be sensitive to environmental considerations. It has been suggested that an increase in the frequency of natural disasters in recent years, specifically catastrophic storms, has resulted from climate change. Global warming may produce financial ruin (R. Sparkes, *The Ethical Investor* (1995), Harper Collins, London, p.99).

[84] S. Schmidheiny, *Changing Course: A. global business perspective on development and the environment* (1992), MIT Press, Cambridge, pp.64–5.

[85] M. Katzman, *Chemical Catastrophes: Regulating environmental risks through pollution insurance* (1985), Richard Irwin, Homewood, Illinois.

insurance companies which held municipal bonds and/or issued insurance to the city.[86] They, in turn, exerted pressure on the city to begin dealing with the smog problem.

In recent years, marine insurance underwriters have been concerned about inadequate government inspection of maritime vessels, particularly those flying 'flags of convenience'. To compensate for this regulatory shortfall, and to ensure that the vessels which they insure are indeed seaworthy, underwriters have engaged their own marine surveyors to inspect the vessels of prospective clients. Similarly, insurance underwriters in the oil and gas industry may engage specialized loss prevention consultants to advise on the insurability of particular activities and on the pricing of specific policies.[87]

In Australia, as a result of legislation, insurance companies may require a certificate of audit before offering environmental liability insurance to corporations.[88] So far, the Australian insurance industry has been slow to respond to this situation, and most Public Liability and Industrial Special Risk policies currently provide only very limited cover for, or even exclude entirely, environmental liability claims. However, as Fowler points out, 'once such special liability cover becomes available in Australia, environmental audits are likely to become a routine prerequisite to the obtaining of such insurance'.[89]

More broadly, general insurance companies: 'have a major role to play in effective management of the environment by helping industries understand the importance of preparing a risk management plan which addresses pollution reduction and avoidance. Without the plan, insurance will be difficult to obtain, and extremely expensive'.[90]

However, insurance is unlikely to realize its potential as an environmental policy tool in the absence of outside intervention. There has been a general withdrawal of cover for environmental impairment

[86] B. Yandle, *The Political Limits of Environmental Regulation* (1989), Quorum Books, New York.

[87] R. Salter, 'Market Credit for Loss Prevention in the Petrochemical Industry' in D. D. Peng (ed.) *Insurance and Legal Issues in the Oil Industry* (1993), Graham & Trotman, London, pp.55–64.

[88] On insurance audits, see Lloyd's List 29 June 1990 at 4; 11 September 1991 at 10; 29 March 1991 at 18; 6 November 1990 at 5; and 26 October 1991 at 12 (via Reuters Textline). J. McDonald, 'Key Issues in Environmental Insurance Litigation' (1991) 8 *Environmental and Planning Law Journal* 145.

[89] R. Fowler 'New National Directions in Environmental Protection and Conservation' in B. Boer, R. Fowler and N. Gunningham (eds.) *Environmental Outlook: Law and Policy* (1994), Federation Press, Sydney.

[90] R. Jones, *Environmental Risk Management* (1996), Paper delivered to 3M Conference, Canberra.

activities deriving from anything other than a sudden and accidental event, except in the case of a very limited number of industries and circumstances. As Freeman and Kunreather have pointed out, currently, most environmental risks do not satisfy the basic conditions of insurability and marketability: the ability to quantify the risk and to set premiums for each individual customer or class of customers.[91] A crucial role for governments is to create the conditions conducive to private insurance functioning effectively. Specifically, this involves 'the design of regulations and the creation of market conditions to permit the insurance industry to play a central role in environmental policy. In large measure, the government can both create and destroy the conditions that would permit insurance to be developed and sold.'[92] For example, if governments set well specified standards and provide the predictability the industry needs then insurance company inspectors can, *inter alia*, inspect against the legal standard and calculate risks in terms of it. Governments can foster a regulatory role for insurance by requiring insurance as a condition of licensing, or as a condition of authorization to engage in activities which pose environmental risk.

As is the case with finance, however, insurance cannot be regarded as a fail-safe instrument for environmental protection. For example, purveyors of crop insurance may also require environmentally inappropriate fertilizers and pesticides as a condition of their policy. Thus, where the scope of risk is narrowly defined, insurance may be environmentally counterproductive.[93] Further, in some settings, insurance may not fulfil its potential as a regulatory instrument. A great deal of very costly insurance litigation arises from disputes between insurer and policyholder over the scope of coverage; this carries no environmental benefit. At the extreme, in the face of accumulating liabilities (and a failure by government to create appropriate conditions), insurers may simply abandon the pollution insurance market. And finally, large commercial entities may choose to self-insure, thereby placing themselves beyond the influence of an insurer.

---

[91] P. Freeman & H. Kunreather, 'The Roles of Insurance and Well Specified Standards in Dealing With Environmental Risks' (1996) 17 *Risk Management and Decision Economics* 513–530 at 530.

[92] P. Freeman & H. Kunreather, 'The Roles of Insurance and Well Specified Standards in Dealing With Environmental Risks' (1996) 17 *Risk Management and Decision Economics* 513–530 at 530.

[93] D. T. Hornstein, 'Lessons from Federal Pesticide Regulation on the Paradigms and Politics of Environmental Law Reform' (1993) 10 *Yale Journal on Regulation* 369–446.

Environmental consultants

In addition to the environmental audit function discussed above, the use of independent environmental consultants to assess and prescribe the environmental performance of firms has been a significant development in recent years. Environmental consultants vary widely in terms of the services which they provide. Some are limited to specific industries, such as mining and agriculture. Others provide specific services, such as audit and compliance monitoring. Larger and more diversified consultants provide a range of services, including risk assessment, training, process engineering, hazardous waste management, and pollution prevention. Although the relationship between firms and consultants differs from other commercial third party situations, in the sense that consultants are, generally, financially dependent on the patronage of firms,[94] consultants can provide firms with significant commercial incentives. Specifically, their professional services are claimed to reduce exposure to litigation and criminal penalties; to improve risk management, operating performance and planning; to reduce costs through recycling, waste minimization and material substitutions (which might otherwise not be identified as viable); and to achieve environmental goals more efficiently and with less application of government resources.[95]

In some cases, the use of independent consultants may be more effective in ensuring compliance with environmental standards than would traditional regulatory instruments. For example, Mitchell[96] has demonstrated that, in the case of reducing oil pollution at sea, classification societies (which effectively act as independent auditors) have been far more successful at enforcing technical specifications for segregated ballast tanks and crude oil washing than governments have in preventing ballast discharges at sea. Mitchell makes the point that classification societies are international corporations whose revenues depend on their public reputation, and as such, they have strong incentives, as well as the means and the authority, to withhold licenses from non-complying ships.

[94] An exception is where audits are required by lending or insurance institutions as a prerequisite for commercial transactions, particularly in response to contaminated site liability legislation (N. Gunningham & J. Prest, 'Environmental Audit as a Regulatory Strategy: Prospects and reform' (1993) 15 *Sydney Law Review* 492–526).

[95] See, generally, N. Gunningham & J. Prest, 'Environmental Audit as a Regulatory Strategy: Prospects and reform' (1993) 15 *Sydney Law Review* 492–526 and footnote 3.

[96] R. B. Mitchell, *International Oil Pollution as Sea*, (1994), Massachusetts Institute of Technology.

In some circumstances, industry will have commercial incentives to use environmental consultants, and will do so voluntarily. In others, they may be disinclined to do so. For example, the result of audits, if made publicly available, could reveal valuable commercial information to competitors, or in the case where regulatory transgressions are discovered, unintentional or not, then this may invite third party litigation.[97] Such concerns may act as a powerful deterrent to the use of environmental audits. It may be necessary, therefore, for government to ensure that the results of purely voluntary audits remain confidential, for example, by making audit results inadmissible in court. In cases where audits are conducted as part of a co-regulatory scheme, or required as a result of regulatory compliance, the results of which are consequently made available to regulatory authorities, then the same regulatory authority may undertake to give participating firms a 'period of grace' in which to rectify any identified problems.[98]

There are also numerous ways in which government can positively encourage the use of environmental consultants, who may then work to improve their clients' environmental performance. Take environmental auditors as an example. First, government may directly subsidize environmental audits conducted, for example, by small and medium sized business that would otherwise lack sufficient financial resources. This approach has been adopted by governments in the United Kingdom and Australia. Secondly, government may provide tax incentives to undergo audits. This would, potentially, target a much wider range of firms, but may not be as an efficient and equitable use of public resources as direct subsidies. Thirdly, through license accreditation systems, government may undertake to regulate more lightly those firms which voluntarily enter an audit scheme. Fourthly, government may provide substantial public relations benefits to firms participating in a voluntary audit scheme, as has occurred under the European Union's Environmental Management and Audit Scheme. Fifthly, government could provide preferential treatment to firms which have conducted an approved audit. This could take the form of preferential government purchasing or tendering, or preferential access to other government programmes, such as business improvement programmes. Sixthly, government and industry could build independent audits into self-

---

[97] N. Gunningham & J. Prest, 'Environmental Audit as a Regulatory Strategy: Prospects and reform' (1993) 15 *Sydney Law Review* 492–526.
[98] *Ibid.*

regulatory or co-regulatory arrangements. For example, self-regulatory environmental covenants in the Netherlands require participating firms to have regular third party audits. Alternatively, co-regulatory agreements which contain provisions for product stewardship may encourage larger firms to audit smaller upstream suppliers and downstream buyers. Seventhly, corporate environmental reporting may include provisions for independent environmental auditing, in a similar fashion to that required for financial reporting. Finally, government may enact strong lender and insurance liability, which would encourage financial institutions to use external audits as a normal part of doing business.

A greater use of independent environmental audits would ease some of the regulatory burden of government and, in particular, free up resources that could more productively be applied to enforcing standards on the worst industry performers. There is a danger, however, that auditors will be subject to the same regulatory capture pressures that have befallen government regulators. Indeed, by being financially dependent on industry, auditors have an added incentive 'not to bite the hand that feeds it'. There are, however, several ways in which the independence of auditors can be reinforced.[99] These include creating a pool of government accredited auditors which are required to meet high independence standards, and including an environmental and/or independent technical expert on audit teams. Other possible measures include:

(i) using government agencies to act as auditors (which will not be subject to the same commercial pressures);
(ii) establishing a body of external verifiers to validate the methodology of accredited independent auditors;
(iii) instituting a system of peer review between auditors; and
(iv) legislating a system of national standards to regulate the activities of auditors.[100]

3. Governing at a distance

In the previous sections, we have argued that both commercial and non-commercial third parties can play important roles in environmental protection. However, institutional actors will not necessarily order

---

[99] See N. Gunningham, 'Who Audits the Auditors?' 1993 11(4) *Environmental and Planning Law Journal* 229–238.
[100] *Ibid.*

themselves to meet specific environmental objectives, and in the absence of external intervention, many of the potential opportunities for third party intervention may never be realized. Thus, there is an essential policy role for government to shape market orderings and to facilitate the constructive activities of non-governmental institutions. That is, at the same time as the state is retreating from many of its traditional regulatory functions, numerous opportunities arise to forge creative new roles, harnessing private institutions and resources in furtherance of public policy.

Governments can, for example, act as facilitators and brokers. Through the judicious use of incentives, or by wielding their own purchasing power, governments are often able to structure a marketplace so that market outcomes fulfil public purposes. In these ways, the behaviour of business can be guided at a distance by governments, and further conditioned by commercial and non-commercial third parties to produce outcomes more advantageous than might be achieved by directions imposed from above.

There are a number of legislative or administrative mechanisms by which the State may harness non-governmental resources in furtherance of regulatory goals.[101] Since we have, so far, referred to these only indirectly, it may be useful to articulate them explicitly here. Governments may:

- conscript third parties to assist with some aspect of compliance. Just as banks are required to report transactions over a certain threshold, so too can institutions be compelled by law to disclose environmental breaches committed by others;

- require that targets of regulation engage the machinery of private institutions. Mandatory environmental audit requirements are perhaps the best example. Similarly, government might require regulated entities to hold liability insurance as a condition of doing business, for example in circumstances of extreme environmental risk;

- with a view to informing markets or other private institutions in a position to foster compliance, require disclosure of certain aspects of a regulatee's activities. This is the basis for toxic release inventories, and CRTK legislation discussed above;

[101] P. N. Grabosky, 'Using Non-governmental Resources to Foster Regulatory Compliance' (1995) 8(4) *Governance, an International Journal of Policy and Administration* 527–550.

- confer entitlements upon private parties, leaving it up to those private parties to enforce those rights. For example, private enforcement provisions in laws which prohibit misleading advertising can be used by environmental groups against 'greenwash' tactics by some corporations. Alternatively, the government may empower third parties to undertake enforcement actions on the part of the state;

- offer incentives directly to targets of regulation to induce compliance, or to engage in a desired course of conduct; or they may also offer incentives to third parties for the co-production of regulatory services. Regulatory authorities may offer incentives for self-regulatory investments, or for the engagement of professional services which would foster compliance. Rewards and bounties to third parties for surveillance and enforcement activity are common in many regulatory systems;

- seek to engage private consultants rather than rely upon information or services from organized interests. The state may also contract out one or more regulatory functions, from specialized testing to an entire regulatory regime. For example, the programme for motor vehicle emissions testing in British Columbia was contracted out to private interests;[102]

- accept standards developed in the private sector and give them official status. In some regulatory systems, the task of developing rules is delegated to private interests. Considerable rule-making function is delegated to professional self-regulatory organizations. Galanter[103] refers to such technologies as 'regulatory endowments'; and

- relinquish a direct regulatory role in deference to market forces. In this case, the role of government is to monitor the behaviour of markets, intervening only in the event of market failure.

4. Instrument and institutional interactions

By now, it will be apparent that instruments and institutions may not be independent, but rather that they often impact upon and influence each other; and there is much to be learned from studying both functional and dysfunctional instrument and institutional interactions. The

[102] E. Baar, 'Contracting Out Regulatory Implementation' (1993), paper delivered at the Canadian law and Society meeting, Ottawa, June 8.

[103] M. Galanter, 'Justice in Many Rooms' (1981) 19 *Journal of Legal Pluralism* 1–47.

following section contributes to our basic framework for the design of regulatory systems, by introducing some of the fundamental forms of instrument and institutional interaction, and analyzing their impact. In so doing, we herald some of the successes and failures of regulatory life which hold lessons for participants in the regulatory process, and which will be discussed in greater detail in chapters four and five.

A typology of interactions

The interaction of regulatory institutions and of the instruments which they command may take a variety of forms. Such interactions can be grouped in three general categories. First, there are those interactions which are generally positive, in which one or both instruments or institutions become active or more effective. Next, there are other circumstances in which they simply co-exist, without directly impacting the performance of each other. And finally, there are those which entail negative impacts, where the effect of one or more instrument or institution is diminished, or functions in a counterproductive manner. Over and above the categories, it should be noted that some instrument interactions will be *contextual*, that is, where the nature of the interaction is largely determined by the overriding policy objectives; while others will be *intrinsic*, that is, where the inherent qualities of instruments dictate the interaction independently of the policy objectives.

1. Complementary interactions

In this category, we examine circumstances in which the use of one instrument, or the role of a particular institution, has a beneficial effect on another instrument or institution. For example, the law of liability, with the ultimate risk of potentially catastrophic losses for insurers, has moved many insurers to impose strict conditions upon policyholders. These, in turn, may undergo environmental audits to ensure that they remain in compliance with the terms of their insurance contract.

A specific form of positive interaction occurs when a particular institution or instrument is stimulated by, contingent upon, or requisite to the functioning of another (activation). For example, Huppes *et. al.* have observed that command and control methods may be a prerequisite for some financial instruments: 'A tax on effluents may only be administered if the installation of piping and measurement apparatus is made obligatory'.[104] This is an example of positive *intrinsic* instrument inter-

---

[104] G. Huppes & R. Kagan, 'Market-Oriented Regulation of Environmental Problems in the Netherlands' (1989) 11(2) *Law and Policy* 215–239.

actions, because the complementary relationship exists irrespective of the particular regulatory context.

Activation occurs when the mobilization of a particular instrument creates a demand for another. As we will see below in chapter four, the establishment of a self-regulatory regime, as in the chemical industry's Responsible Care Program, generated a demand on the part of participating firms for environmental auditing services. The availability of a legal defence of due diligence will stimulate the design of corporate compliance programmes and other self-regulatory initiatives, and may also create a demand for environmental audit services. The likelihood of any of these instruments being mobilized in the absence of the activator is often remote.

Activation can also be produced by positive stimuli. Government purchasing preferences for recycled products or for investment in clean technology may help create and nurture markets when these would not arise or thrive spontaneously. Buying power can thus activate markets for recycled materials. Regulatory enforcement by public agencies might not occur but for the right of private prosecution. Public authorities, reluctant to enforce the law in the normal course of events, may be informally embarrassed or legally compelled to take action as a result of the threat or reality of citizen legal action. In his book on environmental protection in the United States, Yeager observes how citizen suits may actually force executive action.[105] The use of private prosecution can thus activate public enforcement actions when these would not otherwise occur. Other positive forms of interaction occur in which each instrument enhances the effect of the other.

As we will see below in chapters four and five, optimal regulation in both the chemical manufacturing and agricultural sectors requires the use of synergistic combinations of instruments. The conservation of biological diversity, in particular, lends itself to a combination of measures— enhancing those activities which have a positive impact, and minimizing those which have a negative impact.[106] Subsidies for the preservation of remnant vegetation may be combined with penalties for unauthorized clearance. The prospective penalty renders the prospective subsidy that much more attractive at the same time as the prospective subsidy makes

---

[105] P. C. Yeager, *The Limits of Law: the public regulation of private pollution* (1991), Cambridge University Press, Cambridge, p.121.

[106] Organisation for Economic Co-operation and Development (OECD), Group on Economic and Environment Policy Integration, Expert Group on Economic Aspects of Biodiversity, *Economic Incentives for the Conservation of Biodiversity: Conceptual framework and guidelines for case studies* (1994), OECD, Paris, p.13.

the potential penalty that much more burdensome. The carrot becomes even more attractive when the alternative is the stick: punitive instruments are made even more undesirable in the face of an inducement.

For example, this occurs when adherence to specified regulatory standards is made a condition of insurance. The insurance contract thereby reinforces regulatory requirements, which, under a relaxed regulatory regime, might be ignored. Regulatory noncompliance thus entails a risk not only of enforcement action, but also cancellation of insurance. The terms of an insurance contract can thus strengthen the salience of regulatory standards. In the case of what is termed cross-compliance, the provision of support for one objective is made subject to prior compliance with regulatory requirements relating to another. Thus, the eligibility to receive drought relief may be conditional upon having taken specific measures in furtherance of habitat preservation.

2. 'Neutral' interactions

There are some circumstances where instruments or institutions simply co-exist, without impacting upon each other for better or worse. For example, one institution may duplicate the activities of another. The proliferation of public interest groups, often with similar agendas and practices, is a common feature of the contemporary regulatory landscape. An example of a neutral *intrinsic* instrument interaction, as we shall discover in chapter four, is where large multinational chemical companies have voluntarily adopted, or indeed gone well beyond, environmental provisions required under the industry wide self-regulatory programme of Responsible Care.

Many neutral interactions, which might appear to serve no positive function, may result in a net benefit. As we will see, given the flawed nature of most individual instruments, there may, in fact, be good reasons for 'backing up' one instrument with another. For example, while some would regard duplication as inherently wasteful, it is not invariably bad. In some circumstances, it may have particular virtues. Competition in the delivery of public policy, rather than entailing waste, may lead to improved outcomes, or may serve some higher purpose. Again, one should not necessarily lament the fact that three different citizens' groups may independently campaign for the protection of endangered species. Democratic participation often has virtues irrespective of outcome.

In contrast to duplication, where two instruments essentially overlap, there are other circumstances where instruments might be described as adjoining: where one instrument achieves related or residual objectives which remain unmet through the operation of another. For example, in most regulatory settings, informational instruments alone will bring about desired conduct by some actors, but not by others. Those who are not sufficiently motivated by informational instruments may require some form of inducement, or perhaps even threat, before improving their performance. Similarly, if a regulatory strategy—based on negotiation and persuasion—achieves only partial compliance, a complementary strategy of administrative sanctions may win over the remaining noncompliant actors. This is an example where *intrinsic* neutral interactions may be exploited to achieve a common policy goal.

The essence of such complementarity is an efficient division of labour. Cheit notes that comparative institutional advantages may flow from public and private standard setting.[107] He observes complementarity rather than redundancy in the sharing of responsibility for the development of safety standards. Moreover, as we know from our experience with safety systems, a degree of duplication provides insurance against failure. As we shall see, in circumstances where effectiveness is more important than efficiency, policymakers would be wise to consciously build dependability into regulatory design. Consider, for example, the situation of HCFC's where self-regulation is 'backed up' by tradeable permits in the event of the former failing (see chapter six).

3. Counterproductive interactions

Finally, there are circumstances in which one instrument or institution may weaken or block another. One might use the term 'neutralization' to refer to the effect of one instrument in diluting the effects of another. This can be a 'designed-in' feature of regulatory systems: checks and balances may be created intentionally in order to prevent an excessive concentration of power. The goal, in such circumstances, is to produce a creative tension between contending interests, rather than policy gridlock.

More frequently, neutralization occurs unintentionally as the result of independent policies designed to appease contending interests. Indeed, it can occur when instruments are introduced by entirely different regulatory regimes. As we will observe in chapter five, subsidies for certain types of agricultural production and tax deductions for expenditures incurred in land clearance (traditional agricultural

[107] R. Cheit, *Setting Safety Standards: Regulation in the private and public sectors* (1990), University of California Press, Berkeley, p.222.

policies) may coexist with, and effectively neutralize, incentives for the conservation of remnant vegetation. The term 'countervailing subsidies' has been used to refer to this phenomenon.[108] Similarly, price supports, crop subsidies, and tax incentives for the use of pesticides and fertilizers will encourage exploitation of marginal land, and will neutralize instruments deployed in furtherance of conservation.[109] These are examples of *contextual* instruments interactions, where neutralization is a result of contradictory policy objectives rather than the inherent incompatibility of instruments.

Another form of negative interaction occurs when one institution blocks the effects of another, or slows down or impedes the interaction of two others. For example, it might be argued that the use of litigation by companies and/or industry associations, by deterring an environmentalist organization's dissemination of information critical of a particular polluter or regulatory authority, inhibits the influence which the citizens' group's message would otherwise have on regulatory enforcement policy or on the corporate conduct responsible for the adverse environmental impact. Dialogue between citizens' groups and other institutional actors is thus inhibited.

Perhaps the most vivid example of institutional inhibition may be drawn from what have become known as Strategic Lawsuits Against Public Participation (SLAPP).[110] Directed primarily against citizen interest groups, these lawsuits are intended to deter public criticism of questionable corporate or governmental conduct. Causes of action which may serve as the basis of SLAPP suits include business interference, abuse of process, and especially, libel. For example, public concern over use of the pesticide Alar and other agricultural chemicals moved agribusiness interests to promote 'veggie libel' statutes, which make disparagement of certain agricultural products actionable as libel.[111] Targets of successful SLAPP suits may be silenced, if not bankrupted. But the inhibiting effect of SLAPPs can extend well beyond the immediate target. The mere threat of SLAPP litigation undoubtedly

---

[108] J. B. Opschoor & H. B. Vos, *Application of Economic Instruments for Environmental Protection in OECD Countries* (1989), OECD, Paris, p.112.

[109] Organisation for Economic Co-operation and Development (OECD), Group on Economic and Environment Policy Integration, Expert Group on Economic Aspects of Biodiversity, *Economic Incentives for the Conservation of Biodiversity: Conceptual framework and guidelines for case studies* (1994), OECD, Paris.

[110] G. W. Pring & P. Canan, *SLAPPs: Getting sued for speaking out* (1996), Temple University Press, Philadelphia.

[111] *Ibid.* at p. 191.

has a chilling effect on some public protest. As a result, information has less influence on voluntary corporate compliance behaviour or on regulatory enforcement.

Other rules relating to litigation may discourage the collection of information. Rules which enable the results of voluntary environmental audits to be used against a company in a subsequent enforcement action have precisely this effect, with the result that a potentially valuable environmental instrument is far less used than it might be.[112] On other occasions, litigation is used to limit information which would otherwise be employed in furtherance of regulatory prosecution or civil action. In the absence of such information, these instruments are less effective. For example, corporations in Australia sought (unsuccessfully) to invoke the privilege against self-incrimination in order to prevent the results of pollution self-monitoring, mandated by legislation, being used against them in court.[113]

The power of inhibition is by no means limited to coercive instruments. One can also see how subsidies such as tax deductions for the introduction of 'end of pipe' pollution abatement technology might distract attention from policies designed to encourage pollution prevention strategies, for example, the introduction of environmental management systems. Such subsidies can thus lessen the perceived attractiveness of going 'beyond compliance' through the integration of environmental improvement with broader business objectives. This is an example of negative *intrinsic* interactions, in that the measures would be inhibitory irrespective of the particular context.

Challenges for regulatory design

We have provided a basic description of the ways in which instruments may impact upon each other in a regulatory system. We have not sought to provide broader lessons for regulatory design: for this is the theme of the final section of the book. However, the present account may serve to sensitize the reader to some of the complexities involved in answering that question.

In particular, our description underscores the systemic nature of regulatory life. For example, as Harter and Eads have reminded us,

---

[112] See N. Gunningham & J. Prest, 'Environmental Audit as a Regulatory Strategy: Prospects and reform' (1993) 15 *Sydney Law Review* 492–526.

[113] J. McDonald, 'Corporate Confidentiality After Caltex: How safe is your audit?' (1994) 11(3) *Environmental and Planning Law Journal* 193–210.

changes in a given instrument can effect an entire regulatory system.[114] Imposition of command and control regulation, perceived as draconian, may alienate regulated industries, and in the process discredit less controversial instruments or policies administered by the agency merely by association.

Because of this interconnectedness of different instruments and institutions, a particular instrument which may appear attractive, when looked at on its own, may work quite differently when introduced alongside others. At times, this can be highly desirable, as when one instrument provides leverage over another, and, through it, generates preferred outcomes which might otherwise be unattainable. At other times, the impact can be counterproductive, and the outcomes negative. Thus, the attributes of a regulatory package may differ from those of its component instruments.

So too, can the relative strength or salience of a particular instrument affect the properties of the entire system. Vesting a particular interest with the power to veto regulatory policy may impede system effectiveness. Overweighting a system with community consultation may enhance its popular legitimacy, at the expense of efficiency. An instrument which is inefficient, alone or in context, may merit inclusion in a regulatory package if it contributes to the realization of important secondary goals, such as civic education or the building of self-regulatory capacity. Above all, systemic problems are likely to require systemic solutions.

5. Conclusion

In this chapter, we have seen that there is much more to environmental regulation than purely the work of government. Some of the most powerful institutions of corporate social control exist in the private and non-profit sectors. In some cases at least, these functions are performed more effectively, more efficiently, and with greater legitimacy (from the point on view of the regulatee) by non-governmental institutions than by government agencies. We have shown how both industry itself (through self and co-regulation)[115] and commercial and non-commercial third parties have the capacity to act as surrogate regula-

---

[114] P. J. Harter & G. C. Eads, 'Policy Instruments, Institutions, and Objectives: An analytical framework for assessing "alternatives" to regulation' (1985) 37(3) *Administrative Law Review* 221–58.

[115] Above, chapter 2, p.50.

tors and to perform other quasi-regulatory functions in a wide variety of circumstances.

This is not to suggest that government no longer has an important role to play in environmental regulation and policy design, but rather that that role may be changing. Government has a far wider range of options in choosing *how* it intervenes, than is commonly recognized. Some environmental problems may be amenable to command, others to a kind of orchestration, and others still to facilitation. That is, not only can governments intervene directly, but they can also engage in more subtle manipulation of incentives and the creation of opportunity structures ('steering', rather than 'rowing' to use the metaphor popularized by Osborne & Gaebler[116]). There will, inevitably, remain those institutions which must be left to their own devices.[117] Others will entail a combination of design and spontaneity.[118]

We have also described both the opportunities and the pitfalls involved in utilizing combinations of instruments and in utilizing a broader range of social actors. In particular, we have set out a typology of positive, negative, and neutral mixes, emphasized the interconnectedness of different instruments and institutions, and the systemic nature of regulatory life. Above all, we have indicated the complexities of regulatory design.

Against this backdrop, our attention now turns to the principles for the design of regulatory systems, with a focus on that which is theoretically desirable, while being mindful of the constraints imposed by what is politically and socially practicable. We do not, for example, assume an omniscient or omnipotent state with unlimited resources. On the contrary, we recognize the informational asymmetry between industry and government, the often limited reach and competence of regulatory agencies, a political context of considerable fiscal constraint, and a prevalent ideology which is hostile to greater taxation or a larger role for government.

The object of this book is to suggest ways in which governments, operating under such constraints, might at times intervene directly to produce desired environmental outcomes; act to foster constructive activity by non-governmental institutions; and enjoy the benefits of

[116] D. Osborne & E. Gaebler, *Reinventing Government* (1992), Addison Wesley, Reading.

[117] G. Thompson *et. al.* (eds.) *Markets, Hierarchies and Networks: The coordination of social life* (1991), Sage Publications, London.

[118] F. von Hayek, 'Spontaneous ("grown") Order and Organized ("made") Order' pp.292–301 in G. Thompson *et. al.* (eds.) *Markets, Hierarchies and Networks: The coordination of social life* (1991), Sage Publications, London.

non-State institutions functioning independently in constructive ways. More broadly, it is to develop a framework and a broader vision of regulatory design which integrates instruments and parties in a synergistic and complementary fashion in such a way as to optimize the policy mix.

Recognizing that the greatest insights are likely to be generated by a detailed examination of specific contexts or industry sectors, rather than across the board, chapters four and five will seek to envisage what form of regulatory system is most appropriate to minimize environmental harm which results from chemical manufacturing, and from critical aspects of agriculture. There, we explore in more detail, and at a concrete level, the interactions between instruments and actors.

PART II

Redesigning regulation:
A sector specific analysis

4   The Chemical Industry

Neil Gunningham

Introduction

In this chapter, we begin our exploration of sector-specific policy mixes. We provide a brief introduction to the chemical industry, its economic contribution, and its environmental problems, and we identify the key features of that industry that are likely to influence the possibilities for regulatory design. We then summarize the main components and limitations of current regulatory regimes in North America, Western Europe, and Australia, before going on to the main task of the chapter: the design of regulatory policy, harnessing a broader mix of instruments and institutional actors, and tailored to the particular circumstances of the chemical industry.

The problems upon which we focus are, necessarily, a sub-set of the environmental problems confronting the industry as a whole. Our principal focus is on point source pollution, which, together with chemical accidents, has been the major environmental concern with which the industry is associated.[1] As we shall see, this is not without good cause: the chemical industry is, by a large margin, the most polluting industry sector both in the United States and in a number of other countries. The solutions we suggest, however, have resonance far beyond the chemical industry itself.

The chemical industry and its environmental impact

The chemical industry, conventionally defined,[2] is a key manufacturing sector in most of the industrialized world, transforming natural raw

---

[1] For an excellent policy analysis of the latter, see J. Potter, 'Chemical Accident Prevention Regulation in California and New Jersey' (1993) 20 *Ecology Law Quarterly* 755–815.

[2] No classification satisfactorily defines the absolute limits of 'the chemical industry' and national and international industrial classification schemes differ. See, for example, R. Gottlieb (ed.) *Reducing Toxics: A new approach to policy and industrial decision making* (1995), Island Press, Washington DC, p.221. *Chemical and Engineering News*, a leading trade journal published by the American Chemical Society, uses the following categories: organic chemicals; inorganic chemicals; minerals; synthetic fibres; synthetic rubbers; plastics; fertilizers; pesticides; coatings; and aerosols (by end category, such as personal products, and insect sprays) to encompass the industry. This classification does not include 'products of

materials such as metals, minerals, coal, oil, natural gas, vegetable oils, and animal fats into thousands of organic chemicals for commercial use. The chemical industry produces tens of thousands of products whose many applications include raw and basic or intermediate materials for other industries, and finished products for industry, construction, service, agriculture, business, and individual consumers.

During the early part of the twentieth century, the industry expanded substantially in the areas of explosives, synthetic dyes, pharmaceuticals, and petrochemicals, and successfully diffused chemical industry products into many other industrial sectors. In so doing, it established its current dominant role within the manufacturing sector of most developed and many developing countries. More recently, there has been a trend away from bulk chemicals towards higher added value products including pesticides, herbicides, dyestuffs, and biotechnology applications.

Almost all the largest chemical companies are transnationals, most of whom expanded from their original base in North America or Western Europe to establish substantial foreign subsidiaries. Such an expansion was particularly evident from the second half of the 1980s until the 1991 to 1992 recession, during which period such companies opened new markets and built new plants, especially in the Asia-Pacific region. During the same period, world gross output in chemicals grew from US$744 billion to US$1.136 trillion.[3] In addition to a small number of large firms, the industry also includes many smaller operators. These include specialty chemical manufacturers, distributors, and others to whom chemicals are supplied (e.g., upstream suppliers, and buyers for manufacturers downstream).

The chemical industry is a keystone of the United States economy. It has some 1.1 million employees, over $316 billion in sales, and is the

oil companies' and minerals which have little or no chemical industry application (Gottlieb 1995:225)

A useful working definition is that of 'industrial activity', embracing any industrial process in which a basic chemical change/reaction takes place, or in which chemistry is used and chemicals are produced. The industry can be divided into two sub-sectors: 'heavy' (basic chemical sectors engaged in manufacturing the basic inorganic and organic commodity chemicals) and 'light' (clustered according to end products, such as soaps and detergents, dyes, pharmaceuticals, explosives, rubber, plastics and resins, manmade fibres, paints and varnishes, and the paper industry. This classification includes organic industrial minerals production (mining) and processing (primarily associated with fertilizer production) within the chemical process industries (Gottlieb 1995:222).

[3] International Labour Organisation, Chemical Industries Committee, *Recent Developments in the Chemical Industries*, (1995), Geneva, p.10.

second largest manufacturing industry in that country.[4] It is also a leading industry in Western Europe, where it accounts for an estimated one-third of the world turnover of chemical production and 37 per cent of the total European trade balance of manufacturing.[5] In Australia, the chemical industry, similarly, plays an important role, as a key supplier of raw materials to the overall manufacturing industry, and to key export industries such as agriculture and mining.

The chemical industry is a major source of environmental pollution. It is the United States' largest consumer and generator of highly toxic chemical substances.[6] Roughly half of all releases and transfers reported through the TRI, and 80 to 90 per cent of hazardous waste generation reported through the Resource Conservation and Recovery Act, are attributed to the industry.[7] These figures represented a total of three times that of the next major contributor to pollution, the metal industry. The United States chemical manufacturing facilities also dominate individual facilities top-ranked for the largest total emission of hazardous waste.[8] Within most countries in Western Europe, although

[4] Quoted in J. Rees, 'The Development of Communication Regulation in the Chemical Industry' (1997) 19(4) *Law and Policy* (publication of the 1997 issue delayed).

[5] Since the recession of the early 1980s, chemical industry production has expanded by 52 per cent. The industry produces over 70,000 different products and, in 1994, employed 1.06 million people, 5.9 per cent of the manufacturing total. The US chemical industry is the worlds largest, accounting for about 26 per cent of the world total (Chemical Manufacturers Association (CMA), *US Chemical Industry Statistical Handbook 1995* (1995) Chemical Manufacturers Association, Washington DC). In 1993, eighteen out of thirty world chemical majors had their headquarters in Western Europe. The centre of gravity of the chemical industry in Europe remains in Germany, but most European countries, in Western and Eastern Europe, have internationally significant chemical industries. In financial terms, the leading countries include Germany, UK, France, Italy, Netherlands, Switzerland, and the Czech Republic. The European Union boasts approximately 33,000 enterprises involved in chemical production. Approximately 98 per cent of these have fewer than 500 employees and, classified as small or medium enterprises, take 44 per cent of the turnover of the industry and employ 39 per cent of the total workforce (European Chemical Industry Council (CEFIC), Internet site (November 1996) at http://www/innet.net/cefic/cgi-bin).

[6] R. Gottlieb, (ed.) *Reducing Toxics: A new approach to policy and industrial decision making* (1995), Island Press, Washington DC, p.210. According to the EPA Toxic Release Inventory (TRI), the US emits about 20 billion pounds of toxic chemicals annually into the environment (B. Commoner, *Making Peace With The Planet* (1990), Pantheon Books, New York, p.31) However, according to Congress's Office of Technology Assessment, because of under reporting and the omission of data from small establishments, this figure is more likely to be about 400 billion pounds.

[7] US EPA, Toxic Release Inventory (1993), Washington DC, p.60.

[8] In 1991, of the top fifty facilities, more than two-thirds were related to the chemical industry and accounted for almost 40 per cent of the total releases and transfers (R. Gottlieb, (ed.) *Reducing Toxics: A new approach to policy and industrial decision making* (1995), Island Press, Washington DC, p.212).

comparable statistics are lacking, the chemical industry has a broadly similar environmental profile,[9] as indeed it does in a number of other developed nations.[10]

The industry is not only a very substantial contributor to environmental point source toxic chemical *pollution*, but is also, in its capacity as a supplier of intermediate products to other sectors, the most important developer/vendor of toxic chemical *products*, although it is only the former role that has received significant attention. The chemical industry is a contributor to ozone layer depletion and the enhanced greenhouse effect, and its activities have implications for toxic waste management, the transportation of hazardous materials, and the safety of foodstuffs.[11] Finally, there are risks of accidents and explosions to chemical facilities themselves, which can inflict serious damage on local communities as well as broader environmental damage.

It is this last threat, and the consequences of individual dramatic and highly publicized chemical accidents, that have evoked the greatest public outcry and industry response.[12] For example, in 1984, at Bhopal in India, at least 2,000 people were killed and some 200,000 injured when twenty tons of lethal methyl isocyanide escaped from a union carbide chemical plant.[13] A number of other serious accidents have occurred in a wide range of other countries.[14]

---

[9] The Commission of the European Union estimates that environment-related expenditure in 1992 amounted to 3.5 per cent of the turnover of the chemical industry in the EU (International Labour Organisation, Chemical Industries Committee, *Recent Developments in the Chemical Industries* (1995), Geneva, p.34)

[10] For example, in Australia, the chemical industry is also the largest single domestic producer of hazardous wastes (Plastics and Chemicals Industries Association—Chemicals Sector (PACIA), *Reducing Waste: Report on 1994 Waste Survey* (1995), PACIA, Melbourne, p.12.

[11] Since the toxic chemicals emitted into the environment occur in air, drinking water, and food, they readily enter the human body, threatening human health.

[12] R. Gottlieb, (ed.) *Reducing Toxics: A new approach to policy and industrial decision making* (1995), Island Press, Washington DC, p.211. Across the globe, there have been numerous industrial catastrophes involving chemical industry installations (N. A Gunningham, 'Environment, Self-Regulation, and the Chemical Industry: Assessing responsible care' (1995) 17(1) *Law and Policy* 57. See details of accidents internationally on pp.59–60. Also S. Tombs, 'The Chemical Industry and Environmental Issues' in D. Smith, (ed.) *Business and the Environment: Implications of the new environmentalism* (1993), Paul Chapman Publishing, UK, chapter 10 at p.132.

[13] P. Shrivastava, *Bhopal: Anatomy of a crisis* (2nd edn.) (1992), Chapman, London.

[14] Amongst these, are incidents in Seveso, Italy, in 1976; Pasadena, Texas, in 1989; and at Sterlington, Louisiana, in 1991. Similar accidents occurred in Klong Toey, Thailand, in 1991; Hesse, Germany, in 1993; and Shenzhen, China, in 1993 (see J. Withers, *Major Industrial Hazards: Their Appraisal and Control* (1988), Halsted Press, New York; and International Labour Organisation, Chemical Industries Committee (1995) *Recent Developments in the Chemical Industries*, Geneva, p.27.

Responding to public concern and the costs of accidents, both about point-source emissions and accidents, the chemical industry has, during the last decade, significantly improved its environmental performance. Since 1987, the United States chemical industry claims to have reduced by 49 per cent releases of toxic chemicals to the environment.[15] The industry has also reduced disposal in deep-wells by 46 per cent and off-site transfer for treatment and disposal by 56 per cent. A survey by the United States Chemical Manufacturers Association (CMA) showed reductions by its member companies of 16 per cent for releases, 14 per cent for underground injection, and 21 per cent for transfers, excluding transfers for recycling and energy recovery.[16] The industry claims that its environmental control actions have necessitated capital expenditures for pollution abatement and control which have totalled over US$22 billion since 1973.[17] The United States chemical industry pollution abatement spending in 1993 was claimed to be US$4.4 billion. In the year 2000, the CMA, using EPA figures, estimates that it will spend roughly US$6 billion in complying with environmental regulations.[18]

European chemical companies have responded similarly to environmental concerns, with substantial expenditure on improved environmental performance. The Commission of the European Union estimates that environment-related expenditure in 1992 amounted to 3.5 per cent of the turnover of the chemical industry in the European Union.[19] In the United Kingdom, the share of capital spending on environmental protection has risen from 8 per cent in

[15] Chemical Manufacturers Association (CMA), *Fact Sheet: Chemical Industry Halves Toxic Releases* (1996), CMA, Washington DC.

[16] Based on 1993 figures (Chemical Manufacturers Association (CMA) *Fact Sheet: Chemical Industry Halves Toxic Releases* (1996), Washington DC. See also Chemical Manufacturers Association (CMA), '*The year in review, 1995–96' Responsible Care Progress Report*, Washington DC, pp.5–7).

[17] Chemical Manufacturers Association (CMA), *US Chemical Industry Statistical Handbook 1995* (1995), CMA, Washington DC, p.107.

[18] L. Ember, 'Overhaul of Environmental Law Needed for Sustainable Development' (1993) *Chemical and Engineering News*, March 15, p.17, interviewing E. D. Elliott and E. M. Thomas, authors of 'Chemicals' in C. Campbell-Mohn, B. Breen & J. W. Futrell (eds.) *Sustainable Environmental Law* (1993), Environmental Law Institute, St Paul, Minnesota, chapter 17.

[19] International Labour Organisation, Chemical Industries Committee, *Recent Developments in the Chemical Industries* (1995), Geneva, p.34.

1990 to 14 per cent in 1992.[20] The pattern of expenditure in Australia is similar.[21]

Characteristics of the chemical industry

The chemical industry has a number of important characteristics which will be crucially important in designing an appropriate regulatory regime. First, a substantial amount of chemical industry pollution is point source pollution (e.g., from smokestacks or other discharge points) or the result of chemical accidents. Both sources are readily identifiable by regulators and the community and it is, accordingly, difficult for the industry to deny the connection between its activities and their environmental consequences. It is also comparatively easy for regulators to monitor and take action against unlawful emissions or other illegalities by chemical companies.

Secondly, there are many differences amongst chemical producers. As we shall see, these differences have considerable implications for regulatory design. The dominant group are the limited number of large companies (most of them transnationals). These companies all have very high public profiles, and reputations which it is very important for them to protect. As such, they are extremely vulnerable to adverse publicity, to shaming at the hands of public interest groups and others, and to other informal sanctions beyond those imposed by conventional command and control regulation. However, there are also a large number of smaller players involved in the industry, who are particularly difficult to regulate. These essentially fall into two groups, with some limited overlap between them: (i) the specialty chemical manufacturers (who usually produce small volumes of a wide variety of specialty chemicals as demand dictates); and (ii) the distributors, suppliers and buyers

[20] European Chemical Industry Council (CEFIC), Internet site (November 1996) at http://www/innet.net/cefic/cgi-bin. The financial investment which the West European chemical industry makes to support research and technological development is considerable: over 19 billion ECU. in 1994 (D. J. Bricknell, *Response by the Chemical Industry in Europe to the 'Green Paper on Innovation'* (April 1996), SUSTECH Position Paper, CEFIC, Brussels.

[21] For 1995, the chemicals sector quoted an expenditure of approximately US$77 million for the purposes of pollution control and general environment improvements. This figure included a capital spending of approximately US$40 million and in total represented a 10 per cent increase on spending in this area in 1994 (Rust PPK, *International Best Practice in Health, Safety and Environmental Regulation in the Chemicals and Petroleum Industries* (1995), Rust PPK Melbourne, Department of Business and Employment, Victoria, Australia.

of wholesale chemicals. These groups have very different characteristics to the large companies and are likely to respond to very different pressures and incentives. Significantly, with the exception of some distributors and specialty chemicals companies, they are commonly unsophisticated, in some cases economically marginal. In most cases, they trade with, and are to some extent dependent on, the large companies (who, in recent years, have contracted out more work to fewer firms).[22] Both groups of small players present particular problems to regulators.[23]

Thirdly, the long-term viability of the industry probably depends (and is perceived by most large companies to depend) upon its gaining and maintaining the trust of the public. At present, the chemical industry as a whole suffers from a negative public image, not just individual firms, and this image can only be improved (and with it the long-term fortunes of the industry itself) by a substantial improvement in the environmental performance of the industry as a whole. Given the transparency of chemical industry pollution, described above, only demonstrable environmental performance, and not merely better public relations, can deliver improved public trust and credibility.[24]

Fourthly, the industry itself is mature and stable, having been operating on a large scale for many decades. Similarly, given the substantial environmental problems generated by the industry, it was one of the first industry sectors to be subject to regulation, with the result that the regulatory regime which oversees its environmental performance is also a mature one.[25] That regime is also very extensive: the industry is highly regulated across a variety of environmental media.[26]

Fifthly, and related to the last point, there is, in each of the major jurisdictions, a strong industry association with the capacity to exert considerable influence over the behaviour of its member companies. Indeed, for some years, in most developed countries, the industry association has already performed such a role.[27] Related to this, each

---

[22] As we shall see, the buyer-supplier relationship provides substantial opportunities for the large companies to impose pressures on their smaller trading partners to improve their environmental standards. [23] See further, p.227 below.

[24] And the public *is* paying attention. See Frances Irwin *et. al.*, *A Benchmark for Reporting on Chemicals at Industrial Facilities* (World Wildlife Fund, 1995).

[25] See further, p.145 below.

[26] President's Council on Sustainable Development, Eco-Efficiency Task Force, *Chemical Operations Demonstration Project* (February 1995), Washington DC, p.22.

[27] See, for example J. F. Franke & F. Watzold, 'Voluntary initiatives and public intervention regulation of eco-auditing' in F. Leveque, (ed.) *Environmental Policy in Europe* (1996), Edward Elgar, UK, pp.179–181.

industry association is acutely aware that, to the extent it does not put its own house in order in environmental terms, there will be heavy pressure on government to do so. Since government has already regulated the chemicals sector for many years, and there is substantial public support for more stringent regulation, there are, generally, few obstacles to it ratcheting up the severity of that regulation.

Sixthly, the threats caused by chemical industry pollution are likely to inflict damage not only on the natural environment but also on human health, with the result that a broad range of groups might potentially be mobilized to counter such pollution. For example, not just environmental NGOs but also local communities living downwind or downstream from chemical complexes, and perhaps also trade unions, may have a very active interest in curbing harmful emissions.[28] The overlap between occupational health and safety and environmental protection in the chemical industry (for example, what is toxic when emitted outside a plant may also be toxic to workers within it) further enhances the potential for common cause to be established between trade unions and environmentalists (though, to date, there are extremely few concrete examples of such common cause).

Seventhly, the chemical industry is driven by innovation and technological change, which many regard as its very lifeblood.[29] Moreover, processes within the industry are heterogeneous, being so varied and complex as to make sector-wide standards difficult to establish.[30] What is appropriate for large plants may not be appropriate for small ones, what is appropriate for batch chemicals will not be appropriate for continuous processes. Where sector-wide standards are established, they can have a stultifying effect.[31] As a result of these factors, a high priority of individual companies, and of the industry association that repre-

[28] See Jonathon Harr's study of the litigation involving W. R. Grace in *A Civil Action* (1995), Vintage Press, New York.

[29] See, for example, R. Brinkman, S. Jasanoff & T. Ilgen, *Controlling Chemicals: The politics of regulation in Europe and the United States* (1986), Cornell University Press, Ithaca, New York, p.221.

[30] M. Gambel, *US Environment Protection Agency, The Dutch Model: Lessons for the US* (1995), US EPA, Washington, DC, p.2. As a result, in the Netherlands, agreements are reached with individual companies, but against a backdrop of larger environmental goals set for the entire chemical sector.

[31] For example, in the UK, attempts to apply the new regime of Integrated Pollution Control to the fine and contract chemicals sector (which is characterized by complex, multi-purpose batch plant with a need to make products at short notice) has led to problems concerning the requirement that each chemical process obtain a separate authorization. See K. Allott, *Integrated Pollution Control: the First Three Years, Environmental Data Services* (1994), London, UK, p.xiv.

sents them, is to avoid prescriptive regulation or other intrusions into its affairs which might have the effect of inhibiting such innovation.

The regulatory environment and its shortcomings

As indicated earlier, it is the manufacturing phase of production and the regulation of point source pollution that are the principal subject matter of this chapter. Current strategies for addressing point-source pollution by chemical manufacturers necessarily vary from jurisdiction to jurisdiction, according to the political, economic, and cultural characteristics of individual countries. Here is not the place to engage in a detailed description of such regimes, but rather to identify their main features, and their strengths and limitations, as a necessary precursor to the main theme of this chapter: how chemical industry regulation might be redesigned to optimal effect.

This preliminary task need not be an arduous one. Regulation of the chemical industry in almost all developed countries has depended very heavily (though not exclusively[32]) on various forms of command and control. Moreover, in many cases that regulation is much the same as that which has been applied to other industry sectors (though the trend is towards a sector-specific approach).[33] The result is that much of the general critique of direct (and more specifically, command and control) regulation, in chapter two, is directly applicable to the circumstances of the chemical industry.

As we saw in that chapter, governments throughout Western Europe and North America have relied heavily on a regulatory standards approach involving the establishment of technology-based standards for classes of industries or scheduled premises, or some combination of the two. In the United States, (where command and control approaches are most entrenched) the main environmental statutes require the installation of 'best conventional pollutant control technology' or 'best practical control technology currently available' under permitting arrangements. This approach has the advantage of providing 'a

---

[32] For example, in the United States, there is still some residual reliance on common law doctrines to prevent unreasonable air pollution emissions, enforced through civil suits based on personal injury or property damage. For all the reasons identified in chapter two, such liability rules remain a singularly unsatisfactory way of addressing pollution problems. See A. W. Reitze Jnr., 'A Century of Air Pollution Control Law: What's worked ; What's failed; What might work' (1991) 21 *Environmental Law* 1550–1639 at 1554–69.

[33] See p.33.

measure of environmental quality certainty (provided there is adequate monitoring and enforcement), which may be particularly important when potent and toxic substances are being released into the ambient environment'.[34] However, it is inherently biased against technological innovation, which, from an industry perspective, is very unattractive, and provides little ongoing incentive for continuous improvement.

Chemical manufacturing is a complex process involving rapid technological change. As such, it is not well suited to the imposition of highly prescriptive legislation, since technological processes can quickly become outdated. Similarly, the failure under current uniform standards to acknowledge differences among chemical producers, given that technological capacity and sophistication necessarily vary with size and operational circumstances,[35] imposes considerable excess costs without providing demonstrable additional environmental benefits.

The traditional command and control approach has been widely criticized for being too expensive, for interfering too much in private initiative, and for having too many unintended consequences.[36] In the United States, these problems are exacerbated by medium-specific statutes encouraging a 'toxic shell game', which provide incentives simply to transfer hazards from the most highly regulated to the least regulated medium. In that country, where the regulatory regime is also characterized by hostility, distrust and adversarialism, a further result has been a 'progression towards more costly, detailed and intrusive forms of regulation'.[37]

Certainly, there are some exceptions to this characterization of chemical industry regulation: recent experiments intended to transcend these problems. As indicated in chapter two, these include attempts to provide greater flexibility and encourage innovation.[38] These have

[34] J. B. Opschoor & K. Turner, (eds.) *Economic Incentives and Environmental Policies: Principles and practice* (1994), Kluwer Academic Publishers, Dordrecht, p17.

[35] Eco-efficiency Task Force, Chemical Operations Team of the President's Council on Sustainable Development, *Proposed Policy Recommendations For the Chemical Industry* (1995), Washington DC. See also D. J. Fiorino, 'Towards a New System of Environmental Regulation: the case for an industry sector approach' (1996) 26(2) *Environmental Law* 457–489 at 469.

[36] See, generally, D. J. Fiorino, 'Towards a New System of Environmental Regulation: The case for an industry sector approach' (1996) 26(2) *Environmental Law* 457–489 and at 461, who notes that 'air, water and waste issues are managed nationally, and in most states as separate programs', under statutes which do not distinguish chemical sector emissions from those of other industries.

[37] E. Bardach & R. Kagan, *Going by the Book: the problem of regulatory unreasonableness* (1982), Temple University Press, Philadelphia, p.20.

[38] See chapter two, p.47.

received a mixed reception, being praised by some for overcoming regulatory rigidity and for encouraging pollution prevention, while being criticized by others for not going far enough, and for not confronting the central problems of the traditional system.[39] The jury is still out these initiatives. Exhortations from bodies such as the President's Council on Sustainable Development's Chemical Operations Team for the greater use of economic incentives, self-auditing, and risk-based standards are also only slowly and partially eliciting responses.[40]

For example, although much has been written about economic instruments, they have so far been used only to a very limited extent: the most obvious example being the acid rain allowance trading provisions of the 1990 Clean Air Act amendments.[41] In 1991, one commentator summarized the situation admirably as follows: 'For twenty years economic approaches have played a minor role in air pollution control while a very complex command and control system has evolved. When economic approaches have been used in the past they have been discouragingly complex, which may explain the business community's reluctance to participate'.[42] The position has only changed modestly since that date.[43] Notwithstanding some encouraging later successes with tradeable permits in Southern California,[44] the regulatory regime remains, in essence: 'medium-specific, largely command and control, technology-based, and highly prescriptive'.[45]

Since the early 1970s, chemical industry regulation in Canada, most Western European nations, and Australia has also relied largely upon

[39] T. Davies & J. Mazureck, *Industry Incentives for Environmental Improvement: An evaluation of US Federal initiatives* (September 1996), a report to the Global Environmental Management Initiative Resources for the Future, Washington DC.

[40] Eco-efficiency Task Force, Chemical Operations Team of the President's Council on Sustainable Development, *Proposed Policy Recommendations For the Chemical Industry* (February 1995), Washington DC.

[41] Codified as 42 U.S.C. 765lb (1994). For an overview, see W. I. Rogers, *Environmental Law: Air and Water* (1994), West Publishing, St Paul.

[42] A. W. Reitze, 'A Century of Pollution Control Law: what worked; what's failed; what might work' (1991) 21 *Environmental Law* 1549–1646 at 1630.

[43] See, for example, B. Gray, 'Public versus Private Environmental Regulation' (1994) 21 *Ecology Law Quarterly* 434–438,

[44] See, in particular, the experience of the South Coast Air Quality Management District, Southern California RECLAIM program evaluated in P. P. Leyden, *Trading in Southern California* (1997), a paper delivered to American Bar Association 26th Annual Conference on Environmental Law, Keystone, Colorado, March.

[45] D. J. Fiorino, 'Towards a New System of Environmental Regulation: The case for an industry sector approach' (1996) 26(2) *Environmental Law* 457–489 at 480. For a useful general survey of the literature and empirical evidence, see W. E. Orts, 'Reflexive Environmental Law' (1995) 89(40) *Northwestern University Law Review* 1227.

direct regulatory instruments such as prohibitions, permit requirements, standards, and planning obligations.[46] However, regulation in these countries (notwithstanding some significant differences of emphasis in individual jurisdictions) can be distinguished from the United States approach at a number of levels. First, the very processes of rulemaking, standard setting, and enforcement commonly involve much more willingness to compromise and seek consensus than does the United States approach.[47] Secondly, medium-specific approaches are rapidly being replaced by more holistic and integrated approaches, addressing all environmental media within a single statute, and (for individual enterprises) under a single permit or licence.[48] Thirdly, (with the most notable exception of Germany[49]) there is a greater emphasis on performance outcomes, leaving industry with greater freedom in how to reach a particular environmental goal.[50]

Although Western European, Canadian, and Australian chemical industry regulation is, by and large, more responsive than its American counterpart, most governments also increasingly recognize that direct regulation of the chemical industry is reaching the limits of its usefulness, being 'very costly to monitor, inspect and, when necessary, punish those organizations subject to traditional environmental legislation'.[51] It is also acknowledged that often only minimum environmen-

[46] See, for example, E. Rehbinder & R. Stewart, 'Environmental Protection Policy' in M. Cappelletti, M. Seccombe & J. Weiler, (eds.) *Methods, Tools and Institutions* (1986), W. de Gruyter, Berlin.

[47] See, for example, D. Vogel, *National Styles of Regulation: Environmental Policy in Great Britain and the United States* (1986), Cornell University Press, Ithaca, New York; K. Hawkins, *Environment and Enforcement: regulation and the social definition of pollution* (1984), OUP, Oxford; and R. Brinkman, S. Jasanoff & T. Ilgen, *Controlling Chemicals: The politics of regulation in Europe and the United States* (1986), Cornell University Press, Ithaca, New York.

[48] See, for example, the European Union Directive on Integrated Pollution Prevention and Control, Council Directive 96/61 EC (1996).

[49] German industrialists have been 'more comfortable with detailed and precisely worded legislation that spelled out industry's obligations clearly and limited the discretion of German bureaucrats' (R. Brinkman, S. Jasanoff & T. Ilgen, *Controlling Chemicals: the politics of regulation in Europe and the United States* (1986), Cornell University Press, Ithaca, New York, p.232). This is in sharp contrast to the British preference for broad and flexible regulation, allowing for considerable discretion in interpretation by regulatory officials. As Brinkman *et. al.* put it: 'concepts like "reasonable" and "practicable" sum up British regulatory philosophy, a philosophy generally shared by industry' (p.229).

[50] Rust PPK, *International Best Practice in Health, Safety and Environmental Regulation in the Chemicals and Petroleum Industries* (1995), Rust PPK. Melbourne, Department of Business and Employment, Victoria, Australia.

[51] J. F. Franke & F. Watzold, 'Voluntary initiatives and public intervention regulation of eco-auditing' in F. Leveque, (ed.) *Environmental Policy in Europe* (1996), Edward Elgar, UK, p.178.

tal standards can be imposed, and it is difficult to cover all environmental effects—particularly since many new chemicals are invented
and put onto the market each year. Moreover, the sheer volume of regulation to which the chemical sector is subjected to can have a considerable cumulative effect. For example, the German chemical industry
(perhaps the closest European country to the American model) is now
subject to an estimated 2000 different laws.[52]

A further criticism, even of the more flexible forms of chemical
industry regulation, is that it does not encourage continuous improvement. Once an enterprise has achieved the legally prescribed standard
(e.g., an emission concentration of no more than 100 parts per million)
there is no further incentive (unless the standard is anticipated to
change) to further reduce the level of emissions. For this reason, it has
been argued that 'we should be adopting an approach which seeks to
enhance industry competitiveness by driving or luring industry towards
best practice, not in a manner which requires or rewards Health, Safety
and Environment (HSE) best practice, but by creating a regulatory
environment which strives for and allows for excellence in HSE outcomes'.[53]

However, despite the growing recognition of the limitations of traditional styles of regulation, European Union environmental regulatory
reform is a recent process which, notwithstanding the urgings of the
European Union Fifth Action Program 'Towards Sustainability', has
progressed slowly.[54] For example, economic incentives did not play a
significant role until the 1990s, and then only in limited areas.[55] If there
is indeed a trend away from command and control towards 'conduct
regulation' such as voluntary agreements and economic instruments,
then it is still in its very early stages[56] (although the Dutch have

[52] F. Leveque, (ed.) *Environmental Policy in Europe* (1996), Edward Elgar, UK, p.177.

[53] Rust PPK, *International Best Practice in Health, Safety and Environmental Regulation in the Chemicals and Petroleum Industries* (1995), Rust PPK. Melbourne, Department of Business and Employment, Victoria, Australia, p.26.

[54] *ENDS Report*, 'Chemical Release Inventory at the Crossroads' (June 1997) *ENDS Report* No. 269 19–25. See also pledges given by the European Commission to simplify existing legislation on chemicals by focussing on: risk assessment; cost-benefit analysis; and comparison against rules outside the EC (*ENDS Report* (May 1996) No. 256 40), pub-lished by the Environmental Data Service.

[55] See, for example, E. Rehbinder, 'Environmental Regulation Through Fiscal and Economic Incentives in a Federalist System' (1993) 20 *Ecology Law Quarterly* 57–83.

[56] See, generally, F. Leveque, 'The European Fabric of Environmental Regulations' in F. Leveque, (ed.) *Environmental Policy in Europe* (1996), Edward Elgar, UK.

advanced substantially further).[57] Such is also the case in Canada[58] and Australia.[59]

There has however, in almost all the countries under discussion, been a move to supplement command and control with information-based strategies such as CRTK provisions in the United States,[60] the Seveso and Seveso II Directives[61] in Europe, and the proposed introduction of a National Pollutant Inventory in Australia. CRTK provisions, while applying to most categories of industry, have particular implications for the chemical sector, revealing to the public, in graphic and measurable terms, the high percentage of total emissions contributed by that sector, and by individual enterprises within it.[62] The role of community participation is also growing. This is being facilitated by access to information through the mechanisms described above.[63]

Finally, and of very recent origin, both in Europe and the United States, have been attempts to introduce process based regulation emphasizing risk and accident management in respect of uncontrolled

[57] The distinctive Dutch approach is a sector-specific approach to chemicals devised as part of the National Environmental Plan. The vehicle for delivering the goals set in that plan is the environmental covenant: an agreement negotiated between each individual company and the government and underpinned by the force of civil law. It is the covenant that ensures that each company contributes its share towards achieving the sector-specific goal set in the national plan. See, generally, J. M. Van Dunne, (ed.) *Environmental Contracts and Covenants: New instruments for a realistic environmental policy?* (1993), Koninklijke Vermande, Netherlands.

[58] Rust PPK, *International Best Practice in Health, Safety and Environmental Regulation in the Chemicals and Petroleum Industries* (1995), Rust PPK Melbourne, Department of Business and Employment, Victoria, Australia.

[59] For example, countries such as Australia are only taking only their first hesitant steps towards use of economic instruments. The New South Wales Government is proposing to allow tradeable permits among mining companies in the Hunter Valley. See *Environmental Business*, September 1994, p.29.

[60] See chapter two, above. See also California's Proposition 65 (California's Health and Safety Code 25, 249.5–13); and Massachusetts' toxic use reduction legislation (K. Geiser, *Beyond Auditing: Toxic Use Reduction in the United States* (1990), University of Massachusetts, US.

[61] Major-Accident Hazards Directive Involving Dangerous Substances (1997) O.J. L10/13, on December 9, 1996. The new Directive, which entered into force in February 1997, builds on the existing scheme under Directive 82/501/EEC on Major-Accident Hazards of Certain Industrial Activities (1992) O.J. L.230/1.

[62] See discussion on CTRK earlier in this chapter.

[63] However, in other respects, this development is occurring largely irrespective of the legislative provisions. For example, in the United States, Fiorino notes that 'effective citizen (as opposed to interest group) participation in environmental decisions at the local level is not a strength of the current system. Participation often takes the form of public hearings on national standards or decisions made at local or state levels', D. J. Fiorino, 'Towards a New System of Environmental Regulation: The case for an industry sector approach' (1996) 26(2) *Environmental Law* 457–489 at 482.

release of hazardous substances. Both the Seveso II Directive[64] in the European Union and the United States' rule on Risk Management Programs for Chemical Accidental Release Prevention[65] require establishment of systems to oversee implementation of risk management programme elements: a considerable shift of emphasis (albeit only in one particular area) which 'reflects a growing recognition of systems' importance in accident prevention strategy'[66] which we will pursue as a theme later in this chapter.

To summarize: notwithstanding significant differences between the regulatory approaches of different countries (and particularly between the United States and most other developed counties) the regimes for controlling chemical industry pollution are, in each case, based predominantly on forms of direct (usually command and control) regulation. Indeed, the chemical industry, because of its diversity, has attracted a larger number of environmental regulations than probably any other industry.[67] All of these regimes are (though in varying degrees) expensive, cumbersome, time consuming, inflexible, and inefficient.[68] Moreover, they do not encourage industry to go 'beyond compliance' with existing standards. Notwithstanding some significant improvements in recent years, the system of chemical industry regulation still leaves much to be desired, both from an environmental and an economic standpoint.

So where should we go next in terms of environmental policy? According to two leading American commentators, we are: 'poised on the threshold between two fundamentally different stages in the evolution of environmental protection'.[69] In essence, they argue that the old

---

[64] Directive on the Control of Major Accident Hazards Involving Dangerous Substances (96/82/EC).

[65] Accidental Release Prevention Requirements: Risk Management Programs under the Clean Air Act section 112(r) (7).

[66] W. L. Thomas, 'Using ISO 140001 to comply with the Management System Requirements of US EPA's RMP Rule and the EU's Seveso II Directive' *European Environmental Law Review*, December 1998, 335.

[67] L. Ember, 'Overhaul of Environmental Law Needed for Sustainable Development' (1993) *Chemical and Engineering News*, March 15, p.17.

[68] The main limitations of command and control have been usefully summarized by the OECD. in *Alternatives to Traditional Regulation: A Preliminary List* (1994), OECD, Paris, May.

[69] L. Ember, 'Overhaul of Environmental Law Needed for Sustainable Development' (1993) *Chemical and Engineering News*, March 15, p.16. interviewing E. D. Elliott and E. M. Thomas, authors of 'Chemicals' in C. Campbell-Mohn, B. Breen & J. W. Futrell, (eds.) *Sustainable Environmental Law* (1993), Environmental Law Institute, St Paul, Minnesota, US, chapter 17.

command and control way of regulating chemical manufacturing—complicated, reactive and legalistic—'does not allow management of the industry's activities in ways that are compatible with nature and therefore sustainable' and has run its course. They go on to suggest that there are, currently, too few tools to advance environmental policy to the next stage: 'from protection to management, that is, from protection to sustainability'. We concur with this diagnosis, and in the following sections, offer our prescriptions for a cure.

Redesigning regulation: towards efficient and effective policy instruments

In the following sections, we put forward an alternative vision of chemical industry regulation. We explore a range of alternative policy mechanisms, we suggest ways to design complementary combinations of instruments, and we argue the need to harness the resources of a broader range of institutional actors than has so far been the case.

In doing so, it is useful to articulate how we apply our evaluation criteria to point source pollution in the chemical sector. As indicated in chapter one, our main goals are achieving efficiency and effectiveness, while acknowledging that a range of other objectives may also be important in particular circumstances. While efficiency and effectiveness may, commonly, be complementary objectives, this is not always the case. Where conflicts exist and trade offs are inevitable, we place efficiency first, because with point-source pollution (with some exceptions concerning extremely hazardous chemicals) the environment has some assimilative capability.[70] We place pollution prevention before

---

[70] Esty, for example, distinguishes between 'flow' pollution (caused by particles in the air, organic wastes in water, and most solid wastes disposed on land, which degrade rapidly and for which the environment has some absorptive or assimilative capacity) and 'stock' pollutants, such as radioactive materials, heavy metals and some toxic chemicals, which degrade much more slowly. See D. Esty, 'Environmental Federalism' (1996) 95 *Michigan Law Review* 579.

While this assimilative capacity may be substantially less than earlier generations have acknowledged, the fact remains that this capacity enables the use of instruments which, while less dependable than others in delivering environmental outcomes, will do so at less cost. For example, environmental taxes may initially be set at levels too low to achieve the desired environmental outcome. It may, accordingly, take some time to adjust the tax level to one which influences behaviour in the preferred direction and to the preferred degree. In the interim, the environment will continue to be polluted at undesirable levels. However, provided it is sufficiently resilient to tolerate short term abuse, this approach may be preferred (on the grounds of cost effectiveness) to one which, while more dependable in delivering environmental outcomes, imposes higher costs on the parties involved.

pollution control and end of pipe solutions because the latter merely entrench unsustainable practices rather than encouraging industry to pursue sustainability.[71] We also recognize the importance not just of transparency and accountability but also of direct community consultation and involvement in decision-making ('political acceptability' in terms of the criteria identified in chapter one), which, while it may well achieve greater effectiveness, is unlikely to be viewed as 'efficient', given the time consuming nature of this task.

Finally, approaches which encourage polluters to go 'beyond compliance' with existing regulation are preferred to those which aspire merely to prevent polluters dropping below the legal standard. This is represented diagrammatically in Diagram 1 below. The diagram represents the likely range of responses to government environmental regulation by individual firms. This range can be envisaged as a bell curve, with a small tail of laggards not meeting minimum obligations, the bulk of firms located at or near minimum compliance, and a small group of leaders achieving substantially higher levels of environmental performance.[72]

In our view, the goal of chemical industry regulation should be not merely to get all companies up to the minimum legal standard, but to facilitate and encourage companies to move far beyond that standard— to encourage them to go 'beyond compliance' and, in the long term, to develop sustainable business practices. This should be achieved in ways that are flexible and efficient as well as effective in environmental terms. For example, in a range of circumstances, creative regulation can encourage industry to achieve productivity and other gains in tandem with environmental improvements: the classic 'win-win' scenario.[73]

We begin by examining some important innovations in chemical industry regulation. Such regulation, as indeed environmental regulation more generally, is in transition. A number of reforms are in the process of being introduced, while others glimmer on the regulatory horizon. For the most part, these new approaches, at least in their

[71] On pollution prevention in the context of industrial ecology, see René van Berker *et. al.*, 'The Relationship Between Cleaner Production and Industrial Ecology' (1997) 1(1) *Journal of Industrial Ecology*, at 51.

[72] See, generally, N. Gunningham, 'Beyond Compliance: Management of environmental risk' in B. Boer, R. Fowler and N. Gunningham (eds.) *Environmental Outlook: Law and policy* (1994), ACEL, Federation Press, Sydney.

[73] N. A. Gunningham, 'Beyond Compliance: Management of environmental risk' in B. Boer, R. Fowler & N. Gunningham (eds.) *Environmental Outlook: Law and policy* (1994), ACEL, Federation Press, Sydney, and references cited therein.

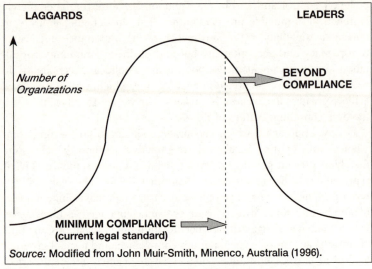

Diagram 1   Responses to environmental regulation

present manifestations, fall far short of delivering optimal policy outcomes. Nevertheless, most of them contain something of value and some contain the seeds of more fundamental change. Our approach is to begin with these innovations and to identify their benefits and limitations before going beyond them to envision the design of instruments and instrument mixes that take advantage of their strengths while compensating for their weaknesses.

The two innovations we examine are: (i) self-regulation, and in particular, the Responsible Care programme; and (ii) systems-based approaches to environmental management and regulation, and, in particular, the International Standards Organisation's EMSs standard, ISO 14001. Responsible Care is a self regulatory scheme designed for, and relating exclusively to, the chemical industry. ISO 14001 is derivative of total quality management (TQM) and systems-based approaches, and is designed for use in any industry sector. As a regulatory mechanism, it can be viewed variously as a means of 'privatising compliance', as a form of process-based regulation and as a vehicle for achieving regulatory flexibility.[74] All are attempts by industry to extri-

[74] On the objectives of 'the Framers', see C. L. Bell, 'Bench Test' (10 November 1997) *The Environmental Forum* at 24 (expounding a restrictive approach toward regulation through ISO 14000).

cate itself from the perceived disadvantages of command and control regulation, and to design alternatives which are more flexible and appropriate to industry needs.[75] As such, they represent radically different approaches to that provided by traditional regulatory regimes. Both of these developments are already now, and in the future will remain, of fundamental importance to chemical industry regulation across a wide variety of nations. As we shall see, they also have considerable implications for the future of environmental regulation generally, and might play crucial roles in broader regulatory mixes.

1. Self-regulation and Responsible Care

In the following sections, we explore the implications for regulation of the Responsible Care programme—an extremely ambitious and very broad self-regulatory scheme which is intended to reduce chemical accidents and pollution and to involve the community in decision-making. Responsible Care operates in forty-one countries and reaches around 88 per cent of the global chemical industry.[76]

Our study is based on empirical work[77] conducted in Australia (one of the first countries to adopt Responsible Care), and to a lesser extent, in the United States and Canada. Many of its conclusions are likely to be applicable to Responsible Care internationally.[78] Moreover, its arguments may have a broader resonance for other schemes involving self-regulation, co-regulation, and innovative regulatory design, both in the environmental arena and in other areas of regulatory policy.

[75] As we shall see, ISO 14001 has many other purposes too, but that of acting as a surrogate for more conventional forms of regulation is certainly one important agenda item.

[76] This figure is based on production volumes. See 'ICCA readies itself for Ottawa Forum' (October 1996) 5 *Careline* 1.

[77] The empirical work involved semi-structured interviews with forty-nine industry participants, self regulators, government regulators and community representatives in Australia, thirty in the United States and thirteen in Canada. Public documents, industry journals, and reports were also relied upon to supplement data gathered elsewhere.

[78] Although David Vogel (D. Vogel, *National Styles of Regulation: Environmental Policy in Great Britain and the United States* (1986), Cornell University Press, Ithaca, New York) rightly alerts us to possible cultural differences between regulatory agencies in different countries, it may nevertheless be that 'certain policy areas are more conducive to private interest government solutions than others' (A. Jacek, 'The Functions of Associations as Agents of Public Policy' in A. Martinelli (ed.), *International Markets and Global Firms* (1991), Sage, London, p.148). Indeed, there is considerable evidence that countries can learn from one another in this regard (see K. Dyson & S. Wilks, (eds.) *Industrial Crisis: A comparative study of the state and industry* (1983), Robertson, Oxford, p.261). Having conducted interviews not only in Australia but the United States and Canada, I am unable to identify cultural distinctions relating to chemical industry regulations of sufficient significance to make my conclusions less relevant to the United States or Canada than they are to Australia.

There is a further reason for examining Responsible Care in some detail, namely that it is a self-regulatory scheme of considerable breadth and scope. Proponents have described it as 'the most ambitious and comprehensive environmental, health and safety improvement effort ever attempted by an industry',[79] as 'an outstanding model for voluntary industry efforts to promote chemical risk management, fulfil the objectives outlined in Agenda 21, and complement environment, health and safety regulatory processes',[80] and as 'a journey of profound cultural change'.[81] Notwithstanding the dangers of overstatement (not least by the chemical industry itself), there can be little doubt that Responsible Care is not only the single most advanced and sophisticated scheme of self-regulation in the environmental area, but it is also one of the most developed and far-reaching regimes of self-regulation to be found anywhere in the western world.[82] Indeed, in the view of many, Responsible Care is likely to be the blueprint for such self-regulatory initiatives that may evolve in other industries in the future.[83]

What is Responsible Care?

Under Responsible Care, chemical companies commit themselves to the improvement of all aspects of their performance which relate to protection of health, safety and the environment. This includes a commitment to improving relations with customers and communities, product use, and overall operation. These goals are to be achieved by two basic mechanisms. The first is the progressive establishment of a number of Codes of Practice. The precise contents of the codes, notwithstanding a common core, varies somewhat from jurisdiction to jurisdiction. For example, in Australia the codes cover: transportation; community awareness and emergency response; waste management;

[79] J. R. Hirl, 'Don't Trust Us, Track Us' (1992), UN 242 No.21 (17 December) *Chemical Marketing Reporter*.

[80] International Council of Chemical Associations Global Status Report on Responsible Care reported in 'ICCA Readies itself for Ottawa Meeting' (October 1996) 5 *Careline* 1.

[81] P. Sandman, *Addressing Scepticism About Responsible Care* (1991), Environmental Communications Research Program, Rutgers University, New Jersey.

[82] See, for example, the assessment of a leading member of the United Nations Environment Agency: 'Care gives industry a leadership role in sustainable development' (July 7/14 1993) *Chemical Week* 20.

[83] See, for example, D. Hunter & R. Mullin, 'Responsible Care: The challenge of communication' (9 December 1992) *Chemical Week 22*. Significantly, a number of industry programmes are already modelling themselves on Responsible Care, including the paint industry's Coatings Care Program and other groups, such as vinyl chloride and chlorinated solvents producers, are in the process of developing such programmes.

warehousing and storage; CRTK; product stewardship; manufacturing; and research and development.[84] These are intended to: 'become the rules (in addition to prevailing legislation) by which member companies operate. Adoption of these rules and compliance with them is a condition of Council membership.'[85] All the codes reflect industry best practice. Taken as a whole, most of the obligations implied by the codes could be discharged through the adoption of a management system approach.[86] However, they also go beyond the adoption of such a system and embrace a broader ethic, implying broader responsibilities, and embodied in a set of guiding principles. See Box 1 below.

The second characteristic of Responsible Care is the commitment to community participation and consultation. In Australia, this is achieved principally through the establishment and functioning of the National Community Advisory Panel (NCAP), in the United States by a National Public Advisory Panel, and in Canada by a National Advisory Panel. For example, the Australian NCAP comprises: 'a cross-section of individual community thought leaders with particular concerns for environmental safety and health issues'.[87] NCAP is intended to provide a vehicle through which the public may play an integral role in shaping the Responsible Care initiative. NCAP members review proposed codes of practice from a public interest perspective, and they alert Australian Chemical Industry Council (ACIC) to other emerging issues of public concern.[88]

Broader public involvement is also contemplated through efforts to accommodate the particular needs of local communities adjacent to manufacturing sites. According to ACIC, specific Codes and operating plans: 'would be sensitive to community concerns, provide information on possible hazards, encourage community involvement in emergency response planning and establish a regular process of positive

[84] In the United States, the codes cover: (i) community awareness and emergency response; (ii) pollution prevention; (iii) distribution; (iv) process safety; (v) employee health and safety; and (vi) product stewardship.

[85] Australian Chemical Industry Council (ACIC), *Annual Report* (1993), ACIC, Melbourne, p.2.

[86] However, note that far from all Responsible Care companies have adopted this approach. For example, in the UK, seven years after the introduction of Responsible Care, only 40 per cent of CIA members have formal environmental management systems (*ENDS Report* (1996), No.257, pp.3–4).

[87] Australian Chemical Industry Council (ACIC), *Annual Report* (1993), ACIC, Melbourne, p.3.

[88] However, it should be noted that, in 1997, these three countries were the only ones of the forty-one nations which have adopted Responsible Care, to have well established, open, public advisory input. See (7 April 1997) *Careline* 2.

Box 1

International Council of Chemical Associations (ICCA)

Responsible Care Principles

- A formal commitment on behalf of each company to a set of Guiding Principles signed, in the majority of cases, by the chief executive officer.

- A series of codes, guidance notes and checklists to assist companies to implement the commitment.

- The progressive development of indicators against which improvements in performance can be measured.

- An ongoing process of communication on health, safety and environmental matters with interested parties outside the industry.

- Provision of fora in which companies can share views and exchange experience on implementation of the commitment.

- Adoption of a title and a logo which clearly identify national programmes as being consistent with and part of the concept of RC.

- Consideration of how best to encourage all member companies to commit to and participate in RC.

- Systematic procedures to externally verify the implementation of the measurable elements of RC by member companies.

Source: CEFIC, 1993, p.5.

---

communication'.[89] The formation of Regional Responsible Care groups is also encouraged. These groups: 'progressively work towards establishing links with local community associations, whilst sharing knowledge on their progress with Responsible Care and the resources available for emergency response situations'.

[89] Australian Chemical Industry Council (ACIC), *Annual Report* (1993), ACIC, Melbourne, p.3.

In all jurisdictions, the scheme promises a commitment to genuine improvement which goes 'beyond compliance' with existing environmental legislation. As the European Chemical Industry Association (CEFIC) summarizes the Responsible Care commitment: 'Chemical Companies are committed in all aspects of safety, health and protection of the environment, to seek continuous improvement in performance, to educate all staff, and work with customers and communities regarding product use and overall operation'.[90]

Can Responsible Care deliver smarter regulation?

The chemical industry has characteristics that could make Responsible Care one of the minority of cases in which industry interest and public interest are sufficiently coincident for self-regulation to be a viable regulatory strategy. Responsible Care is driven by the large, transnational corporations which dominate the chemical industry internationally,[91] and, as we will see, these companies have both the motivation and the capacity to implement the changes to industry practice and culture that the scheme contemplates.

The broader context for the industry's increased environmental sensitivity is the continuing and serious decline of the public image of the industry, closely connected to a series of chemical accidents and wider concerns about the costs of accidents,[92] and the health and environmental effects of chemical production generally.[93] Large multinational corporations are heavily reliant on their corporate image for their commercial success. Union Carbide learnt this lesson the hard way in the wake of the Bhopal disaster. More recently, Exxon also suffered disastrous public relations consequences (not to mention massive financial liability) when the Exxon Valdez ran aground in the previously pristine waters of Prince William Sound. Corporations can respond to these sorts of misfortunes in a variety of ways. One relatively cheap solution is for a company to disassociate itself from potential disasters related to

---

[90] European Chemical Industry Council (CEFIC), *Proceedings of the First International Workshop on Responsible Care in the Chemical Industry*, CEFIC, Brussels.

[91] For example, in Australia, a relatively small number of firms import twenty thousand toxic and hazardous chemicals annually (only 3.4 per cent being manufactured domestically) and thereby control the feedstocks or imports to those processors which produce hazardous wastes (see Plastics and Chemicals Industries Association (PACIA), *Facts and Figures* (1991), PACIA, Melbourne). Twelve companies, out of the ninety or so members of ACIC, have a volume of over about $0.3 billion per year. Of these, ten are transnationals, and two are Australian owned (J. Smith, *Measuring Health, Safety and Environmental Performance: Why, what, and whose?* (1994), summary of a paper presented to the ACIC Convention, 21 February, Leura, NSW.

its activities. In future, we are unlikely to see many oil tankers embla-
zoned with the names of their transnational corporate owners, and
ownership itself may well devolve to subsidiaries, shelf companies, or
independent contractors.

In the case of the chemical industry however, such cheap means of
protecting corporate image are not available to anything like the same
extent. Chemical disasters (and even incidents without serious consequences) tend to be highly visible and readily identified with individual
installations and their corporate owners. Large chemical corporations
usually find that it is not possible to improve the corporate image without changing the reality through improved environmental performance.[94] As one senior executive put it, during the 1980s, the major
chemical companies concluded they: 'just [could not] advertise their
way out of it'.[95]

Of course, there is nothing to prevent individual companies from
improving their own environmental performance without invoking
Responsible Care, and many of them are in the process of doing so.[96]
Here, the main motivators may include not just improved corporate

[92] R. L. Klassen and P. M. McLaughlin, 'The Impact of Environmental Management
on Firm Performance' Management Science, August 1996 at 1199.

[93] Industry polls over the last decade have consistently revealed a high level of public
anxiety and distrust of chemical manufacturers, with companies commonly being
regarded as greedy, rapacious and irresponsible. In the United States, an opinion poll
conducted in 1990 found that the chemical industry's rating of public acceptability had
dropped to 20 per cent—only the tobacco industry has a lower rating. Over 60 per cent
of the public rated the industry as 'very harmful to the environment' (S. J. Lewis, *The Role
and Limits of Volunteerism* (1991), a paper the International Conference on Corporate
Environmental Responsibility, Tutzing, Germany, p.2). Similarly, in Australia, a 1992
survey of community attitudes concluded that the 'chemical industry is associated with
pollution, danger, explosives and possible ill-effects from the use of chemicals and chemical based products. It is also associated with secrecy, lack of public disclosure, possible
dishonesty and lack of ethics' (Motive Market Research Pty Ltd, 'Summary and
Conclusions' (1992) in *ACIC—Monitoring Community Attitudes* (December), pp.11 and 12).
In 1996, the CEFIC presented findings which once again suggested that the public has
a very poor opinion of the industry's environmental credentials and trustworthiness (see
ENDS Report (1996), No.259, p.20.

[94] This is consistent with the very high level of spending by major chemical companies on occupational health and safety, and the low accident rate of such companies. (see
further, H. Genn, *Great Expectations: The role of legacy and employer self-regulation* (1985),
unpublished, Oxford Centre for Legal Studies, Oxford). For a more recent statement of
one leading chemical company's view, see J. Magretta, 'Growth Through Global
Sustainability' (Jan/Feb 1997) *Harvard Business Review* 79–88.

[95] C. Greenert, interview, quoted in 'Responsible Care' (1991) *Harvard Business School
Documents* 9–391–135, 1–26.

[96] See, for example, examples cited in Chemical Manufacturers Association (CMA),
Annual Reports for 1996 and 1997 (1997), CMA, Washington DC.

image and community relations, but also competitive advantage and increased profitability. Firms that take a proactive stance on the environment commonly save substantial sums of money and thereby increase profit directly, for example through improved energy efficiency or recycling.[97] They may also develop the environmental technology to compete more effectively in the global environmental technology market.

However, it is clear that individual initiatives will not be sufficient to give the industry, as a whole, the credibility it badly needs to survive and prosper in the long term. As one industry spokesman pointed out: 'Du Pont and other majors can't rest on their accomplishments. They need to recognise that any incident in the industry destroys the credibility of everyone.' The Canadian Chemical Producers Association President (1991), Jean Belanger, notes that: 'if a paint company or a plating company does something wrong the headlines the next day will scream that chemicals have been wrongly handled and so we will all be tarred by the same brush'. Such an incident also exposes the industry to tougher regulatory requirements, obstacles to development, and community backlash.

A series of such incidents serves to reinforce the industry's very poor public image and results in a host of other problems. In the long term, the chemical industry's very poor public image is likely to result in a loss of public support, a regulatory backlash, extreme difficulty in persuading communities to accept new chemical installations in their locality, and a host of other problems: 'affecting everything from government relations to the recruitment of managerial and scientific talent'. As one industry spokesman put it: 'Businesses can only survive whilst they have society's acceptance for their activities. Once that acceptance is lost, there is only one way to go'.[98] Without a change in public attitudes, the chemical industry's long-term survival is under threat.

What this means, in practical terms, is that each company in the chemical industry must act as its brother's keeper. Thus, a mechanism must be found, nationally and internationally, which enables the industry to continuously improve the environmental performance of all companies, large and small. Such a mechanism must be capable of

---

[97] N. A. Gunningham, *Beyond Compliance: Management of environmental risk* in B. Boer, R. Fowler & N. Gunningham (eds.) *Environmental Outlook: Law and policy* (1994), ACEL, Federation Press.

[98] C. E. Holmes, *Address to Hazardous Waste Conference* (1992), ACIC, Melbourne, p.3.

improving the industry's poor public image,[99] restoring public faith in the industry's integrity and taking the heat out of demands for stricter government regulation.[100] Most importantly, for present purposes, it might also serve as a complete alternative to conventional government regulation, or failing that, at least as an important complement to it. Big companies decided that that mechanism should be Responsible Care. But is it up to that task?

Certainly, the chemical manufacturers associations are in a stronger position than most such bodies to exert pressure for environmental improvement, in part because the industry's characteristics facilitate the development of 'social capital': the development of 'the features of social organisation, such as networks, norms and trust, that facilitate coordination and cooperation for mutual benefit'.[101] As Rees has demonstrated,[102] the industry is an incestuous one in which companies constantly deal with each other. Strategic alliances, product swapping, and technology transfers are the norm rather than the exception. Building on these characteristics of the industry, the chemical industry associations, through Responsible Care, have facilitated the development of trust amongst their members, creating an environment within which people work together, share information, provide mutual aid, and establish policy. Tangible manifestations of this include Responsible Care's leadership groups,[103] workshops, mutual assistance network and implementation guides. As a result, 'by increasing interpersonal trust and reducing uncertainty, the development of community lowers transaction costs and makes collective action easier'.[104]

More broadly, Responsible Care has enabled the development of an industrial morality, a set of norms which generate a sense of obligation,

---

[99] This was acknowledged by ACIC former Chief Executive, Frank Phillips, who said that the plan was developed in response to the industry's poor public image (see R. Smithers, 'Chemical Firms Adopt Code to Clean Up the Industry' (1989) *The Age* 27 September, p.5).

[100] As Canadian Chemical Producers Association President Jean Belanger put it: 'if we could figure out a way of becoming proactive, then we could lessen demands for that degree of regulation' (see R. Mullin, 'Canadian Deadline Approaches: Contemplating continuous improvement' (17 June 1992) *Chemical Week* 128).

[101] R. Putnam, 'The Prosperous Community' (October 1993) *Current*, p.4.

[102] J. Rees, 'The Development of Communication Regulation in the Chemical Industry' (1997) 19(4) *Law and Policy* (publication of 1997 issue delayed).

[103] These groups usually meet quarterly with peers to review progress and to provide and receive assistance. They are, reputedly, a highly effective way of creating peer pressure, and of enlisting corporate leaders to the cause of Responsible Care.

[104] J. Rees, 'The Development of Communication Regulation in the Chemical Industry' (1997) 19(4) *Law and Policy* (publication of 1997 issue delayed).

emphasizing particular values and structuring choice. Such a morality provides:

. . . a form of moral discourse capable of challenging conventional industry practices—"This is the way we always do business around here"—including the economic assumptions underlying many of those taken-for-granted policies and practices. In this way, an industrial morality . . . legitimises aspirations other than profit as a good reason for action. It establishes an alternative moral vocabulary, a rhetoric of organisational motive that competes with (and critiques) the native tongue of the business organisation, the language of profits and losses.[105]

Within such a context, there is also considerable scope for peer group pressure to act as an effective driver of corporate change. For example, the leadership groups, in particular, fulfil this role, bringing together representatives of a number of companies to share their experiences, their progress, and, by implication, their lack of progress.[106]

Similarly, there is the potential for Responsible Care to act as a vehicle for corporate shaming,[107] through the spotlight of public exposure of a polluter's moral failings. Certainly, the performance indicators and verification mechanisms currently being adopted under Responsible Care (described below) could form the basis for identifying recalcitrants and exposing them to the glare of adverse publicity. There is also some anecdotal evidence that, to a modest extent, such shaming already takes place through the leadership groups. In these ways, Responsible Care provides a vehicle for informal social control: regulation from the inside ('moralising social control'[108]), rather than regulation from the outside (based on external constraint).

Overall, the various Responsible Care mechanisms designed to develop mutual trust among competitors; to facilitate mutual aid, information and technology sharing, peer support, and pressure; for

---

[105] See further, N. Gunningham & J. Rees, (1997) *Law and Policy* (publication of 1997 issue delayed).

[106] See T. Posner, *The Engineer* (1992), 5 March, p.20, citing how such a process takes place during meetings of company chief executives. The letters written by ACIC to companies which are not in compliance, which escalate in their formality and moral tone, might also be seen as an attempt at corporate shaming.

[107] There is a recent criminological literature that argues persuasively the importance of a moral dimension to corporate (and individual) behaviour, and documents the considerable extent to which corporations can be 'shamed' into doing the right thing (see J. Braithwaite, *Crime, Shame and Reintegration* (1989), Cambridge University Press, New York).

[108] J. Braithwaite, *Crime, Shame and Reintegration* (1989), Cambridge University Press, New York, pp.9–11.

corporate shaming; and dialogue with local communities, the public and governments, create a climate which can motivate and drive corporate executives to do far more in terms of environmental performance than the law could credibly require. However, despite its considerable potential and strengths, there are also many obstacles to the success of Responsible Care. Of these, the largest is that environmental protection and private profit do not necessarily coincide, and are not perceived to coincide, particularly given the emphasis of most corporations on short-term profitability.[109] For both corporations and individual managers, the essential dilemma is that they will be judged essentially on short-term performance, and if they cannot demonstrate tangible economic success in the here and now, there may be no longer term to look forward to.[110]

Having said that, it is clear that some types of enterprise are in a far better position to take a long-term view and to achieve long-term objectives than others and it is here that the distinction between large and small enterprises becomes crucial.[111] It is clear that those firms which are economically marginal (generally, some SMEs)[112] cannot afford the luxury of a longer term view. For them, the likelihood of sacrificing

[109] Because corporations are judged by markets, investors, and others principally on short-term performance, they have difficulty justifying investment in environmentally benign technologies which may make good economic sense in the long term, but rarely have an immediate or medium-term pay-off. Most areas of reform, including stopping harmful emissions to land, water and air, replacing harmful chemicals with more expensive ones, and cleaning up contaminated land, are vulnerable to these short-term market pressures.

[110] Jackall (R. Jackall, *Moral mazes: The world of corporate managers* (1988), OUP, New York) found that short-term issues overwhelm long term considerations. In Jackall's view: 'Managers think in the short term because they are evaluated both by their supervisors and peers on their short term results'. As one manager put it: 'Our horizon is today's lunch' (Jackall 1988:84). Jackall also found that staff mobility, both within and between corporations (often the result of CEO-inspired reorganizations), meant that those who currently occupy a managerial post might feel no urgency about the environmental consequences of their decisions. This was because the threat of immediate governmental retribution, via the EPA, was most unlikely, and the delays in processing environmental actions through the courts meant that by the time a case was heard, the present incumbents would have moved on, leaving others to deal with the legacy of those decisions (J. E. Rogers Jr., 'Adopting and Implementing a Corporate Environmental Charter' (1992) 35(2) *Business Horizons* 29–33 at 31.

[111] The dichotomy is not invariably appropriate. For example, some small enterprises, particularly those operating in niche markets, have considerable sophistication, technological expertise, and capacity for long-term planning. Nevertheless, the distinction is largely accurate and is a useful one in highlighting divergence of interests within the industry.

[112] See President's Council on Sustainable Development, Eco-Efficiency Task Force, *Chemical Operations Demonstration Project*, (February 1995), Washington DC, p.22.

environmental concerns for short-term profit (or survival) is very high indeed. Many firms must also be most heavily reliant on old, inefficient plant and as a result, most commonly emit the greatest amounts of pollution. It is usually far more expensive to retrofit such plant with advanced pollution technology than it is to incorporate state of the art environmental technology into new plant.[113]

In contrast, in circumstances where companies have substantially higher profit margins and rapidly changing or advanced technology, they are in a far better position to take environmental initiatives which yield only long-term dividends. Larger enterprises and transnationals in particular, by virtue of their market share and other advantages, can usually afford to consider a range of goals in addition to short-term profits.[114] These include the pursuit of long-term strategies of enlightened self-interest. They routinely ask: where do we want to be in ten years time? This connects closely to the question: what are the chemical industry's prospects in the same time frame?

Thus, there is a broad divide between the interests, attitudes and capabilities of large and small firms when it comes to environmental protection and implementing Responsible Care. In essence, for large corporations with a high public profile, the consequences of a poor environmental record are likely to be both substantial and visible, making environment a high corporate priority, which they have both the technological capacity and the economic resources to address. In contrast, many smaller enterprises do not have a public profile (they may indeed never deal with the public directly), and their reputation and profitability may be far less affected by a poor environmental record. Their capacity to address such problems is also often very limited, given the economic and technological constraints within which many of them operate.[115]

---

[113] As one industry observer put it: 'Voluntary actions are likely to be viewed as dispensable extravagances by companies suffering financial difficulties. They may be abandoned over time as management changes or pressure for such efforts fades' (R. Abrams & D. H. Ward, 'Prospects for Safer Communities: Emergency response, community right to know, and prevention of chemical accidents' (1990) 14 *Harvard Environmental Law Review* 135–88).

[114] Moreover, such firms also have the technological capacity and the economies of scale to make environmental improvements both technically feasible and economically realistic (see further, B. P. Pashigan, 'How Large and Small Plants Fare Under Environmental Regulation' September/October 1983) 7 *Regulation* 19–23.

[115] Consistent with this analysis, a 1991 McKinsey survey found that the most constructive responses can be found consistently in multinational companies in highly competitive industries that are close to the consumer and headquartered in cutting-edge regions. Even in the more advanced nations, a much more reactive, or at best receptive, response can still be found in a majority of small and medium-sized companies and in

Indeed, as one industry respondent put it: 'Once organisations start to apply the codes of practice it hits home how much work is involved. It's OK for large companies like "X" which is well down the track anyway, but a lot of cost and effort for many other companies.' Another industry respondent in Australia put it more bluntly: 'Once they realise it will cost the industry three billion dollars, they'll drop it like a hot brick.' There is considerable empirical support for this view, including the fact that the Australian Chemical Specialty Manufacturers Association which represents many of the smaller companies, has withdrawn completely from Responsible Care, citing in part, the excessive costs and burdens that the programme would impose on its members.

The divergence of interests between large and small enterprises raises the first of two very serious obstacles confronting the success of Responsible Care: how to overcome what are known as 'free-rider' and 'mutual assurance' problems, or, generically, as problems of collective action. Left to their own devices, many small companies will continue to inflict substantial environmental damage, which may well in itself defeat Responsible Care's attempt to improve the image of the chemical industry as a whole. If a significant number of smaller companies do not comply, then large companies lose much of the incentive to continue their own voluntary action. If the public fails to distinguish 'good' and 'bad' companies, but rather blames the industry as a whole, for the sins of the worst transgressors, then environmentally responsible companies will suffer the stigma, lack of credibility and public backlash caused by the misdeeds of non-complying companies. As a result, any company spending on Responsible Care, other than as a matter of immediate self-interest (which may include its 'green' credentials), puts itself at a competitive disadvantage to its more pragmatic rivals, who may continue to pay lip-service to Responsible Care, but do little to further its long-term ends; in effect, 'free-riding' on the efforts of others.[116] At the very least, firms are likely to defect from the scheme unless either

industry sectors that are characterized by a high degree of oligopoly or a tradition of government involvement. It would appear that a 'protection' from public scrutiny results in less attention to environmental concerns (J. E. Rogers Jr., 'Adopting and Implementing a Corporate Environmental Charter' (1992) 35(2) *Business Horizons* 29–33 at 30).

[116] The basic free-rider problem is that an enterprise may take advantage of the willingness of other firms to spend on cleaning up the environment, while refraining from doing so itself as a matter of rational, economic self-interest, thereby 'free-riding' on the efforts of others (see M. Olson, *The Logic of Collective Action* (1965), Harvard University Press, Cambridge).

free-riding can be prevented, or firms can be given the necessary assurance that others will contribute their fair share ('mutual assurance').[117]

However, even the resolution of the collective action problem (i.e., overcoming free-riding and mutual assurance issues) will not in and of itself guarantee the fulfilment of Responsible Care's fundamental objective—to change industry behaviour *in ways that secure the trust and confidence of the public.* The second obstacle involves the core problems that beset many self-regulatory schemes—namely that they involve regulation of the industry, by the industry, for the industry, often coupled with limited transparency and accountability. In the case of Responsible Care, we will argue that the 'credibility obstacle' will be insurmountable unless mechanisms are put in place that manifestly give the scheme teeth, and allow for transparency and effective government and third party oversight.

At least in its first phase (until approximately 1996), Responsible Care was based exclusively on *self*-monitoring and *self*-reporting. Individual companies evaluate their own performance in complying with the codes of practice, using mandatory agreed assessment procedures.[118] In terms of enforcement, if moral pressure from peers and the ACIC is ineffective, then 'in cases where members clearly disregard

---

[117] It may be that the assumption that business is invariably rational and self-interested, and, accordingly, will free-ride, is too strict, especially given that Responsible Care represents the recognition by many of the leading players in the industry that 'each must be his brother's keeper'. This suggests that the basic obstacle to effective self-regulation in the circumstances described above is an 'assurance problem' (see C. F. Runge, 'Institutions and the Free-Rider: The assurance problem in collective action' 46 *Journal of Politics* 154–81; and I. Maitland, 'The Limits of Business Self-Regulation' (1985) 27(3) *California Management Review* 132–47 at 134).

[118] Briefly, (using the Australian version of the scheme by way of illustration) the responsibility for the oversight of Responsible Care lies with an industry association (ACIC) Committee, and with the Responsible Care co-ordinators responsible for the scheme's administration. The industry association's oversight role however, is a modest one, which mainly involves issuing self-evaluation forms to participating companies, and following up those companies who do not respond within a stated period. Significantly, the ACIC does not attempt to validate the accuracy of the self-assessments it receives.

In effect, it is the individual member companies which must implement and enforce Responsible Care. The CEO of each participating company pledges the company's commitment by signing the Abiding Principles of the Responsible Care Program. Each company then makes its own arrangements to communicate this commitment to management and all employees (Australian Chemical Industry Council (ACIC), *Responsible Care Program Guide* (1989), ACIC, Melbourne, p.10), and takes responsibility for all relevant monitoring and assessment measures. The primary means of encouraging compliance is moral pressure, which it is hoped will be increased by providing opportunities for senior executives with responsibility for Responsible Care to meet and compare their experiences (ACIC 1989:10).

their obligations in respect of Responsible Care and government expectations, their membership can be terminated'.[119] However, on the basis of behaviour of the industry associations which administer Responsible Care, to date, the likelihood of expulsion is extremely low.[120] As one of our respondents put it: 'the biggest problem with Responsible Care is there are no bodies': no one whom the industry association has demonstrably taken disciplinary action against. And even if a member is expelled, it can still exist profitably outside of the industry association. Some chemical industry associations, indeed, will not even disclose the identity of a firm that withdraws from Responsible Care, and therefore from the association.

This structure raises, in stark form, the crucial issue of accountability. As Peter Sandman notes:

The chemical industry is long past the time when it can say we're doing x, y and z, and have people take its word for it . . . While there is certainly more accountability in Responsible Care than in other industry programs, there is still not enough teeth in it.[121]

Put crudely, while companies are allowed to grade their own exam papers, there is an obvious temptation to fudge the results of their own internal monitoring, and even in the unlikely event that they fail themselves, there are no credible sanctions.

As a result of these limitations, Responsible Care will almost certainly fail to overcome either the collective action/mutual assurance problems or the public trust problems identified above. In terms of collective action, there is overwhelming evidence that moral persuasion alone will be insufficient to bring about effective self-regulation. With nothing to guarantee or enforce the commitment of firms to the self-regulatory scheme, some firms will inevitably defect, and when they do so, the entire social contract on which the agreement of the majority is based

---

[119] Australian Chemical Industry Council (ACIC), *Responsible Care Program Guide* (1990), ACIC, Melbourne, p.20.

[120] For example, in North America, where Responsible Care has been operational for a number of years, there is no documented case of a company's membership being so terminated. This probably reflects the philosophy of the relevant industry associations. As a senior member of the UK Chemical Industry Association (CIA) has put it: 'You can't get acceptance just by jamming things down people's throats', and arm twisting is likely to remain a very rare feature of Responsible Care (T. Posner, *The Engineer* (1992), 5 March, p.20). In 1996, Denmark became the first Responsible Care participant to expel a member for poor environmental performance. The former member is now in the process of suing the Industry Association for doing so.

[121] D. Rotman, 'Pushing Pollution Prevention' (17 July 1991) *Chemical Week* 30 at 33.

is undermined.[122] In these circumstances, firms that comply with Responsible Care risk putting themselves at a competitive disadvantage as against those who do not. The free-rider problems are overwhelming. In terms of gaining public acceptance and credibility, Responsible Care is, at present, equally unconvincing, not only because it lacks effective strategies for monitoring and enforcement, but also because of a serious failure to engage the public in dialogue about its concerns. Industry's progress might usefully be charted according to the categorization developed by Peter Sandman.[123] At stage one (the Stonewall stage), the industry builds a stone wall between itself and the public—maintaining that it knows best, that the public misunderstands chemical risks, and that there is nothing to talk about. At stage two (the Missionary stage), the industry goes out to educate people about chemicals and chemical risks—in effect trying to teach people they were wrong about the chemical industry. Finally, at stage three (the Dialogue stage), the chemical industry openly acknowledges that it does have problems and faults, and is prepared both to provide full information and to listen (a genuine dialogue) rather than talk at the community. On current experience, the industry is now onto the Missionary stage, but occasionally regresses to the Stonewall stage.

Related to this, the industry remains locked into a scientific paradigm which does not connect well to the concerns and values of the groups they are seeking to influence. One commentator has correctly characterized Responsible Care as representing 'the traditional views of an industry with strongly embedded roots in science and the laboratory as the source of truth and correctness'.[124] It is argued that, so long as the industry remains convinced that its own knowledge and expertise is the best, or indeed the only rational way to view the world, then it is destined to fail in its quest to gain the trust of the various publics to which it appeals.

A number of other serious problems threaten Responsible Care's progress. These include: first, the fierce opposition of some of the industry associations responsible for implementing Responsible Care to any kind of government regulation (limiting constructive co-regulation); secondly, the failure of many individual companies to act in the spirit of

---

[122] See I. Maitland, 'The Limits of Business Self-Regulation' (1985) 27(3) *California Management Review* 132–47 at 139.

[123] P. Sandman, *Addressing Scepticism About Responsible Care* (1991), Environmental Communications Research Program, Rutgers University, New Jersey.

[124] J. Ehrenfeld, quoted in *ENDS Report* (August 1996) No.259 21.

CRTK and of some to honour their broader Responsible Care commitments; and finally, the relative ignorance of many small companies, or even middle management and workers of large companies, of what Responsible Care required of them.[125]

Of these, probably the most serious problem is the first. The large majority of non-industry respondents interviewed for this study were of the view that the chemical industry associations, whether in Australia or North America, continue to behave largely as trade associations are prone to behave—as lobbyists, committed to defending the sectoral interests of the industry, as narrowly defined by the most conservative element of the membership. As one industry observer put it:

. . . they think they're reflecting the members' views but they always go for the lowest common denominator. That way they're less likely to be criticised by the membership. It's safer to be conservative . . . its safer to take a lowest common denominator approach.

Such an approach includes resisting proposed government regulation, on behalf of the membership.[126] This raises serious questions as to whether the association responsible for industry public relations and for advocacy can credibly advance the Responsible Care philosophy. As one government regulator in the United States put it: 'Responsible Care is an important initiative but the CMA is absolutely the worst body to implement it.'[127]

However, although Responsible Care, in its present form, is unlikely to deliver many of the environmental benefits it promised, this is no reason for rejecting the scheme in its entirety. To do so would 'be to throw the baby out with the bathwater'. For despite its flaws,

---

[125] See further, N. Gunningham, 'Environment, Self-Regulation, and the Chemical Industry: Assessing Responsible Care' (1995) 17(1) *Law and Policy* 58–109 at 75.

[126] *Ibid.*, 58–109.

[127] Another has argued publicly that: 'One of the problems the Responsible Care program suffers from is its connection with CMA, because CMA plays many roles for the industry. And one of the things CMA does on behalf of the industry is attack regulations. It is viewed as the front line defender of the chemical industry's interests in those regulatory debates. It is difficult for that same organisation to come back and say, in the next breath, "Oh, but we have this Responsible Care program, which is really wonderful, and we want to work with everybody." It's often the case that there are mixed messages. It appears sometimes that the positions CMA is taking in public policy debates are not consistent with Responsible Care. And I think that's a very difficult role for CMA to play— to be the principal advocate of Responsible Care and also serve the other interests of the chemical industry in terms of public policy issues in Washington' (M. Greenwood, Office of Pollution Prevention and Toxics, EPA, quoted in R. Begley, 'Will the Real Chemical Industry Please Stand Up?' (7–14 July 1993) *Chemical Week* 18).

Responsible Care has some considerable virtues, and remains one of the most sophisticated and advanced self-regulatory schemes yet developed. The codes of practice, by comparison with most other such schemes, are both detailed and far-reaching in their effects. There is some genuine coincidence between the self-interest of the industry, in securing its long term future, and the public interest in environmental protection, and many large and influential companies would indeed wish the scheme to succeed. Mechanisms for nurturing peer group pressure, for sharing environmental technology, and for developing trust are also substantially advanced under Responsible Care. Finally, it has the traditional virtues which self-regulation claims over command and control regulation: flexibility, lower costs, and the capacity to encourage cost-effective industry responses.

And Responsible Care has already delivered some important benefits. Certainly, there is evidence of substantial emissions reductions and of continual improvement (as judged by emissions reductions measured by the United States TRI[128] and by the Canadian National Pollutant Release Inventory),[129] an increase in community involvement, and in external evaluation.[130] There is also empirical evidence suggesting that Responsible Care has prompted some important changes in firm organization and practices, and in some cases values. While the response of Responsible Care firms is not uniform, there seems to be more interaction and involvement in environmental issues of corporate managers not typically responsible for environmental management, more interaction with local communities on environmental concerns, and greater discourse with distributors concerning expectations about how their products should be handled and transported. Responsible Care, seemingly, also provides more leverage to community relations and plant managers seeking support for outreach and environmental activities. On the other hand, it has not resulted in ongoing dialogue with environmental groups, training in Responsible Care principles is not

[128] See Chemical Manufacturers Association (CMA), *Responsible Care: Progress Report 1994–95* (1995), CMA, Washington DC, p.23, reporting that, based on 1993 TRI figures, CMA companies have reduced toxic releases by 49 per cent since 1987, while increasing industry production in the same period by 18 per cent.

[129] This inventory was only introduced in 1993, and at the time of writing only three years' results are available. Nevertheless, they do support the industry's own claims and projections in terms of significant and continuing emission reductions. See Canadian Chemical Producers' Association, *Reducing Emissions: 1994 Emissions Inventory and Five Year Projections* (1994), Canadian Chemical Producers' Association, Ottawa.

[130] See Chemical Manufacturers Association (CMA), *Responsible Care: Progress Report 1994–95* (1995), CMA, Washington DC, p.12

widespread, and is seemingly ineffective below management level, and it has not penetrated to product design. And rather than transforming the industry's environmental approach, Responsible Care has served to formalize and institutionalize existing environmental activities. Finally, some of the changes in industry behaviour which the industry associations attribute to Responsible Care, might have come about anyway as a result of other developments.[131] Overall, the record is a very mixed one.[132]

In our view, although Responsible Care may have so many limitations that it is not appropriate for use as a 'stand alone' or single instrument of environmental protection, it may still make an important contribution, achieving far more than conventional regulatory approaches, provided it is used in an *integrated strategy* in conjunction with other instruments and a broader range of institutional actors. Precisely how Responsible Care might be contribute towards an optimal policy mix for the chemical industry sector, is the subject of the following sections. But first, we examine a parallel development, the growth of EMSs, and their relationship with regulation.

2. *Environmental Management Systems (EMSs) and ISO 14001*

Put broadly, EMSs provide a framework for companies to identify, evaluate and manage their environmental risks, enabling them to take a systematic and integrated approach to environmental management. Within that framework, companies introduce their own policies, objectives, programmes, measurement, and assessment methodologies. As we have seen, Responsible Care itself, includes what is essentially a management system, though it also covers a great deal more, (not least product stewardship, community dialogue, chemical distribution and transport safety and various institutional mechanisms to facilitate technological transfer, mutual support, peer group pressure and environmental leadership).

By the mid 1990s, EMSs had become an important policy tool, enthusiastically embraced by a range of international, regional and national bodies, all seeking to develop 'off the peg' management system

---

[131] For example, process based regulations such as OSHA's Process Safety Regulation require changes in behaviour consistent with those of the Responsible Care codes, and broader commitments by companies to TQM programmes might also have led firms to many of the same results.

[132] J. Nash & J. Howard, 'Responsible Care's Mixed Record' (1996) 5(VI) *Tomorrow: Global Environment Business* 12.

standards.[133] The reasons for this enthusiasm are not hard to identify. There is mounting evidence that poor environmental performance is attributable to system failure more than individual failure.[134] The underlying causes of most breaches of health, safety and environmental standards are to be found in factors such as lack of accountability, inadequate monitoring of performance, failures of communication, poor training, and badly maintained equipment: all indicators of a failure to pay systemic attention to environmental performance and to take the policy, organizational and administrative measures necessary for sustained improvement.

EMSs hold out the promise of overcoming such organizational pathologies. A range of studies suggest that those enterprises that adopt such systems can achieve impressive outcomes in terms of environmental performance.[135] Approaches based on techniques of TQM[136] are claimed to be particularly successful. For example, the Global Environmental Management Initiative (GEMI), and a sub-committee of the President's Commission on Environmental Quality[137] have both

[133] The most important of these are the British Standard BS7750, the European Union's Eco-Management and Audit Scheme (EMAS) and the International Standard Organisation's ISO 14001, all discussed below.

[134] For example, the striking evidence produced by organizational theorist Charles Perrow's seminal work on major technological disasters suggests that 80–90 per cent of the failures relate to the management or organizational system and only 10–20 per cent are based on operator error or equipment failure (C. Perrow, *Normal Accidents: Living with high risk technologies* (1984), Basic Books, New York. See also J. Braithwaite, *To Punish or Persuade: Enforcement of coal mine safety* (1985), State University of New York Press, Albany; D. Vaughan, 'The Challenger Disaster' (1995); and P. N. Grabosky, *Wayward Governance: Illegality and its Control in the Public Sector* (1989) Australian Institute of Criminology, Canberra. See also B. Toft and S. Reynolds, *Learning from Disasters* (1994), Butterworths, Oxford; R. Cahill, *Disasters at Sea, Titanic to Exxon Valdez* (1990), Century Press.

[135] The powerful potential of EMSs to achieve dramatic results in improved environmental performance is amply demonstrated by the impressive achievements of a number of companies who took part in demonstration projects (President's Council on Environmental Quality (PCEQ), (Quality Environmental Sub-Committee), *Total Quality Management: A framework for pollution prevention* (1993), Washington DC; and see E. D. Elliott, 'Environmental TQM: Anatomy of a pollution control program that works!' (1994) 92 *Michigan Law Review* 1840 at 1843).

[136] Traditionally, TQM aspires to provide management with a framework 'on which to build "quality" into every conceivable aspect of organisational work'. It is a business discipline and philosophy of management which institutionalizes planned and continuous business improvement (A. Wilkinson & H. Willmott, (eds.) *Making Quality Critical: New perspectives on organizational change* (1995), Routledge, London; and S. Hill, 'From Quality Circles to Total Quality Management' in A. Wilkinson & H. Willmott, (eds.) *Making Quality Critical: New perspectives on organizational change* (1995), Routledge, London, p.33–53).

[137] President's Council on Environmental Quality (PCEQ), (Quality Environmental Sub-Committee), *Total Quality Management: A framework for pollution prevention* (1993), Washington DC.

examined the relationship between TQM and improved environmental performance.[138] On the basis of a number of sophisticated case studies, the latter concluded that: 'TQM and Pollution Prevention are complementary concepts' and that: 'TQM offers an approach that all companies can use to achieve environmental improvements'.[139] It went on to document in considerable detail precisely how TQM tools could be applied to environmental issues.[140]

Worldwide, the most important development towards an EMS approach has been the introduction of the International Standards Organisation's ISO 14000 series of standards, and, in particular, the environmental management standard, ISO 14001 (and in the European Union, the similar but far from identical Eco-Management and Audit Scheme (EMAS)). ISO 14001 is a voluntary standard which is still in its infancy, having been formally endorsed in 1996 and implemented gradually over the next few years. Many fundamentally important questions about the role of this standard are still being addressed. As we shall see, amongst these is the appropriate relationship between ISO 14001 and environmental regulation.

ISO 14001 is based substantially on the ISO 9000 series on quality management. In broad terms, it calls for an understanding and identification of significant environmental issues, the setting of targets, monitoring of progress and continual review of how well the system is working. It involves documentation control, management system auditing, operational control, control of records, management policies, training, statistical techniques, and corrective and preventive action (see Table 1 below). Companies may seek third party certification to this standard if they so wish but are not bound to do so. They may simply use the standard for internal purposes. External pressures, rather than the ISO itself, will determine whether to seek certification.

---

[138] See Global Environmental Management Initiative (GEMI), *Total Quality Environmental Management* (1992), Washington DC, p.ix.

[139] Global Environmental Management Initiative (GEMI), *Total Quality Environmental Management* (1992), Washington DC, p.x.

[140] The perceived advantage of an EMS approach, particularly one that is based on the principles of TQM, is threefold. First, it enables companies themselves to devise ways of reducing or preventing pollution. Rather than being constrained by highly prescriptive government regulations, an EMS-based approach encourages management itself to take the initiative and responsibility for deciding *how* to satisfy regulatory requirements. Secondly, EMS serve to embed an environmental ethic in the organization 'so that systematic environmental management becomes a habit and an inherent part of company culture'. Thirdly, there is the commitment to continuous improvement which TQM implies.

Table 1

ISO 14001 Environmental Management System Elements

1		**Environmental policy**
2		**Planning**
	2.1	Environmental aspects
	2.2	Legal and other requirements
	2.3	Objectives and targets
	2.4	Environmental management programme(s)
3		**Implementation and operation**
	3.1	Structure and responsibility
	3.2	Training, awareness, and competence
	3.3	Communication
	3.4	Environmental management system documentation
	3.5	Document control
	3.6	Operational control
	3.7	Emergency preparedness and response
4		**Checking and corrective action**
	4.1	Monitoring and measurement
	4.2	Non-conformance and corrective and preventive action
	4.3	Records
	4.4	Environmental management system audit
5		**Management review**

A particular attraction of this type of systems-based approach is its perceived capacity to move corporate thinking on environment from the sort of compartmentalization, that characterized the earlier generation of pollution control (vertical standards addressing discrete areas of activity), to a horizontal standard that cuts across the functions of the organization and integrates environmental considerations with other corporate functions. Under the latter approach: 'cost, efficiency, productivity and environmental performance all become part of the same decision making process'.[141]

Moreover, when incorporated into regulation, a systems approach, unlike traditional command and control, can encourage continual improvement and environmental stewardship on the part of industry, and a commitment to go 'beyond compliance' with existing regulation.[142] It also enables firms to devise their own ways to reduce or prevent pollution rather than being constrained by prescriptive government regulations. More broadly, proponents claim than systems-based standards can change the culture of participating enterprises as regards to environmental protection.

Whether, in practice, systems-based approaches to regulation deliver such substantial benefits depends greatly upon the characteristics of the management system itself, on the effectiveness of its implementation, on the political context, and upon a variety of other factors which we examine below through the lens of the ISO 14001 standard. In doing so, we recognize that ISO 14001 is certainly not the only EMS on offer and very possibly not even the best (as we will see below, EMAS is in some respects, much more ambitious). It is, nevertheless, the single management system recognized internationally and the basis on which regulators are most likely to build: overcoming its limitations by adding further components under a process becoming known as ISO 'Plus'.

Can ISO 14001 deliver smarter regulation?

ISO 14001 need not be used as a regulatory instrument. Indeed, it was designed principally as a management tool to improve environmental performance, and at least initially, ISO certification will be used principally to gain an advantage in the international market, where major corporations are likely to insist upon certification as a condition of

---

[141] A. Knight 'International Standards for Environmental Management' (1994) *Industry and Environment*, UNEP, July, p.45.

[142] U. Guntram & P. Winsemius, 'Responding to the Environmental Challenge' (March/April 1992) *Business Horizons* 12.

trade. However, many organizations and their representative bodies do see the ISO standard as having regulatory implications. This perspective is not confined to any particular country or industry sector. Throughout the developed world, there is a considerable industry push for an easing of the regulatory burden. ISO 14001 is seen to provide a considerable opportunity to bring this about.[143] Many regulators too, see attractions in using EMSs as a regulatory tool, both because it promises better environmental outcomes, and because it would place less demands on regulatory resources.

There are a variety of ways in which ISO 14001 might be used either to replace or to complement government regulation.[144] We will see below how international standards can serve as the basis for environmentally preferable commercial influences. But, in general, by far the most important would be its capacity to serve as a surrogate for

[143] For example, in the United States, at least three possible models for integrating ISO 14001 with government regulation are being contemplated: customized (industry specific) environmental regulations for all environmental media, relying (in part) on ISO 14001 certification to confirm that a company is meeting these new multi-media regulations; reduced compliance, reporting and monitoring requirements by government in return for demonstrated commitment to improved environmental performance (one element being ISO certification); and greater EPA flexibility in regulating a specific source 'in exchange for a commitment on the part of the regulated entity to achieve better environmental results than would have been obtained through full compliance with all applicable environmental regulations'.

In the UK, note the resistance of the Environment Agency to industry and government pressure for sites certified to environmental management standards to be given automatic relaxation in regulatory oversight. Rather, the Agency insists that such relaxation be based on a more sophisticated assessment of a site's pollution potential. See 'Agency resists "light touch" for sites with ISO 14001, EMAS' *ENDS Report*, (March 1997) No.266 3.

[144] For example, it might be used as a mechanism for avoiding liability or to justify the mitigation of penalties. In the USA, particular emphasis has been placed on 'compliance assurance' programmes in determining whether penalties should be mitigated. (See W. L. Thomas, 'Using ISO 140001 to comply with the Management System Requirements of US EPA's RMP Rule and the EU's Seveso II Directive' *European Environmental Law Review*, December 1998, 335.) The rationale is that most environmental offences are committed by corporations which, as artificial legal entities, have 'no body to kick and no soul to damn' (J. C. Coffee, 'No Soul to Damn: No Body to Kick: An unscandalized inquiry into the problem of corporate punishment' (1981) 79 *Michigan Law Review* 386). Under what circumstances then, should the misdeeds of individual employees be attributed to the corporation? One answer is to say that the implementation of an adequate compliance assurance programme (of which an environmental management system is an essential component) is a reasonable way for the corporation to stay within the law. If an individual employee breaches the law in contravention of such a programme, liability should, arguably, stay with the individual, and should not be attributed to the corporation. A 'half- way house' would be to make the corporation liable for the misdeeds of the individual but to allow the compliance assurance programme to be pleaded in mitigation at sentencing.

conventional command and control regulation: in effect acting as a form of process-based regulation which would provide regulatees with considerable autonomy. By this, we mean that companies which committed themselves to implementation of ISO 14001 (and the internal company processes and systems it implies) would be exempted from all or part of the regulatory requirements that would otherwise be imposed. For example, a firm which committed itself to adopt ISO 14001 and to meet certain other requirements (perhaps involving community consultation and disclosure of regular environmental audits) might be granted licence fee reductions, an easing off or waiver of regular inspections, or even (most contentious of all) exemption from the sort of detailed prescriptive requirements that characterize United States environmental regulation in particular. This result might be achieved by legislation, as a term of a licence or permit,[145] or through an environmental covenant.[146] The result might be viewed either as a shift from prescriptive regulation to regulatory flexibility implying *de facto* 'privatization of compliance'. As one major player put it: 'Environmental management systems [standards] are an opportunity for moving from the command and control and punish regulatory approach to one of self-responsibility and co-operation'.[147]

Unsurprisingly, there is considerable support from industry, across a range of developed nations, for this sort of approach.[148] In Europe, the

---

[145] Arguably, the best existing example of a broad, flexible licensing requirement on this model is that being developed by the state government of Western Australia (see WA Department of Environment Protection, *Achieving Best Practice Environmental Management* (1996), Discussion Paper, WA Department of Environment Protection, Perth). Also, the Dutch integrated system (see M. Aalders, 'Regulation and In-Company Environmental Management in the Netherlands' (1993) 15(2) *Law and Policy* 75–94).

[146] See the Dutch integrated system (see M. Aalders, 'Regulation and In-Company Environmental Management in the Netherlands' (1993) 15(2) *Law and Policy* 75–94).

[147] S. Newstead, Environmental Coordinator, Exxon, UK, quoted in 'Chemical firms use EMAS, ISO 14001 in push for deregulation' (March 1996) *ENDS Report* No.254 6.

[148] See L. D. De Simone and F. Popoff with World Business Council on Sustainable Development, *Eco-Efficiency: The Business Link to Sustainable Development* (1997), MIT Press. In Germany, regulators have suggested that rigorous implementation of EMAS—the EU's predecessor to ISO 14001—could lead it to relax its regulation of industry, providing greater freedom of action with respect to the approval and inspection of production plants (M. Roberts, 'Fitting in ISO 14000' (November 8 1995) 157(17) *Chemical Week* 46). If the German government defines how verification and accreditation will operate, then EMAS. will come close to becoming law *de facto*. In The Netherlands, system-based regulation is already being implemented, with built in benefits for industry, while in Japan, the intention is to make ISO certification mandatory for companies operating in that country. The chemical industry has been at the forefront of this push towards regulatory flexibility (see also 'From Command and Control to Self-Regulation: The Role

hope of the chemical industry is that those who adopt EMS under either ISO 14001 or under EMAS (with ISO 14001 as a component part of it), coupled with third party certification, will, in return, be offered a relaxation of conventional regulation by government.[149] Similarly, in the United States, so strong has been the push for regulatory flexibility in return for ISO certification, that the CMA has suggested that 'alternatives to command and control—possible regulatory relief from inspections, and reporting—will be a bigger pull [towards certified EMS] in the United States than market pull'.[150]

In essence, this is a plea for substantial decrease in the state's role in regulation. On the positive side, those who argue for this approach are correct that it is the enterprise itself that has the greatest capacity for making a systems approach work to optimal effect. Moreover, enterprises are more committed to rules they write and enforce themselves, and such rules can be tailored to match each enterprise's needs and functions.[151] Given extremely limited inspectoral resources, process-based regulation devolved largely to the industry itself may seem an attractive means of monitoring environmental performance on a continuous basis. However, as indicated earlier in this chapter, experience suggests that regulation entrusted to the industry itself, without outside scrutiny or oversight, is rarely capable either of overcoming the gap between public and private interest, or of providing the credibility necessary for public acceptance.

There are three reasons why ISO 14001 (at least without some forms of external reinforcement) is likely to be less than adequate as a regulatory tool. First, it suffers from a number of serious internal weaknesses, consequent largely on the political compromises involved in its inception.[152] Secondly, there are serious risks of implementation failure.

of Environmental Management Systems' International Environmental Review, March 5, 1997, p.227 (Bureau of National Affairs, Washington DC).

[149] See, for example, 'Chemical firms use EMAS, ISO 14001 in push for deregulation' (March 1996) *ENDS Report* No. 254 5–6.

[150] John Master, consultant to the CMA, quoted in 'Chemical firms use EMAS, ISO 14001 in push for deregulation'(March 1996) *ENDS Report* No. 2546.

[151] See further, I. Ayres & J. Braithwaite, *Responsive Regulation: Transcending the Deregulation Debate* (1992), Oxford University Press, New York, chapter 4.

[152] The ISO 14000 series evolved as a consequence of two events: the Rio Earth Summit in 1992, which brought increasing pressure for new mechanisms to address environmental degradation, and the Uruguay round of GATT negotiations, from 1986 on, which focussed attention on the need to reduce or eliminate non-tariff barriers to trade. Self evidently, these two goals are not necessarily complementary. A central question has become: is it possible to create uniform environmental standards that do not erect trade barriers but instead facilitate trade and remove such barriers? ISO 14000 purports to

Thirdly, the costs of implementing ISO 14001 may exceed the economic benefits, at least in the short term, leaving firms who are offered benefits for embracing it (e.g., regulatory flexibility) with a temptation to merely 'go through the motions'. Moreover, unlike Responsible Care, there is no industry association or peer group pressure to drive genuine environmental improvements. Turning first to ISO 14001's internal weaknesses, these can be summarized as follows:

• Except for committing to continual improvement and demonstrating a commitment to compliance with applicable legislation and regulations, the standard does not establish absolute requirements for environmental performance. The result will be that companies with widely differing levels of environmental performance, even within the same industry sector, may all establish a management system that complies with ISO 14001. As Joe Cascio, Chair of the United States Technical Advisory Group to ISO Technical Committee 207, puts it: 'ISO 14000 isn't about compliance, it's about management. It will make no statement regarding what is desirable for the environment. Neither will it lay out environmental goals, performance levels or technology specifications.'[153]

• Even the commitment to continual improvement must not be taken too seriously, since the standard states that: 'The rate and extent of [continual improvement] will be determined by the organisation in the light of economic and other circumstances . . . the establishment and operation of an EMS will not in itself, necessarily result in an immediate reduction of adverse environmental impact'. Moreover, ISO does not require a commitment to pollution prevention but only

provide an answer to this question, offering a standard that both facilitates trade growth *and* environmental protection. However, the outcome involves a number of compromises which seriously prejudice ISO 14001's standing as a tool for environmental protection. See further, N. Roht-Arriaza, 'Shifting the Point of Regulation' (1995) 22 *Ecology Law Quarterly* 506–507.

[153] G. House, 'Raising the Green Standard' (July 17 1995) 244(14) *Industry Week* 73. This was largely the experience with ISO 14001's predecessor, the ISO 9000 series. As one industry analyst has pointed out: 'the experience in the US has been that ISO 9000 has not done anything good in terms of the quality of products. It has become a documentation process, a paper-based process. It serves the purpose of putting in place a management system to achieve a specified level of quality, but does not say anything about what that level of quality is' (J. Master, consultant to the CMA, quoted in 'Chemical firms use EMAS, ISO 14001 in push for deregulation' (March 1996) *ENDS Report* No. 254 6.

'prevention of pollution', which is a term of art with a much narrower meaning.[154]

- Where conformance by a third party is sought,[155] its credibility will depend substantially upon the qualifications and approach of the third party certification bodies responsible for verifying compliance of an enterprise's EMS against the requirements of ISO 14001.[156] There is a serious danger that many auditors, whose principal training does not relate to environment, but who have either a systems or a quality assurance background, will simply bring their existing skills (and limitations) to accrediting and auditing ISO 14001. This may easily result in a 'box ticking' mentality, and a mechanistic approach which ignores or downplays important areas which only professional judgment, is capable of identifying.[157]

[154] The term 'prevention of pollution' is used in a context whereby it might be possible to satisfy it by end of pipe approaches See N. Roht-Arriaza, 'Shifting the Point of Regulation' (1995) 22 *Ecology Law Quarterly* 505–507.

[155] Although ISO 14001 has been written for third party conformance certification (with an option of self-certification), many enterprises which adopt it may choose not to seek certification unless there is a strong commercial reason for doing so (e.g., marketing advantages, meeting requirements of trading partners, or conceivably, discharging the legal requirement of due diligence). In the absence of such reasons, enterprises are unlikely to seek certification, given the often very considerable expense involved. There is the further possibility, to which we return, of governments requiring or providing incentives for certification, in certain circumstances.

[156] See N. Gunningham, 'Environmental Auditing: Who audits the auditors?' (1993) 10(4) *Environmental and Planning Law Journal*, 229, and note that, in Australia, the Commonwealth Environment Protection Agency (CEPA) and the New South Wales Environment Protection Authority are investigating the feasibility of establishing an environmental auditor certification and registration scheme and a Register of Certified Auditors.

In particular, there is a likelihood of a 'QA takeover' of EMS and audits, resulting in an emphasis on procedures and documentation rather than on environmental performance and technical issues.

[157] For example, in Australia, of the first twelve companies involved in a certification pilot programme, eleven are quality assurance specialists, with only one environmental consultancy. Moreover, the Quality Assurance Society of Australia has the responsibility for registration of environmental auditors. A related concern is that there will be an undue focus on detail, again driven by a quality assurance approach. This has indeed been the experience with the ISO 9000 series of quality assurance standards. It is also noteworthy that at present, it is only organizations that will be accredited, and not the individuals within those organizations, who do the certifying.

Already, tensions are being generated as a result of perceived differences in standards being applied by different types of auditors, or auditors operating in different counties. For example, under EMAS, a disagreement about the stringency of German verifiers, as contrasted with those elsewhere in the European Union, is threatening to call into question the credibility of the whole scheme ((April 1996) *ENDS Report* No. 255 7–9). Comparability can only be achieved from uniform international interpretation of the requirements of ISO 14001 and 14024, consistent instruction of course providers, uniform qualification of auditors, and consistent application of guides.

- ISO 14001 does not require firms to make public their progress in attaining the objectives and targets they set under the standard. In contrast, it is a requirement under the EMAS for participating firms to provide a regular environmental statement detailing their activities, the major environmental issues these activities raise, a summary of pollution emissions and waste generation, and an evaluation of overall environmental performance.[158] Taken together, the verifiers' seal of approval and the validated environmental statement provide the public with two important indicators of, and insights into, the performance of registered companies. The lack of any comparable mechanism under ISO 14001 is a striking omission in terms of transparency and accountability.[159] ISO 14001 is similarly deficient in its lack of any credible requirement for genuine dialogue with the community.[160]

- As a change agent, ISO 14001 is limited by the fact that all normative, or visionary (i.e., consciousness changing) material has been removed from its content at the drafting stage. The result is that 'companies are told to develop objectives and targets, but given no vision of the kind of world that would emerge through meeting these objectives. Admonitions to include environment among the highest priorities of the firm are tempered with qualifications about limiting the boundaries of concern to legal requirements'.[161] There is, for example, only one reference to sustainability in the entire document.

There is no requirement, but merely an option, for an independent third party audit under ISO 14001.[162] This is particularly unfortunate, given the evidence (based on the experience of companies registering

---

[158] It will, generally, include specific performance data, for example, emissions and improvement targets. This statement is intended to inform both the authorities and the public of the firm's activities. It must be verified by a third party. As at November 1995, there were still open issues under EMAS as to exactly what has to be included in the environmental statement.

[159] Under ISO 14001, firms are required to conduct periodic audits, depending on their environmental related activities and the results of previous audits. It is important to note, however, that the audit only addresses the EMS itself, *not* environmental performance *per se*, and that, further, the results of the audit remain confidential.

[160] ISO 14001 requires a procedure for dealing with the public without specifying what it should be. For example, if a company notes and files complaints from members of the public, this might notionally satisfy the requirement.

[161] J. Ehrenfeld, *ISO 14000 and Responsible Care: What Kind of Change Agents Are They?* (1995), paper presented to ISO 14000: Preparing for Change Conference, Houston, Texas, September, p.10.

[162] Certification may be granted either by an internal auditor or externally.

under BS7750 or EMAS), that external audits have very considerable value.[163] Under EMAS, third party verifiers have found that: 'many errors in the calculation and measurement of the factual data presented in environmental statements'[164] further underscore the unreliability of anything short of independent oversight. Whether commercial pressures will push most companies to seek third party audit, rather than self-audit, remains to be seen.

The second problem is that, against the success stories concerning the contribution of EMS described earlier, must be balanced the evidence that these benefits can *only* be obtained if the system is properly implemented. Indeed, superficial or tokenistic attempts to introduce an EMS may well be totally ineffective and even counterproductive.[165] The evidence suggests that any enterprise planning to introduce a TQM system for the control of environmental degradation will need:

- Top down integration with the normal business planning cycle;

- Compatibility with the corporate environmental direction and priorities;

- Meaningful participation by all levels of the organization in plan development;

- Review and correction processes at appropriate organizational levels;

- Planned activities that result in meaningful and measurable tasks and targets at the individual level, forming part of the annual staff performance appraisal; and

- Regular review of plans to ensure adequate completion.[166]

However, the successful incorporation of all these elements into an EMS is problematic, and the dangers of implementation failure must not be underestimated.[167] For example, TQM presents a challenge to conventional management techniques. A lack of understanding, or

[163] See 'Benefits and shortcomings of EMAS' (August 1995) *ENDS Report* 19.

[164] 'Benefits and shortcomings of EMAS' (August 1995) *ENDS Report* 21.

[165] J. C. Coffee, 'No Soul to Damn: No Body to Kick': A unscandalized inquiry into the problem of corporate punishment' (1981) 79 *Michigan Law Review* 386.

[166] N. Burke, *Gaining Organisational Commitments to OH&S by Integrating Safety Onto Your Business Plans* (1994), paper presented at Proactive OH&S Management Conference, Sydney 9&10 March, p.3.

[167] R. Chang, *TQM Fever* (1995), an interview presented by Business Report on ABC National Radio, July.

more likely, a lack of commitment (in terms of effort or finance) to the TQM process amongst management will seriously reduce the likelihood of success. There is also the serious possibility that, in some circumstances at least, enterprises lack the commitment to overcome the initial implementation difficulties—an issue we return to below.

Finally, ISO 14001 has less chance of functioning as an effective self-regulatory or co-regulatory mechanism than does Responsible Care. Responsible Care is structurally, very different from ISO 14001. In the case of the former, the major players came to the conclusion that 'we are only as strong as our weakest link' because a major disaster caused by any one of their members would taint the others and seriously damage the future of the entire industry. So the industry, as a whole, has an interest in making self-regulation work *across the entire industry sector*. Moreover, it has developed a sophisticated set of mechanisms at industry association level (albeit inadequate) for the purposes of delivering such sector wide self-regulation, and for policing the performance of recalcitrants.

None of this is the case with ISO 14001, which is intended for use by individual enterprises, with no wider goal of improving environmental performance across an entire industry sector, and with no mechanism for achieving the latter goal. Some of those to whom it is targeted will have a self-interest in adopting such a system and improving their environmental performance voluntarily. The promise of greater cost efficiencies, of developing and marketing globally, new environmental technology, or the public relations advantages of environmental leadership may be sufficient in some circumstances. However, commonly they will not. For the similar reasons to those we identified earlier in respect of Responsible Care, the gap between short-term objectives, including profit maximization, and long-term environmental goals, will be too large. Specifically, there are many circumstances under which the economic benefits of investing in environmental protection are tenuous or non-existent, and where the costs to business of implementing environmental protection measures (including effective EMSs) will not be offset by any resulting savings from improved economic performance.[168] This leaves firms with the temptation to adopt ISO 14001 in order to gain the benefits of regulatory flexibility, public relations benefits or both, without committing the resources necessary to deliver improved environmental performance.

---

[168] Arguably, the single largest impediment to improved environmental performance is the emphasis of corporations on short-term profitability.

From all of the above, one might reasonably conclude that EMSs, used as a regulatory tool, provides both opportunities and challenges. The opportunities are that, when systems work effectively, they can achieve far greater leaps in environmental performance than are imaginable under conventional regulation—delivering continual improvement, transforming the culture of an organization towards its environmental responsibilities, and taking it beyond compliance with its legal duties. Moreover, because systems address environmental issues very broadly, they will encourage companies to address even many environmental problems which fall between the gaps of existing environmental regulations—in itself a very considerable advantage over conventional regulation.

The challenge is that these gains are not easily achieved. These are considerable pitfalls, not least the dangers that firms may develop mere 'paper systems', which serve the cynical function of keeping the regulators off their backs without delivering the promised environmental benefits, and that even some of those who are genuinely committed to this approach may falter at the point of implementation, again failing to deliver environmental outcomes and perhaps falling below the line set by conventional regulation. As with Responsible Care, the challenge for policy design and regulatory strategy is to find ways of harnessing the considerable promise of this initiative without succumbing to its limitations.

ISO 14001 is the outcome of hard fought negotiations at the international level. Given the depth of the divisions between the United States and the European Union on this issue,[169] the present compromise seems unlikely to be renegotiated, at least for some considerable time ahead. However, the limitations of ISO 14001 need not constrain regulatory reformers. It is entirely realistic to design more flexible, system-based regulation for leading enterprises, specifying parameters far more demanding than those contained in ISO 14001 itself (i.e., ISO 'Plus'). In this way, enterprises that wished to go beyond compliance with existing laws could be offered a more flexible, cost effective systems-based alternative, of which an 'off the peg' management system (including, but not limited to, ISO 14001) could form a part, but not the whole.

In this context, it is important to note that, in the chemical industry sector, considerable thought has already gone into means by which the

[169] N. Roht-Arriaza, 'Shifting the Point of Regulation' (1995) 22 *Ecology Law Quarterly* 506–507.

management system and verification components of Responsible Care might be integrated with the requirements of ISO 14001, thereby avoiding duplication. For example, a number of companies have carried out 'gap' analyses to see what they would have to do under their existing, (Responsible Care driven) management systems to qualify for ISO 14001. There appears to be an emerging consensus that ISO 14001 can be seen as complementary to, and integrated with, Responsible Care (see Box 2 below) and that ISO may be used to implement Responsible Care objectives.[170]

Box 2

Comparing ISO 14001 and Responsible Care

- ISO 14001, like ISO 9001, 2 and 3, is largely about documentation and document control.

- ISO 14001 covers about 20 per cent of the 152 code elements of the Canadian Chemical Producers Association's (CCPA's) Responsible Care, but does not address: employee health and safety; community involvement; Product Stewardship; second party assessments; new product development; transportation; former sites; proactivity in public policy development.

- CCPA's Responsible Care guiding principles, policies, codes and programmes cover and exceed—in intent—all of the elements of ISO 14001.

- ISO 14001 is much more prescriptive than Responsible Care in the areas of: elements of an environmental policy; environmental training; inventories; environmental aspects of operations; document control procedures; management roles and responsibility; the need for setting environmental targets.

- ISO 14001 is designed so that auditors with widely varying backgrounds and experience can consistently audit a wide range of organizations against a clearly defined standard.

---

[170] See, for example, 'The Responsible Care, ISO 14001 intersection' (7 April 1997) *Careline* 8–10. See also John McVaugh's chapter in I. Feldman and T. Tibor (eds.), (1996) *Implementing ISO with ISO 14000: A guide to the new environmental Management Standards*, Irwin, Chicago.

- CCPA's Responsible Care verification process is a much more subjective evaluation of how a company has applied the ethic in its: standard setting, or benchmarking, processes and rationale; documentation systems; auditing processes; resourcing.

- ISO 14001 has the potential to provide added value to CCPA members above what they might choose to do for compliance with phase one of Responsible Care. It can be used as a benchmark for environmental management systems as well as a tool for continuous improvement of a company's EMS process.

Source: Canadian Chemical Manufacturers Association, Primer on Responsible Care and ISO 14001.

The following sections explore the questions of how to design regulation appropriate for those who choose to adopt either a systems-based approach such as ISO 14001 or sign onto Responsible Care (or both). How can regulators maximize the advantages of ISO 14001 (or similar management systems approaches) or Responsible Care, while compensating for their weaknesses? How best can regulators move from adversarialism to partnership and from prescriptive to flexible and responsive regulation?

Towards a broader policy mix

So far, we have argued that traditional approaches to chemical industry regulation have serious shortcomings, both for the industry itself and for the environment. Two major initiatives have evolved: Responsible Care, which is essentially a form of industry association driven self-regulation, and ISO 14001 (and similar standards) which is a management systems approach, functioning at the level of the individual enterprise. If integrated into a regulatory scheme, ISO 14001 would best be categorized as a form of process-based regulation, as an alternative means of achieving compliance implying considerable 'regulatory privatization'. Both Responsible Care and ISO 14001 have a claimed capacity to transcend the limitations of traditional approaches yet, as we have seen, they are also beset with problems so serious that in their present form, and functioning in isolation, neither is likely to deliver substantial environmental benefits.

However, this is far from being the end of the story. In this section, we argue that both of these mechanisms have the potential to make a substantial contribution to environmental policy, and to take the chemical industry 'beyond compliance' with existing legislation and towards sustainability, provided they are integrated into a broader policy mix. Our next task is to identify the appropriate ingredients of that mix and how they may best be combined to achieve optimal economic and environmental outcomes. In doing so, we hope to demonstrate that despite the different origins and different (but overlapping) purposes of Responsible Care and ISO 14001, the means of overcoming their weaknesses and of building on their strengths have much in common.

In redesigning regulation, it is important to recognize that chemical companies are not alike, and that different strategies, and mixes, will be appropriate for different types of enterprise, and circumstances. As indicated earlier, chemical companies fall into one of three broad categories. First, there are the enterprises, many of them transnational corporations, which manufacture and supply chemicals on a large scale. These enterprises are sophisticated and profitable. They have substantial plants, are readily identifiable, and have a high public profile. They have both the capacity and the inclination to think proactively and to recognize the close link between their own future and that of the industry. They recognize, in Joe Rees' terms, that they are 'hostages to each other.'[171] Secondly, there are the small suppliers and buyers who both lack sophistication and size and are closely integrated with and highly dependent upon the first category of companies for their survival. Thirdly, are the specialty chemical manufacturers, independent operators usually using batch rather than continuous processes, and who fill market niches and develop new products, responding quickly to customer specifications.[172] These companies undertake some, but by no means all, of their work, as subcontractors for the larger companies.

We examine strategies for dealing with each group in turn, beginning with the most important, the large corporations which make up the large majority of signatories to Responsible Care and the group

---

[171] J. V. Rees, *Hostages of Each Other: The transformation of nuclear safety since Three Mile Island* (1994), University of Chicago Press, Chicago.

[172] Distributors are harder to categorise than most other groups within the chemical industry. They range from very large and sophisticated companies to very small operators. On the whole, the sector is a very profitable one and the number of economically marginal operators is likely to be very low.

which, by reason of size, is the most likely to consider utilizing a management systems approach under ISO 14001.

Strategies for regulating large chemical companies

Large chemical corporations have long complained that traditional regulation is seriously flawed and, in particular, that it does not facilitate their achieving improved environmental performance at least cost. Viewed as regulatory instruments, both Responsible Care and ISO 14001 are seen by their proponents as mechanisms which can effectively mitigate this problem. While it is unlikely that either mechanism could completely substitute for government regulation, each might nevertheless form the justification for a considerable easing of the regulatory burden (hereafter referred to as 'regulatory flexibility'). Thus, in each case, it is contemplated that business which commits itself to adopting Responsible Care or to implementing ISO 14001 would be given considerable autonomy as regards *how* it achieves improved environmental performance. The central vehicle, intended to ensure that such improvement does indeed result, is the implementation of an EMS—this is the essence of ISO 14001 and an important means of discharging key components of Responsible Care (though Responsible Care, also emphasises community involvement, product stewardship, and an environmental ethic promoted by the industry association).

If commitment to implement a management system were to substantially replace the requirements of conventional regulation, then participating enterprises would be given the flexibility of approach which large business, in particular, has long called for as necessary to achieve cost-effective environmental performance.[173] Moreover, as we have indicated above, EMSs, *whether under Responsible care or ISO 14001* have the potential to achieve continuous improvement in environmental performance, to entrench environmental considerations within the decision-making structure, and to take enterprises 'beyond compliance' with existing regulation. Finally, by transferring considerable responsibility from the regulator to the enterprise itself, this approach has considerable benefits to regulators in terms of freeing up scarce resources. The result would be 'regulating at a distance' without the heavy hand of

---

[173] The Yorktown experiment, described at p.47 above, is the classic example of this approach. The considerable autonomy implied by management-driven approaches also has another important benefit: codes or systems derived by industry have much greater credibility within industry and likelihood of acceptance by it, than those imposed from outside.

highly directive regulation that has characterized past regulator-regulatee interactions.

All this should be attractive on all sides: to enterprises (in terms of autonomy and achieving cost effectiveness) and to regulators, policy-makers, and environmentalists in terms of better environmental outcomes (with fewer regulatory resources). Yet there are considerable pitfalls in this approach, which we have indicated above. Perhaps the greatest danger is that some firms may be tempted to adopt Responsible Care or ISO 14001 to get the regulators off their backs, to gain the benefits of incentives offered for adopting such systems, to obtain public relations benefits, or all of the above.[174] The result may be tokenism and a proliferation of perfunctory 'paper systems' that have little benefit in terms of improved environmental performance. Even worse, it may be very difficult for regulators to distinguish between paper systems and the real thing. Even some enterprises which genuinely embrace a management system approach may do so ineffectively, again failing to deliver the promised environmental outcomes. There are also specific problems with ISO 14001, described in the previous section, to which we will return.

Thus, proposals for regulatory flexibility implying a considerable degree of autonomy and self-regulation (or 'privatization of regulation') inevitably raise concerns from environmentalists, public interest groups, and regulators themselves as to whether such trust placed in business to regulate its own affairs will be betrayed—either deliberately or through incompetence.

Recognizing the serious risks as well as the benefits implicit in proposals for regulatory flexibility, the central challenge is to design a strategy whereby one may gain the maximum benefits of Responsible Care or a management systems approach while minimizing the shortcomings of such approaches. Crucial questions will be: what outcomes should government insist on; how can these be measured; who will do the measuring; to what extent and in what ways will environmental, community and public interest groups be involved in the process; how can the burden on government resources be reduced; what incentives need be provided for industry to embrace regulatory flexibility; and what will happen if enterprises don't live up to their commitments? In the following sections, we address these questions.

---

[174] See above, p.184 on the limits of self-interest in adopting such systems.

We will argue that a number of measures should be seen as prerequisites for government to successfully regulate large companies at a distance, giving them the flexibility they demand, while achieving both improved environmental and economic outcomes, and community acceptance. These are:

- measuring environmental outcomes by independent and transparent performance indicators;

- independent third party oversight underpinned by access to information;

- community empowerment, including the transparency and institutionalized dialogue necessary to bring this about;

- government oversight and an underpinning of effective sanctions; and

- credible incentives for industry participation.

Each of these elements will be examined below.

As a preliminary point, it is important to restate that, in seeking to design an optimal approach, there is no need to be constrained by the limitations of either ISO 14001 or Responsible Care in their present forms. That is, as we shall see, the best way of benefiting from the strengths of these instruments while avoiding their shortcomings includes (but is certainly not limited to) making modifications to, or going beyond them in ways consistent with the public interest. In short, the *quid pro quo* for regulatory flexibility on the part of government will be co-regulation which builds on, but is not limited to, the basic elements of ISO and Responsible Care (what we and others have referred to as ISO or Responsible Care 'Plus').

1. Measuring environmental outcomes under Environmental Management Systems (EMSs)

We begin by examining the potential role of EMSs—the essence of ISO 14001 and an important element of Responsible Care. How can one ensure that EMSs are indeed self-monitoring, self-correcting and self-improving, as their proponents claim? How can one ensure that these systems do not, intentionally or otherwise, produce the trappings of self-regulation without delivering the promised outcomes in terms of a shift in culture, a commitment to continuous improvement, and, as a result, improved environmental performance?

As indicated above, a serious danger of relying on ISO 14001 alone, is that it emphasizes processes but not outcomes. Similarly, Responsible Care, rather than evaluating actual performance, also focuses on progress in implementation of the system itself.[175] That is, it would be possible under both regimes, for enterprises to satisfy the base requirement of system implementation *without improving upon the levels of environmental performance specified by existing regulatory regimes.*

If regulators are to allow a more flexible regulatory approach for those adopting an EMS (and, in the case of Responsible Care, for adopting a range of other commitments too), then they must insist that a fundamental term of the permit, agreement, or other instrument under which the enterprise operates is a commitment to performance outcomes[176] demonstrably better than those required by existing legislation as well as to process. Specifically, to ensure that EMSs (and the Responsible Care codes) do indeed deliver the results of which they are capable, it is essential that governments require participating firms to commit themselves to a number of performance related 'bottom lines'.

This is easier to state in the abstract than to implement in concrete terms, for two reasons. First, there are difficulties in measuring environmental performance (i.e., in specifying appropriate performance indicators), secondly, there are dangers that indicators specified may encourage pollution control and end of pipe solutions rather than pollution prevention and continuous improvement.

Benchmarking and performance indicators   To evaluate actual performance, rather than just progress in implementation of the system or codes of practice, requires the generation and collection of objective data that validates a company's activities against milestones that enable all companies to be compared against each other (often known as 'benchmarking'). This, in itself, will create important incentives for improvement, at least if these figures are made public. It will be equally

---

[175] D. Rotman, 'Pushing Pollution Prevention' (17 July 1991) *Chemical Week* 30 at 33.

[176] The advantages of performance-based reporting have been summarized as being that it: requires clear goals that relate to the issues that the organization exists to deal with and that society expects it to deal with; allows improved accountability, as customers can make judgments about its performance in dealing with those issues; give clear guidance to all levels of the organization as to what they should be trying to achieve (although not how to achieve it); allow and encourage organizational learning and improvement; and enable comparisons between organizations (see C. Meredith, *Process or Outcomes? Defining the most useful measure of environmental performance* (1996), a paper presented at the 1996 Australian Academy of Science *Fenner Conference on the Environment: Linking Environment and Economy Through Indicators and Accounting Systems*, 30 September to 3 October, The University of New South Wales, Sydney, pp.2–3).

important that the relevant data is capable of demonstrating that each participating enterprise is going beyond compliance with outcome-based regulatory requirements. Ideally, the data should also be presented in such a way as to enable a company's performance to be understood by local communities.

So far, only limited progress has been made towards developing and implementing such performance indicators or broader metrics necessary to identify opportunities and assess actual achievements against reduction goals (although the situation is changing rapidly). As the European Chemical Industry Council (CEFIC) acknowledged at its General Assembly in 1996, the lack of comparable data is seriously hampering the industry's search for credibility, but so far, its search for solutions is only in its early stages.[177] In the case of Responsible Care, Union Carbide Chief Executive Officer, Robert Kennedy, summarized the position as follows:

. . . our voluntary reports are a random walk. Companies use different reporting formats, data bases, time frames and definitions. As a result, the work we are doing has not received the recognition it deserves. Ultimately, we need to develop a system of uniform reporting standards around the world, a common vocabulary, accepted definitions and practices, a systems that can be independently verified—plant by plant, country by country—much as financial auditing does for our balance sheets today. It won't be easy, especially when proprietary information is involved. But the value of an independent, certifiable reporting system will far exceed the cost and trouble of developing one.

Performance indicators capable of meeting the criteria identified above have not yet been developed, though considerable effort is being addressed to this goal at the time of writing,[178] including efforts to develop Environmental Performance Evaluation under the ISO 14000 series[179]. Whether it is possible to go further, and to develop a general

[177] *ENDS Report* (August 1996) No.259 21.
[178] See, in particular, the work of the US Multistate Working Group on Environmental Management Systems 'Draft Voluntary Guideline Matrix for Implementation and Evaluation of ISO 14001 Environmental Management Pilot Projects' May 1997. The matrix includes a framework for measuring the results of EMSs in the following categories: environmental performance; environmental conditions; environmental compliance; management framework; pollution prevention; costs and benefits; and stakeholder involvement. The US EPA is considering a second set of measurements to gauge a company's environmental performance. These may include releases of pollution; amount of raw materials used; effectiveness of environmental training of workers; number and frequency of environmental audits; and cost savings accrued from a facility's pollution prevention efforts.
[179] EPE is a process intended to provide organizations with a mechanism for understanding their past and present environmental performance as compared to the intended

measure of environmental performance, applicable to different firms with different processes and products, remains to be seen.[180] However, in their[181] 1997 Report, *Measuring Up*, Ditz and Ranganathan advance this issue significantly, arguing for the adoption of four standards of environmental performance: materials use; energy consumption; non-product output; and pollutant releases that emphasize resource efficiency, pollution prevention and product stewardship, which could be used 'both inside and outside company walls'. In particular, they suggest that: 'Just as a company's financial statement can be relied upon to provide information that is comparable, transparent, and complete, the EIPs [Environmental Performance Indicators] could be used to rate its environmental performance. In this way, EIPs could provide the information necessary to measure and motivate progress towards environment goals'.[182]

Five interim measures are proposed, capable at least of reassuring regulators and others that regulatory flexibility does not result in backsliding. First, one might borrow from proposals in the United States (to develop a regulatory 'cap')[183] and provide that compliance with all 'existing and reasonably foreseeable' regulatory requirements would be the baseline requirement for regulatory flexibility and autonomy[184] or, in the case of new facilities, the lesser of allowable levels of releases or best practices in that industry.[185] Secondly, one might develop indica-

environmental performance of the organization. See ISO 14031 Environmental Protection Evaluation, US SuB Tag 4, Annexes Testing Committee, Draft ATC Report, Sept 1996.

[180] Here, key questions are: what comparisons can be made with data on incidents and impacts of chemical operations and substances; or whom should data be gathered; and what health, safety and environment outcomes should we measure? (see further, J. Smith, *Measuring Health, Safety and Environmental Performance: Why, what, and whose?* (1994), summary of a paper presented to the ACIC Convention, 21 February, Leura, NSW).

[181] D. Ditz & J. Ranganathan, *Measuring Up: Toward a Common Framework for Tracking Corporate Environmental Performance* World Resources Institute, Washington DC, 1997

[182] *Ibid.*, at p.vii.

[183] These approaches contemplate an immediate exit from the current regulatory system for selected major sources, replacing it with contracts tailored to the source's particular circumstances (see W. F. Pederson, 'Can Site Specific Pollution Control Plans Furnish an Alternative to the Current Regulatory System and a Bridge to a New One?' (1995) 25 *Environmental Law Review* 10486).

[184] For example, any project eligible for the XL Program (discussed in chapter two and below at p.47) must be 'able to achieve environmental performance that is superior to what would be achieved through compliance with current and reasonably anticipated future regulation' (60 Fed Reg at 27287).

[185] This is the proposal made by the Aspen Institute Report: *The Alternative Path: A cleaner, cheaper way to protect and enhance the environment* (1996), Program for Energy, the Environment and the Economy, The Aspen Institute, US.

tors based on data required to be reported and measured under exist-ing government programmes. For example, in the United States, the CMA now claims to have external performance measures for five of its six Codes of Practice.[186] These include the toxics release inventory (used as a measure of pollution prevention), Occupational Health and Safety Administration (OSHA) figures (used as a measure of safety per-formance), and the Department of Transportation's hazardous materi-als transportation incident database (as the Distribution Code Performance Measure). Thirdly, agreements may be negotiated at the level of each individual plant or company (if offsetting is allowed)[187] through its licence, permit, or an environmental covenant. Under such agreements, an enterprise, in return for regulatory flexibility, would commit itself (as under some United States state permitting laws)[188] to an implementation schedule for identified and specified source reduc-tions. Fourthly, given that regulatory flexibility could have adverse implications for environmental justice, it should be a requirement that any new proposal demonstrate that it does not pose a significant increase or shift in the risk of adverse effects, or result in a significant relocation of pollution.[189] Finally, the ISO 14000 series contemplates the development of methods of Environmental Performance Evaluation (EPE) which will enable organisations to 'establish processes for mea-suring progress against objectives and criteria relevant to their perfor-mance goals. These methods may be used for benchmarking and other comparative purposes'.[190]

Pollution prevention or pollution control   One of the greatest attractions of management systems approaches is their promise to deliver continuous improvement and environmental performance 'beyond compliance' with existing regulations. Yet there is a danger that performance indicators used to measure achievement will measure outcomes crudely (e.g., levels of discharge to a particular medium). If

[186] Chemical Manufacturers Association (CMA), *Responsible Care: Progress Report 1994–95* (1995), CMA, Washington DC, pp.23–26.

[187] For example, same company be allowed its own 'bubble licence': offsetting gains in one area, inexpensively gained, against losses in another where it would be excessively expensive to achieve change.

[188] Environmental Law Institute, 'New State and Local Approaches to Environmental Protection' (1993), Environmental Law Institute Report to EPA Office of Technology Assessment, Washington DC.

[189] This is the proposal made by the Aspen Institute Report: *The Alternative Path: A cleaner, cheaper way to protect and enhance the environment* (1996), Program for Energy, the Environment and the Economy, The Aspen Institute, US.

[190] G. Crognale at http://www.stoller.com/isofiles/crognale.htm.

they do so, then the familiar problems of encouraging and facilitating enterprises to simply adopt 'end of pipe' solutions (scrubbers rather than cleaner technologies) and to transfer toxins from one media to another, will be further entrenched.

As Atcheson rightly argues, the challenge is to move: 'from single-medium, single-stress, point-source, end of pipe technologies toward whole facility and systemic strategies based on continuous improvement and efficient use of energy and materials, as well as pollution prevention'.[191] Accordingly, relevant indicators must be geared to pollution prevention rather than pollution control, taking account of the raw materials and fuels manufacturers use, and the material and energy intensity of the processes, practices, and procedures they adopt. Having said that, it must be acknowledged that: 'pollution prevention and efficiency approaches . . . are most difficult to verify in any conventional sense'.[192] This indeed, is one reason why regulators are much more comfortable focusing on technologies that can be easily verified—the very end of pipe technology-based approaches we most need to get away from.[193]

There are very few real world examples of how a more flexible regulatory approach utilizing management systems can be made to work in practice or, more particularly, of what indicators may prove appropriate to measure pollution prevention. However, in the United States, Project XL and the Common Sense Initiative are experimenting with 'alternative ways of accomplishing environmental objectives that emphasise performance, allow flexibility, encourage prevention and efficiency at facility level while assuring accountability',[194] and facility planning laws (linking permit requirements to a pollution prevention plan and establishing milestones for performance) are also developing in similar directions.[195] Within the related field of occupational health

---

[191] J. Atcheson, 'Can we Trust Verification?' (July/August 1996) 13(4) *Environmental Forum* 19.

[192] *Ibid.*

[193] For regulators at least, an advantage of old style specification standards is that they are comparatively easy to measure and verify. This is not the case with a more open ended, flexible and outcomes oriented approach, where 'a major issue . . . is to establish feasible and agreed-upon ways to measure and verify facility and sector performance' (D. J. Fiorino, 'Towards a New System of Environmental Regulation: The case for an industry sector approach' (1996) 26(2) *Environmental Law* 457–489 at 478).

[194] J. Atcheson, 'Can we Trust Verification?' (July/August 1996) 13(4) *Environmental Forum* 21.

[195] These are intended to focus resources on pollution reduction goals rather than on completing the burdensome process of achieving several different permits (Environmental

and safety, the Voluntary Protection Program, initiated by the United States OSHA in the 1980s, also provides some guidance as to how this task should be approached.[196] The *Measuring Up* report, considered earlier, makes a substantial advance in identifying indicators which are designed specifically to prevent pollution and resource efficiency.[197]

2. Third party oversight

Independent audits   Having identified what to measure, the next crucial question is: who should do the measuring? Certainly, the adoption of a management system implies that the enterprise will undertake its own continuing monitoring of its performance under that system. However, over and beyond this, such independent and appropriate performance indicators as are developed, must also be independently monitored, for without this, there can be no assurance that the information industry provides is genuine. Moreover, if the monitoring process is to gain community credibility, and be seen as legitimate, it must also be transparent. Both factors are increasingly recognized by the industry itself, as the necessary price for greater autonomy.[198]

Chemical industry associations across a number of countries are now taking active steps to move beyond self-policing of their health, safety, and environmental management procedures. Of course, one option, for larger organizations at least, is to create their own quasi-independent audit team from within the organization. For example,

Law Institute, 'New State and Local Approaches to Environmental Protection' (1993), Environmental Law Institute Report to EPA Office of Technology Assessment, Washington DC).

[196] Under this programme, a company may implement an OHS management system and, in exchange, OSHA will reduce enforcement and inspection requirements. What is striking about this scheme is the extent of the requirements on a firm before it becomes eligible to participate. Under the self-inspection and hazard-correction requirement, an employer must describe its hazard assessment procedures in detail, show how hazard assessment findings are incorporated in planning decisions, training programmes and operating procedures, and agree to provide to OSHA its self-investigation and accident investigation records, its safety committee minutes, its monitoring and sampling results, and its annual safety and health programme evaluation. It also pledges to correct in a timely manner all hazards identified through self-inspections, employee reports or accident investigations, and to provide the results of these investigations to its employees. That is, it is not sufficient for enterprises simply to establish a management system. Rather, there is an insistence that a number of other clearly identified requirements must also be satisfied.

[197] D. Ditz and J. Ranganathan, *Measuring Up: Toward a Common Framework for Tracking Corporate Environmental Performance* World Resources Institute, Washington DC, 1997.

[198] This view has been attributed to US Chemical Manufacturers Association executive J. Davenport.

some transnationals conduct detailed audits on subsidiaries throughout the world, with no prior warning. An advantage of this approach is that the auditors have no commercial vulnerability and are far more likely to be intimately familiar with the firm's operations. Further, the firm itself will find it far more difficult to ignore directions from corporate headquarters than external auditors. However, the disadvantage is the lack of credibility of this approach, for however 'arms length' the audit team may be, its independence may be doubted by the community, whose views will be crucial in this respect.

The favoured form of monitoring and oversight is an audit conducted by an independent professional.[199] As indicated above, such audits can provide systematic, documented, periodic and objective reviews of whether environmental requirements are being met or whether systems are being adhered to.[200] In particular, they involve: 'the structured process of collecting independent information on the efficiency, effectiveness and reliability of the total . . . management system'.[201]

Here, the model is the 'compliance verification system' which the CCPA has adopted, under which a team of four conduct a verification of a member company's operations.[202] In each case, two of these verifiers are people with extensive industry experience, and two are outsiders, one of these being preferably from the company's local

---

[199] An innovative alternative, that has been trialed in Alberta, Canada, is a peer evaluation system whereby each participating company agrees to receive the services of a certified independent auditor from a participating company in the same industry group. Whether such a system would work at least as well as one utilizing auditors from outside the industry itself, whether it would result in collusion, or the converse (auditors from rival firms exploiting opportunities to disadvantage their rivals), it is too soon to say. This is indeed one area whether further empirical evidence is needed and where much may depend on the characteristics of the individual industry.

[200] N. Gunningham & J. Prest, 'Environmental Audit as a Regulatory Strategy: Prospects and reform' (1994) 15 *Sydney Law Review* 492–526, and references therein.

[201] Health & Safety Executive (UK), *Successful Health and Safety Management* HS(G)65, (1991), HMSO, London.

[202] At the time of writing , the Canadian version is stronger than most others. For example, the US CMA is still experimenting with management systems verification to enable a critical assessment of a company's progress, and providing for public participation, while in Australia the current proposal is that a community representative (for example, a technical specialist with links to a local community) will only participate where the company being audited has agreed to their inclusion (J. Smith, *Measuring Health, Safety and Environmental Performance: Why, what, and whose?* (1994), summary of a paper presented to the ACIC Convention, 21 February, Leura, NSW). Clearly, this is a substantial limitation to effective and independent third party oversight and will do little to overcome community scepticism.

community advisory panel. This team seeks evidence as to whether and to what extent the company is in compliance with the guiding principles and codes of Responsible Care. It looks for evidence of a management structure, a bench-marking process, an internal auditing process, and a mechanism for follow-up and continuous improvement.[203] A report is given to company management describing areas where more effective systems may be needed, as well as areas where the company has gone beyond the 'state-of-the-art' of Responsible Care. It is expected that the company will report the results of the verification to its local communities.[204] Three years after its inception, with the first round of verification nearing completion, both companies and verifiers regard the verification process as a qualified success, which in addition to its role in reviewing the performance of individual enterprises, has also served to identify some considerable achievements and limitations of Responsible Care as a whole.[205]

However, what remains strikingly absent even from 'best practices' initiatives such as the Canadian approach, is an independent third party auditing system not merely of whether specified management systems are in place, *but also of a company's environmental performance as a whole, and as to whether it is achieving continuous improvement.* Thus, Responsible Care and ISO 14001 verification, even under recent reforms, share a common and fundamental limitation: the failure to independently measure and report upon environmental performance.[206] Nothing short of this will, in the longer term, satisfy demands for full accountability and reassure governments and communities that firms that gain the benefits of regulatory flexibility are in return, indeed delivering environmental results better than those required by traditional

---

[203] Four verifiers, including two industrial volunteers, a professional auditor, and an environmentalist, studied CCC and Imperial Oil's (Toronto) agricultural chemical groups for a week, which included three to four days of speaking with people of each company. Working from the CEO down, the team verified the management systems ensure that Responsible Care requirements are met. The team was able to examine twenty per cent of the 151 items in depth, quickly checking the others (E. Kirschner, 'New Jersey: State Ambassadors' (1993) 153 *Chemical Week* 40. See also 'CMA Verification Process Kicks Off to Successful Start' (1997) 6 *Careline* 10).

[204] However, this remains a contentious issue. Under the US version, there is no such obligation or expectation as yet. (See also B. Wastle, Vice President, Canadian Chemical Producers Association, letter to the author, November (1993)).

[205] See 'The Verdict on Verification From Canada' (7 April 1997) *Careline* 4.

[206] However, it is understood that, in Canada at least, the next phase of Responsible Care verification will directly address environmental performance (personal communication, B. Wastle, 18 December 1997).

regulation.[207] Thus, in envisioning an optimal regulatory system, we contemplate third party audits by independent experts, involving community and environmental groups, that audit not merely systems but also environmental outcomes in terms of performance indicators, as described in the previous section above.

Of course, audits could instead be conducted by government inspectors (also with community participation) rather than by independent professionals. However, there are considerable attractions in using independent third parties rather than government. Auditing whether an enterprise has genuinely and successfully adopted and implemented a systems-based approach not only requires greater and different skills on the part of government inspectors, but is also extremely demanding of inspectors' time. Most inspectorates currently lack both the time and the technical skills necessary to conduct these tasks. Certainly, those skills could be acquired, but this will often involve hiring more (and more expensive) employees and devoting substantial amounts of additional time to such audits. In an era of fiscal constraint, these options may be impractical or unattractive.

If the audit function were contracted to independent third parties with the specialist skills required (environmental auditors), then these problems could largely be overcome.[208] It is normally a condition of participation in regulatory innovation that it is the enterprise concerned, not government, that bears the cost of third party audit. This approach has the further attractions both of substantially conserving regulatory resources (which can be redeployed so as to focus very largely on those who are still regulated by traditional means), and of satisfying the 'polluter pays' principle.[209]

However, there is a serious difficulty in the strategy of relying upon third party auditors as surrogate regulators, namely ensuring their professional integrity and independence. For there remains the possibility of co-option of the auditors by the firm seeking accreditation—a hazard illustrated by the failure of financial auditors in the financial scan-

---

[207] See, generally, N. Gunningham & J. Prest, 'Environmental Audit as a Regulatory Strategy: Prospects and reform' (1994) 15 *Sydney Law Review* 492–526; and N. Gunningham, 'Environmental Auditing: Who audits the auditors?' (1993) 10(4) *Environmental and Planning Law Journal* 229.

[208] Note the role of auditors under the USEPA's Risk Management Plans programme. See W. L. Thomas 'Using ISO 14001 to comply with the Management System requirements of the USEPA's RMP Rule and the EU's Seveso II Directive' forthcoming in *Hydrocarbon Processing* (1998).

[209] Since the regulated enterprise might wish to conduct such periodic audits for its own purposes, the additional cost to itself may be acceptable.

dals of the 1980s.[210] This problem is exacerbated by the fact that there are no universally agreed standards for carrying out safety audits. Neither is there agreement as regards the professional requirements for auditors, although such a development seems imminent. There are a number of possible ways of dealing with this issue, none of them totally satisfactory. They include nomination of the auditor by the regulator from a pool of accredited auditors, rather than by the regulated enterprise; state regulation of auditors; an auditor accreditation scheme; peer review; civil liability; and the establishment of a set of national standards relating to the quality and scope of audits.[211]

A further problem concerns the circumstances under which audit results should be disclosed, and the issue of transparency, given the tension between the regulator's interests and those of the regulated enterprise. From the regulator's point of view, third party audits work best if the auditor's report is made accessible to the regulatory agency and does not remain confidential as between auditor and enterprise. However, such a requirement is likely to be unattractive to the enterprise itself (which after all, is footing the bill!), which may understandably fear that it is providing the regulatory agency with considerable information (and ammunition, in the event of a prosecution) which would otherwise not be available. There is thus a tension between the regulator's need to be reassured that it will be alerted to unsatisfactory audit results (enabling it to take corrective action) and an enterprise's reticence to adopt a systems-based approach if required to make full disclosure of the audit report.

The community too, is unlikely to trust the outcomes of third party audit unless the results are transparent. If the regulator insists on full disclosure in every case, then an audit approach may become insufficiently attractive for many enterprises to agree to participate.[212] Such an outcome would be counterproductive, and a solution must be found which is acceptable to both sides. The most satisfactory compromise might be one whereby only a overview or summary of the audit is ordinarily supplied to the regulator (and the community) by the auditor,

[210] However, there may be a contrary incentive in the case of at least some environmental auditors: identifying numerous deficiencies in the client's systems in anticipation of gaining the contract to fix them up.

[211] See N. Gunningham, 'Environmental Auditing: Who audits the auditors?' (1993) 10(4) *Environmental and Planning Law Journal* 229.

[212] While self-insurers and those who require a SMS to tender for government contracts might remain within track two, most others might find the remaining incentives insufficient to do so.

indicating the conclusions, but not the details, of the audit. Thus the latter, including any specific identified breaches of the legislation, would remain confidential to the regulated enterprise. The fact that an audit itself is to be treated as a privileged document should be clearly indicated, either in enforcement guidelines or in the legislation itself.[213] However, as indicated below, where the audit summary indicates a generally unfavourable report, or major failings in individual aspects, this should be one circumstance triggering an inspection.

While this solution may serve to alleviate the fears of regulated enterprises, it does far less to assure the regulator that the audit system is working satisfactorily, that the auditors are operating in the public interest, and that they have not been captured by the client enterprise. To overcome these problems, and to ensure the integrity of the audit process, the regulator should have a right to spot check (and verify) a random sample of full audits. Even in this latter circumstance, the information gained from the audit report could not sensibly be used as a basis for enforcement action, for if it were, it would provide a substantial and unnecessary disincentive to adopting an EMS approach. Few companies would agree to participate in the scheme.[214] More appropriately, the agency might undertake to give participating firms qualified privilege[215] and a 'period of grace' to rectify problems revealed by the audit.[216]

CRTK   Another third party oversight mechanism involves engaging and empowering the community to act as a restraint on the behaviour of business. In the case of the chemical industry, the community is a potentially potent force because chemical plant emissions can have the direct effects on human health, and this is widely recognized by communities themselves. Trade unions, local community groups, national environmental groups, and other NGOs can all have a major impact

[213] The one circumstance in which privilege should not be granted is where the duty holder seeks to invoke the audit in defence to a prosecution, in which case the prosecution should have a right to produce other evidence from the audit which counters this.

[214] There is, after all, little incentive to conduct an audit if the information it generates serves to provide a basis for prosecution or other enforcement action.

[215] See N. Gunningham & J. Prest, 'Environmental Audit as a Regulatory Strategy: Prospects and reform' (1994) 15 *Sydney Law Review* 492–526.

[216] It might be necessary to provide statutory guarantees that information gathered in such an audit cannot be used in any subsequent prosecution action. Such a strategy would work most effectively if the relevant inspectorate adopted a diagnostic role—at least in respect of voluntary audits. That is, it would see its primary means of obtaining compliance as the provision of technical assistance to companies in breach of regulatory standards, keeping advice and policing as quite separate functions.

on large corporations, which must, increasingly, protect their environmental credentials and credibility.

However, an essential prerequisite for effective community involvement is access to information about the chemical industry's emissions and activities. Communities that are empowered through information and participation can act as a countervailing force, compensating in part for the inadequacy of regulatory resources, by scrutinizing both industry and agency performance and bringing pressure to bear, and 'shaming industry' where performance is inadequate. Yet, without information, they have great difficulty fulfilling this role. Moreover, as Kleindorfer and Orts put it, information, can serve 'to lesson irrational fears and ideologically driven mistrust among various groups. Improved information about specific issues may increase the chances of a negotiated solution to a problem'.[217]

The chemical industry acknowledged the importance of transparency and information disclosure by its initial adoption (in the United States) of the slogan 'don't trust us, track us',[218] which encapsulates the basic tenet of Responsible Care—namely that the scheme will only gain credibility if the public is enabled through access to information to judge the industry by its actions rather than by its rhetoric. For its part, the industry would prefer that disclosure were provided voluntarily rather than as a result of legislation.[219] However, evidence concerning voluntary approaches suggests that they are of doubtful effectiveness,[220] and, in many respects, a very poor substitute for mandatory disclosure, which conventionally takes the form of CRTK legislation.

The potential benefits of this type of legislation are well known.[221]

[217] P. Kleindorfer and E. Orts, 'Informational Regulation of Environmental Risks' Working Paper, The Wharton School, University of Pennsylvania, 1996.

[218] That slogan turned out to be a public relations disaster (surveys indicated that most Americans remembered only the first part of it) and the Australian ACIC has wisely chosen not to adopt it.

[219] At present, some versions of Responsible Care adopt the former approach. For example, in Australia, a Code of Practice endorses the principle of the community having a right to knowledge concerning hazardous substances stored within members' premises; the processes used at members' premises in manufacture of those products; the transport arrangements for moving those hazardous substances to and from members' premises, and resultant from these activities. The primary mechanism for communicating the relevant information is through local community liaison panels established with the co-operation of local government, State regulatory agencies and prominent local residents (see further N. Gunningham & A. Cornwall, 'Legislating the Right to Know' (1994) 11(4) *Environmental and Planning Law Journal* 274–88).

[220] See N. Gunningham, 'Environment, Self-Regulation, and the Chemical Industry: Assessing Responsible Care' (1995) 17(1) *Law and Policy* 57–109 at 77–80.

[221] See chapter 2, p.63.

Right-to-Know gives community groups insights into the severity of the chemical hazards they face, and, through this, encourages greater public participation. In turn, information about the hazards gives workers and community groups increased potential leverage, enabling them to more effectively pressure polluters to reduce emissions.[222] It can also provide company managers with leverage over internal procedures. With respect specifically to Responsible Care, CRTK, in principle, provides the community groups with a capacity to identify the extent to which individual companies are honouring their responsibilities under the other Codes of Practice.[223]

If Responsible Care is unsatisfactory in terms of information disclosure, ISO 14001 is far worse. American fears about the legal implications of disclosure, and their feelings of discomfort about forms of dialogue which, in Europe, are becoming increasingly common, and the more antagonistic culture between industry and other stakeholder groups in the United States, has resulted (with American success in the negotiating process) in much information under ISO 14001 being treated as confidential, and in almost no effort to encourage dialogue under the standard.[224] As Nash and Ehrenfeld put it:

ISO . . . registration requires very little action that would strengthen a firm's relationships with those outside its fence lines. ISO 14001 companies need only concern themselves with impacts within their immediate "control". They may be passive in their relationships with concerned citizens, simply responding to inquiries instead of actively seeking input from outside.[225]

Unfortunately, American industry resistance to disclosure under ISO 14001 is in no way balanced by a willingness to engage in voluntary disclosure. On the contrary, there is very little evidence that most

---

[222] See further, N. Gunningham & A. Cornwall, 'Legislating the Right to Know' (1994) 11(4) *Environmental and Planning Law Journal* 274–88.

[223] For example, the intention is that member companies will be able to measure performance quantitatively against defined objectives (see Code, section 2.1, and implementation principles).

[224] In contrast, the Coalition for Environmentally Responsible Economies (CERES) principles include a requirement for public disclosure of environmental performance. CERES also requires companies to make information generated through self-audits publicly available—again a sharp contrast to the position under ISO 14001. CERES principles further include commitments from enterprises to report publicly violations of the law, waste management, workplace hazards and to report annually their environmental releases. None of these disclosures on corporate environmental performance is required under ISO 14001. Similarly, EMAS also provides for public disclosure, as does BS 7750, whereby a company must publicly disclose direct as well as indirect significant environmental effects of the manufacturing process.

[225] J. Nash & J. Ehrenfeld 'Code Green' (Jan/Feb 1996) *Environment* 42.

United States companies will voluntarily disclose information to the public, or even to shareholders, concerning their environmental performance, although a handful of firms have opted for much greater transparency, usually through the vehicle of an annual environmental report.[226] In general, however, the public has considerable difficulty obtaining information under voluntary approaches. Significantly, as one community representative argued: 'if it was a law we could compel disclosure. But because its only a voluntary code we have constant problems getting the information we want.'

There is indeed a strong case for government intervention to directly empower the community by requiring statutory disclosure of information concerning emissions. The TRI in the United States, described in chapter two, is a strikingly successful model of how such legislation might be designed. By using the TRI, environmental and public interest groups are enabled to make some independent assessment of progress under Responsible Care and to gain information about the industry's activities and their environmental impact. Companies seeking regulatory flexibility, in return for implementing ISO 14001, should equally be required by law to commit to a similar degree of information disclosure as a term for such flexibility.

3. Broader Stakeholder Involvement: Community participation and dialogue

The chemical industry cannot regain public trust, nor will regulatory flexibility itself be a credible option, unless all stakeholders are directly involved in the process. Means must be found whereby all the relevant communities,[227] including workers/trade unions, local community groups, and national environmental groups, can participate in, oversee, and scrutinize regulatory flexibility. In addition to the role of information and CRTK, such participation could involve an on-going dialogue with those communities 'to identify, address and assess how well the facility is responding to community concerns',[228] community outreach activities and other means of institutionalizing public participation and means of assessing their success.

---

[226] See p.62.

[227] The public is not a homogeneous group—the communities located in close proximity to chemical plants themselves often have very different views from those located at some distance from them.

[228] US EPA, Environmental Leadership Program, *ELP Community Outreach/Employee Involvement* (1996), US EPA, Washington DC, p.1.

In the case of Responsible Care (though not ISO 14001), community input and oversight is currently channelled through the vehicles of national and local advisory councils. For example, in Australia, the National Community Advisory Panel, made up of a variety of community activists and independent technical specialists, has made a major contribution in ensuring that draft proposals are consistent with the public interest goals espoused by Responsible Care. Its most significant role has been in the often substantial modifications it has made to draft Codes of Practice. More broadly, such panels may provide a 'multilateral forum within which problem definition and policy formation could benefit from a direct engagement with alternative perspectives'.[229] Although its views are not binding on the administrators of Responsible Care, the chemical industry has yet to reject them, for to do so would seriously prejudice the credibility of the entire scheme.

Similarly, at local level, there are now a range of local or site liaison committees or committees, which might 'provide the basis for a complementary forum that would foster simultaneously an improved learning capacity at the level of the individual organisation, greater accountability to local publics, and a consequently enhanced legitimacy for the industry's activities'.[230] These groups, whose contribution varies greatly with local circumstances, can, when functioning well, also serve to scrutinizing the performance of companies at a local level.

How effective either national or local groups are, and how much credibility they have, depends substantially on the resources available to them, how their members are chosen, and how genuinely representative they are. While the industry has made recent efforts to attract some of its sternest critics onto the panels, the major environmental groups (in contrast to many local groups) have refused to participate,[231] with the result that individuals on the panel commonly do not represent any broader constituency.

Because ISO 14001 involves individual self-regulation in the absence of any relevant trade association, these mechanisms are not available to

[229] P. Simmons & B. Wynne, 'Responsible Care: Trust, credibility and environmental management: in K. Fischer & J. Schot (eds.) *Environmental Strategies for Industry* (1993), Island Press, US, p.221.

[230] P. Simmons & B. Wynne, 'Responsible Care: Trust, credibility and environmental management' in K. Fischer & J. Schot (eds.), *Environmental Strategies for Industry* (1993), Island Press, US, p.221.

[231] These groups, reportedly, fear that their participation might be perceived as an endorsement of Responsible Care or that, by participating, they might be co-opted and less free to criticize the industry in the future.

underpin community oversight of companies adopting it, and as indicated earlier, ISO 14001 is seriously deficient in terms of community dialogue and disclosure. However, there is no reason, in principle, why regulators should not insist on dialogue with the local community, and disclosure of information as part of the *quid pro quo* for waiving regulatory requirements for ISO 14001 certified companies. Some regulators in the United States are currently contemplating versions of ISO 'Plus' which would do precisely this.[232] Central components of such a strategy are perceived to be: encouraging community participation; institutionalizing public participation; recognizing public knowledge; and utilizing cross-cultural formats and exchanges.[233]

The Australian State of Victoria is already achieving much the same result through the mechanism of Environmental Improvement Plans (EIPs), which form part of the Accredited Licence Scheme, described in chapter two. In return for regulatory flexibility, an accredited company agrees to implement an EMS, to conduct an environmental audit, and implement an EIP. The latter must include a written plan with 'a set of performance measures, monitoring requirements, and improvement proposals which take into account the economics of the company as well as environmental concerns'.[234] Crucially, for present purposes, it must also directly involve their local communities in the development and monitoring of the plan. In so doing, it arguably satisfies 'the multiple objectives of community right-to-know, clearly established milestones, corporate commitment to management system, improved measurement and an increase in trust between all parties'.[235] In the spirit of 'don't trust us—track us', it is arguable that a central component of such a strategy should be the provision by the enterprise to the community (and the regulator) of an annual non-compliance report, disclosing all major breaches during that period. Since workers (also

---

[232] The Environmental Leadership Program of the USEPA, while still evolving, apparently contemplates an environmental management system as its central component, with community outreach and employee involvement as critical elements of that system: a substantial step beyond ISO 14001 in its current form. see also Project XL, referred to at p.47 above.

[233] See National Environmental Justice Advisory Council, Public Participation and Accountability Subcommittee, *The Model Plan for Public Participation* (November 1996), National Environmental Justice Advisory Council, Washington DC.

[234] Environment Protection Authority (Victoria), *A Question of Trust: Accredited licensing concept* (July 1993), a discussion paper, Environment Protection Authority, Melbourne, p.10.

[235] D. Robinson, 'Public Participation in Environmental Decision Making' (1993) 10(5) *Environmental and Planning Law Journal* 320–40.

members of local communities) will commonly be aware of such breaches, the enterprise risks exposure if it under-reports.

However, one fundamental problem with community outreach programmes remains, namely whether community outreach programmes will ever serve to break down the layers of distrust between industrial facilities and those who live near them. The essential problem here is one of fundamental miscommunication between the two groups. Specifically, as Simmons and Wynne point out, the industry remains locked firmly into a paradigm of scientific knowledge as a basis for judgments and decision making (the Missionary stage, above) and fails to take account of the 'culturally embedded basis of public distrust, rooted in a pervasive consciousness of risk that has become characteristic of contemporary industrial cultures'.[236] Indeed, 'as long as the Responsible Care program is founded on the premise that furnishing the public with evidence of its improvement will rebuild trust in the chemical industry, it is unlikely to achieve the recuperation of public confidence that the CIA is hoping for'.[237]

4. Regulating at a distance: government as backstop

As we have indicated, there are serious risks that regulatory flexibility schemes implying greater autonomy for enterprises may be abused. For some who are granted such autonomy, the temptation to pursue short term economic self-interest, to cut corners and minimize costs at the expense of environmental considerations, is simply too great (particularly where commercial incentives to be 'green' are very limited). If these defectors are not appropriately dealt with, then the entire scheme may be undermined.

In the case of Responsible Care, we noted that there are serious free-rider/mutual assurance problems (here referred to as 'collective action' problems), and that the credibility of the programme may be threatened unless firms can be assured that their competitors will implement their obligations. Certainly, third party verification of independent performance indicators could enable companies to compare each others' performance, but moral persuasion such as this, while important, has manifestly proved insufficient to overcome collective action problems of

---

[236] P. Simmons & B. Wynne, 'Responsible Care: Trust, credibility and environmental management' in K. Fischer & J. Schot (eds.), *Environmental Strategies For Industry* (1993), Island Press, US.

[237] J. Ehrenfeld, *ISO 14000 and Responsible Care: What Kind of Change Agents Are They?* (1995), paper presented to ISO 14000: Preparing for Change Conference, Houston, Texas, September, p.10.

this magnitude.[238] So also, community pressure (which relies heavily upon the commitment and cohesiveness and indeed existence of local communities) has had a very uneven impact, and cannot be relied upon in isolation.

The conventional solution to the collective action problem involves coercing those who are unwilling to comply voluntarily.[239] That is, the voluntary compliance of the majority of firms may ultimately depend upon: 'the coercive imposition of the code of conduct on the minority of free-riders'.[240] State intervention is not the only conceivable way to ensure such coercion. It would be possible (as has occurred in the case of the United States nuclear power industry)[241] for the relevant industry association in each jurisdiction to take on a regulatory role—in effect, policing the activities of its members in complying with Responsible Care. However, the chemical industry associations have chosen not to do so, a decision that is most unlikely to be reversed given the hostility of most of their members to such a proposal.

Thus, government intervention will be necessary to ensure that the industry association performs its self-regulatory tasks honestly and effectively; to provide extra leverage where the industry association's efforts and powers are insufficient to change the behaviour of recalcitrants; to regulate the behaviour of those who refuse to participate in the self-regulatory scheme; and to intervene directly where the gap between industry self-interest and the public interest is too large for self-regulation alone to be a credible strategy.

That is, co-regulation, rather than self-regulation, may be the most viable way of preserving the considerable strengths of Responsible Care, while overcoming its collective action problems and restoring public trust. Co-regulation, in this context, means the existence of a degree of government regulation in combination with the self-initiated safeguards introduced by the industry itself under Responsible Care. Minimum (outcome-based) standards would continue to be set by government applying either generally or negotiated individually (e.g.,

---

[238] For example, moral persuasion also formed the basis for environmental responsibility under the Maquila Program, introduced by United States' President Johnson and Mexican President Dias in the 1960s (L. Burton, *Environmental Equity and NAFTA Implementation* (1994), a paper presented to Law and Society Association Meeting, 16–19 June, Phoenix, Arizona).

[239] G. Hardin, 'The Tragedy of the Commons' 162 *Science* 1243–48 at 1247.

[240] I. Maitland, 'The Limits of Business Self-Regulation' (1985) 27(3) *California Management Review* 132–47 at 136.

[241] J. V. Rees, *Hostages of Each Other: The transformation of nuclear safety since Three Mile Island* (1994), University of Chicago Press, Chicago.

pollution prevention measures agreed as a term of a licence, permit, or covenant).[242] Government would reserve the right to impose legal sanctions for breach where enterprises fail to live up to their promises. However, the day-to-day administration of these standards would be the responsibility of industry subject to third party audit, and community scrutiny, as described above.

Under this approach, government leaves to the industry and its association many of the details of how to improve its environmental performance (e.g., the Responsible Care codes of practice), but retains the full powers of the state (including those of enforcement and punishment), invoking them when necessary to deter free-riding or other abuses. Those who genuinely wish to improve their environmental performance beyond the legal norm are encouraged and facilitated to do so with a minimum of government intervention (including a waiver of the inspections and paperwork that firms normally confront, and the provision of incentives, as described in the next section below), but backsliders will continue to face the wrath of the state.

Co-regulation also implies that government must be willing to intervene directly in the affairs of those companies which have not agreed to participate in or defect from the self-regulatory scheme (which, in the case of Responsible Care, includes substantial numbers of smaller operators). It must ensure that non-participating companies are subjected to standards at least as tough as those adopted by participating companies, so that the former do not gain a short-term competitive advantage by refusing to join the self-regulatory programme.[243]

The appropriate approach to the regulatory flexibility bestowed upon those who agree to adopt EMSs, such as ISO 14001, would in many respects be similar. Here, there is no relevant industry association, no credible form of collective self-regulation, and no collective action problems of the type described above. One is dealing with individual enterprises who, in effect, agree to self-regulate in accordance with a management system approach in return for regulatory flexibility. But just as with Responsible Care, so with ISO 14001, there will be risks of abuse such as the adoption of cosmetic 'paper systems' to gain regulatory concessions, public relations, or other perceived advantages.

[242] See p.41.

[243] Consistent with this approach, the Victorian EPA has indicated that it will monitor very closely any company that refused to join Responsible Care or was expelled for failing to come up to standard (R. Smithers, 'Chemical Firms Adopt Code to Clean Up the Industry' (1989) *The Age* 27 September, p.5.

Here, the central policy questions are: how can enterprises be prevented or deterred from abusing regulatory flexibility schemes in this way, and how will regulators or courts be able to distinguish between paper systems and the genuine article? As regards this latter problem, many prosecutors in the United States have doubted 'both the utility of compliance plans and their own ability to distinguish serious efforts at compliance from merely cosmetic plans',[244] at least in the context of a sentence hearing. The problems are readily apparent. For example, in the United States, agreement to introduce corporate compliance plans (including a commitment to a systems-based approach) can lead to a sentence reduction in respect of environmental crime. Here, the experience is that these plans are easily manipulated, with: 'a virtual cottage industry of law firms cranking out compliance plans for their corporate clients (often with the mechanical uniformity of a cookie cutter)'[245] leading one to doubt that adoption of such plans would have much beneficial impact on corporate behaviour, at least until clear minimum criteria are prescribed.

At this stage, we do not have the experience to know how seriously or how extensively firms may abuse privileges given in return for regulatory flexibility under either Responsible Care 'Plus' or ISO 'Plus'. But given the obvious temptations and the experience of related areas, it seems likely that agency strategies to counter this problem will be essential to the successful operation of either approach. This is particularly the case since third party oversight, while important, has its own limitations, identified above. For example, auditors may be less than vigilant, or vulnerable to capture by the very industries they audit; communities may be apathetic, or lacking in any genuine sense; trading partners may settle for formal certification of a management system without insisting on genuine improvements in environmental performance. That is, the additional layers of oversight, scrutiny, and informal social control, which we have argued for, will be important, and capable of taking much of the weight off government, but are likely to be uneven in their impact and less than fully effective. As such, it would be a serious mistake to rely upon them in isolation. Indeed, as we will argue, an underpinning of government control will be absolutely essential to overcome the temptation to cheat.

[244] J. C. Coffee, 'Environmental Crime and Punishment' (1994) *New York Law Journal* (Thursday February 3) 10.

[245] J. C. Coffee, 'No Soul to Damn: No Body to Kick: An unscandalized inquiry into the problem of corporate punishment' (1981) 79 *Michigan Law Review* 386.

When should the regulator intervene to ensure that regulatory flexibility under Responsible Care is working effectively, or that management systems are being complied with, and that an enterprise, through intent, inefficiency, or incapacity, is not failing to discharge its obligations, as measured by agreed performance indicators? And how can such intervention as is needed be designed so as to avoid unnecessary intrusion into the details of how an enterprise conducts itself, while at the same time (given the resources problems indicated earlier) minimizing the burden on regulatory resources, and ensuring that agency intervention is within its budgetary and administrative capability?

To achieve these goals, regulatory design should involve a tiered regulatory response. First, it should encourage enterprises to regulate themselves (for example, one of the prerequisites will be that the EMS is self-referential and self-correcting). Secondly, comes third party oversight, both at the stage of accrediting the system when it is introduced, and through subsequent periodic audits. Thus, the third party audit fulfils a substantial role as surrogate regulator. Communities, empowered with information, direct channels of communication to regulated enterprises, and (at least under Responsible Care) a role in the decision-making process itself, also contribute as a countervailing force, while pressure from trading partners, and peer group pressure, act as informal social control. However, there is also need for a third tier, involving an underpinning of government regulation. This would 'kick in' *as a backup mechanism* in circumstances where there is reason to believe that tiers one and two have not delivered the required outcomes in terms of system-effectiveness and improvements in environmental performance. As a result, enterprises participating in Responsible Care or an EMS, would be spared onerous, time consuming routine inspections.

What circumstances might be appropriate to trigger an inspection? Five are suggested, though others may evolve once a scheme is in operation:

(i)   if a community representative, having exhausted internal procedures, complains that the audit was not, in his/her view, fair and accurate;

(ii)   if the third party audit report itself expresses serious reservations about the effectiveness of the EMS;

(iii) if a regulator's verification of the third party audit (conducted randomly on a small minority of audits) suggests that the audit itself was not fair and accurate;

(iv) if there is a serious accident or incident, or a series of complaints from workers or local communities (although there would need to be safeguards against vexatious complaints); and

(v) if the relevant industry association requests such intervention.

The attraction of the approach we propose is that government retains a role in ensuring that prescribed environmental outcomes are achieved, but does not resort to inflexible, costly, prescriptive, and legalistic mechanisms to do so. Rather, those parts of industry that demonstrate that they can be trusted to self-regulate, are left to decide for themselves precisely how they should improve their environmental performance by devising their own internal regulatory mechanisms best suited to achieve those ends. This has the considerable virtue of encouraging more cost-effective and innovative industry responses than under technology-based 'command and control' regulation.

Thus, government would only regulate 'at a distance', exercising an oversight role rather than directly policing industry performance. This would involve periodic review of the results of companies' self-monitoring,[246] and summaries of the proposed third party audits. The latter would be a crucial independent indicator of whether outcomes are indeed being achieved by individual operators. Government would also take account of complaints against Responsible Care members (or against individual companies who adopt EMS), and of community consultative mechanisms in determining whether self-regulation was working satisfactorily.[247]

Inspections of companies subscribing to Responsible Care or committing to an EMS, would become a low administrative priority or would be discontinued, leaving government free to redeploy its scarce regulatory resources and focus on these companies (often the worst polluters) who have refused to participate in co-regulation under one of these approaches. Government would continue to regulate these companies directly, through regular inspections, reinforced by administrative measures and criminal prosecution.

---

[246] This would include how far the company meets the performance indicators currently being developed under Responsible Care.

[247] In the USA, these include Community Advisory Panels, and, in Australia, community and industry consultative committees.

5. Incentives for enterprise participation in regulatory flexibility

Finally, even if government insists on all the requirements, identified in previous sections, as the *quid pro quo* for granting regulatory flexibility under ISO 14001 or Responsible Care 'Plus', little will be achieved unless enterprises are convinced that the benefits of committing themselves to such approaches are likely to outweigh the costs. Indeed, a number of regulatory redesign initiatives have faltered or failed because there were too few takers.[248] This raises the question: is it necessary or desirable for governments to provide positive incentives to enterprises to participate in regulatory flexibility programmes, and if so, what should those incentives be?

In the case of Responsible Care, there are compelling reasons of industry self-interest (the need to rebuild community trust, maintain legitimacy, and thereby secure the long-term future of the industry) why the industry has devoted considerable resources to establishing and making the programme effective. Moreover, for some companies, Responsible Care has also brought some tangible rewards in terms of reduced waste management, clean up and disposal costs, reduced liability risk, and improved insurance premiums, as well as enhanced community relations. While government can do a great deal to integrate Responsible Care into a broader co-regulatory scheme and to compensate for its weaknesses, government played no significant role in developing the programmr or in encouraging companies to join it. Nor, given the circumstances of its evolution, did it need to. However, if, as we have argued above, regulatory flexibility should be offered to Responsible Care firms not just because they have committed themselves to that programme but also because they have met additional requirements prescribed by government, such as performance outcomes, independent verification, and disclosure (Responsible Care 'Plus') then even these firms may need incentives to participate.

ISO 14001 and EMSs approaches, generally, present a different challenge. As we have indicated, the decision whether to adopt an EMS is one for an individual enterprise without any role or intervention by an industry association. Unlike Responsible Care, there is no sense in which the industry perceives ISO 14001 as a solution to collective

---

[248] For example, the Victorian Accredited Licensing Scheme (which includes a 25 per cent license fee reduction, the offer of a bubble license, and less onerous conventional inspection) had, after 18 months in operation, attracted only a handful of participants, and many of the Reinventing Environmental Regulation initiatives in the USA are experiencing similar problems.

action problems or as a way of addressing the issue of 'communities of shared fate'. It is not, in any sense, a proposed solution to the problem that the industry's reputation and possible future viability 'is only as strong as its weakest link'. Accordingly, the decision whether to adopt such a system is likely to be individual, commercially-based, and driven substantially by trade considerations. And it will be made in the context that ISO certification will cost in the order of US$10,000 to $30,000 a year and involve the commitment of very considerable time and resources within the enterprise. That is, enterprises are only likely to adopt a management systems approach if they perceive it is in their individual self-interest to do so, but not otherwise: peer group and industry association pressure are conspicuously lacking in the case of ISO 14001.

So are incentives for participating in regulatory flexibility programmes necessary? According to one school of thought, the answer is no. On this view, it has now become rational for enterprises not only to comply with existing law but also to move 'beyond compliance' with existing legislation.[249] It is asserted that the business community can combine the objectives of environmental protection and economic growth, and in so doing, not only ease the pressures imposed by regulators, the public and the financial community, but also to increase profits directly and to develop the environmental technology to compete effectively in the global environmental market. That is, according to its proponents, going 'beyond compliance' is both good for business and good for the environment—there is a happy coincidence between private profit and public interest. Companies going down this path will increase profits, enhance their corporate image, position themselves to realize new environment-related market opportunities, generally improve efficiency and quality, foster a greater consumer acceptance of their company and products, and reduce potential legal liability. The fact that ISO 14001 certification may become almost a prerequisite for some forms of international trade should also incline enterprises to adopt the standard voluntarily.

Moreover, if a firm may gain a competitive advantage by embracing regulatory flexibility (e.g., if devising an alternative compliance strategy enables it to compete more effectively on price or quality and capture greater market share), then arguably it must do so for fear that

---

[249] See, generally, N. Gunningham, *Beyond Compliance: Management of environmental risk* in B. Boer, R. Fowler & N. Gunningham, (eds.), *Environmental Outlook: Law and policy* (1994), ACEL, Federation Press, Sydney, and references therein.

otherwise its competitors may recognize this opportunity and gain an advantage by embracing it first.

If all of this is indeed correct, then enterprises have a natural self interest in embracing regulatory flexibility, and in adopting EMSs, whether under ISO or Responsible Care, because of their promise to deliver continuous improvement and 'best practice' environmental management and performance.[250] In particular, a systems-based approach has the capacity to shift enterprises from a purely reactive strategy of, at best, grudging compliance with government regulation, to a proactive response, which involves going 'beyond compliance' and internalizing the environmental challenge as an element of quality management.[251] If so, they should not object to the performance indicators, verification, or other requirements government might impose as a *quid pro quo* for regulatory flexibility (though it should be noted the latter impose requirements well beyond what is required under ISO 14001 certification, and require companies to do much more than will be necessary to use ISO in international trade).

All this sounds too good to be true, and it is. Regrettably, there are limits to the 'win-win' approach and to the natural self-interest of enterprises in going 'beyond compliance' voluntarily. Specifically, there are conditions under which the economic benefits of investing in environmental protection are tenuous or non-existent, and where the costs to business of implementing environmental protection measures (and EMSs) will not be offset by any resulting savings from improved economic performance.

We have already identified the emphasis of corporations, and individual managers,[252] on short-term profitability as being a serious problem.[253] Because corporations are judged by markets, investors, and others principally on short-term performance, they have difficulty justifying investment in environmentally benign technologies or management systems, which usually pay off only in the long term, and sometimes not in ways readily demonstrated in a corporate profit and

---

[250] See further, Australian Manufacturing Council (AMC), Best Practice Environmental Management, (1992), AMC, Melbourne.

[251] This analysis is based on P. Winsemius and U. Guntram, 'The Environmental Challenge' (1992) *Business Horizons*, March/April, p.12.

[252] Individual managers too will be judged essentially on short-term performance, and if they cannot demonstrate tangible economic success in the here and now, there may be no long term to look forward to.

[253] See note 109.

loss account.[254] Moreover, the very process of seeking Responsible Care or ISO 'Plus' recognition under regulatory flexibility will consume very considerable company resources, not least being the time of executives involved in negotiating this, and the additional obligations implied in achieving the 'plus'.

If this analysis is correct, then what role is there for incentives to participate in regulatory flexibility? We are confronted with a situation where enterprises sometimes have a direct incentive to go 'beyond compliance', and others where they do not. Even in the former circumstances, experience suggests that enterprises cannot be relied upon to do what is in both their economic and society's environmental interests.[255] For example, there are a variety of reasons (including bounded rationality,[256] lack of information and appropriate accounting methods,[257] rate of technological change and pursuit of short-term profit) why they may not do so.

If government takes no steps to encourage regulatory flexibility, then experience suggests that only a very limited group of enterprises will opt for this approach. Some may prefer regulatory flexibility because they are already committed to going beyond compliance and such flexibility will better facilitate their doing so, or because of the autonomy that this option promises, or for reasons of improved public profile rather than because of any direct economic return. However, for those seeking to maximize economic returns, the take up rate may be disappointing because most benefits will only manifest themselves in the longer term. Thus many, concerned with short-termism, will be disinclined to grasp the opportunities available, particularly given the start up costs involved (for example, in establishing a management system). And even many firms who might gain a competitive advantage from improved environmental performance will not realize this. Thus, if

---

[254] This indeed, is a major reason why full cost accounting is likely to be crucial to corporations going beyond compliance. Of course, some commitment to environmental priorities will have short-term pay-offs. Improvements in waste reduction, in good housekeeping, in saving energy, in eliminating excessive packaging, even in alternative materials purchase, will feed back directly into corporate profits—but even here, while the first 25 per cent improvement may be quite easily achieved, the next 25 per cent may prove far more challenging.

[255] See J. Romm, *Lean and Clean Management: How to boost profits and productivity by reducing pollution* (1994), Kodansha America, New York; and M. Porter, *The Competitive Advantage of Nations* (1990), Macmillan Press, London, who both provide evidence that there are huge untapped efficiencies to be gained from improved environmental performance.

[256] H. Simon, *Economics, Bounded Rationality and the Cognitive Revolution* (1992) Edward Elgar, UK, p.3.

[257] See p.62.

regulatory flexibility programmes are to not only reward the minority who will do the right thing anyway, but also to induce a much larger, pragmatically minded group, to sign on, it must incorporate a significant range of incentives.

All of this suggests that there remains an important role for government in providing enterprises with financial incentives (which, at the margin, may be crucial), and in other ways encouraging a re-ordering of corporate priorities in order to reap the benefits of improved environmental performance. That is, where it is not necessarily apparent to enterprises whether they are in a win-win situation, government should try and shift the goalposts to achieve this result—by removing the obstacles to improved profitability (greater regulatory flexibility), by providing positive incentives to embrace such flexibility,[258] and by enabling firms to recognize the gains they may make (through information strategies and facilitating full cost accounting[259]). This last role need not be played by government alone, and indeed in some circumstances, is more convincingly played by the private sector.[260]

In particular, we emphasize the role that government can play in designing positive incentives to encourage those at the margin to embrace regulatory flexibility, with its accompanying commitments to systems-based regulation likely to build in continual improvement and cultural change. Without these incentives, many firms may find insufficient reason to 'get over the hump': the initial investment and commitment to a systems-based approach, which may be very considerable. There are a considerable range of credible options for encouraging enterprises to adopt regulatory flexibility, with the obligations that entails, including:

---

[258] Would another option be to make adoption of ISO 1400 mandatory? Such an approach would be highly inappropriate. ISO 14001 has many shortcomings, as described earlier. It was, moreover, designed as a voluntary system, rather than as a regulatory one. Certainly, it might usefully become a component of a broader regulatory approach but to make its use mandatory (for example, for certain sectors or for firms above a certain size) in isolation could achieve little, and would be counterproductive in imposing a straightjacket on those who might prefer to achieve environmental objectives though other means (e.g. Responsible Care). Making ISO 14001 compulsory, even in conjunction with a range of other requirements, would also be overambitious, given the demands on regulatory resources. Nevertheless, there may be circumstances, in respect of particular hazardous industries, where a mandatory systems based approach (which could include but should not be limited to ISO 14001), in conjunction with performance measures and other requirements, may be justified. The safety case regime for off shore oil is such a case.

[259] See chapter two above.   [260] See further chapter five at p.337.

- administrative benefits, such as easing off on regular inspections[261] for enterprises who agree to participate in regulatory flexibility, or blitzing recalcitrants who choose not to;

- logo or other publicity or public relations benefits;

- reduced fees under the licensing system and fast-tracking of permit/licence applications;

- a safe haven for participating enterprises who self-identify breaches of regulation (other than serious breaches involving imminent danger), notify the regulator and make timely correction of deficiencies;

- single multi-media permit for participating facilities (which provides considerable flexibility and efficiencies) and minimize paperwork, or, in the case of specialty manufacturers in particular, less onerous permit requirements each time they begin a new batch chemical process;[262]

- making participation a condition for tendering for major government contracts;

- subsidies to 'kick start' a systems-based approach in firms which, by reason of their size, economic circumstances, or other factors, would otherwise be unlikely to adopt regulatory flexibility (*cf.* Victorian Cleaner Production Partnership Program):[263] and

- reductions in penalties if prosecutions take place, or an option to report and correct deficiencies in lieu of prosecution.

All the above incentives are intended as direct inducements to adopt regulatory flexibility provisions. There are, of course, other types of incentives, which have the broader effect of expanding the category of

[261] For example, participating enterprises might be designated as a low priority for inspections.

[262] One particularly important incentive in the case of specialty manufacturers would be a waiver of the existing requirement to obtain a new permit or permit modification every time they embark upon a new batch process (using chemicals for which they have already been granted a permit) rather than merely notify the agency of the new circumstances. This substantially slows their ability to get a new product to market. Flexibility in this area would provide considerable attractions to such firms.

[263] Note that federal government has been providing financial assistance to SMEs to implement EMS, focussing particularly on cleaner production and waste minimization. See, in particular, the Environment Protection Authority's Cleaner Production Demonstration Program and the National Environment Industries Database.

'win-win' situations, which make it more profitable for business to behave in environmentally beneficial ways.

We examined these mechanisms in chapter two and here refer back to those types of incentives that are compatible with the type of regulatory flexibility regime we propose. These include a range of positive price-based instruments, or supply side incentives, which push back the point at which environmental improvements are no longer financially viable. Supply side incentives refer to direct or indirect payments, including tax concession and subsidies, conditional upon desired conduct. For example, they might include tax concessions for the purchase of environmental preferable technology, tax deductions for the expenses of environmentally responsible activity, and lower taxes for preferred products or materials. The OECD Technology Environment Programme (1995) found that 'natural technological evolution occurring in industry has not forced environmentally protective technologies to be designed or employed. Governments will need to promote cleaner production and products'.[264]

Alternatively, government may invoke negative incentives, such as taxes and charges, which also attach a price signal to environmentally preferable behaviour and/or technologies. Although it is debatable as to whether imposing the potential for new costs actually creates a win-win situation, in terms of the firm's bottom line, price signals should be as equally effective whether they are positive or negative. They may also induce the development of innovative solutions as firms strive to reduce costs. In a similar fashion, the removal of perverse economic incentives can also encourage cost driven environmentally improvements by making it less financially attractive to persist with previously sanctioned harmful behaviour. The extent to which price-based economic instruments foster 'beyond compliance' outcomes will depend on the size of the price signal employed in relation to the prevailing minimum regulatory performance standards.

One way of enhancing the prospects of firms participating in regulatory flexibility arrangements would be to make any positive financial incentives exclusive to 'track two'. Similarly, track two firms could be given exemptions, for example in the form of a tax rebate, from negative price signals.

The various forms of market creation, such as tradeable emission permits, may, in principle, also provide companies with an incentive to

---

[264] OECD 1995 Technologies for Cleaner Production and Products: Towards Technological Transformation for Sustainable Development, OECD Paris.

implement innovative and lateral solutions to pollution reduction. However, it may be difficult or impossible to successfully integrate such instruments where there is an existing sector-specific regulatory regime in place, as is the case with the chemicals sector with its Responsible Care programme and myriad command and control regulations.[265]

Despite the potential difficulties of using tradeable permits in combination with existing policy instruments, in this instance, there are still some useful features related to market-based instruments that could be effectively seconded to the cause of regulatory flexibility. In particular, bubble licences and the ability to net or bank credits within firms could be further incentives offered to track two companies. The level of pollution created by industrial processes will fluctuate in accordance with changing market circumstances, and, for larger firms, across different industrial sites. Providing firms with the ability to accommodate such fluctuations through bubble licenses and/or banking credits overcomes some of the rigidities associated with conventional command and control regulation. They can, further, be used to balance variations across different polluting media.

Disincentives to participate in regulatory flexibility   There is a serious, and as yet, largely unrecognized hazard in designing regulatory innovation, namely that while regulatory flexibility is intended to remove unnecessary, time consuming and costly 'green tape', it may, in practice, replace it with equally demanding alternative requirements. That is, so many new conditions may be imposed as the price for regulatory flexibility as to make the transition from conventional regulation to regulatory innovation, unappealing to business. By making 'the conditions of entry into more flexible regulatory regimes too stringent, regulators risk discouraging entry'.[266] Significantly, a number of regulatory

---

[265] This is because tradeable permit regimes work best when there are large differences in the marginal cost of abatement within and between industrial sectors. That way, there is a stronger incentive for firms to actually engage in trading, thus lowering the overall cost of pollution abatement. The necessary consequence of trading is, however, that some firms, where the marginal cost of abatement is highest, will end up increasing their emissions, relative to the industry average. Such an outcome may well be incompatible with their obligations under Responsible Care or indeed any minimum performance standards that may exist. Finally, it would be difficult and indeed economically undesirable, to distinguish between firms participating in a permits scheme.

[266] For example, Pederson gives the example of proposals for regulatory capping, which would require 'capped' sources to adopt pollution prevention programmes to reduce their emissions over time. He notes that 'the tighter and more detailed the baseline specifications, the fewer caps there will be, and the less room existing caps will allow for pollution prevention' (W. F. Pederson, 'Can Site Specific Pollution Control Plans

innovations have achieved only a very lukewarm reception from the very business community which had called for them.

There are a number of ways in which these problems can be overcome. First, the incentives for participating in regulatory innovation must, demonstrably, far exceed the disincentives. This means ensuring that the stringency of entry conditions required by innovative schemes is not such as to make them unattractive to would be participants. As Pederson argues, to the extent that pollution prevention is more effective than insisting on the letter of existing regulations, then even relatively lenient entry conditions will lead, in the end, to greater overall emission reductions.[267] Secondly, care should be taken by government to provide positive incentives for entry into such schemes (e.g., economic benefits; the award of environmental logos and other public relations benefits; priority under government procurement schemes, as described above). Moreover, the greater the flexibility that government provides within such schemes, the greater will be the opportunity for innovation and cost saving by business. For example, where practicable, government should facilitate the use of bubbles, netting, banking, and other economic related mechanisms geared to providing flexibility. The consultation requirements for entering such a scheme, while important, must also be kept within bounds. Participants in a range of 'reinventing government' initiatives complain of the enormous burden and level of resources required to negotiate such programmes and participation within them. Finally, the disincentives for breach of conventional regulation, including shaming, penalties, and enforcement, must be sufficiently substantial as to encourage business to seek more palatable alternatives. At present, in many jurisdictions, inadequate enforcement currently plays a major part in businesses' lack of enthusiasm for embracing regulatory innovations.[268]

Furnish an Alternative to the Current Regulatory System and a Bridge to a New One?' (1995) 25 *Environmental Law Review* 10486).

[267] W. F. Pederson, 'Can Site Specific Pollution Control Plans Furnish an Alternative to the Current Regulatory System and a Bridge to a New One?' (1995) 25 *Environmental Law Review* 10486.

[268] The Australian approach is found in N. Gunningham, 'Negotiated Compliance— a Case of Regulatory Failure' (1987) 9 *Law and Policy* 69; and D. Farrier, 'Policy Instruments for Conserving Biodiversity on Private Land' in J. Bradstoock, (ed.), *Conserving Biodiversity: Threats and solutions* (1995), Surrey Beatty & Sons, Chipping Norton.

Can commercial third parties reinforce the role of regulatory flexibility?

In chapter three, we identified the potentially very significant and far reaching contributions that commercial third parties can make to environmental protection and indicated the potential roles of the main institutions involved. In this section, we will argue that, although not a prerequisite for 'regulating at a distance', there is much to be gained from harnessing the capacities of commercial entities to act as surrogate regulators. As we shall see, in the context of the chemical industry, commercial actors can exert considerable pressures on each other, in terms of insisting on certain environmental credentials and standards.

Utilizing supply chain pressure

By far the greatest pressure is likely to be exerted by trading partners. For example, large companies, in particular, can insist on their upstream suppliers meeting certain environmental standards. Large companies can thus act as surrogate regulators. They may also bring pressure to bear on downstream purchasers or consumers to use their product in an environmentally responsible manner, as we will see when examining Responsible Care's product stewardship Code of Practice, below.

Here, we are concerned with mechanisms having the capacity to influence the environmental behaviour of large firms and of reinforcing regulatory flexibility. Both Responsible Care and ISO 14001 incorporate such mechanisms. Responsible Care uses not only peer group pressure, mutual support, and the sharing of information, but also the Product Stewardship code to bring commercial pressure to bear from one company to another. We deal with product stewardship in some detail when examining strategies for dealing with small players, below. In the case of ISO 14001, supply chain pressure is a central driver of conformance certification. Indeed, if the experience of its quality standard predecessor, ISO 9000, is repeated, then ISO 14001 certification will become a condition of many customer/client contracts, inducing many enterprises close to the market to embrace ISO 14001 when they might otherwise have chosen not to do so. This may extend to many bilateral and multilateral relations.

This development does not require any intervention from government, except to the extent that government itself is a major customer for many manufacturers, and that governments, no less than private institutions, can choose to use their considerable purchasing power to support ISO 14001 certification by making it a requisite for their suppliers. However, directly or indirectly, government has a close interest in how ISO 14001 and Responsible Care evolve, since these vehicles are likely to be central in delivering effective regulatory flexibility. Given the potentially crucial role that supply chain pressure could play in enhancing the effectiveness of these mechanisms, and in acting as a partial surrogate for government regulation, it is arguable that government should intervene directly, making it a regulatory requirement that major enterprises capable of playing such a role have responsibility to ensure that upstream suppliers and downstream buyers comply with their regulatory responsibilities in respect of those products.

ISO 14001 already requires the certified enterprise to comply with existing legal requirements, and this may serve to pull some suppliers up to the minimum legal standard. It also requires evidence of continual improvement, and, where an enterprise has already signed on to another set of environmental commitments, requires compliance with those principles.[269] It will be interesting to see how seriously certifiers treat these requirements in follow up audits.

However, whether ISO certification will result in a substantial improvement in the environmental performance of those certified is uncertain. To the extent that suppliers treat the establishment of a management system seriously, and provide the resources and the commitment necessary for effective implementation, then environmental improvements are likely to follow, but such a response is by no means guaranteed. Rather, many suppliers may view certification as simply one more hoop through which they must jump to stay competitive. If so, this may produce a more cynical response of simply doing the minimum to gain certification, without the ongoing commitment necessary to bring about substantial organizational and environmental change. Here, the audit capacity of buyers may prove crucial, for it is through this vehicle that they may be capable of subjecting their suppliers to strict scrutiny.

Insurance and financing   Rapidly escalating insurance rates was one of the motivations for introducing Responsible Care in the first place, for the chemical industry's track record of fires and explosions resulted in its being treated unfavourably as a risk.[270] Indeed, several

---

[269] For example, CERES; Responsible Care, etc.

[270] See S. Schmidheiny and F. Zorraquin, *Financing Change: The Financial Community, Eco-Efficiency and Sustainable Development* (1996), MIT Press.

insurance companies had refused coverage for this reason, and the insurance industry, as a whole, has become reluctant to provide gradual pollution coverage (i.e., coverage for environmental impairment liabilities arising from anything other than an accident). However, Responsible Care companies, particularly in Canada, are now receiving favoured treatment from the insurance industry. Rates are being reduced from what they would otherwise have been, and, in one documented case, a major insurer has indicated they will reduce premiums by 50 per cent if sound management systems are in place.[271] The rationale is that such a company will be more likely to be successful and less likely to become liable for damage caused to the environment.

Similarly, the banking industry has been extremely concerned that they might face environmental liability for chemical contamination clean up, a fear that, in the case of the United States CERCLA [272] has already been realized. The result could well be that capital for companies manufacturing or using hazardous chemicals would become either unavailable or extremely expensive. Again, the Canadian experience, at least, is that Responsible Care companies now have 'several points' deducted from their project financing rates.[273]

However, none of these developments flow naturally from market forces, or as a result of Responsible Care alone. Take the case of environmental insurance. For such insurance to be a viable proposition, the insurance industry needs the capacity to identify and quantify the risk: to estimate the probability that individuals and/or the environment will be affected by a particular activity, the severity of those affects, and their legal implications.[274] And it needs to be able to do this in respect of each class of customers[275].

In the past, these conditions have rarely been satisfied and the fragile environmental insurance market has not flourished. Some attention has been given to the role that government could play in creating those conditions. For example, Freeman and Kunreuther have argued that

[271] See Canadian Chemical Producers Association, *Does Responsible Care Work?* (May 1996), Canadian Chemical Producers Association, Ottawa, p7.

[272] Above, pp.116–117.

[273] See Canadian Chemical Producers Association, *Does Responsible Care Work?* (May 1996), Canadian Chemical Producers Association, Ottawa, p.8.

[274] See further P. Freeman & R. Kunreuther, *Managing Environmental Risk Through Insurance* (1997), Kluwer/American Enterprise Institute.

[275] For an account of how insurers might employ environmental performance measurement in risk reduction strategies, see D. A. Henderson 'Lending Abroad: The role of voluntary international environmental management standards' *J. of Commercial Lending*, July 1 1997, at 47.

what is required is that government set well specified standards and give predicability to that market.[276] If the legal conditions are well established and clearly specified and not subject to frequent change then insurers can not only better predict the legal implications (and the costs to themselves) of environmental damage caused by their clients, they can also police those risks more effectively. Thus the insurers' own inspectors can scrutinize their client's compliance and impose sanctions (e.g., they can cancel the insurance policy if the legally prescribed standard have been contravened). In effect, their inspectors can inspect using the legal standard as their yardstick, and calculate the risks in terms of it.

In the case of Responsible Care, the industry associations were unsuccessful in persuading the insurance industry to give discounted premiums to Responsible Care companies on the basis that those companies were likely to be at substantially lower risk than non-member companies. Understandably, the industry was more than reluctant to rely on the only evidence available that that was indeed the case: the self-reporting of Responsible Care companies of their compliance with the programme codes. However, the introduction of independent audits in Canada, as described above, has brought about a significant change in their attitude. The insurance industry (or at least significant parts of it) has now, apparently, been persuaded that there is sufficient *independent* evidence of improved performance on the part of those companies as to either offer insurance where it would not have done so before or to offer substantially discounted premiums to Responsible Care companies.

While there remains the danger that some Responsible Care companies may still not achieve to the performance level the programme anticipates, the introduction of independent audits (even in the absence of demonstrable performance outcomes) reduces this risk substantially. It is not necessary for the insurance industry to be sure that all Responsible Care companies meet the higher standard, merely that *on average* they do, so that, as a class, lower premiums can rationally and profitably be offered to them. However, were better performance indicators to be developed and companies audited against them, as suggested above, then even greater opportunities for reduced premiums for best practice companies would be available.

---

[276] P. Freeman & R. Kunreuther, *Managing Environmental Risk Through Insurance* (1997), Kluwer/American Enterprise Institute.

While ISO 14001, in its current form, may well have too many short-comings for it to be similarly relied upon,[277] it is quite conceivable that ISO 'Plus' (the ISO standard together with sufficient add-ons as to make it a credible alternative regulatory path) could be used in this manner. Banks and insurance companies may, in the future, require ISO certification (with additions) as a requisite to lending and provision of environmental insurance (or discount of premiums) respectively. To the extent that governments can encourage and facilitate such developments by the sorts of means indicated above, then there are strong reasons for their doing so, for as a result, there will be both increased incentives for improved environmental performance by individual enterprises, and a reduced burden on government resources.

Strategies for regulating smaller players

The second and third groups identified earlier, (suppliers, and specialty chemical manufacturers upstream; purchasers and distributors downstream) present particular regulatory problems. Some participants in the chemical products supply chain are small in size, lacking in environmental specialization, skills or even awareness of many of the environmental problems that their handing of hazardous products can cause. Commonly, such firms present the biggest headaches to government regulators. They are so numerous as to be hard to keep track of, and are inspected only very infrequently, yet because of their lack of environmental awareness, skills and specialized resources (coupled in some cases by economic marginality) they are amongst the least likely candidates for effective self-regulation.[278]

Some specialty chemical manufacturers present particular problems. Some of these companies too, have very narrow profit margins. Most are of modest size and some lack economic or technological sophistication. These problems are compounded by the fact that chemical manufacturing is capital intensive. For small firms, there may be insufficient capital available for environmental or other improvements.[279]

---

[277] P. Freeman & R. Kunreuther, 'The Roles of Insurance and Well-Specified Standards in Dealing with Environmental Risks' (1996) 17 *Managerial and Decision Economics* 517–530.

[278] Distributors can be distinguished to some extent: they act rather like regional supermarkets, buying in bulk supplying in smaller quantities within a particular area: in some cases custom blending, and in others, repackaging, for smaller customers. Some of these companies are quite large and the sub-sector, as a whole, is profitable, with few players likely to be experiencing significant economic difficulties.

[279] President's Council on Sustainable Development, Eco-Efficiency Task Force, *Chemical Operations Demonstration Project* (February 1995), Washington DC, p.24.

They are also beset by particular environmental challenges intrinsic in the production of specialty chemicals. To remain competitive, these firms must respond rapidly to requests to customer demand, and the sorts of orders they must fill varies greatly. The result is that they must produce a large number of batch chemicals, adjusting continually in response to their market. Their pattern of raw material usage, equipment configurations, and waste streams is very different from that of the large companies described earlier.[280] And because of their modest size, they have far fewer human and economic resources to deal with the environmental problems this type of production spawns, or to devote to regulatory compliance.[281]

For all these reasons, most of these firms are unlikely candidates for regulatory flexibility programmes (though a minority might be capable of meeting the requirements of such programmes, and may be attracted to them if appropriate incentives are provided.[282] A substantial number of them may, currently, fall below the regulatory standard, let alone industry 'best practice'. Their interest in and capacity to go 'beyond compliance' by developing new and innovative solutions to their environmental problems is, in most cases, very doubtful.[283] They are also less amenable to a number of 'pressure points' which can be utilized successfully against large enterprises. For instance, smaller enterprises will tend to have a much lower public profile than larger firms and will, therefore, be far less susceptible to measures which attempt to harness community pressure.

So how should such groups be regulated and what instrument and policy mix is likely to be most appropriate to their circumstances? It must be acknowledged that government regulation is becoming much more sophisticated in dealing with such groups. In contrast to the older approach, which was characterized by chronic under-enforcement cou-

---

[280] President's Council on Sustainable Development, Eco-Efficiency Task Force, *Chemical Operations Demonstration Project* (February 1995), Washington DC, p.23.

[281] *Ibid.* at p.24.

[282] One particularly important incentive in the case of specialty manufacturers would be a waiver of the existing requirement to obtain a new permit or permit modification every time they embark upon a new batch process (using chemicals for which they have already been granted a permit), rather than merely notify the agency of the new circumstances. This substantially slows their ability to get a new product to market. Flexibility in this area would provide considerable attractions to such firms.

[283] Note their limited ability to identify and implement changes that might take them beyond compliance (e.g., pollution prevention audits, assessment of innovative technologies, systematic self-evaluation) which require both money and expertise.

pled with sporadic and unsophisticated education campaigns, some recent innovations show considerably more promise. These include:

- compliance assistance programmes under which small businesses have regulatory requirements explained in plain English, cost-effective environmental protection and waste reduction opportunities identified, technical assistance provided, and paperwork reduced;[284]

- compliance incentives which recognize that many smaller businesses want to be good citizens, but fear asking for information for fear of possible enforcement action. Incentive programmes provide small businesses which are minor sources of pollution with a grace period of up to six months to correct violations identified by compliance assistance programmes.[285] Environmental audit policies, in particular, can provide incentives for self-policing, encouraging enterprises to identify their environmental problems and opportunities, and to take corrective action;[286]

- compliance plans designed to take account of the fact that: 'improving environmental performance takes time, and not all existing industries will be in a position to implement improvements immediately'.[287] An enterprise may face practical difficulties in complying with a particular provision introduced by new legislation. A compliance plan is intended as a means of ensuring incremental improvements to bring the enterprise up to the legal standard within a given time;[288]

[284] See W. J. Clinton & A. Gore Jr., *Reinventing Environmental Regulation* (1995), White House, Washington DC, p.31.

[285] See W. J. Clinton & A. Gore Jr., *Reinventing Environmental Regulation* (1995), White House, Washington DC, p.30; and US EPA, *Policy on Compliance Incentives for Small Business*, (1996) May 20, US EPA, Washington DC.

[286] See for example, the US EPA's final policy on incentives for self-evaluation and self-disclosure of violations, Federal Register, Dec 22, 1996 (60 FR 66706).

[287] Northern Territory Department of Lands, Planning and Environment, information kit on Draft Waste Management and Pollution Control Bill, December 1996.

[288] To achieve this purpose proposed Australian legislation (see Northern Territory Department of Lands, Planning and Environment, information kit on Draft Waste Management and Pollution Control Bill, December 1996) provides that *pre-existing* industries that can not comply with new legislative requirements made under an Environmental Protection Policy, environment protection order, authorisation, or Regulation, prepare and submit a compliance plan. Such a plan should detail a programme of improvement aimed at achieving compliance within a specified period. Once approved, the compliance plan would have the effect of removing any liability for prosecution for non-compliance with the relevant legislative provisions. Failure to fulfil the requirements contained in the compliance plan would be an offence.

- provision of expert consultancy services, training programmes, and financial incentives and assistance. In this context, the European Commission is developing a uniform methodology for SMEs seeking to establish EMSs,[289] which would enable them to comply with the EMAS at an acceptable cost;[290]

- use of non-mandatory codes of practice in conjunction with performance standards as a means of giving small and medium sized enterprises the concrete guidance they demand, while retaining flexibility[291] (those who do not want to devise their own solutions can simply follow the relevant code, while those who wish to be more innovative can devise other means of achieving the performance standard stipulated in the regulation);

- enabling SMEs to participate in an effluent trading scheme as a means to meet local limits on the levels of discharge into publicly owned treatment works, thereby enabling industrial users to achieve the required overall reduction in pollutant levels more quickly and economically;[292] and

- facilitating hazardous waste exchanges so that materials which cannot be used by the facility that produces them, but could be safely and productively used by another facility, can be exchanged, thereby providing both environmental benefits and economic benefits to both

[289] In the United States, many SOGMA members would claim to have the essential ingredients of a system, but not necessarily one that would satisfy ISO 14001, though it might, in simplified form, contain some of the key components of ISO 14001. None (for reasons of cost) have any intention of formal certification under ISO. There is a trend towards adopting EMSs, but, in many cases, these are, at present, so rudimentary that they would not stand up to external audit and verification.

[290] See President's Council on Sustainable Development, *Towards Sustainability* (1995), Washington DC, p.19.

[291] Such codes are more flexible than regulations in that companies are not compelled to follow them, and non-compliance with the actions specified in a code is not in and of itself an offence. Rather, the onus is on the responsible party to prove, if challenged, that the action was 'as good as' that in the approved code of practice. Thus, companies who have the capacity to devise cost-effective and innovative means of achieving (or going beyond) the performance standard, are encouraged to do so while less advanced organizations have the benefit of specific indications as to how to meet the statutory standards. If the codes of practice adopted under Responsible Care are of a sufficiently high standard (that is, if they represent best practice environmental management) then these codes in themselves might be incorporated by reference into the relevant legislation, becoming the recommended mechanism through which the general duties and performance standards are discharged.

[292] See, in particular, New Jersey Chemical Industry Project, Update 4, US EPA, July, 1997.

parties. Here, the role of government includes setting up or facilitating a clearing house of information and educating enterprises concerning the benefits involved.[293]

However, these are all strategies for dealing with firms who are ready and willing to comply, but do not necessarily know how to do so. There will also be a need to also to address those businesses which are not so willing, or will only comply in the face of credible sanctions. Specifically, given the economic problems facing many smaller enterprises and the lack of resources and incentives which such enterprises face in coming into compliance, there will inevitably remain a role for enforcement of regulations as an underpinning and backstop to more creative and positive strategies. Without such an underpinning, there is, commonly, insufficient incentive for firms to take up more positive and creative strategies.

Here, regulators face particular problems in devising an appropriate enforcement strategy. These include the large relational distance between small companies and regulators, the fact that inspections are necessarily very infrequent, and that, as a result, there is little possibility of negotiating compliance through ongoing visits and dialogue. Because there are so few options, regulators often rely more heavily on deterrence.

So what are the best of the very limited range of options available? Experience in the related area of occupational health and safety suggest that 'a visit [by an inspector] is likely to be relatively effective since small employers are more impressed than are many larger employers by the authority wielded by government inspectors'[294] and that the very fact of an inspector's visit, coupled with some form of enforcement action (e.g., an 'on the spot' fine), may have a significant impact on behaviour, even in circumstances where compliance costs will likely exceed the economic benefits to the employer of compliance. Essentially, this is because such action may serve to refocus employer attention on environmental problems they may previously have ignored or overlooked.[295] From this, one may reasonably conclude that a regulatory agency can achieve a considerable impact by even a limited

---

[293] *Ibid.*

[294] A. Hopkins, *Making Safety Work: Getting Management Commitment to Occupational Health and Safety*, (1995), Allen & Unwin, Sydney, p.177.

[295] J. T. Scholz, 'Cooperation, Deterrence and the Ecology of Regulatory Enforcement' (1984) 18 *Law and Society Review* 1709.

programme of inspections, provided it is reinforced by some degree of formal enforcement action sufficient to bring the problem forcibly to the employer's attention even if the latter is not substantial,[296] and even in the absence of full, or 'wall to wall', inspections.

However, formal enforcement should be seen as a last resort, since positive encouragement and voluntary compliance, to the extent that firms respond to them, is likely to achieve far better results than negative sanctions. Firms should first be provided with assistance and incentives to improve the environmental performance and redeem themselves. Specifically, inspectors could link the provision of other government programmes to encourage environmental protection (as described above) with the execution of the spot fines, using the latter to underpin and to provide an incentive for firms to take advantage of the former. That is, the best strategy is likely to incorporate both carrots and sticks, and to use both instruments that push enterprises to comply as well as those that pull them to do so: and to do so in a manner that integrates these two different types of mechanisms.

Perhaps one of the best illustrations of how this might be done is the agreement signed by the State of Minnesota and the Printing Industry of Minnesota (PIM), a state wide trade association, designed to significantly increase the use of environmental audits by printing firms, many of whom are relatively small operations. It is based on the premise that a clear distinction should be made between firms that have adopted detailed firm environmental compliance and pollution prevention policies and those that take little or no positive initiatives in respect of environmental protection. It seeks: 'to better differentiate the good from the bad actors by increasing the incentives to voluntarily comply with environmental laws and to pursue pollution prevention initiatives'.[297] By encouraging voluntary compliance, the scheme will enable regulatory resources to be redeployed and refocussed on those who are not responsive to voluntary initiatives.

Under the scheme, the PIM Inc established a separate corporation, PIM Environmental Services Corporation, to provide auditing services to PM members. However, it was also necessary to provide some incentive to firms to engage in such audits. Government regulators were

---

[296] There is also some evidence that longer inspections have much greater deterrent effect than superficial inspections which check only the plant's injury records. However, it would be dangerous to generalize from this to conclude that shorter inspections, generally, are less effective.

[297] H. Humphrey III, 'Public/Private Environmental Auditing Agreements: Finding better ways to promote voluntary compliance' (1994) 3 *Corporate Conduct Quarterly* 1 at 2.

reluctant to provide a total amnesty from prosecution for breach of regulations, simply because a firm had engaged in such an audit, for fear of damaging the integrity of their enforcement programme. However, an agreement was reached whereby an auditing firm, which discovers environmental violations and corrects them promptly, will have this fact taken into account when regulators decide whether to initiate any enforcement action, whether an enforcement action should be civil or criminal in nature, and what penalties to impose. Thus 'a company which conducts an auditing program in good faith and makes appropriate efforts to achieve environmental compliance is likely to mitigate the consequences of any violations it discovers'.[298]

The PIM audit agreement demonstrates how the use of audit programmes might be expanded to the smaller players in the chemical industry that, similarly, do not have the resources or sometimes the motivation to conduct environmental audits, but who might be given incentives and encouragement to do so. Such a policy might result not only in voluntary initiatives that substantially improved environmental performance, but also in a far more flexible and cost-effective response on the part of participants than is likely to be achieved through traditional 'command and control' government regulation.

The role of private orderings: Responsible Care and product stewardship

While regulators are in the process of developing increasingly sophisticated strategies for dealing with smaller firms, nevertheless, given the sheer numbers of such firms, there remain serious limits on the capacity of conventional regulation even to reach them, let alone to influence their environmental behaviour. Given the inherent limitations of government regulation, are there other strategies capable of substantially improving the environmental performance of buyers, suppliers, and specialty chemical manufacturers; of complementing government regulation; and compensating for its inadequacies?

In the case of the chemical industry, it would appear, at first sight, that the prospects for private orderings to control the behaviour of smaller players are dim. Suppliers and most specialty chemical manufacturers themselves often have no public reputation to protect, and are far less vulnerable to shaming or to threats to their reputation than the large firms with whom they may deal (so the role of environmental and public interest groups is, therefore, very limited). Moreover, they have

---

[298] *Ibid.* at 23.

less capacity than large firms to take a long-term view of the industry's best interests.

However, that is to see only one side of the coin. In some jurisdictions at least, the relevant specialty chemicals industry association has adopted Responsible Care. For example, in contrast to their Australian counterparts, member companies of the United States Synthetic Organic Chemical Manufacturers Association (SOGMA), are now signatories to Responsible Care. Similarly, chemical distributor associations in Canada, the United States, and the United Kingdom are all exploring means of enhancing chemical distribution safety through the vehicle of some form of partnership with Responsible Care. Driven in part by the need to counter attempts to ratchet up regulation, these initiatives may yet prove valuable. The establishment of mutual assistance networks, for example, enables companies effectively to turn to their peers for information and expertise on how to implement environmental improvements code principles. Such networks can be organized and administered through the relevant industry associations, with the support of government, and may stimulate awareness, technology transfer and encourage innovation and a commitment to environmental protection and waste management.

In the case of distributors, self-regulation has advanced substantially further. In the United States, the Responsible Distribution Process includes a number of codes of practice, including product stewardship,[299] and also a third party verification process. Moreover, the relevant industry association has already taken steps to eject some members who have manifestly failed to move towards implementation of the codes.

However, with the exception of distribution, these initiatives are in their very early stages and it remains an open question whether associations whose members are much less vulnerable to the pressures that generated Responsible Care in the first place (the breakdown of public trust, adverse publicity, and community outrage), and who have far less resources with which to address the problems, will make anything like the same degree of progress.[300] To date, progress has been slow. For

---

[299] According to our respondents, companies do indeed refuse to deliver to others who manifestly do not have appropriate storage facilities for hazardous chemicals. However, we were unable to ascertain how widespread this practice was, or to obtain concrete examples of it.

[300] Small companies find it more difficult. Often, they subscribe to Responsible Care, but they do not have the people and resources to take it to its full extent ((3 March 1996) *Careline* 14).

example, SOGMA members are only gradually adopting the Responsible Care codes and, at the time of writing, it is too soon to say to what extent their behaviour has been influenced by them. They have not, for example, committed to external verification, so self-audit will be the only (and dubious) means of measuring their performance. These companies are also considerably more reluctant to disclose information than their larger counterparts, because their livelihood largely depends on producing a small numbers of chemical mixtures, the ingredients of which are known only to themselves. And while some engage in dialogue with local communities, many others make only token efforts to do so.

However, if participation in, or partnership with, Responsible Care, offers only uncertain opportunities for specialty chemicals manufacturers and suppliers, there remains a second prospect with far more potential for delivering environmental improvements through informal social control, namely supply chain pressure generally,[301] and product stewardship in particular, which Responsible Care companies increasingly see as the most appropriate and effective means of substantially improving the environmental performance of suppliers, buyers, distributors, and specialty chemicals manufacturers.

Product stewardship involves taking responsibility for the health, safety and environmental implications of a product from inception through to final disposition.[302] It necessitates co-operation with customers, distributors and contract manufacturers to ensure the product's safe handling after it leaves the plant and embraces not only the activities of manufacturers, but also those of customers, distributors and suppliers. Its overriding philosophy is that 'everyone in your company, and everyone in your downstream chain is a product steward'.[303] The aim may also extend, where applicable, to upstream suppliers:

. . . to ensure that any relevant health, safety and environment issues that arise in the development, manufacture, storage, transport, marketing, use, recycling

---

[301] On the role of ISO 14001 and supply chain pressure, see above, p.223.

[302] See further, Australian Chemical Industry Council (ACIC), *Product Stewardship: Interim Code of Practice (1994)*, ACIC, Melbourne, p.2; A. D. Veroutis and J. A. Fava, *Elements of Effective DFE Program Management and Product Stewardship*, xx Environmental Quality Management 61 (Autumn 1997); *CMA Measures Product Stewardship*, (April 16 1997) 005 Chemical Week; P. S. Dillon and M. S. Baram, *Forces Shaping the Development and Use of Product Stewardship in the Private Sector*, in K. Fischer and J. Schot (eds.) *Environmental Strategies for Industry: International Perspectives on Research Needs and Policy Implications* (1993), Island Press, Washington.

[303] D. Rotman, 'Pushing Pollution Prevention' (July 17 1991) 148,26 *Chemical Week* 30.

or ultimate disposal of a company's products, packaging and related waste, are dealt with in socially and environmentally acceptable ways which meet with general community expectations, legal requirements and company policy.[304]

To these ends, product stewardship implies a continuous process of risk reduction in development, manufacturing, distribution, handling, use, and disposal, together with improvements in design, monitoring, education, and communication.[305]

While the commitment of large companies to the success of Responsible Care (and their awareness that the industry's prospects and reputation are only as strong as its weakest link) might, arguably, be sufficient to ensure they become effective product stewards, there are additional reasons of self-interest why they may choose to do so, including the threat of legal liability. As one industry insider put it:

. . . we cannot overlook the liability aspects of the chemical industry. We have learned that not only can we be sued whenever we misuse products, we also face liability lawsuits when our customers misuse them. By making our customers better stewards, we have reduced our liability as well.[306]

But legal concerns are not the only driver of effective product stewardship. Dow Chemical Company, the leaders in this field, have found that their product stewardship programme is an important sales tool,[307] and also reduces insurance premiums and improves the company's public profile. Finally, there may be opportunities for large firms to provide commercial consulting services and to profit by marketing their services to downstream customers. Thus, for large firms capable of taking a long-term view, and with the sophistication and skills to implement an effective product stewardship programme, enlightened self-interest may be sufficient to prompt effective product stewardship.

But even if the large companies have the self-interest to make product stewardship work, do they have the power, given that upstream sup-

---

[304] Australian Chemical Industry Council (ACIC), *Product Stewardship: Interim Code of Practice (1994)*, ACIC, Melbourne, p.2.

[305] The key components are said to be 'leadership, continuous improvement of risk management, effective communication of hazards, and forging of partnerships in the supply chain' (L. Tattum, 'Product Stewardship: Old practice, new theory' (7/14 July 1993) 153,1 *Chemical Week* 125–26; and E. Chynoweth & D. Jackson, 'Tour de Force: The Ambassadors' (7 July 1993) *Chemical Week* 126).

[306] S. Patrick, 'Value-Added Product Stewardship' *CMA News*, (September 1996), 25–28.

[307] In effect, Dow promises its customers that, through product stewardship, it will help them to identify and remedy their environmental problems and thereby keep out of trouble (R. Begley, 'Implementing a Philosophy: facing the challenges of the most sweeping code' (1992) *Chemical Week* 17 June 68).

pliers or downstream customers of large chemical companies may be reluctant to embrace these principles voluntarily? The answer is undoubtedly that they do, at least when they are contracting with smaller trading partners, because of the imbalance of power between large companies and their smaller suppliers and customers. The latter are often heavily dependent upon a small number of large trading partners for the large majority of their trade. Some specialty chemicals manufacturers, for example, rely heavily on the work that is contracted to them by major companies. This gives the large companies the leverage to ensure that small companies actually do all that a large chemical manufacturer requires.[308] in other cases, of course (as when chemical companies are supplying to large distributors), the imbalance of size and dependency is far less, and fear of losing a sizeable slice of business may militate against a large chemical manufacturer threatening to withdraw its business in this manner.

Nevertheless, where such imbalance of size exists, then, this leverage which large companies can commonly exert over their small trading partners is crucial, particularly in the absence of any body capable of compelling compliance with self-regulatory standards. This makes product stewardship fundamentally important to the success of Responsible Care—it is the only code capable of inducing non-participants or reluctant participants to comply with its goals. For this reason, many industry figures argue that the code is likely to be substantially more effective than any legislation could be in ensuring that companies dedicate time and resources to health, safety, and environmental concerns.

Specifically, under product stewardship, the environmental practices of small companies can be controlled through a combination of information, customer training, and audit. First, large chemical manufacturers can provide the information which many of their suppliers and customers lack. Secondly, they can educate and train suppliers, customers and their employees on the safe handling, use, and disposal of products,[309] share advanced technology on how to minimize the

---

[308] In the case of the specialty chemical manufacturers, opportunities exist in both directions. For while larger companies can exercise scrutiny over the specialty manufacturers, and offer advice and technical assistance, the latter, in turn, can, consistent with the principles of product stewardship, make detailed enquires and require information concerning the qualities and appropriate precautions concerning the chemicals they are dealing with on behalf of their larger clients.

[309] For example, some companies provide a training kit, and focus on making sure the customer is using the product in the intended way, keeping the customer informed about

hazards, and provide facilities for recycling or reclaiming hazardous products.[310]

To ensure that suppliers and buyers actually implement environmental safeguards, large companies can request information on storage, handling, use and disposal practices, insist on the introduction of appropriate EMSs, and oversee the effectiveness of these practices and systems through periodic audit of the supplier's safety and environmental practices. For example, Dow insists on conducting an audit before it agrees to supply a new customer with hazardous material, and routinely audits its distributors. The audit involves a team visiting the distributor's operations to examine handling, transportation, storage, and terminating techniques and prescribing improvements aimed at achieving environmental standards far in advance of current regulatory requirements.[311]

Many large chemical manufacturers go further and impose specified levels of environmental performance as a condition of contract. They also scrutinize a tenderer's EMSs and past environmental record, and those factors weigh heavily in deciding to whom to award the contract. In effect, many large chemical companies now choose only to deal with firms that can demonstrate satisfactory environmental performance. As one major chemical producer succinctly put it: 'We do not hire the lowest bidder; we hire the carrier least likely to put our products into the Houston Ship Channel'.[312]

Yet, despite its central role, product stewardship is far harder to test, measure or pin down, than any of the other codes of practice. As the CMA acknowledges:

As far as management practice goes, we know we can't define it ahead of time. Since companies are all different they'll have to pick their own unit [of measurement] whether it's a product line or a business unit, but we don't see how it could be facility-based like the other [codes] are.[313]

how the product should be handled, and helping the customer dispose of any hazardous wastes and by-products.

[310] For example, one major company has recently developed a recovery programme for industrial solvents and cleaners, taking in cleaners no longer effective from customers, distilling them to recover the solvent, and safely burning any residue, giving the customer credit for any solvent recovered.

[311] M. Coeyman, 'Making Product Stewardship a Reality' (7 July 1993) *Chemical Week* 37.

[312] This may serve to counter the temptation to which some chemical companies have succumbed in the past, namely to sub-contract some of the dirtiest or most hazardous operations relating to chemical manufacture. See also G. De Morris, 'Whistle Stop Tour Delivers TransCAER Message' (8 December 1993) *Chemical Week* 40.

[313] R. Begley, 'Product Stewardship: Exploring the "How-To"' (11 December 1991) *Chemical Week* 13.

In time, self-evaluations may shed further light on how effectively product stewardship is being implemented—though current efforts focus on perceptions rather than outcomes. For reasons discussed above, it will also be necessary for these self-evaluations to be both accessible to the public and subject to third party audit if they are to have credibility,[314] and for this process to be reinforced by the development of independent performance indicators.

Even if this occurs, product stewardship will continue to face substantial challenges.[315] First, extending it backwards towards upstream suppliers[316] and maintaining control once the product has passed beyond the first point of sale[317] are proving to be extremely difficult and sometimes intractable problems. These problems and others are exacerbated by the competing demands on corporate resources necessary to implement such an all encompassing code.[318] Sometimes, where competition is fierce, a large firm will be most reluctant to sever relations with a small supplier who provides a product at a very good price, but is unwilling to comply with product stewardship, unless it is confident that its competitors are applying the same policy (the problem of 'mutual assurance' again). Secondly, the code's emphasis on disclosing knowledge of how a company's products are actually used is meeting resistance from those who fear it may intrude on a customer's proprietary information. Thirdly, unlike the other codes of practice, there is no obvious location within a company in which to entrench product stewardship, and the sales and marketing units which have direct customer contact have a strong disincentive to promote it, insofar a this will threaten their sales and commissions. Fourthly, the product stewardship code, at least in its present form, only addresses the systems adopted by suppliers and customers, it does not address the environmental outcomes they achieve.

---

[314] Such audits are contemplated at a later date (J. Smith, *Measuring Health, Safety and Environmental Performance: Why, what, and whose?* (1994), summary of a paper presented to the ACIC. Convention, 21 February, Leura, NSW).

[315] M. Coeyman, 'Making Product Stewardship a Reality' (7 July 1993) *Chemical Week* 37: M. Coeyman, 'Responsible Care: Code implementation contracts' (7/14 July 1993) 153(1) *Chemical Week* 14; and M. Coeyman, 'Customers Get New Attention: Product stewardship from the buyer's side' (8 December 1993) 153(22) *Chemical Week* 34.

[316] R. Begley, 'Implementing a Philosophy: facing the challenges of the most sweeping code' (17 June 1992) *Chemical Week* 74.

[317] E. Chynoweth & K. Heller, 'Wanted: A System to Audit Care: Environmentalists and industry forge ahead' (17 June 1992) 150(23) *Chemical Week* 28.

[318] R. Begley, 'Implementing a Philosophy: facing the challenges of the most sweeping code' (17 June 1992) *Chemical Week* 68.

In summary, while product stewardship is still evolving and may have an uneven impact on the behaviour of upstream and downstream links in the supply chain, it holds out the promise of influencing the behaviour of those groups in ways which go far beyond what is available to government regulators. However, given its limitations and uneven impact, it cannot replace regulation, but needs to be utilized in conjunction with it.

This brings us to the final question: what is the most appropriate relationship between product stewardship and government regulation? In our view, government's role should be to facilitate, encourage, and complement product stewardship. Such a strategy involves a number of components. First, it might involve various means of encouraging and rewarding product stewardship practices. For example, companies committing themselves to transparent and accountable forms of product stewardship could be rewarded with various forms of public recognition and public relations benefits. Secondly, as Dillon and Baram argue, governments might identify limits of current initiatives and areas where additional efforts are needed, encouraging voluntary efforts by 'providing industry with the opportunity to apply its expert knowledge of its products and markets to the issues and to the formulation of response strategies.'[319] Thirdly, regulators might create market-based incentives on firms to achieve some product stewardship requirements, such as stimulating technology transfer. Fourthly, small firms themselves, might be subject to differential enforcement policies, dependent upon whether they had signed up for a transparent and accountable form of product stewardship in respect of relevant products. For example, those who had not might be made a higher enforcement priority. Finally, the effectiveness and breadth of product stewardship could be considerably increased by a regulatory requirement for major companies to take on the product stewardship requirements which are currently merely voluntary and unenforceable.[320] Significantly, some

---

[319] P. Dillon & M. Baram, 'Forces Shaping the Development and Use of Product Stewardship in the Private Sector' in K. Fischer and J. Schot, (eds.) *Environmental Strategies for Industry* (1993), Island Press, Washington DC, p.340.

[320] These might include product warnings and labels, education and training programmes; services; access to company personnel and guidance documents, purchasing contract and supply specifications and notification; screening and selection of suppliers; distributors or customers (see P. Dillon & M. Baram, 'Forces Shaping the Development and Use of Product Stewardship in the Private Sector' in K. Fischer and J. Schot, (eds.) *Environmental Strategies for Industry*, (1993), Island Press, Washington DC, pp.329–341).

regulations in Europe and the United States already require companies to engage in some forms of technology transfer.[321]

Broader lessons

Thus far, we have sought to analyse the limitations both of traditional regulation and of more innovative alternatives, such as Responsible Care and ISO 14001, as they relate to the chemical industry. However, recognizing the very considerable merits of the latter approaches, we have suggested a number of ways of building on their strengths, while compensating for their weaknesses. Drawing from that analysis, in this section we seek to identify some broader lessons from the chemicals sector that can be applied to industrial regulatory design.

These themes will be further developed in chapter six. It is important to recognize at the outset, however, that this process is intended to be evolutionary, not revolutionary: we have chosen to build on an existing regulatory framework, in this case self-regulation in combination with command and control, through incremental change, rather than contemplate a wholesale revision of policy direction. This approach necessarily restricts the range of instruments and strategies that might be invoked, as compared to a scenario where there is no pre-existing regulatory framework. By way of contrast, in the following chapter on the agricultural sector, we address the issue of biodiversity conservation on private land, where policymaking is less constrained by existing regulatory requirements.

1. Instrument ordering: towards a 'two-track' regulatory strategy

As we have seen in the chemical sector, there are many different types of companies when it comes to regulatory performance. There are both leaders and laggards, those who are willing to go 'beyond regulation' and those who are not, those who will comply voluntarily, and those who will resist regulation to the extent it is rational to do so. Add to these the irrational and the incompetent and it becomes readily apparent that no single regulatory approach is likely to be appropriate to all regulatees in all circumstances. How then can regulation be designed to accommodate the very different characteristics and motivations of regulatees?

---

[321] See P. Dillon & M. Baram, 'Forces Shaping the Development and Use of Product Stewardship in the Private Sector' in K. Fischer and J. Schot, (eds.) *Environmental Strategies for Industry*, (1993), Island Press, Washington DC, pp.329–341.

The best strategy is to provide incentives for those enterprises which would be willing to do more than the law requires, while also supporting and assisting those, generally smaller, entities who are willing but, at present, incapable of even coming into compliance with existing regulatory requirements. Finally, it is also necessary to have a strategy for dealing with wilful and/or irrational polluters.

We argued earlier that a serious limitation of most existing forms of regulation (in contrast to economic mechanisms) is that they do not encourage firms to go 'beyond compliance'. Yet, some enterprises at least, (particularly in the chemicals sector, given the need for large enterprises to establish their environmental credentials) might be willing to do far more than current regulations require. Indeed, there are some who, while less than perfect, genuinely strive to be regarded as good corporate citizens. To be sure, what we might describe as 'the lure of virtue' is far from universal. One would be naive to suggest that it always triumphs over 'the lure of profit'. But to the extent that a number of chemical manufacturers can be seen to be both doing good and doing well, they set an example for the rest of the industry. They are the 'benchmark' companies. By inspiring imitation of their best practice, and by exerting competitive pressure, they have the potential to foster improved performance by other industry players, both large and small. One important role of best practice environmental regulation should be to facilitate such behaviour, and to nurture virtue by providing a range of incentives.

A necessary first step is to create a legislative framework which harnesses market forces, so as to encourage rather than inhibit commercial drive and innovation. In particular, governments should avoid overly prescriptive regulations and instead confine themselves to setting targets or boundaries, and processes for achieving better results, leaving it to business itself to determine how best to reach those targets. The expectation is that the drive to achieve competitive advantage will stimulate companies to achieve those targets voluntarily, often through technological innovations.[322] Already, some of the largest chemical manufacturers have declared an ultimate goal of zero impact;[323] whilst unrealistic in the short term, it remains a target and exists as a constant reminder of the objective of continuous improvement.

---

[322] M. Porter, *The Competitive Advantage of Nations* (1990), Macmillan Press, London.

[323] R. B. Shapiro, Chairman, Monsanto Company, *Remarks To Society of Environmental Journalists* (28 October 1995), (http://www.monsanto.com/MonPub/InTheNews/Speeches/951028Shapiro_Robert.htm).

The shift from a reactive *ad hoc* approach to pollution control to one where environmental improvement is integrated with an enterprise's core business activities is equally important. EMS is the most appropriate vehicle for achieving this aim. Such systems, when successfully implemented, have proven capacities to achieve continuous improvement, cultural change and substantially improved environmental outcomes. Commonly too, they save money by reducing resource use and achieving other efficiencies. However, there are two important constraints upon the use of systems-based approaches. First, they cannot be successfully forced upon those who have no interest in adopting them (conscripts as contrasted with volunteers).[324] Secondly, they are difficult (though by no means impossible) to adapt to the needs of small and medium-sized enterprises. Accordingly, we do not advocate their incorporation in regulation across the board but only in particular circumstances. From this, we conclude that two distinct types of regulation will be necessary: one for those firms which are willing and able to adopt a systems-based approach (which will be largely, but not exclusively, large firms);[325] and another for those which are not.

This implies the creation of a two-track regulatory system under which firms (or at least firms with certain environmental credentials[326]) are offered a choice between a continuation of traditional forms of regulation, on the one hand (track one), and the adoption of an EMS, on the other (track two). The latter will put primary responsibility on industry itself to find optimal means of achieving environmental performance outcomes, and will involve 'regulatory flexibility' under a partnership between the regulatory agency, the enterprise, and the local community, from which all sides will benefit. Additional incentives to encourage firms to adopt track two will be provided, as described earlier. To prevent abuse, various transparency and accountability mechanisms, and a regulatory underpinning, will also be necessary.

[324] As we have indicated, such an approach has the greatest potential where it would enable enterprises to make economic gains—where, in short, there is a coincidence between what is good for safety and what is good for private profit. Even here, there may be resistance to adopting a systems-based approach, arising either from ignorance, incompetence or irrationality, or from the gap between short-term and long-term gains.

[325] Some small or medium sized firms will also be able to meet the requirements for more flexible regulation. Quite how many will depend largely upon the extent to which EMS. requirements can be modified to meet the needs of such firms and the costs of certification against, say ISO 14001.

[326] A demonstrated record of above average (or 'good') environmental performance and no major violations, is an important 'gateway' requirement which serves the important purpose of denying access to track two regulation to firms who, given their past environmental record, would be most likely to abuse it.

However, while we have emphasized the partnership nature of track two, even track one, which implies a conventional regulatory approach, need not involve an adversarial relationship between regulator and regulated. Rather, there is a case for developing a more co-operative approach, even under traditional regulation, for those who are motivated to comply voluntarily. Provision of advice and technical support holds out the greatest promise for institutionalizing responsibility[327] and is likely to achieve far better results than grudging compliance in the face of negative sanctions.[328] Earlier in this chapter, we suggested a number of specific co-operative strategies to enable smaller firms in particular, to come into compliance, while also noting the considerable potential of industry self-regulation to facilitate mutual assistance— sharing best industry practices, helping companies that lack the technical and organizational capability to implement the codes, and so on.

But it is also the case that a commitment to dialogue, persuasion and co-operative problem solving only makes sense under the right circumstances; namely, when the principal source of non-compliance is not wilful disobedience, but rather a lack of organizational capacity to either understand or implement those norms.[329] In those cases of non-compliance that stem from wilful disobedience, is a different approach necessary? Here, the co-operative approach can all too easily turn into weakness and undue permissiveness. As Ayres and Braithwaite have pointed out: 'The problem with the persuasion model . . . based as it is on a typification of people as basically good—reasonable, of good faith . . . is that it fails to recognise that there are some who are not good, and who will take advantage of being presumed to be so'.[330] For this last group, as we indicated earlier in this chapter, the bottom line must be a deterrence-orientated approach that makes it no longer economically rational for a business to ignore its environmental responsibilities. The appropriate maxim is to 'talk softly, but carry a big stick'.

Thus, good regulation means invoking different strategies, depending upon whether or not business is willing genuinely to embrace reg-

---

[327] See further, N. Gunningham & J. Rees, (1997) *Law and Policy* (publication of 1997 issue delayed).

[328] However, we must acknowledge that most American regulators, imbued in the tradition of adversarial legalism, would disagree.

[329] R. Kagan, & J. Scholz, 'The Criminology of the Corporation and Regulatory Enforcement Strategies' in K. Hawkins and J. Thomas (eds.), *Enforcing Regulation* (1984), Kluwer-Nijhoff, Boston, pp.67–96.

[330] I. Ayres & J. Braithwaite, *Responsive Regulation: Transcending the Deregulation Debate* (1992), Oxford University Press, New York, p.25.

ulatory flexibility and go beyond compliance strategies, and even when it is not, dependent upon whether or not the enterprise is a wilful polluter. This implies an ordering of regulatory responses by the state. The first preference is for enterprises to voluntarily go beyond compliance, with the state encouraging them by providing considerable autonomy and flexibility and other incentives, but subject to certain safeguards, including third party audit and community participation ('track two'). The second preference is for a co-operative and supportive role for the state, facilitating compliance from those who lack the resources or capacity to achieve results in the absence of such positive intervention. The third preference is for a more directive, interventionist, and where necessary, deterrence-oriented approach in order that wilful polluters do not benefit from non-compliance or gain an unfair advantage over those who comply voluntarily.[331]

Having introduced such a 'tiered response', the dilemma for regulators is that it is often not possible to be confident, in advance, of which classification a regulated firm falls into, and still less so to distinguish rational economic actors from the irrational or incompetent. For example, if a regulator assumes that all firms who embrace regulatory flexibility, through Responsible Care or ISO 14001, will devise strategies that will take them beyond compliance with traditional regulatory standards, then it may devise a regulatory strategy that stimulates voluntary action by enlightened enterprises, but which is incapable of effectively deterring those who have no intention of implementing tangible improvements (as opposed to 'paper improvements'). On the other hand, if regulators assumed that all firms fall into the second category, and require threatening with a big stick in order to bring them into compliance, then they will unnecessarily alienate (and impose unnecessary costs on) those who would willingly comply voluntarily.

A solution to this dilemma, suggested by our colleague John Braithwaite, is the regulatory enforcement pyramid.[332] Regulators start at the bottom of the pyramid, assuming that business is willing to comply voluntarily, without any threat from government. However, they also make provision for circumstances where this assumption will be disappointed, by being prepared to escalate up the enforcement

---

[331] To the extent that the irrational do not respond to education and encouragement, they may still respond to penalties. Irrationality is a relative concept. There are few who will not respond to criminal sanctions and these may ultimately face closure, a sanction that even the irrational cannot ignore.

[332] I. Ayres & J. Braithwaite, *Responsive Regulation: Transcending the Deregulation Debate* (1992), Oxford University Press, New York.

pyramid to increasingly deterrence-orientated strategies. Thus, to the extent that departures from compliance come to the attention of regulators, they are met with state response, which has the capacity to escalate or de-escalate depending on the subsequent behaviour of the regulatee. This element of credible enforcement and increasing deterrence, as regulators escalate their response against those unwilling to comply voluntarily, is essential to the success of the enforcement pyramid. Yet, as Braithwaite points out:

> A paradox of the pyramid is that the signalled capacity to escalate regulatory response to the most drastic of measures channels most of the regulatory action to the cooperative base of the pyramid. The bigger the sticks at the disposal of the regulator, the more it is able to achieve results by speaking softly.[333]

In summary, we propose both an ordering of regulatory strategies (with different approaches for those willing to go beyond compliance, those who are willing but not able to comply, and wilful polluters) and also an ordering of regulatory enforcement responses incorporating escalating responses to non-compliance.

2. The limits of 'stand alone instruments': towards co-regulation and tripartism

We have already identified both the strengths and weaknesses of two main alternatives to traditional forms of regulation: Responsible Care and the management systems approach of ISO 14001. For example, we have demonstrated the very rich possibilities for informal social control through Responsible Care and its capacity to achieve many changes in industry attitudes, morality, and behaviour, that are largely beyond the reach of the State, while recognizing that the free-rider and other problems that beset the programme[334] make it a far from adequate 'stand alone' policy instrument. We reached similar conclusions concerning ISO 14001 as a regulatory flexibility tool.

What then are the essential prerequisites for either self-regulation or EMS to function as effective and efficient agents of public policy? What is the most appropriate relationship between either of these approaches and government regulation? And how can we achieve an appropriate integration of government, community, and industry involvement? We

---

[333] J. Braithwaite, 'Responsive Business Regulatory Institutions' in C. A. J. Cody & C. J. E. Sampford, (eds.) *Business, Ethics and Law* (1993), Federation Press, Sydney, p.88.

[334] These include a danger that the regulatory process becomes co-opted by business, that rules in part written by the industry (although endorsed by government) may seek to evade the spirit of the law, and that the Responsible Care co-ordinators will not be sufficiently independent.

address these questions by recognizing the need to integrate these mechanisms into a broader regulatory mix in such a way that their weaknesses can be compensated for and their strengths built upon, and that crucial to doing so will be designing appropriate co-regulatory and tripartite mechanisms.

Based on our analysis of the chemical sector, there are four key components necessary to achieve the successful integration of 'regulatory flexibility' and traditional government regulation (in essence, what we described earlier as a 'two-track' regulatory system), and the meaningful engagement of non-commercial third parties. These are:

(i)   that those enterprises engaging in regulatory flexibility ('track two') should adopt practices and processes that lead to the pursuit of 'beyond compliance' goals and include outcome-based requirements, the achievement of which can be measured through specific performance indicators;[335]

(ii) that there should be independent verification both of the functioning of their management system and of environmental performance under it (e.g., by a third party environmental auditor), with the results or a summary of the results available both to the regulator and third parties such as community groups (transparency);[336]

(iii) that there should be an ongoing dialogue with local communities concerning 'beyond compliance' goals and the means of achieving them (this ensures the credibility and legitimacy of the process and enables third party input and oversight);

(iv) that there should be an underpinning of government intervention, acting as a safety net, which only 'kicks in' when triggered by the failure of the other less intrusive mechanisms, described above. The principle objective of these requirements is to ensure that the forms of regulatory flexibility we have proposed both deliver demonstrable (and measurable) outcomes and gain community credibility.[337]

---

[335] Among the most important features of such systems are: incorporating pollution and waste prevention into core business practices; accounting for the total environmental impact of choices throughout the life cycle of products and services; improving efficiency; considering environmental costs to society in business decisions; employing planning processes to illuminate pollution prevention and product stewardship opportunities; and striving to improve continuously.

[336] But subject to necessary protection: e.g., immunity from prosecutions or a period of grace. See further, N. Gunningham and J. Prest, 'Environmental Audit and Regulatory Strategy: Prospects and Reform' (1993) 15(4) *Sydney Law Review* 492–526.

[337] See here the parallels with the US EPA's Environmental Leadership Program, which anticipates explicit inclusion of compliance assurance, pollution prevention and

This means that not only business and government, but the community too, must be directly involved in decision-making. In the environmental arena, where firms are often unwilling to implement regulation voluntarily, and where regulatory agencies are frequently under-resourced and relatively ineffective, then clearly public interest groups can play an important role, and demonstrably already do so. Thus critical components of a policy mix will be independent third party oversight rather than self-regulation, and tripartism rather than bipartism, and an underpinning of government regulation (co-regulation) acting as a back stop where other mechanisms fail.

3. Surrogate Regulators

Enforcement of environmental regulations is an essential but very time consuming and expensive task. Given that government regulatory resources are already overstretched and, in many jurisdictions, are further contracting, there is a compelling need to use them efficiently. An increasingly legitimate question confronting policymakers, therefore, is whether or not it is possible to identify alternative means by which it might be possible to either replace or complement government regulation. One important strategy for doing so is to delegate regulatory responsibilities to other parties in circumstances where this is a viable option, thereby freeing up resources which can be redeployed to areas where there is no alternative to government enforcement. In addition to relieving some of the fiscal burden on the state, regulatory surrogates my enable the redeployment of scarce resources where no alternatives to state intervention exist.

Before discussing opportunities for recruiting surrogates, there is an important qualification to be made: that they should only be used where doing so will provide overall effectiveness and efficiency gains. This is by no means always the case. For example, in terms of effectiveness, some self-regulatory initiatives are intended more to confuse the public and keep regulators at bay than to genuinely further the goals of environmental protection.[338] Similarly, in terms of efficiency,

community outreach as core components of an environmental flexibility programme built around an environmental management system.

[338] See, for example, J. Braithwaite & B. Fisse, 'Self Regulation and the Costs of Corporate Crime' in C. D. Shearing & P. C. Stenning, *Private Policing* (1987), Sage Publications, Beverley Hills, California; P. Cerexbe, 'Advertising Self Regulation: The Clayton's Codes' (1988) 38 *Consuming Interests* 16–20; M. Blakeney & S. Barnes, 'Advertising Deregulation: Public health or private profit' in R. Tomasic, (ed.) *Business*

the added costs involved in mandatory disclosure of environmental information by business may, in some circumstances, outweigh the efficiency gains that this promises in terms of enhanced enforcement.[339] On occasion, surrogates for government regulation may conflict with other assessment criteria, for example in terms of their equity implications or political acceptability. These too, would need to be mitigated or overcome.

Potential surrogate regulators and their roles

Non-government parties which might, potentially, play the role of surrogate regulators, acting as informal instruments of social control, fall into one of four categories: regulated enterprises themselves, industry associations, commercial third parties, and non-commercial third parties. Each of these groups is discussed briefly below.

First, individual enterprises might regulate themselves. In a modest way, they are often required by law to self-police. For example, it is common for companies to be required to monitor their own releases and report departures from their permit requirements to the authorities. More broadly, initiatives such as Responsible Care and ISO 14001 assume that they will do far more: including implement and administer quite sophisticated codes of practice and environmental management systems. However, without external oversight, there are enormous opportunities and temptations to cheat and even if enterprises do not succumb to these, the community is unlikely to be convinced by their claims to environmental excellence based purely on self-monitoring and self-reporting.

Turning to the second group, there is some scope for the regulation of member companies by industry associations, at least in the case of a programme as sophisticated as Responsible Care. However, effective regulation requires an organized and diligent industry association, with the support of the majority of members for it to take on an enforcement role. Such is rarely the case. Even with Responsible Care, the industry association has not been given sufficient powers to fulfil this role. This serves to emphasize the grave dangers involved in relying on industry association self-regulation alone and the critical roles likely to be played by third parties and an underpinning of government regulation.

Regulation in Australia (1984), CCH. Australia, North Ryde, NSW; and A. C. Page, 'Self-Regulation and Codes of Practice' (1980) *Journal of Business Law* 24–31.

[339] We have addressed the trade offs between efficiency and effectiveness in chapter one.

The third group, commercial third parties, can make a very different, but often more important contribution to environmental protection. As we have witnessed in the chemical sector, they can do so principally through exerting supply-side pressure, where larger firms can both assist and bring pressure upon their smaller vendors to achieve environmental goals. Such assistance could take the form of environmental management expertise, quality control, product design, advice on clean technologies, or regulatory compliance audits. The objective would be to deliver mutually beneficial outcomes: smaller firms gain expertise to improve their environmentally performance in way that reduces compliance costs and improves productivity and larger firms gain a more reliable, cleaner and efficient supplier. The influence exerted by financial institutions such as banks and insurance companies over their clients, and the power of markets (e.g., the power of financial institutions, investors and green consumers over individual companies) is another example of commercial surrogacy. They could, potentially, fulfil monitoring functions reinforced by sanctions, in a manner which can often be more effective than government regulation. Financial markets too, can play an important role in rewarding those firms who demonstrate a commitment to cleaner production, as can independent certification organizations.

The fourth group, non-commercial parties, community, and environmental groups, in particular, have become influential participants in the environmental arena. Extrapolating from the chemical industry, there are at least two opportunities for the community and community groups to encourage an improved industry performance. First, the community can be a powerful motivator for firms to enhance their public image. Local communities, regional and national environmental groups, or even trade unions, could play an important role in scrutinizing the behaviour of firms, and many already do so. Provided they have access to sufficient amounts of relevant and reasonably accurate information, then they can bring pressures on firms through a combination of adverse publicity, whistle blowing, litigation, and local community politics.[340] Secondly, community representatives may directly engage industry in a partnership role.[341] For example, as we have seen,

[340] See p.63.

[341] An outstanding example of such constructive engagement is the work of the Alliance for Environmental Innovation, established by the Environmental Defence Fund and the Pew Charitable Trusts. See the *Green Business Letter* March 1996 1, 7; F. Catherine, 'Advocacy Groups and Business form Enviro Alliance' (March 4–17 1996) Mass High Tech.

the chemical industry has made some moves to involve community representatives in the administration of Responsible Care, through the creation, in Australia at least, of the NCAP.

The use of independent auditors can also be considered a form of non-commercial third party regulatory surrogacy. Although, in many instances, the cost of the audit will be borne by the enterprise, the relationship is 'non-commercial' in the sense that the activity does not relate to the enterprise's normal business activities and there is no ongoing commercial relationship. The certification of management systems adopted under ISO 14001, and subsequent performance in terms of that system, is a typical example.

Sometimes, a combination of these two surrogacy options may be adopted, as under Responsible Care, where firms self-monitor and self-report under the close supervision of their industry association but are also (in some jurisdictions) subject to periodic third party audit.

One major consequence of the use of surrogates is a recasting of the role of government regulators. With far less need for their direct involvement, regulators may take a back seat, intervening only to the extent that surrogacy mechanisms break down in practice, or need external support in order to make them effective. Indeed, as we describe below, a major role for government, in these circumstances, may be that of facilitator or broker (ensuring the effective involvement of appropriate third parties) rather than that of direct participant.

The potential to harness non-government parties as surrogate regulators is, however, not without limits. For example, although local communities may, in principle, exert considerable influence over companies operating in their area, in reality there may be not be any genuine community; or the costs (in time, energy, and opportunity costs) involved in attending meetings, negotiating, or otherwise participating in dialogue with companies may prove overwhelming, with the result that any embryonic community participation soon dissipates. Again, some financial institutions may be preoccupied with the bottom line, rather than with the means of getting there. Despite the considerable attractions of regulatory surrogates, none is likely to be effective as a 'stand alone' instrument and in each case must be integrated with, or function against the backdrop of some continuing form of state intervention. We further explore the implications of integration and principles for the design of policy mixes in chapter six.

4. De-centering the state: government as facilitator, catalyst and activator

Between the polar extremes of deference to spontaneous market orderings, on the one hand, and the 'regulatory state', on the other, there is
often a middle path. Too rarely considered by ideologies of either regulation or deregulation it entails government acting as catalyst, facilitator, and activator rather than as direct regulator. Many of the
regulatory modifications suggested from our analysis of the chemical
sector, in particular the use of regulatory surrogates, require just such
a change of role. Pertinent examples where the state can adopt this new
mantle include:

- Where a state agency chooses to endorse a self-regulatory programme
  such as Responsible Care—or the activities of a particular company
  in compliance with it, by permitting the use of an agency logo or
  other official seal of approval, thereby giving the public greater confidence in the code's credibility.[342]

- Where government provides the conditions conducive to appropriate
  private sector initiative. For example, government might encourage
  supply chain pressure through the incorporation of product stewardship provisions into regulatory flexibility (e.g., as a condition of track
  two regulation) or it might enact legislation making all manufacturers responsible for their products throughout their life-cycle.

- Where government directly influences manufacturers through its purchasing power, making certain environmental requirements conditions of government procurement contracts.[343] In this way,
  government adopts the role of a commercial third party, as opposed
  to a regulator. Because in many markets, government is a dominant
  purchaser, it can provide a leadership role in dictating market preferences for products by developing and implementing a 'green' purchasing policy. For example, governments could support cleaner

---

[342] There is no provision under the Australian Trade Practices Act 1974 (Cth.) which
gives the ACCC the authority to endorse a Code, although the Commission has allowed
this on at least one occasion (see the Australian Scanning Code). Similarly, the New
Zealand Ministry of Consumer Affairs has no statutory power to endorse or sanction any
code officially, nor to give permission for the use of the Ministry's logo in the promotion
of a code. While the Ministry of Consumer Affairs has openly acknowledged its role in
the development of codes, it signed as such in the original EFT code, it has not developed policies or conditions for endorsement of codes (comments received from Bob
Hillier at the New Zealand Ministry of Consumer Affairs (April 1996)).

[343] Provided there is no discrimination against foreign firms.

production by requiring their agencies to select the items with the highest percentage of recovered materials practicable, while at the same time maintaining a satisfactory standard of competition.

- Where government harnesses the influence of financial intermediaries, such as banks and insurance firms, or financial markets, such as investors and consumers. The role of these third parties will be dependent on access to reliable and independent information (based on accurate and shared indicators of environmental performance) to enable them to take environmental performance into account when determining a firm's financial worth, or whether to grant it a loan, or a differential insurance premium. A key role for government is to ensure that the necessary information to influence financial institutions to support the improved environmental performance is readily accessible.[344]

- Where government enables non-commercial third parties to function as an effective countervailing force to the power of industry. For example, 'good neighbour agreements' between chemical firms and local residents are common and potentially effective in both Europe and the United States.[345] Here, the a role for government is to insist on community participation as a condition for regulatory flexibility. For example, it is a requirement, under the United States EPA's Project XL, that community organizations and other local stakeholders have the opportunity to shape and vet a firm's environmental management strategy. It may also mandate the provision of information and technical support as necessary prerequisites to make such a policy effective.

- Where government acts as a clearing house for information, as in the example of 'waste exchanges', where a material that is waste to one facility can be productively used in another and both would benefit but lack the information or opportunity to make such exchanges.

[344] For example, in the United States, it was only once financial markets had access to reasonably accurate indicators of environmental performance (in the form of the government mandated TRI and disclosure requirements imposed by the Securities and Exchange Commission) that the environmental record of individual firms began to be reflected in their stock price.

[345] They feature means by which concerned citizens have access to information relating to regulatory compliance, and the right to inspect facilities and to review compliance and accident plans. With community support, the strategy becomes a legally enforceable contract. Good neighbour agreements can provide firms with a strong incentive to engage in cleaner production activities. However, they are only likely to be appropriate for larger firms with a reasonably high community profile.

Thus, in a wide variety of circumstances, government can function more effectively by 'steering rather than rowing' judiciously facilitating third parties to perform more effectively, many of the functions it performed directly in the past.

5. Accountability, transparency, and consultation

As we have seen, neither Responsible Care nor ISO 14001, or any other management systems-based approach, is likely to function effectively in the public interest in the absence of adequate mechanisms ensuring accountability and transparency. Where an enterprise self-monitors, there will be a temptation to misrepresent the results, providing an overly favourable account of its environmental performance, particularly if there are regulatory or public relations benefits to be gained from so doing. Irrespective of whether firms succumb to this temptation or not, the public will not trust the results.

Moreover, in many countries, and particularly in the United States, where a tradition of adversarial legalism inhibits disclosure, industry has been extremely reluctant to reveal more information about its activities than it has to.[346] Even under Responsible Care, it is only gradually that this resistance to disclosure is being reversed. But substantial parts of the industry itself (at least outside the United States) have now realized that transparency and accountability are essential, for without them it will lack the credibility and legitimacy which are fundamental prerequisites for the granting of regulatory flexibility and greater autonomy of action.

To overcome these temptations and to reassure both regulators and communities that an enterprise is indeed achieving the results that it claims (and in order to bring pressure upon those whose performance is below standard) a number of mechanisms of accountability and transparency might be invoked. As described by Gunningham and Rees, the necessary first step is the promulgation of the principles and practices that the industry accepts as a guide to appropriate conduct (for example, the Responsible Care codes of practice, or the management system requirements under ISO 14001). This is because:

. . . an industry's public commitment to such principles can generate new expectations of accountability, both inside and outside the industry, including demands for more concrete and specific norms . . . [and because] industry, by clarifying the normative standards it sets for itself, including performance indi-

[347] See p.63.

cators and implementation timetables, also provides more precisely defined measures for evaluating and criticizing its performance. With increasing transparency, in short, accountability is more readily maintained.[347]

However, such normative standards will only have value if they measure variables that are important and appropriate indicators of performance. We noted above the importance of establishing independent performance indicators and other matrix. And the results themselves will only have credibility if the data gathering process on which they are based is demonstrated to have integrity. Here, central questions will be who does the monitoring, who pays for it, and who, if anyone, verifies that process.[348]

Finally, the levels of accountability and transparency will be greatly enhanced if there is public disclosure of the results in a form that enables comparison of enterprises against each other and against an independent outside standard (e.g., a regulatory performance standard). In this last respect, both ISO 14001 and Responsible Care fall far short of the ideal in terms of their ability to enhance the accountability of chemical company officials.[349] For example, contrast the very limited progress under Responsible Care, described above, with the achievements of one other advanced self-regulatory body, the Institute of Nuclear Plant Operators (INPO), which has, for some years, ranked nuclear plants in terms of their safety performance, and communicated this information to the industry in such a way as to make industry Chief Executive Officers (CEOs) acutely aware of the relative status of their plants and the implications.[350] This, in itself, is a powerful accountability mechanism capable of: 'institutionalising responsibility and

---

[347] N. Gunningham & J. Rees, (1997) 19(4) *Law and Policy* 363.

[348] The establishment of an independent and transparent audit, certification or verification process, such as is now evolving under the Canadian Responsible Care Program (and is required by the International Council of Chemical Associations as the eighth fundamental feature of Responsible Care), is one means of answering these questions and of achieving credibility. Under ISO 14001, third party certification is optional though not mandatory. However, it may be that firms will prefer such certification to their own in-house audits because of the greater credibility which such 'arms-length' auditing will provide.

[349] In the case of ISO 14001, this limitation is inherent in the standard itself: over and beyond legal compliance, enterprises set their own performance goals and there is no common standard against which they can be measured. In the case of Responsible Care, the indicators so far developed and the data gathering process itself fall seriously short of this goal, which it is not, however, impractical to attain.

[350] J. V. Rees, *Hostages of Each Other: The transformation of nuclear safety since Three Mile Island* (1994), University of Chicago Press, Chicago.

building moral competence into the structure of the enterprise'.[351] Whether Responsible Care will ever develop to this degree of transparency and accountability, remains a moot point.[352] ISO 14001 certainly will not. While some companies are now seeking commercial advantages through voluntary disclosure and transparency (usually through an environmental annual report), they remain the minority and the bulk of enterprises continue to resist such disclosure.[353]

In this context, we have already noted the crucially important role of information disclosure mandated by government, such as CRTK, which is premised on the assumption that public interest groups, if empowered by sufficient information, can act as an effective countervailing force.[354] It has also encouraged introspection, helping firms to identify waste reduction opportunities independent of external pressures. Such regulation through information is made doubly effective if the citizens and commercial actors who have access to information about corporate and government agency pollution are granted the opportunity: (i) to sue regulatory agencies for failure to enforce regulations; and (ii) to sue corporations if the Environment Protection Authority (EPA) is unwilling to file suit itself.

Finally, over and beyond (but closely related to) issues of transparency and accountability, is the role of community participation and dialogue. As we have argued, the active encouragement, and indeed, the institutionalization of public participation, are also crucial not only because of their democratic benefits, (those who have had an opportunity to participate in decisions feel much greater ownership of them) but because without it there can be no genuine partnership in environmental decision-making. Moreover, they can provide important benefits in terms of environmental performance: 'In the long run, the

---

[351] See further N. Gunningham & J. Rees, (1997) 19(4) *Law and Policy* (publication of 1997 issue delayed).

[352] Significantly, under Responsible Care in most countries, even the names of companies who withdraw from the programme (for whatever reason) is not made public, because of a policy of protecting the confidentiality of the industry association's membership. Even the advanced Canadian programme suffers from this serious shortcoming.

[353] Some companies believe transparency can lead to competitive advantage through enhanced access to planning permission, and reduced call for regulation, as well as improved public image. The Monsanto Annual Environmental Report was a leader in this development.

[354] In the United States, CRTK legislation has enabled community groups to construct a league table of polluters—the best, the worst and the most improved. The resulting backlash has prompted a number of major chemical manufacturers to reassess their own operations and to modify their environmental control strategies, even in the absence of government legislation requiring them to do so.

empowerment of local interests and institutions through stakeholder processes should help to find creative solutions and to harmonise national goals to local needs in a sustainable society.'[355]

Under Responsible Care, a number of mechanisms that facilitate consultation are already in place. In addition to information-based strategies already described, they include the role of the National Community Advisory Panel in scrutinizing draft codes and other proposals, and the developing contribution of regional community groups. ISO 14001 makes no comparable attempt to build in community consultative mechanisms. Nevertheless, as we have argued above, ISO 'Plus', or other variations of regulatory flexibility, must necessarily do so.

6. Complementary instrument combinations

What are the broader lessons concerning regulatory mix to be learnt from our study of the chemicals industry? What is perhaps most striking is the extent to which the approach we have marked out relies on complementary combinations of instruments and actors: how the weaknesses of both Responsible Care and ISO 14001, and other management systems, can be compensated for and overcome through a combination of performance indicators, third party audits, community right-to-know, and other forms of community input, and through an underpinning of government oversight. Indeed, there is now almost a convergence of thought amongst those seeking to design various forms of regulatory flexibility in the USA that these are indeed the core ingredients of a successful alternative regulatory approach.[356]

However, over and beyond the importance of designing complementary combinations integrating these components, four additional elements of optimal regulatory mixes must be emphasized: the capacity to achieve better results through activation and reinforcement of one instrument by another; the importance of designing 'push-pull'

---

[355] Aspen Institute Report: *The Alternative Path: A cleaner, cheaper way to protect and enhance the environment* (1996), Program for Energy, the Environment and the Economy, The Aspen Institute, US.

[356] See, for example, the US EPAs Environmental Leadership Program, and Project XL, and the reports of a variety of think tanks including the Aspen Institute's 'The Alternative Path' (1996), the National Environmental Policy Institute's 'Reinventing the Vehicle for Environmental Management' (1995); the Yale Center for Environmental Law and Policy's Next Generation Project and the forthcoming report of the Enterprise for the Environment. More generally, see the approach taken by members of the Risk Management and Decision Processes Center at the Wharton School, University of Pennsylvania.

combinations; the significance of designing complementary enforcement options; and the need to avoid counterproductive combinations with unintended consequences.

Activation and reinforcement

It is both possible and desirable to select combinations of instruments in which one instrument activates and/or reinforces the effect of another. For example, in the context of Responsible Care, the chemical industry had long sought to achieve a reduction in insurance premiums for participants in Responsible Care, both as a means of making the scheme more attractive (perhaps leading to recruitment of new members) and of rewarding better environmental performers. The obstacle was that the insurance industry lacked any independent indicator of the performance of Responsible Care members, and was not willing to rely on self-assessment by individual companies. However, the introduction of independent third party audits in Canada has served not only to increase the credibility of the programme with the public and local communities, but it has also given the insurance industry the independent verification it required in order to provide discounted premiums. Thus, independent verification has served to activate differential insurance premiums which, in turn, increases the economic benefits of Responsible Care and serves as an attraction to participation. And, of course, the promise of differential premiums could serve as an inducement to develop independent audits in the first place. In this respect, the two mechanisms are also mutually reinforcing. In similar fashion, financial market response to environmental performance can be activated by information.[357]

Rather than fulfilling an activating role, some instruments enhance or reinforce others. For example, in the abstract, the codes of practice under Responsible Care are only voluntary measures which are of guidance to Responsible Care members and of no consequence whatsoever to non-members. However, they are important in indirectly shaping the regulatory environment, and in influencing the firm's perceptions of it. In the regulatory context, in many jurisdictions companies have a general legal obligation of 'due diligence', or reasonable care, in the con-

---

[357] Financial markets can play an important role in rewarding firms with a demonstrated good environmental record, but only if they have sufficient independent information to enable them to do so. There is evidence that the introduction of the Toxic Release Inventory had precisely this effect. See S. Feldman, P. Soyka & P. Ameer, *Does Improving a Firm's EMS and Environmental Performance Result in a Higher Stock Price?* (1996), Working Paper, ICF. Kaiser Consulting Group, Fairfax, Virginia, US.

duct of their operations. The definition of 'due diligence' is often imprecise. However, in part, courts go about deciding what it means by asking if a defendant has met the accepted standards of the relevant industry. For the chemical industry, it is highly probable that the courts will look to Responsible Care as a standard not only for Responsible Care members, but also for other chemical companies.[358] Non-participants in Responsible Care are at greater risk of legal liabilities than members. Thus, Responsible Care and due diligence are mutually reinforcing: due diligence becomes more precisely defined as a result of the Responsible Care codes, and the Responsible Care codes become enforceable through due diligence.

There are also a number of other means through which self-regulatory mechanisms such as Responsible Care can be reinforced. For example, we have already observed that compliance with their terms can be made a term and condition of contracts in the supply chain. Government procurement contracts can make participation a prerequisite for tendering, and codes may be cross-referenced with other voluntary and legal regimes (for example, under ISO 14001 a participant who has signed on to a voluntary programme such as the CERES principles or Responsible Care, is required to comply with the terms of that programme in order to obtain ISO 14001 certification). Similar combinations may be equally important at the level of enforcement. For example, both government inspectors and insurers may play important, overlapping, but in important respects, different enforcement roles, which, as a result, are more commonly reinforcing than redundant.

Using combinations which both 'push and pull'

Organizations are commonly complex entities with multiple objectives, and, indeed, multiple selves. As Ayres and Braithwaite put it:

[M]ost business actors are bundles of contradictory commitments to values of economic rationality, law abidingness, and business responsibility. Business executives have profit maximising selves and law-abiding selves; at different moments, in different contexts, the different selves prevail.[359]

As a result, strategies which appeal to different parts of the organization, and to its different motivations, which combine both carrots and

---

[358] See Canadian Chemical Producers Association, *Does Responsible Care Work?* (May 1996), Canadian Chemical Producers Association, Ottawa, p.8.

[359] I. Ayres & J. Braithwaite, *Responsive Regulation: Transcending the Deregulation Debate* (1992), Oxford University Press, New York, p.31.

sticks, and which both pull and push enterprises towards better environmental performance, are likely to be more effective than those which invoke only one of these approaches.

Take the free-rider problem, which we identified above as central to the effective functioning of Responsible Care. As Purchase has argued, there are, essentially, two ways to overcome this problem[360] On the one hand, it can be pursued by employing strategies designed to enhance voluntary compliance (environmental leadership groups, the sharing of technology peer groups, and other forms of mutual support). On the other hand, it can be addressed by having effective monitoring and enforcement mechanisms to deal with non-compliance. Yet neither of these elements alone is likely to be sufficient. The achievement of widespread consensus will be necessary for the successful operation of a voluntary scheme—something which can only be nurtured and attained through the first category of mechanisms. Yet there will inevitably be those who will defect or otherwise abuse a voluntary scheme, making the second category equally essential. Put differently, trust (nurturing virtue) is an essential component of Responsible Care, but it is only when both trust and verification are used together that the scheme becomes a viable one.

A similar point applies in the context of ISO 14001. While we have emphasized the importance of providing a series of incentives for enterprises to participate in regulatory flexibility programmes incorporating ISO 14001 (or ISO 'Plus') those incentives will function much better if the alternatives to participation are also made far less palatable. For example, if non-participants are considered sooner for intensified enforcement activities relative to participants, then there is both the push of negative sanctions as well as the pull of positive rewards, to induce enterprises to join. In the broader context of targeted enforcement strategies generally, the widely acclaimed Maine 200 programme is another example of effectively harnessing combinations of push and pull strategies: offering a partnership role to those willing to improve voluntarily while, in effect, 'blitzing' recalcitrants through a programme of intensified inspections and enforcement action.

---

[360] B. Purchase, *Political Economy of Voluntary Codes* (1996), a draft paper presented at the Voluntary Codes Symposium, Office of Consumer Affairs, Industry Canada and Regulatory Affairs, Treasury Board, Ottawa, September and to be included in Exploring Voluntary Codes in the Marketplace, edited by D. Cohen & K. Webb, Government of Canada, Ottawa, (publication due 1998).

Enforcement though complementary combinations

We have previously emphasized the importance of effective enforcement and means whereby this might be achieved. We have stressed the virtues of looking first to the regulatory capacities of business itself and of third parties, with government's role being principally that of backstop, underpinning other cheaper, and often more effective, private forms of intervention. We will not rehearse these issues further. For present purposes, our point is that even in circumstances where it is indeed possible to invoke private parties as surrogate enforcers of regulation, they are unlikely to be wholly successful in this role unless it is possible for them to take convincing action at every level of the enforcement pyramid, including, crucially, the tip. In the large majority of circumstances, they lack this capacity and, with enforcement as with instrument mixes generally, the best option may well be the design of complementary combinations of institutions and instruments.

Take the case of Responsible Care. Since the industry association lacks ultimate capacity to invoke 'big stick' sanctions at the tip of an enforcement pyramid,[361] the credibility of sanctions at lower levels of the pyramid is also weakened.[362] As a result, it cannot be successfully enforced in isolation. Indeed, this is a common failing of self-regulation and a major reason why there is a compelling need, even with many of the best self-regulatory programmes, to complement self-regulation with some form of government and third party involvement. In a real sense, it is the presence of State and third party institutions which provide the basis for industry self-regulation.

Precisely what form of state (or third party) intervention will provide the most appropriate underpinning is likely to vary with the particular circumstances of the case. However, it is at least possible to identify some of the most commonly important variables, and to illustrate, by example, how co-regulation and tripartism might operate to optimal effect in particular circumstances.

The role of the general law   It is often crucial that self-regulation operates in the shadow of rules and sanctions provided by the general law, for it is these which are the most obvious and visible (but not the

---

[361] For example, even a wider range of sanctions under self-regulation may not work against recalcitrants. Shaming cannot work against firms with no reputation to protect. Expulsion cannot work where firms can still operate effectively outside the industry association.

[362] On pyramid, see, in particular, I. Ayres & J. Braithwaite, *Responsive Regulation: Transcending the Deregulation Debate* (1992), Oxford University Press, New York.

only) means of giving regulatees the incentive to comply with the self-regulatory programme. The relationship between Responsible Care and the laws relating to due diligence, described above, is a good example. Certainly, there is considerable evidence, from a variety of jurisdictions, that it is largely fear of government regulation *and its enforcement* that drives the large majority of self-regulatory initiatives,[363] and it seems unlikely that they will perform well, in the absence of the threat of government intervention, including sanctions at the top of the enforcement pyramid which, in many circumstances, only government has the authority to invoke.

The role of third parties   Third parties acting as surrogate regulators, will often be a useful complement to the role of general law. Indeed, it is arguable that self-regulation is very unlikely to be effective without such involvement.[364] As we have seen, the most obvious third parties with an interest in playing this role are community groups, environmental groups, or NGOs generally. This contribution may be through their use of adverse publicity or in their capacity as potential victims of code malpractice, in taking direct action against firms that breach the self-regulatory programme. There may well be a growing role for private inspection and certification services as alternatives to 'policing' by government agencies or interest groups, with withdrawal of certification as the ultimate sanction.[365] We have, similarly, seen how commercial third parties, such as insurance companies or lenders, may also serve as surrogate regulators, enforcing their interests through such sanctions as the withdrawal or denial of insurance or access the capital. However, once again, since the sanctions available to third parties are very rarely adequate to deal with all circumstances or to escalate to the top of the pyramid, they are usually better viewed as a complement to, rather than as alternative to, enforcement by government.

[363] See Dutch study in M. Aalders, 'Regulation and In-Company Environmental Management in the Netherlands' (1993) 15(2) *Law and Policy* 75.

[364] K. Webb, & A. Morrison, *The Legal Aspects of Voluntary Codes* (1996), a draft paper presented to the *Voluntary Codes Symposium*, Office of Consumer Affairs, Industry Canada and Regulatory Affairs, Treasury Board, Ottawa, September and to be included in *Exploring Voluntary Codes in the Marketplace*, edited by D. Cohen & K. Webb, Government of Canada, Ottawa, (publication due 1998), p.6.

[365] A. Gore, *From Red Tape to Results: Creating a Government that works better and costs less* (1993),US Government Printing Office, Washington DC.

Counter productive mixes and unintended consequences

In Part One of this book, we warned against the dangers of 'smorgasbordism': an approach which uncritically assumes that the more instruments the better, and is the regulatory equivalent of throwing in everything bar the kitchen sink. As we will see, ill considered mixes can easily cause unintended consequences and be counter productive.

For example, liability rules are often advocated by neo-liberal economists as the preferred option in circumstances where the free market alone will not produce optimal results, on the basis that they are less interventionist and more efficient than direct regulation.[366] Yet not only do liability rules have a number of serious limitations, identified in chapter two, they can also be highly counterproductive because of the impact which they have on other policy instruments. For example, we have argued that transparency and accountability are essential aspects of many policy mixes. Yet liability rules (particularly under the adversarial and litigious United States system) provide a considerable disincentive to companies making information about their environmental performance public, for fear of liability entanglements.[367] In the case of the United States chemical industry, there is evidence that companies are deterred from using accident event analysis to gather information aimed at improving safety and environmental performance for fear that the same information will be used against them as a basis for civil liability.[368]

Similarly, we referred earlier to the considerable potential in the chemical industry to facilitate 'waste exchanges', whereby material which is 'waste' to one facility can be used productively by another. Or, to take a simple example, if one small chemical company is discharging an alkali waste and another an acid one, a simple exchange may serve to neutralize many of the problems those chemicals may cause when discharged to sewer. Yet the rigid and onerous requirements of United States legislation regarding hazardous wastes may serve, unnecessarily, to inhibit or prevent, many such transfers. Again, the mandatory disclosure of environmental audits and their use in criminal proceedings can lead to a reluctance to engage in such audits in the first place, yet another clearly counter productive result.

[366] See chapter two, p.78 and references therein.

[367] D. Hunter & E. S. Kiesche, 'US—Implementation Time' (17 June 1992) *Chemical Week* 10.

[368] I. Rosenthal, *Major Event Analysis in the US Chemical Industry: Organisational learning vs liability* (1996), Working Paper, Wharton School of Business, University of Pennsylvania, Philadelphia.

Finally, while we have advocated the virtues of tripartism and empowering community groups and environmental NGOs, it must be acknowledged that an untrammelled right to bring citizen suits can be counter productive. For example, as we noted in chapter three, some incentives for litigation (e.g., bounty hunting provisions) can encourage groups to sue the easiest targets rather than the worst polluters, and even when they do not, such actions threaten to damage long-term negotiated strategies between regulators and industry.

7. Political acceptability: achieving win-win solutions

One of the evaluation criteria for regulatory design, identified in chapter one, was political acceptability. There may well be a tension between achieving this result and what is optimal in terms of efficiency or effectiveness. In the real world, many solutions which fall well short of optimality will, nevertheless, be extremely valuable. Pragmatists reasonably ask: can we find a solution under which none of the main stakeholders are appreciably worse off, and some are better off? Given the many serious defects in most existing systems of regulation, such outcomes should not be too difficult to identify, and in some circumstances it may indeed be possible to go one better and find solutions under which *all* of the stakeholders are better off.

The main proposals we have made for regulatory flexibility and, in particular, for 'track two' regulation building on Responsible Care or ISO 14001, may indeed provide such solutions.[369] For regulators, they promise: enhanced environmental performance (including in areas not covered by regulation), objectively demonstrated; reduced transaction costs (enabling them to redirect scarce resources elsewhere); more timely and better information flow from companies (via the annual audit under ISO); and transfer of monitoring costs to the firm, and increased community involvement. For public interest groups, they promise not just better environmental performance, but also meaningful public consultation and dialogue, including better access to information and better quality information concerning business environmental performance. For business, they offer enhanced credibility (not just with the community, but also with trading partners and with government), greater flexibility and autonomy, positive environmental

---

[369] I am indebted to a current Wharton School project for parts of this list (see also P. Kleindorfer, *Market Based Environmental Audits and Environmental Risks: Implementing ISO 14000* (1996), Working Paper, The Wharton School, University of Pennsylvania, Philadelphia).

and (arguably) economic outcomes,[370] and reduced transaction costs.[371]

Conclusion

The more sceptical reader may be tempted to conclude that the above discussion has been somewhat idealistic, and that political realities preclude significant redesign of industry regulation, particularly in relation to a sector such as chemicals, with a relatively mature regulatory environment. We think not, although we concede that some regulatory systems are more amenable to reform than are others. For example, the adversarial culture which characterizes regulation in the United States, with its associated legislative and political gridlock, makes regulatory reform much more difficult than in the more consensus-based cultures of Northern Europe.[372] But changes have begun to take place in both settings.

Indeed, what is striking is the speed and extent to which the regulatory environment is changing, even during the period of this research. Ideas that four years ago were barely on the agenda, are today part of the political mainstream, and while substantial redesign of the regulatory environment (in the chemicals sector or elsewhere) still seems some way away in all but a very few countries, much else has happened. The proliferation of pilot projects, of experiments at federal, state and local

[370] In addition to facilitating 'win-win' solutions (see M. Porter, *The Competitive Advantage of Nations* (1990), MacMillan Press, London) regulatory flexibility may lead to reduced insurance premiums , reduced risk of litigation, and the flexibility to devise least cost solutions to environmental problems. However, the start up and, indeed, continuing costs of implementing an EMS may be considerable particularly for small companies (see, above, pp.227–228).

[371] While those latter benefits may be significant, it will be crucial that they are coupled with incentives sufficient to offset the accountability and transparency measures which would be a condition of regulatory flexibility. In the final analysis, none of these proposals may be viable unless industry itself is convinced that the benefits (including incentives) substantially outweigh the costs. Significantly, the USEPA in pursuing 'reinventing' initiatives and regulatory flexibility, has been unable and unwilling to extend the benefits that would be necessary for widespread participation in such programs. See D. A. Carr and W. L. Thomas, 'Devising A Compliance Strategy Under the ISO 14000 International Environmental Management Standards' (1997) 15 *Pace Environmental Law Review* 85.

[372] The impact of individual programmes is, similarly, likely to vary substantially. For example, in general, Responsible Care has developed much further in North America and Australia than it has in Western Europe, but even within the latter there are significant differences between countries. It has proven much less popular in Germany (where the dominant approach is 'engineer driven or 'performance oriented' than in the UK, where companies are much more 'management driven').

level, and the whole thrust of 'reinventing environmental regulation' in the United States, or to a lesser extent initiatives sparked by the Fifth Action Program in the European Union, have advanced the regulatory reform debate substantially, and in ways which are largely consistent with (albeit differently conceptualized to) the themes and arguments of this chapter.

Out of this experimentation and re-examination of environmental regulation, the building blocks for successful environmental policy design may gradually be emerging: a managerial and less directive role for government; a broader range of instruments; and the capacity to harness the potential of a wider range of institutions, and the use of combinations of instruments and institutions rather than single instruments or institutions acting alone. However, this is happening *ad hoc*, without coherence, and in the absence of any broader framework or theory of regulatory design within which these developments might be located and better understood, mistakes minimized and opportunities maximized. The aim of the final Part of this book is to provide such a framework and to develop a broader vision of regulatory design which provides principles and processes for the integration of instruments and parties in a synergistic and complementary fashion, in such a way as to optimize (or at least substantially improve) the policy mix.

5 The Agriculture Industry*

Peter Grabosky and Neil Gunningham

Agriculture is one of the world's oldest industries. It is basic to human civilisation, fundamental to human survival, and a major contributor to the economy of many nations. Yet it is also one of the principal causes of environmental degradation. Many contemporary agricultural practices, which have achieved substantially higher yields and lower prices, have also exacted a high environmental cost in terms of land degradation, loss of habitat and biodiversity, and non-point source pollution. At the extreme, unsustainable agriculture poses the danger of irreversible harm which can produce major environmental catastrophe or system collapse.

This chapter examines environmental regulation and policy as it relates to agriculture, focusing on two basic agro-environmental issues: the more general problem of threats to biodiversity (hereafter biodiversity) *on private land*[1] and the more specific topic of agricultural chemicals. We begin by examining some of the ways in which agricultural practices can harm the environment and the characteristics of the agriculture industry itself. We then review the traditional means by which agricultural practices have been regulated. Observing some of the shortcomings which have tended to characterize agricultural regulation, we go on to explore in some detail how particular *combinations* of instruments and institutions might be used to constitute a policy regime

* Some aspects of this chapter relating to biodiversity policy design draw on ideas developed by Neil Gunningham and Mike Young while writing a report to the Australian Government's Department of Environment Sport and Territories (M. D. Young, N. Gunningham, J. Elix, J. Lambert, B. Howard, P. Grabosky, E. McCrone, *Reimbursing the Future: An evaluation of motivational, voluntary, price-based, property-right, and regulatory incentives for the conservation of biodiversity* (1996), Biodiversity Series Paper No. 9, Department of the Environment, Sport and Territories, Biodiversity Unit, Canberra) and previously appeared in N. Gunningham and M. D. Young 'Towards Optimal Environmental Policy: The Case of Biodiversity Conservation' (1997) 24(2) *Ecology Law Quarterly* 244–297. They were also heavily relied upon (with acknowledgment) in OECD, *Saving Biological Diversity: Economic Incentives* (1996), OECD, Paris. The final version of this chapter has particularly benefited from comments on an earlier draft by Lee Breckenridge and Jan Keppler.

[1] We do not purport to address the very different (in policy terms) issue of how to protect biodiversity on public land, for example on reserves or through protected areas.

capable of moving us much closer to the goal of sustainable agriculture.[2] In some circumstances at least, we conclude that the severity of the consequences of policy failure and the limited dependability of any single policy instrument necessitate a regulatory strategy which uses the full suite of instruments available, while in others a much more selective approach is justified.

Section 1: The agricultural industry and its environmental impact

Over the last fifty years, the practice of agriculture has undergone substantial transformation.[3] In the industrialised world, developments in a range of technologies have facilitated a dramatic increase in concentration and specialization. Many small, mixed farms have given way to large specialized enterprises able to benefit from economies of scale. Food and fibre productivity have increased dramatically, due to mechanization, increased chemical use, specialization, and government policies (including price supports and subsidies, which favoured maximizing production).[4] Of particular importance has been the intensification of agriculture, facilitated by the growing use of fertilizers and pesticides.[5]

These changes have allowed fewer farmers, with reduced labour, to produce the majority of the food and fibre required by the consumer. They have led to a shrinking farm population, much larger farms and fields, and the production of a relatively restricted number of crops, often grown in monoculture. The food system in many developed nations has become vertically integrated to an unprecedented extent. As a result, large retailers now have significant influence over primary food production. In some locations, huge surpluses of agricultural commodities have been produced and stockpiled.[6]

---

[2] For a definition of sustainable agriculture, see President's Council on Sustainable Development, *Sustainable America: A New Consensus* (1996), Washington DC, p.125 and following.

[3] University of California Sustainable Agriculture Research and Education Program, *What Is Sustainable Agriculture?* (1996), http://www.sarep.ucdavis.edu/sarep/concept.html.

[4] Recent statistics from FAO give some indication of the magnitude of world agricultural production. Statistics are for the year 1996, in metric tons: Cereals 2,033,380,000; Vegetables 555,070,300; and Fruit 410,280,400.

[5] G. Debailleul, 'Economic Incentives for Biodiversity Conservation in the Agricultural Sector' in OECD, *Investing In Biological Diversity: The Cairns Conference* (1997), OECD, Paris, p.237.

[6] OECD, *Agricultural and Environmental Policies: Opportunities for integration* (1989), OECD, Paris, pp.13–15; OECD, *Towards Sustainable Agricultural Production: Cleaner Technologies* (1994), OECD, Paris, pp.14–16 and 69–71; OECD, *Agricultural and Environmental Policy*

These changes in agricultural production, while contributing to the sustenance of humankind, have also taken their toll on the environment. This is manifest in four basic ways: loss of biological diversity; loss of natural habitats, pollution of off-farm ecosystems; and on-farm pollution occasioning loss of productivity. Closely related are the risks to human health posed by direct or indirect exposure to agricultural chemicals. As we will observe, these problems are themselves interrelated and can inflict multiple harms: pollution is an obvious threat to biodiversity; inappropriate use of agricultural chemicals can impact on biodiversity and damage ecosystems, as well as contaminate produce. Below, we examine in more detail the specific threats that relate most directly to biodiversity conservation on private land and to the use of agricultural chemicals.

Threats to land-based biodiversity

'Biodiversity' refers to the broadly diverse forms into which organisms have evolved and is, generally, considered at three levels. 'Genetic diversity' refers to the variation in genes enabling organisms to evolve and adapt to new conditions. Species diversity refers to the number, types, and distribution of species within an ecosystem. 'Ecosystem diversity' refers to the variety of habitats and communities of different species that interact in a complex web of interdependent relationships.

Biodiversity is essential in the maintenance of human life on earth. Scientists have long acknowledged that the preservation of biodiversity is, by definition, vital for an ecologically sustainable society. Humanity derives all its food, as well as many medicines and industrial products, from domesticated and undomesticated components of biodiversity. Biodiversity is also important as a source of current benefits created by natural ecosystem processes that are not yet fully understood, such as water purification, soil fertilization, and groundwater recharge. Loss of genetic diversity could imperil agriculture.[7]

Integration: Recent Progress and New Directions (1993), OECD, Paris, p.37; D. J. Briggs & F. M. Courtney, *Agriculture and Environment: The physical geography of temperate agricultural systems* (1985), Longman, London, pp.3–6; Y. Hayami & V. W. Ruttan, *Agricultural Development: An international perspective* (1985), The John Hopkins University Press, Baltimore, p.228; and OECD, *Sustainable Agriculture: Concepts, issues and policies in OECD countries* (1995), OECD, Paris, pp.11–16.

[7] E. O. Wilson, *The Diversity of Life* (1992), Harvard University Press, Cambridge, Mass., pp.281–310 (discussing the benefits humanity obtains from biodiversity); Australia and New Zealand Task Force on Biological Diversity, *National Strategy for the Conservation of Australia's Biological Diversity* (1993), Department of the Environment Sports and Territories, Canberra, p.2; E. B. Barbier, J. C. Burgess, & C. Folke, *Paradise Lost? The*

There are many causes of biodiversity loss, including habitat loss and fragmentation, human exploitation, and competition from and predation by introduced species. Currently, it is estimated more than 10,000 species become extinct globally each year.[8] While precise calculation is difficult, it is certain that this rate has increased alarmingly in recent years.

Agriculture, and in particular the agricultural practices which have been developed in recent decades, has been a major cause of biodiversity loss. Indeed, a central purpose of agriculture is 'to reduce biodiversity on the territory it occupies, since it seeks to maximise the yield of a limited number of animal and plant species by weakening the competition to which those species could be exposed from other, unwanted species'.[9]

The filling, draining, channelling, and damming of wetlands and waterways, for example, have had had enormous effects on species such as migratory birds,[10] while surface and groundwater depletion through withdrawals of water for agriculture, and irrigation practices, have also had a serious deleterious impact.[11] But perhaps the most serious threat to land-based biodiversity is habitat destruction resulting from agricultural use. The land on which crops are grown or livestock grazed must be cleared of vegetation. Very little remains of the vegetation which covered the land prior to the advent of modern agriculture. In Bangladesh, only six per cent of the original vegetation remains; forests around the Mediterranean Sea probably covered ten times their current area; and in the Netherlands and Britain, less than four per cent of the lowland raised bogs remain undamaged.[12] In Britain, over fifty

ecological economics of biodiversity (1994), Earthscan Publications, London, p.18: and C. Prescott-Allen & R. Prescott-Allen, *The First Resource: Wild species in the North American Economy* (1986), Yale University Press, New Haven.

[8] Biodiversity Resource Center at the California Academy of Sciences (last visited March 25 1997) <http://cas.calacademy.org/~library/biodiv/biodiv.html> p.1.

[9] G. Debailleul, 'Economic Incentives for Biodiversity Conservation in the Agricultural Sector' in OECD, *Investing In Biological Diversity: The Cairns Conference* (1997), OECD, Paris, p.236.

[10] J. Mummery & N. Hardy, *Australia's Biodiversity: An overview of selected significant components* (1994), Biodiversity Series, Paper No. 2, Biodiversity Unit, Department of Environment Sport & Territories, Canberra.

[11] Commonwealth Department of Environment Sport & Territories, *The National Strategy for the Conservation of Australia's Biological Diversity* (1996), Department of Environment Sport & Territories, Canberra.

[12] World Resource Institute (IUCN. UNEP), *Global Biodiversity Strategy: Guidelines for action to save, study, and use earth's biotic wealth sustainably and equitably* (1992), WRI, Washington DC, p.9.

per cent of ancient woodlands have been cleared since the Second World War.[13] Currently, immense stretches of the Amazon rainforest are being cleared to make way for agriculture.

Clearing vegetation for purposes of agricultural development also serves to fragment the underlying ecosystem.[14] This may alter the microclimate within and surrounding the remaining natural vegetation. For example, the solar radiation associated with the area may change, causing higher daytime temperatures and lower night time temperatures, increasing the risk of frost. In addition, clearing in the course of cultivation or grazing can cause soil degradation through wind and water erosion.[15] Subsequent changes to water balance, in turn, can produce widespread salinity, increased soil erosion, and sedimentation of nearby river systems.[16] Remnant vegetation in salt-affected areas, as well as adjacent lakes, wetlands and rivers, may decay or become permanently altered.[17] Ironically, clearing undertaken to enhance agricultural productivity can also lead to a decline in yield.

Habitat disturbance may also effect wildlife population, concentrations, and movements.[18] Conventional farming requires the application

[13] P. Lowe, G. Cox, M. MacEwen, T. O'Riordan & M. Winter, *Countryside Conflicts: The politics of farming, forestry, and conservation* (1986), Brookfield Publishing, Aldershot, p.56 (B. Howard, 'WA Wheatbelt Case Study' in M. D. Young, N. Gunningham, J. Elix, J. Lambert, B. Howard, P. Grabosky, E. McCrone, *Reimbursing the Future: An evaluation of motivational, voluntary, price-based, property-right, and regulatory incentives for the conservation of biodiversity* (1996), Biodiversity Series Paper No. 9, Department of the Environment, Sport and Territories, Biodiversity Unit, Canberra, (1996), Appendix 2.1, part 2, p.40).

[14] See J. B. Kirkpatrick, 'The Geography and Politics of Species Endangerment in Australia' (1991) 29(2) *Australian Geographical Studies* 246–254.

[15] Beyond the threats which it may pose to biodiversity, soil degradation itself detracts from agricultural productivity. Soil degradation is, arguably, the major environmental problem in some developed countries today and is of serious concern in much of the developing world. P. Gretton & U. Salma, *Land Degradation and the Australian Agricultural Industry* (1996), June, Industry Commission, Canberra; B. Beale & P. Fray, *The Vanishing Continent: Australia's degraded environment* (1990), Hodder & Stoughton, Sydney; and R. D. Grartz, M. A. Wilson & S. K. Campbell, *Landcover Disturbance Over the Australian Continent: A contemporary assessment* (1995), A. report for the Department of the Environment, Sports and Territories, Biodiversity Series, Paper No. 7, Biodiversity Unit, Canberra. For the United States, see G. Gardner, *Shrinking Fields: Cropland Loss in a World of Eight Billion* (1996), Worldwatch Paper No. 131, The Worldwatch Institute, Washington, DC.

[16] D. A. Saunders, R. J. Hobbs & C. R. Margules, 'Biological Consequences of Ecosystem Fragmentation: A review' (1991) 5(1) *Conservation Biology* 18–32.

[17] See D. L. McFarlane, R. J. George & P. Farrington 'Changes in the Hydrologic Cycle' in R. J. Hobbs & D. A. Saunders (eds.) *Reintegrating Fragmented Landscapes* (1993), Springer-Verlag, New York. McFarlane *et al.* observe that agriculture can produce irreversible changes to hydrology.

[18] A. A. Burbidge & K. J. Wallace, 'Practical Steps for Conserving Biodiversity' in R. A. Bradstock, T. D. Auld, D. A. Keith, R. T. Kingsford, D. Lunney & D. P. Sivertsen

of fertilizer and chemicals to control weeds, diseases, and animal pests. These, in turn, when inappropriately applied, can damage ecosystems and enter the food chain, as we describe more fully in the next section below. The intensification of agriculture in particular (relying heavily on these practices), has been responsible for serious reductions both in *in situ* and *ex situ* biodiversity.[19]

Agricultural chemicals: pesticides and fertilizers

Pesticides (a term which we will use broadly to include insecticides, herbicides, and fungicides for controlling weeds, animal pests, and various plant and livestock diseases) can be toxic to humans, domestic animals, and wildlife, as well as to plants. They can cause cancer, neurological damage, and disrupt endocrine systems.[20] Pesticides may persist in soils, groundwater, rainwater, lakes and rivers, and other media, including food and particularly in breast milk. They may become concentrated in the food chain through processes of bioaccumulation.

Pesticides reach soil not only when applied directly, but also when they are washed off foliage or drift during application. Pesticides in soil can affect animals against which they are not directed. Many of these, such as earthworms, mites, and fly larvae, are essential in the breakdown of some kinds of leaf litter and incorporating nutrients into soil. Pesticides may also harm those species which help to control pest populations, including birds and a variety of predatory insects.

Ironically, the very pests which they have been developed to combat may develop resistance to these chemicals. Even where pesticides may succeed in eliminating a pest, new pests may fill the now vacant niche; these new pests may be capable of more harm, and yet may be less tractable than the original target species.

Aquatic systems are frequently contaminated by pesticides. These chemicals reach water by direct application, spray drift, washing from the atmosphere by precipitation, erosion, and run-off from agricultural land. These sources tend to be spasmodic and localized, although usually large and with a more serious environmental impact.

(eds.) *Conserving Biodiversity: Threats and solutions* (1995), Surrey Beatty & Sons, Chipping Norton, NSW.

[19] G. Debailleul, 'Economic Incentives for Biodiversity Conservation in the Agricultural Sector' in OECD, *Investing In Biological Diversity: The Cairns Conference* (1997), OECD, Paris, p.237.

[20] K. Short, *Quick Poison, Slow Poison: Pesticide risk in the lucky country* (1994), Envirobooks, Sydney.

Contamination can also occur by pesticides leaching to groundwater. The more soluble pesticides tend to be washed from aquatic systems relatively quickly. Regardless of solubility, however, the contamination always has an adverse effect on aquatic fauna.

The application of fertilizers may also have serious detrimental environmental impacts. Fertilizer application may change the structure and fertility of the soil. Some forms of fertilizer contribute to soil acidification and may also be toxic to animals and humans. Nitrogen and particulates may contribute to air pollution. Perhaps the most significant environmental harm arising from inappropriate application of fertilizers is their effect on waterways, where they may produce algal growth which has the effect of choking the lake or river in question. Those fertilizers which contribute heavy metal contaminants, such as cadmium, to soils can have adverse effects not only on health and the environment, but also on trade, as contaminated products encounter resistance by overseas regulatory authorities and consumers.

Section 2: Characteristics of the agriculture industry

The structure of contemporary agriculture has significant implications for the design of programmes to foster biodiversity conservation and to minimize the adverse impact of agricultural chemicals. Agriculture is not monolithic: large-scale producers of beef for export exist in a world apart from a small family engaged in market gardening. But it is important to outline the basic industry characteristics and how they must be taken into account when selecting combinations of instruments to improve environmental performance and to reduce the risk of environmental harm.

Arguably, most important is the system of subsidies and price supports which have characterized agriculture in the developed nations for most of the twentieth century. Originally intended to provide producers with some protection against the vagaries of climate and markets, these have encouraged both exploitation of marginal land and use of high chemical inputs.[21] As we will see, the existence of perverse incentives not only sends inappropriate signals to agricultural producers, but also inhibits the design of positive policy instruments.

---

[21] See Organisation for Economic Co-operation and Development (OECD), *Agricultural Policies, Markets and Trade in OECD Countries: Monitoring and evaluation* (1996), OECD, Paris; and K. Allen, (ed.) *Agricultural Policies in a New Decade. Resources for the future* (1990), Washington DC.

Also of great significance is the political culture of farming, which combines a degree of independence of spirit and resistance to regulation with the above mentioned tradition of seeking and receiving subsidies and other benefits from government. Regardless of whether this apparent paradox is understandable or justifiable, it exists, and it may be expected to influence the response of farmers to attempts on the part of government to control their behaviour. In light of these circumstances, if institutions of control can be forged within the agricultural community, their potential impact on the environmental performance of farmers will be greater.

Another aspect of the environment which now impacts significantly upon farmers is globalization. The unprecedented range of choices available to consumers of food and fibre in the industrialized world means that a producer is less able to take the consumer for granted. The increasing importance of export markets to a significant proportion of agricultural producers in many nations means that the stricter standards set by foreign regulators or markets may be more relevant to a producer's livelihood than those which his or her own government might see fit to dictate.

Related to this is the vertical integration of agriculture. The chain of supply from seed to supermarket shelf is more tightly coupled than in the past and the enormous purchasing power of large institutions, such as a major supermarket chains or fast-food franchises, makes them important actors with considerable leverage over their suppliers. Together, these factors are accompanied by increasing commercial pressure to measure and assess environmental performance as a condition of access to markets.

Another important trend (which seems likely to continue unabated) is rationalization to achieve economies of scale. Despite the concentration which began early in the twentieth century, there is in most sectors of agriculture a large number of small producers and a small number of large producers. Variation in size, and with it, variation in economic viability, may influence the producer's capacity to change his or her behaviour. As one industry representative told us, 'There's always a problem at the bottom end.'

Beyond these general patterns, farmers and farming differ not only within and between nations but also between agricultural sectors. In Australia, for example, cattle producers and cotton growers tend to be closely knit and well-organized. Vegetable growers, in contrast, are less cohesive. Such differences have profound implications for the dissemi-

nation of information across a given sector, and for the capacity of producers within that sector to influence each other's environmental performance and for their capacity to resist regulation.

Regulatory space surrounding agro-environmental issues is also populated by a variety of non-governmental institutions. There are those
whose primary concern is agricultural chemicals; others wildlife preservation; others focus on particular ecosystems. They vary in size from
giants, such as Greenpeace and the World Wildlife Fund (WWF), to
small groups of neighbours. Such a rich variety of organisations is
reflected in function and strategy. There are those which are aggres-
sively adversarial and others more low key and co-operative. Some target government or industry directly, while others aim at long-term
consumer attitude change. Others still interact directly with producers.

Special features of biodiversity and agricultural chemical use

Biodiversity, insofar as it has implications for agriculture, has a number
of features which distinguish it from more conventional environmental
protection issues, and which must be taken into account in policy
design. First, in many circumstances, biodiversity loss is irreversible.
Once lost, a species or an ecosystem is lost forever. Secondly, many
species—especially the invertebrates, microbes, and viruses—have yet
to be discovered. As a consequence, much biodiversity is lost before we
even know it is there, and before we know either its ecological role or
its potential contribution to humankind.

Thirdly, ecosystem diversity exhibits threshold effects. The ability of
ecosystems to withstand the stress imposed by environmental degradation is limited. Stressed beyond these limits, ecosystems may collapse.[22]
As a result, any policy which compromises the resilience of ecosystems
may have uncontrollable effects, and even small policy changes can
have dramatic but unforeseen results. The problem is exacerbated by
the fact that information about the responses of species to biodiversity
loss is extremely limited. For example, there is considerable uncertainty
about the nature of ecological thresholds and about the consequences
of transgressing them.

Fourthly, many biodiversity problems cannot be solved merely by
proscribing certain behaviour, but only by ensuring positive ongoing
management: thereby emphasizing the importance of developing a
'custodianship ethic'. Fifthly, much of biodiversity has no immediate

---

[22] E. B. Barbier, J. C. Burgess & C. Folke, *Paradise Lost? The ecological economics of biodiversity* (1994), Earthscan Publications, London, p.184.

economic value, giving rise to substantial tensions between public and private interests. Finally, the causes of genetic, species, and ecosystem losses are extremely diffuse in nature, and involve many different sectors and forms of economic activity. That is, biodiversity is pervasive to social and economic systems, being affected by land and water-use decisions, by pollution, and by economic use generally.[23]

There are special features associated with the use of agricultural chemicals which also have implications for regulatory system design. Perhaps the most significant is the *potential* convergence between the producer's personal interest and a wider public interest. To the extent that chemical inputs can be reduced without detracting from quality and yield, the producer profits and the public wins. However, this may not be perceived to be the case, not only because of a lack of information and education, but also because of the common gap between short-term and transitional problems (increased pests) and longer term gains (greater ultimate profit from sustainable practices).

By contrast, the interest of the farmer in controlling pests may conflict directly with a wider public interest in biodiversity conservation. Doing the right thing for biodiversity may cost the farmer directly in terms of lost productivity. It is commonly the user who gains (in terms of short-term crop yield) and the environment at large that may be damaged from intense pesticide usage.

The salience of commercial relationships to environmental performance is stronger in the domain of chemical use (for example, the importance of supply-chain pressure, referred to above). In contrast, biodiversity conservation often has no immediate economic value to producers, and land clearing issues tend, generally, to lie beyond the reach of market forces.

Although misapplication of chemicals resulting in direct acute injury occurs on occasion, most agricultural pollution is non-point in nature, with the consequence that the origin of the pollution may not be identifiable. This raises particular challenges for monitoring and enforcement.

There are, in addition, a number of characteristics common to both land clearing and the use of agricultural chemicals. In each case, adverse environmental consequences have been aggravated by farmers' low awareness of the impacts of farming practices. The presence of perverse incentives in the form of price supports and subsidies has also,

---

[23] See further, OECD, *Making Markets Work for Biological Diversity: The role of economic incentives measures* (1996), OECD, Paris.

until relatively recently, encouraged both excessive clearing and chemical use. Uncertainties of climate and commodity markets have also militated against environmentally preferable production.

And finally, the political culture of farming bears upon both biodiversity and chemical use. Producers, generally, tend to value autonomy and independence; while they welcome benefits bestowed by governments, they tend to dislike being told what they should or should not do, and they usually have an eye on the bottom line.

Implications for policy design

We have identified a number of specific characteristics of the agriculture industry, of biodiversity (and to a more limited extent), and of agricultural chemical use, which make the achievement of sustainable agriculture a very considerable policy challenge.

In particular, these characteristics serve to emphasize the limitations of single instrument approaches. For example, education and information, long a staple of politically inoffensive agricultural policy, are unlikely to work in the case of economically marginal producers, yet the opposite extreme, command and control regulation, confronts serious problems relating to both political culture and enforceability. Threshold effects and irreversible loss, in the case of biodiversity, also raise the issue of whether it is ever wise to rely on a single instrument approach, given the low dependability of even the best policy instrument acting alone. Because biodiversity is pervasive to social and economic systems, so also must biodiversity conservation policies themselves be pervasive. Similarly, the effectiveness of any new policy instrument may be seriously jeopardized unless attention is first given to the interaction between the new instrument and existing perverse incentives serving also to underscore the importance of recognizing and understanding interactions between policy instruments.

The characteristics identified above also suggest some considerable opportunities for innovative regulatory design, including a greater role for both commercial and non-commercial third parties. For example, the shift towards vertical integration gives rise to possibilities of supply chain pressure for improved environmental performance, while globalization may facilitate greater competition in international markets in terms of clearer production and organic produce. In the case of the use of agricultural chemicals, the potential convergence of interest between the interests of producers and the environmental interest (if less chemicals can still achieve the desired crop yield), in conjunction with increased market demand for less chemical residues, also holds out the potential for public policy to facilitate win-win outcomes.

It will also be apparent that neither the agriculture industry nor the environmental problems it faces are homogenous. For example, what works for large commercial conglomerates may be entirely inappropriate for 'problems at the bottom end'. Similarly, the tools needed to address the extremely diffuse causes of biodiversity loss may be unsuited to deal with issues of agricultural chemicals. For governments, these characteristics imply not only the need to design different policies to meet different problems, but also to do so in such a way as to accommodate the multifaceted nature of many of the problems themselves.

In summary, creation of sustainable agriculture demands a particularly broad array of policy instruments, tailored to the specific sub-sector or environmental threat at issue. It also holds out considerable opportunities for greater constructive involvement by both commercial and non-commercial third parties. In later sections of this chapter, we argue the case not only for particular combinations of instruments, but also for the harnessing of a broader range of institutional actors to implement those combinations. However, before embarking on this central challenge, it is necessary to examine the existing regulatory environment in order to see what works, what doesn't work, and why.

Section 3: The regulatory environment and its shortcomings

Traditionally, regulation of agriculture has been informal, based upon the provision of information and persuasion by government authorities, whose fundamental role has been not to police agricultural producers, but to assist them to do the right thing. For example, in the early days, regulation of agriculture focused on the promotion and development of the industry, and even when environmental concerns were raised this did little to change the basic model of agricultural support rather than regulatory control.[24] The low public visibility of non-compliance further reduced what small risk of detection and sanctioning might have existed. Only relatively recently, and only in the most environmentally progressive countries, has the sanctity of private property and the widely held view that a landowner is free to do whatever he or she

---

[24] N. F. Barr & J. W. Cary, *Greening a Brown Land: The Australian search for sustainable land use* (1992), Macmillan, South Melbourne; and B. R. Davidson, *European Farming in Australia: An economic history of Australian farming* (1981), Elsevier Scientific Publications, Amsterdam.

wishes with their land begun to yield to concerns for a wider public interest. The result is a grudging recognition that even privately owned agricultural land is part of a larger ecosystem. This, in turn, has been accompanied by a partial (but only partial) erosion of the traditional model of agricultural support, and the introduction of a variety of formal and informal constraints on land use and on the use of agricultural chemicals.

Inevitably, the regulatory response has not been uniform across jurisdictions. The particular regulatory configuration has depended upon a number of factors, primarily those relating to the intensity of environmental problems and to the prevailing political culture.[25] In particular, the degree of state intervention has, commonly, varied with the balance of influence wielded by the main stakeholders—environmental and consumer interest groups, on the one hand, and producer interests, on the other. This reflects, in part, the relative salience of agriculture within a jurisdiction's economy; the regime for regulating pesticide use in California is, for example, much more stringent than that prevailing in Iowa.[26] And finally, societies characterized more by consensus than by aggressive adversarialism have, generally, experienced fewer state imposed solutions and more remedies emerging from voluntary co-operation and compromise at the grass-roots. The historical importance of voluntary codes of practice for British agriculture contrast sharply with the prevailing regime of environmental protection in the United States.[27]

For the purposes of this chapter, it is not necessary to delve into the intricacies of regulatory policy in any particular jurisdiction. Rather, we

---

[25] P. Glasbergen, 'Agro-Environmental Policy: Trapped in an iron law?' (1992) 32(1) *Sociologia Ruralis* 30–48. All else equal, where agro-environmental issues are high on the public agenda, and there are fewer competing environmental concerns such as those arising from industrial pollution, one may expect more direct state intervention to regulate agricultural practices.

[26] In 1990, California became the first state to require that all agricultural pesticide use be reported. Today, this includes not only pesticides used on crops but also applications to such sites as parks and golf courses, as well as roadside weed control applications. See http://www.cdpr.ca.gov/noback.htm.

[27] One exception to this generalization is the case of the Netherlands, a nation otherwise characterised by co-operation rather than by command, but which has developed 'the most elaborate and compulsory system of regulations for the use of agricultural nutrients of any country' (P. Glasbergen, 'Agro-Environmental Policy: Trapped in an iron law?' (1992) 32(1) *Sociologia Ruralis* 30–48 at 36. See also M. Wiering, 'Regulating Farmers: Enforcement styles in the environmental regulation of the animal husbandry in the Netherlands' (1996), Paper presented at the Annual Meeting of the Law and Society Association, Glasgow, Scotland, 11 July). This may be explained by the intensity of the nutrient problem in a densely populated environment.

confine ourselves (immediately below) to identifying the main features of existing regulatory regimes as they relate to biodiversity conservation and agricultural chemicals, and (later in this section), to the main limitations of those regimes (while acknowledging differences between them). This is a necessary precursor to our main theme, the re-design of regulatory policy, harnessing a broader mix of instruments and institutional actors tailored to the particular circumstances of the two areas of agriculture upon which we focus.

In the case of biodiversity conservation, the main policy options are: *ex situ* conservation of species (seed banks, botanical gardens, etc.); preserving certain features in their entirety by banning farming there; protecting agricultural land of high natural value; certain forms of reduction in intensiveness of agricultural inputs with a substantial environmental impact; and protecting endangered species and promoting farming practices that use a reduced amount of agrochemical inputs.[28]

The choice of policy options actually invoked in protecting biodiversity has depended, at least in part, upon the threat being addressed and upon the political, cultural, and economic variables identified above. To avoid the exhausting, impractical (and for present purposes), unproductive task of addressing each the individual instruments available,[29] we instead classify the various instruments in terms of a small number of categories which, while informative, are not exclusive.[30] These are: information-based instruments;[31] voluntary instruments;[32] self-

[28] This list is based on G. Debailleul, 'Economic Incentives for Biodiversity Conservation in the Agricultural Sector' in OECD, *Investing In Biological Diversity: The Cairns Conference* (1997), OECD, Paris, p.241.

[29] For a useful general summary, see T. Panayotou, *Economic Instruments for Environmental Management and Sustainable Development* (1994), International Environment Program, Harvard Institute for International Development, Harvard University, Massachusetts, US.

[30] For example, many property right instruments combine regulation, price-based and institutional incentives into a single package.

[31] These are designed to heighten agricultural producers' awareness of the importance of biodiversity conservation for their own interests as well as for the wider public interest. In some cases, they explicitly encourage flora and fauna conservation, as well as land stewardship. In their basic form, they entail many elements of the traditional agricultural extension service, although in some cases, efforts are made to involve the wider community in the production and dissemination of information.

[32] A wide range of voluntary mechanisms have been introduced, with varying degrees of formality, in which co-operative agreements are reached between primary producers and government in furtherance of specific conservation goals. In some jurisdictions, farmers may nominate part of their land as a registered private sanctuary. In general, to the extent that they are widely heralded, voluntary programmes serve a broader, educative purpose beyond the immediate conservation goals at which they are aimed.

regulation; positive incentives;[33] property right, market and price-based instruments (the latter group of which we classified generically as economic instruments in chapter two);[34] and regulation in various forms (e.g., zoning,[35] restrictions on land clearing;[36] and protection of threatened

[33] For example, a number of incentive programmes exist to foster the propagation of endangered species. Scottish Natural Heritage, in an effort to preserve the habitat of the corncrake, an endangered bird species, offers crofters a bounty for the use of special grassland management methods. In return for keeping livestock out of enclosed grasslands between the months of April and July, crofters may receive a bounty of £20 per acre per year for the first 12 acres; £10 per acre per year for the next 12 acres; and £4 per acre per year for the remainder of habitat preserved (A. Cramb, 'Protection Money Will Help Crofters and Corncrakes' (1993) *Reuters News Service*, 24 February).

A variety of other positive incentive instruments may be available for biodiversity conservation, including tax relief, government leasing of environmentally sensitive areas from landowners, and outright grants. In some locations, land containing significant biodiversity value can be purchased outright and set aside for conservation purposes by governments, or non-profit organisations. The most prominent of these is the Nature Conservancy, which controls over 1,500 reserves and manages over one million acres in the United States and elsewhere.

[34] Increasing attention has been accorded regulatory mechanisms involving the creation and transfer of property rights in furtherance of biodiversity conservation. The creation of easements and covenants, which restrict a landholder's ability to exercise certain rights over his or her land, are perhaps the most prominent example. Governments or third parties may also acquire easements or covenants. (M. D. Young, N. Gunningham, J. Elix, J. Lambert, B. Howard, P. Grabosky, E. McCrone, *Reimbursing the Future: An evaluation of motivational, voluntary, price-based, property-right, and regulatory incentives for the conservation of biodiversity* (1996), Biodiversity Series Paper No. 9, Department of the Environment, Sport and Territories, Biodiversity Unit, Canberra, vol 2, p.10). The Wetlands Reserve Program in the United States is a good example of the application of easements. In return for payment, participants agree to set aside wetland over a 30-year period, and implement a conservation plan (Organisation for Economic Co-operation and Development (OECD), *Economic Incentive Measures for the Conservation and Sustainable Use of Biological Diversity: A. Survey of OECD Member Countries* (1994a), Group on Economic and Environment Policy Integration, Expert Group on Economic Aspects of Biodiversity, OECD, Paris).

Market-based mechanisms are also evolving to include such devices as tradeable development rights (analogous to tradeable emissions permits) (T. Panayotou, *Economic Instruments for Environmental Management and Sustainable Development* (1994), unpublished manuscript, Harvard Institute for International Development, Harvard University, Cambridge, MA).

[35] One of the more common regulatory instruments applied to agricultural production is that of zoning, that is, restrictions on where certain types of agricultural activities may take place (P. Glasbergen, 'Agro-Environmental Policy: Trapped in an iron law?' (1992) 32(1) *Sociologia Ruralis* 30–48 at 36). The Netherlands, for example, has specified certain groundwater protection zones, within which stringent requirements for manure management apply. Similarly, the French have water source protection zones, in which certain agricultural practices are prohibited (P. Glasbergen, 'Agro-Environmental Policy: Trapped in an iron law?' (1992) 32(1) *Sociologia Ruralis* 30–48 at 36 and 39). Authorities in the United Kingdom have introduced nitrate-sensitive areas (N. Ward, 'Technological Change and the Regulation of Pollution from Agricultural Pesticides' (1995) 26(1) *Geoforum* 19–33).

[36] In many locations around the world, the issue of land clearing is now a matter of

species[37]). Later, in Section 4 of this chapter, when examining broader instrument combinations, we provide an elaboration and specific examples of the most important of these instruments.

For the present it is sufficient to note that, notwithstanding the quite wide range of instruments available in practice, most governments, in most circumstances, have utilized only a very limited number of them, and these have been, principally: (i) subsidies; and; (ii) piecemeal regulation prohibiting particular acts.[38] Moreover, as we will see in the next subsection below, the former have often proved environmentally counterproductive, while the latter have, commonly, suffered from serious design faults. These limitations have been exacerbated by a failure to realize that complex problems defy simple solutions, and, in particular, by a failure to use a sufficiently broad range of tools in complementary combinations or in conjunction with a broader range of social actors.

In contrast to the range of instruments which are available (albeit not commonly used) to address biodiversity conservation, a much more limited set of instruments have evolved to deal with the problems caused

history. In others, it is of intense contemporary significance. Contrast the European experience, for example, with that of Brazil, where massive clearing of the Amazonian rainforests continues unrelentingly. In the developed world, prohibitions on land clearing have been increasingly common in and near areas of particular ecological significance, such as wetlands. Land use planning systems are common mechanisms of control (D. Farrier, 'Vegetation Conservation: The planning system as a vehicle for the regulation of broadacre agricultural land clearing' (1991) 18(1) *Melbourne University Law Review* 26–59). In other settings, landholders enter into management agreements with governments, and agree to refrain from particular activities (or to engage in certain environmentally beneficial activities), with or without reimbursement (International Institute for Sustainable Development (IISD) International Institute for Sustainable Development (IISD) *Making Budgets Green: Leading practices in taxation and subsidy reform* (1994), IISD, Winnipeg). Within the European Community, landholders receive compensation if they agree to maintain features of the landscape (UNEP, *Measures for the Conservation of Biodiversity and Sustainable Use of its Components* (1994), Global Biodiversity Assessment, UNEP, Nairobi).

[37] Most jurisdictions have legislation to prevent the extinction and to promote the recovery of threatened species, populations and ecological communities. Perhaps the most prominent of these is the United States Endangered Species Act. Passed in 1973 and reauthorised in 1988, the Act regulates a wide range of activities which impact on plants and animals designated as endangered or threatened (C. C. Mann & M. L. Plummer, *Noah's Choice: The future of endangered species* (1996), Knopf, New York; and National Research Council, *Science and the Endangered Species Act* (1995), National Academy Press, Washington, DC).

[38] In the main, species specific measures (mostly the prohibition or limitation of taking) have dominated but note the gradual emergence of a new type of instrument: the threatening process concept. See C. de Klemm 'The Regulation and Management of Destructive Processes' *Environmental Law and Policy* (1997) 27(4) 350–354. See also C. Ford Runge, 'Environmental Protection from Farm to Market' in M. R. Chertow and D. C. Esty, *Thinking Ecologically: The Next Generation of environmental policy* (1997) Yale UP.

by agricultural chemicals (though, as we will see in Section 4, these too can usefully be dealt with in terms of the instrument categories developed above). The modest range of instruments devised to address agricultural chemicals is itself an indication of the relative complexity of these two environmental issues.

At the core of agricultural chemical regulation today are the restrictive regulations which govern the manufacture, distribution, and use of pesticides.[39] In most developed agricultural nations, there are stringent laws governing the marketing and use of agricultural chemicals. Traditionally, these restrictions are based on pre-marketing clearance following item-by-item reviews. The most dangerous substances are prohibited altogether or authorized only for restricted use.[40] Other substances are authorized for more general use. In some jurisdictions, pesticides may only be applied under specified circumstances by licensed applicators. Regulatory authorities can, and do, deregister or impose additional restrictions on the use of a substance when new information comes to light which bears upon safety of the substance in question.[41]

One of the toughest regimes is that of the United States. Thousands of pesticide products have been registered under standards which have evolved in tandem with science and public policy. To ensure that previously registered pesticides measure up to current scientific and regulatory standards, the Federal Insecticide, Fungicide and Rodenticide Act (FIFRA) requires the review and 'reregistration' of all existing pesticides.

Many other counties have followed a broadly similar route in terms of requiring pesticide registration.[42] Within the countries comprising

[39] We use the term 'pesticides' to refer collectively to insecticides, fungicides, rodenticides, and related products.

[40] For an overview of the most dangerous substances, see gopher://gopher. igc.apc.org:70/00/orgs/panna/reports/dozen/dozen_aboutchart.

[41] DDT, once used liberally in many western nations, is largely prohibited. Among the products which have been withdrawn or had further restrictions placed upon their use in recent years by Australian authorities are persistent organochlorines, mercurial fungicides, and dithiocarbamates (Commonwealth of Australia, Department of Primary Industries and Energy, Standing Committee on Agriculture and Resource Management, Agricultural and Veterinary Chemicals Policy Committee, *Australian National Strategy for Agricultural and Veterinary Chemicals*, Draft, 10 April 1997, Department of Primary Industries and Energy, Canberra, p.9).

[42] For example, Australia's current management arrangements for agricultural and veterinary chemicals (Commonwealth of Australia, Department of Primary Industries and Energy, Standing Committee on Agriculture and Resource Management, Agricultural and Veterinary Chemicals Policy Committee, *Australian National Strategy for Agricultural and Veterinary Chemicals*, Draft, 10 April 1997, Department of Primary Industries and Energy, Canberra) consists of three components: a national registration scheme

the European Union, there has been much effort to harmonize and develop programmes for chemical safety, including a substantial number of European Union Directives.[43] Each Member State is obliged to prohibit the marketing or use within its territory of substances or preparations, including imports from non-European Commission countries, which fail to comply with the directives.

However, there is much more to the regulation of agricultural chemicals than merely pre-market certification of substances, and penalties for flagrantly inappropriate use. In recent years, a number of instruments have been and are being developed to complement registration systems and legislative mandates for the reduced use of agricultural chemicals. For example, both Sweden and Denmark[44] have sought to use voluntary targets and mandated reduction to influence the amount of chemical use. In Sweden, an initial reduction target of fifty per cent of the 1981–85 average over five years was imposed in 1985, together with a re-evaluation of existing pesticides, with more stringent criteria for registration. Farmers were not consulted, but now boast of who can achieve the highest yield with the least pesticide. Sweden is now working towards a second reduction target of a further twenty-five per cent of the 1981–85 average by 1996. The targets are legislatively mandated, and supported by a variety of other instruments, including information and industry-based initiatives.[45] In Denmark, a more voluntaristic approach has been adopted.[46] Other initiatives which

which assesses the suitability of a chemical, and authorises its manufacture and supply to the point of sale; regulation of safe and appropriate use which tends to be based on information and education; and traditional regulatory instruments. Residue monitoring programmes are supported by both government and industry sectors, as are various research and development activities.

[43] An European Community Directive is an European Community law binding on the Member States as to the result to be achieved, but the choice of method is left to each individual state. In practice, national implementing legislation in the form deemed appropriate in each Member State is necessary in most cases.

[44] Els Wynen, *Agriculture and the Pesticide Reduction Scheme in Denmark*, Eco Landuse Systems Canberra, August 1994; and Els Wynen, *Agriculture and the Pesticide Reduction Scheme in Sweden*, Eco Landuse Systems, Canberra August 1994.

[45] The Farmers of Sweden, 'We are Creating the World's Cleanest Farming' (1994), IV(4) *Tomorrow: Global Environment Business* 87.

[46] J. A. W. A. Reus, H. J. Weckseler & G. A. Pak, *Towards a Future EC Pesticide Policy: An inventory of risks of pesticide use, possible solutions, and policy instruments* (1994), Centre for Agriculture and Environment, Utrecht, p.32. Authorities in the Netherlands published its Multi-Year Crop Protection Plan in 1991. Central to this plan was a 50 per cent reduction in the use of chemical pesticides by the year 2000. Responsibility for the Plan is shared between four Ministries and other stakeholder groups (e.g., the Netherlands' Society for Nature and the Environment). The most interesting feature of these leading

have also become common include: the provision of basic information about reducing chemical use and techniques of integrated pest management (IPM); voluntary agreements between producers and regulatory authorities for the reduction of chemical inputs; incentives for low input production; various risk-reduction initiatives; and various economic instruments, from taxes and levies, to marketable use rights. Within the European Union, incentive schemes for conversion to organic farming and programmes aimed at the reduction of input use (e.g., integrated pest control management) are being implemented in all Member States as part of agri-environmental schemes.[47]

Although by no means unique to the domain of agricultural chemicals regulation, perhaps most noteworthy of all initiatives are those which entail commercial influences in furtherance of chemical risk reduction. All these will be accorded more extensive treatment in Section 5 of this chapter. But first, we turn to some of the flaws which have characterized the recent history of biodiversity conservation and agricultural chemical control, and which have, commonly, served to undermine the effectiveness of the current regulatory regimes.

Limitations of current regulatory regimes and obstacles to effective policy design

To the extent that the success of existing regulatory regimes can be measured by results, current approaches fall far short of achieving the objectives of sustainable agriculture. To be sure, substantial achievements have been made in some areas, as reflected in the resurgence of the bald eagle and the peregrine falcon in North America, and vastly improved water quality in the Great Lakes. But many agricultural practices remain unsustainable, both ecologically and economically.

As we have noted, more than 10,000 species become extinct globally each year.[48] A significant proportion of this loss results from land clearing for agricultural purposes. Ecosystems continue to be disrupted by wholesale destruction of habitat, or other damaging impacts, such as microclimate change. Removal of vegetation continues to produce

---

edge programmes is their autocratic nature—all were simply imposed by government. The programme envisages that the goals be achieved by voluntary means, but in the event of a shortfall other instruments would be implemented, beginning with a levy on pesticides.

[47] See, for example, Regulation (EEC) No. 2078/92. See also Directive 91/414/EEC. concerning the placing of plant protection crops on the market.

[48] Biodiversity Resource Center at the California Academy of Sciences (last visited March 25 1997) <http://cas.calacademy.org/~library/biodiv/biodiv.html>

salinity, soil erosion, and sedimentation of nearby waterways at an alarming rate.[49]

High-input agriculture produces a variety of adverse environmental impacts.[50] Agricultural runoff is the primary source of pollution of waterways in the United States.[51] Fertilizers contaminate the soil with heavy metals to an extent which is still manifestly unsustainable. Intensive monocropping contributes to soil depletion. And the use of agricultural chemicals continues itself to produce biodiversity loss, as non-target species as well as pests fall victim to pesticides, with consequent disruption of the food chain. In addition to their direct environmental impact, agricultural chemicals continue to damage human health. Groundwater pollution from agricultural chemicals contaminates drinking water supplies in many developed nations. Agricultural workers continue to suffer injury and illness from exposure to chemicals.[52] Consumers in many nations remain at risk from pesticide residues in food.[53]

The structural characteristics of agriculture which contribute to the persistence of these problems, and which have either inhibited the development of, or served to substantially reduce the impact of the large majority of policy instruments so far introduced, are hardly a mystery. Increased agricultural productivity over the past half century has resulted in dramatically improved yields, but at a price. For most of this period, governments have placed a premium on agricultural productivity, at the expense of other considerations, and these priorities have

---

[49] A. Goedmakers, 'Ecological Perspectives of Changing Agricultural Land Use in the European Community' (1989) 27 *Agriculture, Ecosystems and the Environment* 99–106; J. B. Kirkpatrick, 'The Geography and Politics of Species Endangerment in Australia' 29(2) *Australian Geographical Studies* 246–254.; and J. C. Scanlan & E. J. Turner, *The Production, Economic and Environmental Impacts of Tree Clearing in Queensland* (1995), Department of Lands, Brisbane.

[50] Organisation for Economic Co-operation and Development (OECD), *Towards Sustainable Agricultural Production: Cleaner Technologies* (1994), OECD, Paris.

[51] US EPA (1994). For example, in the State of Florida, acreage used in sugar cane production increased by 80 per cent from 1970 to 1990 to a total of 420,000. During this period phosphorous concentrations in runoff water flowing into Lake Okeechobee nearly doubled, with consequent adverse impact on the Everglades ecosystem (South Florida Water Management District, *Lake Okeechobee Water Quality Monitoring Report: October 1984 September 1985* (1986), South Florida Water Management District, Florida).

[52] According to the California Department of Pesticide Regulation there were 1,332 illnesses in 1994 that had a potential or confirmed link to pesticide use (News Release No. 96–39, December 12, 1996).

[53] K. Short, *Quick Poison, Slow Poison: Pesticides Risk in the Lucky Country* (1994), Envirobooks, St Albans, NSW; Heaton, (1994), 46; B. Commoner, *Making Peace with the Planet* (1990), Pantheon Books, New York, p.332.

been reflected in agricultural and regulatory policy.[54] Moreover, the farming and agricultural chemical industry lobbies in many countries are particularly strong and well organized, and have often been successful in heading off regulatory initiatives perceived to threaten their interests. As one Australian environmentalist told us, 'Governments are well meaning, but have failed miserably. They are politically driven, and have probably done more harm than good . . . They seek politically sweet options, such as giving money to committees, and letting them go . . . Command and control has never been used . . . Agriculture is still essentially unregulated.'

These policies, through omission or commission, have contributed to regulatory deficiency in a variety of ways. First, rather than provide incentives for environmental stewardship, they have, at times, provided incentives for conduct harmful to the environment, while failing to assist producers to manage risk in an environmentally benign manner. Secondly, the farming community, lacking awareness of the need for sustainable practices, has maintained its traditional hostility to government intrusion in its affairs. Enforcement of regulation has similarly proved difficult. These problems have been compounded by poor regulatory design and a failure to harness the potential of third parties to act as surrogate regulators. We address each of these problems in turn.

Inappropriate incentives

There has been a lack of incentives under existing regulatory regimes for positive agroenvironmental stewardship that looks beyond short-term profit (or survival) toward an ethic of long-term custodianship of the land. On the contrary, there have often been substantial disincentives to engage in environmentally benign agriculture.

---

[54] A further striking weakness of most agricultural regulatory regimes is the large variety of agencies at various levels of government responsible for oversight and control. The result is often a fragmentation of jurisdiction, and a division of substantive regulatory responsibility which may impede rational regulatory planning. (D. T. Hornstein, 'Lessons from Federal Pesticide Regulation on the Paradigms and Politics of Environmental Law Reform' (1993) 10 *Yale Journal on Regulation* 369–446 at 408) has commented that the system of environmental law in the United States 'increasingly resembles a Rube Goldberg machine'. For example, six federal agencies and at least 25 federal statutes deal with issues relating to the regulation of wetlands M. Grossman, 'Habitat and Species Conservation in the European Union and the United States' (1997) 45(1) *Drake Law Review* 19–49 at 45; See also J. Wargo, *Our Children's Toxic Legacy: How science and law fail to protect us from pesticides* (1996), Yale University Press, New Haven; J. Dryzek, *Ecological Rationality* (1987), Blackwell, Oxford; A. Weale, *The New Politics of Pollution* (1992), University of Manchester Press, Manchester and P. Glasbergen, 'Agro-Environmental Policy: Trapped in an iron law?' (1992) 32(1) *Sociologia Ruralis* 30–48.

For example, agricultural price supports, where governments offer the farmer a guaranteed price per bushel of commodity, constitute an incentive to maximize production. To the extent that higher yields were achievable through monoculture, increased chemical input, and clearing more acreage for cultivation, farmers did just that. In addition to price supports, farmers were the beneficiaries of subsidies and incentives for fertilizer and pesticide use, as well as for land clearing. Australian farmers were, for many years, provided with strong financial incentives for land clearance, with (as we know today) devastating effects on fragile soil and areas of marginal productivity. Drought assistance also encourages continuing cultivation of marginally productive land, at the risk of requiring greater chemical input and further degradation. As well, it subsidizes poor performers at the expense of those farmers who practice water conservation. Environmentalists are critical of policies which compound the problem, rather than contribute to a solution. As one of them told us, 'Keep social welfare things in their place. Welfare is just not good enough'. The serious adverse environmental implications of such policies were becoming obvious by the late 1980s, but the strength of agricultural lobbies in western nations militated against significant reform. We return to the significance of perverse incentives for sustainable agriculture when examining price-based instruments, below.

In addition, the justifications which had been traditionally advanced for price supports, that of providing security for small farmers against the vagaries of climate and world commodity prices, were not always borne out. These instruments failed to ensure sufficient security for small farmers, who remained tempted to reduce the risk of crop failure through increased agricultural inputs and exploitation of marginal land.

Moreover, other policies have had the unintended consequence of discouraging the assumption of additional risk in furtherance of sustainable agriculture. As one agricultural economist told us, 'Insurers are potentially a barrier to change management. IPM methods may entail costs in terms of quality or yield. And this may entail higher premiums'. Indeed, Canadian farmers who refrained from using agricultural chemicals have been denied crop insurance coverage.[55] Any voluntaristic inclinations towards low-input production have thereby been neutralized.

[55] R. MacRae, S. Hill, J. Henning & A. Bentley, 'Policies, Programs and Regulations to Support the Transition to Sustainable Agriculture in Canada' (1990) 5(2) *American Journal of Alternative Agriculture* 76–92 at 80.

Finally, there are the specific problems and benefits which arise where farmers or producers, rather than owning land in fee simple, have a grazing or forestry lease over it. The central problem here is one of inappropriate incentives arising from the relatively short-lived involvement of the lessee, which provides a particular and inappropriate disincentive to long-term custodianship of the land and the temptation to 'flog it to death' for short-term profit. On the positive side however, leases hold out the possibility of imposing restrictive conditions on use (for example, in terms of stock density) and, in the context of native title, may involve shared rather than exclusive use.

Resistance to regulation and compliance

Another major problem is achieving the transition from traditional expectations (that farmers could use their land and conduct their business largely without restrictions) to a much more interventionist approach. After decades of farming under agricultural policies which contributed to environmental degradation, agricultural producers are now being asked to shift direction, often without having developed a full appreciation of the harmful effects of conventional agriculture. One could perhaps understand how a farmer who, having received subsidies for land clearing and pesticide use over a period of decades, only to be told that such practices were now prohibited, might be something less than totally appreciative of new circumstances, or unhesitatingly compliant with new directives.

And agricultural interests have indeed resented and resisted the various regulatory restrictions which governments have sought to impose upon them.[56] The traditional culture of independence which characterizes the agricultural sector is often reflected in resentment of government regulatory intervention, at least those forms of intervention which are perceived to be restrictive or coercive. One can do no better than quote a recent statement from the internet home page of the American Farm Bureau Federation:

Regulatory creep. No, it's not a name you might be tempted to call a broad-shouldered, one-eyebrowed, federal bureaucrat who loves to slap harsh penalties on law-abiding citizens. In fact, it's not a person at all. Regulatory creep, however, is somewhat related to that fictional bureaucrat. Broadly defined, it is

---

[56] Organisation for Economic Co-operation and Development (OECD), *Agricultural and Environmental Policies: Opportunities for integration* (1989), OECD, Paris, pp.32–33.

the tendency of regulations to grow—creep—into areas that Congress never intended for them to address.[57]

Unsurprisingly, in the light of this attitude, resistance to regulation is widespread, and enforcement has, generally, been weak. Non-compliance, except in the most extreme cases (such as pesticide poisoning on a large scale), has tended to be of low visibility, a problem compounded by monitoring costs which, given the spatial distribution of agricultural production, have tended to be prohibitive.[58] As one farmer put it 'it may take an occupying army to regulate the 100,000 farmers in our state'.[59]

Inappropriate applications and their sequelae might not be immediately apparent. What takes place in a far-off field, in a remote location, may escape official attention. Drift from spraying may not effect humans, plants or animals for some time, at which point the cause may be obscure. Even more difficult is the pollution from leaching or runoff. Contamination of groundwater and/or waterways from non-point sources makes it very difficult to assign responsibility to a particular polluter. The common result is encapsulated in the ethos of 'shoot, shovel, and shut up': a response to endangered species legislation that is alive and well, at least in the United States. As one industry spokesperson told us, 'At the end of the day, they can probably get away with something if they want to'.

Inadequate regulatory design

As if the political and economic obstacles to achieving sustainable agriculture were not enough, they have, commonly, been compounded by poor regulatory design, particularly in the case of biodiversity conservation. Here the greatest problem lies in the fact that most legislation seeks to protect individual species from endangerment or extinction despite strong evidence that such an approach is far less effective than

[57] M. Thornton, *Court Wetlands Ruling Halts Regulatory Creep. Focus on Agriculture*, 17 February 1997 (http://www.fb.com/news/focus97/fo0217.html).

[58] Organisation for Economic Co-operation and Development (OECD), *Agricultural and Environmental Policy Integration: Recent progress and new directions* (1993), OECD, Paris, pp.80–88; and Organisation for Economic Co-operation and Development (OECD), *Towards Sustainable Agricultural Production: Cleaner Technologies* (1994b), OECD, Paris. Enforcing those laws which exist to regulate the environmental impact of agriculture is difficult for a number of reasons. Access to private land may be difficult, not only by enforcement officials, but even by biologists seeking to monitor the behaviour of ecosystems.

[59] J. de Witt *Civic Environmentalism* (1994), C Q Press, Washington, p.10.

one that focuses on protecting ecosystems or ecological communities.[60] Endangered species legislation is, commonly, castigated as 'deathbed conservation', an approach which only protects species when they are close to extinction, at a point where the likelihood of actually saving the species is minimal.

Moreover, most species specific legislation suffers from other serious flaws, summarized by Meyers and Temby as follows:

Often . . . the flaw lies in providing too much 'front end' discretion, i.e., for the listing of species. Just as often, legislation . . . fails to mandate habitat preservation as an integral component of species protection efforts, or subjects that duty, or similar duties such as the issuance of conservation orders, to potentially overriding considerations of economic and political factors . . . or fails to include adverse modification of habitat as a form of prohibited 'harm' to species.[61]

In the case of some legislation, the problems of a species-specific approach are exacerbated by a number of other failures of regulatory design. The most well documented example is the United States Endangered Species Act, under which many landowners are unwilling to take action which attracts new endangered species to their land, because the arrival of these species would only invite further restrictions.[62] Indeed, it has been suggested that some landowners deliberately clear unoccupied land before endangered species can nest there and thereby reduce the land's value. The same Act has also been criticized for its inflexibility, its lack of concern for cost, and for the fact that its burdens are borne disproportionately by local interests, in some cases falling more heavily on indigenous minorities.[63]

Further, regulatory solutions to one environmental threat have, at times, served to compound others. Restricting the amount of land which a farmer may place in production might serve the interests of biodiversity conservation, but it can also contribute to agricultural pollution. In order to maximize their yield, farmers may be inclined to use more intensive inputs on that land which they have under cultivation.

---

[60] G. D. Meyers & S. Temby, 'Biodiversity and the Law: A review of the Commonwealth Endangered Species Protection Act of 1992' (1994) 3(1) *Griffith Law Review* 88–89.

[61] *Ibid.*

[62] See also C. C. Mann & M. L. Plummer, *Noah's Choice: The future of endangered species* (1996), Knopf, New York.

[63] *Ibid.*

More generally, complex problems defy simple solutions. For example, where the threat to biodiversity flows from low awareness on the part of those producers, who are also mistrustful of government, a solution may lie in some form of peer to peer education, perhaps reinforced by incentive instruments. Where inappropriate chemical use arises from excessive risk aversion, and where there is insufficient market demand for low input produce, some combination of positive and negative incentives, such as insurance subsidies and a levy on chemical products, may be appropriate. Yet only rarely have different types of instruments been consciously and effectively combined into complementary combinations, geared to overcome the inadequacies of 'stand alone' policies. The problem identified in chapter two: that single instrument approaches are rarely optimal because almost all single instruments have both strengths and weaknesses, is particularly apposite in the case of agri-environmental policy.

Failure to facilitate third party action

Finally, as we will see later, non-governmental institutions might also play a constructive role as surrogate regulators, but at present rarely do so. Banks are, generally, reluctant to impose any terms or conditions upon lending, lest they create a situation adverse to a client's cashflow, and thereby render themselves liable to legal action. In any event, the fundamental basis for a lending decision is the likelihood that the borrower will be able to service, and ultimately repay, the loan. As a result, banks are disinclined to direct clients what to do, except, perhaps, to maximize yield by whatever means are available. Even though a borrower may be engaged in activity which harms the land (which, when it is held as security for the loan, is really the bank's land), or engages in activity adverse to the environment for which they may be subject to negative regulatory sanctions, banks are unlikely to intervene. Insurers, moreover, are concerned more about outputs than inputs, and indeed, may specify chemical application in the terms of an insurance contract.[64]

This raises the crucial question, whether, and how, the energies of these non-governmental institutions can best be utilized in furtherance of sustainable agriculture (or to put it differently, to what extent third

---

[64] Banks too may specify chemical use as a condition of finance. See R. MacRae, S. Hill, J. Henning & A. Bentley, 'Policies, Programs and Regulations to Support the Transition to Sustainable Agriculture in Canada' (1990) 5(2) *American Journal of Alternative Agriculture* 76–92 at 80.

parties can be empowered to take on a such a role). Currently, policy-makers have barely begun to ask, let alone to answer, this question.

Overview

To summarize the obstacles to effective policy design and the short-comings of existing regulatory systems: in the domain of biodiversity conservation, there often remains a divergence of interests between those of the landowner and those of the general public. There exist, moreover, insufficient incentives to compensate for the sacrifices which the appropriate level of environmental stewardship might require on the landowner's part. Of course, regulators may be tempted to resort to coercion of landholders, but in respect of the rural sector in general, and biodiversity in particular, coercion is a particularly blunt instru-ment. These problems have been compounded by the poor design of many regulatory regimes. Farmers are highly resistant to regulation, monitoring is extremely difficult and expensive, and sanctions lack political acceptability. Moreover, in circumstances where what is needed are positive measures to reverse degradation, in conjunction with the development of an ethic of environmental stewardship, then command and control has little to contribute. Even where command and control is practicable, it is not necessarily desirable. Such measures are commonly criticized by economists as being inefficient, unneces-sarily intrusive, and unduly expensive to administer. Some regulations may inhibit innovation and discourage people from searching for new, and more efficient, ways to use a resource.

In the domain of agricultural chemicals, a range of perverse incen-tives have traditionally militated in favour of high input farming. Conditions of agricultural finance and insurance have often required chemical input.[65] The spectre of financial loss arising from crop failure or diminished quality inhibits individual producers from abandoning a risk-averse approach based on generous chemical use. Traditional con-sumer preferences for cosmetically attractive produce have reinforced

---

[65] D. T. Hornstein, 'Lessons from Federal Pesticide Regulation on the Paradigms and Politics of Environmental Law Reform' (1993) 10 *Yale Journal on Regulation* 369–446 at 397–8. The Canadian tax code contained a number of disincentives for sustainable agri-culture, including deductions for fertilizers, and for expenses incurred in bringing mar-ginal land into production. (R. MacRae, S. Hill, J. Henning & A. Bentley, 'Policies, Programs and Regulations to Support the Transition to Sustainable Agriculture in Canada' (1990) 5(2) *American Journal of Alternative Agriculture* 76–92 at 80.) Price support pro-grammes militate against alternative agriculture techniques (C. Ogg, 'Farm Price Distortions, Chemical Use, and the Environment' (1990) 45(1) *Journal of Soil and Water Conservation* 45–47.

the farmer's inclination to use chemical inputs. Hornstein notes that the adverse effects of pesticides tend to be borne not by the farmer, but by others.[66] While the farmer stands to gain from high input practices in the short term, the costs of these practices are borne by neighbours, consumers and the environment, generally. Finally, there is, in many sectors of agriculture, insufficient awareness of the relative cost-effectiveness of alternative methods.

The nature of pollution arising from misuse of agricultural chemicals also poses significant regulatory challenges. Moreover, such regulatory standards as do govern agricultural practices can themselves be unwieldy and difficult to enforce. Uniform standards, while less costly to develop and to administer, fail to account for variations in the robustness of ecosystems. Agricultural practices which are damaging in some contexts may be relatively harmless in others. Differentiated standards, on the other hand, entail greater administrative and enforcement costs.[67] And relevant regulatory responsibilities may be distributed across a number of agencies, including those responsible for air quality, water quality, and food safety. Enforcement problems are exacerbated by difficulties of monitoring and identifying the source of much agricultural chemical pollution.

In agriculture, as in banking, even the threat, or mere suggestion, of impending difficulties may precipitate a self fulfilling prophecy. Restrictions on land clearing may make eminent theoretical sense; the mere possibility of such restrictions, however, can bring about an anticipatory clearing to such an extent that it defeats the purpose of the original instrument. Just as 'panic buying' can produce commodity shortages which would not otherwise occur, so too can 'panic clearing' bring about habitat destruction. As one industry representative told us, 'As soon as draft tree-clearing guidelines were released for discussion, out came the bulldozers'.

Whether in the domain of biodiversity conservation or chemical use, there are limits to what traditional regulatory institutions can deliver. Even the most repressive state is never omnipotent, and the capacity of

---

[66] D. T. Hornstein, 'Lessons from Federal Pesticide Regulation on the Paradigms and Politics of Environmental Law Reform' (1993) 10 *Yale Journal on Regulation* 369–446 at 396.

[67] It has been argued that the EC. Drinking Water Directive imposes unreasonably stringent standards, thereby imposing excessive compliance costs. See also M. G. Faure & J. G. J. Lefevere, *An Analysis of Alternative Legal Instruments for the Regulation of Pesticides* (1994), University of Limburg, Maastricht.

modern democratic government is hardly boundless. This is particularly the case in the current and foreseeable climate of fiscal restraint which characterizes most western democracies.

In both domains, knowledge of environmental risks and remedies is inadequate, particularly on the part of the small, marginal farmer. Attitudes toward government might be characterized as schizophrenic; a culture of dependence on government beneficence coexists ironically with traditional resentment of governmental encroachment on one's autonomy (i.e., they want to capitalize the profits and socialize the losses). And farmers are being urged, if not required, to abandon long-held practices and use new production methods at a very time when the globalization of economic affairs is adding to the uncertainty of rural life.

Whatever the similarities and differences of the many faces of agriculture, it is already abundantly clear that existing systems for agro-environmental regulation have serious shortcomings. Recognizing that both environmental problems and institutional capacities will vary within jurisdictions, as well as between them, what general conclusions might we reach about the most appropriate configuration of regulatory institutions and instruments to minimize the environmentally harmful consequences of agricultural production? What is the potential contribution of non-governmental institutions to environmental policy? How, in what circumstances, and in what combinations, can the main classes of policy instruments be utilized to achieve optimal policy mixes in the case of biodiversity conservation and agricultural chemical use?

Section 4: Assessing instrument options : toward efficient and effective agricultural policy

Our overall objective, in the remainder of this chapter, is to identify instrument and institutional configurations which will function efficiently and effectively to meet the goal of sustainable agriculture. Section 4 examines the roles of the various categories of instruments, Section 5 considers various institutional influences and the roles of third parties, and Section 6 draws from our analysis in the previous two sections to provide some specific principles which are paramount in designing policy mixes for agro-environmental regulation.

We begin, in the present section, by examining, in ascending order of coerciveness, the major categories of instruments of agro-environmental regulation: information, voluntarism, self-regulation, economic instruments, and compulsion.[68] We explore the strengths and limitations of each individual instrument category of policy instruments and the circumstances in which each might most appropriately be used in the agricultural context. More broadly, we indicate how each category of policy instrument can best be integrated into an overall regulatory mix. While efficiency remains our paramount criterion, we recognize that, in the agro-environmental domain, there are circumstances where effectiveness might take precedence. Threats to biodiversity which can entail catastrophic and irreversible damage are the most obvious example.

Overall, we argue that governments need to broaden their repertoire by embracing a much larger range of instruments. Moreover, recognizing that individual instruments all have limitations, they should seek to build on the strengths of individual instruments while compensating for their weaknesses by utilizing a much broader and sophisticated policy mix. However, rather than utilizing as many instruments as possible, the overriding strategy should be to mobilize instruments only when less costly and less coercive measures fail to achieve preferred outcomes. Finally, policymakers need to tailor the precise mix of tools (and institutions) much more closely to the particular environmental and policy context.

Information

The relative isolation of many agricultural producers, their resistance to regulation and to change, and their conservatism, all make information particularly important in this industry sector. Regardless of the agricultural context, or the nature of the environmental risk, information is likely to play a fundamentally important role in achieving sustainable agriculture, providing a very large 'bang for the regulatory buck'. Not only do such instruments impact substantially on attitudes and behaviour,[69] they can also be implemented at modest administrative cost, while frequently repaying substantial dividends in terms of improving management practice. Generally, informational instruments

[68] There are a vast array of policy instruments that might be invoked for biodiversity conservation. To address policy instruments and mixes at a conceptual level, we have developed a sub-set of instrument categories which, while informative, is not exclusive.

[69] See M. D. Young, N. Gunningham, J. Elix, J. Lambert, B. Howard, P. Grabosky, E. McCrone, *Reimbursing the Future: An evaluation of motivational, voluntary, price-based, property-right, and regulatory incentives for the conservation of biodiversity* (1996), Biodiversity Series Paper No. 9, Department of the Environment, Sport and Territories, Biodiversity Unit, Canberra, Vol 1, pp.107–110.

are perceived as equitable, as the information is usually widely disseminated in a non-interventionist manner. Where such instruments provide information that harnesses self-interest, they are also financially attractive, and provide continuing incentives for biodiversity conservation and sustainable agriculture.

Information strategies are most relevant for improving the environmental behaviour of the small, marginal producer, whose lack of environmental awareness is often the basis for noncompliance. Large, professional producers, by contrast, are more likely to be well aware of their responsibilities to the environment, and of the impact of their activities. More generally, information disseminated to the public, to non-governmental organizations and to third parties like financial institutions can enable parties to participate meaningfully in the making and enforcement of agricultural policies.

Information strategies will be particularly productive when the private interests of the farmer and the wider public interest converge. In these circumstances, basic information is occasionally sufficient to bring about voluntary initiatives.[70] This is especially apposite in the case of agricultural chemicals: where the producer is aware that input costs can be reduced without detracting from quality and yield, everyone benefits, without recourse to threat or inducement. Here, it is sufficient for a producer to recognize that excessive chemical input is economically inefficient, and that a reduction in chemical use can improve profit.

In the context of biodiversity conservation, the win-win scenario may occur when the preservation of native vegetation serves to reduce erosion and salinity, although the benefits are likely to be less immediate and tangible than in the pesticide case. Nevertheless, public interest and private interest do at least substantially overlap, and education campaigns which seek to harness the enlightened self-interest of agricultural producers are likely to be a good investment.[71] The success of

[70] For example, there are numerous cases of successful farm enterprises based on methods of Low Input Sustainable Agriculture (LISA), Integrated Pest Management (IPM), and coexistence with thriving biodiversity (J. P. Madden & P. F. O'Connell, 'LISA: Some Early Results' (1990) 45(1) *Journal of Soil and Water Conservation* 61–64; and J. P. Reganold, R. I. Papendick & J. F. Parr, 'Sustainable Agriculture' (1990) June *Scientific American* 72–78). But only if information concerning these successes is widely disseminated may it be possible to overcome the disinclination to change and to break the hold which traditional agricultural practices have had on the farmer: pressure to maximize yield, and the use of chemicals as a means of insuring against risk.

[71] In Australia, The National Farmers' Federation's Property Management Planning process shows farmers that clearing land may involve substantial environmental costs such as erosion and rising salinity. It also indicates that retaining native vegetation can

soil conservation education programmes in the United States, Australia, and elsewhere, are illustrative.[72]

Where win-win scenarios do not apply (such as in circumstances when land clearing or the taking of endangered species would contribute to yield), and agricultural producers are called upon to make sacrifices, information can still play an important, albeit different role. In these circumstances, the provision of information may serve to make coercive forms of intervention more palatable by justifying and legitimizing the sacrifices which producers are called upon to make.[73] Restrictions on agricultural practices become more comprehensible, and thus more acceptable and, more likely to be heeded, when their wider context is understood. These principles apply equally to issues of land clearing and species preservation, as well as to issues surrounding the use of agricultural chemicals.[74] In summary, in some contexts, information serves to activate voluntaristic initiatives, while in others it helps lower a producer's resistance to regulatory edicts.

However, we do not suggest that information is a dependable strategy, particularly where there is a substantial tension between the public and private interests, or that it can be used in isolation (although, exceptionally, it will function effectively in this role). Even when

actually result in higher crop and livestock yields through the benefits of shelter and shade (W. Craik, *IPM—The Way Forward* (1996) Address to The Avcare Annual Convention, Perth, Western Australia, 15 October: http://coombs.anu.edu.au/SpecialProj/NFF/avcare.html). This challenges the traditional premise that land clearing is necessary to increase production.

[72] S. E. Johnson & H. M. Jacobs, 'Public Education for Growth Management: Lessons from Wisconsin's Farmland Preservation Program' (1994) 49(4) *Journal of Soil and Water Conservation* 333; and A. Campbell, *Landcare: Communities shaping the land and the future* (1994), Allen and Unwin, Sydney.

[73] See W. McGuire, (1985) 'Attitudes and attitude change' in G. Lindzey (ed.) *The Handbook of Social Psychology*, 3rd edn, Vol. II, Random House, New York, pp.233–347. See also P. Zimbardo & M. R. Lieppe, *The Psychology of Attitude Change and Social Influence* (1991), Temple University, Philadelphia; and D. Makeswaran & J. Meyers-Levy, 'The Influence of Message Framing and Issue Involvement' (1990) 27 *Journal of Marketing Research* 361.

[74] Programmes such as the Land for Wildlife scheme in the Australian State of Victoria already recognize the central role of information supply. Land for Wildlife produces a series of booklets for landowners which provide constructive advice on matters such as native vegetation management, wetlands and waterway management and weeds control, in addition to assisting in the establishment of wildlife habitats and biodiversity corridors (M. D. Young, N. Gunningham, J. Elix, J. Lambert, B. Howard, P. Grabosky, E. McCrone, *Reimbursing the Future: An evaluation of motivational, voluntary, price-based, property-right, and regulatory incentives for the conservation of biodiversity* (1996), Biodiversity Series Paper No. 9, Department of the Environment, Sport and Territories, Biodiversity Unit, Canberra, p.107).

producers perceive the need for biodiversity conservation, or reduced chemical use, they will not necessarily take appropriate action if this conflicts with other goals and interests. For example, the South Australian experience has been that even when landusers were well informed and were supportive of the need for biodiversity conservation, they were still willing to clear their own land, and only regulation (coupled with compensation) prevented them from doing so.[75] Similarly, the threat of significant crop loss may militate in favour of high chemical input, regardless of the other risks it may entail.

Informational instruments may best be used to narrow or close the gap between the public and private interests or, where this is not possible, to make other, more coercive, strategies more acceptable. As we argue below, it is then desirable to use a mix of voluntary instruments, price-based instruments and regulatory instruments to achieve the dependability that information strategies alone generally lack. Necessarily, the particular mix of instruments at each location and the precise combination of instruments will vary with the ecological, social, economic, and political context.[76] Thus, the approach we recommend is one that makes institutional access to each instrument as wide as possible.[77]

To summarize: information alone will not produce preferred environmental outcomes, whether in relation to chemicals or biodiversity.

---

[75] Personal communication, John Bradsen 5 October 1995.

[76] The case studies contained in appendices 2.1 to 2.7 and summarized in chapter 4 in Young *et al.* (1996) (M. D. Young, N. Gunningham, J. Elix, J. Lambert, B. Howard, P. Grabosky, E. McCrone, *Reimbursing the Future: An evaluation of motivational, voluntary, price-based, property-right, and regulatory incentives for the conservation of biodiversity* (1996), Biodiversity Series Paper No. 9, Department of the Environment, Sport and Territories, Biodiversity Unit, Canberra) illustrate the benefits of, and provide some examples of, this approach.

[77] Ideally, information would be generated from within the agricultural community, or by the market. This will alleviate fiscal pressure on the state, or at least allow limited governmental resources to be conserved for use when voluntaristic or market solutions are not available. Moreover, information from a source close to the farmer will have greater resonance than will information emanating from a source which is relationally distant. (See, generally, D. Black, 'The Epistemology of Pure Sociology' (1995) 20(3) *Law and Social Inquiry* 829.)

Whether, in an era of fiscal constraint, the state will actually play this role, is more problematic. As one agricultural economist, observing the decline in state provided agricultural extension services, told us that: 'There has been enormous change in the last ten years. No longer can the public sector provide the one-on-one interaction and exchange of information that it once might have done. The role of government is now to provide basic information and let others do that'. Realistically, this is a most unlikely prospect with regard to biodiversity conservation issues, and still only occasionally the case in the domain of agricultural chemicals. Where private institutions fail to provide a sufficient base of information, it falls to public interest organisations and ultimately, to institutions of the state, to generate the information in question. Such an investment to compensate

In a few exceptional cases, it may be sufficient to bring about best practice performance on the part of the most professional and civic-minded producers. But more often, it is the foundation for the functioning of other instruments. Where producer interest and public interest diverge, these other instruments may entail elements of inducement or coercion. In those instances where they coincide, the operative instruments will be voluntaristic. To these we now turn.

Voluntarism

As indicated in chapter two, a variety of instruments and mechanisms can be classified under this heading. In the agricultural context, their main characteristics are that the producer has discretion in deciding whether or not to participate. In their purest form, they reflect spontaneous altruism, as the producer chooses to adopt best practice voluntarily. Other forms entail more in the way of dialogue with the state or with third parties, but rely neither on coercion nor substantially on continuing financial inducements. These mechanisms include support for projects undertaken by non-government organizations, community groups, or landholders (where the financial support is partial and there is heavy reliance on voluntary effort for successful completion); and management agreements with the person responsible for managing an area of land (a form of legally binding contract, voluntarily entered into).[78] In the domain of agricultural chemicals, perhaps the most vivid example is the United States EPA's Pesticide Environmental Stewardship Program, (PESP), under which participants agree to devise and implement pesticide reduction strategies.[79]

Among the greatest virtues of voluntary mechanisms are their ability to influence community attitudes. In particular, they have the capacity to build, rather than hinder, the development of a custodial ethic, and to make environmentally sustainable agriculture part of the 'commu-

---

for information failure is a very sound investment, both reducing the need for more interventionist and more costly instruments, and, where these remain necessary, softening their impact.

[78] Grants to facilitate specific projects are also included in this category, notwithstanding that they also provide a financial incentive provided that the grant is intended to provide only partial financial support for the project, which still relies heavily on the voluntary efforts of the recipients for its successful completion. Well targeted, such grants can have high multiplier effects. Because they usually cover only a proportion of the total costs, grants avoid much of the moral hazard associated with management agreements where people have an incentive to falsify receipts and overstate expenditures.

[79] United States, Environmental Protection Agency (EPA), (1996).

nity norm'.[80] Such approaches are particularly important in the agricultural sector where cultural resistance to regulation, and the problem of identifying and monitoring geographically isolated producers, make more coercive approaches problematic. Commitments won by persuasion and based upon mutual agreement are likely to be respected, because each farmer can claim a degree of ownership, and the risk of defiance provoked by more coercive instruments is lacking. Not only are such commitments inherently more flexible than legislation, they may (as the work of Eleanor Ostrom admirably demonstrates[81]), in many instances, preclude the necessity for legislative action. Perhaps most important, they enhance motivation on the part of the farmer.

However, voluntary instruments in the agricultural context suffer from two main problems. First, they can be difficult to target and monitor without incurring high administrative costs, particularly given that agricultural producers are widely dispersed. Secondly, many voluntary agreements (i.e., those without a contractual base) are non-binding. Whatever their virtues, there are those individuals who may fail to abide by them. And with all voluntary agreements, there will be those who, for whatever reason, do not see fit to join them in the first place. Accordingly, they work best where there is a substantial overlap between the public interest and that of private producers. For example, if landowners perceive themselves as having a (short-term as well as long-term) self-interest in soil conservation, voluntarism may be a cost-effective and appropriately non-interventionist strategy.[82] However, even here, voluntarism can only work if resource users appreciate the value of conservation, and their own self-interest in protecting it.[83]

---

[80] A. F. Bennett, 'Conservation and Management on Private Land—Facing the Challenge' in A. F. Bennett, G. Backhouse & T. Clark, (eds.) *People and Nature Conservation: Perspectives on private land use and endangered species recovery* (1995), Surrey Beatty and Sons, Chipping Norton. The most basic process in social change involves developing widespread awareness of and sensitivity to the underlying issue, a process often better fostered and encouraged than imposed.

[81] E. Ostrom, *Governing the Commons: The evolution of institutions for collective action* (1990), CUP, New York.

[82] A. F. Bennett, G. Backhouse & T. Clark, (eds.) *People and Nature Conservation: Perspective's on private land use and endangered species recovery* (1995), Surrey Beatty and Sons, Chipping Norton.

[83] In circumstances such as the above, where the public and private interest substantially coincide, one might imagine that the agricultural community would embrace voluntarism spontaneously, without any prompting from external institutions. However, there are only very limited circumstances where such orderings have evolved independently (see M. Olson, *The Logic of Collective Action: Public Goods and the Theory of Groups* (1965),

Informational and motivational instruments that seek to increase the number of people interested in conservation and that show them how to do this will be extremely important in this respect, again illustrating the point made immediately above: that informational mechanisms can almost invariably reinforce other policy instruments.[84]

Where there is a substantial gap between the public interest and the private interests of individual land users[85] (as is very likely to be the case in the area of biodiversity conservation[86]), then voluntary mechanisms cannot be relied upon in isolation, but need to be reinforced by external stimuli, such as signals from the market or the spectre of more intrusive government regulation (see further, below). For example, whereas many land users may identify with the soil conservation objectives of voluntary land protection schemes, their self-interest in protecting biodiversity is not so readily apparent—at least in the short term. More commonly, there is a perceived tension between maximizing the use of productive land and protecting remnant vegetation. While the preservation of such vegetation may, arguably, provide long-term benefits to land users (acting as a windbreak, reducing dryland salinity, etc.) these benefits are less tangible and immediately realizable than the increase in short-term productivity which remnant removal promises. For land-users who are economically marginal, the evidence is that short-term

Harvard University Press, Cambridge, MA), suggesting the need for external stimuli (in addition to information) to prompt such action. Such stimuli might include signals from the market, or the spectre of more intrusive government involvement, both of which are discussed in greater detail below.

[84] Even when resource users do have full awareness of their self-interest in protecting biodiversity, there is still some danger in relying solely on voluntarism to the exclusion of more interventionist mechanisms. Not all resource users will necessarily behave with rationality. Policy must also take account of the minority who may be irrational, incompetent or intransigent, underlining the need for a regulatory safety net.

[85] See, generally, I. Brotherton, 'On the Voluntary Approach to Resolving Rural Conflict' (1990) 22 *Environment and Planning* 925–939.

[86] The basic problem derives from the fact that private landholders (or indeed other private users of resources) commonly lack any economic incentive to take account of the social costs of their actions. That is, we encounter a classic externalities problem where the direct benefits of biodiversity loss (e.g., increased agricultural production from clearing land) go to individual property owners, whereas the costs (in terms of loss of species, ecosystems, genetic resources and other potential uses) fall on society at large. In collective terms, the problem is that the impact of one landholder clearing their land will make little impact on the overall problem, nor will this individual decision influence the behaviour of other landholders. Accordingly, each landholder will be tempted to take advantage of the willingness of others to protect the environment while continuing to despoil it themselves. See M. Olson, *The Logic of Collective Action* (1965), Harvard University Press, Cambridge, MA.

production pay-offs are often perceived to outweigh possible longer term benefits of conservation.

This suggests a major limitation of voluntaristic approaches to bio-diversity protection, namely that, like information-based instruments, they lack dependability. This limitation raises two important questions in terms of policy design. First, in circumstances where landholders do not have a self-interest in conservation, does voluntarism have any significant role to play? If so, what is that role? The second, (assuming that the answer to the first question is positive) is how voluntary instruments should most appropriately be used in combination with other instruments and institutions.

In terms of the first of these questions, voluntarism can indeed play an important role. Notwithstanding the need to recognize and design policy to take account of self-interest, it must be emphasized that self-interest is not a full explanation of behaviour. On the contrary, altruism and respect for broad conservation objectives may be evident on the part of some, and mechanisms which seek to support and harness such behaviour can play a supporting role in the policy mix, provided they can be justified in cost benefit terms. For example, if limited resources were put into encouraging and supporting landholders willing, in principle, to enter voluntary agreements, this might provide a cost-effective mechanism, even though it is only applicable to a small minority.[87] If it were coupled with appropriate tax concessions (an economic incentive), then many more landholders might be encouraged to participate.

As to the second question, the issue is what combination of instruments can best harness the strengths of voluntarism, while compensating for its weaknesses. Here, policy design must be particularly sensitive to

---

[87] In Australia, such programmes as Land for Wildlife in Victoria have successfully persuaded many landowners to voluntarily manage land as wildlife habitat without offering any direct financial assistance. (See appendix 1 in M. D. Young, N. Gunningham, J. Elix, J. Lambert, B. Howard, P. Grabosky, E. McCrone, *Reimbursing the Future: An evaluation of motivational, voluntary, price-based, property-right, and regulatory incentives for the conservation of biodiversity* (1996), Biodiversity Series Paper No 9, Department of the Environment, Sport and Territories, Biodiversity Unit, Canberra.) Such programmes have the added benefit that they may also promote awareness of biodiversity conservation, thereby contributing to motivational change—a factor acknowledged in the Convention on Biological Diversity. In The Netherlands, voluntary management agreements relating to manner of land use form the basis of a contract with the state. To the extent that these can occur without any threat or inducement, they too are truly voluntaristic, and reliant in part, upon altruism for their success. Thus, the agricultural sector enjoys a long history of voluntarism, which policy makers would be well advised to support and further develop.

the sequence in which such instruments are used, given farmers' resistance to direct government regulation, and the risks of making voluntarism redundant. In any event, on the grounds of efficiency and effectiveness too, less intrusive and less costly instruments should be preferred, provided they achieve the desired environmental goal.

Accordingly, policymakers might begin by introducing information-based strategies, in the hope that individual producers will be inspired to do the right thing without further prompting. This might be done in conjunction with some form of voluntarism or industry self-regulation (the least interventionist next steps), where this is practicable. Where the capacity for this is lacking, however, then these may be reinforced by the use of incentives—those who may be resistant to persuasion or moral guidance, may not be immune to market forces. Ultimately, in the event that less intrusive measures fail, then voluntarism must be superseded by more coercive instruments, including direct regulation, providing the severity of the problem justifies such measures. Indeed, here, when voluntarism fails, it is *replaced* by coercion. In exceptional circumstances, such as where there is a risk of irreversible loss to biodiversity, then, as we indicate below,[88] this sequencing must give way to a different approach, which places effectiveness (in preventing environmental harm) ahead of other considerations.

Even in the latter circumstances, there may be scope for voluntarism in conjunction with direct regulation. For example, one of the most promising initiatives, to overcome the worst flaws of the United States Endangered Species Act, concerns the introduction of voluntary conservation agreements. Welner has described this proposal as follows:

The underlying theory [is] that in order to avoid the prospect of endangered species listings—which can often delay projects and result in extensive, mandatory restrictions on development—landowners and local governments would gladly participate in a voluntary preventative program to protect species and set aside needed habitat. Using this approach, the government could achieve comprehensive habitat protection without needing to list any species.[89]

---

[88] See p.336.

[89] J. Welner, 'Natural Communities Conservation Planning: An ecosystem approach to protecting endangered species' (1995) 47 *Stanford Law Review* 319 at 339. See also M. Bean & D. Wilcove 'Ending the Impasse' 13(4) (July/Aug 1996) *Environmental Forum* 22.

But what is critical to the success of voluntary conservation agreements is the 'hammer' of the Endangered Species Act, which induces landowners to come to the bargaining table. That is, such voluntarism is only effective against the backdrop of tough government regulation, which is likely to be invoked if voluntarism fails.

The precise combination of instruments will necessarily vary with the nature of the threat and with the social, economic, and political context in which it arises. In the domain of agricultural chemicals, for example, information regarding optimal chemical use can serve as the foundation for a voluntary campaign based on the specification of non-binding targets to reduce inputs. Ideally, this would be reinforced by market demand for low input produce. Where market signals are insufficient, some form of price-based instrument, such as a levy on inputs, might be introduced. Proceeds from the levy might, in turn, be used to contribute to a fund to ensure against crop loss or damage.

By contrast, in the domain of biodiversity conservation, information on the merits of biodiversity is the basis for voluntary environmental stewardship. It does not replace voluntarism, but rather inspires and sustains voluntaristic effort. In this sense, it is complementary. Where, as is most often the case, voluntarism entails financial sacrifice, and commercial influences in furtherance of biodiversity are insufficient to prevail, some degree of incentive instruments may be necessary. Where these, in turn, fail to deliver preferred outcomes, a degree of regulatory intervention may be appropriate.

The danger in applying voluntary and regulatory resources in tandem is that the latter may overwhelm or effectively neutralize the value of the former, particularly in the agricultural sector where farmers are sensitive to external regulation. However, in carefully designed systems, this may be avoided either by an enforcement strategy that escalates to regulatory sanctions only where voluntary instruments fail, or in which those who are demonstrably responsible are entrusted to regulate themselves under voluntary codes, leaving regulators free to focus on the irresponsible). Three other approaches that may also overcome the risks of neutralization, while also mitigating the problems of political acceptability inherent in regulating farmers, are sequencing (inviting industry to pursue voluntary measures because of their virtues described above, but recognizing their lack of dependability, and underpinning them with the implicit threat of mandatory action if voluntarism fails[90]); the

---

[90] See p.333.

use of hybrid mechanisms (legislation setting targets, achieved through voluntarism[91]) and partnership arrangements.[92]

Finally, it should be noted that voluntary agreements in the agricultural sector need not always involve government actors. One example of constructive partnership between conservation or consumer groups and farmers is the CORE Values project, a co-operative programme between the New York and New England MacIntosh Growers and the environmental group Mothers and Others. As recently as the 1980s, these groups were adversaries on the Alar issue. Today, apple growers sign a pledge card indicating their intentions to use only IPM practices, which are environmentally preferable.[93] Voluntaristic initiatives may

[91] Legislation can also be used to set general targets, while relying on voluntary approaches as the most desirable vehicle to implement them. For example, in June, 1992, Swedish Farmers pledged to reduce pesticide use by 50 per cent, renounced the use of hormones or antibiotics to influence the growth of animals, and to substantially reduce the leaching of manure by introducing better handling practices. Moreover, they advertised these commitments internationally, (The Farmers of Sweden, 'We are Creating the World's Cleanest Farming' (1994), IV(4) *Tomorrow: Global Environment Business* 87). Similarly, plans to reduce chemical use by an additional 50 per cent by the turn of the century, on a completely voluntary basis, have been announced by the Netherlands Council for Co-operative Business in Agriculture, (B. Sletto, 'Goals Clear, Methods Not' (1995) V(1) *Tomorrow: Global Environment Business* 24–26), while Dutch bulb growers have signed an agreement to refrain from spraying a 1.5 metre buffer strip along waterways (P. Rowland, *Recent Changes in International Crop Protection Practices: The growing trend to reduce pesticide use and pesticide risk* (1995), Bureau of Resource Sciences, Department of Primary Industries and Energy, Canberra, p.26). Crucially, both the Swedish and Dutch initiatives appear to have been introduced in response to legislatively specified targets. In this sense, they were not spontaneously voluntaristic, but rather initiated by government initiative.

[92] Another approach is to develop partnerships between agricultural producers and regulators. In the United States, the Pesticides Environmental Stewardship Program (PESP) is based on voluntary partnerships between producers and the EPA (P. Rowland, *Recent Changes in International Crop Protection Practices: The growing trend to reduce pesticide use and pesticide risk* (1995), Bureau or Resource Sciences, Department of Primary Industries and Energy, Canberra, p.15; and http://es.inel.gov/partners/pest/pest.html). Participating producers agree to implement formal environmental stewardship strategies and report regularly to the agency. In return, they receive personal advice, information, and assurances that their views will be considered in subsequent regulatory decisionmaking. Also in the United States, The Partners for Wildlife Program has involved the co-operation of: Federal, state and local government agencies; conservation organisations; educational institutions; corporations; and almost 13,000 private landowners in furtherance of habitat restoration (*Endangered Species Bulletin* Vol. XXI. No. 1 at http://www.fws.gov/~r9end-spp/esb/96/pfw.html).

[93] C. Petzoldt & J. P. Tette, *Farmers Communicating to Consumers about their Environmental Stewardship* at http://www.nysaes.cornell.edu:80/ipmnet/ny/program_news/Farmers_Comm.html.

also emerge spontaneously in particular regions or from within specific industries.[94]

To summarize, except in those limited circumstances where the public interest in sustainable agriculture and the private interest of producers substantially coincide, and where environmental damage is reversible, voluntary mechanisms should be used to build a stewardship ethic and to supplement other instruments. They cannot, however, be relied upon to work effectively in isolation. In the large majority of cases, they need to be supported by a variety of mechanisms like price and property-right mechanisms, and regulation, (only to be invoked when voluntarism demonstrably fails), that ensure dependability and reduce implementation costs.[95] As indicated earlier, in almost all circumstances, voluntarism will also need to be underpinned by appropriate information.

Self-regulation

The agriculture industry's potential for self-regulation, *industry-wide*, is relatively limited. The diversity of the industry—embracing as it does activities as disparate as woolgrowing and the cultivation of produce from apples to tulip bulbs—defies concerted activity. The contrast on this point with chemical manufacturing is stark. Rather, what one finds in agriculture are a number of discrete industry sectors which exercise various degrees of scrutiny and control over their members. Within at least some of these sectors, however, there arises the potential for credible self-regulation.[96]

---

[94] The Artichoke Research Association, established by California artichoke growers in 1973, developed pest control strategies specific to the crop and to its problem pests. The IPM strategies developed—including pheromone traps, and pest monitoring programmes—helped reduce annual crop losses from 30 per cent to less than 5 per cent, while also reducing insecticide use by as much as 20 per cent. California Department of Pesticide Regulation, Press Release 97–06—*IPM Innovator Awards* January 28, 1997, Department of Pesticide Regulation, Sacramento. See, generally, E. Ostrom, *Governing the Commons: The evolution of institutions for collective action* (1990), CUP, New York.

[95] For example, to avoid the possibility that industry self-regulation becomes a sham, it is necessary for it to be underpinned by external oversight and monitoring. The capacity should exist for government to step in and regulate directly, where self-regulation turns out to be ineffective.

[96] See E. Ostrom, *Governing the Commons: The evolution of institutions for collective action* (1990), CUP, New York; and C. Rose *Property and Persuasion: Essays in History, Theory and Rhetoric of Ownership* (1994), Westview Press, Boulder, Colorado. Ostrom, in particular, examines the effectiveness of self-governing schemes and how this may depend upon the completeness and ecological subtlety of the definition of property rights.

Self-regulatory initiatives are most likely to evolve in contexts entailing an approximation to a community of shared fate.[97] For example, the Australian cattle industry, activated by overseas rejection of Australian export beef tainted by chemical residue, and reinforced by international market demand for best practice product, has introduced a quality assurance programme, Cattlecare.[98] Based, as it is, on certification after third-party audit, the programme provides for withdrawal of certification in cases of non-performance. The fact that the *entire* industry risks losing major export markets if the scheme fails (a 'community of shared fate'), provides a powerful incentive for its success.[99]

Other industry sectors, similarly sensitive to their markets, have also begun to introduce quality assurance or similar programmes intended to protect the reputation of both the entire sector and individual producers. For example, the Dutch pig meat industry has developed an Integrated Quality Assurance System.[100] Similarly, various schemes of organic certification which exist around the world entail provisions for termination in the event that conditions for certification are breached. In the abstract, action at this level would have no consequences of significance for an errant farmer. But when certification is a condition of access to a market, the removal of that certification can be costly indeed. The producer is forced either to find an alternative market, or absorb potentially catastrophic financial loss.

In contrast, biodiversity conservation would appear considerably less amenable to self-regulation. Indeed, one farmer's behaviour, which may be injurious to biodiversity, is unlikely to impact adversely on his peers. Unlike nuclear power operators, farmers are rarely hostages of each other. If one Montana sheep rancher is inclined to shoot wolves venturing onto his property, this does not detract from the marketability of his neighbour's wool. Indeed, the neighbour may be grateful for the rancher's contribution to pest reduction. Similarly, practices which cause runoff and despoil waterways (a classic example of externalities) are equally unlikely to be amenable to self-regulatory solutions.

[97] See above chapter four, p.155. More generally, on the conditions under which self-governing schemes may flourish (see E. Ostrom, *Governing the Commons: The evolution of institutions for collective action* (1990), CUP, New York).

[98] Cattle Council of Australia, *Cattlecare* (1997), Cattle Council of Australia, Sydney at http://www.farmwide.com.au/nff/cattlecouncil/prod05.htm.

[99] See further chapter four, p.155 for a more detailed analysis of self-regulation.

[100] This industry-based certification system enables the tracing of product to specific farms. To the extent that a producer is subject to such a degree of scrutiny, the capacity for social control is that much greater. B. Sletto, 'Goals Clear, Methods Not' (1995) V(1) *Tomorrow: Global Environment Business* 24–26 at 25.

State involvement need not be a necessary condition for the development of a self-regulatory regime. However, the State is strategically positioned to support those self-regulatory regimes which may not be self-sustaining. Even under the most promising circumstances (e.g., where the gap between public and private interest is modest, and the relevant industry association wants the code to work), self-regulation is likely to work best in conjunction with a broader range of policy instruments, which compensate for the weaknesses from which even the best self-regulatory schemes commonly suffer. For example, shaming cannot work against producers with no reputation to protect. Expulsion cannot work where a farmer can still produce and market effectively outside the industry association. If eighty per cent of the industry agrees to comply with a self-regulatory code, but twenty per cent refuse to sign on, a failure to address the misconduct of the latter (which, since they are outside of the code, is beyond the scope of the self-regulatory scheme) will almost certainly result in the failure of the code. Here, government can intervene directly to curb the activities of non-code members.

As an alternative to attracting the attention of the State, producers may be willing to submit to the discipline of industry self-regulation, or may do so as a matter of competitive self-interest. Significantly, the most prominent achievements in self-regulation in agriculture, exist in those mature, cohesive, and professional industry sectors whose members are themselves attuned to the requirements of export markets, and to the elements of international best practice.

The State is also in a position to reinforce self-regulation by positive means. A major contribution of government to self-regulation in agriculture is that of capacity-building.[101] By contributing information about the commercial environment of a specific agricultural sector, and by providing, where necessary, technical expertise in the design of self-regulatory systems, government can assist an agricultural sector to keep its house in order. On a broader level, governments may assist in publicizing exemplary achievements in self-regulation within a particular sector, with a view towards inspiring emulation in other industry sectors.

Again, it may be appropriate for a state agency to endorse a particular code by permitting it to use the agency's logo or other official seal

---

[101] In those political systems where the agriculture sector is less politically influential, the threat of state coercion is more likely to instigate self-regulatory initiatives than provoke industry backlash.

of approval, thereby giving the public greater confidence in the code's credibility. This, in turn, may help the industry sell its product or provide other commercial benefits. In these circumstances, the capacity of the agency to withdraw its endorsement may provide a significant inducement to the target group to self-regulate effectively. Governments may also provide financial incentives, such as tax deductions, for producer investment in self-regulatory activities.

Moreover, all self-regulation operates in the shadow of rules and sanctions provided by the general law, which provide reinforcement for industry controls. For example, misstatements by producers concerning organic certification would breach consumer protection laws governing misleading and deceptive conduct. Miscreants under an industry scheme of self-regulation are thus at risk of suffering sanctions at the hands of the state as well as at the hands of their peers.[102]

There may also be the possibility of facilitating third parties to act as surrogate regulators, policing the code as a complement or as an alternative to government involvement. We were advised of one incident in the Australian State of Queensland in which the gross infestation of one farmer's crop was placing his neighbours' crops at risk. Governments are, generally, reluctant to take the extreme step of issuing and enforcing a crop destruction order, the cost of which is borne by the offending producer. In this instance, the responsibilities were delegated to and carried out by local producers, peers of the offender.

Beyond specialized compliance services and quality assurance (QA) professionals, the most obvious third parties with an interest playing this role of surrogate regulators are consumers themselves. This contribution may be through their direct involvement in administration of the code itself (in which case, it has greater credibility as a genuinely self-regulatory scheme), the detection of violations, or in their capacity as potential victims of code malpractice to take direct action against breaches of the code. Rival producers provide another important group whose self-interest in ensuring a level playing field, and that their competitors do not abuse the code and thereby gain a competitive advantage, can be used to good effect.

---

[102] One Australian farmer was convicted of fraud and sentenced to a term of imprisonment for selling wheat which had been chemically treated as an organic product. The conviction was overturned on appeal (*R* v. *Vebergang*, Supreme Court of Queensland CA No. 398 of 1997, 27 February 1998).

Economic instruments

Despite the utility of the instruments discussed thus far, there will be circumstances when information, voluntary agreements, and self-regulation are insufficient to achieve desired objectives. Foremost among these are win-lose scenarios, where preferred environmental outcomes require real sacrifice on the part of the producer. The market for low-input product may not be sufficient to induce many producers to reduce chemical use, and perceived profits may be higher by using conventional pesticide-intensive methods of production. Similarly, in the case of habitat preservation, the costs of adherence to environmentally preferable methods of agricultural production will, commonly, exceed whatever benefits they may bring to the producer. In such circumstances, mere knowledge of environmentally desirable behaviour may be insufficient to achieve it.

Rather, a range of other instruments, including positive incentives, property rights, and price-based instruments and regulation, might be necessary to encourage farmers to embrace sustainable methods.

Positive incentives

Of these, the least interventionist and the most popular approach with agricultural producers is likely to be positive incentives, consisting of 'programs that seek to get producers to change their land-use, cultivation and livestock raising methods, along with the inputs employed, either permanently or on a temporary basis, in exchange for compensation paid in a lump sum or over time, or else in return for tax benefits for the purpose of achieving environmental objectives'.[103] Such incentives include tax credits, tax deductions, regulatory relief for private landholders who voluntarily protect habitat, and payments to participants in 'safe harbour' co-operative agreements,[104] purchasing of development rights, and other financial inducements for particularly desirable conduct.[105] For example, in the United Kingdom, the

---

[103] G. Debailleul, 'Economic Incentives for Biodiversity Conservation in the Agricultural Sector' in Organisation for Economic Co-operation and Development (OECD) *Investing in Biological Diversity: The Cairns Conference* (1997), OECD, Paris, p.242.

[104] On the latter, see further p.314 below.

[105] These may also include incidental permits for the taking of endangered species (M. Grossman, 'Habitat and Species Conservation in the European Union and the United States' (1997) 45(1) *Drake Law Review* 19–49) and protection from private nuisance suits (R. Moore, 'Controlling Agricultural Nonpoint Source Pollution: The New York experience' (1997) 45(1) *Drake Law Review*, 45 103–124 at 122). See also T. J. Centner, J. E. Houston, C. Fuchs & J. Zeddies, 'Employing Best Management Practices to Reduce

Environmentally Sensitive Areas Scheme provides payment on a per hectare basis for habitat conservation,[106] while within the European Union more generally, the success of increased set-aside in conjunction with a reduction in price support levels, is a clear example of 'how changing the price signals can be the most effective policy option in terms of the short term benefit to the environment'.[107]

Although they violate the polluter pays and user pays principles,[108] and are a drain on the public purse, positive incentives may have particular application in the agricultural sector. For example, where the producers come from low income groups, then subsidies may be more attractive in social welfare terms than taxes or regulation. In addition, the substantial political clout of agricultural communities may make it necessary to offset existing perverse incentives with positive incentives, rather than attempt their immediate removal. In some circumstances, the inclusion of positive incentives in a policy mix might render unnecessary the use of more coercive instruments which may be difficult to enforce in such a geographically isolated sector. On other occasions, positive incentives, for example compensation for income forgone preserving the habitat of a highly endangered species, may sweeten the bitter taste of strict prohibition, when used in combination.[109]

Agricultural Water Pollution: Economics, regulatory institutions, and policy concerns' 45(1) *Drake Law Review* 125–141.

[106] For an overview of incentive instruments see M. D. Young, N. Gunningham, J. Elix, J. Lambert, B. Howard, P. Grabosky, E. McCrone, *Reimbursing the Future: An evaluation of motivational, voluntary, price-based, property-right, and regulatory incentives for the conservation of biodiversity* (1996), Biodiversity Series Paper No. 9, Department of the Environment, Sport and Territories, Biodiversity Unit, Canberra; R. Gale, S. Barg & A. Gillies, (eds.) *Green Budget Reform* (1995), Earthscan Publications, London, p.160.

[107] European Commission, DG. 11, *Towards Sustainability*, (1997) Brussels, section 1.4.

[108] Organisation for Economic Co-operation and Development (OECD), *Agriculture and the Environment in the Transition to a Market Economy* (1993), OECD, Paris, pp.32–4 and 59; Organisation for Economic Co-operation and Development (OECD), *Agricultural Policy Reform: Environmental externalities and public goods in Agricultural Policy Reform: New Appproaches. The role of Direct Income Payments* (1994), Organisation for Economic Co-operation and Development (OECD), Paris; Organisation for Economic Co-operation and Development (OECD), *Agricultural and Environmental Policy Integration: Recent Progress and New Directions* (1993), OECD, Paris, p.33; Organisation for Economic Co-operation and Development (OECD), *Agricultural and Environmental Policies: Opportunities for integration* (1989), OECD, Paris, pp.29–30; and Organisation for Economic Co-operation and Development (OECD), *Sustainable Agriculture: Concepts, issues and policies in OECD countries* (1995), OECD, Paris, pp.17–22.

[109] Where for example, a particular course of action is deemed environmentally preferable, but not essential (such as postponing mowing until the end of the nesting season) an inducement alone may suffice. On the other hand, preserving the habitat of a highly endangered species may require strict prohibition, combined with compensation for producer income forgone.

For present purposes, in terms of achieving sustainable agriculture, there are two particular areas where the use of positive incentives is both attractive and justifiable. First, in the case of responsible chemical use, incentives serve to act as circuit-breakers, enabling producers to overcome the short-term problems of transitioning from conventional pesticide-intensive practices to sustainable ones. Secondly, in the case of biodiversity, there are powerful arguments in favour of compensating or, in prospective terms, rewarding landholders: (i) for environmental stewardship; and (ii) to achieve a transition to a property right regime that protects biodiversity.

Turning to the first of these, we have noted that one of the main impediments to pesticide reduction is the risk of financial loss, especially during the transitional phase. For an individual producer, the transition to low input farming can be difficult. The anxieties and uncertainties that accompany a change in methods may be borne out in weed resurgence, and in an explosive increase in insect pest populations. Properly constructed incentive programmes (which could emanate from either private or public sectors) can help reduce this risk and facilitate conversion to more environmentally benign farming methods.

As illustrated by the case of Campbell Soup, large corporate buyers may be in a position to insure their growers against economic loss.[110] Campbell shielded its growers from financial risk arising from reduction in crop quantity or quality during the initial two years of the programme. Where the absence of a large and willing buyer precludes such support, insurance-based institutions may fill the gap. For example, in Canada, the Saskatchewan Crop Insurance Program offers a higher range of coverage for organic grains, and the Prince Edward Island Department of Agriculture underwrites fifty per cent of any yield reduction associated with transition to low input methods.[111] A number of additional incentive mechanisms suggest themselves, including production subsidies for farmers who rely on low input methods, or transition subsidies during a period of conversion to low inputs. Given the costs of compliance monitoring, one means of enlisting non-government resources could entail a requirement that eligibility for a subsidy be conditional upon membership of an organic certification society.

[110] See chapter three, above p.109; below, p.338.

[111] German farmers in Saarland may receive up to $2,500 compensation for lost income during transition (R. MacRae, S. Hill, J. Henning & A. Bentley, 'Policies, Programs and Regulations to Support the Transition to Sustainable Agriculture in Canada' (1990) 5(2) *American Journal of Alternative Agriculture* 76–92 at 80).

All the above mechanisms may be regarded as circuit-breakers—*short-term* measures which are necessary in order to break to pattern of unsustainable production and to facilitate producers embarking on a new approach; which might not be practicable in the absence of such intervention. But longer term subsidization would be undesirable not only because of the expense involved, but also because of the likelihood that producers become dependent upon them, and disinclined to strive for continuous improvement. Thus, inducements to convert to low-input agriculture should not be open ended, lest they encourage the same degree of dependency that they were designed to overcome. One should also be mindful of the risk that incentive systems can proliferate to the point of redundancy, risking waste of the taxpayer's money and confusion for the producer.[112]

In contrast to the problems of agricultural chemicals, which lend themselves to solutions such as transitional subsidies, the issue of biodiversity loss raises very different questions relating to environmental stewardship. Positive incentives (in the form of reimbursing costs) may be appropriate in two particular sets of circumstances.

The first is where the costs associated with biodiversity conservation cannot be recovered from the market place. Examples of these costs include fencing out an area of value to an endangered species so that it cannot be grazed, and then keeping the area free of vermin. As no market exists for the protection of habitats occupied by most endangered species, it is efficient for the beneficiaries of species protection (taxpayers on behalf of society) to reimburse those who incur the cost of protecting them.[113] As our colleague Mike Young has argued, efficiency criteria would indicate that reimbursement should be only for those costs incremental and in addition to those recoverable through market processes.[114] In practice, such arrangements are also supported

[112] K. Turner, E. Ozdemiroglu & P. Steele, 'Environmentally Sensitive Areas in the United Kingdom: Economic incentives for sustainable farming' (1995) in R. Gale, S. Barg & A. Gillies, (eds.) *Green Budget Reform* (1995), Earthscan Publications, London, pp.119–135 at 129–30.

[113] The World Bank's Global Environment Facility (GEF) describes this concept as one of reimbursing the incremental costs of providing benefits to society. The notion is simply one of paying people to do work which, if they did not do it, would be undertaken by government. Payments should be limited to expenditure which cannot be recovered from the market place. Costs can be reimbursed either by periodic payments or a one-time off payment associated with a conservation covenant, or other similar arrangements that are binding on future land holders.

[114] Young has suggested that this should be called a Beneficiary-Compensates Principle, emphasising that, following an appropriate transition period, payment should be limited to reimbursement of costs incurred in the course of maintaining biodiversity

by provision of periodic advice and a programme that motivates people to feel proud of the contribution they are making to society's biodiversity conservation objectives.

Secondly—on equity grounds and to encourage efficient investment—most developed nations provide a right to compensation for the removal of a right that is being exercised (for example if restrictions are imposed upon the right to clear land). At the same time, however, most nations also reserve the right, from time to time, to redefine the bundle of unfettered economic opportunities embodied in a property-right, and have encouraged people to speculate on the profits and losses associated with them. Thus, establishing a precedent for the payment of compensation for decline in land values should be seen as a very fundamental reform, with immense budgetary implications. If speculation is allowed, then the case for compensation collapses to one of the need to achieve and retain political and community acceptability during the transition period when assumed, but unspecified, property-rights are redefined.[115]

As with voluntary financial instruments for biodiversity conservation on land that remains in private ownership, the role of compensation is largely one of a circuit breaker to bring about the transition to an institutional and property right regime that promotes biodiversity, whilst maintaining motivation, equity, and community acceptance. Administrative costs may be less if the initial policy change is accompanied by a plan to diminish the proportion of compensation payable by, say, twenty per cent per annum. When this is done, the transition is speedier and, as the threat is reduced more quickly, the mix may be more dependable.[116]

Finally, the broader question is whether positive incentives may appropriately be made part of an integrated agricultural policy package. For example, an agricultural variation on the system of accredited licensing (see chapter two) has been proposed in Australia by

values (M. D. Young, N. Gunningham, J. Elix, J. Lambert, B. Howard, P. Grabosky, E. McCrone, *Reimbursing the Future: An evaluation of motivational, voluntary, price-based, property-right, and regulatory incentives for the conservation of biodiversity* (1996), Biodiversity Series Paper No. 9, Department of the Environment, Sport and Territories, Biodiversity Unit, Canberra).

[115] See M. Young & N. Gunningham 'Mixing Instruments and Institutional Arrangements for Optimal Biodiversity Conservation' in Organisation for Economic Co-operation and Development (OECD), *Investing in Biological Diversity* (1996), OECD, Paris, pp.141–167.

[116] *Ibid.*

the Australian Farmers' Federation.[117] The proposed scheme would involve a two-stage process for training landholders in the practices of sustainable production. The first stage would involve self-assessment, in which landholders would test their knowledge and practices of farm planning and sustainable agriculture. Industry associations would be actively involved in the education and training process. They would then seek formal accreditation of land management practices jointly by government and industry authorities. Accreditation would make farmers eligible for a wide range of assistance, including discounts on farm inputs, lower interest rates on bank loans, rate rebates from local government, grants from State governments, and tax incentives. Here, we see a combination of instruments, where the synergies of information and motivation are accelerated by the incentives available to those producers who can demonstrate compliance.

Such positive incentives would thus be appropriately aimed at the highest end of the performance continuum. Directed at the very best performers, they recognize and reward significant achievements. As such, their latent function is to reach more ordinary producers, who might thereby be inspired to realize their potential—short-term subsidies during the period of transition to low input methods are, perhaps, the best example. The celebration of exemplary environmental stewardship will, ideally, attract the attention of lesser performers, who, through nonchalance or through lack of awareness, are failing to comply with regulatory standards.

Despite their advantages in some circumstances, the use of incentives (other than perverse incentives) in the domain of agri-environmental regulation would appear to have suffered from relative neglect thus far.[118] But even if they were to be implemented more widely and with beneficial consequences, they would be unlikely to deliver a perfect world. First, in the majority of circumstances, it is more appropriate to make producers and landholders internalize externalities rather than to subsidize them to change their behaviour—a strategy which, if it became widespread, would also rapidly deplete the public purse. Secondly, there are those who may be irrational, intransigent, or incompetent, and who may lie beyond the reach not only of voluntary, but also of incentive-based mechanisms. Where these informational and positive incentive instruments do not prove effective, the availability

---

[117] D. McGauchie, *The Future of Agricultural Land Use in Australia* (1996), address to the Waite Agricultural Research Institute, Adelaide, South Australia, 26 March.

and use of more negative incentives should cut in. Foremost among these are prices, property instruments, and regulation.

Property-rights and price-based instruments

In the case of biodiversity conservation, market failure is pervasive, while in the case of agricultural chemical use, it is evident in particular circumstances.[119] This failure is caused by, *inter alia*, externalities, the complete absence of markets for some aspects of biodiversity, and inadequately or incompletely defined property rights. The result is that many environmental assets are seriously underpriced and are, therefore, overconsumed. Two particular forms of economic instrument may be invoked to address these problems directly: property rights and price-based instruments. In principal, such instruments have particular advantages in terms of cost effectiveness or economic efficiency.[120]

Property-right instruments with applicability to the agricultural sector include: exclusive-use rights[121] (of which bio-prospecting contracts

---

[118] For a variety of examples of incentives for environmentally appropriate agriculture, see R. Gale, S. Barg, & A. Gillies, (eds.) *Green Budget Reform* (1995), Earthscan Publications, London pp.93–160; and M. D. Young, N. Gunningham, J. Elix, J. Lambert, B. Howard, P. Grabosky, E. McCrone, *Reimbursing the Future: An evaluation of motivational, voluntary, price-based, property-right, and regulatory incentives for the conservation of biodiversity* (1996), Biodiversity Series Paper No. 9, Department of the Environment, Sport and Territories, Biodiversity Unit, Canberra.

[119] Here, one is beginning to observe the emergence of market influences in furtherance of environmentally preferable practices. See p.337, below.

[120] See further, chapter two, above.

[121] Economic theory suggests, controversially, that when people are granted an exclusive right to use and profit from a resource they have a greater incentive to conserve that resource and a lesser incentive to exploit it unsustainably.

The principle of exclusive-use rights, however, is perceived by some people to conflict with the widespread belief that biodiversity is owned collectively by society at large and not available for people to use for profit. The challenge is to decide which areas can be transferred to exclusive private property and which must be managed via closely supervised government processes. In examining exclusive rights mechanisms, it is important to distinguish a right to use a resource as they wish from a right to the exclusive benefit from a resource.

Zimbabwe's CAMPFIRE program (Communal Areas Management Programme for Indigenous Resources) is perhaps the best known and most effective case of this 'exclusive rights' approach to species protection (see E. B. Barbier, 'Community-based development in Africa' in T. M. Swanson and E. B. Barbier (eds.) *Economics for the Wilds* (1992), Island Press, Washington DC; and M't Sas-Rolfes 'Trade in endangered species: Is it a option?' (1994) 14 (3) *Economic Affairs* 2). See also Organisation for Economic Co-operation and Development (OECD), Group on Economic and Environment Policy Integration Expert on Economic Aspects of Biodiversity, *Making Markets Work for Biodiversity: The role of economic incentive measures* (1995), Draft final report, Fourth session 11–13 July, p.24; and R. Eckersley, 'Rationalising the environment: How Much am I Bid?' in S. Rees, G. Rodley and F. Stilwell (eds.) *Beyond the Market: Alternatives to economic*

are a special form[122]); individually transferable property-right mechanisms;[123] covenants and easements;[124] offset arrangements;[125] and leas-

rationalisation (1993), Pluto Press, Leichhardt, NSW, p.245; and B. A. Aylward,
'Appropriating the Value of Wildlife and Wetlands' in T. M. Swanson & E. B. Barbier,
(eds.) *Economics for the Wilds* (1992), Island Press, Washington DC at p.34) and as such,
must be protected by other means.

[122] Bioprospecting contracts are a special form of exclusive right used to maintain
equity and encourage people to maintain a resource in the hope that people will find an
asset which can be marketed. They seek to make biodiversity protection the 'highest and
best use' for a resource.

The most prominent biodiversity prospecting contract is a contract between Costa
Rica's National Biodiversity Institute (INBio) and Merck and Co. Ltd., a large pharma-
ceutical firm (see appendix 1 of M. D. Young, N. Gunningham, J. Elix, J. Lambert, B.
Howard, P. Grabosky, E. McCrone, *Reimbursing the Future: An evaluation of motivational, vol-
untary, price-based, property-right, and regulatory incentives for the conservation of biodiversity* (1996),
Biodiversity Series Paper No. 9, Department of the Environment, Sport and Territories,
Biodiversity Unit, Canberra).

More generally, the intellectual property regime could provide a mechanism for the
equitable re-distribution of exclusive use rights between resource custodians and resource
users such as bio-prospectors. For further discussion, see K. Old, *Utilisation and Conservation
of Australian Plant Genetic Resources: The role of monopoly privilege* (1994), Honours Thesis submitted to the Faculty of Law, Australian National University, October 1994; also M. A.
Gollin, 'An Intellectual Property Rights Framework for Biodiversity Prospecting' in W. V.
Reid, S. A. Laird, C. A. Meyer, R. Gamez, A. Sittenfeld, D. H. Janzen, M. A. Gollin &
C. Juma, (eds.) *Biodiversity Prospecting: Using genetic resources for sustainable development* (1993),
World Resources Institute, US.

[123] These are rights to use specified resources which can be transferred to another person without having to obtain prior consent. The most common case is that of tradeable
permits and licences such as transferable fishing quotas. The strength of tradeable permits and licences is that they offer a dependable means to constrain use within a biodiversity target whilst still giving industry the opportunity to decide how they do that. As
a mechanism, however, they are limited to resources that are relatively homogeneous.
See M. D. Young & B. McCay, *Building Equity, Stewardship and Resilience into Market-Based
Property-Right Systems* (1995), World Bank, Washington DC; and Organisation for
Economic Co-operation and Development (OECD), *Making Markets Work for Biological
Diversity: The role of economic incentives measures*, (1996), OECD, Paris; and D. Farrier, 'Policy
instruments for conserving biodiversity on private land' in J. Bradstock (ed.) *Conserving
Biodiversity: Threats and solutions* (1995), Surrey Beatty and Sons, Chipping Norton.

[124] Covenants (and, in the American terminology, easements as well) are instruments
which restrict a landowner's ability to exercise particular rights over their property; for
example, they can be used to prohibit the clearance of natural vegetation, or to preserve
an area which supports certain types of wildlife.

Because they are negotiated on an individual basis, covenants present the opportunity
for careful targeting. The experience of a number of countries suggests that covenants
and easements offer considerable scope for the 'establishment of buffer zones, wildlife corridors and protected area management' (Organisation for Economic Co-operation and
Development (OECD), *Making Markets Work for Biological Diversity: The role of economic incentives measures*, (1996), OECD, Paris) although the costs of monitoring and enforcing compliance must be weighed against these benefits. Easements are particularly cost effective
when the areas needing special protection are fragmented and the main requirement
is to prevent an action such as clearing. See further, the discussion of the nature

ing and licensing.[126] These types of instruments seek to compensate for, or reverse, market failure through mechanisms which make resource use opportunities consistent with social values. By privatization or similar strategies, they seek to restrain or halt the overconsumption of environmental assets, by making conservation more profitable to the producer.

Applying property rights to unsustainable farming practices can be done by simply extending the private property ownership regime (for example, legalizing ownership of some threatened African species).[127] However, most property rights begin by defining what may be done and then restrict action through various conditions. For example, easements and other legislative arrangements may grant rights to those other than landowners, a conservation covenant may prohibit clearing,

conservancy in the USA in D. Farrier, 'Conserving Biodiversity on Private Land' (1995) 19(2) *Harvard Environmental Law Review* 304–405.

[125] Under these arrangements, industry is given the choice between off-setting the damage they cause or paying an authority to do it on their behalf.

Off setting arrangements with regards to wetlands—known as 'wetlands mitigation'—has been a prominent part of American environment policy for over two decades (White House Office on Environmental Policy, *Protecting America's Wetlands: A. fair, flexible and effective approach* (1993), Washington DC) but grave doubts are held by many as to their value as a means of wetlands protection (see further, D. Farrier, 'Policy Instruments for Conserving Biodiversity on Private Land' in J. Bradstock (ed.) *Conserving biodiversity: Threats and solutions* (1995), Surrey Beatty and Sons, Chipping Norton, pp.304–405).

It has been argued that such means are simply ecologically ineffective, because of insufficient knowledge about the science of creating or restoring wetlands. Even if successful, mitigation efforts can result in fragmented segments of wetlands of far less richness and diversity than the areas which they are intended to replace. Others have criticised the administrative framework used to oversee mitigation projects, claiming that inadequate resourcing has meant that project plans are often not carried out at all or, if they are implemented, are not monitored or maintained. (J. Silverstein, 'Taking Wetlands to the Bank: The role of wetland mitigation banking in a comprehensive approach to wetlands protection' (1994) 22 *Boston College Environmental Affairs Law Review* 129).

There have been some moves to address these regulatory problems with increased use of mitigation banking—which requires the restoration or creation to be performed in advance of the proposed loss (J. Silverstein, 'Taking Wetlands to the Bank: The role of wetland mitigation banking in a comprehensive approach to wetlands protection' (1994) 22 *Boston College Environmental Affairs Law Review* 129) but this does not address the issue of whether such mitigation is ecologically viable.

[126] In their simplest form, licenses, leases and permits combine economic opportunity with a series of restrictions in the form of conditions tailored to a specific location—as such, they have some characteristics of regulation as well as of property rights. Their prime administrative advantage is that they give administrations a periodic opportunity to review progress and use conditions. They are probably the main mechanism used to control activity that has site specific implications for biodiversity (See I. Hodge, 'Incentive Policies and the Rural Environment' (1991) 7 *Journal of Rural Studies* 373–84).

[127] See chapter two, above.

or individually marketable pesticide use or emission rights might control overall chemical use in a region.[128] Where public lands are leased to private agricultural users, conditions of leasehold may require certain action and/or may prohibit specific practices.

In contrast to property-right mechanisms, which indirectly influence prices by changing the cost of certain activities and altogether preventing others, agricultural production prices can be influenced *directly* via price-based mechanisms such as charges, levies, and use fees;[129] tax instruments,[130] and the removal of perverse incentives. Conceptually,

[128] J. A. W. A. Reus, H. J. Weckseler & G. A. Pak, *Towards a Future EC Pesticide Policy: An inventory of risks of pesticide use, possible solutions, and policy instruments* (1994), Centre for Agriculture and Environment, Utrecht, p.79.

[129] These can be used to change the economic signals given to people whose actions threaten biodiversity values. To this end, the OECD has made an important contribution by recommending ways to implement the polluter pays principle and, to a lesser extent, the user pays principle. Collectively, these principles imply that, wherever possible, the costs of supplying access to biodiversity should be recovered from the direct beneficiaries of biodiversity conservation. Similarly, the costs of controlling and preventing direct threats to biodiversity should be recovered from the people who cause those threats. The money collected through the implementation of these mechanisms can be used both as a means to ration use so that it is kept within sustainable limits, and to finance research, management and protection. They can also be used as a means to raise government revenue. Links between management and resource users are strengthened. Political pressure for the administering authority to reduce costs emerges. Cost recovery is now being applied routinely in many industries. See also M. D. Young, N. Gunningham, J. Elix, J. Lambert, B. Howard, P. Grabosky, E. McCrone, *Reimbursing the Future: An evaluation of motivational, voluntary, price-based, property-right, and regulatory incentives for the conservation of biodiversity* (1996), Biodiversity Series Paper No. 9, Department of the Environment, Sport and Territories, Biodiversity Unit, Canberra, chapter 4; and OECD, Group on Economic and Environment Policy Integration Expert on Economic Aspects of Biodiversity, *Making Markets Work for Biodiversity: The role of Economic incentive measures* (1995), Draft final report, Fourth session 11–13 July.

[130] From a tax perspective, biodiversity conservation can be assisted through two mechanisms. The first is by making greater economic use of its attributes. When this occurs, expenditure on biodiversity maintenance is tax deductible because it is expenditure made in the course of earning income. Use of the attributes of biodiversity also shifts the nature of threats faced. Taxation mechanisms can also be used as a mechanism to change the cost of undertaking various activities, and are already used as a means to close the gap between social and private values.

They can also be used as a means to encourage people to contribute to national objectives. The argument for these taxation incentives is that, because they establish an entitlement, people are encouraged to pursue such opportunities without having to prepare submission to and obtain permission from the bureaucracy. They also encourage altruistic behaviour and where there is a national commitment to achieving an objective, like biodiversity conservation, the objective is likely to be achieved at much less cost to government than would be the case if government departments managed all biodiversity conservation of this nature themselves.

However, taxation mechanisms can also work against biodiversity conservation by encouraging people to develop resources rather than conserve. Another argument against

such mechanisms could be used to control most threats to biodiversity, but this is rarely done in practice. For markets to produce efficient solutions, it is necessary for transactions to be reversible in that any item consumed can be replaced. In the case of biodiversity, however, many habitats can never be recreated. Efficient markets need to be able to revise prices continuously through time and across space. In the case of biodiversity, a system is required that enables government institutions to constantly monitor and, when appropriate, change the prices they set. As a result, price-based instruments are not useful 'across the board' for protecting biodiversity. Nevertheless, in selected circumstances, pricing mechanisms do have a significant role in revealing the cost of preventing and controlling adverse impacts on biodiversity. As the OECD points out:

. . . biodiversity is arguably different as an environmental and economic resource because its fate depends on many decisions made in many different economic sectors. That is, it is pervasive to the economic system, being affected by land and water use decisions, by pollution and by economic activity generally. As such, biodiversity conservation policies must themselves be pervasive, i.e., they must be capable of filtering through the entire economic system.[131]

In particular, there is a strong case for the removal or modification of perverse incentives that significantly raise the cost of biodiversity conservation. Such incentives are more prevalent in respect of agriculture and the environment than perhaps any other area of regulation. At the global level, Panayotou[132] has estimated that ninety cents in every dollar invested in biodiversity conservation is spent on tasks such as undoing the unintended effects of government subsidies and of protecting people from competition. 'Countervailing subsidies' have encouraged land clearing and chemical use, while price supports, generally, have operated to neutralize other instruments intended to encourage environmentally friendly production.[133] However, to remove such

these mechanisms is that, when not channelled through a well developed non-government organisation or screening mechanism, they are prone to taxation rorts.

[131] Organisation for Economic Co-operation and Development (OECD), *Making Markets Work for Biological Diversity: The Role of Economic Incentives Measures* (1996), OECD, Paris.

[132] T. Panayotou, *Reducing Biodiversity Expenditure Needs: Reforming perverse incentives* (1996), paper presented to an OECD Conference on Incentive Measures for Biodiversity Conservation and Sustainable Use, Cairns, Australia, March 1996.

[133] Organisation for Economic Co-operation and Development (OECD), *Agricultural and Environmental Policies: Opportunities for integration* (1989a), OECD, Paris, p.112; and see R. Gale, S. Barg & A. Gillies, (eds.) *Green Budget Reform* (1995), Earthscan Publications, London pp.93–160.

subsidies risks imposing significant financial losses on producers, in a manner not likely to win their hearts and minds to the cause of environmentally preferable agriculture. For this reason, a gradual withdrawal of subsidies, or a shift in the nature of those subsidies (so they are no longer perverse in environmental terms), or their combination with incentives for environmentally desirable conduct, may be preferable to simply terminating them all at once.[134]

For example, contemplated reforms to the European Union's Common Agricultural Policy include reduced reliance on market price support compensated by direct aid measures, partly linked to environmental conditions; the monitoring of effects; and reporting. Arguably, the redesign of subsidies (tying them to positive environmental objectives) provides a powerful policy tool for environmental protection, whereas their complete removal might in some circumstances, produce more intensive and environmentally destructive activities.[135] Indeed, a strong case can be made for payments to economically marginal producers to assist them in leaving the land, thereby allowing more successful (and, potentially, more environmentally competent) producers to acquire their holdings. Such a programme was part of an Australian rural adjustment policy in 1997.

In contrast with the very limited appropriateness and use of price-based instruments (other than the removal of perverse incentives) to protect biodiversity, the use of charges and levies on agricultural chemicals is commonplace. These encourage the producer to search for lower cost (and, presumably, lower input) alternatives.[136] Similarly, water pricing policies may be geared to reduce water consumption and encourage irrigation practices that reduce chemical runoff.[137] Their rel-

[134] With the phasing out of farm subsidies which began during the Clinton administration, the predictions of free market environmentalists about the likely benefits of terminating farm subsidies may ultimately be subject to empirical verification.

[135] R. Soufi & M. Tudderham, 'Reform of the Common Agricultural Policy' in R. Gale, S. Barg & A. Gillies, (eds.) *Green Budget Reform* (1995), Earthscan Publications, London; and K. Turner, E. Ozdemiroglu & P. Steele, 'Environmentally Sensitive Areas in the UK: Economic incentives for sustainable farming' in R. Gale, S. Barg & A. Gillies, (eds.) *Green Budget Reform* (1995), Earthscan Publications, London.

[136] J. A. W. A. Reus, H. J. Weckseler & G. A. Pak, *Towards a Future EC. Pesticide Policy: An inventory of risks of pesticide use, possible solutions, and policy instruments* (1994), Centre for Agriculture and Environment, Utrecht, p.73.

[137] The Environmental Defence Fund has proposed an incentive based system to reduce agricultural run-off which would specify a pollution reduction goal, then give farmers the flexibility to decide how best to meet that goal (Environmental Defence Fund, 'Economic Incentives Could Reduce Water Pollution From Agriculture' (1994) Vol. XXV (September) *EDF Letter* 5). EDF also recommends more efficient irrigation

ative ease of administration and revenue generating potential make them even more attractive to governments in an era of fiscal restraint. However, these instruments encounter serious problems when dealing with diffuse pollutants and groundwater contamination. The key to their success is the ability of administrators to get the incentives right. Ultimately, the feasibility of such instruments will depend upon the farmer's bottom-line (and the viability of alternative agricultural practices and/or business inputs). A doubling in the price of a chemical may still pale in comparison to the loss of income which could result from a decline in quality or yield. For a producer concerned about the prospect of significant economic loss, a significant increase in input costs may be a small price to pay for security.

The extent to which property-right and pricing mechanisms can make a positive contribution to biodiversity conservation and the reduction of agricultural chemical pollution is likely to depend substantially on the particular contexts in which they are applied,[138] the threats to which they are addressed,[139] and the particular attributes of individual instruments.[140] For example, in addressing problems such as pesticide pollution, property rights through tradeable permits commonly suffer from the size of the tradeable market, the inability to accurately monitor trading, the complexity of transactions, and problems associated with non-uniform mixing from point source.

More broadly, price-based approaches may be less appropriate than other instruments in addressing two key characteristics of biodiversity. These are that biodiversity loss is often irreversible, and that ecosystems have limits and, if stressed beyond those limits, they will collapse. Nevertheless, property-right and price-based instruments may contribute positively to an integrated policy package. The latter may be

technologies to minimize agricultural runoff (http://www.edf.org/pubs/AnnualReport/1982/g_agbase.html).

[138] Compare, for example, commercialization of wildlife, performance bonds and tradeable permits, discussed above at note 121.

[139] For example, instruments which are appropriate to address pollution may work very differently when applied to other threats to biodiversity.

[140] For example, management agreements coupled with reimbursement can fulfil a particular function (for which regulation or other instruments are no substitute). Similarly, some property rights mechanisms have the distinctive characteristic of providing the land user with an incentive to protect the environment, and in doing so encourage positive custodianships of biodiversity and support for biodiversity objectives. Experience with the effectiveness of property rights based mechanisms however, is mixed. In particular, the effectiveness of property-right mechanisms is dependent upon the capacity of the institutional mechanisms used to develop, review and enforce them.

expected to interact with informational instruments relating to the virtues and profitability of low input methods, making the latter even more attractive. Lest these taxes on inputs be perceived as punitive or unfairly directed at farmers, the revenue generated by them may be hypothecated[141] for a variety of purposes, including research and development, water quality enhancement, or subsidies for low input farmers.

As we have observed, the coupling of positive and negative incentives can also be a complementary and effective strategy, which allows the former to become more palatable to the farmer. This is well illustrated by the successful scheme introduced in the German State of Baden-Wurttemburg, which combines direct compensation to farmers for reduced use of nitrates and pesticides with a charge for water use.[142] The linked instruments each address a different factor underlying non-point source pollution; farmers whose pollution problems arise from inappropriate use of water are influenced by the charges. Those who apply chemicals in excess are encouraged by the subsidy to reduce input. Producers targeted by both instruments experience less of a financial burden because of the combined use of stick and carrot.

Property-right and price-based instruments, despite their considerable virtues, still lack dependability, particularly in relation to the conservation of biodiversity, and for this reason may, at times, require some degree of underpinning by regulation. The extent to which regulatory intervention is justified (often in conjunction with voluntary and/or motivational instruments), and the form it might take, will depend upon, *inter alia*, whether there is a danger of irreversible biodiversity loss, and whether that loss gives rise to the possibility of a major environmental catastrophe or system collapse, matters to which we will return.

---

[141] One mechanism often used to increase acceptance of charges and levies is to give those whose incomes are affected by the charge or levy a say in determining how the resultant money is spent. Alternatively, a government can promise to commit the money collected to a cause. Known as hypothecation, this mechanism is used to underscore the point that communities should contribute directly to the financing of programmes that improve the environment (Department of Finance, *Submission to HORSCERA: Inquiry into management arrangements for inscribed World Heritage Areas* (1994) AGPS, Canberra; and M. D. Young, N. Gunningham, J. Elix, J. Lambert, B. Howard, P. Grabosky, E. McCrone, *Reimbursing the Future: An evaluation of motivational, voluntary, price-based, property-right, and regulatory incentives for the conservation of biodiversity* (1996), Biodiversity Series Paper No. 9, Department of the Environment, Sport and Territories, Biodiversity Unit, Canberra, p.124).

[142] W. Rudig & R. A. Kraemer, 'Networks of Cooperation: Water Policy in Germany' (1994) 3(4) *Environmental Politics* 52–79.

Coercive sanctions

In the domain of biodiversity conservation, the main regulatory instruments are well known[143] and include zoning,[144] land-use restrictions,[145] standards,[146] and bans,[147] as well as some licences[148] and

[143] Regulatory approaches utilize either: (i) spatially defined (exclusionary or zonal); (ii) species, ecosystem or community specific; or (iii) threat specific triggers, to address biodiversity conservation, including that which is agriculture-based.

[144] Traditionally, zoning is used to define what activities take place in certain areas but can be used to create and protect a wide range of public amenities. Zoning can be used in conjunction with other measure, such as offsetting arrangements, cross-compliance, and development rights to create incentives (M. D. Young, N. Gunningham, J. Elix, J. Lambert, B. Howard, P. Grabosky, E. McCrone, *Reimbursing the Future: An evaluation of motivational, voluntary, price-based, property-right, and regulatory incentives for the conservation of biodiversity* (1996), Biodiversity Series Paper No. 9, Department of the Environment, Sport and Territories, Biodiversity Unit, Canberra, vol. 1, p.26).

[145] In Australia, each state has legislative controls aimed at protecting native vegetation. Clearing controls vary from state to state in their design and application. No state has totally banned clearing of native vegetation but stringent controls exist South Australia, Victoria and Western Australia. Both Commonwealth and state governments are involved with fisheries management (M. D. Young, N. Gunningham, J. Elix, J. Lambert, B. Howard, P. Grabosky, E. McCrone, *Reimbursing the Future: An evaluation of motivational, voluntary, price-based, property-right, and regulatory incentives for the conservation of biodiversity* (1996), Biodiversity Series Paper No. 9, Department of the Environment, Sport and Territories, Biodiversity Unit, Canberra, vol. 1, chapter 2).

[146] Direct regulations can play a particularly vital role in preventing and eliminating those actions which under present arrangements could result in losses that are either totally irreversible or only irreversible at unacceptably high costs. In such situations, the conventional approach is to recommend that a safer minimum standard be set. For biodiversity conservation, however, we often don't know what the safe minimum standard is. Indeed for a significant number of areas in Australia that point may have been passed and the need is for species recovery plans and rehabilitation of ecosystems (M. D. Young, N. Gunningham, J. Elix, J. Lambert, B. Howard, P. Grabosky, E. McCrone, *Reimbursing the Future: An evaluation of motivational, voluntary, price-based, property-right, and regulatory incentives for the conservation of biodiversity* (1996), Biodiversity Series Paper No. 9, Department of the Environment, Sport and Territories, Biodiversity Unit, Canberra, vol. 1, chapter 6).

[147] Regulation's strength, in some circumstances, is the certainty it provides, particularly where it takes the form of direct bans on destructive activity, supported by sanctions. It is true that there will remain a temptation to cheat, particularly where breaches are not transparent. For example, a ban on clearing is likely to be more effective than a ban on killing endangered species because the administrative costs of monitoring clearing are lower than those of watching the fate of a species. The American experience is that when an endangered species is present, the maxim 'shoot, shovel and shut up' still prevails despite regulation. How strong this temptation will be, and how likely people are to succumb to it, will depend in part on the perceived legitimacy of the regulation (reinforcing the need for education and motivation) and, in part, on the likelihood of detection and severity of sanctions (C. Perrings & D. Pearce, 'Threshold Effects and Incentives of the Conservation of Biodiversity'(1994) 4(1) *Environmental and Resource Economics* 13–28).

[148] One traditional mechanism used by governments is to issue licences, leases, and permits to use natural resources. Examples explored in the case studies undertaken in this report include licences to shoot kangaroos, pollution permits, licences to collect native

quotas.[149] For agricultural chemicals, they include outright prohibition, pre-market approvals, conditions of use, and certification of user.[150]

In contrast to price-based instruments, regulation directly controls or restricts environmentally damaging activities by mandating the reduction or restriction of harmful activities. As such, it is much more prescriptive. Moreover, legislation proscribing certain activity has a moral dimension that is lacking in economic instruments, sending a clear message as to what is socially unacceptable behaviour. However, the moral influence of law, while important, is also variable, and is likely to be substantially reinforced by the provision of adequate information and education. Regulation often lacks the flexibility associated with market-based approaches, and is commonly criticized by economists for being inefficient, unnecessarily intrusive, and expensive to administer.[151]

plants, and leases to graze rangelands. In their simplest form, these permits combine economic opportunity with a series of restrictions in the form of conditions tailored to a specific location. Their prime administrative advantage is that they give administrations a periodic opportunity to review progress and review use conditions. As such, they are probably the main mechanism used to control activity that has site specific implications for biodiversity. In theory, a high degree of dependability is offered. In practice, unless careful attention is given to institutional arrangements, administrators are easily captured by licence and permit holders with the consequence that official objectives are poorly achieved. They are, however, a mechanism used routinely by private enterprise and, in countries where non-government is actively involved in biodiversity conservation, by these organizations.

A problem with many existing systems is that all the pressure for change is placed on new licence holders and not those whose conditions are fixed. Another is a failure to allocate rights and conditions on an ecosystem basis so that the total impacts of all licences is kept within sustainable limits (M. D. Young, N. Gunningham, J. Elix, J. Lambert, B. Howard, P. Grabosky, E. McCrone, *Reimbursing the Future: An evaluation of motivational, voluntary, price-based, property-right, and regulatory incentives for the conservation of biodiversity* (1996), Biodiversity Series Paper No. 9, Department of the Environment, Sport and Territories, Biodiversity Unit, Canberra, vol. 1, chapter 6).

[149] Individual Transferable Fishing Quotas have been implemented in Australia and around the world with varying degrees of success. The Southern Bluefin Tuna system, introduced in 1984, provided individuals with rights to harvest a given quota of stock. The sum of all quotas represented the Total Allowable Catch (TAC) which was, theoretically, equivalent to the species maximum sustainable yield. Difficulties in estimating the maximum sustainable yield, and therefore the TAC, meant the system has not been successful at maintaining species (Bureau of Industry Economics, *Environmental Regulation: The economics of tradeable permits—a survey of theory and practice* (1992), Research Report 42, AGPS, Canberra).

[150] See above, p.283.

[151] As we saw in chapter two, some regulations limit innovation and discourage people from searching for new, more efficient ways to achieve the intent of a regulation. Moreover, regulatory instruments may be inequitable, and difficult to revise as new information becomes available. Again, while regulation may serve to bring people up to a prescribed minimum standard, or prevent damage below a threshold, it is not well equipped to bring about continuous improvement, to influence behaviour above the threshold or

Nevertheless, direct regulation may sometimes be necessary because, although the less coercive instruments discussed above can make significant contributions to sustainable agriculture, there are still circumstances in which they may fail to deliver preferred environmental outcomes, or indeed, may fail to prevent serious environmental damage. Given these risks, and the possibility of irreversible harm to some ecosystems, there remains a place for coercive sanctions in agro-environmental regulation.

Even if the vast majority of producers do the right thing, there is always the chance that the irrational, the incompetent, or the intransigent individual will produce serious harm. No less than in other walks of life, there are those farmers who are quite simply resistant to new ideas. There are others who, because of educational disadvantage, are unable to process information which is readily available to them and to their peers. While relatively small, these minorities cannot be ignored.

When the intransigent, the incompetent, or the recalcitrant lie beyond the reach of voluntary, property-right, and financial incentives, more intrusive means might offer the most efficient way of protecting the environment at least administrative cost.[152] As we were told by one farmer, 'What will attract interest is a prosecution'. This was echoed by another of our respondents, a representative of a marketing authority, who said simply, 'In the end, you need a big stick'. The well-documented experience of land clearing control in South Australia also supports this conclusion.[153] Neither information, incentives, nor compensation, were sufficient to halt widespread clearance of what small proportion of unspoilt habitat remained in that state. Only the

to achieve on-going management and environmental stewardship. See further, B. A. Ackerman & R. B. Stewart, 'Reforming Environmental Law' (1985) 37 *Stanford Law Review* 1333.

[152] Of course, the recalcitrant, incompetent, or intransigent could also ignore regulation. However, for a variety of reasons, they are far less likely to do so. The techniques that regulators can invoke to achieve compliance are far more compelling than those available for other categories of instruments (see J. F. Dimento, *Environmental Law and American Business: Dilemmas of compliance* (1986), Plenum Press, New York). As to the literature which examines the suggestion that regulatory law deters violations in ways superior to other approaches, see R. Kagan & J. T. Scholz, 'The "Criminology of the Corporation" and Regulatory Enforcement Strategies' in K. Hawkins & J. M. Thomas, (eds.) *Enforcement Regulation* (1984), p.67.

[153] J. Bradsen, (1994) 'The "Green Issues": Biodiversity Conservation in Australia' in B. Boer, R, Fowler & N. Gunningham (eds.) *Environmental Outlook: Law and Policy*, Federation Press, Sydney.

introduction of regulation (made politically palatable by combining it with transitional compensation arrangements) achieved this effect.[154]

Having said that, the more coercive instruments should be used with caution, given the cost entailed in implementing them, the uncertainty involved in mobilizing them successfully, and the risk that if their use is perceived to be unjust, or unreasonable (particularly the agricultural sector, with its long history of resistance to regulation), they can trigger a backlash which can only work to the detriment of the environment. Following the principles set down by Ayres and Braithwaite,[155] coercive sanctions should be used as a last resort, in response proportionate to the compliance performance of the regulated entity. In this way, the application of discretion in enforcement often enables regulation to function as an effective safety net, in conjunction with other more flexible and constructive instruments.[156] For example, Pratt *et al.* describe how the Texas State Soil and Water Conservation Board seek a voluntary solution to problems of nonpoint source pollution, and only when the problem persists do they refer the matter to the state Natural Resource Conservation Commission for enforcement action.[157]

Generally, regulatory approaches provide an effective means to stop actions which need to be completely prevented or excluded across large areas, such as land clearing. In the case of biodiversity regulation, it has a particular role to play when biodiversity loss has proceeded so far that

[154] A firm response to flagrant misconduct is important for three reasons. First, it is necessary as a deterrent to future harm doing. Unsurprisingly, compliance will be greater if recalcitrant offenders are penalized severely and publicly so that the effectiveness and the attractiveness of less interventionist and more financially desirable instruments is maximized. Secondly, where visible damage is inflicted on an ecosystem, the public often demands a firm response as a reaffirmation of environmental values. Thirdly, given that the infliction of environmental damage can also be regarded as an offence against those who have done the right thing, often at substantial personal sacrifice, a firm response suggests to them and to others that their sacrifices were not in vain. The appearance of a level playing field may be an essential prerequisite to the success of the sort of positive, less interventionist approach which we envisage for the large majority of circumstances.

[155] I. Ayres & J. Braithwaite, *Responsive Regulation: Transcending the deregulation debate* (1992), Oxford University Press, New York.

[156] However, escalation up an enforcement pyramid, as advocated by Ayres and Braithwaite (I. Ayres & J. Braithwaite, *Responsive Regulation: Transcending the deregulation debate* (1992), Oxford University Press, New York) requires a continuing relationship between regulator and regulatee, under which the regulator applies a 'tit for tat' strategy. Such a strategy will have no application in the case of 'one off' events, such as land clearing, though it may be considerably more valuable where there is a commitment to ongoing management, and sanctions and rewards can be applied depending upon the regulatees past behaviour.

[157] S. J. Pratt, L. Frarey, A. Carr, 'A Comparison of US and UK Law Regarding Pollution From Agricultural Runoff' (1997) 45(1) *Drake Law Review* 159–196.

any further loss is deemed unacceptable. In principle, the strength of regulation in these circumstances is the greater certainty it provides, particularly where it takes the form of direct bans on destructive activity, supported by sanctions. In practice, the most common form of regulation has been to ban an activity, but to provide for exceptions (e.g., for those who obtain a licence). Past experience in many jurisdictions is that the exemptions are so routinely granted as to undermine the conservation objectives of the ban itself.[158] Nevertheless, the South Australian experience, referred to above, suggests that when regulation is not so constrained, it can be very effective in preventing clearing.

As with other instruments, the relative effectiveness of regulation is likely to be context specific. For example, there are limits to the extent to which regulation reinforced by sanctions can serve to achieve biodiversity maintenance on privately managed semi-natural systems. As Bowers demonstrates: 'where maintaining biodiversity requires people to perform actions that are not economic, sanctions will not in general work since primary operators (farmers or foresters who work the land) are likely to respond by abandoning management altogether'.[159]

In contrast, when the aim is to preserve a natural system by preventing use, a regulatory sanction may be much more effective than any other single instrument because it prevents certain types of land-use change. Because land-use change usually 'cannot be brought about by doing nothing, the landholder . . . cannot frustrate the intentions of the controlling authority by passive resistance',[160] and defiance can be both identified and punished by law. However, even here, it must be acknowledged that some positive management will be necessary to protect biodiversity from feral animals and other threats, and that for

[158] For example, the experience under New South Wales endangered species legislation, at least until the issue of State Environmental Planning Policy 46 in August 1995, was that licences were very commonly granted, thereby defeating the biodiversity aims of the legislation to a significant extent. Even without the licensing exception, it is true that there will remain a temptation to cheat, particularly where breaches are not transparent. How strong this temptation will be, and how likely people are to succumb to it, will depend in part on the perceived legitimacy of the regulation (reinforcing the need for education and motivation) and, in part, on the likelihood of detection and the severity of sanctions.

[159] J. Bowers, *Incentives and Mechanisms for Biodiversity: Observations and Issues* (1994), CSIRO Division of Wildlife and Ecology, Canberra, p.13. However, note that, in the USA, the Endangered Species Act has effectively induced the formulation of long-term management arrangements, including the hiring of trained managers, enforced as conditions in permit for development activity.

[160] J. Bowers, *Incentives and Mechanisms for Biodiversity: Observations and Issues* (1994), CSIRO Division of Wildlife and Ecology, Canberra, p.14.

reasons stated below,[161] management agreements can achieve such protection in a way that regulation alone cannot.

As we have seen, conventional command and control regulation in the agricultural sector has been, traditionally, handicapped by information costs. Non-compliance may not be immediately apparent, and evidence necessary to sustain the imposition of penalties may be difficult and costly to collect. Developments in technology may well provide at least a partial solution to this problem. The ability of government to monitor the environmental consequences of agriculture may be expected to grow significantly, and the costs of such monitoring may be expected to decrease. Greater surveillance capability will enhance the capacity to identify, and ultimately to interdict, harm to the environment. Progress in detection and measurement technology will enhance the potential to identify habitat degradation and the sources of non-point pollution. Governments have already begun to invest in remote sensing technology to measure tree cover.[162]

At the end of the day, there is a place for command and control instruments to regulate both chemical use and biodiversity conservation. They are best reserved for wilful, egregious misconduct, or activity resulting in serious environmental damage. The mobilization of sanctions should be done in a manner which avoids creating the impression that all agricultural producers are bad citizens. To this end, the celebration of virtue should accompany the chastisement of wrongdoing. Here, the enforcement principles enunciated by Ayres and Braithwaite and encapsulated in their title *Responsive Regulation*, are most apposite.[163] To the extent that departures from compliance come to the attention of regulatory authorities, they are met with response which can escalate or de-escalate, depending upon the subsequent performance of the regulatee.

The role of precautionary regulation

There is one other role for regulation: to guide administrative process and warn when greater precaution is necessary. In the face of the uncertainty and complexity that characterizes both biodiversity and agricultural chemicals, regulations and the standards associated with

---

[161] J. Bowers, *Incentives and Mechanisms for Biodiversity: Observations and Issues* (1994), CSIRO Division of Wildlife and Ecology, Canberra, p.37.

[162] Australian Bureau of Agricultural and Resource Economics (1995).

[163] I. Ayres & J. Braithwaite, *Responsive Regulation: Transcending the deregulation debate* (1992), Oxford University Press, New York.

them can be used to indicate the need for existing institutions to use different administrative processes. Consequently, in the case of biodiversity conservation, rather than seeing regulations as offering a 'safe minimum standard' it can be more useful to envisage a continuum beginning with a precautionary regulation (such as a requirement to obtain a permit), which is used to indicate the presence of an irreversible threshold; precautionary standards which indicate the need to change administrative procedures; and ending with minimum standards and targets. The same principles would apply to the registration of agricultural chemicals.

Precautionary standards offer an effective means to trigger the adoption of different instruments and administrative procedures. As such, they should not imply a need to choose between regulation and other instrument categories, but rather an opportunity for complementary combinations of instruments. For example, a precautionary regulation, such as a requirement to apply for a clearing permit, might result in approval of clearing in one area conditional upon a conservation covenant being placed on another area, supported by a management agreement that would reimburse the landholder for the cost of completing special fencing requirements.[164] Similarly, agricultural

---

[164] Direct regulations can play a particularly vital role in preventing and eliminating those actions which under present arrangements could result in losses that are either totally irreversible or only irreversible at unacceptably high costs. In such situations, the conventional approach is to recommend that a safer minimum standard be set. For biodiversity conservation, however, we often don't know what the safe minimum standard is. Indeed, for a significant number of areas in Australia, that point may have been passed, and now the need is for species recovery plans and rehabilitation of ecosystems.

Faced by uncertainty and the need for dependability, regulations can contribute to biodiversity by signalling where precaution is necessary. The recently introduced Western Australian and New South Wales clearing controls provide examples of the approach. In each case, a *precautionary regulation* requires people to obtain a clearing permit before they clear significant areas of vegetation.

Where there is a *possibility* that a development might have irreversible consequences for biodiversity, the Precautionary Principle would suggest that the onus is on the proponent to demonstrate that this is not the case. In the land clearance examples listed above (p.325), the prohibition, however, is not absolute. Consistent with the precautionary principle, permission to clear native vegetation can still be obtained providing the proponent shows that clearance will not have unacceptable effects on the environment or biodiversity values. The onus of proof is shifted from the government to the proponent. These precautionary standards provide a second function of indicating areas where expenditure on recovery and rehabilitation might be justified. Recognition of these characteristics, coupled with recognition of the importance of seeking dynamic and continuing improvement, suggests that periodic review of these precautionary regulations and standards is necessary to ensure that they are set at appropriate levels. This is particularly important, for most decisions to permit further biodiversity loss decreases the margin of safety left in the system. Regulatory mechanisms that are not reviewed periodically are unlikely to be

chemicals can be registered with conditions imposing restrictions on the circumstances under which a particular substance can be applied.

Instrument interactions

In this section, we explore the overall role of various instrument types in the broader policy mix, and the optimal relationship between them. Our particular focus is on the overall relationship between property-right, price-based, and regulatory instruments, which we have not so far explored. However, for the sake of completeness, we begin by briefly recapping on the role of information, voluntarism, and self-regulation.

We begin with information, which, as we have observed, is the foundation on which all other instruments rest. When the interests of the producer and those of the general public coincide, awareness of environmental risk and knowledge of how to do the right thing will foster stewardship. In other settings, where a degree of sacrifice is required on the part of the farmer, information will lower impediments to improved performance. However, information is necessary, but usually not sufficient, to achieve preferred agro-environmental outcomes. Information can energize voluntaristic and self-regulatory initiatives, foster the efficient functioning of markets and incentive schemes, and help legitimize command and control regulation. As such, it should be regarded as an important underpinning to all other classes of instruments, serving to reinforce and enhance their impact.

Voluntary instruments have the virtue of being non-coercive, and because they are in a sense 'owned' by the regulated entity or industry, are likely to be embraced with a degree of enthusiasm unlikely to be elicited by other instruments. The advantages of voluntarism are by no means limited to matters of legitimacy. The psychological investment which voluntarism requires on the part of the producer can strengthen commitment to principles of sustainability. Because of the commitment which voluntarism requires on the part of the producer, such instruments help develop a custodial ethic, and can contribute to peer education. At times, voluntaristic initiatives may be inspired and sustained by market demand. In other situations, a degree of stimulus from the State may be essential. Voluntarism is not universally applicable, however. Where the

dependable (M. D. Young, N. Gunningham, J. Elix, J. Lambert, B. Howard, P. Grabosky, E. McCrone, *Reimbursing the Future: An evaluation of motivational, voluntary, price-based, property-right, and regulatory incentives for the conservation of biodiversity* (1996), Biodiversity Series Paper No. 9, Department of the Environment, Sport and Territories, Biodiversity Unit, Canberra, p.132).

costs of voluntarism are high, the mobilization of incentives, whether positive or negative, will be required. Even where it is applicable, it has low dependability, and for this reason, like information, it should not be used in isolation but, in virtually all cases, should be supported by other instruments, most notably price and property-based instruments, or regulation.

Self-regulation has many of the same virtues as voluntarism, including its non-coercive nature, its legitimacy and the fact it is 'owned' by the industry. It may also produce willing commitment to achieve far more than regulation, and has considerably more flexibility. Yet, as we have seen, it is only likely to be viable in limited circumstances, and even here commonly requires an underpinning of government regulation and third party oversight to compensate for its inherent weaknesses.

Incentive instruments also have the virtue of being non-coercive, and their existence within a comprehensive policy package may lessen the likelihood of resistance which might arise from the presence of less palatable components of a regulatory mix. Incentives can, moreover, help overcome impediments to sustainable practice arising from inertia or from prohibitive cost. Of equal if not greater importance is the capacity-building function of those incentive instruments which take the form of awards and recognition. To the extent that producers can see something of themselves in a recognized exemplar, they may develop a feeling of competence and self-efficacy which will permit them to engage in voluntaristic initiatives. The celebration of exemplary environmental performance may also be expected to stimulate the search for information on the part of some producers, thereby enhancing the effect of information-based strategies.

Moving up the scale of intrusiveness, we turn next to property rights and price-based instruments and to their relationship with regulation. Property-right mechanisms, by either constraining or expanding the opportunities available to resource users, can be a powerful controlling influence on agro-environmental performance. Where markets for these rights can be created, often change can be achieved with less cost to society and with greater equity than is achievable under other mechanisms. A particular strength of property-right instruments is their lack of intrusiveness, and the fact, in some circumstances, that they can be tailored to site specific problems in an administratively efficient manner.[165] These considerable virtues of property-right instruments suggest that they should play a central role in most policy mixes.

---

[165] See T. Panayotou, *Economic Instruments for Environmental Management and Sustainable Development* (1994), unpublished manuscript, Harvard Institute for International

Similarly, price-based instruments, such as user charges and levies, can be an important way of changing the economic signals given to those whose actions threaten the environment, and are an important embodiment of the user pays and polluter pays principles. But should property right and price-based instruments be combined solely with voluntary and/or motivational instruments, or do they also require underpinning by regulation?

This last question is central, because while price-based instruments have considerable virtues, they lack dependability. For example, a key characteristic of some price-based approaches is that a price is set and the market then decides how much biodiversity conservation to deliver or how much chemical input to use. This encourages people to find efficient ways to profit from this trade-off and seek ways to do more or less damage, depending upon the way that the instrument operates. However, setting prices at the optimal level to influence behaviour is a 'hit and miss' approach, with the result that if the price is set too low (which may only be apparent with hindsight), it will not have the anticipated effect on behaviour.[166]

A further problem with relying on prices, rather than regulatory compulsion, is that prices are not well suited to dealing with the wide range of responses people make to the same price signal. It may be that only those 'at the margin' respond in the preferred direction. But for a variety of reasons indicated earlier, ranging from incompetence or ignorance to intransigence, there is likely to be a minority who, in the absence of more directive or even coercive policies, will continue to behave in a manner which threatens conservation.[167]

This minority cannot be ignored. If left unchecked, it will have a substantial impact on biodiversity or agricultural chemical use, not just directly through its own behaviour, but also through its impact in demotivating other target group members—particularly in respect of voluntary mechanisms. For example, there is evidence that landusers

Development, Harvard University, Cambridge, MA, pp.15–20. Note that tradeable rights systems only work in regions where there are enough fungible goods and actors to make up a market. On the other hand, other property right systems, e.g., site specific easements or land trust arrangements, are a good way to deal with site specific problems.

[166] As Lee Breckenridge points out (personal communication November 1997) price-based instruments will only be effective if there is a mechanism in place for making rolling adjustments based not only on changing economic conditions, but also on discovery of new scientific information.

[167] The existence of such a minority was acknowledged by a wide diversity of stakeholders during the consultation process.

and others who contribute to voluntary programmes, such as the Australian Landcare programme, may become dispirited if others are free to continue to degrade adjoining land. In many circumstances, the creation of a level playing field may be an essential prerequisite to the success of the sort of positive, less interventionist approach that we envisage for the large majority of circumstances.

Regulatory approaches mitigate both the uncertainty and irrationality problems. They decide what conduct is required and then let the market reveal the economic consequences of doing this. In the domain of biodiversity conservation, the regulatory approach is often preferred over pricing policies, as it is changes in physical processes and quantities, not prices, that affect ecosystems most directly. Arguably, there is more dependability when ecological constraints are set and then price, demand and technological forces are allowed to work themselves out. Management agreements (under which landholders are paid to protect biodiversity) and regulations both do this. Financial incentives, such as the former, have the disadvantage, however, of creating an atmosphere where people are only prepared to conserve biodiversity when they are paid to do so, and implying that they are entitled to destroy it irrespective of social expectations. Moreover, because such instruments create the impression that people have a right to destroy biodiversity, incentive-based approaches may be ignored. Where they are effective, they can be expensive. They are also inconsistent with the polluter pays principle.

By combining instruments together, however, these weaknesses can be overcome. Initially, information and voluntary initiatives would be deployed, followed by some form of inducement for biodiversity stewardship. Ultimately, clearing of native vegetation, for example, may be banned by regulation, transitional compensation offered to those adversely effected by this measure, and management agreements used to reimburse the costs of any new management procedures that may be required. At the same time, any perverse incentives that encourage biodiversity loss, like some land rating systems do, might be removed.[168]

In summary, where persuasion and education fail, where enterprises are unwilling to improve their environmental performances voluntarily,

---

[168] In Australia, local government is funded partially from revenue raised from a tax on the unimproved value of land. In assessing the amount of tax to be paid, land is assessed at its value if it was being used for its highest and best use in the market place. Thus, those who have not cleared there land are forced to pay tax as if they had cleared it. This gives them a clear and unintended signal that this land should be cleared irrespective of its biodiversity value.

and where economic instruments or voluntarism lack dependability, then regulation may be the only technique capable of exerting pressure and compelling resource users and others to protect the environment. Thus, even those who do not behave with economic rationality and respond to economic instruments can still be persuaded to halt destructive practices. A further advantage of regulation that it has a moral and educational influence which economic incentive-based strategies lack. In some circumstances, the very fact that certain behaviour is proscribed by law may be sufficient to create moral inhibitions against engaging in that behaviour, though this is not necessarily the case.

Our conclusion is that there is a tension between achieving dependability (which implies a need for regulation), on the one hand, and cost-effectiveness, flexibility and non intrusiveness (through property-right and price-based instruments and voluntarism), on the other. How should this tension be resolved?

The extent to which property-right or price-based instruments mechanisms (often in conjunction with voluntary and/or incentive-based instruments) need to be underpinned by regulation will depend on whether, in the circumstances to be addressed, there is a danger of irreversible harm, and whether that harm may produce threshold effects giving rise to the possibility of a major environmental catastrophe or system collapse.[169] In the latter circumstance, any policy which compromises the resilience of ecosystems may have uncontrollable effects, and even small policy changes can have dramatic but unforeseen results. Therefore, dependability becomes the *most* important objective when irreversibility or threshold breach is at stake, but not otherwise.

In these circumstances, we conclude that financially attractive instruments are rarely adequate on their own and often need to be underpinned by precautionary instruments, and ultimately by a regulatory safety net to deal with recalcitrant producers (who in well designed systems should be few in number). We explore the implications of this conclusion further in the section on design criteria, below.

To summarize the discussion, this section has moved through a series of arguments that began by pointing out the need for instrument mixes and how the strengths of each instrument can be harnessed to build a framework that is as dependable as possible in terms of preventing irreversible losses and, within this constraint, trades-off criteria like efficiency, equity, precaution, dynamism, administrative costs, and com-

---

[169] E. B. Barbier, J. C. Burgess, & C. Folke, *Paradise Lost? The ecological economics of biodiversity* (1994), Earthscan Publications, London, p.184.

munity acceptability. We have argued first for dependability, which implies the need for precautionary regulations and precautionary standards, underpinned by a firm regulatory safety net that prohibits irreversible actions. However, we have also emphasized the importance of mechanisms that build community support. To achieve such support, mechanisms must be both equitable and have acceptable administrative costs.

Finally, the importance of using property rights, price-based, and regulatory instruments in a *complementary* manner has been emphasized. In particular, the mere fact that the state makes clear its willingness to escalate to regulation if voluntary, property-right, and price mechanisms fail, means that the latter are likely to work more effectively, since agricultural producers' decisions concerning the use of voluntary and property-right instruments will be coloured by their knowledge of the existence of a background of regulation. So paradoxically, the backdrop of regulation is likely to render positive instruments more attractive— and thus more effective—to industry, by presenting them with an unpalatable alternative.

Section 5: Institutional influences: the role of third parties

As we argued in chapter three, optimal policy design involves not just the use of a broader range of instruments, but also either harnessing a broader range of institutions or empowering them to act autonomously and creatively. These include a range of third parties, both commercial and non-commercial. The role of public and environmental interest groups is widely recognized,[170] but far less so is the potentially crucial contribution of commercial third parties. These non-governmental institutions, to the extent that they are able to exert a controlling influence on the environmental performance of agricultural producers, can relieve the state of some regulatory burdens which might otherwise prove insurmountable, given the inherent limitations of command and control regulation and the fiscal constraints which beset most governments today. The limited resources of the state may thus be reserved for those contexts where they are essential, and most productive.

Commercial institutions, supply side pressure and sustainable agriculture

Some of the most significant influences in furtherance of sustainable agriculture arise from commercial relationships. But the beneficial

[170] See p.350, below.

effect of commerce on agricultural practice is not uniform. What works for pesticide reduction does not extend to preventing land clearing. Here, we explore some examples of constructive commercial influences, identify their strengths and limitations, and suggest what other instruments might be introduced to enhance their positive effects.

There is great potential to harness market forces, or indeed, to *create* market forces as surrogate regulators of agricultural chemicals. Crucial here are the influences which large buyers exert on their upstream suppliers. We have already noted the achievements realized by Campbell Soup and its growers in reducing chemical input.[171] In the late 1980s, the Campbell Soup Company sought to reduce pesticide application by its growers by 50 per cent. By 1994, the company exceeded this goal for three crops, without any reduction in crop yield or quality. In some locations, farmers were able to achieve significant profit improvements by reducing input costs. Campbell's is not alone in imposing such pressures on its growers, and the indications are that an increasing number of other enterprises are contemplating similar action.[172]

The case of the Beech-Nut company is illustrative of a growing trend of supply chain pressure being exerted in support of 'green markets'. Beech-Nut, a North American manufacturer of baby foods, among other products, claims to be particularly conscientious about minimizing pesticide residue in its products.[173] The company's marketing claims that residue levels in their baby food products are negligible to non-detectable, and thus 'comparable to those containing organically grown fruits and vegetables'. The company boasts of a rigorous Pesticide Residue Control Program which limits the use of pesticides 'from seed to shelf'. Contracts with growers are based on compliance with exacting company standards, including complete prohibition of many pesticides, and limited use of approved chemicals during key growth periods. Producers are subject to rigorous inspection, and rejection when they fail to meet company standards. Beech-Nut has an extensive laboratory testing programme, and compiles an extensive database on each fruit or vegetable it uses. Future purchasing decisions are based on analyses of quality and safety data.

---

[171] See p.313.

[172] For example, the Gerber Company, a manufacturer of baby foods, has required its contract growers to provide detailed pesticide application records before the crops are purchased (World Wildlife Fund, *Reducing Reliance on Pesticides in Great Lakes Basin Agriculture* (1995), World Wildlife Fund, Washington DC, pp.2 and 15).

[173] Beech-Nut, *Beech-Nut Pesticide Residue Control Program* (1997), at http://www.family internet.com/beech-nut/res.htm.

Producers and manufacturers are not the only ones who, in pursuit of a comprehensive 'green' image, are bringing supply chain pressure to bear. Growing demand in the United States for low input foods has inspired the creation of natural foods supermarkets, which specialize in meats and vegetables raised without pesticides or chemicals. Even those supermarkets which do not specialize in organic produce are strategically situated to influence the environmental performance of their suppliers, and a number of major chains are now doing so.[174] Some now review suppliers' audit records, to determine the nature, amount, and timing of chemical application on the produce considered for purchase.[175] Environmental marketing programmes can also exist at the wholesale level. Matteson *et al.* discuss how, in the Netherlands, wholesale produce marketers contribute to 'green' continuity in the supply chain.[176] They require certain standards on the part of their suppliers, and, in turn, affirm these standards in marketing their produce to retailers downstream.[177] As a representative of the British Agrochemical Association put it, 'If you want to supply Sainsbury's you have to meet their standards'.[178] Coercive though they may be, market forces tend to be regarded as more legitimate than government dictates. As one of

[174] Major French supermarket chains, such as Monoprix and Carrefour, sell some organic produce. Sainsbury's, in the UK, has announced its intention that all of its food from all over the world be produced under IPM regimes (P. Rowland, *Recent Changes in International Crop Protection Practices: The growing trend to reduce pesticide use and pesticide risk* (1995), Bureau or Resource Sciences, Department of Primary Industries and Energy, Canberra, pp.5–6; and Sainsbury's has a web page devoted to the environment: http://www.j-sainsbury.co.uk/environment/).

[175] The largest supermarket chain in the Netherlands, Albert Heijn, has an in-house Controlled Cultivation Program. The company, which has a 28 per cent national market share, sets progressively higher environmental guidelines for its suppliers (P. Matteson, L. den Boer & J. Proost, 'Green Labels in The Netherlands: Careful Negotiations and Clearer Choices' (1996) 6(4) (December) *Global Pesticide Campaigner*). So too, do such North American chains as Wegman's, which prides itself on its environmental policy, and which now sells produce bearing an IPM label. The IPM label programme was developed by a partnership between Wegmans, Comstock Michigan Fruit, which supplies Wegmans' produce, and Cornell University. The University extension programme assists Comstock's growers in developing their IPM programmes. See http://www.nysaes.cornell.edu:80/ipmnet/ny/program_news/labels.html.

[176] P. Matteson, L. den Boer & J. Proost, 'Green Labels in The Netherlands: Careful Negotiations and Clearer Choices' (1996) 6(4) (December) *Global Pesticide Campaigner* 16.

[177] See also A. M. Moodie, 'Control System Helped Food Firm Trace Problem' (1996) (8 November) *Australian Financial Review* 61.

[178] Pike relates that Sainsbury's competitor Tesco requires farmer-financed audit reports as a condition of supply. A. G. Pike 'Pesticide Risk Reduction: The Role of the UK Pesticides Forum' Presented at the National Pesticide Risk Reduction Workshop, Bureau of Resource Sciences, Department of Primary Industries and Energy, Canberra, Australia, 16 April 1997.

our respondents put it, 'There's increasing acceptance that that is in the nature of the game. Farmers see a reason for doing it if it's through the market.'

Market forces can influence the production of fibre, as well as food. A number of prominent apparel manufacturers have begun to use organic cotton in their product, thus increasing demand for chemical-free raw materials.[179] In 1995, the North American outdoors clothing company Patagonia decided to use only organic cotton in its cotton products. Requiring that its raw materials be grown without the use of pesticides or herbicides, the company purchased 500,000 pounds of organic cotton in 1996 at twice the cost of conventionally grown cotton. The nonprofit NGO Pesticide Action Network is advising the company on alternative growing techniques, which are then communicated to suppliers upstream. By taking up a significant proportion of the available supply of organic cotton, the company, through its competitors, may stimulate wider demand for organically grown cotton. Here is an example of how public interest collaboration with the private sector can catalyse buyer-supplier relations and help influence production practices upstream.

Efforts to measure and assess the environmental performance of suppliers and growers are assisted by the technique of quality assurance, long a fixture in manufacturing and service industries. In the past, classification of produce tended to be based on aesthetic considerations. While these remain significant (as anyone who has recently visited a Japanese supermarket can attest) they are being rivalled by other considerations, not the least of which pertain to chemical residue. Indicative of this shift in perspective is the fact that some large food manufacturers and retailers now maintain their own testing laboratories, enabling them to exercise substantial upstream influence. As one agricultural consultant told us, 'The power of individual companies in some of these industries (such as horticulture or meat) is becoming huge. If Woolworths (a major supermarket chain) identifies a product attribute that they don't like, it affects the whole industry.'

[179] Innovators in organic cotton production have been recognized by the United Nations Environment Program (UNEP). See organically grown naturally colored cotton UNEP-WGD-SPD NEWSFAX, (1996) Issue 3 (6 April) at http://unep.frw.uva.nl/UnepHome/newsfax/newsfax3.html. The large manufacturer Levi Strauss has ordered 2,300 bales of organic or transitional cotton from the 1997 crop in the United States. (*Green Business Letter*, April 1997). The Gap, a three billion dollar company with 1,300 retail stores in the United States, Canada and the UK, is making a commitment to using organic cotton in their products at http://www.organic.com/Non.profits/F2F/Features/who.organic.html.

In Wisconsin, an experiment is currently taking place to apply another important quality control system—the technique of total quality management—to the potato growing industry. This is being achieved through the vehicle of ISO 14001 in conjunction with Integrated Pest Management. Again, the driving force is commercial buyers: over 50 per cent of potatoes grown in Wisconsin go to the production of french fries. This gives the large wholesale buyers of those potatoes enormous leverage over the growers, leverage which is currently being used to achieve radical changes in their approach to pesticide use and sustainable farming. The other crucial driver in the Wisconsin approach is consumer pressure. While it is unclear whether or to what extent consumers are willing to pay more for potatoes with less pesticide residue, if prices are comparable between those and other potatoes, then the former will likely gain market share. The influence of consumer preference may be enhanced by a basic 'green' marketing message, but arguably even more so if an accreditation or certification is invoked.

Independent compliance professionals are another group that have a constructive and increasingly important role to play in improving the environmental performance of the agriculture sector—including a contribution to monitoring and supply-chain pressure. As one of our informants told us, 'with the retraction of government services, consultants have become a much more important resource'. This role, however, differs somewhat from that of their counterparts in manufacturing industry. The institution of environmental auditing has, as yet, a smaller role in agricultural production, although a formal assessment of economic potential which may accompany an application for finance and insurance may address aspects of environmental impact. On the other hand, farm management consultants and their counterparts in other areas of agriculture are in a position to profoundly influence the environmental impact of large producer operations—and their influence is likely to percolate through vertical markets and, in some cases, through modelling and example.

By assisting producers to minimize input costs, and to adopt methods of best agricultural practice, consultants are strategically positioned to facilitate regulatory compliance on the part of their clients (assuming there are existing regulations in place to begin with). Specialists in integrated pest management and waste conversion technologies, for example, are in a position to promise their clients cost savings, which translates into a better bottom line, as well as minimizing compliance difficulties, and 'keeping them honest'. As one of them boasted to us, 'We've had guys who have reduced their application by 40 to 50 per cent and improved their yield'. By virtue of their professional status, and the fact that their services are engaged for a fee, their advice is likely to be perceived as more valuable, and thus more likely to be heeded, than 'free' advice emanating from sources outside the industry.[180] As we were told, 'Farmers will get more benefit from advice if they pay for it. You value what you pay for.'

What is especially noteworthy about the above examples of supply chain pressure and monitoring of environmental performance is that they occur largely beyond the ambit of government. To be sure, the state provides a basic legal framework for commercial activity, and minimum standards of food safety and hygiene. Ideally, the state would also provide mechanisms for penalizing misleading and deceptive marketing claims. But the achievements noted above are all market-driven, and based on standards of conduct far in excess of that which any government would command. At the same time, because they emanate from the market rather than from the state, they are regarded as more legitimate than state control.

Nevertheless, there is no doubt that market instruments can be further enhanced by government and independent third party activity and that an optimal regulatory design would seek to further facilitate, support, and expand such market driven initiatives. Through awards and recognition, governments can celebrate exemplary practices, and thereby give a valuable marketing boost to 'green' produce. Through preferential procurement practices, governments can themselves amplify market signals in furtherance of best environmental practice. Governments can also contribute to the establishment and maintenance of certification and labelling schemes, although, as we shall soon observe, non-state actors have begun to play an important role in this regard.

---

[180] To the extent that the state withdraws from its traditional role as the provider of extension services, commercial compliance professionals have the potential of substituting for them. The agricultural consulting industry is poised to fill a vacuum about to be created by current trends in public sector service delivery. The movement in most western societies towards privatization of governmental functions has begun to include agricultural extension services. Whether the privatization of these functions will contribute overall to improved environmental performance remains to be seen. Marginally viable agricultural enterprises may be unable to afford the services of professional consultants; in such cases, industry associations may be able to provide services at minimal cost.

Indeed, in the case of these commercial pressures, the potential role of public interest groups is likely to be more important than that of government. In particular, the marketing of products made from low-input ingredients can be reinforced through oversight exercised by public interest third parties. In Europe, consumer interest groups test purported organic cloth for any traces of chemical residues. Retailers who falsely advertise their products as chemical free are liable to action for fraud. The retailer Esprit guarantees a paper trail of certification for their organic cotton and has set an industry standard by giving funds to help establish an organic certification programme.

Public interest groups can also play an increasingly important role in the development of consumer demand for products raised in an environmentally benign manner. By calling attention to the hazards of high input agriculture, and by heralding those commodities which have been produced by sustainable means, interest groups can contribute significantly to the generation of market forces.

Additional pressures may emanate from consumer preferences and regulatory requirements in overseas export markets. Japanese authorities raised the issue of chemical residues in order to limit imports of Australian rice. Regardless of whether the basis of this resistance was protection of the Japanese consumer, or rather protection of the Japanese farmer, from foreign competition, Australian rice growers were moved to improve their environmental performance. State of the art production and storage technologies to ensure zero residues were introduced by Australian rice growers, who now have access to the Japanese market.

Third party accreditation also plays an important role in supporting supply chain pressure. Suppliers, buyers and consumers need some form of independent guarantee that a product labelled 'green' is indeed what it purports to be. Any failure at this level will bring an entire 'green' industry into disrepute. While, in principle, governments could play this role, in practice the most important contribution is that of specialized companies which offer independent testing and quality assurance services. Some provide an entire range of services, from consulting, to field sampling, to pesticide residue testing, to furnishing documentation, and certification of test results. When properly delivered, such quality assurance services can 'pay for themselves' by maximizing the market potential of clients' products.[181] It should also be

---

[181] For an example of one such service, see http://www.primuslabs.com/primus/overview.html.

noted that some commercial quality assurance services trade on their ability to anticipate and address any regulatory compliance problems which a client might encounter, thus providing peace of mind for the client and precluding any conflict which might arise between the client and government regulatory agencies.

Depending on location in the supply chain, certification may occur under the auspices of commercial laboratories, or producers' associations. In Italy, a farmers' organization, the Confederazione Nazionale Coltivatori Diretti, grants a certificate to farmers who comply with prevailing pesticide regulations. In France and Belgium, at the regional level, labels for IPM fruit production have been introduced.[182] Governments too may develop certification standards, although the difficulties inherent in a government sponsored eco-labelling scheme have been discussed above, in chapter two. Regardless of their location and institutional sector, many certification organizations throughout the world now seek accreditation by IFOAM—the International Federation of Organic Agriculture Movements. This accreditation should facilitate access by organic products to international markets. There seems little doubt that some form of formal certification can only serve to accelerate the effect of consumer power on production methods.

Key to all of this, of course, is the definition of the standard in question. Standards which are too permissive will fail to discriminate between environmental performers. They will do little to encourage improvement above the existing low threshold. Unreasonably strict standards, on the other hand, will be met by only a handful of producers, and ignored by the rest.

It will also be important to ensure that consumer decision-making does not become confused by the proliferation of labelling and certifying schemes. It may be necessary for government to introduce some degree of coherence.[183] Given the rapid globalization of the economy, it would seem that some supra-national authority, whether intergovernmental (such as FAO) or nongovernmental (such as IFOAM), may well come to play an important role. The state must also maintain its traditional role, providing an underpinning of regulation where other,

---

[182] J. A. W. A. Reus, H. J. Weckseler & G. A. Pak, *Towards a Future EC Pesticide Policy: An inventory of risks of pesticide use, possible solutions, and policy instruments* (1994), Centre for Agriculture and Environment, Utrecht, p.81.

[183] D. Dumaresq & R. Greene, *From Farmer to Consumer: The future of organic agriculture in Australia* (1997), Rural Industries Research and Development Corporation, Canberra.

less intrusive options, are unsuccessful or unavailable. That is, there will remain producers who may lack the knowledge and/or the capacity to do the right thing. A degree of regulatory control, focused most closely on high risk situations, will be essential to compensate for the absence of controlling influences of a commercial nature. For example, in the absence of non-State institutions with the capacity to protect against indiscriminate chemical use, strict vigilance over the registration and application of chemicals will remain an important public function.

Institutions of finance and insurance

Institutions of agricultural finance might also play a more active role in fostering low input agriculture.[184] Ordinary commercial loan applications have already begun to entail scrutiny of potential environmental liability, to the point of requiring a satisfactory environmental audit report as a condition of loan approval. Loan approvals, moreover, are subject to requirements that the borrower comply with existing regulatory requirements. These controls can as easily be extended to the environmental performance of agricultural producers. However, this is most unlikely to happen until such time as financial institutions either perceive a direct and positive connection between a borrower's commitment to sustainable agriculture and its prospective financial viability, or that their clients may be vulnerable to substantial damages as a result of environmental liability.

Only the latter seems credible, and here much will depend upon the relevant liability regime. At present, liability rules have a far greater influence on financial institutions in the United States than in most other jurisdictions. Here, concerns about environmental liability may move lenders to require environmental audit as part of their loan review, and may make credit for certain facilities, such as chemical and fertilizer storage, more difficult to obtain.[185] This could have an overall educative effect on producers, with positive consequences for environmental performance.

The availability of insurance against loss of or damage to crops could also enhance the attractiveness of low input agriculture. In the absence of such insurance, many producers will continue to use chemicals to manage risk. This raises the question: is it possible to foster an

---

[184] M. Farrell, 'Raising Capital For An Organic Grower' (1996) 18(6) *In Business* 34; and 'Agri Finance, Checking Out Organic Farming' (1994) 36(3) *Agri Finance* 33.

[185] M. Boehlje, M. Duncan & D. Lins, *Agricultural and Rural Finance Policy* (1996) at http://ianrwww.unl.edu:80/farmbill/finance.htm.

insurance market for low input producers? In the absence of a natural emergence of such a market, some degree of state subsidization might be both desirable and (in comparison with other options) a cost-effective policy intervention. Such a form of intervention would not be novel or inconsistent with other policy interventions. A rich variety of finance and insurance subsidy programmes exist in the industrialized world. Subsidized loans for small business, and mortgage assistance for military veterans, are among the most common. The Canadian province of Ontario provides malpractice insurance premium subsidies for local physicians.[186] Government subsidies for general crop insurance are a fixture in the United States.[187] Governments concerned to reduce the risk entailed in the transition to low input agriculture could elicit considerable support from financial institutions.

Commercial institutions, third parties, and biodiversity

The salience of commercial influences and institutions to the control of agricultural chemicals stands in stark contrast to issues of biodiversity conservation, such as agricultural land clearing. For the most part, there is relatively little opportunity to involve commercial third parties in this area: almost all the circumstances, identified above, which influence their behaviour in respect of chemicals are absent.[188] There is much less opportunity to benefit from 'green' markets, and little leverage to be gained from supply chain pressure. Nor can insurance contribute much in the way of a solution, as land clearing is less driven by issues of risk management than by those of productivity.

For the time being, the preservation of native vegetation and species' habitat depends upon instruments other than 'green' commercial influences.[189] Although many environmentalists object to certain retail fast

---

[186] http://www.oma.org/pcomm/pressrel/1996/pp061896.htm.

[187] See United States General Accounting Office, *Crop Insurance: Opportunities exist to reduce government costs for private-sector delivery (1997)* RCED-97-70 April 17, at http://www.gao.gov/new.items/rc97070.pdf. The principle could easily be extended to low input or transitional production.

[188] We do not address the issue of eco-tourism, which is only marginally related to the issue of agricultural land clearing.

[189] However, potentially, there is quite a role that could be played with regard to biodiversity and habitat conservation in situations where liabilities were firmly defined or the prospect of asset loss clear. For example, insurers already play a key role in keeping development and other activities out of flood prone areas by refusing to insure or exacting high premiums. If farmers' liability for damages to wildlife were more firmly set out in tort or regulatory laws, then presumably, insurers and even banks could play a role within the umbrella of that liability scheme. Personal communication, Lee Breckenridge, November 1997.

food products on the grounds that rainforests have been cleared for grazing land from which the ingredients are produced, these objections generate no discernible market pressures impacting on land use. The day may well arrive when the biodiversity impact of agricultural produce will become a widespread marketing criterion, but this will require a much greater level of environmental consciousness than exists today.

There are, nevertheless, some significant recent developments which are suggestive of how commercial institutions might foster biodiversity conservation. The most notable has been consumer resistance to rainforest timber and preference for sustainable forest products. The Forest Stewardship Council, established in 1993, seeks to foster demand for products of sustainably managed forests by accrediting certification schemes.[190] What can be done for forests can, arguably, be done for other agricultural products.[191] With the development of quality assurance programmes such as those in The Netherlands, where, as we noted, thirty per cent of all pig meat can be traced to specific individual farms, accountability for the environmental impact of producer performance may well reach a degree of precision previously thought unattainable.[192]

Again, the first steps in this direction would best be taken by producers (or producer associations) themselves, as genuine commitment on the part of the individual is more likely to flow from circumstances in which producers themselves share a sense of ownership. But this is most unlikely to occur in the absence of an external activator. Producers' motivation will be that much greater when environmental NGOs can raise public consciousness and public opinion to the extent that consumer preferences become loud and clear. Ultimately, sourcing and marketing practices of large retailers can both reflect and stimulate

---

[190] E. Meidinger, *Look Who's Making the Rules: The roles of the forest stewardship council and international standards organisation in environmental policy making* (1996), paper prepared for the Colloquium on Emerging Ecological Policy: Winners and Losers, Oregon State University, Corvallis, 23 September.

[191] See, for example, the successful campaign for dolphin-friendly tuna. The British supermarket chain Sainsbury's proudly claims to source only dolphin-friendly tuna (http://www.j-sainsbury.co.uk/environment/report.html). The Rainforest Action Network advertises a wide variety of products derived from sustainable forests. (http://www.ran.org/ran/info_center/products.html#pagetop). This could be the embryonic form of biodiversity-friendly commerce. The Portland, Oregon-based Pacific Rivers Council (PRC) is seeking to introduce a labelling system for produce and other goods produced in a way that doesn't harm salmon through chemical runoff (*Green Business Letter*, July 1997).

[192] B. Sletto, 'Goals Clear, Methods Not' (1995) V(1) *Tomorrow: Global Environment Business* 24–26 at 25.

consumer demand. Another activator of producer associations is the spectre of government regulation, which can be a powerful inducement to initiate some form of self-regulation sufficiently credible to head off that threat.

Institutions of finance, in collaboration with governments, may contribute to biodiversity conservation in one important respect. 'Debt for nature swaps', where a government or private organization agrees to purchase another nation's debt on the secondary debt market, is the basic model.[193] One could envisage a domestic application of 'debt for nature' exchange, where a secondary market could be created from the sale by banks of their farm mortgage income streams. A prospective purchaser would seek out farms with serious repayment problems and which contained areas of significance for the conservation of biodiversity. The purchaser might also write off some of the debt in return for a conservation easement. Arrangements of this kind may be satisfactory from the banks' point of view as they would be off-loading their riskiest debt. In return, governments or NGOs would be picking up conservation easements at discount prices.

On a more modest scale, but one with considerable potential, banks are becoming increasingly aware of the relationship between agricultural and ecological sustainability. We were told that 'more and more banks are using a range of information to determine whether properties are sustainable—how good a risk they are in terms of investment. Banks are now employing agronomists to do evaluations of loan applications.'

Finally, there is the issue of bioprospecting, which may prove to be an important exception to the general rule that commerce has very little role to play in influencing biodiversity conservation, in respect of land clearing. Bioprospecting is the search of an ecosystem for products of potential commercial value.[194] Prospecting agreements provide remuneration to a country (often through a public research institution) for the right of access to that country's biodiversity and consideration for the commercialization of such resources. They provide an incentive to conserve biodiversity through the direct payment (often paid in

---

[193] M. D. Young, N. Gunningham, J. Elix, J. Lambert, B. Howard, P. Grabosky, E. McCrone, *Reimbursing the Future: An evaluation of motivational, voluntary, price-based, property-right, and regulatory incentives for the conservation of biodiversity* (1996), Biodiversity Series Paper No. 9, Department of the Environment, Sport and Territories, Biodiversity Unit, Canberra, vol. 2, p.39).

[194] Organisation for Economic Co-operation and Development (OECD), *Contracting for Genetic Resources* (1994), Group on Economic and Environment, OECD, Paris.

advance), the royalties, as well as the services and technology that is transferred.

The most prominent biodiversity prospecting contract is a contract between Costa Rica's National Biodiversity Institute (INBio) and Merck & Co Ltd, a large pharmaceutical firm. In 1991, Merck agreed to pay INBio US$1.13 million for the right to screen samples from INBio's biotic collection. If the screening results in a commercial application for Merck, INBio will share royalties on product sales.[195] A set amount of the direct payment (ten per cent) to INBio, and fifty per cent of any royalties, must be returned to conservation projects or National Parks under the agreement. Another firm, Biotics, has negotiated contracts with suppliers in three countries, including New Zealand. However, these contracts only provide for a share of royalties and do not include an up-front payment.[196]

As with the example of debt for nature, biodiversity prospecting contracts too may be 'writ small' and apply to individual landholders.

The limits of supply-chain pressure and 'green' markets

Notwithstanding the potential for some commercial influence on biodiversity conservation in limited circumstances, identified above, for the most part, commercial influences are unlikely to have a significant positive effect. In this area, the role of incentives, of price-based and property-rights instruments, supported by regulation, as described earlier, will remain crucial.

Even in the much more promising context of agricultural chemicals, market driven commercial institutions may not always have the capacity to deliver environmentally favourable outcomes. Large scale buyers, commonly, require continuity of supply, in terms of both quantity and quality of product, which may be more difficult to achieve with no chemical input. Organic produce tends to be more expensive, which may discourage buyers and consumers for whom cost is a dominant consideration in purchasing. As one of our respondents, not inclined to understate matters, put it, 'Organic Farming is over. It's gone. It's a trivial market. The future of agriculture is in high yield. You can't feed the world on organic produce. And affluent consumers don't want it either.'

---

[195] UNEP, *Measures for the Conservation of Biodiversity and Sustainable Use of its Components* (1994), Global Biodiversity Assessment, UNEP, Nairobi.

[196] Organisation for Economic Co-operation and Development (OECD), *Economic Instruments for the Conservation of Domestic and Global Biodiversity: Project proposal* (1993), Expert group on Economic Aspects of Biodiversity, Environment Policy Committee, OECD, Paris.

Small scale producers, moreover, particularly those in sectors of agriculture where there is little vertical integration of marketing arrangements, may be less exposed to environmentally favourable commercial influences. And the complexities of food production may defeat efforts to identify content, in some cases. Soy-based ingredients are found in a vast array of food products. It may be difficult for a consumer to act on a preference for or against a particular variety of genetically altered soybeans when their contribution to the finished product is peripheral.

This is another example of the point already made in a number of contexts, namely there are limits to the appropriate use of all instruments and institutions, and we must choose wisely and well between them, and that what we choose is highly context specific. This is a theme we explore further in the next section on design criteria.

The contributions of environmental interest groups

Environmental interest groups will continue to play key roles in agro-environmental policy. One uses the plural here quite deliberately, as the variety of interest groups, and the approaches which they take, are diverse indeed.[197] In some cases, environmental interest groups can supplement, and in others, even replace, activities of the state. Although space does not permit a full exposition of interest group activity in the agro-environmental context, we suggest some of the main contributions which they are in a position to make.

Perhaps the most important function performed by interest groups concerned in whole or in part with agro-environmental issues is the provision of information.[198] By calling public attention to biodiversity loss and to the risks posed by agricultural chemicals, public interest groups have already contributed significantly to heightened public awareness about the adverse environmental and health impacts of agriculture, and appropriate means for dramatic remedial action. Depending on its content, the information which they produce may be directed at farmers, governments, or the general public. Depending on the organization's

---

[197] There exists a rich variety of organisations concerned with environmental and human health risks posed by agricultural chemicals (for an overview, see G. Ekstrom (ed.) *World Directory of Pesticide Control Organisations* (1996), Crop Protection Publications, London; and for an overview of biodiversity-oriented interest groups, see Commonwealth Department of the Environment Sport and Territories, Biodiversity Information Sources http://www.erin.gov.au/other_servers/category/Biodiversity.html.

[198] J. C. Pierce, M. A. E. Steger, B. S. Steel & N. Lovrich, *Citizens, Political communication and Interest Groups: Environmental organisations in the United States* (1992), Praeger, Westport, CT.

strategic objectives, the information can have a positive or negative tone. While some organizations publicize the damage inflicted by agricultural chemicals and other threats to biodiversity, others extol the virtues of sustainable agriculture and species preservation.

Some organizations, such as Greenpeace, are more explicitly adversarial, involving considerable reliance on non-violent direct action.[199] Similarly, the Pesticide Action Network, founded in 1982, launched a campaign in 1985 to abolish the use of some of the most dangerous agricultural chemicals. The 'Dirty Dozen' campaign, as it came to be known, entailed the collation and dissemination of information to the general public and to government agencies.[200] Of no less significance is the role of local grass-roots activists in publicizing examples of acute environmental damage, and exerting pressure on regulatory authorities to require higher standards of performance on the part of producers. We noted above how one of the producer representatives we interviewed now expects a fish kill occasioned by a misapplication of chemicals to be followed by a prosecution, because the public would expect nothing less.

Among the most significant manifestations of information conveyed with a positive tone are the products of organizations such as the World Wide Fund for Nature (WWF) and the National Audubon Society in the United States.[201] Another example of information in a positive key is that which sensitizes consumers to environmentally preferable produce. This, as we have seen, has had significant upstream influence

---

[199] Greenpeace, for example, has targeted particular producers of agricultural chemicals by means of dramatic aerial photography with a view towards discrediting them publicly (D. King, 'It's Clean, It's Green, and It'll Feed the World' (1997), 2 (vii) (March/April), *Tomorrow* 10–12. Greenpeace's strategic posture is by no means limited to adversarial activities. Their constructive engagement in planning the Sydney 2000 Olympic Games and in the development of a CFC-free refrigerator are illustrative).

[200] In addition, the campaign monitors registration of exceptionally toxic chemicals around the world. The organization lobbies governments as well as marge financial institutions such as the World Bank and the IMF (A. Schonfield, W. Anderson & M. Moore, 'PAN's Dirty Dozen Campaign—The View at Ten Years' (1995), 5(3) September, *Global Pesticide Campaigner*, Pesticide Action Network North America, San Francisco, CA).

[201] Both of these organizations seek to raise general public awareness about threats to biodiversity. The approach of WWF and Audubon to governments and to industry is based more on negotiation and consultation rather than confrontation. These and other organizations also contribute sophisticated policy analysis to government decisionmaking fora (P. Faeth, *Growing Green: Enhancing Environmental and Economic Performance in US Agriculture* (1995), World Resources Institute, Washington). As an interviewee from one NGO told us: 'We've played a major role in shifting the debate. We have had a lot of input into major government inquiries and studies' (http://www.panda.org/forests4life/forests4life.htm; http://www.audubon.org/).

on retailers, wholesalers, and producers. On a sub-national level, the Midwest Organic Alliance is a non-profit organization in the United States which encourages the reduction of enviromentally harmful agri-cultural chemicals in food production.[202] It promotes the environmen-tal and economic benefits of certified organic production to farmers, processors, distributors, retailers, and consumers.

A related approach is to forge coalitions with other interests. For example, the 'Green Scissors Program', developed by Friends of the Earth in the United States, targets US federal programmes on the grounds of fiscal extravagance and adverse environmental impact.[203] In so doing, it appeals both to fiscal conservatives and to environmental-ists, who might otherwise be regarded as strange bedfellows. Among the targets of the Green Scissors campaign are price supports for tobacco, sugar, peanuts, and cotton, as well as irrigation subsidies, all of which encourage exploitation of marginal land and high chemical input.

Aside from the provision of information, public interest organizations may be involved in wielding, singly or in collaboration with government or industry actors, many if not most of the regulatory instruments we have discussed. Citizen enforcement in particular, (given the limited resources of government agencies) is likely to play an important con-tinuing role in the regulatory process. Defenders of Wildlife has been especially prominent in mounting legal challenges to what it perceives to be inaction on the part the US Department of the Interior and the Fish and Wildlife Service (FWS) in failing to protect habitat.[204] The US Environmental Protection Agency (EPA) has also been the target of legal action to prevent the use of an unregistered pesticide.[205] Vigilance of this kind, reinforced by litigation, helps prevent regulatory inaction where a degree of state intervention may be warranted. Provided they are empowered to do so, citizen groups can also take action against sec-ond parties, such as landholders and others. For example, they may sue private developers where their activities threaten endangered species.

Ideally, citizens would complement, not replace, enforcement by government agencies. The challenge is to harness the constructive ele-ments of private enforcement, neutralize those elements which might be counterproductive, and combine them systematically with public

---

[202] http://www.midwestorganic.org/.

[203] http://www.foe.org/eco/scissors97/index.html.

[204] http://www.defenders.org/pr120496.html_;http://www.defenders.org/action44. html.

[205] gopher://gopher.igc.apc.org:2998/0PESTIS/r.877057768.4469.12.

enforcement. The optimal ordering for citizen enforcement would entail some provision for private actions. A degree of citizen involvement will complement the finite resources of government, without sacrificing coherent enforcement policy in favour of uncontrolled and opportunistic bounty hunting.[206]

One model of how to achieve these competing goals is through the controlled use of private enforcement along the lines of that authorized in the United States under a variety of statutes which allow for a degree of private initiative, subject to safeguards against abuse.[207] And short of direct involvement in the enforcement process, one might envisage enlisting the assistance of private citizens in the regulatory process by inviting them to report incidents of environmental offending to appropriate regulatory or law enforcement authorities.[208] This can be reinforced by offering rewards for information leading to conviction, such as those which are made available in the United States under the Endangered Species Act.[209]

---

[206] Notwithstanding the importance of preventing frivolous or vexatious citizen action, it is important that safeguards avoid a chilling effect on citizen speech or action. For example, as we noted above in chapter two, public concern over use of the pesticide Alar and other agricultural chemicals moved agribusiness interests to promote 'veggie libel' statutes, which make disparagement of certain agricultural products actionable as libel (G. Pring & P. Canan, *SLAPPs: Getting sued for speaking out* (1996), Temple University Press, Philadelphia, p.191). By 1996 twelve states in the United States had enacted agricultural disparagement statutes (R. Finn, 'Libel Concerns Are A Reality For Scientists Who Speak Out In Public' (1996) 10(6) (March 18) *The Scientist* 15).

[207] The False Claims Act permits private citizens who discover fraud against the government to initiate a private civil action on behalf of the United States. If successful, the private plaintiff receives a proportion of the damage award. Procedural safeguards significantly reduce the risk of frivolous or vexatious actions (see E. Caminker, 'The Constitutionality of Qui Tam Actions' (1989) 99 *Yale Law Journal* 341–388). Regulations under the Surface Mining Control and Regulation Act allow citizens to request an inspection by federal regulatory authorities. The citizen must submit a signed written statement which would give regulatory authorities reason to believe that a violation exists. The citizen may accompany the inspector in the course of the inspection, and is entitled to receive a copy of the inspector's report In the event that no inspection is conducted, the citizen is entitled to a written explanation for the decision in question (see N. Shover, D. Clelland & J. Lynxwiler, *Enforcement or Negotiation: Constructing a regulatory bureaucracy* (1986), State University of New York Press, Albany). A wide variety of US environment statutes such as the Clean Air Act, the Clean Water Act, The Endangered Species Act and the Resource Conservation and Recovery Act, all have citizen suit provisions.

[208] In a small, close-knit community, this may not be easy. As one producer told us, 'When you know your neighbour's doing the wrong thing, and your kids are going to the same school as his, it's hard to dob him in.' On the other hand, agricultural workers, and the growing number of newcomers to the land may be less inhibited. We are indebted to Professor Laureen Snider for this observation.

[209] See also P. N. Grabosky, 'Regulation by Reward: On the Use of Incentives as Regulatory Instruments' *Law and Policy*, 17, 3, (July, 1995) 256–281.

The context most appropriate for citizen action of this kind would involve the most blatant examples of environmental misconduct—negligent applications of chemicals resulting in injury to humans or ecosystems; fraudulent misrepresentation of product; or, in the case of biodiversity, wilful destruction of species or habitat.

Although, in some circumstances, the objectives of the public interest sector may be best served by an adversarial posture, including litigation vis à vis producers and/or the state, there are other circumstances in which a more co-operative approach is appropriate. This is particularly the case in encouraging voluntaristic initiatives. Partnerships between environmentalists and producers, based on co-operation rather than conflict, have the potential to produce significant achievements, and win-win outcomes.[210] The Core Values Project, an example of constructive engagement between apple growers and pesticide reduction activists in New York State, is illustrative, as are some of the more successful Landcare groups in Australia.[211] The New South Wales Farmers' Federation, the WWF, and the State Government have formed a partnership to foster the fencing of remnant vegetation. As a representative of one nation's peak environmental body told us, with regard to achieving significant improvement in the environmental performance of farmers, 'You can't take them on. You've got to bring them with you. You have to deal with the industry productively.'

Some environmental organizations are in a position to wield price-based instruments in furtherance of biodiversity conservation, while others proffer incentives in furtherance of pesticide risk reduction. Groups such as the Nature Conservancy and the Audubon Society acquire acreage (or covenants) on the private market, creating, in effect, private nature reserves.[212] A number of recipients of the prestigious Goldman Environmental prize have been recognized for their efforts to arrest land clearing.[213] Defenders of Wildlife, a national nonprofit conservation organisation in the United States, offers financial compensation to ranchers for stock taken by wolves and grizzly bears.[214] They also offer a reward of $5,000 cash to landowners who permit a wolf to den and raise pups on their property.[215]

---

[210] L. A. Thrupp, New Partnerships for Sustainable Agriculture (1996), World Resources Institute, Washington.

[211] S. Lockie & F. Vanclay, (eds.) *Critical Landcare* (1997), Centre for Rural Social Research, Charles Sturt University, Wagga Wagga, NSW.

[212] http://www.tnc.org/.   [213] http://www.goldmanprize.org/goldman/.

[214] http://www.defenders.org/pr081397.html; http://www.defenders.org/pr091297.html.   [215] http://www.defenders.org/adopt.html.

Public interest organizations are also in a position to activate commercial influences in furtherance of low input agriculture and biodiversity conservation. The campaigns for dolphin-friendly tuna and sustainable forest products were almost entirely the work of public interest organizations. Groups such as Mothers and Others and The Midwest Organic Alliance are active in developing consumer demand for organic foods.[216]

To the extent that the governments adopt a less active role in environmental protection, one may expect environmental interest groups to become even more visible. The scope of this role, in any event, will depend on the political and legal culture of the jurisdiction in question. In a number of Western nations, the environmental NGO sector commands a degree of expertise which may match or even exceeds that employed by the state or the private sector. Government and industry alike are beginning to realize the potential for leveraging resources from environmental interest groups. In many places, direct government grants or tax incentives for charitable contributions have helped sustain an active public interest sector. In the United States, private philanthropy is an important source of support. But growing public appreciation of the need for sustainable agriculture suggests that regardless of its configuration, the non-profit sector seems destined continue to play a major role in the policy process.

Section 6: Design considerations

Having outlined the main instrument categories, the roles of third parties, and the interactions between them, in general terms, it remains to address more specific design principles. In this final section, we will argue that, drawing from the above analysis, six guidelines are paramount in designing policy mixes for agro-environmental regulation.

1. Instrument ordering

Even assuming that complementary instruments are available, and that an instrument mix is preferred to single instrument approaches, there may be reasons for *ordering* the introduction of the various instruments, rather than introducing them at the same time. For example, it would seem sensible to remove or neutralize existing perverse economic incentives first, since these would otherwise distort or reduce the effectiveness

---

[216] http://www.ozemail.com.au/~kkaos/index.html#list   http://www.ext.vt.edu/vvac/bgvp/bgvp.html.

of new policy instruments. Where a tax concession is inducing unacceptable vegetation clearance, then it is more economically efficient to remove the tax concession than to attempt to prohibit clearing.

Again, where more than one instrument or combination of instruments might achieve the intended policy outcome, and dependability is not of the essence, it would also be appropriate to introduce less intrusive and interventionist instruments before more intrusive ones, or where it is only practicable to introduce instruments concurrently, then enforcement discretion should, similarly, be nuanced so as to nurture virtue, escalating to more interventionist responses only when less intrusive responses prove ineffective.[217]

A policy instrument is more likely to produce both improved environmental performance and a positive attitude change if it is perceived as noncoercive. This is particularly important in the agriculture sector, given its traditional antipathy to command. It therefore follows that instruments should be no more coercive than circumstances require. Following Ayres and Braithwaite, coercive response should be escalated or de-escalated depending on the compliance performance of the regulated entity.[218] To this end, we recommend the sequenced mobilization of instruments in ascending order of coerciveness. Voluntary instruments are likely to be preferred by resource users over direct regulation because they are often more flexible, and they grant individuals greater freedom and opportunities to innovate. By offering a choice, they are likely to be perceived as more legitimate, thus facilitating compliance. There are also more positive reasons for preferring noncoercive responses, (and for decentralizing decision-making): specifically, to draw on farmer's expertise and on-the-ground management skills in searching for ways to combine agriculture with biodiversity, and tailor pesticide and fertilizer use to local conditions.

More generally, less interventionist incentive mixes, underpinned by regulations to prevent and exclude irreversible actions, are likely to deliver more efficient outcomes than more interventionist mixes. The reason for this is that less interventionist incentives permit trade-offs and encourage innovation. They also address underlying causes of environmental threats which, if removed or countered by a compensating mechanism, make further administrative action rarely necessary. Of no

---

[217] I. Ayres & J. Braithwaite, *Responsive Regulation: Transcending the deregulation debate* (1992), Oxford University Press, New York.
[218] *Ibid.*

less importance is their greater political acceptability and lower likelihood of eliciting defiance and resistance.

Voluntaristic initiatives for pesticide reduction undertaken by European farmers through their study groups and other forms of peer collaboration are a good example. When operating effectively, they preclude the necessity for state regulatory enforcement.

2. Institutional mixes: utilizing third parties

Implicit in the use of a broader range of instruments, is the use of a larger range of actors to implement them. Expanding the field of participation means not only the involvement of governments (first parties), landholders, or other users (second parties), but also a range of other interested actors (third parties). In this context, it is important to note that scrutiny on the part of citizens' and public interest organizations can exceed vigilance by government agencies. It is important to take advantage of both the democratic benefits which direct stakeholder participation can bring, and the enhanced legitimacy and leverage in implementation which broader third party engagement can provide.

As we have observed, there are circumstances in which the influence wielded by non-government institutions, particularly in furtherance of responsible chemical use, far exceeds the power of the State. This is especially apposite in relation to that part of the agriculture sector comprised of a large number of small producers, who would otherwise pose formidable problems of surveillance for regulatory authorities. In particular, if institutions of control can be forged from *within* the agricultural community, their potential impact will be greater. The resonance of information imparted by a fellow farmer, and the influence of one's peer group, may surpass that of the State in terms of impact and perceived legitimacy. These non-governmental instruments of social control can, in turn, be reinforced by commercial influences.

The role of third parties in contributing to the improvement of agro-environmental outcomes is destined only to expand. Public interest groups contribute to raising the general level of public awareness of agro-environmental issues, and have begun engaging producer associations in constructive partnerships. The activities of public interest groups in fostering consumer demand for low input produce is perhaps most noteworthy. Public interest groups can play other roles too. For example, the credibility and balance of biodiversity audits[219] would be

---

[219] Biodiversity audits would involve a small audit team containing scientific and other expertise and including respected members of the local community. Their role would be

considerably strengthened if the audit team included not only scientific experts, and local resource users, but also a representative of a community group or other appropriate NGOs. Similarly, if clearing restrictions are challenged by landholders, who wish to argue a case for further clearing beyond the legislative threshold, then third parties such as environmental groups, should have a right of standing, thereby acting as a countervailing force. For example, in the United States, the right to bring 'citizen suits' can enable local conservation groups to sue private land-users where their activities threaten endangered species. This approach has the particular virtue of compensating for lack of resources, and sometimes lack of political will, on the part of government enforcement agencies, and of leveraging substantially increased enforcement capability. The 'whistle-blower' or 'dob-in' factor is also an important one, capable of being harnessed in the public interest, although it may be of only limited value where illegal activity largely corresponds with local community mores.

Commercial influences in furtherance of sustainable agriculture appear destined to play an increasingly important role in the regulatory process. As consumer demand for environmentally preferable produce increases, upstream institutions will not only strive to meet that demand, but will market their produce and services in a manner designed to increase that demand. Moreover, one can expect to see more large institutions exercise upstream influence on growers. Commercial drivers of sustainable agriculture have already begun to rival, indeed in some cases, to surpass, regulatory interventions.

As a general principle, if adequate solutions are achievable without state intervention, governments should defer to these alternative orderings. However, such spontaneous market orderings are still the exception rather than the rule. In circumstances where commercial institutions are not functioning optimally (in public policy terms) in that role now, but have the potential to do so, the lesson for regulatory design is that they should be encouraged and facilitated by the state. In particular, the state may use its influence to foster or enhance those commercial influences which contribute most constructively to agro-environmental performance. As we have seen, governments can pre-

to assess the biodiversity significance of land in the area (see further M. D. Young, N. Gunningham, J. Elix, J. Lambert, B. Howard, P. Grabosky, E. McCrone, *Reimbursing the Future: An evaluation of motivational, voluntary, price-based, property-right, and regulatory incentives for the conservation of biodiversity* (1996), Biodiversity Series Paper No. 9, Department of the Environment, Sport and Territories, Biodiversity Unit, Canberra pp.109–11).

serve the integrity of markets by ensuring that markets are informed, and that deceptive practices are identified and punished. It can also use its own formidable buying power to foster demand for environmentally appropriate produce. This can also entail the provision of technical assistance to producers, and providing resources for public interest third parties to contribute constructively to policy.

Where non-state institutions fail to deliver, however, it is the job of government to provide a safety net, particularly where there are threshold effects and environmental harm is irreversible. The resources of governments are not unlimited. For this reason, they should be marshalled with care. One should look first to market solutions. Where these do not emerge, governments can seek to stimulate them. Where these efforts are unsuccessful, incentives targeted directly at producers may be necessary. Should the above still fail to deliver preferred outcomes, a degree of coercive intervention will be required. The role of the state is necessary, but by no means sufficient.

3. Economic and structural setting

The organizational context of agriculture will also influence the choice of regulatory instruments. As we have noted, agricultural production in the industrialized world has become more centralized. Most nations have a small number of very large producers and a large number of very small producers. The former, especially to the extent that they operate in mature, cohesive industry sectors, are likely to have the capacity (though not necessarily the willingness) to manage their chemical use in an environmentally appropriate manner. They will already command, or have ready access to, the best information about cost-effective input methods. They will have the ability to engage state of the art expertise and technology, such as geo-positioning for precise chemical application, and specialized management consultants. They will have the capacity to engage in voluntaristic and self-regulatory initiatives.[220]

Whether they also have the motivation to engage in environmentally responsible chemical practices will depend upon a number of factors. The extent to which they are integrated into a supply chain, leading to discerning regulatory systems and consumers abroad, is likely to be particularly important. And they will be most sensitive to market signals,

---

[220] This is not to suggest that some small producers are not exceptionally innovative. Some can respond to new challenges fare more rapidly than their counterparts with entrenched cultural attitudes.

both domestic and international. While these factors are by no means guarantors of exemplary environmental performance, the ability of many agricultural producers around the world to meet the most exacting standards imposed by importing countries and large commercial buyers suggests that commercial pressures are quite significant.

In contrast, small producers, particularly those who are economically marginal, may lack the knowledge, the resources, or the capacity to comply.[221] This situation will be even more difficult to the extent that they are not well integrated in cohesive producer associations and in supply chains that have constructive downstream influences. It is this latter group where carrots and, ultimately, sticks, may be necessary to achieve preferred environmental outcomes.

In essence, different mixes will be appropriate in different socio-economic circumstances. All else being equal, voluntary mechanisms and management agreements will be more attractive to the economically secure primary producer. By contrast, transferable tax credits and subsidies will be more appealing to those (such as the subsistence farmer) who are 'up to their ears in red ink' and receive little or not taxable income. Accreditation and labelling schemes will be more applicable to those interests which may be influenced by purchasing power. And coercive strategies will be reserved for the intractable minority.

4. Design for precaution

To account for irreversibility and lack of knowledge, regulatory packages which build in dependability, and involve more rather than fewer instruments, will be necessary. This is particularly apposite in the case of biodiversity conservation, where the existence of threshold effects poses a risk of catastrophic harm. So too, has it become the foundation of agricultural chemical regulation, characterized in recent years by increasingly stringent pre-marketing approval and registration.

In the case of biodiversity, Perrings and Pearce have argued that the existence of irreversible threshold effects (and often fundamental ignorance about the implications of crossing a threshold) introduces uncertainty, which renders the development of economic instruments to

---

[221] However, as Ostrom, (*Governing the Commons: The evolution of institutions for collective action* (1990), CUP, New York) suggests, on occasion, it is the small producers that are most keenly motivated by their dependence on local conditions to take long range and co-ordinated measures to ensure sustained productivity by protecting underlying resources, rather than 'mining' them for short term profit.

achieve biodiversity conservation objectives problematic.[222] If price-based instruments do not work as predicted, it may be too late to save the ecosystems or species concerned. Perrings and Pearce argue that, in such situations, regulation is probably the most dependable strategy. However, most tradeable right systems use regulations to place limits on acceptable behaviour.

Unfortunately, economists, such as Perrings and Pearce, may well have an over optimistic view of the virtues of regulation in this context. For while regulation does have considerable advantages over the sorts of incentive-based mechanisms discussed above, regulations are not dependable enough to rely upon alone. Regulatory failure is not uncommon. Effective implementation and enforcement are crucially important to regulation's dependability: yet failures at this level are well documented and widespread.[223] In circumstances of biodiversity protection, where valued attributes are widely dispersed, enforcement resources are thin on the ground, and regulation is often not supported by the local community, the possibility of regulatory failure is substantial.

Our view is different to Perrings and Pearce. Recognizing that the agriculture sector is comprised of many diverse sub-sectors, we do *not* suggest that regulation alone—or indeed any other policy instrument—has sufficient dependability to act as an effective safety net in its own right. On the contrary, we see regulation as a last line of defence, which is fallible. Accordingly, one of the functions of other instruments and mechanisms, in concert with astute institutional arrangements, is to dissuade resource users from actions that, with minor mis-judgement, could result in an irreversible change in an ecosystem type, the demise of a species, or the loss of genetic traits.[224] Regulation in this context is

[222] This is, in part, because threshold effects invalidate the normal test for efficiency in the allocation of resources. See C. Perrings & D. Pearce, 'Threshold effects and incentives for the conservation of biodiversity' (1994) 4 *Environmental and Resource Economics* 13–28.

[223] For a general review, see N. Gunningham, 'Negotiated non-compliance: A case study of regulatory failure' (1987) 9(1) *Law and Policy* 69–97 and references therein. Much of the existing legislation is supported by grossly inadequate budgets, leaving enforcement agencies with an almost complete incapacity to discharge some of their statutory functions. When this problem is compounded by a lack of political will and a desire on the part of politicians not to offend rural constituencies, then the impact of the legislation may be very modest indeed. On the other hand, in South Australia, where the law is clear, simple and well known, it has had a very substantial impact and may well have succeeded, over time, in making the prohibition of broad acre clearing acceptable to local communities.

[224] In the context of uncertainty, it is very difficult to know if a threshold is being approached. A precautionary approach would be to prohibit clearing unless those proposing it could prove it did not have threshold effects.

rather like an elastic safety net with holes in it: the greater the weight imposed on the safety net, the larger the holes become. One role of other instruments is to keep the weight off the safety net, because in the case of biodiversity conservation, the greater the expectation of regulation, the less effective regulation is likely to be.

Accordingly, given the severity of the consequences of policy failure and the limited dependability of regulation, we argue for a mixed approach *which uses the full suite of instruments available.* The logic is similar to that applied to aircraft design. Because the consequences of the failure of a single system, without backup, would be catastrophic, aircraft design deliberately incorporates multiple systems to compensate for the possible failure of any one in particular (*fail-safe mechanisms*).

Setting administrative cost issues to one side, generally, those mixes that involve more rather than fewer instruments are likely to be more effective in preventing irreversible loss. Put differently, emphasis on dependability and precaution means that the most effective instrument mix will include mechanisms and instruments that appear to be redundant but are there because, from time to time, others are expected to fail. Under this approach, the role of non-regulatory instruments is to increase dependability by reducing the need for regulatory mechanisms to be used as the first line of defence.

5. The first mover problem and moral hazard

Lack of public knowledge about the environmentally harmful impacts of agriculture gives rise to opportunistic behaviour on the part of individuals. This militates in favour of measures which, in concert, make the incentive for (most) individuals to act in the public interest greater than the incentive to pursue private gain.

This problem is at its most acute in the case of biodiversity conservation. Against the backdrop of considerable uncertainty about the consequences of biodiversity loss, and ignorance about its extent, how can one best deter opportunistic behaviour which could inflict irreversible damage? As a public good, there is often a large gap between private values and the public interest in protecting biodiversity. Moreover, because of the lack of information about biodiversity, administrators are not always aware of the size of this gap. As Bowers has pointed out, from time to time unforeseen contingencies may arise which offer opportunities for profit at the expense of biodiversity.[225] These situa-

---

[225] J. Bowers, *Incentives and Mechanisms for Biodiversity: Observations and Issues* (1994), CSIRO Division of Wildlife and Ecology, Canberra, p.19.

tion will give rise to a special case of the *First Mover Problem,* namely: if others seize private opportunities and seek to profit from them by masking public values from the control authority, then they may damage biodiversity before the authority responsible for protecting biodiversity can act.

If, for example, a farmer discovers that remnant vegetation on his or her property contains an endangered species or, more seriously, one thought to be extinct, then unless there is a guarantee of compensation, he or she has a strong financial incentive to hide this fact from the community.[226] Similarly, there is a strong temptation for a person who applies for a clearing permit to omit to note the presence of an endangered species within the area covered by the application, or for a forester to shoot an endangered animal and remove all evidence of this in the area he or she wishes to log.[227]

There are two means of dealing with the first mover problem. The *first* is for governments to invest in detection, monitoring, and information gathering so as to reduce the risk of the first mover losses occurring. Given the limited capacity of most bureaucracies to anticipate and respond quickly to change, however, this strategy is not a dependable one. Moreover, the collection of more information takes time to implement. By the time the information is collated, an irreversible biodiversity conservation threshold may have been passed.

The *second* means is to introduce control instruments which, in concert with one another, make the incentive for (most) individuals to act in the public interest greater than the incentive to mask it in pursuit of private gain. Management agreements that encourage people to renegotiate the contract when circumstances change are the most common method used to reduce the first-mover problem. Another common method is to offer compensation for the value of the income opportunity lost as a result of the discovery of a public interest greater than the expected private one. This is consistent with the culture of dependency on subsidies which has characterized the agricultural sector in a number of nations. This latter option, however, runs the risk of encouraging people to hold out for bigger and bigger rewards.[228] The idea of a 'safe harbour' under the United States Endangered Species Act,

---

[226] *Ibid.* at p.13.

[227] In the United States of America the expression that accompanies this practice is 'Shoot, shovel and shut-up'.

[228] J. Bowers, *Incentives and Mechanisms for Biodiversity: Observations and Issues* (1994), CSIRO Division of Wildlife and Ecology, Canberra, p.19.

whereby regulators offer future land use assurances to a landowner in return for the landowner's commitment either to enhance habitat or to maintain for a period habitat that may eventually be used by endangered species, also goes some way towards alleviating the first mover problem by this method. If it were combined with a tax credit for the costs associated with maintaining the habitat of endangered species, or the capacity to sell safe harbour rights to other landowners, then it would go even further.[229]

A related issue which illustrates the unreliability of regulations is the issue of 'moral hazard'. Moral hazard arises from the fact that, for biodiverse resources, the chance of being detected breaching a regulation or agreement can be very low. One means of dealing with the moral hazard problem is to build institutional capacity and responsibility for preserving biodiversity at the industry and local level. If, through co-management and astute property-right arrangements, biodiversity conservation is seen as a community and industry responsibility then, arguably, the risk of discovery will be greater, and hence the incentive to cheat less. Industry and community responsibility can be developed further via the use of motivational instruments such as the issuance of prizes, awards, and accreditation that give status to those who are seen as one's peers.

Another means of dealing with the moral hazard problem is to link reward to performance of the actual objective being sought. Thus, a management agreement might, for example, pay people for the number of birds breeding in an area and not the cost of getting them to breed there. Under such an agreement, the work required to attract and retain birds would not be specified, and hence the moral hazard problem would not arise.

6. Financially attractive

Where ongoing and active contributions to the sustainable agriculture are required, financially attractive instrument mixes should be preferred to ones that reduce the welfare of producers.[230] This is particularly the case given the 'bottom line' focus of most producers, and the cultural heritage of subsidization which has characterized western agriculture, where incentives became a way of life in the late twentieth century.

---

[229] See, generally, M. Bean and D. Wilcove 'Ending the Impasse' (1996) 13(4) *Environmental Forum* 22.

[230] We define a financially attractive mix as one that, at the point of introduction, has the potential to increase the wealth or income of those who participate.

The overall success of a policy regime will be substantially higher and the prospects for sustainable agriculture will be greater if direct regulatory approaches are overlain with a web of mechanisms that create a financially attractive and voluntary atmosphere encouraging co-operation and the sharing of information. For reasons described below, only the latter approach is likely to induce resource users and communities to actively contribute to sustainable practices.

There are a variety of ways in which financially attractive instrument mixes can be created. For example, in many countries, it has become common to use financial instruments to close the gap between the private and public demands for biodiversity conservation. Often, the incentive offered is less than the full cost of an action. For example, in Western Australia, landholders are offered fifty per cent of the cost of fencing out remnant native vegetation and, if they sign a thirty-year memorandum of understanding to maintain that remnant, a significant local government rate rebate will apply. Also in Western Australia, sharefarming arrangements have been developed whereby farmers receive an annuity for allowing the state or private forestry companies to grow and harvest timber on their land. Sustainable management of such timber resources will help conserve biodiversity and arrest soil degradation.

In the domain of agricultural chemicals, incentives for moving from traditional methods to low-input production would be an attractive alternative, or at least complement, to a levy imposed on inputs. Cross-compliance, where eligibility for a benefit is conditional upon compliance with regulatory requirements, is preferable to simple direction.

One important use of financial inducements is to act as a 'circuit breaker' during a transition to a new regime. This principle extents to biodiversity conservation as well as chemicals regulation. In South Australia, the introduction of widespread clearing controls was made politically palatable by coupling it with the provision of compensation; in turn, this compensation provision was removed after an transitional period in which the land clearing controls gained a widespread acceptance.[231] Subsidies during the period of transition to low input agriculture are similarly illustrative.

---

[231] For details see M. D. Young, N. Gunningham, J. Elix, J. Lambert, B. Howard, P. Grabosky, E. McCrone, *Reimbursing the Future: An evaluation of motivational, voluntary, price-based, property-right, and regulatory incentives for the conservation of biodiversity* (1996), Biodiversity Series Paper No. 9, Department of the Environment, Sport and Territories, Biodiversity Unit, Canberra, p.122.

Financial inducements may achieve even more when initial participation is voluntary, because in these circumstances community acceptance of the circuit-breaking change to a new regime is strengthened.
The result, even when financial support is removed or phased out, is a
more genuine and more durable attitude change. Once agreement has
been reached over the new regime, however, the mix can involve significant penalties.

Financially attractive mixes are particularly important where there is
a need to encourage ongoing management of a resource: a situation
where, as we will see, negative regulation is likely to be particularly ineffective. Another key to ensuring ongoing management of resources is
some mechanism (for example, a covenant or easement) to ensure that
protection does not cease with the termination of the management
agreement. Policy instruments which merely halt existing biodiversity
loss are important, particularly in gaining breathing space during which
more constructive policies can be developed, but they do not in themselves ensure that resources will be appropriately managed so as to preserve biodiversity. For example, although the South Australian
experience[232] suggests that compensation backed by legislation can
have considerable success, even this mix remains, in one aspect, seriously inadequate. The South Australian model is, essentially, one of
prohibition on clearance coupled with compensation, with only very
modest provision for management of land subject to clearance controls.[233] For this reason, it is likely to be far more successful in preventing clearance than in ensuring effective ongoing care of native
vegetation and woodland habitat on private land.

Farrier, in particular, has argued that those who are forcibly
constrained from clearing land are unlikely to be enthusiastic land man-

---

[232] See, in particular, the South Australian approach under the Native Vegetation
Management Act 1985 (subsequently repealed by the Native Vegetation Act 1991)
described in J. Bradsen, 'The Green Issues: Biodiversity Conservation in Australia' in
B. Boer, R. Fowler & N. Gunningham (eds.) *Environmental Outlook: Law and Policy* (1994),
Federation Press, Sydney.

[233] A permit is required to clear native vegetation, which is likely to be refused in a
very large majority of cases. Payment of compensation, which was automatic under the
Native Vegetation Management Act 1985, is no longer so under the 1991 legislation.
Nevertheless, the system still contemplates the offering of financial incentives for forego-
ing development rights, and financial assistance with the management of reserved stands
of native vegetation and planned revegetation (M. D. Young, N. Gunningham, J. Elix,
J. Lambert, B. Howard, P. Grabosky, E. McCrone, *Reimbursing the Future: An evaluation of
motivational, voluntary, price-based, property-right, and regulatory incentives for the conservation of biodiversity* (1996), Biodiversity Series Paper No. 9, Department of the Environment, Sport
and Territories, Biodiversity Unit, Canberra, p.25).

agers, and that for this reason, regulation must be combined with adequate financial instruments but that 'these should take the form of forward looking payments for management rather than backward looking compensation'.[234] He suggests a re-ordering of current land protection initiatives as a possible way of meeting this objective. In his view:

The priorities of these initiatives need to be adjusted to ensure that greater emphasis is placed on the retention of existing native vegetation rather than replanting, and that restructuring in local communities is not based exclusively on short term productivity concerns, but also takes into account the much longer term economic interest that the community has in conserving biodiversity.[235]

The final element, in terms of ensuring ongoing management of resources, is some mechanism (e.g., a covenant or easement) to ensure that protection does not cease with the termination of the management agreement.

To summarize the lessons of this section: instrument mixes which are net, financially attractive, maximize acceptance, are largely self-enforcing, and create a dynamic incentive to search for more cost-effective solutions. Often, they also provide a continuing incentive to improve beyond the target.[236] They are essential where there is a need to ensure ongoing management of a resource.

There may be a tension between the need to maintain net, financially attractive instrument mixes, and the need for sustainable agriculture to be achieved at least cost to government. In cases where a permanent financial incentive is offered, particular questions of efficiency and administrative feasibility need to be addressed. The case for continuing use of financial instruments is dependent upon the gap between public concern and private interest and opportunities to close that gap via the use of other instruments. As indicated above, the greater that gap, the greater the need for financial instruments to encourage ongoing management. Recognizing that the administrative costs of any scheme involving annual payments are high, in many cases

---

[234] D. Farrier, 'Conserving Biodiversity on Private Land' (1995) 19(2) *Harvard Environmental Law Review* 304–405.

[235] *Ibid.*

[236] T. Schelling (ed.) *Incentives for environmental protection* (1983), Massachusetts Institute of Technology Press, Cambridge, US; and P. N. Grabosky, 'Regulation by Reward: On the Use of Incentives as Regulatory Instruments' *Law and Policy*, 17, 3 (July 1995) 256–281.

it may be more cost-effective to change property-rights, either with or without a compensation payment, than to pursue annual payments.

The goal of cost effectiveness is particularly challenging in the area of property-rights. Property-rights are often incompletely specified. Governments, on behalf of the community, usually retain the right to respecify the rights and obligations associated with a property entitlement. Where property-rights are unclear, the introduction of financial payments can act to turn a property-right still held by society into one held by a title holder. Several Australian states, for example, have introduced regulations that require people to obtain a permit to clear native vegetation. Prior to the introduction of these regulations, most landholders thought they had a right to clear land.

Recognition of these issues has led Young to the conclusion that it is critical to distinguish between: *reimbursement* of non-marketable costs associated with protecting biodiversity values for society by, for example, fencing an endangered habitat; *compensation* for lost property-rights, like the right to graze an area; and *pricing policies* that either internalize or subsidize the costs of controlling and preventing threats to biodiversity associated with economic activity.[237]

Conclusion

In this chapter, we have seen that the environmental threats posed by the use of agricultural chemicals, and the threats which current agricultural practices pose for biodiversity conservation, are unlikely to be solved under existing regulatory and policy regimes. Many of the most serious problems of contemporary approaches: the inability to overcome entrenched resistance from powerful agricultural interests; the difficulties of monitoring and ensuring compliance; the enormously damaging impact of perverse incentives; and that the low level of awareness, which characterizes some small producers, cannot be overcome by modest modifications to the *status quo*. Sustainable agriculture will require much broader and innovative policy prescriptions.

Because the threats to biodiversity conservation, in particular, are complex and multifaceted, they do not lend themselves to single or simple answers, and in this chapter we do not purport to provide any. Nor do we claim that redesigning instruments and policy mixes *alone* will be

---

[237] Young argues in particular for reimbursement of nonmarketable costs, and limiting compensation for a transitory period. See the discussion and references at p.75 above.

sufficient to achieve all our environmental and economic goals in respect of agriculture. However, we do argue that we are likely to move much closer to the goal of sustainable agriculture if we seek to use (along with other policies beyond the scope of this book) complementary combinations of policy instruments, and to harness the contribution of a broader range of parties.

Precisely what this will involve necessarily varies with the context and content of the problem to be addressed. We have shown that the sorts of combinations of instruments and parties, that may work best in curbing the use of agricultural chemicals, may be very different from those which are optimal for addressing the challenge of land-based biodiversity conservation. For example, while there is very considerable potential to enable commercial third parties to act as surrogate regulators in the case of agricultural pesticides, much less opportunity exists with regard to biodiversity conservation.[238] And even within each of these categories, much will depend upon the particular economic, social, and political context, and upon the nature of the threat itself. For example, different solutions are called for in addressing problems of irreversible biodiversity loss than in other circumstances. Similarly, viable policy options vary greatly, depending upon whether one is dealing with 'win-win' or 'win-lose' scenarios, large agribusiness as opposed to the subsistence farmer, and upon whether the benefits of investing in sustainable practices are short term or long term.

How then should we go about the task of designing context-specific policy mixes? In this chapter, we have emphasized not only the nature of the major environmental problems confronting the agricultural sector, but also the changing nature of agriculture itself, and the challenges to and opportunities for policy-making that this presents. For example, the shift to concentration and specialization and the accompanying trend to vertical integration present exciting possibilities for utilizing the tightly coupled chain of supply from seed to supermarket shelf in the cause of sustainable agriculture. Here, increasing consumer awareness of environmental issues, in conjunction with the leverage which wholesale buyers and retailers have over producers, is critically important in harnessing market forces in furtherance of agricultural chemical control.

---

[238] Although, as Breckenridge (personal communication November 1997) points out, there are possibilities for developing better methods of audit and certification for some crop management that could address aspects of biodiversity (e.g., efforts to encourage growing coffee beans under a canopy of trees).

We have argued that effective policy prescriptions must be capable of addressing the very considerable problems confronting existing regulatory and policy regimes. In designing mixes, we have emphasized, for example, the need to address such major obstacles as the resistance of the agricultural lobby (or what we termed, in chapter one, the objective of political acceptability). Our proposals for the design of financially attractive instrument mixes, for the judicious combination of positive and negative instruments, and for further use of mechanisms, such as the Californian partnerships approach, were amongst our suggestions to overcome this obstacle. Again, the existence of perverse incentives permeates agricultural policy in many jurisdictions, and recipients of such incentives (commonly subsidies) are unlikely to be enthusiastic supporters of their demise. Addressing this problem, our proposals include reshaping such subsidies, in the short term, so that they produce environmentally benign consequences, rather than seeking to abolish them. Innovative solutions are also available to deal with the problem of noncompliance, not least of which is cross-compliance, which in the agricultural sector has enormous potential, by tying government subsidies to compliance with other regulatory requirements.

We also emphasized the counterproductive nature of some existing regulatory approaches (e.g., the way in which the United States Endangered Species Act unintentionally encourages landowners to destroy habitat that might become the home of an endangered species), and proposed more constructive alternatives. Similarly, we have suggested how incentives for chemical use can be replaced by incentives for low input production methods. To the extent possible we sought to achieve 'win-win' solutions, while recognizing that such solutions are not always possible.

And we attempted to grapple with such thorny issues as the first mover problem and the need to make biodiversity conservation cost effective. The critical importance of providing positive incentives to landholders to adopt a stewardship ethic, and the impracticality of them doing so without reimbursement for incremental costs, was also emphasized, while seeking to balance this against the political implausibility, and sometimes undesirability, of permanent, ongoing compensation. In the case of agricultural pesticides, we further explored the roles of constructive engagement between consumer, environmental, and commercial interests.

Throughout, we argued that there are a variety of instruments that can make an important contribution to achieving the goals of sustainable agriculture. In broad terms, we categorized these as informational, voluntary, self-regulatory, price-based, property-based, and regulatory. Yet for the most part, these instruments have not realized their potential, largely because single policy instruments, generally, have both strengths and weaknesses, and are unlikely to successfully achieve a number of different policy goals. Accordingly, their use as 'stand alone' policy tools is seriously sub-optimal, yet this is precisely how these instruments have often been used.

In the large majority of circumstances, the multiple objectives of sustainable agriculture will be achieved most effectively through a mix of instruments and mechanisms targeted to the suite of threats extant at any location. An optimal strategy will harness the strengths of individual mechanisms, while compensating for their weaknesses by the use of additional and complementary policy instruments. We have sought to indicate the circumstances in which each category of instruments might most appropriately be used, and to suggest optimal instrument combinations suited to particular contexts. For example, while regulation is an important instrument of last resort, it is also a particularly blunt one, and wholly unsuited for dealing with either first mover problems or those which require positive and ongoing future management of a resource. The comparative virtues of positive custodianship management agreements, and the considerable promise of the Californian experiments in partnerships, are obvious.

Finally, we stressed the potentially very positive and creative role of third parties in achieving sustainable agriculture. The role of environmental groups and other NGOs is well rehearsed, as are the means by which they might play such a role. However, the even greater potential of commercial third parties is as yet only dimly understood and seriously underexploited. We showed how a number of commercial institutions: banks, insurance companies, wholesalers, and retailers, might play important and constructive roles as *de facto* regulators, and how governments can actively support, enlist, and facilitate such efforts. In doing so, we have sought to move beyond the market-government dichotomy to devise better ways of achieving environmental protection at an acceptable economic and social cost. As we have seen, this approach would still involve government intervention, but selectively and in combination with a range of market and non-market solutions.

In seeking to design optimal combinations of instruments and actors, the greatest obstacle is the fact that it will be necessary for the mix to accommodate a vast array of ecological, political, social, and economic contexts. For example, so complex and various are the causes of biodiversity loss and the circumstances in which they arise that no single instrument, and indeed no single mix of instruments, could conceivably be successful in addressing all or even most of them. As a result, generalizations are extremely hazardous. In short, the complexities of social, economic, and ecological processes preclude simple broad-brush solutions.[239] *The only answer to the question: 'what is the optimal combination of instruments and mechanisms?' is: 'it all depends, and that the optimal combination will change with time and context'.*[240] As one recent study put it: '*a priori* rules are inferior to case-by-case analysis'.[241] Rather than seeking to identify optimal mixes in the abstract, a context[242] and threat-specific approach is preferable. We have adopted precisely such an approach in this chapter, but in order to go beyond a case-specific approach, we also sought to identify a set of design criteria which, we believe, should be paramount in constructing policy mixes more generally. In the final chapter we hope to take this one step further by developing a process and principle-based approach to the design of optimal policy mixes.

---

[239] K. Turner & H. Opschoor, 'Environmental Economics and Environmental Policy Instruments: Introduction and overview' in H. Opschoor and K. Turner (eds.) *Economic Incentives and Environmental Policies: Principles and practice* (1994), Kluwer Academic Publishers, Dordrecht.

[240] For example, tradeable rights can operate effectively where natural resources are not site-specific and where 'acceptable overall-impacts can be determined', but they are not appropriate where resources are site-specific, as is commonly the case with habitats or ecosystems.

[241] H. Opschoor & K. Turner, *Economic Incentives and Environmental Policies: Principles and practice* (1994), Kluwer Academic Publishers, Dordrecht, p.35.

[242] The OECD suggests that the key variables include: the structure of existing conservation laws, regulatory techniques, and property rights to land and resource use; the distribution of the benefits and costs of biodiversity across key target groups; government administrative structure and capacity; public awareness of biodiversity values; characteristics of the biodiversity values to be conserved (local or national public good; relative importance of use and passive use values); and characteristics of uncertainty, potential for threshold effects, and the need for safe minimum standards and 'threshold' instruments. See OECD, *Saving Biological Diversity: Economic Incentives* (1996), OECD, Paris.

PART III

Conclusion: 'Smart' Regulation

6 Designing Environmental Policy

Neil Gunningham and Darren Sinclair

Introduction

Threats to the environment take many forms. They range from global issues, such as ozone depletion and the enhanced greenhouse effect, to localized matters, such as point-source pollution, toxic waste disposal or agricultural chemical run-off. Just as the causes of major environmental problems are many and various, so too are their solutions. From this we conclude that strategies to address environmental degradation are context-specific.[1] What sorts of policies work will be highly dependent upon the characteristics of the environmental issue under consideration. As a result, it would be futile to attempt to construct a single optimal regulatory solution that would be applicable to a wide variety of circumstances. Moreover, there are so many possible permutations of instrument and institutional interactions as to make the task of producing a general causal model of relationships between the multiple variables impractical even if problems of context specificity were overcome.[2]

Does this mean that nothing of value can be said at a general and abstract level and that the most we can ever do is focus on solutions to particular types of problems (point-source pollution, land-clearing, soil degradation, etc.) with little hope of learning any broader lessons or of extrapolating from one policy area to another? We believe that such a conclusion is too bleak, and that, notwithstanding the context-specific nature of most environmental problems, it is possible to build a *process and principle based framework* for designing environmental regulation in any given circumstances. By this, we mean an approach which, while falling short of providing determinative regulatory solutions, leads policymakers to ask the crucially important questions (processes) and assess

---

[1] For a similar conclusion, see J. B. Opschoor & R. K. Turner (eds.) *Economic Incentives and Environmental Policies: Principles and Practice* (1994), Kluwer Academic Publishers, Dordrecht.

[2] As Bressers and Klok put it 'theories based on the joint influence of possible combinations of circumstances rather than the isolated influences of individual circumstances tend to become tremendously complex' (H. Bressers & P. J. Klok 'Fundamentals for a Theory of Policy Design' (1988) 15(3/4) *International Journal of Social Economics* 22.

their decisions against a set of design criteria (principles) which form the basis for reaching preferred policy outcomes.[3]

Specifically, we seek to demonstrate that there is a middle path. This path involves drawing lessons from both the theoretical literature on regulation and from empirical study of what works and what doesn't work in specific contexts (drawing, in particular, on our case studies of the chemical industry and agriculture) to provide a series of policy prescriptions of broad application. These are intended to guide policymakers seeking to design regulatory or policy solutions to any given environmental problem, on how best to approach that task.

In this chapter, we address the three major components we believe are crucial to successful regulatory design. First, and briefly, we examine *regulatory design processes*: the preliminary steps which policymakers must go through in identifying their objectives, the characteristics of the environmental problem they confront, the available policy options, and issues of consultation and participation. These processes can be mechanistic, except if they are used in an open-ended way to challenge assumptions and fully explore possibilities. While the questions making up the processes are not new they are essential, and a failure to undertake them commonly causes policy failure.

Secondly, we identify a series of *regulatory design principles*. We argue that adherence to these principles is at the very heart of successful policy design. Not least, we argue that policymakers should take advantage of a number of largely unrecognized opportunities, strategies and techniques for achieving efficient and effective environmental policy. These include:

- the desirability of preferring complementary instrument mixes over single instrument approaches while avoiding the dangers of 'smorgasbordism' (i.e., wrongly assuming that all complementary instruments should be used rather than the minimum number necessary to achieve the desired result);

---

[3] A benefit of this approach is that policy-makers will avoid expending scarce resources by exploring in detail inappropriate and unproductive regulatory strategies at the early stages of the design process, thus reserving resources for a more detailed assessment once the available options have been refined down to a short-list. For example, McGarity refers to a 'phased system of reducing options' whereby regulators begin with 'a large number of options initially' and 'as options are rejected, the remaining options should be analysed with increasing thoroughness' (O. R. McGarity, 'Regulatory Analysis and Regulatory Reform' *Texas Law Review* (1987) vol. 65:1243).

- the virtues of parsimony: why less interventionist measures should be preferred and how to achieve such outcomes;

- the benefits of an escalating response up an instrument pyramid (utilizing not only government but also business and third parties) so as to build in regulatory responsiveness, to increase dependability of outcomes through instrument sequencing, and to provide early warning of instrument failure through the use of 'triggers';

- empowering third parties (both commercial and non-commercial) to act as surrogate regulators, thereby achieving not only better environmental outcomes at less cost, but also freeing up scarce regulatory resources which can be redeployed in circumstances where no alternatives to direct government intervention are available; and

- maximizing opportunities for win-win outcomes, by expanding the boundaries within which such opportunities are available, and encouraging business to go 'beyond compliance' with existing legal requirements.

Thirdly, we stress the crucial importance of *designing instrument combinations* and discuss how such permutations might be inherently complementary, inherently counterproductive, or essentially context-specific in nature. We also explain how instrument combinations can be sequenced in order to avoid dysfunctional results and so as to expand the range of circumstances in which particular combinations will be complementary rather than counterproductive.

The purpose of the design processes and principles is to guide policymakers in developing an optimal policy mix to achieve *a given environmental goal* (or goals), not to determine what that goal should be. Fundamentally, the design processes and principles do *not* address the issue of how governments should establish environmental policy goals. Rather, it is assumed that government has already determined a specific environmental goal or goals. It is only after this goal has been articulated that our set of design processes/principles can come into play.

It is also important to note some further issues we do not address. In particular, we are not directly concerned with the debate on compliance. The extent to which different instruments are capable of being, or under a particular enforcement approach likely to be, effectively enforced, is obviously an important consideration in relation to their effectiveness and efficiency. However, it is not necessary to enter into this debate in order to address our central concerns, identified above. Nor do we find it necessary to enter the debate concerning the prevailing regulatory culture of different jurisdictions and their relative effectiveness although this too, is likely to influence regulatory outcomes.[4] As we will see, our design principles can be applied successfully against the backdrop of a variety of enforcement practices and across a range of cultures, without need to engage with the details of either of these debates.

Regulatory design processes

There are a number of steps in the design of optimal policy mixes which are crucial to the delivery of desired policy outcomes. And although these process orientated prescriptions can appear pedestrian, it is important to emphasize their relative contribution, especially if they are used as a rigorous tool of analysis and to structure the application of the regulatory principles outlined below.[5] A thorough assessment of the regulatory terrain, including a clear understanding of overriding policy goals, an identification of the nuances and particularities of different environmental circumstances, and a consideration of the full range of potential regulatory actors, are fundamental prerequisites to the advancement of environmental policy outcomes. Yet (notwithstanding a growing trend to develop checklists for regulatory decision-making[6]), the all too frequent neglect of such basic processes causes, demonstrably, dysfunctional policy design.[7]

Neglect of process-based issues will, hopefully, become less frequent as consciousness of their importance increases. In particular, a 1997 OECD review of related issues in the context of Regulatory Impact Analysis,[8] is itself likely to raise awareness substantially.[9] The role of Regulatory Impact Analysis is outlined in Box 3 below.

[4] See, for example, D. Vogel *National Styles of Regulation: Environmental Policy in Great Britain and the United States* (1986) Ithaca, NY Cornell UP.

[5] Others too have recognized the need for procedural guidelines in regulatory design. For example, the OECD has developed a reference checklist for regulatory decision-making (OECD, Puma/Reg (1994)6) and the Treasury Board of Canada has produced a step by step guide assessing regulatory alternatives. See 'Assessing Regulatory Alternatives', Treasury Board of Canada Secretariat (1994), Ottawa.

[6] See n.7 above and n.10 below.

[7] See, for example, M. K. Landy, *The Environmental Protection Agency: Asking the wrong questions* (1994), Oxford University Press, New York, especially pp.239–241.

[8] *Regulatory Impact Analysis: Best Practices in OECD Countries* Organisation for Economic Co-operation and Development, Paris, 1997.

[9] The contribution that RIA makes as a policy tool will depend on the commitment

Box 3: Regulatory Impact Analysis

While practice often falls short of ideal, the goal of RIA is the optimization of policy to maximize benefits and minimize costs. There is a move, especially in a number of OECD countries, to fully integrate RIA with government policy processes. RIA should contribute to better informed decision making and more open and transparent government processes. Countries vary in the questions asked in RIA,[10] but common elements include:

1. **What is the nature of the problem being addressed?**

2. **What is the objective of intervention? What are the specific goals being pursued?**

3. **What are the options for dealing with the problem? As well as regulation, are there other alternatives?**

4. **Analyse the impacts that the different policy options will have on different groups in society. Rank proposed options according to the benefits and costs they generate and how these benefits and costs are distributed across those who are affected by the problem and its solution. Identify data sources and assumptions used in making these assessments.**

5. **Consult widely to ensure all important considerations have been brought to bear.**

6. **Confirm the preferred policy solution, and bring together all the factors that have led to that solution.**

7. **Explain how the policy will be implemented and reviewed this strategy at a later date to ensure objectives have been achieved.[11]**

made to it and the quality of the analysis conducted under each process. Amongst a number of performance criteria identified by the OECD for an RIA system, is included a commitment to make maximum use, within cost constraints, of quantitative data and rigorous empirical methods. This should maximize objectivity and comparability across alternative policy options.

[10] See T. D. Hopkins (1997) 'Alternative Approaches to Regulatory Analysis: Designs from Seven OECD Countries' in *Regulatory Impact Analysis: Best Practices in OECD Countries*,

Since we are not alone in recognizing the importance of process issues, we will address them very briefly, as a necessary precursor to our core concerns with regulatory design principles and policy mixes. Suffice it to say, that the processes listed below are compatible with RIA, and those aspects which are particularly relevant to our purposes are highlighted and expanded. It should also be noted that the *design principles* which we describe in a subsequent section could be embedded within a RIA framework. For example, the analysis of instrument mixes and the selection of the best policy option could take place via questions 3 and 4 contained in Box 1.

Process 1. Identify the desired policy goal(s) and the trade-offs necessary to achieve it

A crucial initial step will be to accurately identify the relevant environmental policy goal.[12] That is, precisely what is the intended outcome and over what time frame. We recognize that, in some circumstances, it may be difficult to quantify the environmental goal, and in others it may be expected that the goal will change over time, particularly when scientific information is less than complete at the time of the policy's inception and as the costs and benefits of achieving the goal become apparent. Notwithstanding these potential difficulties, it is imperative that policymakers strive to pin down the exact nature of the government's policy goals to the maximum extent possible, because only then is effective policy design practicable.[13]

PUMA, OECD, Paris, and T. O. McGarity *Reinventing Rationalite: The Role of Regulatory Analysis in the Federal Bureaucracy*, (1991) Cambridge University Press.

[11] These questions form the basis of the RIA conducted in Australia by the Commonwealth Government. See Office of Regulation Review (1997) *A Guide to Regulation*, Australia, October.

[12] We recognize, of course, that in the political process, policy goals sometimes only gradually evolve, but even so, policy-makers should still endeavour to identify them to the extent practicable. In addition to clearly defining the policy goal, it would also be useful to determine the broader motivations behind the policy goal such as the scientific rationale. This will be pertinent in particular to the application of voluntary based and information based policy instruments.

[13] Whilst we assume that, in the vast majority of circumstances, it will be government that is setting the policy goals, we acknowledge that, in certain instances, parties other than government may set such goals, for example industry associations in the case of pure industry self-regulation or environmental organizations in the case of specific consumer campaigns. That is, there is no reason, in theory, why the design principles could not be equally applied by non-government interest to achieve their environmental objectives. In practice, however, it most likely government that will have the necessary resources and

How that goal is achieved will depend on the weighting given to a number of evaluation criteria, which, in some circumstances, will be in tension, and may require policy trade-offs. We refer here, in particular, to the criteria listed in chapter one, particularly effectiveness, efficiency, and equity.[14] The ranking of these criteria in addressing a particular policy goal will have a profound impact on the nature of subsequent policy design.

For example, if the policy goal was to prevent irreversible loss (such as the demise of a species on the verge of extinction), effectiveness might well take precedence over efficiency or equity. That is, the priority would be upon achieving a dependable result (getting it right first time, because there are no second chances) even if this was not efficient. In contrast, if the government's policy goal was, for example, to reduce point source emissions of sulphur dioxide from industry by 50 per cent in increments of 10 per cent over a five-year period in order to limit the incidence of acid rain, then efficiency might be given a much greater prominence. This is because the nature of the goal is incremental and accumulative, and even if industry does not meet its target in any one year, the longer term goal may still be achieved.[15] Considerations of equity will also be crucial at this stage. What will be the distributive impact of a given approach? It is necessary, therefore, for policymakers to clearly establish what their policy priorities are at the outset. It is only after the overriding policy goal has been clarified, and competing objectives weighed and prioritized, that a suitable policy mix can be formulated.[16]

---

iauthority to recruit a range of instruments and participants for an optimal regulatory solution.

[14] See above, p.25.

[15] That is not to say that reductions in point source emissions could not require absolute adherence to rigid phase out schedules; governments may, for example, be committed to a binding international environmental treaty, as in the case of ozone depleting substances under the Montreal Protocol. The point is that, for a variety of reasons, different policy priorities will be attached to different environmental goals.

[16] There is a broader debate concerning the most appropriate level at which to design policy goals and in particular as to whether these need to be approached at a broad and integrated level. One of the major handicaps of existing environmental policy is its failure to establish integrated policy goals that engage actors and activities across a range of sectoral and institutional groupings. The European Union has emphasized the need for long term policy goals that balance ecological and economic and social objectives, estimate the risks and are based on good science. For example, regional management plans may be developed using risk-based assessment which aims to identify and prioritize the sources of environmental harm and the assimilative capacity of the local environment to

Process 2. Identify the unique characteristics of the environmental problem being addressed

Since no single policy mix is likely to be successful when applied to all environmental problems, the next step in the design process is to identify the distinguishing characteristics of the relevant environmental issue in order to facilitate the selection of appropriate combinations of instruments and participants.[17]

Not surprisingly, there are many defining characteristics that could influence regulatory design for a particular environmental problem. These include: whether the source of pollution or environmental degradation is point-source or diffuse; whether there are large numbers of potential regulatees; whether these regulatees are large and highly visible, or small and relatively obscure; whether there is a tension between public and private interests; whether there is well organized industry representation; whether there are significant costs faced by the regulatees; whether there are pre-existing regulations in place; whether the environmental problem is multifaceted; and the prevailing political or regulatory culture.[18]

cope with that harm. Once these parameters have been established, an integrated plan that targets the respective contributors in the context of the region's overall environmental limitations and priorities is conceived and implemented. For example, a reduction in fossil fuel consumption of the transport sector is far more likely to be achieved through an integrated transport policy which recognizes the synergies and trade-offs between different modes of transport than a policy approach with treats each mode in an *ad hoc* and compartmentalized fashion. This, it may be argued, is putting the principles of ecological sustainable development into practice. In focussing on how regulation can be best designed to achieve pre-determined environmental goals, we do not underestimate the importance of how environmental goals are established. We consider that optimal policy design and the pursuit of integrated environmental goals are not mutually exclusive. That is, having better, more integrated environmental goals does not remove the need for good regulatory design and vice versa. Consequently, even if a greater emphasis is placed on environmental goal setting, improving regulaory design will remain an important and worthwhile exercise in itself.

Policymakers should, however, be wary of an overly reductionist approach to designing policy mixes. That is, although some environmental goals will necessarily be compartmentalized into smaller, more manageable discrete policy units, it is desirable to achieve the highest level of commonality of such policy units practicable. This is because the greater the level of commonality, the greater the opportunity to build in synergistic instrument and institutional combinations.

[17] For another analysis see 'Assessing Regulatory Alternatives', Treasury Board of Canada Secretariat, (1994) Ottawa. In particular, questions 4 (what are the behaviours that are creating or contributing to the problem?), 5 (who are the key players?), 6 (what is their behavioural profile?) and 7 (what external factors are influencing the behaviours?).

[18] The Sustainable Industries Division of the United States EPA has adopted a particular version of this approach under the guise of 'backward mapping': a process which,

Undertaking the task of identifying the particular characteristics of each individual environmental challenge, as it applies to a particular area or industry sector, makes apparent that, in almost all cases, policy design must be fundamentally shaped by these defining characteristics. For example, in addressing chemical industry pollution, there are large, highly visible players, vulnerable to public pressure from local communities and national environmental groups, both of whom have a strong interest in the industry's environmental performance. The sources of pollution are readily identifiable, easily monitored and regulated, and there is considerable potential for supply side pressure exerted by large manufacturers on their smaller buyers and suppliers.

In contrast, in confronting agricultural run-off, there are many geographically isolated small rural producers, whose activities are not easily monitored or policed. There is considerable cultural resistance to regulation amongst those producers, who form a significant political lobby. While environmental NGOs have relatively little influence, there may be very considerable potential to enlist the support of commercial third party suppliers as surrogate regulators. As we saw in chapters four and five, the range of instruments and strategies that has been, and is likely to be, valuable in regulating the two groups, is very different.

Process 3. Identify the range of potential regulatory participants and policy instruments

In chapter three, we argued that policymakers have often artificially limited the range of participants in the regulatory process to that of government regulator and industry regulatee. On the contrary, as we pointed out, there is, in fact, a much greater choice of potential participants, including a wide range of commercial and non-commercial third parties.[19] Given the context specific nature of most environmental issues, the ability to recruit various parties will inevitably vary. An important step in the regulatory design process, therefore, is to identify which parties have the capacity/potential to contribute to regulatory

---

in essence, refers to a comprehensive identification of the drivers and barriers that determine environmental performance, and as a consequence, the key decision making leverage points within firms. That is, at the outset of policy design in respect of any given industry sector, an attempt is made to learn about the relevant characteristics of the selected industry, including current economic and technological trends, demographics, and prevailing organizational culture—all traits that may promote or hinder environmental improvements. Backward mapping is also intended to engage affected parties in seeking to define policy parameters and potential solutions.

[19] See further, p.93 below.

policy in a particular environmental circumstance. This exercise has the benefit of not only formally discounting options which are not viable, but more importantly, *of ensuring that the full range of options has been considered*. It would also be judicious at this point to assess (at least in a preliminary fashion) the preparedness and/or willingness of these parties to fulfil any possible regulatory role.

The presence or absence of particular parties will necessarily dictate, from the full suite of instruments we outlined in chapter two, those which might be used in a particular environmental circumstance. For example, the use of insurers as quasi-regulators is not an option if the insurance industry has either no capacity or no incentive to intervene in the circumstances of the case. Similarly, there would be little point in contemplating the application of commercial pressure by 'green' consumers, if it were discovered that the public had no reliable way of distinguishing an environmentally preferred product from other less desirable examples. The object of this exercise is not to determine the parties and instruments that should form the basis of a preferred policy mix, merely to establish at the outset the range of available options that might make up that mix. In essence, this will be a mechanistic process, with policymakers, to the extent possible, deferring qualitative judgments. This does not exclude, however, determining the relative size of potential contributions.

A useful example of this process can be drawn from chapter five, where we examined the protection of remnant vegetation on the private property of farmers. Here, the range of parties which might credibly and constructively be involved are: (i) industry, in the form of individual farmers; (ii) government agencies, in the form of resource and environmental departments; and (iii) non-commercial third parties, in the form of NGOs and community groups.[20] In contrast, commercial third parties, such as banks and insurers, have little direct input into the protection of remnant vegetation, and may indeed prefer its removal in the interest of short-term profitability. It would take a very substantial shift in incentives and perceptions to turn this around, ren-

---

[20] Non-commercial third parties may have a variety of roles. Community groups are in position to engage in voluntary activities, along with NGOs, whilst the latter may also take legal action through third party standing provisions. They both could have a role, along with government, in the provision of education and information. Farmers themselves can distribute information and expertise through peer group networking (this can be formalized through mechanisms such as the Land Care Program in Australia).

dering the use of commercial third parties impractical at this time.[21] Similarly, it is difficult to imagine supply chain pressure being exercised through retailers or 'green' consumers when there is no tangible relationship between the quality or properties of farm produce and the protection of remnant vegetation.

Having established the range of potential parties relevant to the issue of remnant vegetation, the next step is to identify the applicability (not preferability) of particular policy instruments that those parties might employ. For example, in the case of possible government roles, a short list can be compiled with relative ease. Government agencies have at their disposal command and control instruments, including a range of planning controls. More radically, they can modify property rights (removing the unencumbered right of farmers to clear their land). They have the ability to offer positive incentives, principally in the form of subsidies, and may also remove any existing perverse incentives, such as tax concessions for land clearing, and generate information and disseminate it to industry groups and third parties. An additional option is the use of price-based incentives. In contrast, the lack of a 'community of shared fate'[22] means that self-regulation by farmers is unlikely to be a viable option.

Process 4. Identify opportunities for consultation and public participation

The broader benefits of consultation and public participation in regulatory policymaking have been more than fully articulated elsewhere and need only be summarized here. As the OECD has put it, such participation:

contribute[s] to regulatory quality by: (i) bringing into the discussion the expertise, perspectives and ideas for alternative actions of those directly affected; (ii) helping regulators to balance opposing interests; (iii) identifying unidentified effects and practical problems; (iv) providing a quality check on the administration's assessment of costs and benefits; (v) identifying interactions between regulations for various parts of government. Consultation processes can also enhance voluntary compliance, reducing reliance on enforcement and sanctions.[23]

---

[21] Limited exceptions would exist if farmer's liabilities for damages to wildlife were set out firmly in tort or regulatory laws, because then insurers and even banks might play a role under the umbrella of the liability scheme.

[22] See J. V. Rees, *Hostages of Each Other: The transformation of nuclear safety since Three Mile Island* (1994), University of Chicago Press, Chicago.

[23] OECD Recommendation of the Council of the OECD on Improving the Quality of Government Regulation OECD, Paris, 1995, p.18.

Put differently, public participation provides a watchdog role on the performance of industry and government regulators (addressed in design principle three below), an under-utilized source of expertise and advice, and a source of legitimacy for industry self-regulation. Such participation is normally essential to achieving early consensus and agreement on objectives and outcomes. In the United States in particular, a number of recent initiatives have sought participation, consensus, or a partnership approach to environmental policymaking.[24]

Building in opportunities for participation and consultation is an important step for a variety of reasons. First, it is a means of ensuring that equity considerations are not lost in the broader quest for effectiveness and efficiency. In this context, equity, as a minimum, might dictate that reforms 'must not result in a significant increase in risk to any exposed population or shift risks appreciably from one population to another'.[25] Secondly, it may result in decisions that are more effective, because policies are usually more easily implemented when people understand the reasons behind them. Thirdly, it will usually result in decisions that gain greater political acceptability (not least because solutions may not appear legitimate to those affected by them unless those groups have been involved in the decision-making process itself).

It is doubtful however, whether greater public participation will enhance efficiency. On the contrary, it is likely to result in delays, and, commonly, consumes very considerable resources on the part of all those involved.[26] But this must be balanced against the advantages identified above and, in particular, the likelihood that where affected parties play a meaningful role in setting goals, defining priorities, and crafting policies, the outcomes are likely to be both more administratively workable and politically acceptable.[27]

As we saw in chapter four through the example of the chemical industry, government has a central role to play in activating the process of public participation. It can do this by means such as: (i) providing community groups or individuals with greater information; and by (ii)

---

[24] These include the Pollution Prevention Pilot Project, the EPA's Common Sense Initiative, and Project XL.

[25] *The Alternative Path: A Cleaner Cheaper Way to Protect and Enhance the Environment*, Aspen Institute, 1996, Washington DC.

[26] See, for example, Blueprint for Environmental Partnerships, Environmental and Natural Resources Law Program, Stanford University, USA, (publication due 1998).

[27] B. Crabtree, 'A viable framework for stewardship' *Perspectives*: Vol. 9 No. 3 (1995) World Business Academy, citing successful Dutch and New Zealand experiments which incorporate these elements.

actively engaging community groups in the policymaking process, at least in the early stages of regulatory design.

The application of all the processes identified in this section are essentially mechanistic prerequisites to the more complex and evaluative task of selecting from the range of available options to design successful policy combinations. It is to this more challenging task of establishing regulatory design principles that we now turn.

Regulatory design principles

In this section, we identify the core principles which should underpin regulatory design. Although these do not purport to prescribe specific solutions to specific environmental threats, our principles provide the guidelines and roadmaps which will enable policymakers to arrive at those solutions. The five principles described below are intended to be addressed sequentially.

We begin by arguing the virtues of using combinations of instruments, while for resources and other reasons, avoiding an unnecessary proliferation of such combinations. Secondly, we emphasize that, in choosing those combinations, there are compelling reasons of efficiency, effectiveness, and political acceptability for preferring the least interventionist combinations that will work. Thirdly, recognizing that it is not always apparent in the abstract whether a particular measure will work or not, we argue the virtues of an escalating response up an instrument pyramid in order both to achieve more responsive regulation and to achieve greater dependability of outcomes. Fourthly, we suggest the benefits of invoking a broader range of parties (most notably business and commercial and non-commercial third parties) as surrogate regulators, both because they will often be more effective than governments and because they enable government resources to be redeployed in areas where they could be better used. Finally, we demonstrate ways in which it is possible to redesign regulation to achieve win-win outcomes and to move the goalposts in such a way as to broaden the range in which such outcomes are achievable.

Principle 1. Prefer policy mixes incorporating a broader range of instruments and institutions

There are very few circumstances where a single instrument is likely to be the most efficient or effective means of addressing a particular environmental problem.[28] Certainly, such circumstances exist. For example, a ban on the manufacture of certain highly toxic substances may be a highly effective way of preventing their use, without the need to invoke additional instruments to achieve this effect.[29] Similarly, many economists would argue that a central virtue of replacing 'the tragedy of the commons' with clearly defined property rights is that the new owners are provided with appropriate incentives for responsible land management *without need for external and continuing* government intervention.[30]

However, in the very large majority of circumstances, we have demonstrated in previous chapters that individual instruments have both strengths and weaknesses and that none are sufficiently flexible and resilient to be able to successfully address all environmental problems in all contexts.[31] For example, command and control regulation has the virtues of high dependability and predicability (if adequately enforced), but commonly proves to be inflexible and inefficient. In contrast, economic instruments tend to be efficient but, in most cases, not dependable. Information-based strategies, voluntarism and self-regulation have the virtues of being non-coercive, unintrusive, and (in most cases) cost-effective, but also have low reliability when used in isolation. They are also less likely to be successful, the greater the gap between the public and private interest.

Our general conclusion is that the best means of overcoming the deficiencies of individual instruments, while taking advantage of their strengths, is through the design of combinations of instruments (and, as we will see below, also involving a wider range of institutional actors). However, as we have argued earlier, it is important not just to explore a broader range of regulatory and policy instruments, but to consider *systematically* the benefits of their mutual application. In particular, in the large majority of circumstances, it is crucial not only to go beyond 'single instrument' or 'single strategy' approaches[32] but to design a *complementary* mix of instruments tailored to specific policy goals. We elaborate on this latter issue in the later section on the design of instrument combinations.

---

[28] See chapter two.

[29] However, even here it might be argued that the ban will be more effective if it is accompanied by an information campaign to inform manufacturers of their obligations.

[30] See chapter two.   [31] See chapters two, four and five.

[32] T. Swanson, 'Book Reviews: J. B. Opschoor & R. K. Turner (eds.) *Economic Incentives and Environmental Policies: Principles and Practice* (1994)' (1995) 4(1) *Review of European Community and Environmental Law (RECIEL)* 85.

Similar arguments for regulatory pluralism apply with regard to institutions. We argued in chapter three that regulation has, in most jurisdictions, been artificially restricted to government and industry, and that this reinforces outmoded notions of government as an omnipotent source of regulatory authority. A greater range of institutional actors, including commercial third parties, such as banks, insurers, consumers, suppliers and environmental consultants, and non-commercial third parties, can assist in taking the weight off government intervention. We saw in chapter five, for example, the great potential to harness market forces as surrogate regulators of the use of agricultural chemicals. Thus government can redirect is limited resources to those companies which are genuinely recalcitrant, and increasingly assume the mantle of facilitator and broker of third party participation in the regulatory process. The additional benefits of broadening the regulatory net to include third parties are that a multiplicity of regulatory signals have the potential to be mutually reinforcing, and that, in many cases, surrogate regulators are far more exacting than direct government intervention.

If one accepts this general approach of using combinations of instruments and institutions, then there may be a temptation to succumb to a 'kitchen sink' approach to policy design,[33] throwing in every conceivable policy instrument and institution on the assumption that the severity of the environmental problems we confront, and their likely consequences for humankind, are such as to justify almost any level of resource input. However this approach, which we have described as 'smorgasbordism', is likely to be seriously sub-optimal for a variety of reasons.

First, there are practical limits to the capacity of industry to comply with a large range of regulatory and quasi-regulatory requirements. Regulatory overload is now a well recognized phenomenon.[34] There comes a point where further imposition of regulation may be counterproductive. The sheer weight of regulation may make it difficult for an enterprise even to identify all its regulatory obligations, and this in itself may inhibit compliance. Moreover, the administrative demands on industry of a multiplicity of different regulatory instruments may become so heavy as to impose substantial additional costs on the individual firm. This, in turn, may prompt a political backlash

---

[33] R. Hahn, 'Towards a New Environmental Paradigm' (1993) 102 *Yale Law Journal* 1719.

[34] D. Osborne & E. Gaebler, *Reinventing Government* (1992), Addison Wesley, Reading, MA.

from industry that results in substantial deregulation and the removal of good regulation as well as bad. Therefore, it is better to select those combinations that are likely to achieve the greatest return, the 'biggest bang for the regulatory buck', rather than to impose such a multiplicity of different regulations as may prove both economically and politically counterproductive. The additional design principles described below assist us in deciding how much regulation is appropriate to deal with a particular problem.

Secondly, the imposition on the public purse and the demand on public resources, from smorgasbordism, would also be excessive. There are both practical and political reasons why governments limit their degree of intervention in the affairs of business. The introduction of a substantial array of new instruments would, inevitably, impose an administrative and resource burden upon regulatory agencies which they are increasingly ill-equipped to discharge. Smarter regulation, as governments increasingly recognize, does not necessarily mean more regulation.[35]

There is a third and compelling reason to avoid smorgasbordism when designing policy mixes. This is that not all combinations of instruments or institutions are likely to be complementary. On the contrary, as we demonstrate later in this chapter, a considerable number of combinations are either inherently, or in particular contexts, counterproductive, duplicative, or at the very least, sub-optimal. This can occur as a result of poor design at the policy level or through political misfortune.[36] Given these pitfalls, it is critically important to establish principles which enable the design of combinations that are complementary.

The following design principles, therefore, examine in some detail: how to develop more sophisticated, complementary mixes of policy instruments; how to engage a much wider group of parties in the regulatory process; where it is necessary to escalate up to higher levels of

---

[35] D. Osborne & E. Gaebler, *Reinventing Government* (1992), Addison Wesley, Reading, MA.

[36] Braithwaite gives an example of the latter: '[suppose] there are two coherent policy packages on offer: ABCD and WXYZ ('Responsive Regulation in Australia' in P. Grabosky & J. Braithwaite *Business Regulation and Australia's Future* (1993) Australian Institute of Criminology, Canberra, p.92). One constituency lobbies for the first because it likes features A and B of this package. Another constituency lobbies for the second because it likes Y and Z. The politicians then try to give everyone what they want by opting for a policy package ABYZ. Unlike the original two policy packages, ABYZ turns out to be totally incoherent. For example A and Z are mutually contradictory: the purpose of A is defeated when it is put together with Z'.

coerciveness and intrusiveness; and how to design for certainty whilst maximizing the potential for economically beneficial outcomes. These tasks are challenging ones, to which far too little attention has been given in the regulatory and policy literature.

Principle 2. Prefer less interventionist measures

First, it is important to define what we mean by 'intervention', a term which has two principal components: *prescription* and *coercion*. Prescription refers to the extent to which external parties determine the level, type and method of environmental improvement. Coercion, on the other hand, refers to the extent to which external parties or instruments place negative pressure on a firm to improve its performance. By way of example, it may argued that industry self-regulation is higher in terms of its prescriptiveness than its coercion. That is, firms may be required to address specific issues and adopt certain behaviours, as prescribed under codes of practice, but there is little by way of external enforcement to ensure that their obligations are met.

In contrast, some economic instruments, such as taxes and charges, are high on coercion and low on prescription. That is, coercion is exercised through a price signal, which firms by and large cannot avoid. How they respond to that price signal, however, is independent of outside influence—they may choose to pay the higher tax or change their behaviour so as to limit its impact. If they choose the latter, then they also have total control over the type of remediation implemented. Ranking instrument categories according to the level of intervention therefore requires a balancing or assessment of the respective contributions of the two constituent components, prescription and coercion.[37]

[37] Even within the seemingly highly interventionist category of adversarial command and control, it is possible to make distinctions. For example, there are two alternative command and control approaches to limiting automobile emissions. First, most developed countries mandate that vehicle manufacturers fit catalytic converters to their automobiles (which remove air pollutants such as nitrous oxide and carbon monoxide). This is a highly interventionist technology based standard: it is both coercive, i.e., enforced by law, and prescriptive, i.e., the technological solution is pre-determined. Secondly, a number of countries have instituted clean air policies for automobiles. Here, the law requires manufacturers to only sell automobiles which emit low levels of pollutants. In the case of California, a certain percentage of sales must be devoted to automobiles with very low levels of polluting emissions. These two policy strategies provide an interesting contrast: they are both command and control, and they both are highly coercive. Where they differ is in the level of prescriptiveness. The second approach (based on performance standards) is low on prescription—there is no restriction on the way in which manufacturers comply. It may be argued, then, that this is less interventionist overall than the technology based standard.

There are a variety of reasons why, all else being equal, less interventionist approaches should be preferred to more interventionist ones. Most of these can be understood in terms of the evaluation criteria we referred to earlier. Specifically, highly interventionist measures rate badly in terms of at least three of those criteria: efficiency; effectiveness; and political acceptability.[38]

In terms of *efficiency*, highly coercive instruments usually require substantial administrative resources in terms of monitoring and policing, without which they are likely to be ineffective. Highly prescriptive instruments lack flexibility and do not facilitate least cost solutions. Traditional command and control regulation has both of these characteristics, and many of the most severe criticisms of this approach, identified in chapter two, are a consequence of this.

Highly interventionist strategies may also result in the unnecessary deployment of resources to policing those who would be quite willing to comply voluntarily under less interventionist options. Regulated enterprises may, similarly, be forced to spend large amounts of money satisfying highly prescriptive requirements which do not provide the least cost solution to the environmental problem at hand. Good environmental performers, in particular, may suffer under highly interventionist approaches, which may inhibit them from going beyond compliance with regulation. For all these reasons, highly interventionist approaches are generally less efficient than viable alternatives.

High intervention is also unlikely to be as *effective* as alternative approaches, essentially because conscripts generally respond less favourably than volunteers. Regulatees are much more receptive to positive economic incentives, such as subsidies and tax credits, than to negative ones such as taxes and charges. Indeed, measures which are highly coercive can be counterproductive. In particular, they may cause resentment and resistance from those who regard them as an unjustifiable and intrusive intervention in their affairs, rather than the constructive resolution of environmental problems. In respect of command and control, in particular, much depends upon the response of the relevant regulatory agency. For example, adversarial legalism of the kind that characterizes many American enforcement agencies may spawn a culture of regulatory resistance.[39] The result may be the consumption

---

[38] See chapter 1, p.25.
[39] R. Kagan, 'Regulatory Enforcement' in D. Rosenbloom & R. Schwartz (eds), *Handbook of Regulation and Administrative Law* (1994), Dekker, New York.

of large amounts of regulatory (and enterprise) resources in wholly unproductive administrative and legal challenges.[40]

Unsurprisingly, high intervention also tends to score very badly in terms of *political acceptability*. This is particularly the case in sectors such as agriculture, with a history and culture of independence from, and a strong resentment of, government regulatory intervention. We saw, in chapter five, the considerable resistance which taxes and clearing controls can produce in the agricultural sector, and it is extremely difficult to monitor and enforce direct regulation, given the low visibility of the behaviour and the spatial distribution of agricultural production. For these reasons, and because of the powerful lobbying power of agricultural producers, policymakers have sought to avoid highly interventionist measures and, until recently, routinely preferred the provision of information and persuasion to direct intervention.

In contrast to the problems of high interventionism, described above, low interventionist options, to the extent that they are viable, have the considerable advantages of providing greater flexibility to enterprises in their response, greater ownership of solutions which they are directly involved in creating, less resistance, greater legitimacy, greater speed of decision-making, sensitivity to market circumstances, and lower costs.[41] There is considerable evidence that a policy instrument is more likely to produce both compliance and a positive attitude change if it is perceived as non-coercive.[42] It is 'far better if the public values of a regulatory system are internalised as the private values of firm managers— that they act in accordance with [low intervention] because it is the "right thing to do" '.[43] From a regulator's perspective, a focus on less interventionist approaches also has the attraction of freeing up scarce regulatory resources which may be redeployed against those who are unwilling or unable to respond to such measures and against whom

---

[40] E. Bardach & R. Kagan, *Going by the Book: the problem of regulatory unreasonableness* (1982), Temple University Press, Philadelphia.

[41] See, generally, J. A. Sigler & J. E. Murphy, *Interactive Corporate Compliance: An alternative to regulatory compulsion* (1989), Quorum Books, New York.

[42] W. K. Muir, 'Under what circumstances can law bring about attitude change?' in J. B. Grossman & M. H. Grossman (eds.) *Law and Change in Modern America* (1967), Goodyear Publishing, Pacific Palisades, California.

[43] D. Cohen, 'Voluntary Codes: The Role of the Canadian State in a Privatised Regulatory Environment', a draft paper presented at the Voluntary Codes Symposium, Office of Consumer Affairs, Industry Canada and Regulatory Affairs, Treasury Board, Ottawa, (1996) September and to be included in *Exploring Voluntary Codes in the Marketplace*, edited by D. Cohen & K. Webb, Government of Canada, Ottawa, (publication due 1998), p19.

there is no viable alternative to the deployment of highly intrusive instruments.

Implicit in this principle of 'starting with the least interventionist policy measure' is the assumption that the measure *actually works*. That is, the instrument must be capable of delivering the identified environmental outcomes.[44] In some cases, this will mean that 'what works' requires a relatively high level of intervention, but even in such cases it should still be possible to apply the principle of least intervention. Thus, the principle does not imply our endorsement, for example, of self-regulation or free-market solutions *per se*. Indeed, as one of us has argued elsewhere, both these mechanisms have serious shortcomings and are only likely to be viable in a very limited number of contexts.[45] However, to the extent that, and in the circumstances which they are viable, the principle implies we should prefer them to more interventionist alternatives.

Applying the principle of low interventionism

Having established the reasons why policymakers should prefer less interventionist policy mixes, we now turn our attention to how this might be achieved in practice. Broadly speaking, policy instruments can be located on a continuum from the least to the most interventionist. For example, the paradigm case of the latter is command and control regulation in the American mould: highly prescriptive and enforced coercively. At the other extreme, are instruments such as pure voluntarism, education, and some information based approaches. In between (in escalating degrees of intervention), lie mechanisms such as free market environmentalism, self-regulation and economic instruments.[46]

This, however, is a very broad brush approach. In practice, it is often necessary to examine individual instruments rather than merely instrument categories because the level of intervention can vary quite dramatically within each category. For example, changes to property rights are relatively non-interventionist when rights are bestowed on private parties over resources which were previously part of the commons, but

[44] For example, as we indicated in chapter 2, tradeable permits are only likely to be effective when they can be readily monitored and verified, and there are good trading prospects.

[45] N. Gunningham & J. Rees, 'Industry Self-Regulation' (1997) 19(4) *Law and Policy* (publication of 1997 issue delayed).

[46] Of course, it is easier to weigh the relative merits of different instruments categories at the extremes of the interventionism continuum than those located close together in the middle.

highly interventionist when property rights which previously existed are withdrawn (as when farmers are denied rights to clear remnant vege- tation). Similarly, not all information-based instruments can be located close to the non-interventionist pole of the continuum. On the contrary, the United States EPA's Toxic Release Inventory (which comes under the umbrella of community right to know) is quite coercive in requir- ing companies to estimate emissions and disclose this information. That is, there is a higher level of coerciveness associated with a specific mea- sure located within a wider category that is generally perceived to involve low interventionism. The level of intervention may also vary greatly in terms of how a given instrument is used. For example, enforcement of environmental regulation in the United Kingdom is much less coercive than it is in the United States.[47]

Secondly, in applying the principle of least intervention, policy- makers should bear in mind the capacity to raise the level of interven- tion, if and when required, with various instruments and/or instrument combinations. That is, it is not necessarily a matter of choosing one instrument in preference to another in a static sense, but rather that of invoking a temporal sequence of instruments, as described in the next principle below. Alternatively, firms may be segregated into different streams of regulatory intervention; for example, as we argued in the case of the chemical industry, one might introduce a 'green track' of low intervention regulation for leading edge environmental performers, while retaining a more conventionally interventionist regulatory track for those firms which are merely complying with minimum standards or are recalcitrant.[48]

Principle 3. Ascend a dynamic instrument pyramid to the extent necessary to achieve policy goals

We asserted, in the previous principle, that preference should be given to the least interventionist measure(s) that will work. However, it is not always apparent to policy designers whether a particular measure they contemplate using will work or not, principally for two reasons. First, a given instrument may be effective in influencing the behaviour of some, but not of others (suggesting the need for regulation to be responsive to the different behaviour of different regulatees). Secondly, a particular instrument which, prior to its introduction, seemed likely to be viable

---

[47] D. Vogel, *National Styles of Regulation: Environmental Policy in Great Britain and the United States* (1986), Cornell University Press, New York.
[48] Chapter four at p.137.

in its entirety, may, in the light of practical experience, prove not to be so (suggesting the need for instrument sequencing to increase dependability). The strategies required to address both these concerns invoke a broader mix of instruments and harness a wider range of parties than traditional regulatory design.

Building in regulatory responsiveness

A window into the first problem is provided by John Braithwaite, whose enforcement pyramid (described more fully in chapter four and set out at Figure 1 below) conceives of responsive regulation essentially in terms of dialogic regulatory culture in which regulators signal to industry their commitment to escalate their enforcement response whenever lower levels of intervention fail.[49] Under Braithwaite's model, regulators begin by assuming virtue (to which they should respond by offering co-operation) but when their expectations are disappointed, they respond with progressively punitive and deterrent oriented strategies until the regulatee conforms.

Central to Braithwaite's model are the need for: (i) gradual escalation up the face of the pyramid; and (ii) the existence of a credible peak or tip which, if activated, will be sufficiently powerful to deter even the most egregious offender. The former (rather than any abrupt shift from low to high interventionism) is desirable because it facilitates the 'tit for tat' response on the part of regulators which forms the basis for responsive regulation.[50] The latter is important not only because of its deterrent value, but also because it ensures a level playing field in that the virtuous are not disadvantaged. As one regulator put it: 'you're an idiot to [comply] if nobody else does, so to be credible, regulators have to be seen to be effective in punishing cowboys'.[51]

---

[49] I. Ayres & J. Braithwaite, *Responsive Regulation* (1992), Oxford University Press, UK.

[50] Under this strategy, the regulatory agency approaches each firm in a co-operative, flexible manner, but turns to punishment if and when the firm clearly defects from co-operation. Once the firm begins to co-operate again, the agency does so too. It should be noted that the enforcement pyramid is based on a repeat player prisoner's dilemma, under which the regulator's response (up or down the pyramid) depends upon the previous response of the regulatee.

[51] Enforcement at the peak of the pyramid also serves to focus the minds of corporate decisionmakers, in a manner which, given bounded rationality, is otherwise unlikely. For example, in Australia, it was the imprisonment of one egregious offender for environmental crime, rather than the mere existence of environmental regulation, which caused a rush to develop environmental audits and other means of establishing a due diligence defence. As one senior regulator put it: 'its a mind set, not at plant level but at board level—the culture isn't there, and without the leverage of legislation, it won't get done'.

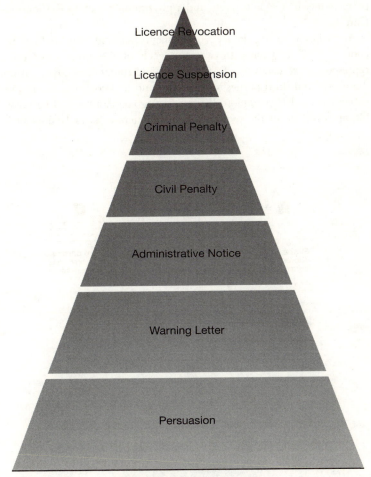

Figure 1 Enforcement pyramid.

For present purposes, it is possible to reconceptualize and extend the scope of the pyramid. The Braithwaite pyramid is concerned with the behaviour of, and interaction between, only two parties: state and business, with only the former acting as regulator and enforcer, and the latter solely in the role of regulatee. Yet it will apparent from what we said in previous chapters that there is also very considerable scope for third parties, both commercial and non-commercial, to act as quasi regulators. Similarly, second parties, (specifically business) may themselves perform a (self) regulatory role under programmes such as Responsible Care.

Accordingly, a regulatory enforcement pyramid can usefully be conceived of as having three faces: each of the three faces each representing respectively: first parties (government); second parties (business); and third parties (commercial and non-commercial). In our expanded model, escalation (i.e., increasing coercion) would be possible up any face of the pyramid, and not merely (as in Braithwaite's

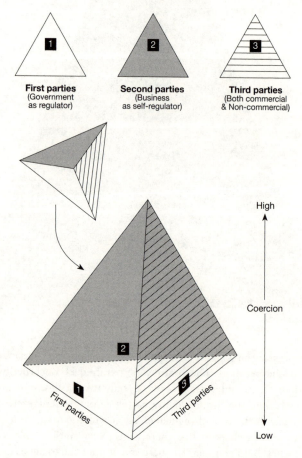

Figure 2 Regulatory pyramid—expanded model

model) in terms of government action.[52] That is, escalation would also be possible up the second face (through self-regulation), or up the third face (through a variety of actions by commercial or non-commercial third parties or both).[53]

To give a concrete example of escalation up the third face, the developing Forest Stewardship Council (FSC) is a global environmental standards setting system for forest products.[54] The FSC will both establish standards that can be used to certify forestry products as sustainably managed and will 'certify the certifiers'. Once operational, it will rely for its 'clout' on changing consumer demand and upon creating strong 'buyers groups' and other mechanisms for institutionalizing 'green' consumer demand.[55] That is, its success will depend very largely on influencing consumer demand. While government involvement, for example through formal endorsement or though government procurement policies which supported the FSC, would be valuable, the scheme is essentially a free standing one: from base to peak (consumer sanctions and boycotts) the scheme is entirely third party based. In this way, a 'new institutional system for global environmental standard setting'[56] will come about, entirely independent of government.

In summary, the Braithwaite pyramid enforcement responses are based on state regulation, rather than with how best to employ a range of instruments *and parties*. In contrast, our pyramid conceives of the

[52] Although, in his broader writing, he recognizes the important contributions of self-regulation and tripartism involving NGOs (see I. Ayres & J. Braithwaite, *Responsive Regulation: Transcending the regulation-deregulation debate* (1992), Oxford University Press, UK).

[53] Our conception of the three dimensional pyramid was first mooted in N. Gunningham 'Codes of Practice: The Australian Experience', a draft paper presented to the *Voluntary Codes Symposium*, Office of Consumer Affairs, Industry Canada and Regulatory Affairs, Treasury Board, Ottawa, September 1996 and is to be included in *Exploring Voluntary Codes in the Marketplace*, D. Cohen & K. Webb (eds.), Government of Canada, Ottawa, p.1: and in N. Gunningham & J. Rees 'Industry Self-Regulation' (1997) 19(4) *Law and Policy* (publication of 1997 issue delayed).

[54] The FSC is largely generated by the World Wide Fund for Nature (WWF). It is based on a coalition for environmental groups, timber traders, indigenous peoples groups, foresters and community forestry groups.

[55] Very little has been written on the FSC. We are indebted for this account to E. Meidinger, 'Look Who's Making the Rules: The roles of the Forest Stewardship Council and International Standards Organisation in Environmental Policy Making' (1996), a paper presented to Colloquium on Emerging Environmental Policy: Winners and Losers, Oregon State University, Corvellis, Oregon, September 23.

[56] E. Meidinger, 'Look Who's Making the Rules: The roles of the Forest Stewardship Council and International Standards Organisation in Environmental Policy Making' (1996), a paper presented to Colloquium on Emerging Environmental Policy: Winners and Losers, Oregon State University, Corvellis, Oregon, September 23.

possibility of regulation using a number of different instruments implemented by a number of parties (or faces of the pyramid). It conceives of escalation to higher levels of coerciveness not only within a single instrument, but also across several different instruments. That is, our model of three dimensional regulation holds out the possibility of escalating degrees of coercion through the interaction of different but complementary instruments and parties. Thus, one might begin with a less intrusive instrument such as business initiated voluntarism or education (i.e., using second parties), but then recruit another instrument if the first exhausts its responsive potential (e.g., third party audit or government mandated community right to know), and end up (where all else fails) with highly coercive instruments, such as government enforcement of command and control regulation or third party foreclosure of a loan. Ideally, one would use a combination of instruments in sequence to achieve a co-ordinated and gradual escalation up one or more faces of the pyramid from base to peak. Only if the different levels of the pyramid are connected in such a way as to enable a strategic escalation to the top where less coercive measures fail, will this approach work effectively.[57]

A graphic illustration of exactly how this can indeed occur is provided by Joe Rees' analysis of the highly sophisticated self-regulatory programme of the INPO, which, post Three Mile Island, is probably amongst the most impressive and effective such schemes worldwide.[58] However, even INPO is incapable of working effectively in isolation. There are, inevitably, industry laggards, who do not respond to education, persuasion, peer group pressure, gradual nagging from INPO, shaming, or the other instruments of informal social control at its disposal.

After some years of achieving very little progress in changing the behaviour of this minority, INPO faced a dilemma: 'a significant number of plants were ignoring the problems INPO had identified, yet get-

---

[57] Of course, it is conceivable, as we indicate in principle four below, that spontaneous orderings may arise without government purview, though these are likely to be a minority of cases.

[58] See J. V. Rees, *Hostages of Each Other: The transformation of nuclear safety since Three Mile Island* (1994), University of Chicago Press, Chicago, US. Collective action problems were minimized because most of the limited number of nuclear power operators clearly recognized that there is a 'community of fate' (one nuclear accident involving any facility will likely destroy the viability of the entire industry) and, for reasons of self-interest, have willingly acquiesced in a self-regulatory structure capable of delivering 'mutual assurance'.

ting tough seemed out of the question because that might drive the recalcitrants out of the association'.[59] INPO's ultimate response, after five years of frustration, was to turn to the government regulator, the Nuclear Regulatory Commission (NRC).[60] The result was the effective dismissal of top executives, plant shutdown, and substantial improvements in safety. All this was achieved only by invoking the power of the NRC (which alone had the capacity to bring criminal proceedings and to shut the plant down). Had effective action not been taken against the recalcitrant few, and in the longer term, had free riders been allowed to flourish without sanction, then INPO's authority over other firms would have been jeopardized. That is, the effective functioning of the lower levels of the pyramid may depend substantially upon invoking the peak, which in this case, only government could do. As Rees puts it: 'INPO's climb to power has been accomplished on the shoulders of the NRC'.[61]

This case also shows the importance of integration between the different levels of the pyramid. The NRC did not just happen to stumble across, or threaten action against recalcitrants, rather there was considerable communication between INPO and the NRC which facilitated what was, in effect, a tiered response of education and information, escalating through peer group pressure and a series of increasingly threatening letters, ultimately to the threat of criminal penalties and incapacitation, the latter being penalties government alone could impose, but the former being approaches which, in these circumstances at least, INPO itself was in the best position to pursue. Thus, even in the case of one of the most successful schemes of self regulation ever documented, it was the presence of the regulatory gorilla in the closet, that secured its ultimate success.

Another example of integrated escalation up an instrument pyramid is the two track regulatory system we proposed in chapter four. Here, the essential idea is not to respond to individual enterprises by being

---

[59] N. Gunningham & J. Rees, 'Industry Self-regulation' (1997) 19(4) *Law and Policy* (publication of 1997 issue delayed).

[60] For example, Rees describes how, in one case, INPO sent a letter to the CEO of one company (twelve pages plus seventeen attachments) documenting its persistent failure to address a number of very serious safety concerns, and insisting that the CEO pass a copy of the letter to his own board and the NRC (J. V. Rees, *Hostages of Each Other: The transformation of nuclear safety since Three Mile Island* (1994), University of Chicago Press, Chicago).

[61] J. V. Rees, *Hostages of Each Other: The transformation of nuclear safety since Three Mile Island* (1994), University of Chicago Press, Chicago.

more or less punitive, depending on their previous response (as under Braithwaite's model), but rather to offer different but standardized regulatory paths to those with different environmental credentials and motivations. The regulatory track offered to 'best practice' performers will be considerably more flexible and attractive than that offered to their more pedestrian rivals, and will use a combination of instruments: self-regulation utilizing environmental management systems; independent third party audit; community dialogue; oversight; and transparency. However, responsiveness is built in, in that a failure to live up to the commitments required of 'green track' performers will result in a demotion to 'conventional track' regulation, which is more restrictive, prescriptive, and coercive.

However, we do not wish to give the impression that a co-ordinated escalation up one or more sides of our instrument pyramid is practicable in all cases. On the contrary, controlled escalation is only possible where the instruments in question lend themselves to a graduated, responsive and interactive enforcement strategy and where regulators have access to credible instruments. The two instruments which are most amenable to such a strategy (because they are readily manipulated) are command and control and self-regulation. Thus, it is no coincidence that our first example of how to shift from one face of the pyramid to another as one ascends and of how to invoke the dynamic peak, was taken from precisely this instrument combination. However, there are other instruments which are at least partially amenable to such a response, the most obvious being insurance and banking.

A combination of government mandated information (a modestly interventionist strategy at the middle levels of the pyramid) in conjunction with third party pressure (at the higher levels of the pyramid) might also be a viable option. For example, government might require business to disclose various information about its levels of emissions under a Toxic Release Inventory,[62] leaving it to financial markets, insurers (commercial third parties), and environmental groups (non-commercial third parties) to use that information in a variety of ways to bring pressure on poor environmental performers.[63]

In contrast, in the case of certain other instruments, the capacity for

[62] See N. Gunningham & A. Cornwall, 'Legislating the Right to Know' (1994) 11 *Environmental and Planning Law Journal* 274–288 and chapter two above.

[63] J. T. Hamilton 'Pollution as News: Media and stockmarket reactions to the Capital Toxic Release Inventory Data' (1995) *Journal of Environmental Economics and Management* 98–103.

responsive regulation is lacking, either because an individual instrument is not designed to facilitate responsive regulation (i.e., its implementation is static rather than dynamic and cannot be tailored to ascend or descend depending on the behaviour of specific firms) or because there is no potential for co-ordinated interaction between instruments. For example, economic instruments have both these characteristics. In essence, either an economic instrument is in place and must be responded to, or it is not. An environmental tax (or the level of tax), for example, cannot be imposed depending upon whether or not an enterprise has responded positively to less intrusive instruments, but rather, is intended as a uniform price signal which will apply to all members of the target group equally, irrespective of their past behaviour. By the same token, there are significant limits to the extent to which broad based economic instruments, such as pollution taxes and tradeable emission permits, can be designed to interact in a co-ordinated and complementary fashion with other instruments,[64] except by means of temporal sequencing, as described below.

Another limitation, for those aspiring to a co-ordinated and gradual escalation of instruments and coerciveness, is the possibility that, in some circumstances, escalation may only be possible to the middle levels of the pyramid, with no alternative instrument or party having the capacity to deliver higher levels of coerciveness. Or a particular instrument or instrument combination may facilitate action at the bottom of the pyramid and at the top, but not in the middle levels, with the result that there is no capacity for gradual escalation. For example, lender liability gives banks and other financial institutions a considerable incentive to scrutinize the environmental credentials of their clients very closely before lending them money, and at this stage they may counsel a client towards improved environmental performance. However, subsequent to providing the loan, the only available sanction may be to foreclose, without credible intermediate options.[65] In any of

---

[64] Again, an environmental tax would be inconsistent with the use of certain other instruments, e.g., performance or specification standards. Rather than mandating a particular response, an environmental tax offers the target group a choice either to pay the tax (and stay dirty) or improve their environmental performance, to minimize it. It is not possible to escalate up from an environmental tax, to other more coercive instruments, for those who choose to stay dirty.

[65] Moreover, once the money has been lent, then the lender's control over the client, and its capacity to threaten further sanctions, is seriously limited by practical considerations. For example, early termination of the loan may threaten the financial viability of the borrower.

these circumstances, our proposed dynamic instrument pyramid still has some value but it will operate in a less than complete fashion.

In the substantial range of circumstances when co-ordinated escalation is not readily achievable, a critical role of government will be, so far as possible, to fill the gaps between the different levels of the pyramid. In doing so, it will seek to compensate for either the absence of suitable second or third party instruments, or for their static or limited nature, either through direct intervention or, preferably, by facilitating action or acting as a catalyst for effective second or third party action, as described in design principle five. In effect, a major role for government is thus to facilitate second and third parties climbing the pyramid.

Finally, there are two general circumstances where it is inappropriate to adopt an escalating response up the instrument or enforcement pyramid, irrespective of whether it is possible to achieve such a response. First, in situations which involve a serious risk of irreversible loss or catastrophic damage, then a graduated response is inappropriate because the risks are too high: the endangered species may have become extinct before the regulator has determined how high up the pyramid it is necessary to ascend in order to change the behaviour of the target group. In these circumstances, a horizontal rather than a vertical approach may be preferable: imposing a range of instruments, including an underpinning of regulation, simultaneously rather than sequentially.[66] Secondly, a graduated response is only appropriate where the parties have continuing interactions—it is these which makes it credible to begin with a low interventionist response and to escalate (in a tit for tat response) if this proves insufficient. In contrast, where there is only one chance to influence the behaviour in question (for example, because small businesses can only very rarely be inspected), then a more interventionist first response may be justified, particularly if the risk involved is a high one.

Instrument sequencing to increase dependability

In the event that an instrument (or instrument combination) that seems viable in its entirety[67] turns out not to be so, our proposed solution is to introduce instrument sequencing: enabling escalation from the pre-

---

[66] See chapter five above and N. Gunningham & M. D. Young, 'Towards Optimal Environmental Policy: The Case of Biodiversity Conservation' (1997) 24 *Ecology Law Quarterly* 243–298.

[67] As distinct from the first category, where the focus was on instruments which work against some regulatees but not against others.

ferred least interventionist option, if it fails, to increasingly more interventionist alternatives. For example, a particular industry sector may be allowed to conduct a voluntary self-regulation scheme *on the proviso* that if it fails to meet the agreed objectives, mandatory sanctions will be introduced. Similarly, drawing on the Braithwaite model, a single firm which is persistently recalcitrant may be exposed to a graduated escalation of policy responses. Such solutions are not only consistent with design principle three above, they also avoid a slide into smorgasbordism: rather than using all instruments and participants simultaneously, it is only when the least interventionist (viable) instrument(s) have demonstrably failed that one climbs up the pyramid and invokes a broader range of instruments and parties, and even then, only to the extent necessary to achieve the desired goal.

The precise nature of sequencing arrangements will be determined by the level of discretion that is associated with their implementation. That is, some sequencing arrangements will entail the automatic application of more interventionist measures if and when earlier measures fail, thus reducing the level of discretion, while others will require some further action by first, second, or third parties prior to their implementation, thus increasing the level of discretion. Minimizing the amount of discretion, once certain defined parameters have been breached, sends a powerful message to industry to deliver on less interventionist forms of regulation. Of course, this does not preclude lobbying by business, but this is less likely to succeed if government has already publicly committed itself to a specified course of action. The following scenarios illustrate how the level of, for example, government discretion can vary when addressing entire industry sectors.

• The United States Climate Action plan aims to reduce the level of greenhouse gas emissions. The plan is based on a series of low intervention voluntary agreements with industry. Implicit in the plan is a commitment to legislated targets if industry does not deliver on its promises. This provision contains a high level of discretion because the threat is: (i) implicit not explicit; (ii) undefined; and (iii) linked to a particular administration.

• The New Zealand government has made similar voluntary arrangements with industry to reduce greenhouse gas emissions. It has, however, implemented a sequencing provision with far less discretion. If industry fails to achieve pre-specified reduction targets, a carbon tax will be introduced. This provision contains far less discretion because (i) it is explicit; and (ii) it is defined. It is, however, still linked to a particular administration.

- The Australian response to phasing out the use of ozone depleting hydrochlorofluorocarbons (HCFCs) is similarly based on an industry wide voluntary self-regulation scheme. The sequencing provision, in this case, is in the form of a legislated tradeable quota scheme. If industry fails to meet pre-specified HCFC reduction targets, the tradeable quota scheme automatically comes into effect. This provision contains even less discretion than either of the previous two examples because (i) it is explicit; (ii) it is defined; and (iii) it is included in legislation, thus reducing opportunities for further political discretion. It would still be possible for a subsequent government to amend the relevant legislation. However, this is likely to require the expenditure of considerable political capital.

The particular circumstances of different environmental problems will dictate the extent and discretion of sequencing provisions. The greater the environmental threat, the tougher sequencing provisions should be. In the case of irreversible environmental threats, such as the loss of biodiversity, it may be that sequencing is inappropriate.

Triggers and buffer zones

Our proposed methods of sequencing are dependent on *triggers* to warn the authorities when less interventionist measures have failed. For example, under a scheme of self-regulation, the industry itself may invite government intervention.[68] Alternatively, government and industry may agree to defined performance benchmarks. A failure to comply with these benchmarks would automatically trigger tougher regulations (for example, HCFC self-regulation in Australia). Or it may be that public interest groups would be able to identify serious breaches which would warrant intervention from governments or other third parties, possibly insurers.

In order to increase the dependability of sequencing provisions, several possible triggers would be preferable, though precisely which ones are most appropriate will depend upon the particular context. In broad terms, appropriate triggers might include: random government inspections; independent auditors; mechanisms for industry association

---

[68] See the example of INPO, discussed above.

reporting (see the INPO example above); in-house whistle blowers; community oversight; and compulsory firm reporting.

In relying on triggers to invoke sequencing, it is important that the triggers pre-empt unacceptable levels of environmental harm. That is, there needs to be a *buffer zone* between the point at which a trigger is set off and the level of environmental harm that is being monitored. For example, with Australia's self-regulatory scheme to phase out the use of HCFCs, the level at which mandatory quotas kick-in is well below that which is required to meet our international commitments under the Montreal Protocol—creating an effective buffer zone. The greater the degree of effectiveness that is required for a particular environmental issue, the greater the size of the buffer zones. This is similar to the concept of 'precautionary regulation', where tougher regulation acts as a safety net if and when other policies fail. The regulation is enacted, but the expectation is that it will not be used.

Circuit breakers

Another strategy, related to that of sequencing, is the use of *circuit breakers*. A circuit breaker is an instrument which is introduced as a short-term measure (and ultimately withdrawn), its purpose being to pre-empt the anticipated failure of another instrument. Circuit breakers tend to be low intervention instruments introduced in anticipation that certain high intervention instruments, introduced in isolation, have a high chance of failure. For example, a ban on land clearing in South Australia was regarded as essential to halt widespread environmental degradation, but was also politically unacceptable and largely unenforceable in the absence of some complementary positive inducement. Compensation was introduced for those who were refused a permit to clear, in order to overcome both these problems and to facilitate the cultural change that was needed in the long term (i.e., from a belief that all landowners had an unencumbered right to clear, to a commitment to sustainable land use). Once this had been achieved (or at least that opposition to clearing bans had been largely overcome), the right to compensation was withdrawn.[69]

Circuit breakers are similar to sequencing in that there is an ordering of policy responses, beginning with less interventionist and then moving up to more intrusive regulations. The difference is that, with sequencing, escalation up the enforcement pyramid occurs only when

[69] See N. Gunningham & M. D. Young, 'Towards Optimal Environmental Policy: The Case of Biodiversity Conservation' (1997) 24 *Ecology Law Quarterly* 243–298.

lower policies fail, whereas, with circuit breakers, there is an expectation that they are only a short-term measure, eventually to be replaced by other more conventional policy responses. It is important to recognize that the use of circuit breakers is a direct violation of the polluter pays and/or user pays principles (it may, nevertheless, be consistent with the precautionary principle). In some circumstances, however, this pragmatic approach may be necessary to achieve real progress in areas where regulatory resistance is high and external monitoring is difficult.

Principle 4. Empower participants which are in the best position to act as surrogate regulators

We argued in chapter three that there are a range of second and third parties, both commercial and non-commercial, which may play valuable roles in the regulatory process, acting as quasi-regulators. These range from industry associations (administering self-regulatory programmes) through financial institutions to environmental and other pressure groups. All too often, however, policymakers have avoided or ignored the potential contributions of such parties, treating government as the sole regulatory provider.[70] Yet, by expanding the regulatory 'tool box' to encompass additional players, many of the most serious shortcomings of traditional regulatory approaches may be overcome.

There are several reasons why the recruitment of third parties into the regulatory process may provide for improved outcomes. First, in some instances third party quasi-regulation may be far more potent than government intervention. For example, the threat of a bank to foreclose a loan to a firm with low levels of liquidity is likely to have a far greater impact than any existing government instrument. Secondly, it may be perceived as more legitimate. For example, as we indicated in chapter five, farmers are far more accepting of commercial pressure to reduce chemical use than they are of any government mandated requirements. Similarly, participation by community groups, in partic-

---

[70] For example, in the UK, a move to a more determinative style of regulation decision-making whereby policy goals are prescribed by legislation and the role of the regulator is essentially to implement these goals has removed much discretion from the regulatory process. Thus, even though greater rights for public participation have been introduced, because many of the environmental standards the regulator must enforce have largely been predetermined at the legislative level, expectations of what can be achieved through community participation may well be frustrated (R. McCrory, *Loaded Guns and Monkeys Responsible: Environmental Law* (1994), Imperial College Centre for Technology, UK.)

ular, may well be crucial in terms of political acceptability. Thirdly, government resources are necessarily limited, particularly in an era of fiscal constraint. Accordingly, it makes sense for government to reserve its resources for situations where there is no viable alternative to direct regulation. The potential for Responsible Care to supplement government regulation of the chemical industry is a case in point.[71] Fourthly, even if resources were more readily available, governments are not omnipotent. There are many areas of commercial activity which impact on the environmental performance of industry where direct government influence is impractical. For example, where there are a myriad of small players, such that it is impossible even for government to identify, let alone regulate all of them.

Finally, and more broadly, it is desirable to work with markets rather than against them. This is not to be interpreted as a retreat into 'free market environmentalism'. Rather, it is a recognition of the latent power of markets to change industry behaviour and the extent to which this potential influence remains unexploited.[72] In many cases, harnessing the power of markets will, necessarily, be achieved through the vehicles of second and third parties rather than by direct government regulation.

Applying the principle of empowerment

As we identified in earlier chapters, the participation of second and third parties, particularly commercial third parties, in the regulatory process is unlikely to arise spontaneously, except in a very limited range of circumstances where public and private interests substantially coincide.[73] Such parties may have little existing interest in environmental performance, lack the necessary information even if they did, or indeed may have a commercial interest in maintaining or accelerating environmental degradation. For example, banks are unlikely to promote the conservation of remnant vegetation on farms where they perceive the clearing of land to provide increased earnings, nor are they likely to oppose the running of extra stock where this increases the ability to repay loans. There remains, therefore, a significant role for government

---

[71] See chapter four above, and N. Gunningham, 'Environment, Self-Regulation, and the Chemical Industry: Assessing Responsible Care' (1995) 17(1) *Law and Policy* 58–109).

[72] OECD Draft Council Recommendation on the use of Economic Instruments in Environmental Policy, Env/EC (90) 23.

[73] N. Gunningham & J. Rees, 'Industry Self-regulation' (1997) 19(4) *Law and Policy* (publication of 1997 issue delayed).

in facilitating, catalyzing and commandeering the participation of second and third parties to the cause of environmental improvement. Thus, in the case of the chemical industry, we saw how government could play important roles in providing information and rights of legal challenge to NGOs, and how it could reinforce the potential of supply chain pressure by requiring that larger firms, in particular, ensure that upstream suppliers and downstream buyers conform to ISO 140001 standards, with their promise of continuous improvement and cultural change.

Another powerful illustration of this principle can be drawn from Mitchell's work on pollution by oil tankers at sea.[74] Mitchell demonstrates how the imposition by the state of penalties for intentional oil spills (pursuant to an international treaty) was almost wholly ineffective, due in no small part to difficulties of monitoring, and, in some cases, to a lack of either enforcement resources or political will. Nor, in the absence of government intervention, did third parties have incentives to contribute significantly to the reduction of oil spills. However, all this changed when a new regime was introduced, requiring tankers to be equipped with segregated ballast tanks. Despite the increased cost of the new equipment, this regime has been extremely successful, a fact owed substantially to the role played by a range of powerful third parties. In particular, the new regime facilitated coerced compliance by non-State classification societies, ship insurers, and ship builders. As Mitchell demonstrates, shipowners were critically dependent upon each of them. Together, and in conjunction with state action, they achieved far more than State action alone was ever likely to.[75]

There are a variety of mechanisms through which government may seek to engage second and third parties more fully in the regulatory process. An obvious starting point is the provision of adequate information. Reliable data on the performance of industrial firms, enables third parties (e.g., investors and banks), which may be in a position to exert influence to make objective judgments about preferred company profiles. For example, it was only when government mandated collation and disclosure of toxic releases that financial markets were able to factor this information into share prices, thereby rewarding good environmental performers and disadvantaging the worst performers.[76]

---

[74] R. Mitchell, *International Oil Pollution at Sea: Environmental Policy and Treaty Compliance* (1994), MIT Press, Massachusetts.

[75] *Ibid.* at chapter 8.

[76] J. T. Hamilton, 'Pollution as News: Media and stockmarket reactions to the Capital

Some strategies for empowering third parties will be specific to particular target groups. For example, government may facilitate the activities of non-commercial third parties, such as NGOs, through the provision of funding support, the enactment of community right to know legislation, and the provision of legal standing.[77] In seeking to target banks, government might increase lender liability for a range of environmentally destructive behaviours. Insurers as regulators may be invoked by making insurance a condition of licence, or a condition of authorization to engage in activities which have a high environmental risk.

Governments could also harness the very considerable power of supply chain pressure, whereby large firms put pressure on their smaller suppliers/buyers to improve environmental performance. For example, governments may make it a condition of regulatory flexibility that firms over a certain size not only adopt environmental management systems (a form of process based regulation) but also ensure that their major suppliers also conform to a simplified version of the system. Alternatively, such a condition could be included in an industry wide self-regulation programme, as is already the case under the Product Stewardship code of practice of Responsible Care.[78]

Consistent with our design principles, the preferred role for government is to create the necessary preconditions for second or third parties to assume a greater share of the regulatory burden, rather than engaging in direct intervention. This will also reduce the drain on scarce regulatory resources and provide greater ownership of environmental issues by industry and the wider community. In this way, government acts principally as a catalyst or facilitator. In particular, it can play a crucial role in orchestrating a co-ordinated and gradual escalation up an instrument pyramid (described in principle three), filling any gaps that may exist in that pyramid and facilitating links between its different layers.

This role can be illustrated by example. Insurance has the potential

Toxic Release Inventory Data' (1995) *Journal of Environmental Economics and Management* 98–103.

[77] For example, Hobert points out that 'without legal standing, and actionable statutory standards—two fundamental structural characteristics of the pluralist regime—environmental groups simply could not have exercised the policy leverage that they obtained in the 1970s. Legal power is the single most important political resource available to environmental groups' (G. Hobert *Pluralism by Design* (1992), Praeger, NY, p.9).

[78] See chapter four above and N. Gunningham, 'Environment, Self-Regulation, and the Chemical Industry: Assessing Responsible Care' (1995) 17(1) *Law and Policy* 58–109.

to be a useful instrument in the middle layers of the pyramid. Insurers have the capacity to conduct site visits, engage independent auditors, vary the size of premiums, and, if necessary, withdraw their services altogether. Insurers are, however, dependent on the availability of reliable information on which to make their initial and subsequent assessments of firm performance, but, commonly, have great difficulty obtaining relevant information over and beyond that required to be disclosed by their clients.[79] As a consequence, there is a possible role for government (at the middle layers of the pyramid) to ensure that this information is accessible, for example, through the provision of compulsory pollutant inventory reporting by industry. It may also be that insurers lack the necessary muscle at the top of the pyramid to deal with unrepentant recalcitrants. In such circumstances, insurers may advise government regulators of a firm's transgression and invite the full force of the law to be applied (whether they choose instead simply to cancel the insurance policy may depend substantially on the competitiveness of the market). Thus, we have a combination of third party and government regulation co-ordinated between the different layers of the pyramid to provide the opportunity for co-ordinated enforcement escalation.

To assert the desirability of greater involvement by second or third parties is not to imply that all available such parties should be mobilized in all circumstances.[80] To do so would be to neglect the benefits of parsimony, identified above, and to violate design principle two. Indeed, there is a strong case to be made for the judicious selection of third parties in many regulatory scenarios. It is useful at this stage to refer back to our central evaluation criteria of efficiency and effectiveness. Where efficiency takes priority, then it makes sense to avoid smorgasbordism because having too many quasi-regulators may increase the regulatory load on individual firms to the point at which it becomes counterproductive. There is also little point in unnecessarily imposing

---

[79] P. Freeman & H. Kunreather, 'The Roles of Insurance and Well Specified Standards in Dealing With Environmental Risk' (1996) 17 *Risk Management and Decision Economics* 513–530.

[80] In the case of mine site remediation, it is difficult to envisage a viable role for second or third parties as surrogate regulators. The long lead times involved, often in the region of twenty to thirty years, and the likelihood of geographical isolation, mean that there is no obvious mechanism for invoking commercial or non-commercial third parties. Similarly, once a mine has been exhausted of its mineral wealth there is little incentive for firms to respond to self-regulatory initiatives—they have no ongoing interest in the mine site. In the absence of second or third party opportunities, it is incumbent upon government to intervene.

a regulatory burden on a range of third parties. And even if government does not directly pay for the cost of third party participation, it, and industry, may indirectly pay through the encroachment of economic inefficiencies and market distortions. Accordingly, in these circumstances, governments should carefully select and empower those third parties which a likely to deliver the greatest 'bang for the buck', and ensure that the benefits of third party intervention clearly outweigh the costs.

In contrast, in the limited range of circumstances where effectiveness is of the essence, for example in cases of potential irreversibility or catastrophic loss, and where no single instrument has sufficient dependability, the weighting should be in favour of as large as possible a number of third parties capable of acting an a constructive *and complementary* capacity. This will provide added robustness to the regulatory process.

It is important to emphasize that where second and third party participation is inappropriate, then (assuming the problem is sufficiently serious) there may be no alternative to direct government intervention, which might take the form of either command and control or the application of economic instruments.[81]

Principle 5. Maximize opportunities for win-win outcomes

As we discussed in chapter two, major criticisms of much conventional regulation are the lack of incentives for firms to continuously improve their environmental performance[82] (for example, an emission standard of 100 ppm gives no rewards for companies to substantially reduce this level) and the failure to encourage firms to adopt pollution prevention measures over end-of-pipe solutions (the same standard can be met by putting scrubbers on the chimney rather than developing cleaner technology).

The opportunities for both continuous improvement and pollution prevention will be considerably enhanced to the extent that firms can

---

[81] This is not to imply that third party involvement and economic instruments are necessarily counterproductive, as market instruments themselves may be enhanced by third party activity.

[82] This is a standard criticism of both specification standards (which encourage or mandate firms to adopt a particular technology and, in practice, often discourage alternative, more innovative and effective solutions) and of performance standards (which mandate a particular outcome but do not provide any encouragement to exceed it). Contrast these standards with economic mechanisms, which do provide incentives to continuing improvement.

achieve higher levels of environmental performance at the same time as increasing productivity and/or profits: the classic win-win scenario.[83] A key challenge for policymakers, therefore, is to ensure that regulatory solutions optimize the opportunity for win-win outcomes and facilitate and reward enterprises for going 'beyond compliance', while also maintaining a statutory baseline and a ratcheting up of standards.

Will firms voluntarily go beyond compliance?

It is increasingly argued that it is in a business's own self-interest to move *beyond compliance* with existing legislative requirements and adopt a 'proactive' stance on the environment, voluntarily exceeding mandated minimum performance standards.[84] According to its proponents, firms going down this path may (in addition to improving profitability) enhance their corporate image, position themselves to realize new environment-related market opportunities, generally improve efficiency and quality, foster a greater consumer acceptance of their company and products, and reduce potential legal liability.[85] Moving beyond compliance also gives firms the incentive to develop new environmental

[83] When we discuss win/win, in this context, we are confining the discussion to the perspective of the firm, not the economy as a whole. That is, an individual firm increasing its productivity, or at least not reducing it, through environmental improvements. This should be distinguished from the concept of 'no-regrets' which is commonly used in the discussion of policy options to reduce greenhouse gas emissions. 'No-regrets', in this context, refers to policies which produce a net economic benefit, or are at least economically neutral, across the economy as a whole. That is, even though some firms and indeed sectors may suffer as a result of environmental policy, this loss of economic activity will be more than compensated for by an upswing in other sectors and/or firms. 'No-regrets' quite literally means, having introduced a policy that brings about net economic growth, policy makers will have no-regrets at having done so even though the original environmental objective may no longer apply. In this sense, 'no-regrets' is promoted as the most appropriate policy response when there is a high degree of scientific uncertainty associated with an environmental problem. It is thus a qualification of the Precautionary Principle. Further, we note in our discussion that win/win outcomes can, in fact, go beyond a narrow definition of profitability, to include less tangible benefits, such as improved community relations. Of course, for economically marginal firms, enhanced profitability will be the bottom line. Note that it is arguable that beyond compliance and win-win outcomes are not necessarily the same thing, i.e., going beyond compliance may not necessarily be profitable, but if we apply our broader definition of win-win, then for the purposes of our discussion they can be treated as equivalent terms.

[84] The 'cleaner production' literature, for example, proposes a systematic and comprehensive integration of pollution prevention and waste reduction activities into a firm's core decision making processes in order to maximize profit making opportunities.

[85] There are a number of broader reasons why it might be rational to go beyond compliance. For example, increased public scrutiny in the United States through the Toxic Release Inventory has induced firms to self-impose stricter emission reduction targets

technologies which can be sold into the rapidly growing and lucrative global market for environmental goods and services.[86]

And yet, despite the apparent benefits which may flow from improved environmental performance, the large majority of enterprises in the large majority of jurisdictions have taken very few steps to take advantage of them or to position themselves as environmental leaders.[87] Assuming that considerable win-win opportunities do indeed exist (that is, even if proponents of this position may overstate the benefits, their basic position is sound[88]), why have the majority of enterprises adopted a position which is, on the face of it, irrational? The most plausible answers are an emphasis on short-term profits, and bounded rationality.[89]

(S. Aora & T. N. Cason 'An Experiment in Voluntary Regulation: Participation in EPA's 33/50 Program' (1995) 28 (3), *Journal of Environmental Economics and Management* 271). There is evidence to suggest that firms may choose to segment consumer preferences by competing on grounds of high environmental quality (F. Cairncross *Costing the Earth: The challenge for governments, the opportunities for business* (1992), Harvard Business School Press, Boston, Massachusetts). Another motivation for going beyond compliance could be as a means of delaying or avoiding tighter government regulations. Firms may even over-comply to encourage tougher regulations in order to gain an advantage over existing competitors and restrict new entrants. Going beyond compliance may also occur inadvertently through large, one-off investments in new plant and equipment that are substantially less polluting than existing technology. Finally, multinationals may find it more efficient to standardize industrial processes across national borders, even when their operations may substantially exceed the regulatory requirements of some jurisdictions.

[86] On current OECD projections, for example, the global market for environmental goods and services will be $US 600 billion in the year 2000. See N. A. Gunningham, 'Beyond Compliance: management of environmental risk' in B. Boer, R. Fowler & N. Gunningham (eds.) *Environmental Outlook: law and policy*, ACEL, Federation Press, Sydney and references cited therein.

[87] Guntram & Winsemius argue that there are four development stages in corporate environmental policy: reactive, receptive, constructive and proactive. There is a broad consensus that the majority of business, even in the most advanced industrialised countries, has not moved beyond stage 2 or, at best, stage 3 (U. Guntram & P. Winsemius, 'Responding to the Environmental Challenge' (1992) March/April *Business Horizons* 12).

[88] M. E. Porter & C. van der Linde, 'Green and Competitive' (Sept–Oct 1995) *Harvard Business Review*, 120–134; and discussion 'The challenge of going green' (July–Aug 1994) *Harvard Business Review*, 37–50. For a more comprehensive critique, see J. C. Robinson, 'The Impact of Environmental and Occupational Health Regulation on Productivity Growth in US Manufacturing' (1995) 12 *Yale Journal of Regulation* 388. See also N. Gunningham 'Beyond Compliance: management of environmental risk' in B. Boer, R. Fowler & N. Gunningham (eds.) *Environmental Outlook: law and policy* (1994), ACEL, Federation Press, Sydney.

[89] Broader reasons for failing to exploit the economic advantages of going beyond compliance include: insufficient technical expertise; lack of information; middle management inertia; ignorance of marginal cost curves; insufficient resources to focus on anything other than core business functions; a reluctance to borrow capital; and uncertainty about future returns (M. Jacobs, *The Green Economy* (1991) Pluto Press, UK;

The former is probably the single largest impediment to improved environmental performance.[90] Crucially, most environmental investments will only pay off in the medium to long term, while the up-front investment is primarily short term. Because corporations are judged by markets, investors, and others principally focussing on short-term performance, if they cannot demonstrate tangible economic success in the here and now, there may be no long term to look forward to.[91]

Bounded rationality may also explain business' failure to adopt proactive environmental policies even when it is in their economic interests to do so. Bounded rationality assumes not that people are irrational (although they sometimes are) but rather that they have neither the knowledge nor the powers of calculation to allow them 'to achieve the high level of optimal adaptation of means to ends that is posited by economics'.[92] For example, it is widely accepted that there are substantial energy efficiency improvements which industry could profitably adopt. And yet, most firms fail to take advantage of them. Only where energy is a large component of business input costs, have substantial investments in energy efficiency been made. In the least energy efficient industries, where energy costs are only a minor component of overall business costs, energy efficiencies have been almost entirely ignored. This is bounded rationality at work: management focuses on core business functions and ignores lesser costs, even though these costs could be reduced through environmentally beneficial behaviour.

N. Gunningham, 'Beyond Compliance: management of environmental risk' in B. Boer, R. Fowler & N. Gunningham (eds.) *Environmental Outlook: law and policy* (1994), ACEL, Federation Press, Sydney.

[90] A. Rappaport and M. Flaherty, 'Multinational Corporation and the Environment' (1991), Centre for Environmental Management, Tufts University.

[91] Of course, some commitment to environmental priorities will have short-term pay-offs. Improvements in waste reduction, in good house-keeping, in saving energy, in eliminating excessive packaging, even in alternative materials purchase, will feed back directly into corporate profits—but even here, while the first 25 per cent improvement may be quite easily achieved, the next 25 per cent may prove far more challenging. But beyond this, the extent to which a firm may be willing to sacrifice short-term profit for long-term dividends will depend on a number of factors. See generally, N. Gunningham, 'Beyond Compliance: Management of Environmental Risk' (1994) in *Environmental Outlook*, B. Boer, R. Fowler and N. Gunningham (eds.), (1994), ACEL, Federation Press, Sydney, pp.254–281.

[92] H. Simon, *Economics, Bounded Rationality and the Cognitive Revolution* (1992), Edward Elgar, UK, p.3. Two factors which undermine rationality are not knowing in advance the desired outcome, and not knowing how to achieve the desired outcome even when it is known in advance. Given these constraints on rational behaviour, there is an important role for government in providing incentives for firms to go beyond compliance.

The role of government

On this analysis, the market, unaided, cannot be relied upon to deliver win-win outcomes. That is, a number of opportunities which would yield such outcomes are not, under present conditions, being taken up. Arguably, there is a role for government intervention to increase the uptake within firms of existing economically rational environmental improvements: in effect, seeking to compensate for both the inadequacy of markets (unaided) and of business rationality in order to maximize both the public (environmental) and private (economic) benefits.

But what form should this intervention take? Of course, government could simply mandate improved levels of business environmental performance. However, because there is a coincidence between self-interest and environmental improvement, other less interventionist measures should have a high chance of success, rendering prescriptive forms of intervention unnecessary or even counterproductive (see principle two above). Accordingly, the most appropriate role for governmental regulation lies in nudging firms at the margin towards cleaner production, heightening their awareness of environmental issues, and encouraging the re-ordering of corporate priorities in order to reap the benefits of improved environmental performance.

One way of increasing the chances of win-win outcomes is through the provision of information (e.g., cleaner production demonstration projects, technical support, databases, and clearinghouses). A related strategy would be to encourage full cost accounting, on the assumption (for which there is much support) that unless business knows the environmental costs and benefits of its current practices, its unlikely to change them.[93] Such strategies may be particularly important in addressing the problem of bounded rationality. Not only can government provide information to industry, but other non-government sources of information can also be harnessed and, in some cases, may be more effective.[94]

[93] Current accounting methods allocate environmental costs to overhead accounts, whereas full cost accounting not only quantifies these costs but allocates them to the production processes or product lines that are responsible for their creation (M. Bennett & P. James, 'Environment-Related Management Accounting: Current practice and future trends' (1997) 17 *Greener Management International* 32–52.

[94] For example, in buyer-supplier relations, manufacturers of pesticides, herbicides, and fertilizers may be persuaded to provide information on the best ways to avoid run-off. Similarly, power utilities may supply information to electricity consumers on the best ways to improve energy efficiency. It is sometimes more cost-effective for power utilities to invest in energy efficiency services than to invest in additional power plants. Information can also be dispersed through instruments such as labelling. For example,

Sometimes, because of institutional inertia, even when firms are made aware of potential cost savings they still will not exploit win-win opportunities. In such cases, information alone is not enough, but is a necessary prerequisite. Here, information strategies can be supplemented by other voluntary promotional schemes which attempt to elicit and formalize a commitment from management to cost-effective environmental improvement. Examples include government sponsored schemes such as Golden Carrots and Green Lights in the United States and the PRISMA project in the Netherlands, described in chapter two. These programmes employ voluntary commitments on the part of industry to achieve improvements in areas such as energy efficiency and pollution prevention, and thereby bestow important public relations benefits on participants.[95]

Finally, arguably at a higher level of intervention, governments might consider some form of financial inducements to 'nudge' firms in the right direction, so overcoming narrow short-termism and bounded rationality. For smaller firms which may not have the internal resources and expertise to identify and implement win/win outcomes, government may subsidize the cost of external consultants preparing an environmental audit and management plan which seeks to exploit profitable environmental improvements. Again, once firms become aware of how to achieve win-win outcomes, and can easily access the consulting expertise and internal systems necessary to achieve them, they are far more likely to take positive action. Smaller firms may also require some assistance to cover up front costs and to more easily access capital.[96]

However, it makes sense to target any financial inducements at those firms which are genuinely going beyond compliance rather than those which are merely going to comply with the minimum standards. One

the energy efficiency performance of industrial plant and equipment may be disclosed (on a voluntary or mandatory basis), so that purchasers are more able to factor in energy running costs.

[95] The ability of public recognition to foster better environmental outcomes is another measure that may by harnessed by government. This could take the form of positive incentives, such as awards, labelling and honour rolls, or negative incentives such as peer pressures, community right to know, and public shaming. See chapter two above.

[96] Government could assist such firms by, for instance, offering soft-loans at reduced interest rates for investments designed to achieve specific environmental objectives, or by offering in particular circumstances to act as guarantor for commercial loans. Another approach would be to offer a revolving grant scheme to cover up-front costs—once the investment returns a profit, the grant is repaid and passed onto another firm. Government purchasing policy and tendering guidelines for government contracts may provide additional avenues for encouraging firms to strive for higher environmental standards.

way of achieving this is via a two-track, parallel regulatory system that provides incentives to those firms committed to higher levels of environmental performance which go substantially beyond compliance. Such incentives might include—increased flexibility, autonomy, and public relations benefits less demanding administrative requirements, reduced licence fees, preferential purchasing, etc. The intention is to attract as many firms as possible to the 'green track', but to maintain the conventional track as a fall back mechanism. Under this scenario, it is not necessary for government to know the level of win/win opportunities available to each firm. Ultimately, it is up to each firm to determine whether financial benefits, or lack thereof, of minimal compliance are outweighed by the benefits of being a 'green track' firm with higher levels of environmental performance. Firms should be able to move between tracks, but if they are placed on green track first, then deliberately fail to meet expectations, they should be regulated more harshly than if they had started off on the conventional track.

Moving the goal posts: turning win-lose into win-win

It is inevitable that even the most progressive companies will eventually reach a point at which win-win is no longer a viable option, and where any further spending on environmental protection will directly threaten corporate profits. Specifically, there are many circumstances under which the economic benefits of investing in environmental protection are tenuous or non-existent, and where the costs to business of implementing environmental protection measures will not be offset by any resulting savings from improved economic performance.[97]

At this point, two strategies are available to government. The first is to recognize the tension between environmental protection and corporate profit, and to design policy instruments and enforcement responses accordingly. Here, we simply restate the importance of a pyramidal enforcement response such as we advocated at principle three above. Regulators start at the bottom of the pyramid, assuming that business is willing to comply voluntarily. However, they also make provision for circumstances where this assumption will be disappointed, by being

---

[97] The greater the nexus between environmental improvement and costs, the greater the incentive to comply with minimum standards only. In many cases, there will be a progressive rise in the marginal cost of abatement. This may result in firms implementing the cheap options first, then gradually reaching a point where going beyond compliance is no longer attractive. See N. Walley & B. Whitehead, 'Its Not Easy Being Green' (May–June 1994) *Harvard Business Review* 46–52.

prepared to ascend the enforcement pyramid to increasingly deterrence-orientated strategies. Critically, at the peak of the pyramid will be a deterrence-orientated approach that makes it no longer economically rational for firms to avoid their environmental responsibilities.

A second strategy is for government to push back the point at which win-win becomes win-lose.[98] One area where such potential exists relates to the establishment and exploitation of new markets for environmental technology, where enormous business opportunities exist both to provide environmental benefits and to increase corporate profits.[99] While such markets may evolve in the absence of government intervention, their scope and success can be influenced very directly by such action. But again, this raises the question: what particular forms of intervention are appropriate? According to Michael Porter, and contrary to conventional wisdom, the most potent form of government action is the enactment and enforcement of more stringent environmental regulation to provide firms with a *competitive advantage* in these nascent markets.[100]

Porter's empirical work suggests that countries that have the most rigorous environmental requirements often lead in exports of affected products. For example, Germany has had perhaps the world's tightest regulations in stationary air pollution control, and German companies

[98] At first sight, a number of such opportunities might seem to be available. Government could, for example, provide subsidies to firms to engage in environment related research and development, or tax concessions or enhanced depreciation arrangements for environmentally beneficial plant and equipment. However, these and similar options will achieve only zero sum outcomes. Subsidies and tax concessions, for example, can only be provided at a cost to the public purse. Moreover, they violate the polluter pays principle and put subsidized firms at an unfair advantage. Alternately, governments might impose higher environmental taxes. Pollution taxes, for example, have the potential to provide a continuous financial incentive to improve environmental performance beyond minimum standards. Once these are in place, there will be a larger range of situations in which it is 'win-win' to implement environmental improvements. However, it would be spurious to suggest that this produces genuine win-win outcomes for industry. On the contrary, this puts industry in a considerably worse financial position than it was in immediately prior to the imposition of the tax. And there is the added danger that such taxes would need to be much higher than merely a break-even financial proposition for environmental improvement. For example, one study of sewage discharge fees in the UK demonstrated that even a 400 per cent increase in fees, which in many cases made the introduction of available alternative technology economically very attractive, did not result in any such take up of this technology (M. Jacobs, *The Green Economy* (1991), Pluto Press, London, UK, p.157).

[99] Although there may be no immediate productivity benefits to be gained from environmental improvement, additional profits may be derived from the sale of innovative environmental technologies in international markets.

[100] M. Porter, 'America's Green Strategy' (1991) April, *Scientific American* 168.

appear to hold a wide lead in patenting—and exporting—air pollution and other environmental technologies.[101] Conversely, those who weaken their regulations will fall behind in environmental exports. Thus, as the United Kingdom's environmental standards have lagged, so to has its 'ratio of exports to imports in environmental technology fallen from 8:1 to 1:1 over the past decade'.[102] However, Porter is at pains to emphasize that not all standards will lead to desirable trade outcomes, and that we need regulations that aim at outcomes rather than methods (that is, performance based rather than technology based standards), that are flexible and cost effective and which encourage companies to advance beyond their existing control technology. It must also be acknowledged that Porter's views have been strongly challenged from a variety of sources,[103] and that empirical support for his position is somewhat tenuous.[104]

We agree with Porter that there is much that governments can and should do to encourage firms to develop environmental technologies and to harness environmental services markets. However, we note that traditional command and control regulation is not necessarily the only or indeed the best means of achieving this outcome. Rather, there are a variety of other, less intrusive policy options using not just government, but also second and third parties, which could also serve to drive environmental technological innovation and serve to create or expand global opportunities and markets for environmental services. As we argued earlier, such less-interventionist solutions have considerable attractions in terms of costs, effectiveness and legitimacy. Accordingly, in our view, the Porter solution (since it comes at the peak of an instrument pyramid) should be regarded as a last rather than a first resort.

Take for example, the issue of pollution from the chemical industry. While it would certainly be viable, following Porter, to mandate tough standards, it would also be possible to adopt a self-regulatory scheme, as is the case with Responsible Care (with a proviso that if the scheme was not demonstrably achieving certain performance outcomes within

---

[101] *Ibid.*

[102] *Ibid.*

[103] See, for example, N. Walley and B. Whitehouse, 'Its Not Easy Being Green' (May–June 1994) *Harvard Business Review* 46. Also, arguably, only the top 10 per cent of firms will respond in the way that Porter predicts. The other 90 per cent, by implication, have little to gain.

[104] See, for example, J. C. Robinson, 'The Impact of Environmental and Occupational Health Regulation on Productivity Growth in US Manufacturing' (1995) 12, *Yale Journal of Regulation* 388–434.

a given period, government would intervene more directly). Such a scheme might be coupled with external audit, and government might itself require disclosure of results, enabling commercial third parties and, to a lesser extent, consumers and public interest groups to bring pressure on those who were achieving poorest results. Besides being less interventionist than the Porter solution, co-regulation has additional advantages of providing greater flexibility, giving industry ownership of the solution, and of avoiding much of the culture of resistance that may accompany government regulation.[105]

Instrument mixes

Throughout the book, we have highlighted the importance, in terms of achieving effectiveness and efficiency, of using combinations of instruments and parties to compensate for the weakness of stand-alone environmental policies. It cannot be assumed, however, that all instrument combinations will automatically be complementary. Some instrument mixes may indeed be counterproductive, while the outcome of others may be largely determined by the specific contexts in which they are applied. Unfortunately, the practical task of identifying which particular combinations are complementary, which counterproductive, and

---

[105] Even if these purported solutions proved unsuccessful, the logical next step is not necessarily to move directly towards the regulatory peak, but rather (to the extent that they are viable in the circumstances of the case) to use economic mechanisms in preference to more stringent standards precisely because they provide more flexibility, incentives for innovation and cost-efficiency, and less intrusiveness and coercion. In any event, Porter's paradigm case is pollution control, and the solution he proposes, whatever its merits in dealing with point-source pollution, is manifestly inapplicable to a range of other environmental problems, such as biodiversity. For example, much biodiversity (with limited exceptions such as biotechnology) has no immediate economic value, property rights are incompletely specified, and there are very few technological spin-offs capable of providing global environmental market opportunities. Even in the case of pollution control, it is only a modest minority of highly innovative and imaginative entrepreneurs (the leaders rather than the laggards) who are likely to position themselves to improve environmental technology and take advantage of global market opportunities in the way Porter suggests. He offers no prescriptions in respect of the laggards (except to the extent that they will be beneficiaries of any new technologies that leaders now have the incentive to develop and sell—again, for reasons which relate to economies of scale and the size of home markets which are the first base for many new environmental technologies, it may not be viable for small countries to adopt the Porter strategy. It is no coincidence that his major examples are the USA, Japan and Germany). In contrast, our own process and principle based proposals are capable of addressing a very wide range of both environmental problems and the behaviour of all, rather than a minority, of environmental players.

which context specific, is especially daunting. Not only is there an extremely large number of potential instrument combinations, but the answers to the question 'which ones are complementary or otherwise, and why?' are themselves both complex and qualified. To engage in the encyclopaedic task of exploring the full implications of all instrument combinations would not only be impractical but would not, we suspect, make for riveting reading.

Instead, we have chosen to provide a much shorter (and we hope more digestible) account of instrument interactions, which analyses the most important combinations and their implications without attempting an exhaustive categorization. From this, we derive a practical set of recommendations for instrument combinations that will guide policymakers in the application of our previous design processes and principles. The table below summarizes the main observations

For the purposes of analysis, we divide the plethora of potential instrument combinations into the following categories:

(i) mixes that are inherently complementary;
(ii) mixes that are inherently incompatible;
(iii) mixes that are complementary if sequenced; and
(iv) mixes the complementarity or otherwise of which is essentially context specific.

In examining instrument combinations, a preliminary question to resolve is the level of generality with which to approach this issue. If we engage at too abstract a level, we risk making broad generalizations that lack utility because they are incapable of addressing more subtle distinctions within instrument categories. For example, if we seek to treat economic instruments as a single category, then we may miss or seriously misunderstand the important differences between, for example, taxes and liability rules. On the other hand, if we address the issue of instrument categories at a high level of specificity, then we must deal with so many categories of combinations as to make the entire enterprise unworkable. We have sought to steer between these two extremes, breaking up the most important and complex categories of instruments: command and control regulation (performance based, process based, and technology based) and economic instruments (broad based economic instruments, supply side incentives, and liability) into a number of parts, while treating self-regulation, voluntarism, and informational strategies largely as single entities. Similarly, while we treat government and self-regulatory bodies as single institutions, we felt it necessary to distinguish between a number of different types of third parties, the most important distinction being between commercial and non-commercial institutions. Box 4 below provides a summary of the instrument categories used in the following discussion (a more detailed analysis of the various categories can be found in chapter two).

Box 4 Policy Instrument Categories

Command and control regulation. The various types of command and control standards have fundamentally different *modus operandi*. For example, *technology standards* prescribe an approved technology for a particular industrial process or environmental problem.[106] Such a standard 'is defined in terms of the specific types of safeguarding methods one must use in specific situations and . . . places great emphasis on the design and construction of these safeguards'.[107] In contrast, *performance standards* define a firm's duty in terms of the problems it must solve or the goals it must achieve. That is, performance standards are outcome-focused and avoid overt prescriptions. *Process standards* address procedures and parameters for achieving a desired result; in particular, the processes to be followed in managing nominated hazards.[108] They are most used in respect of hazards that do not lend themselves to easy measurement, such as safe working practices, or environmental management systems.[109]

Economic instruments. For present purposes, we distinguish between three types of economic instruments. First, we refer to

---

[106] In some versions, the regulatee is notionally given considerable discretion to select the most appropriate technology to their circumstances, but in practice, those who depart from the one approved technology run a considerable 'regulatory risk' that the regulatory authority will not deem their choice of technology as complying with the statutory requirement. See J. Atcheson, 'Can We Trust Verification?' (July/August 1996) *Environmental Forum* 16 at 17.

[107] P. W. McAvoy, *OSHA Safety Regulation: Report of the Presidential Task Force* (1977), American Enterprise Institute, Washington DC.

[108] See, for example, J. Potter, 'Chemical Accident Prevention Regulation in California and New Jersey' (1993) 20 *Ecology Law Quarterly* 755–815.

[109] Industry Commission, *Work, Health & Safety: Inquiry into occupational health and safety* (1995), Volume I. Report No 47, AGPS, Canberra, p.38; and N. Gunningham 'From Compliance to Best Practice in OHS: The role of specification, performance and systems based standards' (1996) 9(3) *Australian Journal of Labour Law* 221–246.

broadbased economic instruments as tradeable emission/resource permits and pollution/resource taxes which apply to industry as a whole, that do not distinguish between sectors and/or preferred technological solutions, nor impose performance limits on individual firms. That is, apart from government setting the overall level of the tax or number and value of permits, the market is left to operate freely. Secondly, we refer to *supply side incentives*, which, in essence, are subsidies provided by government for particular types of technology and/or specific types of industrial activity. These are distinguished from broad-based instruments in that there is a much higher level of government prescription. The third and final category is that of *legal liability*, whereby firms can be held financially responsible for previous cases of environmental harm.

Self-regulation. This is not a precise concept, but, for present purposes, self-regulation may be defined as a process whereby an organized group regulates the behaviour of its members.[110] Most commonly, it involves an industry-level organization (as opposed to the government or individual firms) setting rules and standards (codes of practice) relating to the conduct of firms in the industry. One can further categorize industry self-regulation in terms of the degree of government involvement (for 'pure' self-regulation, without any form of external intervention, is uncommon).[111]

Voluntarism. In contrast to self-regulation, which entails social control by an industry association, voluntarism is based on the individual firm undertaking to do the right thing unilaterally, without any basis in coercion. Commonly, voluntarism is initiated by government, and may involve government playing the role of

---

[110] Organisation for Economic Co-operation and Development (OECD), *Meeting on Alternatives to Traditional Regulation* (1994) May, OECD, Paris, p.7.

[111] Rees, for example, suggests that industry self-regulation might take one of three forms. First, voluntary, or total self-regulation involves an industry or profession establishing codes of practice, enforcement mechanisms, and other mechanisms for regulating itself, entirely independent of government. Secondly, mandated self-regulation involves direct involvement by the state whereby it requires business to establish controls over its own behaviour, but leaves the details and enforcement to business itself, subject to state approval and/or oversight. Finally, mandatory partial self-regulation involves business itself being responsible for *some* of the rules and their enforcement but with the over-riding regulatory specifications, though not the details, being mandated by the State. (J. V. Rees, *Reforming the Workplace: A study of self-regulation in occupational health and safety* (1988), University of Pennsylvania Press, US, p.9.)

co-ordinator and facilitator. At a general level, this category embraces voluntary agreements between governments and individual businesses taking the form of 'non-mandatory contracts between equal partners, one of which is government, in which incentives for action arise from mutual interests rather than from sanctions'.[112] However, the variety of such agreements makes precise classification difficult.[113]

Information strategies. The range of educational and information-based instruments is broad, and, in many cases, these instruments may overlap. For present purposes, information strategies may be taken to include: education and training;[114] corporate environmental reporting;[115] community right to know and pollution inventories;[116] and product certification.[117]

---

[112] Organisation for Economic Co-operation and Development (OECD), *Meeting on Alternatives to Traditional Regulation* (1994) May, OECD, Paris, p.7.

[113] The words 'non-mandatory' are fundamental, for to the extent that such agreements contain a coercive element (for example, there are strong pressures to enter into it) they might legitimately be regarded as an innovative form of command and control, or co-regulation.

[114] Environmental information is commonly delivered through government sponsored education and training programmes. Education and training can be tailored to meet the needs of industry, and in particular, to address information gaps that hamper the environmental performance of small and medium sized businesses. A key function of these instruments is to internalize environmental awareness and responsibility into corporate decision-making.

[115] Corporate environmental reports are a way for firms to disseminate information about the environmental record, either as part of an annual report or as a stand alone document. Corporate environmental reporting is still in its infancy, however developments include the use of 'eco-balance sheets' and full-cost accounting which measure all business inputs and outputs, establish performance indicators, and calculate environmental efficiency per unit of production.

[116] A number of countries around the world have introduced laws compelling disclosure of pollution and chemical hazard information. Commonly referred to as 'community right to know' (CRTK), such legislation is intended to inform the community of the environmental impact of a firm's activities and of a firm's pollution abatement policies The most prominent is the Emergency Planning and Community Right to Know Act (the EPCRA) introduced in the United States in 1986.

[117] Surveys indicate that many consumers take environmental considerations into account when they purchase goods and services. There is evidence, however, that unassisted markets do not provide accurate information to consumers and, in some cases, may mislead them about the environmental performance of specific products. Product certification and eco-labelling schemes are intended to inform the public about the environmental 'soundness' (or otherwise) of various consumer products.

A summary of instrument mixes

The table below provides a succinct reference vehicle for policy-makers contemplating various instrument combinations. We recommend that what we describe below as negative instrument interactions should be avoided, if at all possible, in the design of optimal environmental regulation. Policy-makers, or indeed any other interested parties, should seek to invoke positive and complementary instrument interactions to gain maximum utility out of the design processes and principles described earlier in this chapter. Particular attention should be paid to the application of sequenced instrument combinations as a way of avoiding negative interactions, and in the process, adding considerable dependability to the policy mix as a whole. It is also necessary to emphasize the importance of comprehensively identifying the key contextual features of the environmental issue being addressed (see design processes above), as the nature of the interaction of a number of instrument combinations will be determined by these features.

Inherently complementary combinations

Certain combinations of instruments are inherently complementary. That is, their effectiveness and efficiency will be significantly enhanced by using them in combination, irrespective of the circumstances of the relevant environmental issue. As such, policymakers can be confident in choosing these combinations over others.

Information and all other instruments

Information is a critically important instrument of environmental protection, not least because of serious asymmetries of information that exist in the absence of intervention (for example, between regulator and regulatee, between large and small firms, between the community and business, and between buyers and suppliers). Information strategies can be designed to rectify or compensate for these asymmetries. The provision of information is also an essential prerequisite for continuous improvement in environmental performance, for only with adequate information can decisionmakers at all levels arrive at decisions which maximize returns and do not lead to unintended consequences.

However, information alone is very unlikely to be a dependable policy instrument[118] and, for this reason, is best used in combination with

---

[118] Predictably, instruments within this category will also be more effective in some circumstances than others. CRTK, for example, relies heavily on the energies of local

Table: Summary of Instrument Mixes

	information & education	voluntarism	self-regulation	supply side incentives[1]	broad based economic instruments[2]	liability	property rights[3]	process standards	performance standards	prescription standards
information & education	Positive	Positive	Positive	Positive	Positive	Positive	Positive	Positive	Positive	Positive
voluntarism	Positive		Contextual	Positive	Contextual	Positive	Positive or duplicative	Positive	Positive, if beyond compliance	Positive
self-regulation	Positive	Contextual		Positive	Negative, but positive if sequential or targeting different activities	Positive or duplicative	Negative	Positive or duplicative	Positive if beyond compliance or duplicative	Negative or duplicative
supply side incentives	Positive	Positive	Positive		Negative	Positive	Contextual	Positive	Positive	Duplicative
broad based economic instruments	Positive	Contextual	Negative, but positive if sequential or targeting different activities	Negative		Negative	Duplicative	Positive	Negative, but positive if sequential or targeting different activities	Negative

liability	Positive	Positive	Positive or duplicative	Positive	Negative	Duplicative	Negative	Negative	Positive	Positive
property rights	Positive	Positive or duplicative	Negative	Contextual	Duplicative	Negative	Contextual	Contextual	Negative	Negative
process standards	Positive	Positive	Positive or duplicative	Positive	Positive	Negative	Contextual		Positive	Negative
performance standards	Positive	Positive, if beyond compliance[4]	Positive if beyond compliance or duplicative	Positive	Negative, but positive if sequential or targeting different activities	Positive[5]	Negative	Positive		Negative
prescription standards	Positive	Positive	Negative or duplicative	Duplicative	Negative	Positive	Negative	Negative	Negative	

---

[1] Supply side incentives comprise subsidies, in the form of, for example, tax concessions or soft loans for environmentally preferred technologies. These are distinguished from broad based instruments in that there is a higher level of government prescription.

[2] Broad based economic instruments comprise economic measures, such as pollution taxes or tradeable emission permits, which apply to industry as a whole, do not distinguish between sectors and/or preferred technological solutions, nor impose performance limits on individual firms. That is, apart from government setting the overall level of the tax or number and value of permits, the market is left to operate freely.

[3] We refer here to the creation of property rights over natural resource were none previously existed, as proposed by free-market environmentalists, not too the manipulation of existing property rights such as easement restrictions.

[4] That is, the voluntary component requires firms to exceed minimum performance standards.

[5] Provided the standard under tort law is higher than that under regulation.

other instruments. In this role, as we will see immediately below, information is a crucially important complement to all the other main types of policy instrument.

Information is essential to the effectiveness of command and control regulation, both flowing from the regulatee to regulator and vice versa. For example, monitoring and disclosure requirements are crucial to ensure adequate compliance and are, therefore, often built into the legislation itself.[119] Information instruments designed primarily for other purposes may also be of value to regulators, enabling them to target toxic 'hot spots' or worst performers. Conversely, as we saw in chapters four and five, information provided by a regulator to industry may reduce the prospects of regulatory resistance and facilitate best practice.

Information is equally important to successful self-regulation. Because of the distrust that industry self-regulation almost inevitably generates among local communities and national environmental groups, the legitimacy and credibility of such schemes is likely to depend heavily upon their accountability and transparency and, underpinning both, the availability of independent performance information.[120] Information will, similarly, serve to complement voluntarism, which itself relies largely upon harnessing enlightened self-interest or altruism.[121] In either event, the provision of information is usually

communities in using the information and pressuring enterprises to improve their environmental performance. Where an environmental hazard involves no immediate threat to human health, or where there is no identifiable local community, or where we are dealing with non-point source pollution, not readily measured and traced back to its origins, then this instrument has far less to offer. Similarly, corporate environmental reporting is dependent upon the willingness of public interest groups to follow through on its results and to both shame bad performers and praise good ones. Finally, eco-labelling relies upon the willingness of consumers to buy 'green' products and upon their capacity to distinguish between these and other classes of product.

[119] For example, enterprises may be required to self-monitor their emissions and disclose the results to the regulatory authority. In most instances, legislation will also compel the regulatee to give access to government inspectors in order for them to identify whether or not the regulatee is in compliance.

[120] The use of independent verifiers (overcoming the limitations of industry self-reporting) under Responsible Care is one example. Such information is also essential to government, for independent evidence of the success of such schemes is part of the *quid pro quo* for government providing regulatory flexibility and autonomy to participating enterprises. Under effective self-regulatory schemes, information is also likely to flow freely between member companies as to ways of more successfully delivering on their environmental goals. For example, under Responsible Care, there are quite extensive provisions for technology sharing, for leadership groups, and for mentoring small suppliers to educate them as to how to achieve higher standards of environmental performance.

[121] As, for example, the Australian Landcare programme, which is designed to gen-

necessary to draw the attention of communities or individuals either to their own self-interest or to the wider environmental merits of a particular course of action.[122] Information flow from participants in voluntary agreements to regulators will be equally important.[123]

Market mechanisms, including economic incentives, also depend heavily for their success upon the availability of sufficient information to enable economic actors to make rational decisions in their self-interest. Indeed, one of the most common failings of pure free market approaches, such as the creation of property rights,[124] is the lack of access to information by the main parties, and their consequent inability to make rational decisions in the absence of such information. In the case of economic instruments, information is of such fundamental importance that, in almost every case, its provision will enhance the functioning of individual instruments.[125] For example, recent commentators on regulation in developing countries have pointed out that: 'it would be pointless, and ultimately counterproductive, to advocate large-scale implementation of pollution charges or tradeable permits under conditions [of very limited information] which practically guarantee their failure'.[126] Indeed, information instruments, such as full cost accounting, may be fundamental in ensuring that firms do respond rationally to economic incentives.[127]

erate voluntary action from the rural community concerning issues such as soil erosion (see chapter five).

[122] For example, only if farmers become aware of the longer term consequences of destructive agricultural practices, such as the need for wildlife sanctuaries is clearly demonstrated, are they likely to modify them and voluntarily contribute to this goal.

[123] For example, 'without high quality information on current and projected technologies and markets, regulators will be unable to judge whether the offers coming from industry will achieve the desired environmental objectives. Nor [in the case of sector-specific voluntary agreements] would they be in a position to judge if a particular industry sector was making sufficient efforts, in comparison with other sectors' (D. Wallace, *Environmental Policy and Industrial Innovation* (1995) Earthscan, London, p.249).

[124] See above, chapter two, p.37.

[125] For example, taxes, charges or other price based instruments may be imposed by government, in order to give firms greater incentives for improved environmental performance, but unless an enterprise is aware of the extent of its environmental discharges, and has an accounting system that identifies which area of the firm's operations is responsible (and which managers), then the economic instruments may not have their desired effect on behaviour.

[126] S. Afsah, B. Lapante & D. Wheeler 'Controlling Industrial Pollution: A. new paradigm' (1996) October, *Policy Research Working Paper*, World Bank, Policy Research Department, p.5.

[127] Similarly, most small and medium sized firms, in particular, barely know what questions to ask, or who to address them to, let alone what the possible solutions. Even in large firms, where information access is easier, such information may not be acquired.

Our conclusion is that (except in a very small number of cases where the provision of information would be demonstrably counter-productive[128]), information should be seen as a potentially important complement to all other instrument categories. However, this is not to say that it should be invoked in all circumstances. On the contrary, information instruments cost time and money to implement (to government, to business or to others), and should only be invoked where the benefits outweigh the costs. Compare, for example, the considerable costs incurred in establishing an environmental labelling strategy, and the very modest benefits such a strategy has commonly delivered,[129] with the modest costs of, and very considerable dividends provided by a Toxic Release Inventory or similar instrument.[130]

Voluntarism and command and control regulation

Voluntarism will complement most forms of command and control regulation, particularly where levels of environmental performance 'beyond compliance' are desired. In the case of performance based command and control regulation, a minimum performance benchmark is established, with voluntary based measures encouraging firms to achieve additional improvements. The United States EPA's 33/50 programme is a good example of this approach.[131] Under the 33/50 pro-

Bounded rationality, the lack of capacity to comprehend and address a wide variety of complex issues, may result in a failure to access or act on information, even when it is rational (and profitable) to do so. Only to the extent that these problems can be overcome through information, education, and training will economic instruments be capable of achieving their desired impact on behaviour.

[128] For example, a duty to disclose the results of voluntary environmental audits (which might then be used against the enterprise, either by governments or by third parties such as environmental groups), would produce a disincentive to conducting audits in the first place. Such an outcome is highly undesirable, given the very considerable benefits such audits can produce in terms of improved environmental performance. A requirement for mandatory disclosure of commercial in confidence information would also be counterproductive, for similar reasons. Information disclosure by businesses can make them vulnerable to civil actions. This is a major reason why US firms opposed transparency provisions in the ISO 14001 Environmental Management Systems standard. In relation to information, liability rules can also be counterproductive. For example, in the USA (where information disclosure can make firms vulnerable to civil action, and where litigation is frequent), companies are very resistant to providing information on their own performance for fear that this will subsequently be used against them in civil litigation.

[129] S. Dawson & N. Gunningham, 'The More Dolphins There Are The Less I Trust What They're Saying' (1996) 18 (1) *Adelaide Law Review* 1–34.

[130] N. Gunningham & A. Cornwell, 'Legislating The Right To Know' (1994) 11 *Environmental and Planning Law Journal* 274–288.

[131] S. Aora & T. N. Cason, 'An Experiment in Voluntary Regulation: Participation

gramme, firms are encouraged to reduce the levels of their toxic chemicals releases, often at substantial cost, on a purely voluntary basis. Existing command and control regulations that apply to toxic chemical releases remain in force, with the 33/50 programme delivering additional benefits.

The combination of the two instruments means that participating firms go beyond the command and control baseline, but that non-participating firms must still comply with this baseline. If voluntarism were introduced alone, then there would be no guarantee that non-participating firms would not increase their levels of toxic chemical releases, thus free-riding on those committed to higher standards. The combination of voluntarism and performance based command and control, in this instance, has produced environmental improvements additional to that which could have been achieved if either were employed in isolation. It is important to note that, in contrast to beyond compliance activities, if voluntarism and performance based standards were targeting the *same* level of behaviour then, at best, they would be a duplicative combination, and, at worst, counterproductive.

Voluntarism may also work well with process based command and control regulation, for example, where the adoption of environmental management systems, such as ISO 14001, have been mandated.[132] Because process based prescriptions tend to be qualitative in nature, and therefore more difficult to measure quantitatively than performance or technology based standards, their full potential is difficult to enforce externally unless the regulated firm is committed to the concept. Voluntary based measures which seek to change the attitude of managers and the corporate culture may serve to reinforce a commitment to process based standards.

In contrast, technology based command and control regulation is unlikely to produce complementary outcomes when used in combination with voluntary measures. This is because technology based standards are highly prescriptive—firms can either comply or not, resulting in little room for beyond compliance achievements. In effect, technology based standards restrict the way in which firms respond to an environmental imperative, in terms of the method of environmental

in EPA's 33/50 Program' (1995) 28 (3) *Journal of Environmental Economics and Management* 271.

[132] W. L. Thomas, 'Using ISO 14001 to comply with the Management System Requirements of US EPA's RMP Rule and the EU's Seveso II Directive' (1988) *European Environmental Law Review* 335.

improvement, whereas voluntary measures are, in principle, designed to provide additional regulatory flexibility.

Self-regulation and command and control

As with voluntary measures, self-regulation that targets environmental performance that is beyond mandatory minimum standards, will also be inherently complementary with command and control regulation. The complementarity arises because the two instruments are targeting different levels of environmental performance, and because the command and control standard is not prescribing how the standard must be achieved (see also voluntarism and command and control for a similar conclusion). In these circumstances, as we saw in chapter four, regulation will be the rising floor that follows the vanguard of self-regulatory responses to environmental challenges, rather than the ceiling that gets imposed ahead of, and which limits, the voluntary responses.[133]

If, on the other hand, self-regulation and performance based (or indeed technology or processbased) command and control regulation were targeted at the same level of environmental performance, then, as we indicate below, the self-regulatory component would be redundant. However, later, we also demonstrate how the sequencing of command and control with self-regulatory instruments can be used to avoid such redundancy and build on their mutual strengths.

Command and control regulation (or self-regulation) and supply side incentives

Economic instruments in the form of supply side incentives, such as tax concessions or soft loans for environmental preferred technologies, will complement command and control regulation or self-regulation which target environmental performance directly related to those technologies.[134] For example, performance based regulation which requires firms to reduce their contribution to greenhouse gas emissions will obviously be assisted by incentives for firms to purchase more energy efficient industrial motors and drives or co-generation facilities. In the case of biodiversity conservation, the European Union has had particular success using a combination of grants and subsidies with regulation.[135]

---

[133] We are indebted to Brian Wastle for this metaphor.

[134] Although it could distort the choice of means.

[135] For example, in protected areas, regulations should be used to prevent site damage, while subsidies should encourage positive management of protected land.

Similarly, technology based standards, which could be mandated by government or take the form of self-regulatory codes of practice, are more likely to be complied with if there is an additional financial incentive associated with the purchase of the relevant technologies. However, the latter combination of instruments is probably a case of 'policy overkill', and is such a clear violation of the polluter pays principle that it could probably only be justified as a transitional arrangement where industry faces onerous competitive pressures. The complementary link between process based standards and supply side incentives is less obvious than that for the other forms of regulation. This is because process based standards do not necessarily entail a change in technology, particularly end-of-pipe technology. Rather, the emphasis is on developing systems which manage environmental issues better and, ideally, avoid problems before they arise, for example, through pollution prevention initiatives.

Command and control (or self-regulation) and broad based economic instruments (which target different aspects of a common problem)

Although the underlying rational of regulation, in the form of command and control or self-regulation, is fundamentally different to that of broad based economic instruments, their joint application may be complementary if they are used to target different aspects of a common environmental issue. The example of phasing out leaded fuel provides a good example. In Australia, all vehicles, post-1985, were required to be fitted with catalytic converters which necessarily entailed the use of engines which only operated on unleaded fuel (a conventional technology based command and control measure). The Federal Government also introduced a (phased) price differential on the price of fuel such that leaded fuel became more expensive than unleaded fuel (a broad based economic instrument, in the form of a pollution tax). The reason these two radically different policy approaches complement each other is that by addressing different contributory aspects of the same problem, they provide the market with mutually supportive signals—the technology based standard is directed at the vehicle manufacturer, while the pollution tax is directed at the consumer (contrast the situation described below, when they are used to address the same contributory activities).

Liability rules and command and control (or self-regulation)

Some forms of liability rules will complement command and control regulation (or self-regulation). Specifically, where the standard imposed under tort law is higher than that imposed by regulation, then the latter will act as a baseline, leaving the possibility that the courts will provide for higher standards in particular circumstances. However, one potentially undesirable side-effect will be that an individual court decision may destroy the uniformity provided by the regulation.[136]

Complementarity is also possible at the level of enforcement, provided that the negligence rule in torts is equal to or less stringent than the statutory standard.[137] As Simmons and Cowell argue: 'civil liability does not substitute for a strong regulatory framework. Yet strong regulation depends on a context that promotes a degree of compliance readiness on the part of the regulated community. Liability provides a powerful incentive . . . [and] complement[s] command and control and economic instruments'.[138] Similarly, concern about civil liability can result in increased self-regulation or voluntarism 'and stimulate innovative activity at the level of the firm'.[139] However, if the tort system imposes standards that are higher than those under regulation, then 'it undermines the notion that the regulatory system sets standards where benefits are balanced against costs. Under such conditions the two systems work at cross-purposes'.[140]

Broadbased economic instruments and compulsory reporting and monitoring provisions

Much of the early literature on economic instruments and on regulation assumes that these mechanisms should be treated as alternatives. Some economists, for example, begin by listing the shortcomings of command and control regulation before going on to argue that it should be replaced, in all except extreme cases, by economic instruments and other market-based mechanisms. However, this mutually exclusive treatment of economic instruments and regulation hides far more than it reveals.

---

[136] S. Rose-Ackerman, 'Public Law versus Private Law in European Regulation' (1996) 4(4) *RECEIL* 312 at 315.

[137] S. Rose-Ackerman, 'Public Law versus Private Law in European Regulation' (1996) 4 (4) *RECEIL* 312 at 315.

[138] P. Simmons & A. Cowell, 'Liability and the environment' (1993) in *Clean Production Strategies: Developing preventive environmental management in the industrial economy*, T. Jackson (ed.), Lewis Publishers, Boca Raton, p.364.

[139] *Ibid.*, p.364. The authors point out that liability rules do much more than just create a threat of financial penalty and thereby create incentives for improved environmental performance. In particular, 'they also create an added layer of horizontal control [e.g., transactional monitoring is extended to include environmental performance] reinforcing the effect of regulatory and market policy instruments'. *Ibid.* p.362.

[140] S. Rose-Ackerman, 'Public Law versus Private Law in European Regulation' (1996) 4 (4) *RECEIL* 312 at 315.

In practice, many economic instruments rely on a substantial underpin-ning of government regulation for their effective implementation.[141]

Most, if not all, broadbased economic instruments (such as pollution taxes and tradeable emission permits) require a certain level of com-mand and control in order to function effectively and equitably. Of par-ticular importance, in this regard, are compulsory reporting and monitoring provisions. For example, a tax on the level of effluent being discharged into a stream will only be a viable instrument if government (or conceivably a third party) can accurately measure the amount of discharge. Therefore, the economic instrument, in this instance, will need to be employed in conjunction with compulsory requirements for measuring and reporting the level of discharge, thus forming a com-plementary instrument combination.[142]

Similarly, tradeable permit schemes require that firms actually adhere to the requirements of the permit they have purchased (or have been granted), which necessarily entails the application of the com-mand and control performance standard inherent in the value of the permit. In addition, each time a trade takes place, the government (or conceivably a third party) must be kept informed in order to maintain accurate record keeping of the location and monetary value of permits, thus necessitating compulsory reporting requirements. There is a cru-cial distinction to be made between the application of command and control instruments, in this instance, which are essentially ancillary to broad based economic instruments, and those which are designed to address the same activities as economic instruments (see below).

Inherently counterproductive instrument combinations

Certain combinations of instruments are either inherently counterpro-ductive or, at the very least, sub-optimal. That is, their efficiency and effectiveness is significantly diminished when they are employed in combination. As with complementary combinations, we consider that the counterproductive or sub-optimal nature of these interactions is not context specific. This is not to suggest that such combinations should

---

[141] More recent and sophisticated studies recognize the substantial extent to which many economic instruments depend upon pre-existing traditional regulation, and the extent to which they will, as commonly, complement other policy instruments rather than replace them (e.g., OECD Draft Council Recommendation on the use of economic instruments in environmental policy, Env/Ec (90)23).

[142] G. Huppes, E. van der Voet, G. H. Vonkeman & P. Maxson, *New Market-Orientated Instruments for Environmental Policies* (1992), Graham and Trotman, London.

never be considered, but there would need to be some other overriding imperative (such as differences in regional assimilative capacities, discussed below) in order to justify the loss of regulatory efficiency. Some combinations, however, are so manifestly incompatible or antithetical (e.g., the free market environmentalism/property rights approach and command and control[143]) that policymakers are unlikely to ever contemplate them, and these merit no further discussion. However, other combinations are more complex and their implications less clear. These we explore below.

Command and control regulation and broad-based economic instruments (which target the same aspects of a common problem)

Most command and control instruments, specifically performance based standards and technology based standards, seek to impose predetermined environmental outcomes on industry. That is, even if the standards are not uniform (in that different requirements apply to different sectors, or indeed, different firms) individual firms are not free to make independent judgments as to their preferred method of environmental improvement (in the case of technology standards) or their overall level of environmental performance (in the case of performance standards). Economic instruments, in contrast, seek to maximize the flexibility of firms in making such decisions—government influences the overall level of environmental performance by providing a price signal relative to the level of pollution or resource consumption, or by creating a purchasable right to pollute or consume resources.[144]

If a command and control instrument were to be super-imposed on an economic instrument that targets the same behaviour, or vice versa, then to the extent that the command and control instrument limits the choice of firms in making individual decisions, the economic instrument will be compromised. That is, there will be a sub-optimal regulatory outcome. This is because, as we pointed out in chapter two, economic instruments are designed to exploit differences in the marginal cost of

[143] The creation of property rights over the use of natural resources, such as water or wildlife, where access was previously available to all, will be undermined by most forms of command and control regulation. This is because a central purpose of the property rights approach is to allow the unfettered operation of market forces, which the imposition of specific directives by government will necessarily inhibit (see chapter two for further discussion).

[144] Many economic instruments tend to work with gradations and continuously defined variables that give no place for people to 'dig in their heels'. See T. Schelling, *The Strategy of Conflict* (1960), Harvard University Press, Cambridge.

abatement between firms.[145] It makes economic sense for those firms which can reduce their levels of pollution most cheaply to carry a greater share of the abatement burden, and for those where it is most expensive, to carry a lesser share of the same burden. The result is that the net cost of reducing the overall level of pollution (or resource consumption) will be lessened, or, for a given level of expenditure, a greater level of pollution reduction will be achieved. By simultaneously applying a prescriptive command and control instrument, for example a performance standard which mandates levels of energy efficiency for firms in tandem with a broad based carbon tax, free market choices would be artificially restricted, thus undermining the basic rationale of the economic instrument.

Another example of where economic instruments and performance based command and control have been uneasy bedfellows is the case of load-based licensing. Introduced in several jurisdictions internationally, load-based licences set a maximum level of pollution output which is determined by the regulatory authorities. Such licences are often portrayed as another form of pollution tax. Firms are provided with an economic incentive for reducing pollution, via a reduction in licence fees, which is often combined with a mandatory maximum level of permissible pollution. In effect, regulators are taxing higher levels of pollution at the same time as imposing a command and control minimum performance standard.

By imposing the minimum performance standard, authorities are compromising the efficiency of the load-based licence fees. In the interests of efficiency, they should remove the minimum performance standard and allow those firms with a lower marginal cost of abatement to deliver the majority of the pollution reduction (and conversely, allow those with higher marginal costs to pay a higher tax, polluting at levels which may exceed the maximum contemplated under a licensing system). If the overall level of pollution remains too high, then the regulators should simply increase the size of the fee. If the fee is not set at a level sufficient to deliver the desired net outcome, and in many instances this will be the case, then, by implication, it is not acting as an effective economic instrument.[146] Sometimes, producers will be

---

[145] The 'marginal cost of abatement' is the cost for each firm or industry to reduce emissions of a particular pollutant by a given unit from their current level of emissions.

[146] For example, it may be that the load-based licence fee is, in essence, a revenue raising measure or principally symbolic in nature—one industry interviewee stated that the primary motivation for his firm's preference of load based licences was not financial,

unresponsive to higher fees (i.e., high inelasticity). Then, the policy-maker must either choose a more effective instrument or question whether the costs involved in achieving the environmental goal out-weigh the benefits.

There is, however, an extenuating circumstance which may justify the sub-optimal outcome in regulatory efficiency resulting from the combination of broad based economic instruments with prescriptive command and control. Where pollutants have highly localized impacts, through, for example, differences in assimilative capacities or proximity to local communities, effectiveness and equity issues may override the efficiency considerations. Localized impacts can be contrasted with global pollutants such as ozone depleting substances, greenhouse gas emissions, and to a lesser extent, sulphur dioxide emissions. In the case of highly localized pollutants, such as the run-off of agricultural chemicals into local river systems, it may be necessary to impose minimum levels of performance on firms/individuals in highly sensitive regions, or indeed a variety of different levels tailored to local conditions, even if there was a more general economic instrument in place. Although this would reduce the overall efficiency of the economic instrument, through the restriction of free market choice, this loss of efficiency may be justified on the grounds of effectiveness or equity.

Just as economic instruments are designed to maximize the choice of firms in determining their level of environmental performance, so too are they designed to maximize choice in the method of environmental improvement. In this sense, technology based standards which dictate the method of environmental improvement will necessarily be in conflict with such economic instruments. That is, the capacity of economic instruments to drive innovative improvements in environmental performance will be undermined by the predetermination of preferred solutions by regulatory authorities. In contrast, process based standards, which seek to bring about a systems-based improvement to environmental management, are unlikely to conflict with economic instruments as they neither seek to impose specific levels of environmental performance nor particular technologies for environmental improvement. On the other hand, if firm management responds rationally to the price signal provided by economic instruments, then it may be argued that process based standards would be redundant. However, as we have

rather it was to gain recognition for consistently exceeding minimum performance standards.

pointed out elsewhere, for a variety of reasons, firms are unlikely to be purely rational actors.[147]

Self-regulation and broad-based economic instruments

To the extent that self-regulatory measures mimic the impact of command and control instruments, then they too would be incompatible with broadbased economic instruments. If, for example, self-regulation required that firms meet uniform performance targets, then economic instruments designed to exploit differences in the marginal cost of abatement would be compromised. If self-regulation was used to impose industry-wide targets, thus leaving individual firms to determine the level of their contribution, then the effect of undermining broad-based economic instrument would be lessened. However, variations in the average marginal cost of abatement between sectors, would still compromise the efficiency of the economic instrument to the extent that it was prevented from exploiting these cost differences.

For example, the sector specific voluntary agreements that have been introduced in the Netherlands establish different targets for different sectors. Unless these agreements were established on the basis of perfect information, it is highly likely that they would not, in fact, accurately reflect the differences in the marginal cost of abatement between the sectors, let alone individual firms, nor would they be able to adapt to changes in those difference over time. As such, it would be counterproductive to combine them with a broad based economic instrument, because the latter does not discriminate between sectors.

A pertinent example of the incompatibility of self-regulation and broad-based economic instruments can be drawn from the policy mix used to phase out the use of ozone depleting substances, in particular CFCs, in Australia. Under the National Ozone Strategy, the Federal Government introduced a national cap on the production and importation of CFCs, with firms allowed to trade individual CFC quotas they had been allocated under the cap, in effect, a system of tradeable

---

[147] Contrary to the assumption of many neoclassical economists, industry is not composed of fully informed, flawlessly calculating individuals. In reality, people never have all the information they need, and yet they are unable to process all the information they have, rather they can only do one or a few things at a time, and can only attend to a small part of information recorded as memory or presented by the environment (most commonly, the situation is less than fully understood, not all options are recognized or fully assessed, and there is insufficient time to overcome these limitations) (see H. Simon, *Economics, Bounded Rationality and the Cognitive Revolution* (1992), Edward Elgar, England).

permits. Subsequently, however, the Federal and State governments negotiated a number of sector specific self-regulatory agreements with industry to phase out the use of CFCs. These agreements contained different timetables, both across different industrial sectors, and across different types of ozone depleting gases.

The incompatibility of these two approaches being used in combination is obvious. If the tradeable permits were to realize their efficiency potential, those firms which faced the highest cost of abatement, irrespective of the particular industry they belonged to, or the particular gas they used, should have been allowed to purchase the necessary CFC permits (albeit indirectly through the various importers and manufacturers of CFCs). This would have forced up the market price, thus encouraging those firms, again, irrespective of their industry sector, with lower abatement costs to reduce their consumption of CFCs. By imposing predetermined outcomes on the various industry sectors, the self-regulatory strategy effectively prevented such an outcome. Not surprisingly, the tradeable quota programme failed, with only one recorded trade having taken place.[148]

Technology based standards and performance based standards

In the United States, in particular, much command and control regulation has taken the form of technology based standards, such as BAT standards. And although, strictly, these do not mandate particular technological solutions, the practical result is that firms are unwittingly coerced into choosing specific technologies.[149] In addition, regulators may also employ technology specific regulations which mandate particular solutions. These are often used in relation to product standards. For example, in the case of vehicle safety in the United States, all new vehicles are required to be fitted with air bags for the front passengers. In contrast, performance based standards aim to avoid prescriptive technological solutions, leaving the method of compliance to individual firms (using the vehicle safety example, a performance based standard would simply require vehicle manufacturers to meet predetermined benchmarks—this may or may not involve the use of air bags[150]).

---

[148] In fairness, it should be pointed out that there were other contributory factors, in particular, the fact that the size of the overall quota was probably too large.

[149] See chapter two for further details.

[150] For example, the German automobile company, Audi, devised a mechanical system, based on cables, that shifted the engine and other dangerous components away from a vehicle's occupants in the event of a frontal collision, but was forced to resort to air bag technology in the face of, *inter alia*, United States safety legislation.

Although the differences between technology based and performance based standards may, in some instances, be an unintended outcome of regulatory practice, it is difficult not to conclude that they are fundamentally incompatible policy approaches. In the case of the former, regulators maintain a high degree of control over the direction and actuality of technological solutions. In the case of the latter, regulators are not concerned with the way in which firms run their industrial processes, rather the focus is on the level of environmental performance. It is highly unlikely that these two approaches can operate successfully simultaneously, and indeed, it may be argued that some of the difficulties associated in particular with United States' style command and control regulation is the result of authorities failing to adequately recognize their mutual incompatibility, and the merits of applying them in different circumstances.

For example, the United States EPA's Project XL initiative, which is designed to give firms much greater flexibility through the adoption of less prescriptive, performance orientated regulation, has failed to attract a substantial number of participants, due, at least in part, to the concern of firms that pre-existing BAT regulations may still apply. Thus, even if firms participating in Project XL reach agreement with regulatory authorities to put into place a performance and process based environmental management strategy, they may still be subject to Federal prosecution if they fail to comply with the Clean Air Act or the Clean Water Act.[151]

The clash of regulatory styles between technology based and performance based standards is exacerbated by the advent of multi-media, facility wide permits and bubble licences. Not only do such instruments avoid prescriptive technological solutions, they also allow them to aggregate their environmental performance across more than one media and more than one site. Residual BAT standards may thus undermine the potential benefits to be derived from such approaches.

Incentive based instruments and liability rules

The purpose of incentive based instruments is to allocate regulatory costs to those who can bear them most efficiently, thereby providing a search by regulatees for innovative ways to minimize environmental

---

[151] A. D. Carr & W. L. Thomas 'Devising a Compliance Strategy Under the ISO 14000 International Environmental Management Standards' (1997) 15 *Pace Environmental Law Review* 85.

damage. Pollution fees, tradeable pollution rights, offsets, and 'bubbles' all fall into this category. If such incentives are in operation at the same time as liability rules, then this will be either redundant or counterproductive. As Rose Ackerman points out: 'tort judgments will undermine such a regulatory scheme, especially if courts applied a strict liability standard, the type of standard which some United States judges have found least 'regulatory'. Thus, incentive-based statutes should include a provision clearly pre-empting tort actions'.[152]

Sequencing instrument combinations

One way of avoiding potentially dysfunctional results that can arise when applying incompatible instruments simultaneously (and of expanding the operational possibilities of compatible combinations) is to sequence their introduction.[153] That is, certain instruments would be held in reserve, only to be applied if and when other instruments demonstrably fail to meet pre-determined performance benchmarks. One type of sequencing is when an entirely new instrument category is introduced where previous categories have failed. Another version is when only the enforcement component of a pre-existing instrument is invoked to supplement the shortcomings of another. Logically, such sequencing would follow a progression of increasing levels of intervention.[154] The benefit of this approach is that considerable utility can be derived from otherwise counterproductive instrument combinations, and in the process, the overall dependability of the policy mix can be improved.

Self-regulation and sequential command and control

One way of bolstering the credibility of self-regulation is to underpin its purported targets with a back-drop of command and control regulation (commonly referred to as 'co-regulation'). That is, if and when it could be demonstrated that an individual firm or industry sector had failed to deliver the promised benefits, then the regulatory authorities could step in to impose mandatory requirements. Thus, the two instruments are applied sequentially: it is only when the first fails that the latter kicks in. As an added incentive to effective self-regulation, those mandatory

---

[152] S. Rose-Ackerman, 'Public Law versus Private Law in European Regulation' (1996) 4 (4) *RECEIL* 312 at 317.

[153] See further earlier discussion on instrument sequencing under principle three.

[154] See design principle two for further details.

requirements could be more onerous than if the firm had never participated in the self-regulatory scheme in the first place. Such a complementary combination has the added benefit to participating firms of minimizing the incidence of firms 'free-riding' on the efforts of others.

By sitting in reserve, to be imposed only when self-regulation fails, command and control, in the form of performance standards, can play an important complementary role in improving the operation of self-regulation. As we saw earlier, performance based standards form a natural partnership with self-regulation, with the former specifying a minimal level of performance based compliance, and the latter delivering results over and above this minimum. Process based standards may also be mutually reinforcing, or at worst, duplicative, to self-regulation (this is because process based standards, by requiring firms to take greater responsibility for environmental performance through the adoption of management systems, already have several features in common with self-regulation). Technology based standards, on the other hand, may be duplicative, or potentially even counterproductive, if used in simultaneous combination with self-regulation (for example, where a mandated technological solution is inconsistent with proposed self-regulatory solutions or where industry reacts defensively to external intervention).

Self-regulation and sequential broad-based economic instruments

A similar analysis to the above applies to the relationship between self-regulation and broad based economic instruments, namely that they are complementary when applied sequentially but not otherwise. However, in this case, the economic instruments are imposed when it is deemed that the entire self-regulatory regime has failed, rather than when an individual enterprise within that regime has failed to discharge its responsibilities under it. This provides an element of certainty and credibility to self-regulatory initiatives.

An example of this type of instrument sequencing can be drawn from a policy introduced in New Zealand, previously discussed, to reduce the emissions of greenhouse gases by industry. Under this policy, industry agreed to self-regulate a 5 per cent reduction in greenhouse gas emissions. However, the government announced in advance that if self-regulation failed, it would implement a broad based carbon tax. Similarly, in Australia, industry agreed to voluntarily phase-out the use of HCFCs through a programme of self-regulation, but on the clear understanding (included in legislation) that if it fails to meet pre-specified phase-out targets, then a tradeable quota scheme would automatically be introduced.[155]

Combinations where the outcome will be context-specific

While we have been able to identify a number of inherently compatible and inherently incompatible combinations, there will be other instrument combinations where it is not possible to state in the abstract whether the outcome will be positive or negative. Rather, much will depend on the particular context in which the two instruments are combined. For example, this is the case with combinations of voluntarism and self-regulation. These two instrument categories overlap to a substantial extent, and indeed, the borderline between them is significantly blurred—the main distinction, for our purposes, being that self-regulation entails social control by an industry association, whereas voluntarism is based on the individual firm undertaking to do the right thing unilaterally, without any basis in coercion. There is no inherent reason why these two instrument categories should be used in combination with each other, but equally no compelling reason why they should not.

Similarly, it is not easy to determine in advance the likely outcome of combinations using both the free market and self-regulation. In principle, self-regulation might appear to resonate with free market approaches—both (at least in their pure form), sharing an antipathy with government regulation. Yet in practice, self-regulation has often been used to achieve purposes quite antithetical to the ideals of the market—as in the many documented examples when it has resulted in collusive conduct and as a vehicle for restrictive trade practices.

The relationship between voluntarism and economic instruments is also likely to be context specific—it is difficult to generate broad lessons in the absence of specific details. Although strict economic theory would appear to make voluntarism redundant in the face of effective price signals, the relationship between the two in practice is less clear. To the extent that firms behave in less than fully rational ways (and there is considerable evidence of this[156]), then voluntarism might be complementary to economic instruments by bringing to the attention of managers opportunities for environmental improvement that would not have occurred if relying on price signals alone. For example, energy taxes will make many energy efficiency improvements financially

---

[155] Interestingly, the performance benchmarks agreed to by industry to avoid the introduction of tradeable quotas were significantly tougher than those required for Australia to meet its international obligations under the Montreal Protocol.

[156] See above, p.415.

advantageous, but as energy costs remain a minor component of many firms' overall costs structures, they may go unnoticed. Voluntary programmes may, however, encourage firms to actively seek out and exploit such opportunities. On the other hand, to the extent that voluntary measures mimic the effects of command and control regulation or self-regulation in interfering with the free operation of the market, that is by allowing pollution from those firms with higher marginal costs of abatement to be compensated by reductions in pollution from those with the lower costs, then the combination will, similarly, be counterproductive.

In light of these conclusions, it is important for policymakers to distinguish between different instruments combinations that are inherently antagonistic, and those instruments combinations which are dysfunctional essentially as a result of the contextual features surrounding their application. In many cases, the *latter* will arise because of the existence of competing policy goals (rather than any inherent incompatibility of the instrument combinations themselves). For example, in the case of biodiversity conservation in Australia, the introduction of policies to preserve biodiversity have, historically, been undermined by incentives for clearing native vegetation on private land. Also in Australia, the introduction of voluntary agreements with industry to reduce greenhouse gas emissions are compromised by the existence of generous tax subsidies for the use of diesel fuel. Where such conflicts exist, a priority for policymakers will be the removal of such perverse incentives.

Multi-instrument mixes

So far, we have confined our discussion to bipartite mixes. There is, of course, no reason why mixes should not be multipartite, and they commonly are. The benefit of our examination of bipartite mixes has been to identify complementary and counterproductive mixes, with the result that we know, in the case of multipartite mixes, what combinations to avoid, and which complementary combinations we might build upon. The possible permutations of multipartite mixes are very large indeed, and having given a detailed examination of bipartite mixes, it is neither necessary nor practicable to examine all or even most such combinations here. Instead, we make two general points about such mixes, giving examples to illustrate our arguments.

First, there are often additional synergies to be derived from mixing larger numbers of complementary instruments, resulting in a return which is greater than with a simple bipartite mix. For example, in some cases environmental insurance could, potentially, act as a considerable incentive to improved environmental performance, but, in practice, is often either unavailable or available only at very high premiums. Commonly, such insurance is unavailable because insurance companies lack access to reliable, independent information upon which to base their premium structures. For example, in the case of the chemical industry's Responsible Care initiative, the mere existence of the self-regulatory scheme was insufficient to convince the insurance industry to give discounted premiums to Responsible Care companies (i.e., insurance and self-regulation were unable to function as complementary combinations). However, in Canada, with the gradual introduction of verification by independent third parties of the environmental performance of individual enterprises, the insurance industry changed its position and is now beginning to provide substantial discounts to best practice companies. This, in turn, has created a further incentive for companies to enter Responsible Care and subject themselves to such verification.[157]

Secondly, the sequence in which the various components of multi-partite combinations are introduced may be crucial to their success. For example, there may be substantial efficiencies in offering regulatory flexibility to better environmental performers, but that the *quid pro quo* for this should include commitments by the enterprise to deliver environmental performance levels which go beyond compliance, independent indicators against which performance is measured, verified by an independent third party, disclosure to and dialogue with the community, and a set of triggers which, if activated, result in government intervention.[158] However, it is crucial to the success of this arrangement to order these various instruments. In particular, it is essential that government regulation serves as a backstop, only being invoked if other instruments fail to achieve the desired effect. It is this which enables government to 'regulate at a distance', providing industry (until it defects) with the autonomy and flexibility it demands, while saving scarce regulatory resources for other purposes.

Conclusion

In this final chapter, we have built upon the empirical and theoretical analysis presented in the previous chapters to identify broader lessons

---

[157] See chapter 4, above.   [158] *Ibid.*

concerning regulatory mix and the design of integrative environmental policy. More particularly, we have sought to identify a series of processes and principles which are central to optimal regulatory design, and to specify the circumstances under which particular combinations of instruments will facilitate successful policy outcomes. Before articulating how this has advanced the regulatory debate, it may be helpful to take stock, and summarize the arguments that have led us to this point.

We began, in Part One, by tracing the less than satisfactory performance of both the main government and market approaches to environmental protection, and by examining the arguments for utilizing a broader range of instruments and parties. In the case of instruments, we concluded that not only was the capacity of individual instruments to curb environmental degradation highly threat and context specific, but that rarely was a single instrument alone capable of delivering optimal policy outcomes. In respect of parties, we argued that not only first parties (government), but also second parties (business) and third parties (both commercial and non-commercial) could play important quasi-regulatory roles and contribute to achieving desired policy outcomes, far beyond that which has been contemplated to date.

Our general conclusion was that not only is it desirable to use a broader range of policy tools, but also to match the tools: with particular environmental problems; with the party or parties best capable of implementing them; and with each other. That is, it was in *combinations* of instruments and actors that the greatest hope lay of building on the strengths of individual mechanisms, while compensating for their weaknesses. And it was with government actively facilitating second and third party involvement that their potential as quasi-regulators was most likely to be realized.

Thus, the crucial policy question became: how, in what circumstances, and in what combinations, can the main classes of policy instruments and actors be used to achieve optimal policy mixes? In chapters four and five, we sought to address this question through our detailed studies of the chemical industry and agriculture. In doing so, we saw the myriad and complex ways in which instrument and institutional interactions can play out in the context of specific environmental and policy problems.

In chapter four, we paid particular attention to the potential of self-regulation (in the form of Responsible Care) and of process-based regulation (in the form of ISO 14001 or other management systems) to bring about cultural change and continuous improvement. We showed how these approaches did indeed have the capacity to deliver smarter regulation, but that in neither case were they likely to do so in isolation. Strikingly, both these approaches suffered from limitations which could only be overcome through integrating them with a variety of other instruments and institutions. In particular, integrated policy design, in the context of the chemical industry, implied the need for independent measures of environmental performance, third party oversight through independent audits, and community right to know. More generally, there was a role for broader stakeholder involvement, the introduction of incentives for regulatory flexibility, and government as backstop rather than as primary regulator.

We also emphasized the need to design different regulatory strategies for different types of firms. For example, we argued the value of a 'two track' regulatory system: one for best practice performers who should be encouraged and facilitated in going 'beyond compliance' with existing regulation, and another for laggards, who need to be brought up to the existing legal standards by a variety of other strategies. We sought to identify a variety of strategies appropriate for small enterprises, not least being a much expanded role for third party oversight and supply chain pressure though mechanisms such as product stewardship. Finally, we explored the roles of co-regulation and tripartism, of accountability, transparency, and consultation, and of 'de-centering the state' so that it acts more as facilitator, catalyst and activator, and less as direct regulator.

In chapter five, we studied the very different environmental challenges confronting the agriculture industry, and in particular, biodiversity conservation and agricultural chemicals. In agriculture, unlike the chemical industry, command and control regulation usually plays only a modest supporting role, and the favoured policy tools are more likely to be subsidies and education. Moreover, the environmental threats themselves, and the obstacles to effective social control, are radically different from those confronting the chemical industry. Consequently, in terms of regulatory design, the solutions are also radically different.

Here too, we argued the case for an integrated approach, though one using very different instrument mixes from those contemplated for the chemical industry. We stressed the imperative of complementary combinations, using positive incentives, price-based instruments and property rights, backed under specific circumstances, by coercive sanctions, and underpinned in all circumstances by information and voluntarism.

Crucial to our analysis was the impact of institutions on instrument implementation. Here, we focussed on the critically important, but commonly unrecognized regulatory role, of a variety of third parties, and on how commercial institutions, supply side pressure, and institutions of finance and insurance, can contribute to the cause of sustainable agriculture.

From this analysis, we identified a number of design considerations which are crucial to achieving sustainable agriculture. These include:

(i)   the importance of instrument ordering (for example, only *after* the removal or neutralization of subsidies will other instruments function effectively);

(ii) the need to use institutional mixes (for scrutiny on the part of public interest groups or a range of financial institutions can exceed the vigilance of government agencies);

(iii) the significance of the economic and structural setting (for different mixes will be appropriate in different socio-economic circumstances);

(iv) the need to design for precaution (for the consequences of irreversible species loss necessitates using the full suite of instruments available);

(v)   the importance of addressing the first mover problem and moral hazard; and

(vi) the need to design mixes that are overall, financially attractive (for where ongoing contributions to sustainable agriculture are required, negative mechanisms alone are incapable of ensuring appropriate land management or of engendering the necessary custodial ethos).

Returning to this final chapter, we have attempted to transcend our previous sector-specific analysis to derive more widely applicable lessons about how policymakers should proceed in designing integrative environmental policy. We have done so under three broad headings. First, we demonstrated the need for policymakers to engage in a series of preliminary *process based* questions in order to identify the desired policy outcomes and the trade-offs necessary to achieve it, the unique characteristics of the environmental problem being addressed, and the range of potential regulatory participants (and policy instruments). In this section, our main concern was to underscore the importance of these processes and the dire consequences of failing to address them.

In the second section, we argued that successful regulatory design depended crucially upon adhering to a number of *regulatory design principles* which have hitherto not featured prominently, if at all, on the policy agenda. We argued for a substantial reconceptualization of some ideas which have already permeated the regulatory debate (e.g., mechanisms intended to achieve responsive regulation and the role of an instrument pyramid) and for the introduction of a number of others which have yet to influence that debate. For example, policy discussion of instrument use is now advancing beyond the stage where different groups simply argue the supremacy of individual approaches (e.g., *either* economic instruments *or* direct regulation) to one where it is now acceptable to incant the need for policy mixes. However, the crucial next stage, of articulating what the implications of this may be, and of identifying precisely *how* successful policy mixes should be designed, has barely begun. One aim in this book has been to advance that debate.

In doing so, we have counselled policymakers to adhere to a number of guiding principles geared to ensuring that the combinations they choose are not only efficient and effective, but to the extent possible, politically acceptable and equitable (while recognizing the possible tensions between these criteria). For example, we stressed the importance of preferring the least interventionist measures *that will work*, because highly interventionist alternatives perform badly in terms of at least three of our evaluation criteria. Of equal importance, we indicated what it would mean to apply this principle across a broad range of circumstances, and the dynamic rather than static nature of its successful application.

The heuristic device of a three sided pyramid was introduced, thereby encapsulating not only the Braithwaitian concept of a graduation to higher levels of intervention (in response to regulatory resistance) but more importantly, of achieving this through interactions between different, but complementary instruments *and* parties. We also emphasized the potential of instrument sequencing, a largely unrecognized technique which enables a temporal response to regulatory performance and builds in dependability. To this analysis, we add the features of triggers (designed to warn the authorities when less interventionist measures have failed and to invoke sequencing), buffer zones (designed to pre-empt unacceptable levels of environmental harm before a trigger is set off), and circuit breakers (designed to pre-empt the anticipated failure of another instrument by providing short-term reinforcement until political obstacles are overcome or cultural change achieved).

Consistent with the pursuit of pluralistic regulatory policy, we argued for the importance of harnessing resources *outside* the public sector by empowering third parties which are in the best position to act as surrogate regulators. In doing so, we recognized that the regulatory potential of many third parties is unlikely to be realized spontaneously, and it is only if the state is prepared to intervene, acting as catalyst, activator, or facilitator, that they are likely to perform successfully in a quasi-regulatory capacity.

Finally, we addressed one of the most crucial contemporary debates about the future of regulation: the extent to which it is possible to design policy in such a way as to encourage and facilitate industry in going 'beyond compliance' with existing regulation. Here, we argue not only the importance of state intervention in nudging industry towards win-win solutions, but also the largely unrealized potential to 'move the goalposts' so that, at the margin, win-lose situations are transformed into win-win.

Our last challenge, and the third of the main tasks we addressed in this chapter, was that of designing successful policy mixes. Given the very large number of possible permutations, this task can all too easily become encyclopaedic. To avoid both the impracticality of this approach and the indigestion of the reader, we steered a more modest course, identifying the most important combinations and explaining, in each case, why they are variously complementary or counterproductive (or, in some cases, why the answer is context specific), and why it matters.

At the end of the day, we hope that our contribution to the process of regulatory design will not only assist policymakers to achieve 'smarter' regulation, but also that, in some small way, it will move industry further along the path towards environmental sustainability.

Selected Bibliography

Aalders, M., 'Regulation and In-Company Environmental Management in the Netherlands' (1993) 15(2) *Law and Policy* 75–94.

Abrams, R. & Ward, D. H., 'Prospects for Safer Communities: Emergency response, community right to know, and prevention of chemical accidents' (1990) 14 *Harvard Environmental Law Review* 135–88.

Ackerman, B. A. & Hassler, W. T., *Clean Coal/Dirty Air or How the Clean Air Act became a Multibillion-Dollar Bail-Out for High-Sulfur Coal Producers and What Should Be Done About It* (1981), Yale University Press, New Haven.

Ackerman, B. A. & Stewart, R. B., 'Reforming Environmental Law' (1985) 37 *Stanford Law Review* 1333.

Adams, P. & Ruchel, M., *Unlocking the Factory Door* (1992), Report of the Coode Island Review Panel by the Hazardous Materials Action Group, Melbourne.

Afsah, S., Lapante, B. & Wheeler, D., 'Controlling Industrial Pollution: A new paradigm' (1996) October, *Policy Research Working Paper*, World Bank, Policy Research Department.

'Agri Finance, Checking Out Organic Farming' (1994) 36(3) *Agri Finance* 33.

Allan, L., Kaufman, E. K. & Underwood, J. D., *Paper Profits: Pollution in the pulp and paper industry* (1972), MIT Press, Cambridge.

Allen, K. (ed.), *Agricultural Policies in a New Decade. Resources for the future* (1990), Washington, DC.

Allott, K., *Integrated Pollution Control: The first three years* (1994), Environmental Data Services, London.

Alm, A. L., 'A Need For new Approaches: Command-and-control is no longer a cure-all' (May–June 1992) *EPA Journal* 6–11.

Anderson, T., 'At Home on the Range with the Wolves: Making a Liability into an Asset' (1995) 2 (June) Ecoworld.com.

Anderson, T. L. & Leal, D. R., *Free Market Environmentalism* (1991), Westview Press, Boulder, Co.

—— 'Free Market Versus Political Environmentalism' (1992) 15 *Harvard Journal of Law and Public Policy* 297–310.

Anhang, G., 'Cleaning Up the Lender Management Participation Standard under Comprehensive Environmental Response Compensation and Liability Act 1980 in the Aftermath of Fleet Factors' (1990) 15 *Harvard Environmental Law Review* 235.

Anon, 'Ruckelshaus Worried Citizen Suits Will Reveal Poor Enforcement Record' (1984), May 11, *Inside EPA*, United States Environment Protection Agency.

Arora, S. & Cason, T. N., 'An Experiment in Voluntary Environmental Regulation: Participation in EPA's 33/50 Program' (1995) 28(3) *Journal of Environmental Economics and Management* 271.

Aspen Institute *The Alternative Path: A cleaner, cheaper way to protect and enhance the environment* (1996), Program for Energy, the Environment and the Economy, The Aspen Institute, US.

Atcheson, J., 'Can We Trust Verification?' (1996) 13(4) *Environmental Forum* 19.

Austin, J., 'The Rise of Citizen Suit Enforcement in Environmental Law: Reconciling the private and public Attorney-General' (1987) 81 *Northwestern University Law Review* 220–62.

Australia and New Zealand Environment and Conservation Council (ANZECC), *Revised Strategy for Ozone Protection in Australia* Report No. 30 (1994), AGPS, Canberra.

Australia and New Zealand Task Force on Biological Diversity, *National Strategy for the Conservation of Australia's Biological Diversity* (1993), Department of the Environment Sports and Territories, Canberra.

Australian Chemical Industry Council (ACFIC), *Responsible Care Program Guide* (1989), ACIC, Melbourne.

—— 'Summary and Conclusions' *ACIC—Monitoring Community Attitudes* (December 1992) 11.

—— *Annual Report* (1993), ACIC, Melbourne.

—— *Product Stewardship: Interim Code of Practice* (1994), ACIC, Melbourne.

Australian Manufacturing Council (AMC), *Best Practice Environmental Regulation* (1993).

Aylward, B. A., 'Appropriating the Value of Wildlife and Wetlands' (1992) in T. M. Swanson & E. B. Barbier, (eds.) *Economics for the Wilds*, Island Press, Washington DC.

Ayres, I. & Braithwaite, J., *Responsive Regulation: Transcending the deregulation debate* (1992), Oxford University Press, New York.

Baar, E., 'Contracting Out Regulatory Implementation' (1993), paper delivered at the Canadian Law and Society meeting, Ottawa, June 8.

Bakkenist, G., *Environmental Information: Law, policy and experience* (1994), Cameron May, London.

Barbier, E. B., 'Community-based development in Africa' (1992) in T. M. Swanson & E. B. Barbier (eds.) *Economics for the Wilds*, Island Press, Washington DC.

Barbier, E. B., Burgess, J. C. & Folke, C., *Paradise Lost? The ecological economics of biodiversity* (1994), Earthscan Publications Ltd, London.

Bardach, E. & Kagan, R., *Going by the Book: The problem of regulatory unreasonableness* (1982), Temple University Press, Philadelphia.

Barr, N. F. & Cary, J. W., *Greening a Brown Land: The Australian search for sustainable land use* (1992), Macmillan, South Melbourne.

Baumol, W. & Oates, W., *The Theory of Environmental Policy* (1988) (2nd edn.), Cambridge University Press, Cambridge.

Beale, B. & Fray, P., *The Vanishing Continent: Australia's degraded environment* (1990), Hodder & Stoughton, Sydney.

Bean, M. & Wilcove, D., 'Ending the Impasse' (July/Aug 1996) 13(4) *Environmental Forum* 22.

Becker, G. S. & Stigler, G. T., 'Law Enforcement, Malfeasance, and Compensation of Enforcers' (1974) 3(1) *Journal of Legal Studies* 1.

Beech-Nut, *Beech-Nut Pesticide Residue Control Program* (1997), at http://www.familyinternet.com/beech-nut/res.htm.

Begley, R., 'Product Stewardship: Exploring the "How-To" ' (11 December 1991) *Chemical Week* 13.

—— 'Implementing a Philosophy: facing the challenges of the most sweeping code' (17 June 1992) *Chemical Week* 68.

—— 'Will the Real Chemical Industry Please Stand Up?' (7–14 July 1993) *Chemical Week* 18.

Bell, C. L., 'Bench Test' (10 November 1997) *The Environmental Forum* at 24.

Bennett, A. F., Backhouse, G. & Clark, T., (eds.) *People and Nature Conservation: Perspective's on private land use and endangered species recovery* (1995), Surrey Beatty and Sons, Chipping Norton.

Bennett, M. and James, P., 'Environment-Related Management Accounting: Current practice and future trends' (1997) 17 *Greener Management International* 32–52.

Berkes, F., 'Marine Inshore Management in Turkey' in National Research Council, *Proceedings of the Conference on Common Property Resource Management* (1986), National Academy Press, Washington DC.

Berle, G., *The Green Entrepreneur* (1991), Liberty Hall Press, New York.

Bernstein, J., *Alternative Approaches to Pollution Control and Waste Management— Regulatory and Economic Instruments* (1993), The World Bank, Washington DC.

Black, D., 'The Epistemology of Pure Sociology' (1995) 20(3) *Law and Social Inquiry* 829.

Blakeney, M. & Barnes, S., 'Advertising Deregulation: Public health or private profit' (1984) in R. Tomasic (ed.) *Business Regulation in Australia*, CCH Australia, North Ryde.

Blumm, M. C., 'The Fallacies of Free Market Environmentalism' (1992) 15 *Harvard Journal of Law & Public Policy* 371–89.

Boehlje, M., Duncan, M. & Lins, D., *Agricultural and Rural Finance Policy* (1996) at http://ianrwww.unl.edu:80/farmbill/finance.htm.

Bonyhady, T., *Places Worth Keeping: conservationists, politics and law* (1993), Allen & Unwin, Sydney.

Botlain, D. B., *Discordant Harmonies* (1990), Oxford University Press, New York.

Bowers, J., *Incentives and Mechanisms for Biodiversity: Observations and Issues* (1994), CSIRO Division of Wildlife and Ecology, Canberra.

Boyer, B. & Meidinger, E., 'Privatising Regulatory Enforcement: A preliminary assessment of citizen suits under Federal environmental laws' (1985) 34 *Buffalo Law Review* 833–964.

Bradsen, J., 'The "Green Issues": Biodiversity Conservation in Australia' (1994) in B. Boer, R. Fowler & N. Gunningham (eds.) *Environmental Outlook: Law and Policy*, Federation Press, Sydney.

Braithwaite, J., *To Punish or Persuade: Enforcement of coal mine safety* (1985), State University of New York Press, Albany.

—— *Crime, Shame and Reintegration* (1989), Cambridge University Press, Cambridge.

—— 'Policies for an Era of Regulatory Flux' (1991) in B. Head & E. McCoy (eds.) *Deregulation or Better Regulation?*, Macmillan Press, Melbourne.

—— 'Responsive Business Regulatory Institutions' (1993) in C. Cody and C. Stampford (eds.), *Business, Ethics and Law*, Federation Press, Sydney.

Braithwaite, J. & Fisse, B., 'Self Regulation and the Costs of Corporate Crime' in C. D. Shearing & P. C. Stenning *Private Policing* (1987), Sage Publications, Beverley Hills.

Braithwaite, J. & Makkai, T., 'Trust and Compliance' (1994b) 4 *Policing and Society* 1.

Bressers, H. & Klok, P. J., 'Fundamentals for a Theory of Policy Design' (1988) 15(3/4) *International Journal of Social Economics* 22.

Breyer, S., *Regulation And Its Reform* (1982), Harvard University Press, Cambridge.

—— *Breaking the Vicious Circle: Toward effective risk regulation* (1993), Harvard University Press, Cambridge.

Bricknell, D. J., *Response by the Chemical Industry in Europe to the 'Green Paper on Innovation'* (April 1996), SUSTECH Position Paper, CEFIC, Brussels.

Briggs, D. J. & Courtney, F. M., *Agriculture and Environment: The physical geography of temperate agricultural systems* (1985), Longman, London.

Brinkman, R., Jasanoff, S. & Ilgen, T., *Controlling Chemicals: The politics of regulation in Europe and the United States* (1986), Cornell University Press, Ithaca.

Brotherton, I., 'On the Voluntary Approach to Resolving Rural Conflict' (1990) 22 *Environment and Planning* 925–939.

Brown, L. R., Flavin, C. & Postel, S., *Saving the Planet: How to shape an environmentally sustainable global economy* (1991), W. W. Norton, New York.

Browner, C. in W. E. Orts 'Reflexive Environmental Law' (1995) 89(4) *Northwestern University Law Review* 1227.

Brunet, E., 'Debunking Wholesale Private Enforcement of Environmental Rights' (1992) 15 *Harvard Journal of Law & Public Policy* 311–24).

Buchanan, J., 'Politics without Romance' (1994) in J. Buchanan & R. Tollison (eds.) *The Theory of Public Choice—II*, University of Michigan Press.

Burbidge, A. A. & Wallace, K. J., 'Practical Steps for Conserving Biodiversity' (1995) in R. A. Bradstock, T. D. Auld, D. A. Keith, R. T. Kingsford, D. Lunney & D. P. Sivertsen (eds.) *Conserving Biodiversity: Threats and solutions*, Surrey Beatty & Sons, Chipping Norton.

Burchell, G., 'Civil Society and the System of Natural Liberty' (1991) in G. Burchell, C. Gordon & P. M. Miller (eds.), *The Foucault Effect: Studies in governmentality*, Harvester Wheatsheaf, London.

Bureau of Industry Economics, *Environmental Regulation: The Economics of Tradeable Permits—A survey of theory and practice*, Research Report 42, (1992), AGPS, Canberra.

Bureau of National Affairs (Washington DC), 'From Command and Control to Self-Regulation: The Role of Environmental Management Systems' *International Environmental Review*, March 5, 1997 227.

Burke, N., *Gaining Organisational Commitments to OH&S by Integrating Safety Onto Your Business Plans* (1994), paper presented at Proactive OH&S Management Conference, Sydney 9–10 March.

Burton, L., *Environmental Equity and NAFTA Implementation* (1994), a paper presented to Law and Society Association Meeting, 16–19 June, Phoenix, Arizona.

Business and the Environment, 'Alliance for Environmental Innovation to Start First Projects This Spring' (1996) VII(3) (March) *Business and the Environment*.

Cahill, R., *Disasters at Sea, Titanic to Exxon Valdez* (1990), Nautical Press, Texas.

Cairncross, F., *Costing the Earth: The challenge for governments, the opportunities for business* (1992), Harvard Business School Press, Boston.

Calavita, K. & Pontell, H. N., 'The State And White Collar Crime: Saving the Savings and Loan' (1994) 28(2) *Law and Society Review* 297–324.

Caminker, E., 'The Constitutionality of Qui Tam Actions' (1989) 99 *Yale Law Journal* 341–388.

Campbell, A., *Landcare: Communities shaping the land and the future* (1994), Allen and Unwin, Sydney.

Campbell-Mohn, C., Breen, B. & Futrell, J. W. (eds.), *Sustainable Environmental Law* (1993), Environmental Law Institute, St Paul, Minnesota, US.

Canadian Chemical Producers' Association, *Reducing Emissions: 1994 Emissions Inventory and Five Year Projections* (1994), Canadian Chemical Producers' Association, Ottawa.

—— *Does Responsible Care Work?* (May 1996), Canadian Chemical Producers Association, Ottawa.

Cappelletti, M., Seccombe, M. & Weiler, J. (eds.), *Methods, Tools and Institutions* (1986), W de Gruyer, Berlin.

Careline 'ICCA readies itself for Ottawa Forum' (1996), 5 *Careline* 1.

—— 'The Responsible Care, ISO 14001 intersection' (7 April 1997) *Careline* 8–10.

—— 'The Verdict on Verification From Canada' (7 April 1997) *Careline* 4.

Carr, D. A. & Thomas, W. L., 'Devising A Compliance Strategy Under the ISO 14000 International Environmental Management Standards' (1997) 15 *Pace Environmental Law Review* 85.

Catherine, F. 'Advocacy Groups and Business form Enviro Alliance' (March 4–17 1996) Mass High Tech.

Cattle Council of Australia, *Cattlecare* (1997), Cattle Council of Australia, Sydney at http://www.farmwide.com.au/nff/cattlecouncil/prod05.htm.

Centner, T. J., Houston, J. E., Fuchs, C. & Zeddies, J., 'Employing Best Management Practices to Reduce Agricultural Water Pollution: Economics, regulatory institutions, and policy concerns' 45(1) *Drake Law Review* 125–141.

Cerexbe, P., 'Advertising Self Regulation: The Clayton's Codes' (1988) 38 *Consuming Interests* 16–20.

Chang, R., *TQM Fever* (1995), an interview presented by Business Report on ABC National Radio, July.

Cheit, R., *Setting Safety Standards: Regulation in the private and public sectors* (1990), University of California Press, Berkeley.

Chemical Manufacturers Association (CMA), *Responsible Care: Progress Report 1994–95* (1995), CMA, Washington DC.

—— *US Chemical Industry Statistical Handbook 1995* (1995), CMA, Washington DC.

—— *Fact Sheet: Chemical Industry Halves Toxic Releases* (1996), Washington DC.

—— '*The year in review, 1995–96' Responsible Care Progress Report* (1996), Washington DC.

—— *Annual Reports for 1996 and 1997* (1997), CMA, Washington DC.

—— *US Chemical Industry Statistical Handbook 1995* (1995), Chemical Manufacturers Association, Washington DC.

Chemical Week 'Care gives industry a leadership role in sustainable development' July 7–14 (1993) *Chemical Week* 20.

—— *CMA Measures Product Stewardship*, 16 April 1997 *Chemical Week*.

Chisholm, A. G. & Moran, A. J. (eds.) *The Price of Preservation*, Tasman Institute, Melbourne, 1993.

Chynoweth, E. & Heller, K., 'Wanted: A System to Audit Care: Environmentalists and industry forge ahead' (17 June 1992) 150(23) *Chemical Week* 28.

Chynoweth, E. & Jackson, D., 'Tour de Force: The Ambassadors' (7 July 1993) *Chemical Week* 126.

Clinton, W. J. and Gore, A. Jr., *Reinventing Environmental Regulation* (1995), White House, Washington DC.

'CMA Verification Process Kicks Off to Successful Start' (1997) 6 *Careline* 10.

Coeyman, M., 'Customers Get New Attention: Product stewardship from the buyer's side' (8 December 1993) 153(22) *Chemical Week* 34.

—— 'Making Product Stewardship a Reality' (7 July 1993) *Chemical Week* 37.

—— 'Responsible Care: Code implementation contracts' (7/14 July 1993) 153(1) *Chemical Week* 14.

Coffee, J. C., 'Environmental Crime and Punishment' (3 February 1994) *New York Law Journal* 10.

—— 'No Soul to Damn: No Body to Kick: An unscandalised inquiry into the problem of corporate punishment' (1981) 79 *Michigan Law Review* 386.

—— 'Rescuing the Private Attorney General: Why the model of the lawyer as bounty hunter is not working' (1983) 42 *Maryland Law Review* 215–288.

Cohen, D. S., 'The Regulation of Green Advertising: The state, the market and the environmental good' (1991) 25 *University of British Columbia Law Review* 225.

—— 'Voluntary Codes: The Role of the Canadian State in a Privatised Regulatory Environment' (1996), a draft paper presented at the Voluntary Codes Symposium, Office of Consumer Affairs, Industry Canada and Regulatory Affairs, Treasury Board, Ottawa, September.

Cohen, M. & Rubin, P., 'Private Enforcement of Public Policy' (1985) 3(1) *Yale Journal on Regulation* 167–194.

Cohen, S., 'EPA: A Qualified Success' in S. Kamieniecki, R. O'Brien & M. Clarke (eds.), *Controversies in Environmental Policy* (1986), State University of New York Press, Albany.

Cohen, D. S. & Webb, K. (eds.), *Exploring Voluntary Codes in the Marketplace*, Government of Canada, Ottawa (due to be published in 1998).

Commission of the European Community (CEC), *Towards Sustainability* Fifth Action Program of European Union (1992), Brussels.

Commoner, B., 'Failure of the Environmental Effort' (1988) 10 *Environmental Law Reporter* 195.

—— *Making Peace with the Planet* (1990), Pantheon Books, New York.

Commonwealth of Australia Department of Environment Sport & Territories, *The National Strategy for the Conservation of Australia's Biological Diversity* (1996), Department of Environment Sport & Territories, Canberra.

Commonwealth of Australia Department of Finance, *Submission to HORSCERA: Inquiry into management arrangements for inscribed World Heritage Areas* (1994) AGPS, Canberra.

Commonwealth of Australia, Industry Commission, *Work, Health & Safety: Inquiry into occupational health and safety* (1995), Volume I Report No. 47, AGPS, Canberra.

Commonwealth of Australia, Department of Primary Industries and Energy, Standing Committee on Agriculture and Resource Management, Agricultural and Veterinary Chemicals Policy Committee, *Australian National Strategy for Agricultural and Veterinary Chemicals* (10 April 1997), Department of Primary Industries and Energy, Canberra.

Commonwealth of Australia Ecologically Sustainable Development Steering Committee, *National Strategy for Ecologically Sustainable Development in Australia* (1992), AGPS, Canberra.

Commonwealth of Australia Ecologically Sustainable Development Working Group, *Intersectional Issues Report* (1992), AGPS, Canberra, in M. D. Young *et al.*, 'Feedlots and Water Quality' (1994) 11 *Australian Journal of Environmental Management* 52.

Commonwealth of Australia, Office of Regulation Review (1997) *A Guide to Regulation*, AGPS, October.

Conveyancer & Property Lawyer, 'Digging Deep: Re-using Contaminated Land' (191), 87 *Conveyancer & Property Lawyer* 249.

Crabtree, B., 'A viable framework for stewardship' (1995) 9(3) *Perspectives* 6.

Craik, W., *IPM—The Way Forward* (1996) Address to The Avcare Annual Convention, Perth, Western Australia, 15 October: http:// coombs. anu.edu.au/SpecialProj/NFF/avcare.html).

Cramb, A., 'Protection Money Will Help Crofters and Corncrakes' (1993) *Reuters News Service*, 24 February.

Cushman, J. R., 'Virginia Seen as Undercutting US Environmental Rules' (1997) *New York Times* 19 January 11.

Davidson, B. R., *European Farming in Australia: An economic history of Australian farming* (1981), Elsevier Scientific Publications, Amsterdam.

Davies, T. & Mazurek, J., *Industry Incentives for Environmental Improvement: Evaluation of US Federal Initiatives* (1996) A Report to the Global Environmental Management Initiative Center for Risk Management, Resources for the Future, Washington DC.

Davy, B., *Essential Injustice: When legal instruments cannot resolve environmental and land use disputes* (1997), Verlag Springer, Vienna.

Dawson, S. & Gunningham, N., 'The More Dolphins There Are the Less I Trust What They're Saying: Can green labelling work?' (1996) 18(1) *Adelaide Law Review* 1.

De Klemm, C., 'The Regulation and Management of Destructive Processes' (1997) 27(4) *Environmental Law and Policy* 350–354.

De Morris, G., 'Whistle Stop Tour Delivers TransCAER Message' (1993) *Chemical Week* 8 December: 40.

De Simone, L. D. & Popoff, F. with World Business Council on Sustainable Development, *Eco-Efficiency: The Business Link to Sustainable Development* (1997), MIT Press, Cambridge.

De Witt, J., *Civic Environmentalism* (1994), C Q Press, Washington.

Debailleul, G., 'Economic Incentives for Biodiversity Conservation in the Agricultural Sector' in OECD, *Investing In Biological Diversity: The Cairns Conference* (1997), OECD, Paris.

Deegan, C., 'Corporate Environmental Reporting in Australia—a review and critical assessment' (1996), a paper presented at the 1996 Australian Academy of Science *Fenner Conference on the Environment: Linking Environment and Economy Through Indicators and Accounting Systems*, 30 September–3 October, The University of New South Wales, Sydney.

Deloitte Touche Tohmatsu International, *Coming Clean: Corporate environmental reporting* (1993), Deloitte Touche Tohmatsu International, London.

Dezalay, Y. & Garth, B. G., *Dealing In Virtue: International commercial arbitration and the construction of a transnational legal order* (1996), University of Chicago Press, Chicago.

Di Iulio, J., Garvey, G. & Kettl, D., *Improving Government Performance* (1993), The Brookings Institution, Washington DC.

Dieker, C., *Lessons from Uncle Sam: Regulation v economic incentives* (1997), a paper delivered at 16th Australian National Environmental Law Conference, Adelaide, April.

Dillon, P. & Baram, M., 'Forces Shaping the Development and Use of Product Stewardship in the Private Sector' (1993) in K. Fischer and J. Schot (eds.), *Environmental Strategies for Industry*, Island Press, Washington DC.

Dimento, J. F., *Environmental Law and American Business: Dilemmas of compliance* (1986), Plenum Press, New York.

Ditz, D. & Ranganathan, J., *Measuring Up: Toward a Common Framework for Tracking Corporate Environmental Performance* (1997), World Resources Institute, Washington DC.

Dovers, S., 'Information, Sustainability and Policy' (1995) 2(3) *Australian Journal of Environmental Management* 149.

Dowie, M., *Losing Ground: American environmentalism at the close of the twentieth century* (1996), MIT Press, Cambridge.

Dryzek, J., *Ecological Rationality* (1987), Blackwell, Oxford.

Dumaresq, D. & Greene, R., *From Farmer to Consumer: The future of organic agriculture in Australia* (1997), Rural Industries Research and Development Corporation, Canberra.

Dyson, K. & Wilks, S. (eds.), *Industrial Crisis: A comparative study of the state and industry* (1983), Robertson, Oxford.

Easterbrook, G., *A Moment On The Earth: The coming of age of environmental optimism* (1995), Viking Press, New York.

Eckersley, R., 'Rationalising the environment: How Much am I Bid?' in S. Rees, G. Rodley & F. Stilwell (eds.) *Beyond the Market: Alternatives to economic rationalisation* (1993), Pluto Press, Leichhardt.

—— *Markets, the State and the Environment* (1995), Macmillan Press, Melbourne.

—— (ed.), *Markets, the State and the Environment* (1995), Macmillan Press, Melbourne.

Ehrenfeld, J., *ISO 14000 and Responsible Care: What Kind of Change Agents Are They?* (1995), paper presented to ISO 14000: Preparing for Change Conference, Houston, September.

Ehrlich, E., *Fundamental Principles in the Sociology of Law* (1912) Harvard University Press, Cambridge.

Ekstrom, G. (ed.) *World Directory of Pesticide Control Organisations* (1996), Crop Protection Publications, London.

Elkington, J., Knight, P. & Hailes, J., *The Green Business Guide* (1992), Victor Gollancz, London.

Elliott, E. D., 'Environmental TQM: Anatomy of a pollution control program that works!' (1994) 92 *Michigan Law Review* 1847.

Elliott, E. D. & Thomas, E. M., 'Chemicals' (1993) in C. Campbell-Mohn, B. Breen & J. W. Futrell (eds.) *Sustainable Environmental Law*, Environmental Law Institute, St Paul, Minnesota.

Ember, L., 'Overhaul of Environmental Law Needed for Sustainable Development' (1993) *Chemical and Engineering News* 17.

Endangered Species Bulletin Vol. XXI No. 1 at http://www.fws.gov/~r9end-spp/esb/96/pfw.html).

Environment Canada Multi-Stakeholder Advisory Committee *National Pollutant Release Inventory for Canada* (1992), Environment Canada, Ottawa.

Environment Policy and Law 'Environmental Covenants' (1994) 24(4) *Environment Policy and Law* 191.

Environmental and Natural Resources Law Program, Stanford University, *Blueprint for Environmental Partnerships*, Stanford University, US (publication due 1998).

Environmental Business, September 1994, 29.

Environmental Data Services, 'Benefits and shortcomings of EMAS' (August 1995) *ENDS Report* No. 19.

—— 'Sustainable Development Advisors Take Government To Task' (1997) 264 *ENDS Report* No. 264 7–8.

—— 'Chemical Firms use EMAS, ISO 14001 in push for deregulation' (March 1996) *ENDS Report* No. 254(6).

—— 'Chemical Release Inventory at the Crossroads' (June 1997) *ENDS Report* No. 269 19–25, published by the Environmental Data Service.

—— 'Sustainable Development Advisors Take Government To Task' (1997) *ENDS Report* No. 264 p.7.

Environmental Defence Fund, 'Economic Incentives Could Reduce Water Pollution From Agriculture' (1994) Vol. XXV (September) *EDF Letter* 5.

Environmental Law Institute, 'New State and Local Approaches to Environmental Protection' (1993), Environmental Law Institute Report to EPA Office of Technology Assessment, Washington DC.

—— *Brazil's Extractive Reserves* (1995), Environmental Law Institute, Washington DC.

Esty D., 'Environmental Federalism' (1996) 95 *Michigan Law Review* 579.

European Chemical Industry Council (CEFIC), *Proceedings of the First International Workshop on Responsible Care in the Chemical Industry*, CEFIC, Brussels.

European Commission, *Towards Sustainability* (1997) Brussels, section 1.4.

Fadil, A., 'Citizen Suits Against Polluters: Picking up the pace' (1985) 9 *Harvard Environmental Law Review* 23–82.

Faeth, P., *Growing Green: Enhancing Environmental and Economic Performance in US Agriculture* (1995), World Resources Institute, Washington.

Fahey, P., 'Advocacy Group Boycotting of Television Advertisers, and its Effect on Programming Content' (1992) 140 *University of Pennsylvania Law Review* 647–709.

Farrell, M., 'Raising Capital For An Organic Grower' (1996) 18(6) *In Business* 34.

Farrier, D., 'Vegetation Conservation: The planning system as a vehicle for the regulation of broadacre agricultural land clearing' (1991) 18(1) *Melbourne University Law Review* 26–59.

—— 'Conserving Biodiversity on Private Land' (1995) 19(2) *Harvard Environmental Law Review* 304–405.

—— 'Policy instruments for conserving biodiversity on private land' in

J. Bradstock (ed.), *Conserving Biodiversity: threats and solutions* (1995), Surrey Beatty & Sons, Chipping Norton.

Faure, M. G. & Lefevere, J. G. J., *An Analysis of Alternative Legal Instruments for the Regulation of Pesticides* (1994), University of Limburg, Maastricht.

Feldman, S., Soyka, P. & Ameer, P., *Does Improving a Firm's EMS and Environmental Performance Result in a Higher Stock Price?* (1996), Working Paper, ICF Kaiser Consulting Group, Fairfax, Virginia.

Finn, R., 'Libel Concerns Are A Reality For Scientists Who Speak Out In Public' (1996) 10(6) *The Scientist* 15.

Fiorino, D. J., 'Towards a New System of Environmental Regulation: the case for an industry sector approach' (1996) 26(2) *Environmental Law* 457–489.

Fischer, K. & Schot, J. (eds.) *Environmental Strategies for Industry: International perspectives on research needs and policy implications*, Island Press, US (1993).

Fisse, B. & Braithwaite, J., *Corporations, Crime and Accountability* (1993), Cambridge University Press, Sydney.

Fitzpatrick, P., 'Law and Societies' (1984) 22 *Osgoode Hall Law Journal* 115–138.

Flavin, C., 'The Legacy of Rio' in Worldwatch Institute, *State of the World 1997* (1997), Earthscan Publications, London.

Foucault, M., 'Governability' in G. Burchell, C. Gordon & P. M. Miller (eds.) *The Foucault Effect: Studies in governmentality* (1991), Harvester Wheatsheaf, London.

Fowler, R. 'New Directions in Environmental Protection and Conservation' in B. Boer, R. Fowler & N. Gunningham (eds.) *Environmental Outlook: Law and Policy*, Federation Press, Sydney, 1994.

Franke, J. F. and Watzold, F., 'Voluntary initiatives and public intervention— the regulation of eco-auditing' (1996) in F. Leveque (ed.) *Environmental Policy in Europe*, Edward Elgar, UK.

Freeman, P. & Kunreuther, H., 'The Roles of Insurance and Well-Specified Standards in Dealing with Environmental Risks' (1996) 17 *Managerial and Decision Economics* 517–530.

—— *Managing Environmental Risk Through Insurance* (1997), Kluwer/American Enterprise Institute.

Friedman, M., 'Consumer Boycotts: A conceptual framework and research agenda' (1991) 47(1) *Journal of Social Issues* 149–168.

Funk, W., 'Free Market Environmentalism: Wonder drug or snake oil?' (1992) 15 *Harvard Journal of Law and Public Policy* 511–12.

Galanter, M., 'Justice In Many Rooms' (1981) 19 *Journal of Legal Pluralism* 1–47.

Gale, R., Barg, S. & Gillies, A. (eds.), *Green Budget Reform* (1995), Earthscan Publications, London.

Gambel, M., *US Environment Protection Agency, The Dutch Model: Lessons for the US* (1995), US EPA, Washington DC.

Gardiner, J. & Balch, G., 'Getting People to Protect Themselves: Information facilitation, regulatory and incentives strategies' (1980) in J. Brigham & D.

Brown (eds.) *Policy Implementation: Penalties or incentives*, Sage Publications, Beverly Hills.

Gardner, G., *Shrinking Fields: Cropland Loss in a World of Eight Billion* (1996), Worldwatch Paper No. 131, The Worldwatch Institute, Washington, DC.

Geiser, K., *Beyond Auditing: Toxic Use Reduction in the United States* (1990), University of Massachusetts, US.

Genn, H., *Great Expectations: The role of legacy and employer self-regulation* (1985), unpublished, Oxford Centre for Legal Studies, Oxford.

Gerits, R. & Hinssen, J., 'Environmental Covenant for the Oil and Gas Producing Industry: A valuable policy instrument?' (1994) 24(6) *Environment Policy and Law* 323.

Gilfedder, L. & Kirkpatrick, J. B., *A Survey of Landholder Attitudes and Intentions Towards the Long Term Conservation of Native Lowland Grasslands* (1995), Report to the Grasslands Ecology Unit, Australian Nature Conservation Agency, Canberra.

Gilpin, A., *An Australian Dictionary of Environment and Planning* (1990), Oxford University Press, Melbourne.

Glasbergen, P., 'Agro-Environmental Policy: Trapped in an iron law?' (1992) 32(1) *Sociologia Ruralis* 30–48.

Global Environmental Management Initiative (GEMI), *Total Quality Environmental Management* (1992), Washington DC.

Goedmakers, A., 'Ecological Perspectives of Changing Agricultural Land Use in the European Community' (1989) 27 *Agriculture, Ecosystems and the Environment* 99–106.

Gollin, M. A., 'An Intellectual Property Rights Framework for Biodiversity Prospecting' in W. V. Reid, S. A. Laid, C. A. Meyer, R. Gamez, A. Sittenfeld, D. H. Janzen, M. A. Gollin & C. Juma (eds.) *Biodiversity Prospecting: Using genetic resources for sustainable development* (1993), World Resources Institute, US.

Goodin, R., 'Making Moral Incentives Pay' (1980) 12 *Policy Sciences* 131.

Gore, A., *From Red Tape to Results: Creating a Government that works better and costs less* (1993), US Government Printing Office, Washington DC.

Gottlieb, R. (ed.), *Reducing Toxics: A new approach to policy and industrial decision making* (1995), Island Press, Washington DC.

Grabosky, P. N., 'Citizen Co-Production and Corruption Control' (1990) 5 *Corruption and Reform* 125–51.

—— 'Green Markets: Environmental regulation by the private sector' (1994) 16(4) *Law and Policy* 419–448.

—— 'Regulation by Reward: On the Use of Incentives as Regulatory Instruments' (1995) 17(3) *Law and Policy* 256–281.

—— 'Using Non-governmental Resources to Foster Regulatory Compliance' (1995) 8(4) *Governance, an International Journal of Policy and Administration* 527–550.

—— *Wayward Governance: Illegality and its Control in the Public Sector* (1989) Australian Institute of Criminology, Canberra.

Grabosky, P. & Braithwaite, J., *Business Regulation and Australia's Future* (1993) Australian Institute of Criminology, Canberra.

Grabosky, P. N. & Braithwaite, J., *Of Manners Gentle: Enforcement strategies of Australian business regulatory agencies* (1986), Oxford University Press, Melbourne.

Grartz, R. D., Wilson, M. A. & Campbell, S. K., *Landcover Disturbance Over the Australian Continent: A contemporary assessment* (1995), A report for the Department of the Environment, Sports and Territories, Biodiversity Series, Paper No. 7, Biodiversity Unit, Canberra.

Gray, B., 'Public versus Private Environmental Regulation' (1994) 21 *Ecology Law Quarterly* 434–438.

Green Business Letter, 'Grand Alliances: A new network of nonprofits is helping environmental partnerships grow and prosper' (1996) (March).

Greenert, C. Interview, quoted in 'Responsible Care' (1991) *Harvard Business School Documents* 9-391-135.

Greenpeace, *Community Right-to-Know and the Myth of Self-Regulation* (1994), Greenpeace, Melbourne.

Gretton, P. & Salma, U., *Land Degradation and the Australian Agricultural Industry* (1996), June, Industry Commission, Canberra; B. Beale & P. Fray, *The Vanishing Continent: Australia's degraded environment* (1990), Hodder & Stoughton, Sydney.

Greve, M., 'Environmentalism and Bounty Hunting' (1989) 97 *The Public Interest* 15–29.

Greve, M. S. & Smith, F. L., *Environmental Politics: Public costs, private rewards* (1992), Praeger, New York.

Grodsky, J. A., 'Certified Green: The law and future of environmental labelling' (1993) 10(1) *Yale Journal on Regulation* 147.

Grossman, M., 'Habitat and Species Conservation in the European Union and the United States' (1997) 45(1) *Drake Law Review* 19–49.

Gunningham, N., *Pollution, Social Interest And The Law* (1974), Martin Robertson, UK.

—— 'Negotiated Non-Compliance: A case study of regulatory failure' (1987) 9(1) *Law and Policy* 69–97.

—— 'Public Choice: Advancing the economic analysis of law' (1992) 21(1) *Federal Law Review* 117.

—— 'Who Audits the Auditors?' (1993) 11(4) *Environmental and Planning Law Journal* 229–238.

—— 'Beyond Compliance: Management of environmental risk' (1994) in B. Boer, R. Fowler & N. Gunningham (eds.) *Environmental Outlook: Law and policy*, Federation Press, Sydney.

—— 'Environment, Self-Regulation, and the Chemical Industry: Assessing Responsible Care' (1995) 17)(1) *Law and Policy* 58–109.

Gunningham, N., 'Issues and Options in Designing an NPI' (1995) in Minter Ellison (eds.) *Final report to the Environment Protection Agency for the Development of Legislative Modelling for the National Pollutant Inventory and Associated Community Right to Know in Australia*, Minter Ellison, Melbourne).

——— 'From Compliance to Best Practice in OHS: The role of specification, performance and systems-based standards' (1996) 9(3) *Australian Journal of Labour Law* 221.

——— 'From Compliance to Best Practice in OHS: The role of specification, performance and systems based standards' (1996) 9(3) *Australian Journal of Labour Law* 221.

Gunningham, N. & Cornwell, A., 'Legislating the Right to Know' (1994) 11(4) *Environmental and Planning Law Journal* 274–288.

Gunningham, N. & Prest, J., 'Environmental Audit as a Regulatory Strategy: Prospects and reform' (1993) 15 *Sydney Law Review* 492–526.

Gunningham, N. & Rees, J., 'Industry Self-regulation' (1997) 19(4) *Law and Policy* 363.

Gunningham, N. & Young, M. D., 'Towards Optimal Environmental Policy: The Case of Biodiversity Conservation' (1997) 24(2) *Ecology Law Quarterly* 244.

Guntram, U. & Winsemius, P., 'Responding to the Environmental Challenge' (March/April 1992) *Business Horizons* 12.

Hahn, R., *A Primer on Environmental Policy Design* (1989), Harwood Academic Publishers, London.

——— 'Towards a New Environmental Paradigm' (1993) 102 *Yale Law Journal* 1719.

Hahn, R. & Stavins, R., 'Incentive-Based Environmental Regulation: A new era from an old idea?' (1991) 18(1) *Ecology Law Quarterly* 1.

Hamilton, J. T., 'Pollution as News: Media and stockmarket reactions to the Capital Toxic Release Inventory Data' (1995) *Journal of Environmental Economics and Management* 98–103.

Hamilton, K. & Cameron, G., 'Simulating the Distributional Effects of a Canadian Carbon Tax' (1994) XX(4) *Canadian Public Policy: Analyse de Politiques* 385.

Hardin, G., 'The Tragedy of the Commons' 162 *?Science* 1243–48.

Harlow, C. & Rawlings, R., *Pressure Through Law* (1992), Routledge, London.

Harper, M. C., 'The Consumer's Emerging Right to Boycott: NAACP v Claiborne Hardware and its implications for American Labor Law' (1984) 93(3) *Yale Law Journal* 409–454.

Harr, J., *A Civil Action* (1995), Vintage Books, New York.

Harris, R. A. & Milkis, S. M., *The Politics of Regulatory Change: A tale of two agencies* (1989), Oxford University Press, New York.

Harter, P. J. & Eads, G. C., 'Policy Instruments, Institutions, and Objectives: An analytical framework for assessing "alternatives" to regulation' (1985) 37(3) *Administrative Law Review* 221–58.

Harvard Business School Documents 'Responsible Care' (1991) *Harvard Business School Documents*, 9-391-135, 1–26.

Harvard Law Review, 'Note: Harnessing Madison Avenue: Advertising and products liability theory' (1994), 107 *Harvard Law Review* 895–912.

Hawkins, K., *Environment and Enforcement: regulation and the social definition of pollution* (1984), OUP, Oxford.

Hayami, Y. & Ruttan, V. W., *Agricultural Development: An international perspective* (1985), The John Hopkins University Press, Baltimore.

Health & Safety Executive (UK), *Successful Health and Safety Management* HS(G)65, (1991), HMSO, London.

Henderson, D. A., 'Lending Abroad: The Role of Voluntary International Environmental Management Standards' (July 1997) *Journal of Commercial Lending* 47.

Hill, S., 'From Quality Circles to Total Quality Management' in A. Wilkinson & H. Willmott (eds.) *Making Quality Critical: New perspectives on organizational change* (1995), Routledge, London.

Hinchy, M., Thorpe, S. & Fisher, B. S., *A Tradeable Emissions Permit Scheme* (1992), ABARE Research Report 93.5, ABARE, Canberra.

Hines, J., Hungerford, H. & Tomera, A., 'Analysis and Synthesis of Research on Environmental Behaviour: A meta-analysis; (1987) 18(2) *Journal of Environmental Education*.

Hirl, J. R., 'Don't Trust Us, Track Us' (1992), UN 242 No. 21 (17 December) *Chemical Marketing Reporter* 16.

Hobert, G., *Pluralism by Design* (1992) Praeger, New York.

Hodge, I., 'Incentive Policies and the Rural Environment' (1991) 7 *Journal of Rural Studies* 373–84.

Hodgson, J., 'Third Party Appeals in South Australia 1972–1993' (1996) 13(1) *Environmental and Planning Law Journal* 8–28.

Holmes, C. E., *Address to Hazardous Waste Conference* (1992), ACIC, Melbourne.

Holmes, J., *Managing into the 1990s—Manufacturing and the Environment: An executive guide* (1992), Department for Enterprise (DTI), London.

Hopkins, A., *Making Safety Work: Getting Management Commitment to Occupational Health and Safety* (1995), Allen and Unwin, Sydney.

Hopkins, J. M. & Saunders, D. A., 'Ecological Studies as a Basis for Management' (1987) in D. A. Saunders, G. W. Arnold, A. A. Burbidge & A. J. M. Hopkins (eds.) *Nature Conservation: The role of remnants of native vegetation*, Surrey Beatty and Sons, Chipping Norton.

Hopkins, T. D. (1997) 'Alternative Approaches to Regulatory Analysis: Designs from Seven OECD Countries' in *Regulatory Impact Analysis: Best Practices in OECD Countries, OECD*, Paris.

Hornstein, D. T., 'Lessons from Federal Pesticide Regulation on the Paradigms and Politics of Environmental Law Reform' (1993) 10 *Yale Journal on Regulation* 369–446.

House, G., 'Raising the Green Standard' (July 17 1995) 244(14) *Industry Week* 73.

Howard, B., 'WA Wheatbelt Case Study' in M. D. Young, N. Gunningham, J. Elix, J. Lambert, B. Howard, P. Grabosky, E. McCrone, *Reimbursing the Future: An evaluation of motivational, voluntary, price-based, property-right, and regulatory incentives for the conservation of biodiversity* (1996), Biodiversity Series Paper No. 9, Department of the Environment, Sport and Territories, Biodiversity Unit, Canberra (1996), Appendix 2.1, part 2 p.40.

Howse, R., Pritchard, J. R. S. & Trebilcock, M. J., 'Smaller Or Smarter Government?' (1990) 40 *University of Toronto Law Journal* 498.

Humphrey, H. III, 'Public/Private Environmental Auditing Agreements: Finding better ways to promote voluntary compliance' (1994) 3 *Corporate Conduct Quarterly* 1.

Hunter, D. & Kiesche, E. S., 'US—Implementation Time' (17 June 1992) *Chemical Week* 10.

Hunter, D. & Mullin, R., 'Responsible Care: The challenge of communication' (9 December 1992) *Chemical Week* 22.

Huppes, G. & Kagan, R., 'Market-Oriented Regulation of Environmental Problems in the Netherlands' (1989) 11(2) *Law and Policy* 215–239.

Huppes, G., van der Voet, E., Vonkeman, G. H. & Maxson, P., *New Market-Oriented Instruments for Environmental Policies* (1992), Graham and Trotman, London.

Iles, A. T., 'Adaptive management: Making environmental law and policy more dynamic, experimentalist and learning' (1996) 13(4) *Environmental and Planning Law Journal* 288.

Intergovernmental Panel on Climate Change (IPPC), *Climate Change: Second Assessment* (1996), Cambridge University Press, Cambridge, UK.

International Council of Chemical Associations, *Global Status Report on Responsible Care* reported in 'ICCA Readies itself for Ottawa Meeting' (October 1996) 5 *Careline* 1.

International Institute for Sustainable Development (IISD), *Making Budgets Green: Leading practices in taxation and subsidy reform* (1994), IISD, Winnipeg.

International Labour Organisation (ILO), Chemical Industries Committee (1995) *Recent Developments in the Chemical Industries*, Geneva.

Irwin, F. et. al., *A Benchmark for Reporting on Chemicals at Industrial Facilities* (1995), World Wildlife Fund.

Jacek, A., 'The Functions of Associations as Agents of Public Policy' (1991) in A. Martinelli (ed.), *International Markets and Global Firms*, Sage, London.

Jackall, R., *Moral mazes: The world of corporate managers* (1988), Oxford University Press, New York.

Jacobs, M., *The Green Economy* (1991), Pluto Press, United Kingdom.

——— 'Sustainability and the "Market": A typology of environmental economics' in R. Eckersley (ed.), *Markets, the State and the Environment* (1995), Macmillan Press, Melbourne.

James, D., *Using Economic Instruments for Meeting Environmental Objectives: Australia's experience* (1993), Department of the Environment, Sport and Territories, Canberra.

Jasch, C., 'Environmental Information Systems in Austria' (1993) 13(2) *Social and Environmental Accounting* 7.

Johnson, S. E. & Jacobs, H. M., 'Public Education for Growth Management: Lessons from Wisconsin's Farmland Preservation Program' (1994) 49(4) *Journal of Soil and Water Conservation* 333.

Joliffe, H., 'EU Fifth Action Program: progress report on implementation of "Towards Sustainability"' (1996) 5(4) *Review of European Community and Environmental Law (RECIEL)* 342.

Jones, L. R. & Baldwin, J. H., *Corporate Environmental Policy and Government Regulation* (1994), JAI Press, Greenwich, Connecticut.

Jones, R., *Environmental Risk Management* (1996), Paper delivered to 3M Conference, Canberra

Joyner, C., 'The Transnational Boycott as Economic Coercion in International Law: Policy, place and practice' (1984) 17(2) *Vanderbilt Journal; of Transnational Law* 206–286.

Kagan, R., 'Regulatory Enforcement' in D. Rosenbloom & R. Schwartz (eds.), *Handbook of Regulation and Administrative Law* (1994), Dekker, New York.

Kagan, R. A., Axelrad, L., & Ruhlin, C., 'Convergence and Divergence in National Modes of Regulation: Multinational Corporations and American Adversarial Legalism' (1996) A paper presented to the *Annual Meeting of the Law and Society Association*, Glasgow, July 10–13.

Kagan, R. & Scholz, J., 'The Criminology of the Corporation and Regulatory Enforcement Strategies' in K. Hawkins & J. Thomas (eds.) *Enforcing Regulation* (1984), Kluwer-Nijhoff, Boston.

Kato, K., 'The New Frontiers of Environmental Policy in Japan' (1991) in P. Thomas (ed.) *Environmental Liability*, International Bar Association Section on Business Law, 7th Residential Seminar on Environmental Law, Graham and Trotman, London.

Katzman, M., *Chemical Catastrophes: Regulating environmental risks through pollution insurance* (1985), Richard Irwin, Homewood, Illinois.

Kelman, S., 'Economic Incentives and Environmental Policy: Politics, ideology, and philosophy' in T. Schelling (ed.), *Incentives for Environmental Protection* (1983), MIT Press, Cambridge.

Kenny, M., 'Use of Marketplace Incentives in California to Improve Air Quality' (1997), a paper delivered to *American Bar Association 26th Annual Environmental Law Conference*, Keystone, Colorado, March 1997.

Kettl, D. F., *Sharing Power: public governance and private markets* (1993), Brookings Institution, Washington.

Keystone Center, *Keystone National Policy Dialogue on Ecosystem Management*, Final Report (October 1996), Keystone Center, Colorado.

King, D., 'It's Clean, It's Green, and It'll Feed the World' (1997), 2(vii) (March/April), *Tomorrow* 10–12.

Kinrade, P. in R. Eckersley (ed.) *Markets, the State and the Environment: Towards Integration*, Macmillan Education Australia, Melbourne, 1995.

—— 'Towards Ecologically Sustainable Development: The Role and Shortcomings of Markets' in R. Eckersley (ed.) *Markets, The State and The Environment: Towards Integration* (1995) Macmillan Education Australia, Melbourne, p. 86.

Kirkpatrick, J. B., 'The Geography and Politics of Species Endangerment in Australia' (1991) 29(2) *Australian Geographical Studies* 246–254.

Kirschner, E., 'New Jersey: State Ambassadors' '(1993) 153 *Chemical Week* 40.

Klassen, R. L. & Curtis, P. McLaughlin 'The Impact of Environmental Management on Firm Performance', *Management Science*, August 1996 at 1199.

Kleindorfer, P., *Market Based Environmental Audits and Environmental Risks: Implementing ISO 14000* (1996), Working Paper, The Wharton School, University of Pennsylvania, Philadelphia.

Knight, A., 'International Standards for Environmental Management' (1994) *Industry and Environment*, UNEP, July.

Kohn, R., 'When Subsidies for Pollution Abatement Increase Total Emissions' (1992) 59(1) *Southern Economic Journal* 77.

Krier, J. E., 'The Tragedy of the Commons, Part Two' (1992) 15 *Harvard Journal of Law & Public Policy* 325–47.

Kuttner, R., *Everything For Sale: The virtues and limits of markets* (1997), Alfred A. Knopf, New York.

Land Use Consultants, *Countryside Schemes and Nature Conservation* 91994), London, UK.

Landes, W. & Posner, R., 'The Private Enforcement of Law' (1975) 4 *Journal of Legal Studies* 1.

Landy, M., *The Environmental Protection Agency: Asking the wrong questions* (1994), Oxford University Press, New York.

—— 'National Regulation in a Global Economy: The dynamics of interdependency' (1997), a paper delivered at University of California, Berkeley, February.

Landy, M. K. & Hague, M., 'The Coalition for Waste: Private interests and Superfund' (1992) in M. S. Greve & F. L. Smith Jr., (eds.) *Environmental Politics: Public costs, private rewards*, Praeger Publishers, New York.

Lash, J. A., *A Season of Spoils: The Reagan administration's attack on the environment* (1984), Pantheon Books, New York.

Latin, H., 'Ideal versus Real Regulatory Efficiency: Implementation of uniform standards and "fine tuning reforms" ' (1985) 37 *Stanford Law Review* 1267.

Lazarus, J. R., 'The Tragedy of Distrust in the Implementation of Federal Environmental Law' (1991) 54 *Law and Contemporary Problems* 363–364.

Leone, R., *Who Profits? Winners, Losers and Government Regulation* (1986), Basic Books, New York.

Leveque, F. (ed.) *Environmental Policy in Europe* (1996), Edward Elgar, UK.

—— 'The European Fabric of Environmental Regulations' (1996) in F. Leveque (ed.), *Environmental Policy in Europe*, Edward Elgar, UK.

Lewis, S. J., *The Role and Limits of Volunteerism* (1991), a paper the International Conference on Corporate Environmental Responsibility, Tutzing, Germany.

Leyden, P., 'Trading in Southern California' (1997), a paper delivered to *American Bar Association 26th Annual Conference on Environmental Law*, Keystone, Colorado, March.

Lockie, S. & Vanclay, F. (eds.), *Critical Landcare* (1997), Centre for Rural Social Research, Charles Stuart University, Wagga Wagga.

Lohman, L. S., 'Economic Incentives in Environmental Policy: Why are there white ravens?' (1994) in H. Opschoor & K. Turner (eds.), *Economic Incentives and Environmental Policies: Principles and practice*, Kluwer Academic Publishers, Dordrecht.

Long, F. K. & Arnold, M. B., *The Power of Partnerships* (1995), Harcourt Brace, New York.

Lowe, P., Cox, G., MacEwen, M., O'Riordan, T. & Winter, M., *Countryside Conflicts: The politics of farming, forestry, and conservation* (1986), Brookfield Publishing, Aldershot.

M't Sas-Rolfes 'Trade in endangered species: Is it an option?' (1994) 14(3) *Economic Affairs* 2.

MacRae, R., Hill, S., Henning, J. & Bentley, A., 'Policies, Programs and Regulations to Support the Transition to Sustainable Agriculture in Canada' (1990) 5(2) *American Journal of Alternative Agriculture* 76–92.

Madden, J. P. & O'Connell, P. F., 'LISA: Some Early Results' (1990) 45(1) *Journal of Soil and Water Conservation* 61–64.

Magretta, J., 'Growth Through Global Sustainability' (Jan/Feb 1997) *Harvard Business Review* 79–88.

Maitland, I., 'The Limits of Business Self-Regulation' (1985) 27(3) *California Management Review* 132–47.

Makeswaran, D. & Meyers-Levy, J., 'The Influence of Message Framing and Issue Involvement' (1990) 27 *Journal of Marketing Research* 361.

Manes, C., *Green Rage: Radical Environmentalism and the Unmaking of Civilisation* (1990), Little Brown, Boston.

Mann, C. C. & Plummer, M. L., *Noah's Choice: The future of endangered species* (1996), Knopf, New York.

Mansbridge, J., 'A Deliberative Theory of Interest Representation' (1992) in M. Petracca (ed.) *Interest Groups in the Political Process*, Westview Press, Boulder.

Marcus, A., *The Adversary Economy: Business responses to changing government requirements* (1980), Quorom Books, Westport CT.

Matteson, P., den Boer L. & Proost, J., 'Green Labels in The Netherlands: Careful Negotiations and Clearer Choices' (1996) 6(4) (December) *Global Pesticide Campaigner* 8.

Mayer, M., *The Greatest Ever Bank Robbery: The collapse of the savings and loan industry* (1992), Collier Books, New York.

McAvoy, P. W., *OSHA Safety Regulation: Report of the Presidential Task Force* (1977), American Enterprise Institute, Washington DC.

McCrory, R. *Loaded Guns and Monkeys Responsible: Environmental Law* (1994), Imperial College Centre for Technology, UK.

McDonald, J., 'Key Issues in Environmental Insurance Litigation' (1991) 8 *Environmental and Planning Law Journal* 145.

—— 'Corporate Confidentiality After Caltex: How safe is your audit?' (1994) 11(3) *Environmental and Planning Law Journal* 193–210.

McFarlane, D. L., George, R. J. & Farrington, P., 'Changes in the Hydrologic Cycle' (1993) in R. J. Hobbs & D. A. Saunders (eds.) *Reintegrating Fragmented Landscapes*, Springer-Verlag, New York.

McGarity, T. O., 'Regulatory Analysis and Regulatory Reform' (1987) 65 *Texas Law Review* 1243).

—— 'Four Dimensions of Health and Environmental Regulation' (undated), an unpublished paper, University of Texas Law School.

McGarity, T. O. & Shapiro, S. A., *Workers At Risk: The failed promise of occupational safety and health administration* (1993), Praeger, Westport.

McGauchie, D., *The Future of Agricultural Land Use in Australia* (1996), address to the Waite Agricultural Research Institute, Adelaide, South Australia, 26 March.

McGuire, W. (1985) 'Attitudes and attitude change' in G. Lindzey (ed.) *The handbook of social psychology*, 3rd edn., Vol. II, Random House, New York.

McKean, M., *Environmental Protest and Citizen Politics in Japan* (1981), University of California Press, Berkeley.

McVaugh, J. 'Implementing ISO 14000' in T. Tibor & I. Feldman *ISO 14000: A guide to the new environmental management standards*, Irwin, Chicago, 1996.

Meadows, D. H. & Randers, J., *Beyond the Limits: Confronting Global Collapse: Envisioning a Sustainable Future* (1992), Post Mills VT, Chelsea Green.

Meidinger, E., 'Look Whose Making the Rules: The roles of the Forest Stewardship Council and International Standards Organisation in Environmental Policy Making (1996), a paper presented to Colloquium on Emerging Environmental Policy: Winners and Losers, Oregon State University, Corvellis, Oregon, 23 September.

Mendeloff, J., 'Overcoming Barriers to Better Regulation' (1993) 18 *Law and Social Inquiry* 711.

Menell, P., 'The Limitations of Legal Institutions for Addressing Environmental Risks' (1991) 5(3) *Journal of Economic Perspectives* 93.

—— 'Educating Consumers about the Environment: Labels versus Prices' in E. Eide & R. van den Bergh (eds.), *Law and Economics of the Environment* (1996), Juridisk Forlag, Oslo.

Meredith, C., *Process or Outcomes? Defining the most useful measure of environmental performance* (1996), a paper presented at the 1996 Australian Academy of Science *Fenner Conference on the Environment: Linking Environment and Economy Through*

Indicators and Accounting Systems, 30 September to 3 October, The University of New South Wales, Sydney.

Meyers, G. D. & Temby, S., 'Biodiversity and the Law: A review of the Commonwealth Endangered Species Protection Act of 1992' (1994) 3(1) *Griffith Law Review* 39.

Miller, A. S., 'The Origins and Current Directions of United States Environmental Law and Policy: an overview' (1994) in B. Boer, R. Fowler & N. Gunningham (eds.), *Environmental Outlook: Law and Policy*, Federation Press, Sydney.

Miller, J., *Citizen Suits: private enforcement of Federal pollution control laws* (1987), John Wiley, New York.

Mitchell, R., *International Oil Pollution at Sea* (1994), MIT Press, Cambridge.

Moodie, A. M., 'Control System Helped Food Firm Trace Problem' (1996), 8 November, *Australian Financial Review* 61.

Moore, R., 'Controlling Agricultural Nonpoint Source Pollution: The New York experience' (1997) 45(1) *Drake Law Review* 103–124.

Moran, A., 'Tools of Environmental Policy: Market instruments versus command and control' (1995) in R. Eckersley (ed.), *Markets, the State and the Environment*, Macmillan Press, Melbourne, p.73.

Motive Market Research Pty Ltd, 'Summary and Conclusions' (1992) in *ACIC—Monitoring Community Attitudes* (December), pp. 11 and 12.

Mueller, D., *Public Choice II* (1989), Cambridge University Press, Cambridge, New York.

Muir, W. K., 'Under what circumstances can law bring about attitude change?' in J. B. Grossman & M. H. Grossman (eds.) *Law and Change in Modern America* (1967), Goodyear Publishing, California.

Mullin, R., 'Canadian Deadline Approaches: Contemplating continuous improvement' (17 June 1992) *Chemical Week* 128.

Mummery, J. & Hardy, N., *Australia's Biodiversity: An overview of selected significant components* (1994), Biodiversity Series, Paper No. 2, Biodiversity Unit, Department of Environment Sport & Territories, Canberra.

Nash, J. & Ehrenfeld, J., 'Code Green' (Jan/Fen 1996) *Environment* 42.

Nash, J. & Howard, J., 'Responsible Care's Mixed Record' (1996) 5(VI) *Tomorrow: Global Environment Business* 12.

National Law Journal (USA), *1993 Corporate Counsel Survey*, Aug 30, 1993.

Netherlands National Environmental Policy Plan 2: 'The Environment, Today's Touchstone', SDU Uitgeverij Plantignstraat, 1995, p.1.

Organisation for Economic Co-operation and Development, *Agricultural and Environmental Policies: Opportunities for integration* (1989), OECD, Paris.

——— *Draft Council Recommendations on the Use of Economic Instruments in Environmental Policy* (1990), ENV/EC OECD, Paris.

——— *Guidelines for the Use of Economic Instruments in Environmental Policy* (1990), October, OECD, Paris.

Organisation for Economic Co-operation and Development, *Environmental Labelling in OECD Countries* (1991), OECD, Paris.

—— *Environmental Policy: How to Apply Economic Instruments* (1991), OECD, Paris.

—— *The State of the Environment* (1991), OECD, Paris.

—— *Agricultural and Environmental Policy Integration: Recent Progress and New Directions* (1993), OECD, Paris.

—— *Agriculture and the Environment in the Transition to a Market Economy* (1993), OECD, Paris.

—— *Economic Instruments for the Conservation of Domestic and Global Biodiversity: Project proposal* (1993), Expert group on Economic Aspects of Biodiversity, Environment Policy Committee, OECD, Paris.

—— Group on Economic and Environment Policy Integration, Expert Group on Economic Aspects of Biodiversity, *Economic Incentives for the Conservation of Biodiversity: Conceptual framework and guidelines for case studies* (1994), OECD, Paris.

—— *Alternatives to Traditional Regulation: A Preliminary List* (1994), OECD, Paris.

—— *Applying Economic Instruments to Environmental Policies in OECD and Dynamic Non-Member Economies* (1994), OECD, Paris.

—— *Agricultural Policy Reform: Environmental externalities and public goods in Agricultural Policy Reform: New Approaches. The role of Direct Income Payments* (1994), OECD, Paris.

—— *Contracting for Genetic Resources* (1994), Group on Economic and Environment, OECD, Paris.

—— Group on Economic and Environment Policy Integration, Expert Group on Economic Aspects of Biodiversity, *Economic Incentives for the Conservation of Biodiversity: Conceptual framework and guidelines for case studies* (1994), OECD, Paris.

—— *Meeting on Alternatives to Traditional Regulation* (1994), OECD, Paris.

—— *Reducing Environmental Pollution: Looking back, thinking ahead* (1994), OECD, Paris.

—— *Towards Sustainable Agricultural Production: Cleaner Technologies* (1994), OECD, Paris.

—— *Technologies for Cleaner Production and Products: Towards Technological Transformation for Sustainable Development* (1995), OECD, Paris.

—— *Recommendation of the Council of the OECD on Improving the Quality of Government Regulation* (1995), OECD, Paris.

—— Group on Economic and Environment Policy Integration Expert on Economic Aspects of Biodiversity, *Making Markets Work for Biodiversity: The role of economic incentive measures* (1995), Draft final report, Fourth session 11–13 July.

—— Group on Economic and Environment Policy Integration, Expert Group on Economic Aspects of Biodiversity, *Biological Diversity: Economic incentive measures for conservation and sustainable use* (1995), OECD, Paris.

—— *Recommendation of the Council of the OECD on Improving the Quality of Government Regulation*, (1995), OECD, Paris.

—— *Sustainable Agriculture: Concepts, issues and policies in OECD countries* (1995), OECD, Paris.

—— *Environmental Data 1995: Compendium*, November 1995, OECD, Paris.

—— *Making Markets Work for Biological Diversity: The role of economic incentives measures* (1996), OECD, Paris.

—— *Agricultural Policies, Markets and Trade in OECD Countries: Monitoring and evaluation* (1996), OECD, Paris.

—— *Saving Biological Diversity: Economic Incentives* (1996), OECD, Paris.

—— *Evaluating Economic Instruments for Environmental Policy* (1997), OECD, Paris.

—— *Regulatory Impact Analysis: Best Practices in OECD Countries* Organisation for Economic Co-Operation and Development (1997), OECD, Paris.

Ogg, C., 'Farm Price Distortions, Chemical Use, and the Environment' (1990) 45(1) *Journal of Soil and Water Conservation* 45–47.

Old, K., *Utilisation and Conservation of Australian Plant Genetic Resources: The role of monopoly privilege* (1994), Honours Thesis submitted to the Faculty of Law, Australian National University, October 1994.

Oldeman, L. R. *et. al.*, *World Map of the Status of Human-Induced Soil Degradation: an explanatory note* (1991), 2nd edn., International Soil Reference and Information Centre & United Nations Environment Programme, Wageningen, Netherlands and Nairobi.

Olson, M., *The Logic of Collective Action: Public Goods and the Theory of Groups* (1965), Harvard University Press, Cambridge.

Opschoor, J. B. & Vos, H. B., *Application of Economic Instruments for Environmental Protection in OECD Countries* (1989), OECD, Paris.

Opschoor, J. B. & Turner, K., *Economic Incentives And Environmental Policies: principles and practice* (1994), Kluwer Academic Publishers, Dordrecht.

Orts, W. E., 'Reflexive Environmental Law' (1995) 89(40) *Northwestern University Law Review* 1227.

Osborne, D. & Gaebler, T., *Reinventing Government* (1992), Addison-Wesley, Boston.

Ostrom, E., *Governing the Commons: The evolution of institutions for Collective action* (1990), Cambridge University Press, New York.

Owen, D., 'A Critical Perspective on the Development of European Corporate Environmental Accounting and Reporting' (1996), a paper presented at the 1996 Australian Academy of Science *Fenner Conference on the Environment: Linking Environment and Economy Through Indicators and Accounting Systems*, 30 September to 3 October, The University of New South Wales, Sydney.

Page, A. C., 'Self-Regulation and Codes of Practice' (1980) *Journal of Business Law* 24–31.

Pain, N., 'Third Party Rights Public Participation Under the Environmental Planning and Assessment Act 1979 (NSW): Do the floodgates need opening or closing?' (1989) 6(1) *Environmental and Planning Law Journal* 26–35.

Palmquist, P., 'Pollution Subsidies and Multiple Local Optima' (1990) 66 *Land Economics* 394–401.

Panayotou, T., *Economic Instruments for Environmental Management and Sustainable Development* (1994), unpublished manuscript, Harvard Institute for International Development, Harvard University, Cambridge.

—— *Reducing Biodiversity Expenditure Needs: Reforming perverse incentives* (1996), paper presented to an OECD Conference on Incentive Measures for Biodiversity conservation and Sustainable Use, Cairns, Australia, March 1996.

Papadakis, E., *Politics and the Environment: the Australian experience* (1993), Allen & Unwin, Sydney.

Pashigan, B. P., 'How Large and Small Plants Fare Under Environmental Regulation' (September/October 1983) 7 *Regulation* 19–23.

Patrick, S., 'Value-Added Product Stewardship' (September 1996) *CMA News* 25–28.

Pease, W. S., 'Chemical Hazards and the Public's Right-to-Know: How effective is California's Proposition 65?' 30(10) *Environment* 9.

Pederson, W. F., 'Can Site Specific Pollution Control Plans Furnish an Alternative to the Current Regulatory System?' (1995) 25 *Environmental Law Reporter* 10486.

Perrings, C. & Pearce, D., 'Threshold Effects and Incentives of the Conservation of Biodiversity' (1994) 4(1) *Environmental and Resource Economics* 13–28.

Perrow, C., *Normal Accidents: Living with high risk technologies* (1984), Basic Books, New York.

Petzoldt, C. & Tette, J. P., *Farmers Communicating to Consumers about their Environmental Stewardship* at http://www.nysaes.cornell.edu:80/ipmnet/ny/program_news/Farmers_Comm.html.

Pierce, J. C., Steger, M. A. E., Steel, B. S. & Lovrich, N., *Citizens, Political communication and Interest Groups; Environmental organisations in the United States* (1992), Praeger, Westport.

Pike, A. G., 'Pesticide Risk Reduction: The Role of the UK Pesticides Forum' Presented at the National Pesticide Risk Reduction Workshop, Bureau of Resource Sciences, Department of Primary Industries and Energy, Canberra, Australia, April 16 1997.

Plastics and Chemicals Industries Association (PACIA), *Facts and Figures* (1991), PACIA, Melbourne.

Plastics and Chemicals Industries Association—Chemicals Sector (PACIA), *Reducing Waste: Report on 1994 Waste Survey* (1995), PACIA, Melbourne.

Platt, N., 'The Rise of the Eco-Consumer Has Big Business Seeing Green' (1992) *Reuters News Service*, 25 May.

Polinsky, M., 'Private versus Public Enforcement of Law' (1980) 9 *Journal of Legal Studies* 105.

Porter, M., *The Competitive Advantage of Nations* (1990). Macmillan Press, London.

—— 'America's Green Strategy' (1991) April, *Scientific American* 168.

Porter, M. E. & van der Linde, C., 'Green and Competitive' Sept–Oct 1995 *Harvard Business Review* 120–134.

Posner, T., *The Engineer* (5 March 1992), 20.

Potter, J., 'Chemical Accident Prevention Regulation in California and New Jersey' (1993) 20 *Ecology Law Quarterly* 755.

Pratt, S. J., Frarey, L. & Carr, A. 'A Comparison of US and UK Law Regarding Pollution From Agricultural Runoff' (1997) 45(1) *Drake Law Review* 159–196.

Prescott-Allen, C. & Prescott-Allen, R., *The First Resource: Wild species in the North American Economy* (1986), Yale University Press, New Haven.

Pring, G. W. & Canan, P., *SLAPPs: Getting sued for speaking out* (1996), Temple University Press, Philadelphia.

Project 88, *Project 88—Round II: Incentives for Action* (1991), Washington DC.

'PUMA/OECD, 'Choices of Policy Instruments' (20 March 1997), 15th Session of Public management Committee, PUMA/OECD, Paris.

Purchase, B., *Political Economy of Voluntary Codes* (196), a draft paper presented at the Voluntary Codes Symposium, Office of Consumer Affairs, Industry Canada and Regulatory Affairs, Treasury Board, Ottawa September, and to be included in 'Exploring voluntary codes: the marketplace', D. Cohen & K. Wess (eds.), Government of Canada, Ottawa, due in 1998.

Purdue, M., 'Integrated Pollution Control in the Environmental Protection Act 1990: A Coming of Age in Environmental Law?' (1991) 54 *Modern Law Review* 534.

Putnam, R. 'The Prosperous Community' (October 1993) *Current* 4.

Quarles, J., *Cleaning up America: An insider's view of the Environmental Protection Agency* (1976), Houghton Mifflin, Boston, US.

Rae, M., 'Why Do Corporate Environmental Reporting? If You Don't, Your Company Will Die!' (1996), a paper presented at the 1996 Australian Academy of Science *Fenner Conference on the Environment: Linking Environment and Economy Through Indicators and Accounting System*, 30 September–3 October, The University of New South Wales, Sydney.

Raffle, B. I. & Mitchell, D. F. *Effective Environmental Strategies: Opportunities for innovation and flexibility under Federal environmental laws*, Executive Summary, Amoco, Chicago, 1993.

Ramsay, R. & Rowe, G. C., *Environmental Law and Policy in Australia* (1995), Butterworths, Australia.

Rappaport, A. & Flaherty, M., 'Multinational Corporation and the Environment', Centre for Environmental Management, Tufts University, 1991.

Rees, J. V., *Reforming the Workplace: A study of self-regulation in occupational health and safety* (1988), University of Pennsylvania Press, Philadelphia.

——— *Hostages of Each Other: The transformation of nuclear safety since Three Mile Island* (1994), University of Chicago Press, Chicago.

——— 'The Development of Communication Regulation in the Chemical Industry' (1997) *Law and Policy* (publication delayed) 19(4).

Reganold, J. P., Papendick, R. I. & Parr, J. F., 'Sustainable Agriculture' (1990) June *Scientific American* 72–78.

Rehbinder, E., 'Environmental Regulation Through Fiscal and Economic Incentives in a Federalist System' (1993) 20 *Ecology Law Quarterly* 57–83.

Reilly, W., *Aiming Before We Shoot: The quiet revolution in environmental policy* (1990), address to the National Press Club, Washington DC, September 26.

Reitze, A. W. Jnr., 'a Century of Pollution Control Law: What worked; what's failed; what might work' (1991), 21 *Environmental Law* 1549.

Reus, J. A. W. A., Weckseler, H. J. & Pak, G. A., *Towards a Future EC Pesticide Policy: An inventory of risks of pesticide use, possible solutions, and policy instruments* (1994), Centre for Agriculture and Environment, Utrecht.

Reuters News Service 'It's Green for Go in Boots the Chemist' (1992), 13 June.

—— 'New York City Fund Wants Green Stance from Four Companies' (1992), 10 December.

Rhone, G. T., *Canadian Standards Association Sustainable Forest Management Certification System* (1996), Industry Canada, Ottawa.

Roberts, M., 'Fitting in ISO 14000' (November 8 1995) 157(17) *Chemical Week* 46.

Robinson, D., *Pollution Control and Public Interest Litigation* (1991), Environmental Defender's Office, Sydney.

—— 'Public Participation in Environmental Decision Making' (1993) 10(5) *Environmental and Planning Law Journal* 320–40.

Robinson, J. C., 'The Impact of Environmental and Occupational Health Regulation on Productivity Growth in US Manufacturing' (1995) 12(2) *Yale Journal of Regulation* 388.

Robinson, N., 'International Initiatives on Greenhouse' in B. Boer, R. Fowler, & N. Gunningham (eds.), *Environmental Outlook No. 2* (1996), The Federation Press, Sydney.

Rogers, J. E. Jr., 'Adopting and Implementing a Corporate Environmental Charter' (1992) 35(2) *Business Horizons* 29–33.

Rogers, W. I., *Environmental Law: Air and Water* (1994), West Publishing, St Paul.

Roht-Arriaza, N., 'Shifting the Point of Regulation' (1995) 22 *Ecology Law Quarterly* 506–507.

Romm, J., *Lean and Clean Management: How to boost profits and productivity by reducing pollution* (1994), Kodansha America, New York; and M. Porter, *The Competitive Advantage of Nations* (1990), Macmillan Press, London.

Rose, C., *Property and Persuasion: Essays in History, Theory and Rhetoric of Ownership* (1994), Westview Press, Boulder.

Rose, N. & Miller, P., 'Political Power Beyond the State: problematics of government' (1992) 43 *British Journal of Sociology* 173.

Rose-Ackerman, S., 'Public Law versus Private Law in Environmental Regulation: European Union proposals in the light of the United States experience' (1995) 4(4) *Review of European Community and International Environmental Law (RECEIL)* 312.

—— 'Public Law versus Private Law in European Regulation' (1996) 4(4) *RECEIL* 312.

Rosenthal, I., *Major Event Analysis in the US Chemical Industry: Organisational learning vs liability* (1996), Working Paper, Wharton School of Business, University of Pennsylvania, Philadelphia.

Rotman, D., 'Pushing Pollution Prevention' (17 July 1991) *Chemical Week* 30.

Rowland, P., *Recent Changes in International Crop Protection Practices: The growing trend to reduce pesticide use and pesticide risk* (1995), Bureau of Resource Sciences, Department of Primary Industries and Energy, Canberra.

Rudig, W. & Kraemer, R. A., 'Networks of Cooperation: Water Policy in Germany' (1994) 3(4) *Environmental Politics* 52–79.

Runge, C. F., 'Institutions and the Free-Rider: The assurance problem in collective action' 46 *Journal of Politics* 154–81.

—— 'Environmental Protection from Farm to Market' (1997) in M. R. Chertow & D. C. Esty, *Thinking Ecologically: The Next Generation of Environmental Policy* (1997) Yale University Press, London.

Rust PPK, *International Best Practice in Health, Safety and Environmental Regulation in the Chemicals and Petroleum Industries* (1995), Rust PPK Melbourne, Department of Business and Employment, Victoria.

Salter, R., 'Market Credit for Loss Prevention in the Petrochemical Industry' In D. D. Peng (ed.) *Insurance and Legal Issues in the Oil Industry* (1993), Graham & Trotman, London.

Samson, T., *An Important Step But No Giant Leap: An assessment of the Victorian Accredited Licensing System* (1996), October, Australian National University Honours Thesis, Australian National University, Canberra.

Sandman, P., *Addressing Scepticism About Responsible Care* (1991), Environmental Communications Research Program, Rutgers University, New Jersey.

Saunders, D. A., Hobbs, R. J. & Margules, C. R., 'Biological Consequences of Ecosystem Fragmentation: A review' (1991) 5(1) *Conservation Biology* 18–32.

Saunders, M., 'Farmer Jailed for Duping Food Giant on Organic Wheat' (1997) *The Australian*, 2 October, p.5.

Scanlan, J. C. & Turner, E. J., *The Production, Economic and Environmental Impacts of Tree Clearing in Queensland* (1995), Department of Lands, Brisbane.

Schauzenbacher, B., *Economic Instruments as Policy Instruments for Environmental Management and Sustainable Development* (1995), UNEP, Environment and Economics Unit, Nairobi.

Schelling, T., *The Strategy of Conflict* (1960), Harvard University Press, Cambridge.

—— (ed.), *Incentives for Environmental Protection* (1983), Massachusetts Institute of Technology Press, Cambridge.

Schmidheiny, S., *Changing Course: A global business perspective on development and the environment* (1992), MIT Press, Cambridge.

Schmidheiny, S. & Zorraquin, F., *Financing Change: The Financial Community, Eco-Efficiency and Sustainable Development* (1996), MIT Press, Cambridge.

Schneider, S. H., *The Planetary Gamble We Can't Afford to Lose* (1997), Basic Books, New York.

Scholz, J. T., 'Cooperation, Deterrence and the Ecology of Regulatory Enforcement' (1984) 18 *Law and Society Review* 1709.

Schonfield, A., Anderson, W. & Moore, M., 'PAN's Dirty Dozen Campaign— The View at Ten Years' (1995), 5(3) September, *Global Pesticide Campaigner*, Pesticide Action Network North America, San Francisco.

Schuler, S., 'New Jersey's Pollution Prevention Act of 1991 A regulation that even the regulated can enjoy' (1992) 16 *Seton Hall Legislative Journal* 814–832.

Shapiro, R. B., *Remarks To Society of Environmental Journalists* (1995), October 28.

Shearing, C. & Stenning, P., *Private Policing* (1987), Sage Publications, Beverly Hills.

Short, K., *Quick Poison, Slow Poison: Pesticide Risk in the Lucky Country* (1994), Envirobooks, St Albans.

Shover, N., Clelland, D. & Lynzwiler, J., *Enforcement or Negotiation: Constructing a regulatory bureaucracy* (1986), State University of New York Press, Albany.

Shrivastava, P., *Bhopal: Anatomy of a crisis* (2nd edn.) (1992), Chapman, London.

Shughart, W. F. II, *Antitrust Policy and Interest-Group Politics* (1990), Quorum Books, New York.

Sigler, J. A. & Murphy, J. E., *Interactive Corporate Compliance: An alternative to regulatory compulsion* (1989), Quorum Book, New York.

Silverstein, J., 'Taking Wetlands to the Bank: The role of wetland mitigation banking in a comprehensive approach to wetlands protection' (1994) 22 *Boston College Environmental Affairs Law Review* 129.

Simmons, P. & Cowell, A., 'Liability and the environment' (1993) in T. Jackson (ed.), *Clean Production Strategies: Developing preventive environmental management in the industrial economy*, Lewis Publishers, Boca Raton.

Simmons, P. & Wynne, B., 'Responsible Care: Trust, credibility and environmental management' (1993) in K. Fischer & J. Schot (eds.) *Environmental Strategies for Industry*, Island Press, US.

Simon, H., *Economics, Bounded Rationality and the Cognitive Revolution* (1992) Edward Elgar, UK.

Sletto, B., 'Goals Clear, Methods Not' (1995) (1) *Tomorrow: Global Environment Business* 24–26.

Smith, J., *Measuring Health, Safety and Environmental Performance: Why, what, and whose?* (1994), summary of a paper presented to the ACIC Convention, 21 February, Leura, NSW.

Smith, M. C., *Morality and the Market: Consumer pressure for corporate accountability* (1990), Routledge, London.

Smithers, R., 'Chemical Firms Adopt Code to Clean Up the Industry' (1989) *The Age* 27 September, p.5.

Soufi, R. & Tudderham, M., 'Reform of the Common Agricultural Policy' in R. Gale, S. Barg, & A. Gillies, (eds.) *Green Budget Reform* (1995), Earthscan Publications, London.

South Florida Water Management District, *Lake Okeechobee Water Quality Monitoring Report: October 1984* (1986), South Florida Water Management District, Florida.

Sparkes, R., *The Ethical Investor* (1995), Harper Collins, London.

Squillace, M. 'Innovative Enforcement Mechanisms in the United States', Australian Institute of Criminology (AIC), Conference Proceedings No. 26, 1–3 September 1993, *Environmental Crime*, N. Gunningham, J. Norberry & S. McKillop (eds.), IAIC, Canberra, 1995.

Stewart, R., 'Models for Environmental Regulation: Central planning versus market-based approaches' (1992) *Boston College Environmental Affairs Law Review* 547.

Stone, C., 'Choice of Target and Other Law Enforcement Variables' in M. Friedland (ed.), *Sanctions and Rewards in the Legal System* (1989), University of Toronto Press, Toronto.

Stuart, G., 'Marketing Reports on Environmental Concerns in the Packaging Industry' (1992) *Reuters News Service*, 20 August.

Sunstein, C., 'Paradoxes of the Regulatory State' (1990) 57 *University of Chicago Law Review* 407.

—— *After the Rights Revolution: Reconceiving the Regulatory State* (1990), Harvard University Press, Cambridge.

Surrey, S., 'Tax Incentives as a Device for Implementing Government Policy: A comparison with direct government expenditures' (1970) 83(4) *Harvard Law Review* 705.

Swanson, T., 'Economic Instruments and Environmental Regulation: A critical introduction' (1995) 4(4) *Review of European Community and International Environmental Law* 287.

—— *Intellectual Property Rights & Biodiversity Conservation: An interdisciplinary analysis of the values of medical plants* (1995), Cambridge University Press, New York.

—— Book Reviews: J. B. Opschoor & R. K. Turner (eds.) *Economic Incentives and Environmental Policies: Principles and Practice* (1994) (1995) 4(1) *Review of European Community and Environmental Law (RECIEL)* 85.

Swanson, T. M. & Barbier, E. (eds.), *Economics for the Wild: Wildlife, wildlands, diversity and development* (192), Earthscan, London.

Tattum, L., 'Product Stewardship: Old practice, new theory' (7/14 July 1993) 153(1) *Chemical Week* 125–26.

Teubner, G., 'Substantive and Reflexive Elements in Modern Law' (1983) 17 *Law and Society Review* 239–286.

—— Farmer, L. & Murphy, D. (eds.), *Environmental Law and Ecological Responsibility* (1994), Wiley, UK.

The Farmers of Sweden, 'We are Creating the World's Cleanest Farming' (1994), IV(4) *Tomorrow: Global Environment Business* 87.

Thomas, W. L., 'Using ISO 140001 to comply with the Management System Requirements of US EPA's RMP Rule and the EU's Seveso II Directive' *European Environmental Law Review*, December 1998, 335.

Thompson, G. *et. al.* (eds.), *Markets, Hierarchies and Networks: The coordination of social life* (1991), Sage Publications, London.

Thornton, M., *Court Wetlands Ruling Halts Regulatory Creep. Focus on Agriculture*, 17 February 1997 (http://www.fb.com/new/focus97/fo0217.html).

Thrupp, L. A., *New Partnerships for Sustainable Agriculture* (1996), World Resources Institute, Washington.

Tibor, T. & Feldman, I., *ISO 14000: A Guide to the New Environmental Management Standards* (1996), Irwin, Chicago.

Tietenberg, T. H., 'Economic Instruments for Environmental Regulation' (1990) 6(1) *Oxford Review of Economic Policy* 17.

Toft, B. & Reynolds, S., *Learning from Disasters* (1994), Butterworths, Oxford.

Tombs, S., 'The Chemical Industry and Environmental Issues' in D. Smith (ed.) *Business and the Environment: Implications of the new environmentalism* (1993), Paul Chapman Publishing, UK.

Trade Practices Commission (TPC) (Australia), *Self-regulation in Australian Industry and the Professions* (1988), AGPS, Canberra.

Treasury Board of Canada Secretariat, 'Assessing Regulatory Alternatives' (1994), Ottawa.

Turner, K., Ozdemiroglu, E. & Steele, P., 'Environmentally Sensitive Areas in the United Kingdom: Economic incentives for sustainable farming' (1995) in R. Gale, S. Barg, & A. Gillies (eds.) *Green Budget Reform* (1995), Earthscan Publications, London.

United Nations Commission on Environment and Development (UNCED), *Agenda 21: Programme of action for sustainable development*, Section 1 Chapter 8(B) *Providing and Effective Legal and Regulatory* Framework (1992), United Nations Conference on Environment and Development, UNCED, Geneva.

United Nations Environment Programme (UNEP), Advisory Committee on Banking and the Environment (1992), UNEP, Nairobi.

—— *Measures for the Conservation of Biodiversity and Sustainable Use of its Components* (1994), Global Biodiversity Assessment, UNEP, Nairobi.

—— *Environmental Effects of Ozone Depletion: 1994 Assessment* (1994), UNEP, Nairobi.

United States General Accounting Office, *Crop Insurance: Opportunities exist to reduce government costs for private-sector delivery* (1997) RCED-97-70 April 17 at http://www.gao.gov/new.items/rc97070.pdf.

University of California Sustainable Agriculture Research and Education Program, *What Is Sustainable Agriculture?* (1996).

—— *US Chemical Industry Statistical Handbook 1995* (1995), Chemical Manufacturers Association, Washington DC.

US Environment Protection Agency, *EPA Acid Rain Program* (1996), Update No. 3 Technology and Information, EPA, Washington DC.

US Environmental Leadership Program, *ELP Community Outreach/Employee Involvement* (1996), US EPA, Washington DC.

US National Environmental Justice Advisory Council, Public Participation and Accountability Subcommittee, *The Model Plan for Public Participation* (November 1996), National Environmental Justice Advisory Council, Washington DC.

US President's Council on Environmental Quality (PCEQ), (Quality Environmental Sub-Committee), *Total Quality Management: A framework for pollution prevention* (1993), Washington DC.

US President's Council on Sustainable Development, *Towards Sustainability* (1995), Washington DC.

—— *Sustainable America: A New Consensus* (1996), Washington DC.

—— Eco-Efficiency Task Force, *Chemical Operations Demonstration Project* (February 1995), Washington DC.

—— Eco-efficiency Task Force, Chemical Operations Team *Proposed Policy Recommendations For the Chemical Industry* (1995), Washington DC.

Van Berke, R. *et. al.*, 'The Relationship Between Cleaner Production and Industrial Ecology' (1997) 1(1) *Journal of Industrial Ecology* 51.

Van Dunne, J. (ed.), *Environmental Contracts and Covenants: New instruments for a realistic environmental policy?* (1993), Koninklijke Vermande, Netherlands.

Vaughan, D., *The Challenger Launch Decision: Risky Technology, Culture, and Deviance at NASA* (1996) University of Chicago Press, Chicago.

Veroutis, A. D. and Fava, J. A., 'Elements of Effective DFE Program Management and Product Stewardship' (1997i), 10 Environmental Quality Management 61.

Victorian Environment Protection Agency, *A Question of Trust: Accredited licensing concept* (July 1993), a discussion paper, Environment Protection Authority, Melbourne.

—— *Accredited Licenses* (1994), Publication 423, VGPS, Melbourne.

Vogel, D., *Lobbying the Corporation: Citizen Challenges to Business Authority* (1978), Basic Books, New York.

—— *National Styles of Regulation: Environmental Policy in Great Britain and the United States* (1986), Cornell University Press, Ithaca.

von Hayek, F., 'Spontaneous ("grown") Order and Organized ("made") Order' (1991) in G. Thompson *et. al.* (eds.) *Markets, Hierarchies and Networks: The coordination of social life*, Sage Publications, London.

Wallace, A., *Eco-Heroes: Twelve Tales of Environmental Victory* (1993), Mercury House, San Francisco.

Wallace, D., *Environmental Policy and Industrial Innovation* (1995), Earthscan, London.

Wallace, K. L. & Moore, S. A., 'Management of Remnant Bushland for Nature Conservation in Agricultural Areas of South-Western Australia—Operational and Planning Perspectives' (1987) in D. A. Saunders, G. W. Warnold, A. A. Burbidge & A. J. M. Hopkins (eds.) *Nature Conservation: The role of remnants of native vegetation*, Surrey Beatty and Sons, Chipping Norton.

Walley, N. & Whitehead, B., 'Its Not Easy Being Green' (1994) May–June, *Harvard Business Review*, 46–52.

Ward, B., 'Now at BAT' (July 1997) 14(4) *Environmental Forum* 38.

Ward, N., 'Technological Change and the Regulation of Pollution from Agricultural Pesticides' (1995) 26(1) *Geoforum* 19–33.

Wargo, J., *Our Children's Toxic Legacy: How science and law fail to protect us from pesticides* (1996), Yale University Press, New Haven.

Washington Lee Law Review 'Regulation Symposium' (1988), 45 *Washington and Lee Law Review* 1245.

Weale, A., *The New Politics of Pollution* (1992), University of Manchester Press, Manchester.

Webb, K. & Morrison, A., 'The Legal Aspects of Voluntary Codes' (1996), a draft paper presented to the *Voluntary Codes Symposium*, Office of Consumer Affairs, Industry Canada and Regulatory Affairs, Treasury Board, Ottawa, September.

Welner, J., 'Natural Communities Conservation Planning: An ecosystem approach to protecting endangered species' (1995) 47 *Stanford Law Review* 319.

Western Australia Department of Environment Protection, *Achieving Best Practice Environmental Management* (1996), Discussion Paper.

White House Office on Environmental Policy, *Protecting America's Wetlands: A fair, flexible and effective approach* (1993), Washington DC.

Wiering, M., 'Regulating Farmers: Enforcement styles in the environmental regulation of the animal husbandry in the Netherlands' (1996), Paper presented at the Annual Meeting of the Law and Society Association, Glasgow, Scotland, 11 July.

Wilcox, M., 'The Role of Environmental Groups in Litigation' (1985) 10 *Adelaide Law Review* 41–8.

—— 'Retrospect and Prospect' in T. Bonyhady (ed.) *Environmental Protection and Legal Change* (1992), Federation Press, Sydney.

Wilkinson, A. & Willmott, H. (eds.) *Making Quality Critical: New perspectives on organizational change* (1995), Routledge, London.

Wilson, E. O., *The Diversity of Life* (1992), Harvard University Press, Cambridge, Massachusetts.

Wilson, J. Q., *Political Organisations* (1973), Basic Books, New York.

Winsemius, P. & Guntram, U., 'The Environmental Challenge' (1992) *Business Horizons*, March/April, p.12.

—— 'Responding To The Environmental Challenge' (1992) *Business Horizons*, March–April 12.

Withers, J., *Major Industrial Hazards: Their Appraisal and Control* (1988), Halsted Press, New York.

World Bank, *China: Southern Jiangsu Environmental Protection Project* (1993), Staff Appraisal Report 11370-CHA, Washington DC.

World Commission On Environment And Development, *Our Common Future* (1987), Oxford University Press, Oxford, UK.

World Conservation Monitoring Centre, *Global Biodiversity—Status of the Earth's Living Resources* (1992), Chapman and Hall, London.

World Meteorological Organisation, *Scientific Assessment of Ozone Depletion: 1994* (1995), WMO, Geneva.

World Resource Institute, *Global Biodiversity Strategy: Guidelines for action to save, study, and use earth's biotic wealth sustainably and equitably* (1992), WRI, Washington DC.

—— *World Resources 1994–95: A guide to the Global Environment* (1994), Oxford University Press, New York.

—— *World Directory of Country Environmental Studies* (1996), WRI, Washington, DC.

World Wildlife Fund, *Reducing Reliance on Pesticides in Great Lakes Basin Agriculture* (1995), World Wildlife Fund, Washington DC.

Yandle, B., *The Political Limits of Environmental Regulation* (1989), Quorum Books, New York.

Yeager, P. C., *The Limits of Law: The public regulation of private pollution* (1991), Cambridge University Press, Cambridge.

Yeager, R. & Miller, N., *Wild Death Land Use and Survival in Eastern Africa* (1986), State University of New York Press in association with the African-Caribbean Institute, Albany, New York.

Young, M. D. & Gunningham, N., 'Mixing Instruments and Institutional Arrangements for Optimal Biodiversity Conservation' in OECD, *Investing in Biological Diversity* (1996), OECD, Paris.

Young, M. D., Gunningham, N., Elix, J., Lambert, J., Howard, B., Grabosky, P. & McCrone, E., *Reimbursing the Future: An evaluation of motivational, voluntary, price-based, property-right, and regulatory incentives for the conservation of biodiversity* Part 1 and Part 2 Appendices (1996), Department of the Environment, Sport and Territories, Biodiversity Unit, Biodiversity Series, Paper No. 9, Canberra.

Young, M. D. & McCay, B., *Building Equity, Stewardship and Resilience into Market-Based Property-Right Systems* (1995), World Bank, Washington DC.

Zimbardo, P. & Lieppe, M. R., *The Psychology of Attitude Change and Social Influence* (1991), Temple University Press, Philadelphia.

Index